The **Rough Guide to**

The Dordogne and the Lot

written and researched by

Jan Dodd

with additional contributions from

Laura Bennitt, Janet Cintas and Hugh Cleary

ROUGH GUIDES

www.roughguides.com

Contents

◀◀ Geese in the sunlight ◀ Detail on the fountain at the Monument aux Girondins

Introduction to

The Dordogne and the Lot

It was in the green, secluded valleys of the Dordogne and Lot region that prehistoric people penetrated deep into limestone caves to paint the world's earliest masterpieces of pot-bellied ponies, mammoths and muscular bison. Later occupants of the area expressed their faith in the Romanesque churches to be found on many a hilltop, and in the array of abbeys and towering cathedrals, while the legacy of a more bellicose era lies in the medieval fortresses perched on pinnacles of rock. A more intimate link with the past is recorded among the ancient farmhouses tucked into the landscape's folds.

In addition to this richly layered history, the Dordogne and Lot is endowed with a tremendous variety of scenery, from the dry limestone plateaux of the *causses*, sliced through with narrow gorges, to the wooded valleys of the Périgord Noir and the Bordeaux vineyards' serried ranks. Through these landscapes slide the great rivers that unify and define the region: the **Dordogne**, which flows 500km from the Massif Central west to the Atlantic coast, and further south the **Lot**, writhing across country on its way to join the **Garonne**, which, along with its tributaries, the **Tarn** and **Aveyron**, marks this region's southern border.

It is a region best savoured at its own unhurried pace; there is always something to catch the eye, some forgotten corner to stumble upon, a market or a village *fête*. That isn't to say the region is undiscovered – indeed, some sights number amongst the most visited in France – but its heartland is still steeped in what the French call the *douceur de vivre*, the gentle way of life.

Where to go

The principal western gateway to the Dordogne and Lot region, and its only major city, is **Bordeaux**, whose sprawling suburbs belie a core of elegant eighteenth-century townhouses, superb restaurants and a vibrant cultural life. The surrounding vineyards, whose profits paid for much of the city's expansion, are just as distinguished.

Fact file

- The **area** covered by this guide amounts to some 30,000 square kilometres and has a **population** of under two million. Of these, around 750,000 live in Bordeaux, the region's main industrial centre, while elsewhere the economy is based primarily on agriculture and tourism.
- The most famous product is undoubtedly **wine**. It's the vineyards around Bordeaux that really put this region on the map – they extend over 1000 square kilometres and are divided into 57 different *appellations*. The average annual output is 700 million bottles produced by 6400 producers representing 12,600 individual châteaux.
- The Dordogne and Lot boasts three individual **World Heritage Sites** – the Vézère valley, with its prehistoric cave art, Bordeaux's entire old town, and the town and vineyards of St-Émilion – in addition to a dozen or so sights listed under the pilgrims' route to Santiago de Compostela in northern Spain.

▶ Bordeaux at night

Northeast lies **Périgueux**, where an extraordinary Byzantine-style cathedral stands above a tangle of medieval lanes. The city is the capital of a broad sweep of rolling pasture and woodland known as **Périgord Vert** (Green Périgord). This region's loveliest river is the Dronne and its most appealing town water-bound **Brantôme**, known for its rock-cut sanctuaries and plethora of restaurants. East of here is castle-country: **Château de Puyguilhem** stands out for its elegant Renaissance architecture, while the **Château de Hautefort** is one of the grandest castles in the Dordogne and Lot.

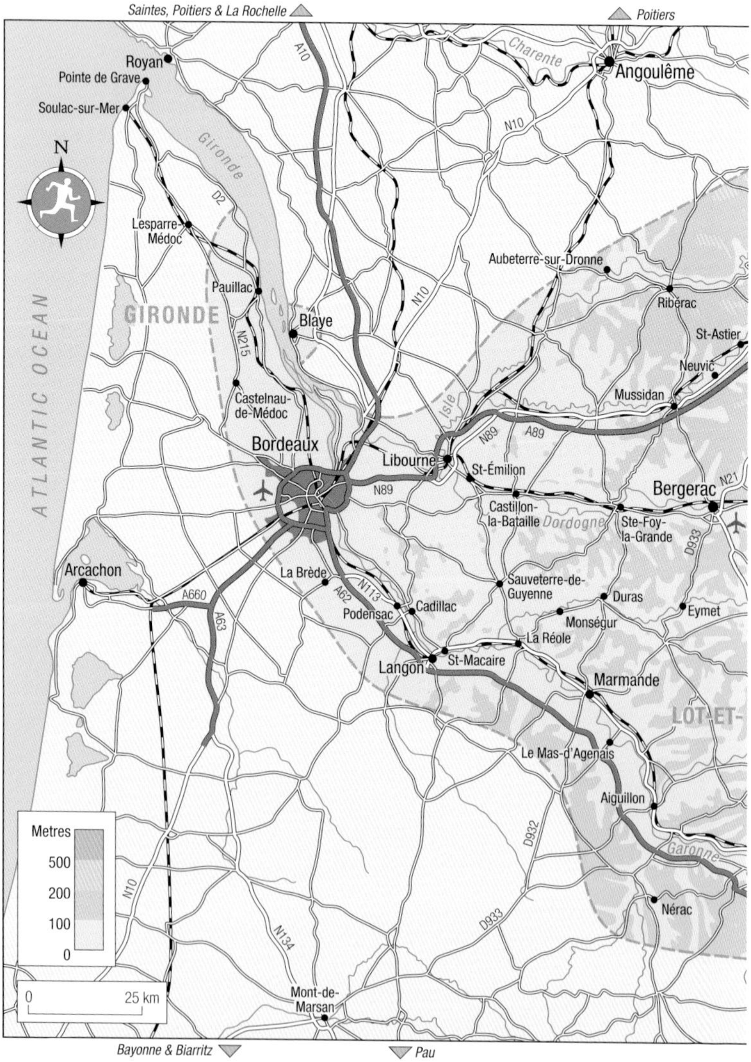

South of Périgueux, in an area known as **Périgord Pourpre** (Purple Périgord) thanks to its wine production, vines cloak the slopes of the lower Dordogne valley around the pleasant riverside town of **Bergerac**. The star of this area is the river itself, which loops through two immense meanders near **Trémolat** to create a classic Dordogne scene.

East of Trémolat the colour-scheme changes again as you enter the **Périgord Noir** (Black Périgord), named for the preponderance of evergreen oaks with their dark, dense foliage. Here you'll find the greatest concentration of Périgord cottages with their steep,

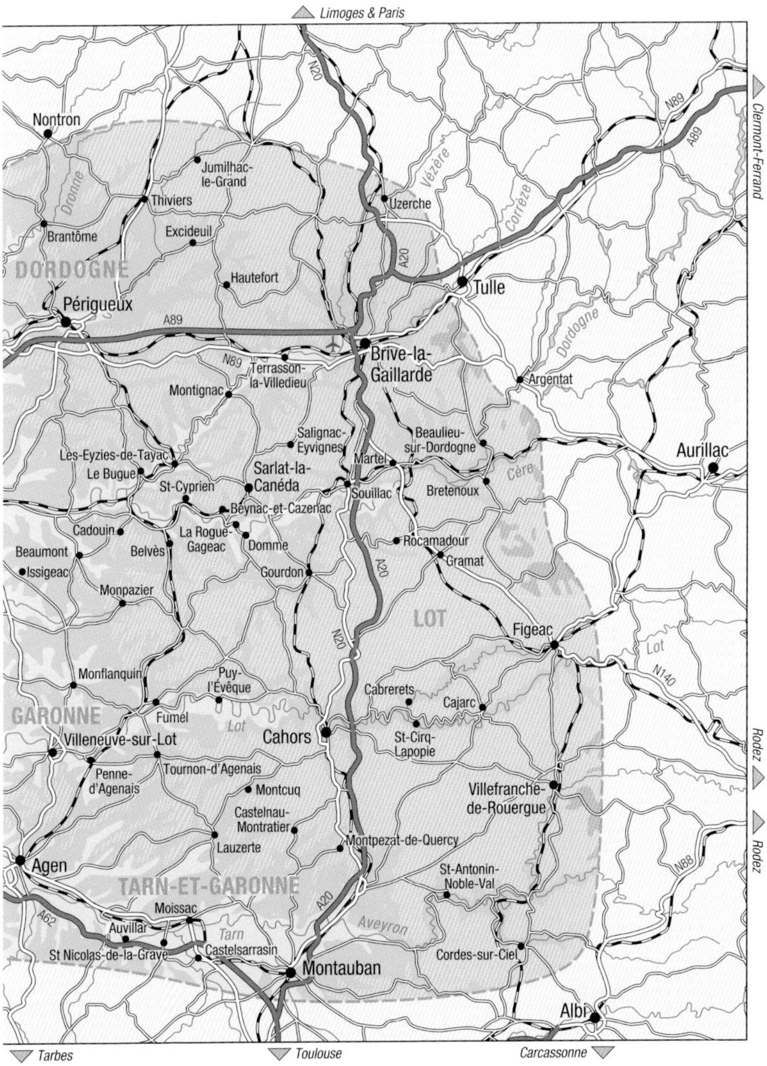

◀ Château Milande, Périgord Noir

stone-covered roofs, and dramatic fortresses perched high above the river. Here, too, are the walnut orchards and flocks of ducks and geese, the source of so much of the produce featured in the region's markets. Of these the most vivid is **Sarlat's**, held among the fine medieval and Renaissance houses built in honey-coloured stone. Close by, the beetling cliffs of the **Vézère valley** are riddled with limestone caves where prehistoric artists left their stunning legacy.

Upstream from Sarlat, the abbey-church of **Souillac** offers remarkable Romanesque carvings, while the nearby pilgrimage town of **Rocamadour**, set halfway up a cliff-face, is equally compelling. Further east is the **Château de Castelnau**, a supreme example of medieval military architecture, and the Renaissance **Château de Montal**, with its exquisite ornamental detailing.

Shadowing the Dordogne to the south, the Lot flows through comparatively wild country where, even in high summer, it's possible to find quiet corners. The departmental capital, **Cahors**, is home to France's best surviving fortified medieval bridge, while upstream the perched village of **St-Cirq-Lapopie** provides the valley's most dramatic sight. From near here the pretty Célé valley cuts northeast to **Figeac**, which boasts a highly rewarding museum dedicated to the man who unravelled the mystery of hieroglyphics. West of Cahors, the atmospheric villages of **Monflanquin** and **Monpazier** represent outstanding examples of *bastides*, the "new towns" of the Middle Ages, built on a grid plan around arcaded squares.

The highlights of the Garonne valley to the south are the Romanesque carvings of the abbey-church at **Moissac** and the river's dramatic gorges around the attractive old town of **St-Antonin-Noble-Val** and the evocative ruined fortress of **Najac**.

When to go

Winters are wet and mild, with little snow or frost - on sunny days it's possible to sit outside even in December. **Spring** can be very variable: some years see glorious weather; in others it's cold and wet. Temperatures begin to pick up around May and can reach the mid-30s in high **summer**, though usually hover in the mid-20s. **Autumn** is similar to spring, though brings slightly more sunshine.

▲ The gardens at Château de Hautefort

Bridge at Bourdeilles

The most important factor in deciding when to visit is the **holiday seasons**. By far the busiest period is mid-July through August, peaking in the first two weeks of August, when hotels and campsites are bursting at the seams and top-rank sights absolutely heaving. Conversely, from November to Easter many places close down completely. Overall, the **best time to visit** is September and early October, with May and June coming a close second.

Average daily temperature and rainfall

	Jan	Feb	Mar	Apr	May	Jun	Jul	Aug	Sep	Oct	Nov	Dec
Bordeaux												
Temp. max (ºC)	9	11	14	16	20	23	26	26	24	19	13	10
Temp. min (ºC)	2	3	4	6	10	12	14	14	12	9	5	3
Rainfall (mm)	100	84	78	75	79	58	48	57	76	85	88	100
Sarlat												
Temp. max (ºC)	8	10	13	16	19	23	26	25	23	18	12	9
Temp. min (ºC)	1	2	3	6	9	11	14	13	12	9	4	2
Rainfall (mm)	78	78	76	80	92	78	59	64	65	79	78	79

15 things not to miss

It's not possible to see everything that the Dordogne and Lot has to offer in one trip – and we don't suggest you try. What follows is a selective and subjective taste of the region's highlights: spectacular castles, delectable food and drink and eye-catching architecture. They're arranged in five colour-coded categories to help you find the very best things to see, do and experience. All entries have a page reference to take you straight into the Guide, where you can find out more.

01 **Canoeing** Page **39** • Drifting along in a canoe is a good way to get some gentle sightseeing done.

02 Rocamadour Page **239** • Cliff-side pilgrimage town which will take your breath away if you avoid the peak-season crowds.

03 Prehistoric caves Page **201** & ***Cave art* colour section** • The caves and rock shelters around Les Eyzies contain stunning examples of prehistoric art.

04 The gardens of Manoir d'Eyrignac Page **199** • Explore these ornate gardens dating back to the eighteenth century.

05 Bordeaux Page **57** • The elegant eighteenth-century architecture of the Place de la Bourse is typical of the buzzing city of Bordeaux.

06 Bastide towns Page **305** • Monpazier is one of the region's best-preserved *bastide* towns, built in the typical grid-style, with many buildings dating from the thirteenth century.

07 Festivals Page **38** • From the ancient tradition of the Jurade in St-Émilion, to atmospheric Baroque concerts in local churches, to jazz in Bergerac and Monségur.

08 Vineyard visits Page **59** • From household names like Margaux to tiny, family-run concerns, a visit and obligatory tasting at any of the wine châteaux around Bordeaux provides a memorable experience.

09 Local produce Page **34** & ***A Taste of Périgord* colour section** • Famous gastronomic treats from the region include foie gras, walnut oil and truffles – the famously expensive "black diamonds".

10 Cadouin Abbey Page **187** • The astonishing Cadouin Abbey was once a major pilgrimage site.

11 Château at Najac Page **344** • The fairy-tale château of Najac set on top of a hill with an impressive view dominates the Aveyron.

12 St-Antonin-Noble-Val Page **340** • See St-Antonin-Noble-Val and the medieval houses from its glorious heyday sheltering under towering limestone cliffs.

13 Pont Valentré Page **273** • The Pont Valentré in Cahors is an outstanding example of a fortified medieval bridge.

14 Sarlat Page **193** • Lose yourself in Sarlat's old centre – an intriguing maze of narrow medieval lanes.

15 Cordes Page **342** • The picturesque medieval hill-town of Cordes-sur-Ciel, the pearl of the *bastides*, perches on a rocky pinnacle.

Basics

Basics

Getting there

The quickest way to reach the Dordogne and Lot from most parts of the United Kingdom and Ireland is by air. From southern England, however, the Eurostar provides a viable alternative, making the journey from London to Paris via Lille in under three hours, from where you can connect to the fast and efficient TGV services south to Bordeaux. The Channel Tunnel is the most flexible option if you want to take your car to France, though the cross-Channel ferries are often cheaper. It's also worth bearing in mind that if you live west of London, the ferry services to Roscoff, St-Malo, Cherbourg, Caen and Le Havre can save a lot of driving time. From the US and Canada you'll usually be routed though Paris, or another European hub, with onward connections. There are direct flights to Paris and other European hubs from Australia and New Zealand, though in general the cheapest air fares are via Asia. From South Africa, connections are usually made through Paris or Amsterdam.

Fares increasingly depend on how far in advance you can book: the earlier the cheaper. But they will also depend on the **season**, with the highest prices around early June to the end of August, when the weather is best; fares drop during the "shoulder" seasons – roughly September to October and April to May – and you'll get the best prices during the low season, November to March (excluding Christmas and New Year when prices are hiked up and seats are at a premium). Flying at weekends is generally more expensive; price ranges quoted below assume midweek travel.

It's worth noting that a **Rail pass** (see p.21) may be useful if you are visiting France as part of a longer European trip.

Flights from the UK and Ireland

Flying is by far the most popular means of reaching Dordogne and the Lot. The cheapest fares are likely to be with one of the **low-cost airlines**, a number of which operate direct flights to southwest France. New routes are opening all the time (and some closing), but at the time of writing **Ryanair** flies from London Stansted to Bergerac, Biarritz (roughly 100km south of Bordeaux) and Rodez (60km southeast of Figeac), from Luton to Bergerac and Limoges (80km north of Périgueux) and from Dublin to Biarritz; **easyJet** links Luton and Bristol with Bordeaux; and **bmibaby** flies from Manchester to Bordeaux and from Manchester to Toulouse. Fares fluctuate dramatically depending on how far in advance you book and how flexible you are about days and times, but booking over a month in advance and being prepared to fly at inconvenient times, single fares start at around £30 including taxes. With most of these airlines, tickets – or certainly the cheapest ones – can only be purchased online.

It's always worth checking out the **traditional carriers**, such as British Airways, Air France, Flybe and Aer Lingus. The cheapest tickets usually require you to stay over on a Saturday night and don't allow any amendments. Again, the further ahead you book, the better, but low-season return fares to Bordeaux start at around £110 from London, £170 from Edinburgh and €250 from Dublin.

Air France, and its partner airlines, offer reasonably priced fares to Bordeaux and Toulouse from London, Dublin and various regional airports, though they always involve a change at Paris Charles de Gaulle airport (CDG). **British Airways** flies direct from Gatwick to Bordeaux and Heathrow to Toulouse; they also fly to Paris CDG from Heathrow, Birmingham, Bristol, Edinburgh, Glasgow and Manchester. From Northern Ireland, you'll be routed through London. Flybe is an excellent bet for flying from smaller airports; it serves Bergerac and Bordeaux from a dozen regional airports across Britain, though flights are less frequent. **Aer Lingus** has direct flights from Dublin to Bordeaux and Toulouse. It also flies from Dublin and Cork to Paris CDG.

Flights from the US and Canada

The only direct **flights** from the US or Canada to the Dordogne and Lot region is the weekly Montréal to Bordeaux service offered by **Air Transat**. However, most major airlines operate scheduled flights to Paris, from where you can take a domestic flight (check there's no inconvenient transfer between Charles de Gaulle and Orly airports) or transfer to the rail network. **Air France** has the most frequent and convenient service, with daily flights from half a dozen US cities, but their fares tend to be pricey. Other airlines offering services to Paris from a variety of US cities include: **American Airlines** from New York, Boston, Chicago, Dallas and Miami; **Continental** from New York and Houston; **Delta** from Atlanta, Cincinnati, Houston and New York; **Northwest** from Detroit; and **United** from Chicago, Philadelphia and Washington DC. **Air Canada** offers non-stop services to Paris from Montréal and Toronto. Another option is to take one of the other **European carriers**, such as British Airways, Iberia or Lufthansa, from the US or Canada to their home base (London, Madrid and Frankfurt respectively), then continue on to Paris or direct to Bordeaux.

Thanks to such intense competition, transatlantic **fares** to France are fairly reasonable. A typical return fare to Paris, flying midweek outside peak season, costs around US$700 from Houston or Los Angeles and US$550 from New York. From Canada, prices to Paris start from Can$850 from Montréal and Toronto or Can$950 from Vancouver. Air Transat's return fares on the non-stop Montréal–Bordeaux route start at around Can$900.

Flights from Australia, New Zealand and South Africa

There are scheduled flights to Paris from Sydney, Melbourne, Brisbane, Perth and Auckland, all of which involve at least one stop en route. Alternatively, you can fly via another European hub and get a connecting flight to Bordeaux from there. Flights via Asia or the Gulf States with a transfer or overnight stop in the airline's home port are generally the cheapest option. The cheapest return **fares** start at around Aus$1700 from Sydney, Perth and Darwin and NZ$2300 from Auckland.

From South Africa, both South African Airways and Air France operate daily non-stop flights from Johannesburg to Paris. With other airlines you'll be routed through another European hub such as London, Amsterdam, Madrid or Frankfurt, from where you can pick up a connecting flight to Bordeaux. From South Africa, you're looking at anything upwards of R7500 from Johannesburg and R9000 from Cape Town.

Travelling with pets from the UK

For information about travelling with pets from the UK to France, consult Ⓦwww.defra.gov.uk/wildlife-pets/pets/travel/pets/index.htm or contact the Pet Travel Scheme (PETS) helpline (Ⓣ0870/241 1710).

Six steps to a better kind of travel

At Rough Guides we are passionately committed to travel. We feel strongly that only through travelling do we truly come to understand the world we live in and the people we share it with – plus tourism has brought a great deal of **benefit** to developing economies around the world over the last few decades. But the extraordinary growth in tourism has also damaged some places irreparably, and of course **climate change** is exacerbated by most forms of transport, especially flying. This means that now more than ever it's important to **travel thoughtfully** and **responsibly**, with respect for the cultures you're visiting – not only to derive the most benefit from your trip but also to preserve the best bits of the planet for everyone to enjoy. At Rough Guides we feel there are six main areas in which you can make a difference:

- Consider what you're contributing to the **local economy**, and how much the services you use do the same, whether it's through employing local workers and guides or sourcing locally grown produce and local services.
- Consider the **environment** on holiday as well as at home. Water is scarce in many developing destinations, and the biodiversity of local flora and fauna can be adversely affected by tourism. Try to patronize businesses that take account of this.
- Travel with a purpose, not just to tick off experiences. Consider **spending longer** in a place, and getting to know it and its people.
- Give thought to how often you **fly**. Try to avoid short hops by air and more harmful night flights.
- Consider **alternatives to flying**, travelling instead by bus, train, boat and even by bike or on foot where possible.
- Make your trips "**climate neutral**" via a reputable carbon offset scheme. All Rough Guide flights are offset, and every year we donate money to a variety of charities devoted to combating the effects of climate change.

Trains from the UK

Eurostar operates high-speed passenger trains daily from St Pancras International to the Continent via the **Channel Tunnel**; most but not all services stop at either Ebbsfleet or Ashford in Kent (30min from London). Services depart roughly every hour (from around 5.30am to 8pm) for Paris Gare du Nord (2hr 20min), most of which stop at Lille (1hr 30min). You can connect with TGV trains to the southwest at either station.

Standard **fares** from London to Paris start at £59 for a non-refundable, non-exchangeable return. "Semi-flexible" tickets, which can be exchanged but not refunded, start at £135. Otherwise, you're looking at up to £310 for a fully refundable ticket with no restrictions. Ticket prices are often significantly lower for those under 26, and all tickets go on sale three months in advance – you need to be quick to snap up the cheapest fares.

Tickets can be bought online or by phone from Eurostar (add £5 per booking), as well as from travel agents and mainline train stations. Note that Inter-Rail, Eurail and Eurodomino **rail passes** (see below) entitle you to discounts on Eurostar trains. For information about taking your **bike** on Eurostar, see p.29.

The websites listed on p.24 are helpful for working out times and prices for Eurostar tickets, plus onward connections within France. Booking far enough in advance with Rail Europe, for example, a return all the way from London to Bordeaux currently costs £190.

Rail passes

Rail Europe (ⓦwww.raileurope.fr) issues a number of **rail passes** for travel within France and for trips combining France with other European countries. Note that these passes must be purchased in your home country.

If you plan to visit several countries and are a European resident, the best bet is an **Inter-Rail Pass**, which entitles you to unlimited travel within the specified period and geographical area. The passes come in over-26 and (cheaper) under-26 versions, and cover 29 European countries plus Morocco. For non-European residents there are various Eurail passes, covering either several countries or just France. The France Rail Pass, for example, allows between three and nine days of unlimited travel within a month (€170 for three days, €25 for each additional day); first-class passes and cheaper passes for children, young people and seniors are also available.

Ferries from the UK and Ireland

Though slower than travelling by plane or via the Channel Tunnel, the ferries and catamarans plying the waters between Dover and Calais offer the cheapest means of travelling to France **from the UK** and are particularly convenient if you live in southeast England, from where the quickest crossings take less than two hours. Even if your starting point is west of London, it may still be worth heading to one of the south-coast ports and catching a ferry to Brittany or Normandy. If you're coming from the north of England or Scotland, you could consider the overnight crossings from Hull and Rosyth to Zeebrugge (Belgium) operated by P&O Ferries and Norfolkline respectively. Another option is taking a ferry from Portsmouth to Santander (with Brittany Ferries) or Bilbao (P&O Ferries) in northern Spain. Crossing times are long (20–34hr), but the route north into the Dordogne, by car or train, is a relatively short one – it's roughly 200km from Bilbao to Bordeaux. By comparison, it takes at least eight hours by motorway from Calais to Bordeaux, a journey of around 870km.

From Ireland, putting the car on the ferry from Cork or Rosslare (near Wexford) to Cherbourg or Roscoff in Brittany cuts out the drive across Britain to the Channel. The crossing takes around thirteen hours from Cork and eighteen hours from Rosslare. Again, you'll need to add another eight hours or so for the drive down to Bordeaux.

One-way **fares** for a car and up to five passengers are available for as little as £22 with Norfolkline on the Dover-Dunkirk route, while return fares on the Dover-Calais route start at around £35, again for a car and four passengers. The voyage from the south coast to northern Spain costs around £700 return for a car and four people. From Ireland return fares for a car and two adults start at around €300 on the Cork to Roscoff route. Most ferry companies also offer fares for foot passengers, typically around £20 return on cross-Channel routes; accompanying bicycles can usually be carried free in the low season, though there may be a small charge during peak periods.

An easy way to compare prices and get an overview of possible routes is via Ferry Savers (Ⓣ0844/576 8835, Ⓦwww.ferrysavers.com) and EuroDrive (Ⓦwww.eurodrive.co.uk), both of which offer cut-price fares; the latter caters only for people taking their cars across the Channel.

The Channel Tunnel

It's a long drive south to the Dordogne and Lot from the north coast of France (upwards of eight hours using the motorways as far as possible), but if you do want to take your car – and don't fancy a long sea journey and a short drive into the region from northern Spain (see opposite) – the simplest way is to load it on to one of the drive-on drive-off shuttle trains operated by **Eurotunnel** (Ⓣ0870/535 3535, Ⓦwww.eurotunnel.com).

The service runs continuously between Folkestone and Coquelles, near Calais, with up to three departures per hour at peak times (one every two hours from midnight to 6am) and takes 35min (slightly longer at night), though you must arrive at least 30min before departure. It is possible to turn up and buy your ticket at the check-in booths, but you'll pay the highest rate on the day. Standard **fares** start at £49 one-way if you book far enough ahead and/or travel offpeak, rising to £150 on the day. Fully refundable and changeable FlexiPlus fares cost £199 return.

If you don't want to drive too far when you've reached France, you can take advantage of SNCF's **motorail**, booked through Rail Europe's Motorail department (Ⓣ0844/848 4050, Ⓦwww.raileurope.co.uk). This involves putting your car on the train in Calais for the journey south to Brive or Toulouse. The service operates only in summer, with one train per week between May and September, and is a relatively expensive option: Calais–Brive, for example, costs from around £350 one way for a car and up to six adults travelling in the low season, rising to over £560 at peak times (Aug).

Buses

Eurolines, the association of European national bus and coach networks, (UK Ⓣ0871/781 8181, Ⓦwww.eurolines.com) runs regular bus-ferry services from London Victoria to Bordeaux, and also to Brive, Souillac, Cahors, Montauban and Toulouse in summer. Adult return **fares** start at £78 for Bordeaux if you book at least thirty days in advance, with a journey time of roughly eighteen hours. Regional return fares from the rest of England and Wales are available, as are student, youth and seniors' discounts.

Airlines, agents and operators

There are a vast number of travel agents and tour operators offering holidays in Dordogne and the Lot, with options varying from luxury château-based breaks to adventure trips involving cycling and canoeing. In addition to the **specialist tour operators** listed below, bear in mind that most of the ferry companies and airlines (see p.24 & below) also offer their own travel and accommodation deals. You'll also find operators listed on the Holiday France website (Ⓦwww.holidayfrance.org.uk), run by the Association of British Tour Operators to France.

Airlines

Aer Lingus Ⓦwww.aerlingus.com.
Air Canada Ⓦwww.aircanada.ca.
Air France Ⓦwww.airfrance.com.
Air New Zealand Ⓦwww.airnz.co.nz.
Air Transat Ⓦwww.airtransat.com.
American Airlines Ⓦwww.aa.com.
bmibaby Ⓦwww.bmibaby.com.
British Airways Ⓦwww.ba.com.
Cathay Pacific Ⓦwww.cathaypacific.com.
Continental AirlinesⓌwww.continental.com.
easyjet Ⓦwww.easyjet.com.
Emirates Ⓦwww.emirates.com.
Flybe Ⓦwww.flybe.com.
Gulf Air Ⓦwww.gulfairco.com.
Iberia Ⓦwww.iberia.com.
KLM Ⓦwww.klm.com.
Korean Air Ⓦwww.koreanair.com.
Lufthansa Ⓦwww.lufthansa-usa.com.
Malaysia Airlines Ⓦwww.malaysiaairlines.com.
Northwest Ⓦwww.nwa.com.
Qantas Ⓦwww.qantas.com.
Singapore Airlines Ⓦwww.singaporeair.com.
Ryanair Ⓦwww.ryanair.com.
South African Airways Ⓦwww.flysaa.com.
Thai Airways Ⓦwww.thaiair.com.
United Airlines Ⓦwww.united.com.
US Airways Ⓦwww.usair.com.
Virgin Atlantic Ⓦwww.virgin-atlantic.com.

Agents and operators

Adventure Center US Ⓣ1-800/228-8747, Ⓦwww.adventurecenter.com. American hiking and "soft adventure" specialists. Their eight-day "Dordogne Discovery" includes a bit of canoeing, walking and cycling, while "Flavors of the Dordogne" is a deluxe gastronomic experience.
Arblaster & Clarke UK Ⓣ01730/263 111, Ⓦwww.winetours.co.uk. Treat yourself to a luxury tour of the Bordeaux vineyards with Britain's biggest wine-tour specialist.
Backroads Ⓣ1-800/462-2848 or 510/527-1555, Ⓦwww.backroads.com. Luxury cycling and walking tours of the Bordeaux vineyards and the Dordogne and Vézère valleys.
Cycling for Softies UK Ⓣ0161/248 8282, Ⓦwww.cycling-for-softies.co.uk. An easy-going cycle holiday operator. Accommodation and restaurants tend to be top-end, with several Michelin-starred restaurants on the itineraries.
Cyclomundo US Ⓣ1-212/504 8368, Ⓦwww.cyclomundo.com. Defines itself as the "bike rider's travel agency", specializing in custom-made "biking à la carte" trips for serious cyclists.
Equine Adventures UK Ⓣ0845/130 6981, Ⓦwww.equineadventures.co.uk. Offers horseback holidays worldwide, including in the Dordogne and the Bordelais vineyards.
Eurocamp UK Ⓣ0844/406 0402, Ⓦwww.eurocamp.co.uk. Self-drive, go-as-you-please holidays with tent or mobile home.
France Afloat US Ⓣ0870/011 0538, Ⓦwww.franceafloat.com. French canal and river cruising specialist,Canal latéral à la Garonne around Moissac and Agen and the Canal du Midi.
French Affair UK Ⓣ020/7381 8519, Ⓦwww.frenchaffair.com. Offers a range of luxury,

villa-style self-catering accommodation in the Dordogne and Lot.

French Travel Connection Australia ⓣ02/9966 1177, ⓦwww.frenchtravel.com.au. Australia-based online agent offering everything to do with travel to and around France, including accommodation, canal boats, walking tours, train travel, cookery classes, car rental and more.

Grape Escapes UK ⓣ08456/430 860, ⓦwww.grapeescapes.net. Tailor-made holidays exploring the Bordeaux vineyards.

HF Holidays UK ⓣ0845/470 7558, ⓦwww.hfholidays.co.uk. Walking and cycling specialist offering guided trips around Sarlat and independent tours along the Dordogne and Lot valleys.

The International Kitchen US ⓣ1-800/945-8606 or ⓣ312/467-0560, ⓦwww.theinternationalkitchen.com. "Cooking school vacations" in a Bordeaux wine château or in the Dordogne or the Quercy.

North South Travel UK ⓣ01245/608 291, ⓦwww.northsouthtravel.co.uk. Friendly, competitive travel agency, offering discounted fares worldwide – profits are used to support projects in the developing world, especially the promotion of sustainable tourism.

Peregrine Adventures Australia ⓣ03/8601 444, ⓦwww.peregrine.net.au. Small-group adventure specialist offering guided and independent walking and cycling holidays in the Dordogne.

STA Travel US ⓣ1-800/781-4040, UK ⓣ0871/230 0040, Australia ⓣ134 782, New Zealand ⓣ0800/474 400, South Africa ⓣ0861/781 781; ⓦwww.statravel.com. Worldwide specialists in low-cost flights and tours for students and under-26s, though other customers are welcome.

Rail contacts

Europrail International Canada ⓣ1-888/667-9734, ⓦwww.europrail.net.

Eurostar UK ⓣ0870/518 6186, ⓦwww.eurostar.com.

International Rail UK ⓣ0870/084 1410, ⓦwww.international-rail.com.

Rail Europe UK ⓣ0844/8484 064, ⓦwww.raileurope.co.uk; US ⓣ1-800/622 8600; Canada ⓣ1-800/361-7245, ⓦwww.raileurope.com; Australia ⓦwww.raileurope.com.au.

Rail Plus Australia ⓣ1-300/555 003, New Zealand ⓣ09/377 5415; ⓦwww.railplus.com.au.

Trainseurope UK ⓣ0871/700 7722, ⓦwww.trainseurope.co.uk.

World Travel ⓦwww.world-travel.co.za.

Ferry contacts

Brittany Ferries UK ⓣ0871/244 0744, ⓦwww.brittany-ferries.co.uk; Republic of Ireland ⓣ021/427 7801, ⓦwww.brittanyferries.ie.

Condor Ferries ⓣ0845/609 1024, ⓦwww.condorferries.co.uk.

Irish Ferries Republic of Ireland ⓣ0818/300 400, UK ⓣ+353 818 300 400; ⓦwww.irishferries.com.

LD Lines UK ⓣ0844/576 8836, ⓦwww.ldlines.co.uk.

Norfolkline UK ⓣ0844/847 5022, ⓦwww.norfolkline.com.

P&O Ferries UK ⓣ0871/664 5645, ⓦwww.poferries.com.

Sea France ⓣ0871/222 2500, ⓦwww.seafrance.com.

Getting around

France has the most extensive train network in Western Europe. The nationally owned French train company, the SNCF (Société Nationale des Chemins de Fer), runs fast, modern trains between all the main towns in the Dordogne and Lot, and even between some of the minor ones. In rural areas where branch lines have been closed, certain routes (such as Agen to Villeneuve-sur-Lot) are covered by buses operated by the SNCF or in partnership with independent lines. It's an integrated service, with buses timed to meet trains and the same ticket covering both. To really do the region justice, however, you'll need your own transport.

By rail

SNCF has pioneered one of the most efficient, comfortable and user-friendly railway systems in the world. Pride and joy of the French rail system is the high-speed **TGV** (*train à grande vitesse*; Ⓦwww.tgv.com). Bordeaux is reachable in three hours by regular TGV trains from Paris Montparnasse, some of which continue on along the main line to Agen (4hr 15min) and Montauban (4hr 45min). Elsewhere, the majority of trains you will use here are designated TER (*Train Express Régional*) which cover shorter distances and stop at more and smaller stations. Around Bordeaux, useful lines run into the Médoc, Entre-deux-mers and to St-Emilion. A scenic branch traces much of the Dordogne valley linking Bordeaux with Bergerac and Sarlat, while three north–south axes cross the Dordogne and Lot valleys (Périgueux–Agen, Brive–Cahors–Montauban and Brive–Figeac–Toulouse). In all these cases, schedules are thin, with gaps of several hours between trains, so it's imperative to check timetables in advance either by phone (Ⓣ36.35; €0.34 per min) or by consulting Ⓦwww.voyages-sncf.com. Paper copies of **timetables** are available free at most stations. *Autocar* (often abbreviated to *car*) at the top of a column means it's an SNCF bus service, on which rail tickets and passes are valid.

Tickets

Tickets for all SNCF trains can be bought online with a credit card through Ⓦwww.sncf.com, which has an English-language option, or by phone and at any train station (*gare SNCF*). At stations, it's easiest to use the yellow touch-screen machines (in English), though note that these only accept payment by card. Alternatively, you can use the ticket office, though there are sometimes long queues. If boarding at a smaller station (such as Le Bugue), which has neither machines nor a ticket office, you can buy your ticket from the guard on the train. All tickets – but not passes or internet tickets printed out at home – must be **validated** in the orange machines located at the entrance to the platforms; it is an offence not to follow the instruction *Compostez votre billet* (Validate your ticket).

Fares

Fares are cheaper if you travel off-peak (*période bleue* or blue period) rather than during peak hours (*période normale* or *période blanche*, normal or white period) – in general, peak period means Monday mornings and Friday and Sunday evenings. A leaflet (*le calendrier voyageurs*) showing

Left luggage

As part of the "Vigipirate" anti-terrorist campaign, left-luggage facilities at the vast majority of train and bus stations have been closed. In this region, only the gare St-Jean in Bordeaux still has a left-luggage service. Apart from carrying your bags with you, the only option is to leave them at your hotel.

the blue and white periods is available at train stations. For longer journeys it's worth checking the advance special discount offers, known as *tarifs Prem's* (one-way fares from €22 on TGVs), on the SNCF website (see p.25). A limited number of these are available on some main lines and can be bought online between two months and two weeks in advance. Even cheaper internet-only TGV fares (from €19 one-way) can be purchased through ⓦwww.idtgv.com on services from Paris to Bordeaux and Toulouse; tickets go on sale four months before departure and you'll have to be able to print out your ticket. Try to book in advance for all TGV trains, as **seat reservations** are obligatory, and are included in the ticket price, though note that you will have to pay extra for them if you are travelling on an Inter-Rail pass. Anybody under 26 is entitled to a discount of 25 percent off all blue-period trains in France.

Those planning on spending a longer period in France to live or work should look into the SNCF's own discount cards: the **carte 12–25** for young people costs €49 and gives an extra discount of 25 percent off all fares, while the **carte escapade**, for those over 26, costs €85 and offers similar reductions. The special tourist trains in the region, such as those running in summer between Bergerac and Sarlat (see p.200) and Martel and St-Denis (see p.247) have their own separate ticketing systems.

By bus

The most convenient **bus services** are those operated as an extension of rail links by SNCF, which run between train stations and serve areas not accessible by rail. In addition to SNCF buses, private, municipal and departmental buses can be useful for local and some cross-country journeys, though be prepared for early starts and careful planning – the timetable is often constructed to suit market and school hours – if you want to see much outside the main towns.

Timetables for SNCF services are available at ⓦwww.sncf-voyages.fr, but times for services run by private companies can be frustrating to track down. ⓦwww.france-week-end.com has links to bus timetables by department, and ⓦwww.mopy.fr is a good source for the south of the region, but it's frankly easiest just to ask at the local tourist office, or in the case of large towns such as Bordeaux, at the bus information centre.

Larger towns usually have a *gare routière* (bus station), often next to the *gare SNCF*. However, the private bus companies don't always work together and you'll frequently find them leaving from an array of different points (here, too, the local tourist office should be able to help).

One final thing to note is that many rural bus services only operate *sur réservation* or "on demand". This means that you need to phone the operating company by 6pm the day before you wish to travel (or by 6pm on Friday for travel on Monday). Such services are usually indicated by a telephone icon in the bus timetable.

By car

Driving in the Dordogne and Lot can be a real pleasure – and is often the only practical means of reaching the more remote sights. There are three **autoroutes** in the area: the A20 cuts south from Limoges to Toulouse via Cahors; the A62 runs along the Garonne from Bordeaux to Toulouse; and the A89 links Bordeaux with Périgueux and Brive. Motorway **tolls** are payable in cash or by credit card (get in the lane marked CB) at the frequent tollgates (*péages*). The Michelin website (ⓦwww.viamichelin.fr) details the cost of tolls on any particular journey – as an example, the tolls for a car from Bordeaux to Périgueux (100km) total €8.90 and €12.00 from Bordeaux to Montauban (200km), less for a motorbike. Slower and more congested are the toll-free national roads (marked, for example, N21 or RN21 on signs and maps). The smaller *routes départementales* (marked with a D) are generally uncongested and make for a more scenic drive, though may occasionally be in relatively poor condition.

For up-to-the-minute **information** regarding traffic jams and roadworks on *autoroutes*, ring the 24hr, multilingual service Autoroutel (ⓣ08.92.70.70.01; 00.34 per min) or consult ⓦwww.asf.fr. Traffic information for other roads can be obtained from the Bison Futé recorded information service

(Ⓣ08.00.10.02.00; free, Ⓦwww.bison-fute.equipement.gouv.fr) in French only.

There are times when it's wiser not to drive, most obviously in Bordeaux, where **parking** can be difficult and expensive; if you're renting a car here, it's best to do so at the airport, to avoid the city centre. The region's other towns and cities are all of a manageable size – just follow signs for *centre ville* or the tourist office and you'll normally find a car park nearby. The cost of **fuel** can be a discouraging factor. At the time of writing, petrol prices were hovering around €1.40 a litre for unleaded (*sans plomb*), slightly more for four-star (*super*) and €1.20 a litre for diesel (*gazole* or *gasoil*); you'll find prices lowest at out-of-town hypermarkets. Note that in rural areas most petrol stations close at night, on Sundays and on bank holidays, and some may also close on Mondays. Some stations are equipped with 24hr pumps, but these only work with French bank cards.

If you run into **mechanical difficulties** you'll find garages and service stations in the Yellow Pages of the phone book under "*Garages d'automobiles*"; for **breakdowns**, look under "*Dépannages*". If you have an accident or theft, you should contact the local police – and keep a copy of their report in order to file an insurance claim. Within Europe, most vehicle **insurance** policies cover taking your car to France; check with your insurer. However, you're advised to take out extra cover for motoring assistance in case your vehicle breaks down; contact your insurer or one of the motoring organizations listed below for a quote.

Rules of the road

US, Canadian, Australian, New Zealand and all EU **driving licences** are valid in France, though an International Driver's Licence makes life easier. The minimum driving age is 18 and you must hold a full (not a provisional) licence. Drivers are required to carry their licence, insurance papers and vehicle registration document (*carte grise*) with them in the car.

Since the French drive on the right, drivers of right-hand drive cars must adjust their **headlights** to dip to the right. This is most easily done by sticking on black glare deflectors, which can be bought at motor accessory shops and at the Channel ferry ports or the Eurostar terminal. Motorcyclists must drive with their headlights on, and must also wear a **helmet**.

All non-French vehicles must display their **national identification letters** (GB, etc), either on the number plate or by means of a sticker. Even if your car has flashing **hazard-warning lights**, it is compulsory to carry a red triangle and fluorescent jacket in case the lights fail or you break down on a blind corner. **Seat belts** are compulsory front and back, and children under 10 years are not allowed to sit in the front of the car. It is illegal to use a hand-held **mobile phone** while driving.

The law of *priorité à droite* – **giving way** to traffic coming from your right, even when it is coming from a minor road – has largely been phased out. However, it still applies on a few roads in built-up areas and the occasional roundabout, so it pays to be vigilant at junctions, especially in rural areas where old habits die hard. A sign showing a yellow diamond on a white background gives you right of way, while the same sign with a diagonal black slash across it warns you that vehicles emerging from the right have priority. *Stop* signs mean you must stop completely; *Cédez le passage* means "Give way".

Unless otherwise indicated, **speed limits** are: 130kph (80mph) on *autoroutes*; 110kph (68mph) on dual carriageways; 90kph (55mph) on other roads; and 50kph (31mph) in towns. In wet weather, and for drivers with less than two years' experience, these limits are 110kph (68mph), 100kph (62mph) and 80kph (50mph) respectively, while the town limit remains constant. The legal blood **alcohol limit** is 0.05 percent alcohol (0.5 grams per litre), and police frequently make random breath tests, while saliva tests for drugs are becoming increasingly common. There are increasingly stiff **penalties** for driving violations, which can mean fines of up to €75,000, your licence confiscated on the spot and a prison sentence in the most serious cases.

Car rental

Car rental in France costs upwards of €50 for a day and €200 for a week, but is usually cheaper if arranged before you leave home or online. You'll find the big firms represented in Bordeaux and most major towns, with addresses detailed throughout the Guide. Local firms can be cheaper but most don't offer one-way rentals and you need to check the small print carefully. It is difficult to rent cars with automatic transmission in France. If you can't drive a manual, try to book an automatic well in advance, possibly before you leave home, and be prepared to pay a much higher price for it.

The **cost** of car rental includes the minimum car insurance required by law. Under the standard contract you are liable for an excess (*franchise*) for any damage to the vehicle. This starts at around €500 for the smallest car and can be covered by credit card. You should return the car with a full tank of fuel or face paying an exorbitant fuel charge.

To rent a car in France you must be over 21 and have driven for at least one year; some companies stipulate two. Most companies charge **drivers under 25** an extra insurance premium, typically €25 per day.

Car rental agencies

Alamo Ⓦwww.alamo.com.
Argus Car Hire Ⓦwww.arguscarhire.com.
Auto Europe Ⓦwww.autoeurope.com.
Avis Ⓦwww.avis.com.
Budget Ⓦwww.budget.com.
Dollar Ⓦwww.dollar.com.
Enterprise Ⓦwww.enterprise.com.
Europcar Ⓦwww.europcar.com.
Europe by Car Ⓦwww.europebycar.com.
Hertz Ⓦwww.hertz.com.
Holiday Autos Ⓦwww.holidayautos.com.
National Ⓦwww.nationalcar.com.
SIXT Ⓦwww.e-sixt.com.
Thrifty Ⓦwww.thrifty.com.

By scooter and motorbike

Scooters are relatively easy to find and, though they're not built for long-distance travel, are ideal for pottering around the local area. You also don't need a licence to drive them, just a passport or some form of ID. Places that rent out bicycles often also rent out scooters; you can expect to pay at least €40 a day for a 50cc machine, less for longer periods. For anything more powerful you'll need a full **motorbike** licence. Rental prices are around €70 a day for a 125cc bike. Expect to leave a hefty deposit by cash or credit card – over €1000 is not unusual – which you may lose in the event of damage or theft. Crash helmets are compulsory on all bikes, and the headlight must be switched on at all times.

Cycling

Bicycles (*vélos*) have high status in France, where cyclists are given respect both on the roads and as customers at restaurants and hotels. In addition, local authorities are actively promoting cycling, not only with urban cycle lanes but also with comprehensive networks in rural areas (frequently using disused railways). Bordeaux and the Gironde region have been particularly active in this respect and produce a free booklet called *Les Pistes Cyclables de Gironde*, available from tourist offices in the region. Elsewhere, tourist offices can usually provide maps of local routes.

Hotels are nearly always obliging about looking after your bike, even to the point of allowing it into your room. Most towns have well-stocked retail and **repair shops**, where parts are normally cheaper than in Britain or the US. However, if you're using a foreign-made bike with nonstandard metric wheels, it's a good idea to carry spare tyres.

The **train** network runs various schemes for cyclists, all of them covered on the website Ⓦwww.velo.sncf.com. It's possible to take your bike for free on all TER trains in the region – make sure you arrive in good time to get a slot in the bike rack. Longer distance trains are more problematic: on some TGVs you can reserve a slot in advance (€10; call Ⓣ36.35), but not all lines offer this service; the Paris-Bordeaux line rarely does. In these cases, the options are to dismantle your bike and pack it in a bike bag measuring no more than 120cm by 90cm (which means you can carry it on board like an ordinary piece of luggage), or to send your bike in one piece as registered baggage through Sernam, the SNCF's baggage service. Call Ⓣ36.35 to reserve; delivery takes two days and costs €49 from door to door or €39 from one Sernam agency to another.

Eurostar allows you to take your bicycle as part of your baggage allowance, provided it's dismantled and packed in a bike bag, again measuring no more than 120cm by 90cm. However, the company encourages people to register their bikes and send them unaccompanied with their registered baggage service, Esprit Europe (Ⓣ08705/850 850, Ⓦwww.espriteurope.co.uk) for £20 one-way, with a guaranteed arrival time of 24 hours; you can register your bike, which does not need to be dismantled, from ten days before departure. **Ferries** usually carry bikes free (though you may need to register it), as do some **airlines** such as British Airways, while others now charge – check when making your booking.

Bikes – either mountain bikes (*vélos tout-terrain* or VTT) or hybrid bikes (*vélos tout-chemin* or VTC) – are often available to **rent** from campsites and hostels, as well as from specialist cycle shops and some tourist offices for around €15 per day. The bikes are often not insured, however, and you will be presented with the bill for its replacement if it's stolen or damaged; check your travel insurance policy for cover.

As for **maps**, a minimum requirement is the IGN 1:100,000 series (see p.46) – the smallest scale that carries contours. The UK's national cyclists' organisation, the CTC (Ⓣ0844/736 8451, Ⓦwww.ctc.org.uk), can suggest routes and supply advice for members (£36 a year, or £58.50 for a family of four and £12 for under 18s and students under 26 years). They run a particularly good insurance scheme. Companies offering specialist bike touring **holidays** are listed on p.23. For **guidebooks** aimed at cyclists, see p.370.

All cyclists are required by law to wear a reflective safety jacket at night outside urban areas and in the daytime during periods of poor visibility, or risk being fined up to €35.

By boat

Boating is a leisurely way to explore the Lot and Garonne valleys. From April to September the **River Lot** is navigable for motorboats from St-Cirq-Lapopie downstream to Luzech (65km), and from Fumel down to its confluence with the Garonne (78km). There are plans to make the river between these two stretches accessible to pleasure craft, making it navigable right across the *département* by 2012. From October through to March the current is too swift and the river too high to be safe. But the Lot is a capricious river at any time, so it pays to follow the guidelines provided by rental companies carefully.

The other option is to potter along the **Canal latéral**, which tracks the Garonne eastwards from Castets-en-Dorthe, near Langon, to Toulouse (190km), where it joins the Canal du Midi. You can also combine the Canal latéral with the River Lot and the **River Baïse** south to Nérac.

Boats are usually rented by the week, though shorter periods are also available outside the July and August peak. **Rates** range from €800 to €2500 per week for a four- to six-person boat, depending on the season and level of comfort. No licence is required, but you'll receive instruction before taking the controls. You should also be given a **carte de plaisance**, guaranteeing that the boat is insured and in good working order.

Boat rental companies in the Lot

Babou Marine Ⓣ05.65.30.08.99, Ⓦwww.baboulene-jean.fr.
Crown Blue Line France Ⓣ04.68.94.52.72, Ⓦwww.crownblueline.com.
Locaboat Plaisance Ⓣ03.86.91.72.72, Ⓦwww.locaboat.com.
Lot Navigation Ⓣ05.53.84.52.50, Ⓦwww.lot-navigation.com.
Nautic Ⓣ04.67.94.78.93, Ⓦwww.nautic.fr.
Nicols Ⓣ02.41.56.46.56, Ⓦwww.nicols.com.

Accommodation

At most times of the year you can turn up in any town in the Dordogne and Lot region and find a room or a place in a campsite, but it's best to book in advance. In general you'll be able to get a simple double for around €40, though sometimes with shared facilities, while €50 should secure a reasonable level of comfort. As a general rule the areas around train stations have the highest density of cheap hotels.

Problems may arise between mid-July and the end of August, when the French take their own vacations en masse. During this period, hotel and hostel accommodation can be hard to come by – particularly in the most popular towns, such as Sarlat – and you may find yourself falling back on local tourist offices for help. Some offer a **booking service**, though they can't guarantee rooms at a particular price, and all provide lists of hotels, hostels, campsites and bed-and-breakfast possibilities. With **campsites**, you can be more relaxed about finding an empty pitch somewhere for a tent, though it may be more difficult with a caravan or camper van.

Hotels

Most French hotels are **graded** from zero to five stars. The price more or less corresponds to the number of stars, though the system is rather simplistic, having more to do with ratios of bathrooms-per-guest and so forth than genuine quality, and some of the unclassified and single-star hotels can actually be very good. A new certification, called HotelCert (Ⓦwww.hotelcert.org) aims to reward more meaningful criteria, such as friendliness of staff and cleanliness of rooms. What you get for your money varies enormously between establishments. Paying under €40, you take your chances somewhat: there won't be soundproofing and the showers (*douches*) and toilets (WC or *toilettes*) may well be communal (*dans le palier*). However, you should have your own bidet and washbasin (*lavabo*), often partitioned off from the rest of the room in an area referred to as a *cabinet de toilette*. The shared showers down the hall are usually free but sometimes you'll be charged a couple of euro per shower. Over €40 should get you a room with its own bath or shower though not necessarily toilet, and, though the decor may not be anything to write home about, comfortable furniture. For around €50 you should expect a proper, separate bathroom (*salle de bain*) and TV, while at over €85 you'll find something approaching luxury. Hotels with one star or above have a telephone in the rooms, though some phones can only receive calls. **Single rooms** – if the hotel has any – are only marginally cheaper than doubles, so sharing always slashes costs, especially since most hotels willingly provide rooms

Accommodation price codes

All the hotels and *chambres d'hôtes* listed in this book have been price-coded according to the following scale. The prices quoted are for the cheapest available double room in high season, although remember that many of the cheap places will also have more expensive rooms with more facilities. In the case of a hostel, we give the price of a dormitory bed.

① €40 and under	④ €61–80	⑦ €121–150
② €41–50	⑤ €81–100	⑧ €151–200
③ €51–65	⑥ €101–20	⑨ €201 and over

with **extra beds** for three or more people at good discounts.

Breakfast, which is not normally included, will add between €6 and €15 per person to a bill, sometimes more – though there is no obligation to take it. The cost of eating **dinner** in a hotel's restaurant can be a more important factor to bear in mind when picking a place to stay. It's actually illegal for hotels to insist you take half-board (*demi-pension*), though a few do, especially during the summer peak. This is not always such a bad thing, however, since you can sometimes get a real bargain. Some hotels also offer an especially good deal on week nights called a *soirée étape* – dinner, bed and breakfast at a heavily discounted rate. It's really aimed at business travellers rather than tourists, so you might not be offered it directly, but it's worth looking out for.

Note that many family-run hotels close down for two or three weeks a year. In smaller towns and villages they may also close for one or two nights a week, usually Sunday or Monday. Details are given where possible in the Guide, but dates change from year to year and some places will close for a few days in low season if they have no bookings. The best precaution is to phone ahead to be sure.

A useful option, especially if you're driving and looking for somewhere late at night, are the modern **chain hotels** located at motorway exits and on the outskirts of major towns. Among the cheapest (from around €35 for a three-person room with communal toilets and showers) are the one-star Formule 1 chain (Ⓣ08.92.68.56.85, €0.34 per min; Ⓦwww.hotelformule1.com) and the sightly more comfortable Etap Hotel (Ⓣ08.92.68.89.00, €0.34 per min; Ⓦwww.etaphotel.com).

Aside from the chains, there are a number of **hotel federations** in France. The biggest and most useful of these is **Logis** (formerly Logis de France); 83 av d'Italie, 75013 Paris; Ⓣ01.45.84.83.84, Ⓦwww.logis-de-france.fr), an association of over 3000 hotels nationwide; standards are generally good, though are sometimes bit erratic. The organization produces a free annual guide, which you can obtain from your nearest French tourist office (see p.48), from Logis itself or from member hotels. Two other, more upmarket federations worth mentioning are the Châteaux & Hôtels Collection (84 av Victor-Cresson, 92441 Issy-les-Moulineaux; Ⓣ01.72.72.92.02, Ⓦwww.chateauxhotels.com) and Relais du Silence (17 rue d'Ouessant, 75015 Paris; Ⓣ01.44.49.90.00, Ⓦwww.silencehotel.com).

Bed-and-breakfast and self-catering

Predominantly in country areas, in addition to hotels, you will come across *chambres d'hôtes*, **bed-and-breakfast accommodation** in someone's house, château or farm. If you're lucky, the owners may also provide traditional home cooking and a great insight into French life. In general, prices range between €40 and €100 for two people including breakfast; payment is almost always expected in cash. Some offer meals on request (*tables d'hôtes*), usually evenings only, while others are attached to *fermes auberges*, farm-restaurants serving local produce (see p.34). Again, we've detailed a number of *chambres d'hôtes* throughout the Guide and tourist offices will also be able to provide lists.

If you're planning to stay a week or more in any one place it might be worth considering renting **self-catering accommodation**. This will generally consist of self-contained country cottages known as *gîtes* or *gîtes ruraux*. Many *gîtes* are in converted barns or farm outbuildings, though some can be quite grand.

You can get lists of both *gîtes* and *chambres d'hôtes* from **Gîtes de France** (Ⓣ01.49.70.75.75, Ⓦwww.gites-de-france.com). They also publish annual guides such as *Nouveaux Gîtes Ruraux*, *Chambres et Tables d'Hôtes* and *Chambres d'Hôtes de Charme* (€20–22), and more comprehensive regional or departmental guides that include photos (€5–20). All these guides are available online or from departmental offices of Gîtes de France (see p.32), as well as from local bookstores and tourist offices. Tourist offices will also have lists of places in their area that are not affiliated to Gîtes de France.

You'll also find self-catering accommodation, much of it foreign-owned, on Ⓦwww.frenchconnections.co.uk, Ⓦwww.cheznous.co.uk and Ⓦwww.bvdirect.co.uk; or try one of the agents listed in the Travel Shop section of the official French tourist office website, ⓦwww.franceguide.com.

Departmental Offices of Gîtes de France

Aveyron/Lot/Tarn et Garonne Château de Bernussou, 12200 Villefranche de Rouergue ⓣ05.65.75.55.66, ⓔinfo@gitesdefrance-reservation-altg.com.
Corrèze Immeuble Consulaire, BP 30, 19001 Tulle ⓣ05.55.21.55.61, ⓔgites-de-france@correze.chambagri.fr.
Dordogne 25 rue Wilson, BP 2063, 24002 Périgueux ⓣ05.53.35.50.24, ⓔdordogne.perigord.tourisme@wanadoo.fr.
Gironde 17 cours Xavier Arnozan, 33082 Bordeaux ⓣ05.56.81.54.23, ⓔresa@gites-de-france-gironde.com.
Lot-et-Garonne 11 rue des Droits-de-l'Homme, 47000 Agen ⓣ05.53.47.80.87, ⓔgites-de-france.47@wanadoo.fr.

Hostels, foyers and gîtes d'étape

At around €15 per night for a dormitory bed, usually with breakfast thrown in and the opportunity to prepare your own meals in a shared kitchen, **youth hostels** – *auberges de jeunesse* – are invaluable for single travellers on a budget; per-person prices of dorm beds are given throughout the Guide.

Most hostels are run either by the municipality or by the French **hostelling association**, the Fédération Unie des Auberges de Jeunesse (FUAJ); see opposite. Many can be reserved online through the FUAJ website; see opposite. To stay at FUAJ hostels you normally have to show a current HI (Hostelling International) **membership card**. It's usually cheaper and easier to join before you leave home, provided your national Youth Hostel association (see opposite) is a full member of HI. Alternatively, you can purchase an HI card in certain French hostels for €15.30 (€10.70 for those under 26), or buy individual "welcome stamps" at a rate of €2.90 per night; after six nights you are entitled to the HI card. The only exception is Bordeaux, whose private hostel doesn't require membership.

Unfortunately, there aren't that many youth hostels in the Dordogne and Lot region. Sometimes, as is the case in Villefranche-de-Rouergue and Périgueux, hostel accommodation is provided in workers' hostels (**Foyers de Jeunes Travailleurs**). These tend to be functional and centrally located, with good canteens. Other hostels, most notably that at Cadouin, are more beautifully sited, though you might have to factor in the cost of a taxi in order to get there.

In the countryside, hostel-style **gîtes d'étape** are aimed primarily at hikers and long-distance bikers. Often run by the local village or municipality, they are less formal than hostels and provide bunk beds, primitive kitchen and washing facilities from around €10. They are marked on the large-scale IGN walkers' maps and listed in the individual Topo guides (see p.370). For more information check out the Gîtes de France booklet *Gîtes d'Étapes et de Séjours* (€10), and in *Gîtes d'Étape et Refuges*, published by Rando Éditions, downloadable at ⓦwww.gites-refuges.com; €5 for the southwest region.

Youth hostel associations

France

Fédération Unie des Auberges de Jeunesse (FUAJ), 27 rue Pajol, 75018 Paris ⓣ01.44.89.87.27, ⓦwww.fuaj.org.

UK and Ireland

Youth Hostel Association (YHA) England & Wales ⓣ01629/592 700, ⓦwww.yha.org.uk.
Scottish Youth Hostel Association ⓣ01786/891 400, ⓦwww.syha.org.uk.
Irish Youth Hostel Association ⓣ01/830 4555, ⓦwww.anoige.ie.
Hostelling International Northern Ireland ⓣ028/9032 4733, ⓦwww.hini.org.uk.

US and Canada

Hostelling International-American Youth Hostels ⓣ301/495-1240, ⓦwww.hiayh.org.
Hostelling International Canada ⓣ1-800/663 5777, ⓦwww.hihostels.ca.

Australia and New Zealand

Australia Youth Hostels Association ⓣ02/9565 1699, ⓦwww.yha.com.au.
Youth Hostelling Association New Zealand ⓣ0800/278 299 or 03/379 9970, ⓦwww.yha.co.nz.

Camping

Practically every village and town in France has at least one **campsite** to cater for the thousands of people who spend their holiday under canvas. Most sites open from around Easter to September or October. The vast majority are graded into four **categories**, from one to four stars, by the local authority. One- and two-star sites are very basic, with toilets and showers (not necessarily with hot water), but little else, and standards of cleanliness are not always brilliant. At the other extreme, four-star sites are far more spacious, have hot-water showers and electrical hook-ups. Most will also have a swimming pool – sometimes heated – washing machines, a shop and sports facilities, and will provide refreshments or meals in high season. At three-star sites you can expect a selection of these facilities and less spacious plots. A further designation, **Camping Qualité** (Ⓦwww.campingqualite.com), indicates those campsites with particularly high standards of hygiene, service and privacy. For those who really like to get away from it all, **camping à la ferme** – on somebody's farm – is a good, simple option. Lists of sites are available at local tourist offices.

Though **charging systems** vary, most places charge per pitch and per person, usually including a car, while others apply a global figure. As a rough guide, a solo camper without a car will pay between €5 at a simple municipal site and €15 at a four-star in prime location; equivalent rates for a family of four with a tent and car would be €10–35. In peak season and if you plan to spend a week or more at one site, it's wise to book ahead, and note that many of the big sites have caravans and chalet bungalows for rent.

If you're planning to do a lot of camping, it's worth getting hold of an **international camping carnet** (CCI), which gives discounts at member sites and serves as useful identification. Many campsites will take it instead of making you surrender your passport during your stay, and it covers you for third party insurance when camping. You can obtain the carnet from national motoring organizations or, in the UK, from the Camping and Caravanning Club (Ⓣ0845/130 7701, Ⓦwww.campingandcaravanningclub.co.uk; £4.95).

The Fédération Française de Camping et de Caravaning (Ⓣ01.42.72.84.08, Ⓦwww.ffcc.fr) publishes an annual guide (€16.80) covering 10,000 campsites. Another good source for information on a large number of sites is the excellent Camping France website Ⓦwww.campingfrance.com. If you'd rather have everything organized for you, a number of companies specialize in **camping holidays**, including Eurocamp (listed on p.23).

Lastly, a word of **caution**: never camp rough (*camping sauvage*, as the French call it) on anyone's land without first asking permission. If the dogs don't get you, the guns might – farmers have been known to shoot first and ask later. On the other hand, a politely phrased request for permission will as often as not get positive results. Camping on public land is not officially permitted, but is widely practised by the French, and if you are discreet you're not likely to have problems.

Food and drink

The cuisine of the Dordogne and Lot region is predominantly simple, country cooking (*cuisine de terroir*), revolving around duck and goose, garlic, a host of mushrooms, walnuts and whatever else the land has to offer. It's the sort of cuisine best sampled in little family-run places, where it's still possible to eat well for €15 or less. That said, every restaurant worth its salt offers a *menu du terroir*, featuring local specialities. Expensive *gastronomique* restaurants throughout the region, and most mid-priced establishments, also offer a smattering of fish dishes. But real fish and seafood fanatics should head for Bordeaux – a city famed for the range and quality of its restaurants – and the towns and villages along the Gironde estuary. See *A Taste of Périgord* colour section for more on the region's speciality food and drink. The food glossary is on p.378.

Breakfast and light meals

A croissant or *pain au chocolat* (a chocolate-filled, light pastry) with hot chocolate or coffee in a café-bar is generally the most economical way to eat **breakfast**, costing around €4–5. The standard hotel breakfast comprises bread and/or pastries, jam and a jug of coffee or tea, and orange juice if you're lucky, from around €6. More expensive hotels might offer a buffet comprising cereals, fruit, yogurt and the works.

At **lunchtime**, and sometimes in the evening, you'll find places offering a *plat du jour* (daily special) at between €9 and €12, or *formules*, a limited menu, typically offering a main dish and either a starter or dessert for a set price. *Croques-monsieur* and *croques-madame* (variations on the toasted-cheese sandwich), along with *frites*, *gaufres* (waffles) and fresh-filled baguettes are good lunchtime snacks. You could also try a **crêpe** (pancake with a filling) – the savoury buckwheat variety (*galettes*) are the main course; sweet, white-flour crêpes are dessert. **Pizzerias**, usually *au feu de bois* (wood-fired), are also very common.

For **picnics**, the local outdoor market or supermarket will provide you with almost everything you need. Cooked meat, prepared snacks, ready-made dishes and assorted salads are also available at charcuteries (delicatessens), which you'll find in some villages, and in most supermarkets. Boulangeries (bakers) provide bread and sometimes double as patisseries, selling a mouthwatering array of cakes and pastries.

Restaurant meals

There's no difference between restaurants (or *auberges* or *relais* as they sometimes call themselves) and brasseries in terms of quality or price range. The distinction is that **brasseries**, which resemble cafés, serve quicker meals at most hours of the day (as late as 11pm or midnight in Bordeaux), while **restaurants** tend to stick to the traditional meal times of noon to 2pm, and 7pm to 9pm or 9.30pm. In touristy areas in high season, and for all the more upmarket places, it's wise to make reservations – easily done on the same day in most cases.

When hunting for places to eat, don't forget that **hotel restaurants** are open to non-residents, and can be very good value. In country areas keep an eye out for **fermes auberges**, farm restaurants where the majority of ingredients are produced on the farm itself. These are often the best places to sample really traditional local cuisine at very reasonable prices; a four-course meal for between €15 and €35 is the norm, including an apéritif and wine, but reservations are a must.

Prices, and what you get for them, must be posted outside. Normally there's a choice between one or more *menus fixes* – with a set number of courses and a limited choice – and choosing individually from the *carte* (menu). **Menus fixes**, often referred to simply as *menus*, are normally the cheapest option, typically around €12–15 at lunchtime (*le déjeuner*) for a three- or four-course menu, rising to €20–30 or more at dinner (*le dîner*). Going **à la carte** offers greater choice and, in the better restaurants, unlimited access to the chef's inventiveness – though you'll pay for the privilege.

In the vast majority of restaurants a **service charge** of fifteen percent is included in prices listed on the menu – in which case it should say *service compris* (*s.c.*) or *prix nets*. Very occasionally you'll see *service non compris* (*s.n.c.*) or *servis en sus*, which means that it's up to you whether you leave a tip or not. Wine (*vin*) or a drink (*boisson*) is sometimes included in the cost of a *menu fixe*. Otherwise, the cheapest option will be the house wine, usually served in a jug (*pichet*) or carafe; you'll be asked if you want *un quart* (0.25 litre), *un demi* (0.5 litre) or *un litre* (1 litre).

One final note is that you should always call the waiter or waitress *Monsieur* or *Madame* (*Mademoiselle* if a young woman), never *Garçon*.

Vegetarian food

Vegetarians can expect a lean time in the Dordogne and Lot region – there are very few specifically vegetarian restaurants, though crêperies, pizzerias and Chinese or North African restaurants can be good standbys. Otherwise the best you can hope for is an omelette, salad or plate of vegetables – often tinned – at an ordinary restaurant. Occasionally they'll be willing to replace a meat dish on the fixed-price menu (*menu fixe*); at other times you'll have to pick your way through the *carte*. Remember the phrase "*Je suis végétarien(ne); est-ce qu'il y a quelques plats sans viande?*" (I'm a vegetarian; are there any non-meat dishes?). **Vegans**, however, should probably forget about eating in restaurants and stick to self-catering.

Drinking

In France **drinking** is done at a leisurely pace whether it's a prelude to food (*apéritif*), or a sequel (*digestif*), and cafés are the standard places to do it. Every bar or café has to display its full price list, including service charges. You normally pay when you leave, and it's usually perfectly acceptable to sit for hours over just one cup of coffee. Note that the minimum age for buying alcohol is 18, though younger teenagers may drink wine in a restaurant if with their parents.

Wine

Though consumption has declined since the days when public information campaigns urged French labourers to keep their intake below three bottles per day, **wine** (*vin*) is still drunk at just about every meal or social occasion. Red is *rouge*, white *blanc* and rosé *rosé*. The house wine served in restaurants can be very good value in this wine-producing region, or opt for a bottle of AOC (*appellation d'origine contrôlée*) wine if you want a more sophisticated taste. You can buy a very decent bottle of wine for €6 in a shop or from the producer, while €10 and over will get you something worth savouring. A glass of wine in a bar will typically cost around €3 to €6.

The best way of **buying wine** is directly from the producers (*vignerons*) at their vineyards or at Maisons or Syndicats du Vin (representing a group of wine-producers), or Coopératifs Vinicoles (producers' co-ops). At all of these you can usually sample the wines first. The most interesting option is to visit the vineyard itself, where the owner will often include a tour of the *chais* in which the wine is produced and aged. The most economical method is to buy *en vrac*, which you can do at some wine shops (*caves*), filling a plastic five- or ten-litre container (generally sold on the premises) straight from the barrel. Supermarkets often have good bargains, too.

There are strict limitations on the extent to which wine-growers can interfere in the natural process – it's illegal even to water vines. The result is that, far more than in other countries, French wines are the product of a very specific bit of land or *terroir*, and there will often be significant differences in taste between the wines of two neighbouring producers. This makes tasting wines a real joy, and even if you're not an expert, it's well worth trying to establish which grape types you particularly like or dislike, and whether you like your wine fruity or dry, light or heavy. Waiters and wine producers are usually delighted to give you advice in making a choice.

For basic wine vocabulary, see p.384.

Beer

Light Belgian and German **beers**, plus various French brands from Alsace, account for most of the beer you'll find. Draught beer (*à la pression*) – very often Kronenbourg – is the cheapest drink you can have next to coffee and wine; *une pression* (usually 0.33 litre) will cost around €3 to €4. For a wider choice of draught and bottled beer you need to go to special beer-drinking establishments such as the English- and Irish-style pubs found in larger towns and cities. A small bottle at one of these places can cost up to twice as much as a *demi* in an ordinary café-bar. Buying bottled or canned beer in supermarkets is much cheaper.

Spirits and liqueurs

Strong alcohol, including **spirits** (*eaux-de-vie*), such as cognac and armagnac, and **liqueurs** such as locally made walnut liqueurs (*vins de noix*), are always available. Refreshing *pastis* – the generic name for aniseed drinks such as Pernod or Ricard – is served diluted with water and ice (*glace* or *glaçons*). Among less familiar names, try Poire William (pear brandy), or Marc (a spirit distilled from grape pulp). Measures are generous, but they don't come cheap: the same applies for imported spirits such as whisky (*Scotch*). Two drinks designed to stimulate the appetite – *un apéritif* – are Pineau (cognac and grape juice) and Kir (white wine with a dash of cassis – blackcurrant liqueur – or with champagne instead of wine for a Kir Royal). For a post-meal *digestif*, don't miss out on armagnac, oak-aged brandy from the south of the Garonne but available in bars and restaurants throughout the region. **Cocktails** are served at most late-night bars, discos and clubs, as well as at upmarket hotel bars; they usually cost at least €5.

Soft drinks

On the **soft drink** front, you can buy cartons of unsweetened fruit juice in supermarkets, although in cafés, the bottled (sweetened) nectars such as apricot (*jus d'abricot*) and blackcurrant (*cassis*) still hold sway. Fresh orange or lemon juice (*orange/citron pressé*) is a much more refreshing choice on a hot day. Other soft drinks to try are syrups (*sirops*) of mint, grenadine and other flavours mixed with water. The standard fizzy drinks of lemonade (*limonade*), Coke (*coca*) and so forth are all available. Bottles of **mineral water** (*eau minérale*) and spring water (*eau de source*) – either sparkling (*gazeuse*) or still (*plate*) – abound. But there's not much wrong with the tap water (*l'eau de robinet*) which will always be brought free to your table if you ask for it.

Coffee, tea and hot chocolate

Coffee is invariably espresso – small, black and very strong. *Un café* or *un express* is the regular; *un crème* is with milk; *un grand café* or *un grand crème* are large versions. In the morning you could also ask for *un café au lait* – espresso in a large cup or bowl filled up with hot milk. *Un déca* is decaffeinated. Ordinary **tea** (*thé*) – Lipton's nine times out of ten – is normally served black (*nature*) or with a slice of lemon (*au citron*); to have milk with it, ask for *un peu de lait frais* (some fresh milk). *Chocolat chaud* – **hot chocolate** – unlike tea, lives up to the high standards of French food and drink and is available at any café. After meals, **herb teas** (*infusions* or *tisanes*), are offered by most restaurants – most commonly *verveine* (verbena), *tilleul* (lime blossom), *menthe* (mint) and *camomille* (camomile).

The media

French newspapers and magazines are available from newsagents (maisons de la presse) and, in larger towns, from side-street kiosks. A limited range of English-language newspapers and news magazines are on sale in Bordeaux and in larger towns in the rest of the Dordogne and Lot region.

Newspapers and magazines

Of the **French daily papers**, *Le Monde* (Ⓦwww.lemonde.fr) is the most intellectual; it is widely respected, but somewhat austere, even though it now carries such frivolities as colour photos. *Libération* (Ⓦwww.liberation.com), founded by Jean-Paul Sartre in the 1970s, is left-wing, pro-European, independent and more colloquial, with good, if slightly narrow, coverage. Rigorous left-wing criticism of the French government comes from *L'Humanité* (Ⓦwww.humanite.fr), the Communist Party paper, though it is struggling to survive. The other nationals are all firmly right-wing in their politics: *Le Figaro* (Ⓦwww.lefigaro.fr) is the most widely read. The top-selling tabloid, predictably more readable and a good source of news, is *Aujourd'hui*, while *L'Équipe* (Ⓦwww.lequipe.fr) is dedicated to sports coverage. The widest circulations are enjoyed by the **regional dailies**; in this area, *Sud Ouest* (Ⓦwww.sudouest.com) and *La Dépêche* (Ⓦwww.ladepeche.com), based in Bordeaux and Toulouse respectively. For visitors, they are mainly of interest for their listings, and for their free supplements covering events in the area during July and August.

Weeklies of the *Newsweek/Time* model include the wide-ranging and socialist-inclined *Le Nouvel Observateur* (Ⓦwww.nouvelobs.com), its right-wing counterpoint *L'Express* (Ⓦwww.lexpress.fr) and the centrist with bite, *Marianne* (Ⓦwww.marianne-en-ligne.fr). Comprising mainly translated articles, *Courrier International* (Ⓦwww.courrierinternational.com) offers an overview of what's being discussed in the media around the globe. The best investigative journalism is in the weekly satirical paper *Le Canard Enchaîné*, while *Charlie Hebdo* is a sort of *Private Eye* or *Spy Magazine* equivalent. There's also *Paris-Match* (Ⓦwww.parismatch.com) for gossip about stars and royalty. **Monthlies** include the young and trendy *Nova* (Ⓦwww.novaplanet.com), which has good listings of cultural events.

The large number of Brits living in France has also led to an active English-language press in the country. Two monthly newspapers in English are *The Connexion* (Ⓦwww.connexionfrance.com) and the broadsheet *The French Paper* (Ⓦwww.thefrenchpaper.com).

Moral censorship of the press is rare. On the newsstands you'll find pornography of every shade alongside knitting patterns and DIY. The politicisation of the press, however, is becoming an increasingly thorny topic in France, particularly due to President Sarkozy's wide-ranging media connections and apparent influence on many publications. *Libération*, radical but respected, has attracted the wrath of the Sarkozy government, and has been openly attacked for making critical revelations about the president.

Radio

If you've got a **radio**, you can tune into English-language broadcasts. The websites of the BBC (Ⓦwww.bbc.co.uk/worldservice), Radio Canada (Ⓦwww.rcinet.ca) and Voice of America (Ⓦwww.voa.gov) list their world service frequencies around the globe. The French equivalent is Radio France International (RFI; Ⓦwww.rfi.fr), which broadcasts on 89 FM and 738 MW in French and various foreign languages including English. For news in French, there's the state-run France Inter (89.7 FM), Europe 1 (183 LW or various FM frequencies) or round-the-clock news on France Info (105.5 FM).

Television

French terrestrial TV has six channels: three public (France 2, France 3 and Arté/France 5); one subscription (Canal Plus – with some unencrypted programmes); and two commercial (TF1 and M6). Of these, TF1 (Ⓦwww.tf1.fr) and France 2 (Ⓦwww.france2.fr) are the most popular channels, showing a broad mix of programmes. In addition there are any number of cable and satellite channels, which include CNN, BBC World, BBC Prime, Eurosport, MTV, Planète, which specializes in documentaries, Ciné Classics and Jimmy (*Friends*, *The X-Files* and the like in English). The main French-run music channel is MCM. The evening French **news** broadcasts are at 8pm on TF1 and France 2.

Festivals

It's hard to beat the experience of arriving in a small French village, expecting no more than a bed for the night, to discover the streets decked out with flags and streamers, a band playing in the square and the entire population out celebrating the feast of their patron saint. As well as the country-wide Fête de la Musique (June 21) and Bastille Day (July 14), there are any number of festivals – both traditional and of more recent origin – throughout the Dordogne and Lot.

In such dedicated **wine** country, there are inevitably festivals coinciding with the grape harvest, when each village stages its own celebrations. The biggest wine jamboree is Bordeaux's Fête du Vin, which takes place in alternate years, while St-Émilion's Jurade hosts a more stately procession in spring to announce the judging of the new wines and in autumn to kick off the harvest.

The region's cathedrals, churches and châteaux make superb venues for festivals of **music** and **theatre**. All the major towns, and many of the smaller, put on at least one such festival a year, usually in summer, when you can often catch free performances in the streets. Anyone interested in contemporary theatre should make a beeline for Périgueux in early August, when international mime artists gather for Mimos, one of France's most exciting and innovative festivals.

Popular local culture is celebrated in the Félibrée, a festival established in 1903 to promote and safeguard the local *Occitan* (or *Oc*) language and culture. The **Félibrée** takes place on the first Sunday in July, when there is a procession, an *Occitan* Mass and – of course – a blow-out Périgordin meal. Nowadays the celebrations also continue for around ten days either side of the Félibrée itself in the form of folk concerts, crafts demonstrations, theatre and so forth. It takes place in a different town in the Dordogne *département* each year; contact the tourist office in Périgueux for the latest information.

More recent introductions are the **historical spectaculars** held at places such as Castillon-la-Bataille, where the final battle of the Hundred Years' War is re-enacted by hundreds of local thespians. Such events may be touristy, but the atmosphere – most are held at night – and general enthusiasm more than compensate.

For details of the region's most important and interesting festivals, see the boxes at the beginning of each chapter of the Guide.

Sports and outdoor activities

The Dordogne and Lot region offers a wide range of sports, with outdoor activities including hiking, cycling, trekking and waterborne diversions such as canoeing. As for spectator sports, you can watch local teams play big-league sports such as football, but you might find that locally popular games such as rugby are more worthwhile seeking out.

Walking

Walking undoubtedly is the best way to enjoy this region of France. Well-maintained long-distance paths known as *sentiers de grande randonnée*, or simply **GRs**, cut across country, signed with red and white waymarkers and punctuated with campsites and *gîtes d'étapes* (see p.32) at convenient distances. Some of the main routes in the region are the GR6, linking Ste-Foy-la-Grande in the west to Figeac; the GR36, which wanders southeast from Périgueux via Les Eyzies and Cahors to the Gorges de l'Aveyron; and the GR65, the great pilgrimage route passing through Figeac, Cahors and Moissac on the way to Santiago de Compostela in Spain.

The entire GR65 and parts of the GR36 and GR6 are described in a **Topo-guide** (available outside France in good travel bookshops), which gives a detailed account of the route, including maps, campsites, refuges, sources of provisions, etc. In France, the guides are available from bookshops and some tourist offices, or direct from the principal French walkers' organization, the Fédération Française de la Randonnée Pédestre (see p.41 for details).

In addition, many tourist offices produce guides to their local footpaths; where there is no tourist office, try asking at the *mairie*. Particularly noteworthy are the guides produced by Sarlat tourist office detailing walks in the Périgord Noir, and the free pamphlets describing various options in the Gironde. For recommendations on walking **maps**, see p.46.

Cycling

The region's minor roads and demarcated **cycling** routes provide plenty of opportunities for cyclists; it's best to avoid main roads if you want to enjoy yourself, particularly in the high season. Again, many tourist offices can provide details of cycle paths in their area. Among the long distance routes, there's the "Grand Traversée du Périgord" running 180km from Mareuil in the far northwest via Brantôme, Périgueux and Les Eyzies to Monpazier. In the Lot-et-Garonne, the "Véloroute" follows the River Lot 80km from Aiguillon northeast to Fumel and Bonaguil. And in the Gironde a disused railway has been converted into a cycle – and walking – route stretching from just outside Bordeaux to Sauveterre-de-Guyenne in the Entre-Deux-Mers. Even Bordeaux itself has an impressive network of cycle lanes. For more on cycling in France, see p.28. For recommendations on cycling **maps**, see p.46.

Canoeing

Canoeing is hugely popular in the Dordogne and Lot region, and in the summer months every navigable river has outfits renting canoes and organizing excursions. Those along Dordogne itself are the busiest, particularly the stretch between La Roque-Gageac and Beynac, where you pass beneath some of the region's most dramatic castles, and the Vézère, where you can stop off at various points to visit the valley's prehistoric sights. Other, quieter options include the River Lot, through the Aveyron gorges and the smaller Dronne, Dropt and Célé rivers.

You can **rent** two- to three-person canoes and single-seater kayaks on all these rivers; every tourist office also stocks lists of local operators. Although it's possible to rent by the hour, it's best to take at least a half-day and simply cruise downstream. The company you book through will provide transport as required. Prices vary according to what's on offer, but you can expect to pay €15–20 per person for a day's rental.

On the Dordogne and Lot rivers you can make **longer excursions** of up to two weeks, either accompanied or on your own, sometimes in combination with cycling or walking. Various tour operators offer canoeing packages or you can book direct with the local company. Two of the biggest along the Dordogne valley are Canoes Loisirs (ⓣ05.53.28.23.43, ⓦwww.canoes-loisirs.com) and Copeyre Canoë (ⓣ05.65.37.33.51, ⓦwww.copeyre.com), both of which maintain a number of bases between Argentat and Beynac.

The length of the canoeing **season** depends on the weather and the water levels. Successive droughts have caused some rivers almost to dry up in recent summers. Better to come in spring or early summer to be on the safe side. Most operators function daily in July and August, on demand in May, June and September, and close between October and April when the rivers are too high for inexperienced canoeists. One or two, however, stay open throughout the year. All companies are obliged to equip you with lifejackets (*gilets*) and teach you basic safety procedures. You must be able to swim.

Horseriding

Horseriding is an excellent way of enjoying the countryside. Practically every town in the Dordogne and Lot, and many farms, have equestrian centres (*centres équestres*) where you can ride with a guide or unaccompanied – depending on your level of experience – on the marked riding trails that span the region. Local and departmental tourist offices can provide details, or you can contact the Comité National du Tourisme Équestre (overleaf).

Rock climbing and caving

In the limestone regions of the Dordogne and Lot **rock climbing** (*escalade*) and **caving** (*spéléologie*) are popular activities. Several local canoe rental outfits, such as Couleurs Périgord and Kalapaca offer beginners' courses and half-day or full-day outings. Again, further information is available from tourist offices or the appropriate national federation.

Swimming

There are several pebbly beaches which give access to the water along the Dordogne and Lot rivers, but it's often too shallow or fast-flowing to be ideal for **swimming**. An alternative is to head for one of the real or artificial lakes, which pepper the region. Many have leisure centres (*bases de plein airs*) at which you can rent pedaloes, windsurfers and dinghies, as well as larger boats and jet-skis (on the bigger reservoirs). It's worth noting, however, that in high summer, when the water is at its lowest, pollution warnings have been issued on rivers and lakes in the region. Check with local tourist authorities for the current situation. Many hotels and campsites also have their own swimming pools for guests to make use of. One thing to be aware of is that some impose strict rules on what sort of swimming costumes can and can't be worn: for men, long or baggy swimming shorts are often outlawed.

Football and rugby

By far the most prominent **football** team in the region is Bordeaux's **FC Girondins** (ⓦwww.girondins.com), whose home ground is Stade Chaban-Delmas, in the city's southwestern suburbs. Illustrious players such as Zidane, Deschamps, Wiltord and Lizarazu – all members of France's winning 1998 World Cup squad – all played for Bordeaux at one time or another. 2009 was a particularly successful year for the club, under the inspiration of France's World Cup-winning captain, Laurent Blanc. Tickets to see the Girondins start at just €10, going up to €50 for the best seats in the ground.

Despite the influence of France's footballing prowess, **rugby** remains the most important and closely followed field game throughout this region. In season (mid-September to mid-May) virtually every town worth its salt boasts a team and if you go along to a match you'll soon get swept up in the camaraderie; unless it's a final, tickets are easy to buy at the gate and are reasonably priced (around €15). The top teams to look out for are Brive and Montauban, who both play in the First Divison (Top 14) and attract international players. Bordeaux, represented by Stade Bordelais, and Agen rank in the Second Division (Pro D2).

Boules

Once the preserve of elderly men in berets, **boules**, and its variant *pétanque* (in which contestants must keep both feet on the ground when throwing), has been growing in popularity in recent years and broadening its appeal to include more young people and women. There is even a world championship and talk – not all of it in jest – of getting *boules* recognised as an Olympic sport.

National sports federations

Canoeing Ⓦ www.ffck.org.
Caving Ⓦ www.ffspeleo.fr.
Cycling Ⓦ www.ffct.org.
Golf Ⓦ www.ffg.org.
Riding Ⓦ www.ffe.com.
Rock climbing Ⓦ www.ffme.fr.
Walking Ⓦ www.ffrandonnee.fr.

Shopping and markets

The quickest and most convenient places to shop are the hypermarkets and supermarkets you'll find in and around every major town. Even some villages have a "superette". But more interesting by far are the specialist food shops and, of course, the markets which are still held at least once a week in towns throughout the region.

Many of these **markets** have been held on the same day for centuries. One of the region's biggest and best is that at Sarlat, but the competition is fierce and it's worth including several market days in your itinerary. In recent years the hordes of visitors in summer have meant an inevitable increase in the volume of generic tack sold at the biggest markets, but they still boast more than enough enticing local produce and genuine craftsmanship to be unmissable.

In winter time, you'll also find most towns in the Dordogne and Lot hold *marchés aux gras* when whole fattened livers of duck and goose are put up for sale alongside the other edible bits of the fowl. Often these events double up as truffle markets and are one of the few places in France where **bargaining** is acceptable. For a list of the region's most important and interesting markets, see the boxes at the beginning of each chapter of the Guide.

Boutiques in Bordeaux and the other main towns are good for **clothes** and shoe shopping and also for perfumes and cosmetics.

Travel essentials

Costs

Although prices have been rising steadily in recent years, the Dordogne and Lot is not an outrageously expensive place to visit, at least compared to the rest of northern Europe, largely because of the relatively low cost of accommodation and eating out. When and where you go, however, will make a difference: in prime tourist spots hotel prices can go up by a third during July and August.

Average costs

For a reasonably comfortable existence, including a double room in a mid-range hotel, a light restaurant lunch and a proper restaurant dinner, plus moving around, café stops and museum visits, you need to allow around €100/£90/US$135 a day per person. But by counting the pennies, staying at youth hostels or camping, and being strong-willed about extra cups of coffee and doses of culture, you could manage on €50/£45/US$70 a day each, to include a cheap restaurant meal. It's possible to survive on less, by living off street snacks and not doing much, but you'd be missing out on a lot of what the region has to offer.

Youth and student discounts

Once obtained, various official and quasi-official youth/student ID cards soon pay for themselves in savings. Full-time students are eligible for the **International Student ID Card** (ISIC; Ⓦwww.isic.org or www.isiccard.com), which entitles the bearer to special air, rail and bus fares and discounts at museums, theatres and other attractions. It also gives you access to a free 24-hour helpline to call in the event of a medical or legal emergency. You have to be 26 or under to qualify for the **International Youth Travel Card**, while teachers are eligible for the **International Teacher Card**, offering similar discounts. They are available through universities and student travel specialists such as STA Travel, USIT and Travel CUTS.

Taxes

The majority of goods and services in France are subject to **value added tax** (*taxe sur la valeur ajoutée* or *TVA* in French), usually at a rate of 19.6 percent, which is included in the price. Most local authorities also levy a **tourism tax** on hotel and *chambre d'hôte* accommodation – called a *taxe de séjour* – generally not more than €1 per person per night depending on the category; in some areas this tax only applies in peak season. While the tax is not included in room rates, it must be clearly indicated as a separate item.

Crime and personal safety

In the more rural parts of the Dordogne and Lot region crime is extremely rare. However, petty theft is a problem in Bordeaux and, to a lesser extent, in other major towns; you should also be careful in crowds, especially during festivals. In urban areas and at prime tourist spots cars with foreign number plates also face a high risk of break-ins. Vehicles are rarely stolen, but luggage makes a tempting target.

It obviously makes sense to take the normal **precautions**: don't flash wads of notes around; carry your bag or wallet securely; never leave cameras, mobile phones or other valuables lying around; and park your car overnight in a monitored parking, garage or, at the very least, on a busy and well-lit street. It's wise to keep a separate record of cheque and credit card numbers, and the phone numbers for cancelling them. Finally, make sure you have a good insurance policy (see p.45).

There are two main types of **police** in France – the Police Nationale and the Gendarmerie Nationale. The former deals with all crime, parking and traffic affairs within large and mid-sized towns, where you will find them in the Commissariat de Police. The Gendarmerie Nationale covers the rural areas.

Emergency numbers

Police ⓣ17; Ambulance ⓣ15; Fire ⓣ18. Or call ⓣ112 for all emergencies.

If you need to **report a theft**, go to the local Gendarmerie or Commissariat de Police (addresses of commissariats are given in the Guide for the major towns), where they will fill out a *constat de vol*. The first thing they'll ask for is your passport, and vehicle documents if relevant. Although the police are not always as cooperative as they might be, it is their duty to assist you if you've lost your passport or all your money.

If you have an **accident** while driving, you must fill in and sign a *constat d'accident* (declaration form) or, if another car is also involved, a *constat aimable* (jointly agreed declaration); these forms should be provided with the car's insurance documents. The police can impose on-the-spot fines for minor **driving offences** and take away your licence for anything more serious (see p.27 for more).

Drugs

Drug use is just as prevalent in France as anywhere else in Europe – and just as risky. People caught smuggling or possessing drugs, even just a few grams of marijuana, are liable to find themselves in jail. Should you be **arrested** on any charge, you have the right to contact your consulate, though don't expect much sympathy.

Racism

Unfortunately, **racist attitudes** are not uncommon in France, particularly towards the country's Arab and black communities. Visitors to the Dordogne and Lot are extremely unlikely to experience any aggression or open hostility, but may encounter an unwelcome degree of curiosity or suspicion from shopkeepers, hoteliers, bar and club owners and the like. The police in Bordeaux and the larger towns such as Périgueux and Montauban may demand to see your papers or even to search you. Carrying your passport at all times is a good idea.

If you suffer a **racial assault**, contact the police, your consulate or one of the local anti-racism organizations (though they may not have English-speakers): SOS Racism (29 rue Bergeret, 33000 Bordeaux; ⓣ05.56.31.94.62, Ⓦwww.sos-racisme.org); and Mouvement contre le Racisme et pour l'Amitié entre les Peuples (MRAP; Paris ⓣ01.53.38.99.99, Ⓦwww.mrap.asso.fr).

Electricity

The **electricity** supply in France is almost always 220V, using plugs with two round pins. If you need a transformer, it's a good idea to buy one before leaving home, though you can find them in big department stores.

Entry requirements

Citizens of European Union (EU) countries can travel freely in France, while those from Australia, Canada, New Zealand and the United States, among other countries, do not need a visa for a stay of up to ninety days. However, the situation can change and it's advisable to check with your nearest French embassy or consulate before departure.

All non-EU citizens who plan to remain longer than ninety days should apply for a **long-stay visa**, for which you will have to show proof of – among other things – a regular income or sufficient funds to support yourself and medical insurance. For further information about visa regulations consult the Ministry of Foreign Affairs website: Ⓦwww.diplomatie.gouv.fr.

The website Ⓦwww.embassyworld.com has a list of embassies and consulates in France.

Gay and lesbian travellers

In general, France is more liberal on homosexuality than many other European countries. The legal age of consent is 16 and civil unions between same-sex couples were made legal in 1999. That said, gay couples are not allowed to adopt children and same-sex marriages remain illegal. In 2004 Noël Mamère, the controversial mayor of Bègles, near Bordeaux, created quite a furor by conducting the country's first gay marriage. The courts annulled it the following year, but an active movement is nevertheless building behind the campaign for gay marriages to be permitted.

On a day-to-day level, the French mostly consider sexuality to be a private matter and homophobic assaults are extremely rare. In the Dordogne and Lot region there's a thriving gay and lesbian community in Bordeaux and smaller groups in Cahors and in other towns and cities. Nevertheless, **gays** tend to be discreet outside specific gay venues, parades and the prime gay areas of Bordeaux. **Lesbians** tend to be extremely discreet. You can expect to be received with tolerance, but not necessarily a warm welcome.

Useful contacts

Dykeplanet Ⓦ**www.dykeplanet.com.** Sells *Le dykeGuide*, a French-language guidebook (€13) published annually and aimed at lesbians primarily. Available at FNAC stores and major booksellers or from the publishers.

France Gay et Lesbien Ⓦ**www.petitfute.com.** Annual, French-language guidebook (€18) published by Petit Futé. Available at FNAC stores and major booksellers or from the publishers.

Spartacus International Gay Guide Ⓦ**www.spartacusworld.com.** Has an extensive section on France and contains some info for lesbians.

Têtu Ⓦ**www.tetu.com.** France's best-selling gay/lesbian magazine, with events listings and contact addresses; you can buy it in bookshops, newsagents or through their website, which is also an excellent source of information.

Health

Visitors to the Lot and Dordogne region have little to worry about as far as health is concerned. No vaccinations are required, there are no nasty diseases to be wary of and tap water is safe to drink. The worst that's likely to happen is a case of sunburn or an upset stomach from eating too much rich food – or a hangover from all that wonderful wine. If you do need treatment, however, you should be in good hands: the French healthcare system is rated one of the best in the world.

Under the French health system, all services, including doctor's consultations, prescribed medicines, hospital stays and ambulance call-outs, incur a charge which you have to pay upfront. **EU citizens** are entitled to a refund (usually between 70 and 100 percent) of medical and dental expenses, providing the doctor is government registered (*un médecin conventionné*) and provided you have a European Health Insurance Card (EHIC; *Carte Européenne d'Assurance Maladie*). Note that everyone in the family, including children, must have their own card, which are free. In the UK you can apply for them online through the Department of Health website (Ⓦwww.dh.gov.uk), by phone (Ⓣ0845/606 2030) or by post – forms are available from post offices. Even with the EHIC card, however, you might want to take out some additional insurance to cover the shortfall. A stay in hospital, for example, can still leave you with a hefty bill. All **non-EU visitors** should ensure they have adequate medical insurance cover.

For minor complaints go to a **pharmacie**, signalled by an illuminated green cross. You'll find at least one in every small town and even some villages. They keep normal shop hours (roughly Mon–Sat 9am–noon & 3–6/7pm), though some stay open late and, in larger towns, at least one (known as the *pharmacie de garde*) is open 24 hours according to a rota; details are displayed in all pharmacy windows.

For anything more serious you can get the name of a **doctor** from a pharmacy, local police station, tourist office or your hotel. Alternatively, look under "Médecins" in the Yellow Pages (*Pages Jaunes*) phone directory. The consultation fee is in the region of €21–25. You'll be given a statement of treatment (*Feuille de Soins*) for later insurance claims. Any prescriptions will be fulfilled by a pharmacy and must be paid for; little price stickers (*vignettes*) from each medicine will be stuck on the *Feuille de Soins*.

In serious **emergencies** you will always be admitted to the nearest general hospital (*centre hospitalier*). Phone numbers and addresses are given in the Guide for all the main cities. The national number for calling an ambulance is Ⓣ15.

Insurance

Even though EU citizens are entitled to health care privileges in France, it's advisable

Rough Guides travel insurance

Rough Guides has teamed up with WorldNomads.com to offer great **travel insurance** deals. Policies are available to residents of over 150 countries, with cover for a wide range of **adventure sports**, 24hr emergency assistance, high levels of medical and evacuation cover and a stream of **travel safety information**. Roughguides.com users can take advantage of their policies online 24/7, from anywhere in the world – even if you're already travelling. And since plans often change when you're on the road, you can extend your policy and even claim online. Roughguides.com users who buy travel insurance with WorldNomads.com can also leave a positive footprint and donate to a community development project. For more information go to Ⓦ**www.roughguides.com/shop**.

to take out an insurance policy before travelling to cover against theft, loss and illness or injury. Before paying for a new policy, however, it's worth checking whether you are already covered: some all-risks home insurance policies may cover your possessions when overseas, and many private medical schemes include cover when abroad. In Canada, provincial health plans usually provide partial cover for medical mishaps overseas. Students will often find that their student health coverage extends during the vacations and for one term beyond the date of last enrolment.

A typical **travel insurance policy** usually provides cover for the cost of medical treatment and damage caused by accidents, as well as cancellation or curtailment of your journey. Cover for lost or stolen cash, cheques and possessions usually costs a little extra. Most policies exclude so-called dangerous sports unless an extra premium is paid: in the Dordogne and Lot this would include rock climbing and pot-holing and sometimes such apparently benign activities as canoeing, so it's best to check the small print carefully. Many policies can be chopped and changed to exclude coverage you don't need.

If you need to **make a claim**, you should keep receipts for medicines and medical treatment, and in the event you have anything stolen, you must obtain an official statement from the police (called *un constat de vol*).

Laundry

Laundries are still reasonably common in French towns – just ask in your hotel, or the tourist office, or look in the phone book under "*Laveries automatiques*" or "*Laveries en libre-service*". They are usually unattended, and whilst some have machines for changing notes, it's prudent to come armed with small change. Washing powder (*la lessive*) is always available on site. Machines are graded in different wash sizes, costing in the region of €4 to €5 for 7kg. Most hotels forbid doing any laundry in your room, though you should get away with just one or two small items.

Mail

French **post offices**, known as La Poste and identified by bright yellow-and-blue signs, are generally open from around 9am to 5pm or 6pm Monday to Friday, and 9am to noon on Saturday. Those in smaller towns and villages usually also close from noon to 2pm.

You can receive mail using the **poste restante** system available at the central post office in every town. It should be addressed (preferably with the surname first and in capitals) "Poste Restante, Poste Centrale", followed by the name of the town and its postcode. You'll need your passport to collect your mail and will have to pay €0.56 per item. Mail is only kept for two weeks.

Stamps (*timbres*) are sold at *tabacs* and newsagents as well as post offices. For information on postal rates, among other things, log on to the post office website Ⓦwww.laposte.fr.

You can also change money at post offices, send faxes and do photocopying. To post your letter on the street, look for the bright yellow **postboxes** – make sure, where necessary, to put your letter in the box marked "étranger" (abroad).

Maps

In addition to the **maps** in this guide and the various free town plans you'll be offered along the way, the one extra map you might want is a good, up-to-date road map of the region. The best are the regional maps produced by Michelin (1:300,000) and IGN (1:250,000; ⓦwww.ign.fr). In both cases you'll need to buy three maps (Aquitaine, Midi-Pyrénées and Auvergne-Limousin) to cover the entire area encompassed by the Guide. Alternatively, both companies issue large spiral-bound road atlases covering the whole of France at around the same scale.

If you're planning to walk or cycle, it's well worth investing in the more detailed IGN maps. The Carte de Randonnée (1:25,000) series is specifically designed for walkers, while the Carte de Promenade (1:100,000) is ideal for cyclists.

Money

France's currency is the **euro** (€), which is divided into 100 cents (also called *centimes*). There are seven notes – in denominations of 5, 10, 20, 50, 100, 200 and 500 euros – and eight different coins: 1, 2, 5, 10, 20 and 50 cents, and 1 and 2 euros.

At the time of writing **exchange rates** were somewhat volatile but stood at around €1.10 to the pound, €0.73 to the US dollar, €0.63 to the Canadian dollar, €0.56 to the Australian dollar, €0.45 to the New Zealand dollar and €0.10 to the South African rand. For the most up-to-date exchange rates for these and other currencies, consult ⓦwww.xe.com.

The best way to access money in France is to use your **credit** or **debit card** to withdraw cash from an **ATM** (known as *un distributeur de billets* or *un point argent*); most machines give instructions in several European languages. Note that there is often a transaction fee, so it's more efficient to take out a sizeable sum each time rather than making lots of small withdrawals.

Credit and debit cards are also widely accepted in shops, hotels and restaurants, though some smaller establishments don't accept cards, or only for sums above a certain threshold. Visa – called Carte Bleue in France – is almost universally recognized, followed by MasterCard (also known as EuroCard). American Express ranks a bit lower.

You can **change cash** at most banks and main post offices, though only the latter will change traveller's cheques. There are money-exchange counters (*bureaux de change*) at French airports, major train stations and usually one or two in city centres as well, though they don't always offer the best exchange rates.

Opening hours and public holidays

Basic **hours of business** are 9am to noon and 2pm to 6pm. Many shops and other businesses in Bordeaux stay open throughout the day, as do most tourist offices and museums throughout the region in July and August. Otherwise, almost everything closes for a couple of hours at midday, sometimes longer. Small food shops often don't reopen till halfway through the afternoon, closing around 7.30pm or 8pm, just before the evening meal. Supermarkets also tend to stay open to at least 7pm.

The standard **closing day** is Sunday, though some food shops, particularly bakeries (boulangeries), and newsagents are open in the morning. Some shops and businesses, particularly in the rural areas, also close on a Monday.

Core **banking hours** are Monday to Friday 9am to noon and 2 to 4.30pm. Some

Public holidays

January 1 New Year's Day
March/April Easter Monday
Ascension Day (forty days after Easter)
Pentecost or Whitsun (seventh Sunday after Easter)
May 1 Labour Day
May 8 Victory in Europe (VE) Day 1945
July 14 Bastille Day
August 15 Assumption of the Virgin Mary
November 1 All Saints' Day
November 11 Armistice Day 1918
December 25 Christmas Day

branches close on Monday, while others stay open at midday and may also open on Saturday morning. All are closed on Sunday and public holidays (see box opposite).

Museums tend to open around 9 or 10am, close for lunch from noon until 2pm or 3pm, and then run through to 5pm or 6pm. In summer some stay open all day and close later. Museum closing days are usually Monday or Tuesday, sometimes both. Many state-owned museums have one day of the week or month when they're free or half price.

Churches are generally open from around 8am to dusk, but may close at lunchtime and are reserved for worshippers during services (times of which will usually be posted on the door). Country churches are increasingly kept locked; there may be a note on the door saying where to get the key, usually from the priest's house (*le presbytère*) or someone else living nearby, or from the *mairie*.

France celebrates eleven **public holidays** (*jours fériés*), when banks and most shops and businesses (though not necessarily restaurants), and some museums, are closed.

Telephones

You can make domestic and international **phone calls** from any telephone box (*une cabine*) and can also receive calls – look for the number in the top right-hand corner of the information panel. The vast majority of public phones require a **phone card** (*une télécarte*), available from *tabacs* and newsagents; they come in 50 and 120 units (€7.50 and €15 respectively). You can also use **credit cards** in many call boxes.

Alternatively, you can pick up one of the many phone cards (*cartes téléphoniques*) that operate with a unique **code** on sale at post offices, *tabacs*, newsagents and many supermarkets, which can be used from both public and private phones. At the time of writing, Symacom (Ⓦwww.symacom.fr) gave the best rates and quality of service with its "Continental" cards priced at €7.50 and €15. Note, though, that you pay a substantial charge on each connection, so these are only good value for a couple of long calls, not for many short ones.

French **telephone numbers** have ten digits. Numbers beginning with Ⓣ080 are free-dial numbers; those beginning Ⓣ081 and Ⓣ086 are charged as a local call; anything else beginning Ⓣ08 is premium-rated. Numbers starting Ⓣ06 are mobile numbers and therefore also expensive to call.

Mobile phones

If you want to use your **mobile/cell phone** in France, contact your phone provider before leaving home to check whether it will work locally, and what the call charges are – they tend to be pretty exorbitant, and remember that you're likely to be charged extra for incoming calls.

French mobile phones operate on the European GSM standard, so many **US cellphones** won't work in France unless they are "tri-band". The quickest and cheapest option is probably to change your phone and/or service provider.

If you're going to be in France more than just a couple of weeks and making a lot of local calls, it may be worth buying a French **SIM card** and a prepaid phone card. For this you'd have to make sure your phone is

Calling home from abroad

Note that the initial zero is omitted from the area code when dialling the UK, Ireland, Australia and New Zealand from abroad.

Australia international access code + 61
New Zealand international access code + 64
UK international access code + 44
US and Canada international access code + 1
Republic of Ireland international access code + 353
South Africa international access code + 27

"unlocked", in other words it will work with other providers. Again, you'll get a local number. You can buy the kits (upwards of €15 for a starter kit including a SIM card and around €5 worth of calls credited to your account) in France at one of the high street shops run by the three main French operators, the largest of which are Orange and SFR, followed by Bouygues Télécom.

Smoking

Smoking is banned in all enclosed public spaces, including museums, restaurants, bars and nightclubs.

Time

France lies in the **Central European Time Zone** (GMT+1). This means it is one hour ahead of the UK, six hours ahead of Eastern Standard Time, and nine hours ahead of Pacific Standard Time. Between April and October France is eight hours behind eastern Australia and ten hours behind New Zealand; from November to March it is ten hours behind southeastern Australia and twelve hours behind New Zealand. Daylight Saving Time (GMT+2) in France lasts from the last Sunday of March to the last Sunday of October.

Tipping

Hotels and almost all restaurants include a **service charge** of fifteen percent in their prices (*service compris*). It's therefore not necessary to leave an additional cash **tip** at restaurants unless you feel you have received service out of the ordinary; if so, an extra two or three percent is plenty. It's customary to tip porters, tour guides and taxi drivers one or two euros, and to leave the small change at cafés.

Tourist information

The French Government Tourist Office (Maison de la France, Ⓦwww.franceguide.com) increasingly refers you to their website for information, though they still produce a number of useful brochures, alongside stock items such as the Logis book (see p.31). For information specific to the Dordogne and Lot region, contact the regional or departmental tourist offices (see opposite) before you leave home.

Tourist offices

In the Dordogne and Lot region you'll find a tourist office – usually an **Office du Tourisme** (OT) but sometimes a **Syndicat d'Initiative** (SI) – in practically every town and many villages (addresses, contact details and opening hours are detailed in the Guide). For the practical purposes of visitors, there is little difference between them; sometimes they share premises and call themselves an OTSI. In small villages where there is no OT or SI, the *mairie* (town hall) will offer a similar service.

All these offices can provide specific local information, including listings of hotels and restaurants, leisure activities, bike rental, bus times, markets, laundries and countless other things; many can also book accommodation for you. If asked, most offices will provide a town plan (for which you may be charged a nominal sum), and many will have maps and local walking guides on sale. In Bordeaux and the larger towns you can usually also pick up free events guides or at least a list of summer festivals, while those in the wine regions will additionally provide information on local vineyards, and in peak season may also conduct vineyard tours.

Regional and departmental tourist offices

Aquitaine Ⓣ05.56.01.70.00, Ⓦwww.tourisme-aquitaine.info.
Aveyron Ⓣ05.65.75.55.75, Ⓦwww.tourisme-aveyron.com.
Corrèze Ⓣ05.55.29.98.78, Ⓦwww.vacances-en-correze.net.
Dordogne Ⓣ05.53.35.50.24, Ⓦwww.dordogne-perigord-tourisme.fr.
Gironde Ⓣ05.56.52.61.40, Ⓦwww.tourisme-gironde.fr.
Lot Ⓣ05.65.35.07.09, Ⓦwww.tourisme-lot.com.
Lot-et-Garonne Ⓣ05.53.66.14.14, Ⓦwww.tourisme-lotetgaronne.com.
Midi-Pyrénées Ⓣ05.61.13.55.48, Ⓦwww.tourisme-midi-pyrenees.com.
Tarn-et-Garonne Ⓣ05.63.21.79.09, Ⓦwww.tourisme-tarnetgaronne.com.

Government websites

Australian Department of Foreign Affairs Ⓦwww.dfat.gov.au, Ⓦwww.smartraveller.gov.au.

British Foreign & Commonwealth Office Ⓦwww.fco.gov.uk.
Canadian Department of Foreign Affairs Ⓦwww.international.gc.ca
Irish Department of Foreign Affairs Ⓦwww.foreignaffairs.gov.ie.
New Zealand Ministry of Foreign Affairs Ⓦwww.mft.govt.nz.
US State Department Ⓦwww.travel.state.gov.
South African Department of Foreign Affairs Ⓦwww.dfa.gov.za

Travellers with disabilities

The French authorities have been making a concerted effort to improve facilities for disabled travellers. Though haphazard parking habits and stepped village streets remain serious obstacles for anyone with mobility problems, ramps and other forms of access are gradually being added to hotels, museums and other public buildings. All but the oldest hotels are required to adapt at least one room to be wheelchair accessible, and a growing number of *chambres d'hôtes* are doing likewise. Accessible hotels, sights and other facilities are gradually being inspected and, if they fulfil certain criteria, issued with a "Tourisme & Handicap" certificate.

Most **train stations** now make provision for travellers with reduced mobility. Spaces for wheelchairs are available in first-class carriages of all **TGVs** for the price of the regular, second-class fare; note that these must be booked in advance. For other trains, a wheelchair symbol in the timetable indicates services offering special on-board facilities, though it's best to double-check when booking. SNCF also runs a scheme called Accès Plus, through which they assist travellers with disabilities, as long as you get in contact with them 48 hours in advance. Full details are in the free booklet *Accès Plus* or on the website Ⓦwww.accesplus.sncf.com.

Drivers of **taxis** are legally obliged to help passengers in and out of the vehicle and to carry guide dogs. Specially adapted taxis can be arranged in Bordeaux through Mobibus (Ⓣ05.56.16.61.66, Ⓦwww.mobibus.fr) as long as you give at least a week's notice. Elsewhere, such services are generally only available to local residents, but ask at the local tourist office or *mairie* for further information. All the big **car rental** agencies can provide automatic cars if you reserve sufficiently far in advance, while Hertz offers cars with hand controls on request – again, make sure you give them plenty of notice.

As for finding suitable **accommodation**, listings produced by Logis (see p.31) and Gîtes de France (see p.31) indicate places with specially adapted rooms. It's essential to double check when booking that the facilities meet your needs.

If you can read French, there are some other excellent guides to make use of. The association Vacances Accessibles, La Borde Rouge, 46150 La Bastide du Vert (Ⓣ06.13.72.86.20, Ⓔdupirejonathan@yahoo.fr, Ⓦwww.handiplage.fr) can provide the outstanding **guidebook**, *Le Guide de Globe Roller; Voyages Accessible dans le Lot* (2006), by local resident and wheelchair user Jonathan Dupire. It details accessible accommodation, transport, attractions and other tourist facilities graded according to the level of mobility. The same organisation also produces a booklet called *Handi-plus Aquitaine*, which outlines suitable itineraries across the whole region. *Handitourisme*, published annually by Petit Futé (Ⓦwww.petitfute.com) covers the whole of France.

For general **information** about accessibility, special programmes and discounts contact one of the organizations listed below before you leave home.

Contacts for travellers with disabilities

Access Tourisme Service 8 rue St-Loup, 45130 Charsonville Ⓣ02.38.74.28.40, Ⓦwww.access-tourisme.com. Organised and customized holidays for people with special needs including adapted vehicle rental, accessible hotels and even travel companions if required.

Access Travel 6 The Hillock, Astley, Lancashire M29 7GW Ⓣ01942/888 844, Ⓦwww.access-travel.co.uk. Tour operator that can arrange flights, transfer and accommodation. This is a small business, personally checking out places before recommendation.

Accessible Journeys 35 West Sellers Ave, Ridley Park, PA 19078 Ⓣ1-800/846-4537 or 610-521-6959, Ⓦwww.disabilitytravel.com. Well-established travel agent offering both group tours and advice on independent travel for disabled travellers.

APF (Association des Paralysés de France) 17 bd Auguste Blanqui, 75013 Paris ⓣ01.40.78.69.00, ⓦwww.apf.asso.fr. National association that can answer general enquiries and put you in touch with their departmental offices.

Work and study in Dordogne and the Lot

EU citizens are free to work in France on the same basis as a French citizen. This means you don't have to apply for a residence or work permit except in very rare cases – contact your nearest French consulate for further information. **Non-EU citizens**, however, will need a work permit (*autorisation de travail*) and a residence permit; again contact your nearest French consulate or, if already in France, your local *mairie* or *préfecture* to check what rules apply in your particular situation. Whatever your nationality, once you have a work permit, you are entitled to exactly the same conditions as French workers, including the national **minimum wage** (SMIC), currently set at €8.71 per hour.

When **looking for a job**, a good starting point is to read one of the books on working abroad published by Vacation Work (ⓦwww.vacationwork.co.uk). You could also try the websites ⓦwww.monster.fr and www.jobs-ete.com, which focuses on summer jobs for students. Once in France, you'll find "Offres d'Emploi" (Job Offers) in the national and regional papers, while the Centre Régional d'Information Jeunesse Aquitaine in Bordeaux (see p.64) has information about temporary jobs in the region. The national employment agency, pôle emploi (ⓦwww.pole-emploi.fr), with offices all over France, advertises temporary jobs in all fields. Non-EU citizens will have to show a work permit to apply for any of their jobs.

A degree and a TEFL (Teaching English as a Foreign Language) or similar qualifications are normally required for **English-language teaching** posts. The *E L Gazette Guide to English Language Teaching Around the World* (ⓦwww.elgazette.com; latest edition 2005) provides lists of schools and other practical information. The same company also publishes the monthly *E L Gazette*, which carries some job advertisements. Other useful resources are *Teaching English Abroad*, published by Vacation Work, and the TEFL website ⓦwww.tefl.com.

Foreign students pay the same as French nationals to enrol for a course and you'll be eligible for subsidized accommodation, meals and all the student reductions. French **universities** are fairly informal, but there are strict entry requirements, including an exam in French, for undergraduate degrees, but not for postgraduate courses. For full details and prospectuses, contact the Cultural Service of any French embassy or consulate.

Embassies and consulates can also provide details of **language courses** at French universities and colleges, which are often combined with lectures on French "civilization" and usually very costly. Numerous private language schools also offer French language courses, particularly in Bordeaux, which are often cheaper than those run by the universities.

Further contacts

AFS Intercultural Programs ⓦwww.afs.org. Opportunities for high-school students to study in France for a term or full academic year, living with host families.

Alliance Française ⓦwww.alliance-bordeaux.org.

Campus France ⓦwww.campusfrance.org. Government-run agency set up to promote French higher education abroad.

Erasmus ⓦwww.british-council.org/erasmus or contact their university's international office. EU-run student exchange programme enabling students at participating universities in Britain and Ireland to study in one of 31 European countries. Grants available for three months to a full academic year.

Language Courses Abroad ⓦwww.languagesabroad.co.uk.

WWOOF ⓦwww.wwoof.fr. Volunteer to work on an organic farm in return for board and lodging.

Guide

Guide

1

Bordeaux and its vineyards

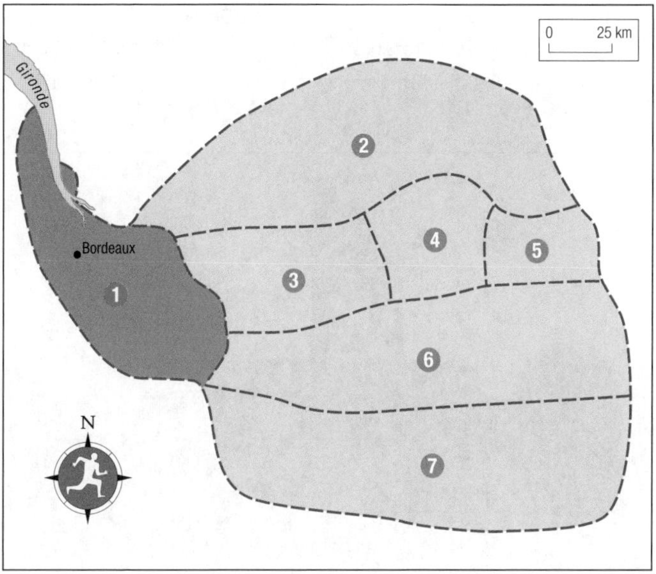

CHAPTER 1

Highlights

* **Bordeaux** Lively, stylish city whose wealth of elegant eighteenth-century architecture takes some beating. **See p.57**
* **Médoc vineyards** Explore the vineyards that produce some of the world's most famous wines. **See p.82**
* **Sauternes** Sample the sweet Sauternes wine evocatively described as "bottled sunshine". **See p.96**
* **Château de Roquetaillade** One of the region's most impressive and well-preserved fortresses features fairy-tale interiors. **See p.100**
* **Entre-deux-Mers** Its rolling hills dotted with Romanesque churches, this is without doubt the prettiest of Bordeaux's wine regions. **See p.101**
* **La Sauve-Majeure** Twelfth-century sculptors illustrated biblical stories in engaging detail on the capitals of this semi-ruined abbey church. **See p.101**
* **St-Émilion** Although best known for its wine, the town of St-Émilion has enough of beauty and interest to attract a wider audience than wine-lovers. **See p.111**

▲ The ruins of La Sauve-Majeure

1

Bordeaux and its vineyards

France's second largest Atlantic port, **Bordeaux**, is at heart a trading city, built on revenues from wine exports and from the expansion of colonial trade in the eighteenth century. The legacy of this wealth is a city centre dignified by grand avenues, civic monuments and graceful rows of townhouses. For many, the architecture alone provides sufficient attraction but Bordeaux also boasts several rewarding museums, any number of superb restaurants and a thriving cultural and nightlife scene. It is also the area's principal administrative centre – capital of both the Aquitaine *région* and the Gironde *département* – and, with its European air services and good train connections, a major gateway to the Dordogne and Lot region.

Before setting off into the Dordogne heartland, however, there are the Bordeaux **vineyards** – one of the world's foremost wine-producing regions – to explore. Neatly tended rows of vines stretch down the Médoc peninsula in the north and then south and east of Bordeaux along the Garonne and Dordogne valleys for more than fifty kilometres. The northern peninsula is the place to start. The countryside may not be the most enticing – the **Médoc** vineyards are flat and monotonous – but the châteaux – Margaux, Palmer, Mouton-Rothschild and Lafite – are world-famous, and there are also any number of lesser-known producers to visit. Some have established wine-related museums as an added attraction. Just across the estuary at **Blaye**, the wines remain good, if cheaper, and the citadelle is worth a visit in its own right. Médoc wines are mostly reds, while to the southeast of Bordeaux the **Graves** is also known for its dry white wines and the **Sauternes** for sweet, golden-coloured whites, some of which, such as those of Château d'Yquem, are amongst the most highly sought-after wines in the world. There are, however, a couple of non-wine-related diversions in the region as well: the moated fourteenth-century **Château de la Brède**, home of the philosopher Montesquieu, and in the very south of the region the **Château de Roquetaillade**. Although dating from the same period, the latter is of particular interest for its exuberant late-nineteenth-century makeover by architect Viollet-le-Duc.

Heading north across the Garonne from the Sauternes, the **Entre-Deux-Mers** may not be the most prestigious of Bordeaux's wine regions but it is by far and away the prettiest. The vineyards here are interspersed with pasture, orchards and woodland across rolling hills topped with sun-soaked villages. Many of these settlements, such as the well-preserved **Sauveterre-de-Guyenne** and

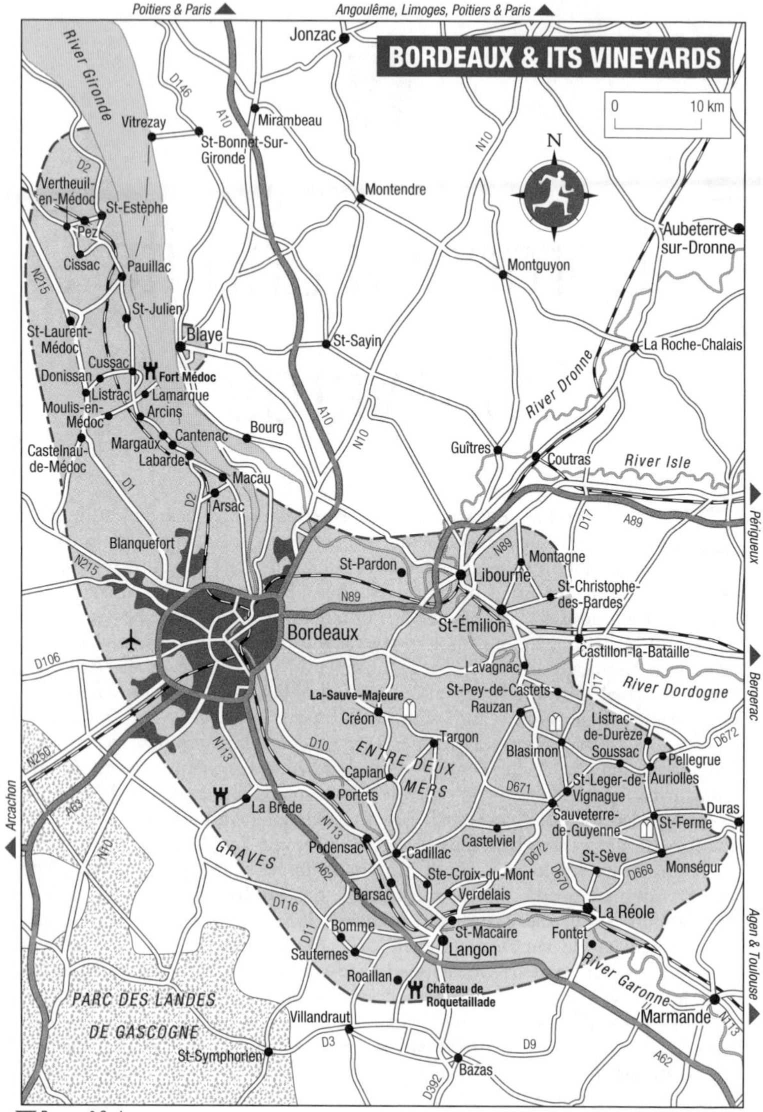

Monségur, are *bastides*, medieval new-towns built on a strict grid-pattern around a central market square (see box, p.306). The Entre-Deux-Mers is also home to a number of once-wealthy abbeys in various states of ruin. The best is the twelfth-century **La Sauve-Majeure**, in the west of the region, where fragments of wall shelter the most beautiful array of carved capitals.

Religion and wine come together again in **St-Émilion**, north of the Entre-Deux-Mers. The enchanting wine-town sits on a south-facing slope overlooking the Dordogne valley, a huddle of grey-white houses, towers and spires encircled by vines. St-Émilion largely owes its existence – and certainly its name – to an eighth-century hermit whose cave, and the vast subterranean church next door, now provide the town's most compelling sights. Not forgetting, of course, the surrounding wine châteaux.

The Bordeaux region is relatively well covered by **public transport**. There are train services along the Garonne and Dordogne valleys, though the latter is rather sporadic, and a branch line north through the Médoc. Rather more comprehensive are the buses, though here, too, services are being cut back all the time. Some routes duplicate the trains, while others cut across country to places such as Sauveterre-de-Guyenne, Monségur and La Sauve. If you intend to use the buses a lot, pick up a Trans-Gironde route-map and the relevant timetables from the Tbc information booth in Bordeaux (see p.65). That said, to make the most of the region, and particularly when it comes to visiting the vineyards, you will need your own transport. Renting a car is the obvious solution, but **cycling** is also an option. Outside Bordeaux, the backroads are pleasant to cycle on and the departmental authorities have established a number of dedicated cycle paths, of which the most useful is that from Bordeaux to Sauveterre in the Entre-Deux-Mers.

Bordeaux

Big and obviously wealthy, with a population of around three quarters of a million, **BORDEAUX** is very much an Atlantic city, characterized by a monumental, Parisian-style grandeur and sophistication. The French novelist Stendhal called it "the most beautiful town in France". That's perhaps overstating it a bit, but Bordeaux has undergone a transformation in recent years and it's possible once again to see what he meant. Many of the magnificent eighteenth-century buildings have been cleaned of their grime and the banks of the Garonne river, for centuries the key to Bordeaux's success, have been reclaimed for pedestrians.

Especially attractive is the relatively compact and unusually homogeneous centre, constructed and paid for by the expansion of colonial trade in the eighteenth century. The **architecture** grabs your attention, notably the marvellous ironwork and sculptural embellishments found on the more bourgeois residences. Here and there remnants of an older city survive, including a few fragments of what the Romans called Burdigala and some fine churches, of which **Cathédrale St-André** is by far the most outstanding.

Some history

Bordeaux was founded by the Bituriges Vivisci, a local Gaulish tribe, some time around the third century BC. In 56 BC it was absorbed peacefully into the Roman Empire as the capital of the Aquitania administrative region. Successive Germanic invasions in the third century AD prompted the construction of stout defensive walls, following the route of present-day cours de l'Intendance, rue des Remparts and cours d'Alsace-Lorraine, but the city nevertheless fell to the Visigoths in 409. After peace was finally re-established in the tenth century, Bordeaux came into the hands of the counts of Poitou, later titled the **dukes of Aquitaine**, who ruled a vast area stretching from the Loire to the Pyrenees. In 1152 the then Duchess Eleanor of Aquitaine (see box, p.356) married Count Henry of Anjou, and when he was crowned King Henry II of England two years later, Bordeaux began three centuries under **English rule**. Though the local lords – an unruly lot – initially balked at the takeover, they were soon won

The wines of Bordeaux

Along with Burgundy and Champagne, the **wines of Bordeaux** form the "Holy Trinity" of French viticulture. Despite producing as many whites as reds, it is the latter – known as claret to the British – that have graced the tables of the discerning for centuries. The countryside that produces them encircles the city, enjoying near-perfect climatic conditions and soils, ranging from limestone to sand and pebbles. The region now produces around 5.5 million hectolitres, equal to some 700 million bottles, of AOC (*Appellation d'Origine Contrôlée*) wines, of which just under a third are exported. The vast majority of this is red wine.

Some history

It was the **Romans** who introduced vines to the region during the first century AD. In the early thirteenth century, after a long period of decline the **English**, accompanied by local Benedictine monks, began planting new vineyards around Bordeaux, precipitating a golden era for producers and merchants. Wine bound for England went tax-free and the volume exported in 1307 – around 700,000 hectolitres in total for the whole region – was not reached again until the 1950s. The next great boost came in the mid-seventeenth century when the **Dutch** started draining the marshy land north of Bordeaux, giving rise to the Médoc vineyards. They also invented the technique of burning sulphur inside barrels to disinfect and preserve the wood that, coincidentally, also helped to preserve the wine. Since it no longer deteriorated after six months or so – to the benefit of vineyards further from Bordeaux – the merits of ageing were soon discovered, first in the cask and then, during the eighteenth century, in the bottle. By this time all the great Bordelais vineyards had been planted, ushering in a period of prosperity, which lasted until **phylloxera** (see p.364) hit in the late nineteenth century. On the whole, the Bordeaux vineyards weathered the crisis reasonably well and the top names continue to dominate the world's quality wine market despite increasing competition from New World wines.

In the lower echelons, however, things are not so rosy. Europe's "**wine lake**" is now estimated at over 1.5 million hectolitres, a combination of overproduction, falling consumption and increasing competition; in France, some would also add charges of complacency and arrogance as local wine producers sat on their laurels and failed to adapt to new methods and new markets. Recent years have seen some measures aimed at addressing the problems of the ailing industry, including tentative attempts to reduce production (although, understandably, nobody is volunteering to grow less) and rather more enthusiastic efforts on the part of wine producers to develop exports to new markets – particularly Russia and China – and to diversify into "wine tourism", the latest buzzword among the Bordelais. Amongst a variety of initiatives, you'll find more châteaux now open their doors to the public; some offer wine-tasting or cooking classes, others upscale accommodation or wine-related museums.

The financial crisis of 2008–2009 gave the wine industry a further buffeting, turning up the heat on the already struggling smaller producers but also providing a sharp shock to the top-end names who had thought their niche market untouchable. In 2009 Bordeaux merchants for the first time threatened to boycott the biggest names unless they brought down their prices, and in a general backlash against €500 bottles, industry leader Pierre Castel problematically declared that he personally considered any price over €50 to be a waste of money.

Classification

The **classification** of Bordeaux wines is an extremely complex affair. At the lowest level, the AOC label is a guarantee of both origin and quality found throughout France. In the Bordeaux region there are 57 *appellations*, starting with the general Bordeaux and Bordeaux Supérieur, which can come from anywhere in the Gironde *département*. Within this broad category, districts producing better wines, such as

Graves and Haut-Médoc, are entitled to use their more specific *appellation*. Finally, come the villages and communes known for the very finest wines – Margaux, Pauillac and Sauternes, to name but three.

In addition, some individual vineyards around Bordeaux were classified in 1855. What were then considered the region's best wines were graded into five **grands crus**, or "great growths", based largely on the prices the wines had fetched over the previous century. Of the reds, only the Médoc wines and a single wine from the Graves (Haut-Brion) were deemed worthy of consideration and of these, just four were voted Premiers Grands Crus Classés: Margaux, Lafite, Latour and Haut-Brion. Of the sweet Sauternes wines, which were classified at the same time, Château d'Yquem alone merited the title Premier Cru Supérieur. With the exception of Château Mouton-Rothschild, which moved up a class to become the Médoc's fifth Premier Cru in 1973, there have been no official changes since, so divisions between the Grands Crus should not be taken too seriously. Since then, additional categories, such as Crus Bourgeois and Crus Artisans, have been devised, both of which include some excellent wines. Rather unjustly, St-Émilion wines were not classified until 1954.

Nearly all Bordeaux wines are blended; in other words they contain at least two, usually three, **grape varieties**. To a large extent the type of grapes grown depends on local soil conditions. There is enormous skill in deciding the exact proportions required – which varies from year to year and is almost always done after vinification – to bring out the best in the wines. Bordeaux reds comprise a blend of Cabernet Sauvignon, the oldest of the Bordeaux grapes, Cabernet Franc, Merlot and, in smaller proportions – if at all – Malbec and Petit-Verdot. The whites, on the other hand, can contain only Sémillon, Sauvignon and Muscadelle grapes.

For more on Bordeaux's most important individual wine regions see the following: **Médoc** p.82; **Graves** p.92; **Sauternes** p.96; **St-Émilion** p.111. Details of introductory **wine-tasting courses** can be found on p.81, p.90 and p.113 for Bordeaux, Pauillac and St-Émilion respectively.

Vineyard visits

Touring the vineyards around Bordeaux and sampling a few local wines is a pleasure not to be missed. Many of the larger producers now offer properly organized **visits** – often in English if you ring ahead – of their vinification plant and ageing cellars (*chais*), but rarely inside the château itself. They increasingly charge a fee, usually in the region of €5 to €7, though this generally includes **tastings**. In a few cases you have to make an **appointment** several days, or even weeks, in advance, sometimes in writing. Other producers are happy for you just to roll up within specified hours. It is advisable to phone ahead, especially outside the main summer season, to ensure someone will be there if you want to visit a particular château, otherwise you can just drive around any of the main wine areas and look out for signs hung outside saying "ouvert" ("open"). Note, though, that the majority of producers don't accept visitors during **harvest time** (generally late Sept to early Oct).

Where the **smaller vineyards** are concerned, the visits are a lot more ad hoc. Some charge, but may waive the fee if you make a purchase, while others offer them free. Nevertheless, it's worth bearing in mind that these are commercial operations and that, while there's no compulsion to buy, the purchase of just one or two bottles will be much appreciated – and seems fair recompense for the time spent showing you round.

In the Guide we recommend vineyards open to visitors in each of Bordeaux's wine regions. There are, of course, hundreds more. The local **Maison du Vin** will be able to provide you with detailed lists and will often offer advice or help make appointments. For those without their own transport the simplest thing is to take one of the **guided tours** offered by tourist offices in each of the wine districts.

over when they found themselves at the heart of a very profitable business exporting wine to England.

Bordeaux boomed as a result. A succession of new walls had to be built in the thirteenth and fourteenth centuries to encompass the expanding city – some of

Festivals, events and markets

As you might imagine, the majority of **festivals** and **events** in the Bordeaux region revolve around wine. Nearly all the different *appellations* have at least one *portes ouvertes*, usually at a weekend, when you can visit participating châteaux without an appointment and sample some of their wares for free. Then in autumn, most villages celebrate the end of the grape harvest with a *fête des vendanges* in mid- to late-October. This normally takes the form of a big meal (to which members of the public are welcome, though you'll have to reserve in advance) and some form of entertainment, followed by dancing. Contact the tourist office of the relevant town for further information.

First weekend in April Médoc: Les Portes Ouvertes dans les Châteaux. Some eighty châteaux and wine cooperatives representing the Médoc's eight *appellations* offer free tastings over two weekends.

Late April or early May St-Émilion: Portes Ouvertes dans les Châteaux. Around eighty châteaux open their *chais* and offer free tastings over a long weekend.

Third Sunday in May Pauillac: La Fête de l'Agneau et du Vin. A weekend dedicated to Pauillac lamb, raised on the surrounding salty meadows. Events include herding the sheep to the summer pastures, sheepdog trials and a special Mass.

Mid-June to mid-July Entre-Deux-Mers: Festes Baroques Ⓦwww.festesbaroques.com. Tremendous programme of early music concerts held mainly in wine châteaux and village churches. Some concerts are free, others cost between €12 and €30.

Late June or early July Bordeaux: Fête du Vin Ⓦwww.bordeaux-fete-le-vin.com. In even-numbered years the city celebrates its wine heritage with a massive, four-day jamboree on the esplanade de Quinconces. There are introductory tasting lessons, concerts, street performers and a wine auction, amongst other events. The festival culminates in a spectacular fireworks display over the river. In odd-numbered years there's a more modest Fête du Fleuve with nautical parades, regattas, concerts and, of course, wine and food stalls along the quays (Ⓦwww.bordeaux-fete-le-fleuve.com).

Third Sunday in June St-Émilion: Fête de Printemps. Members of the Jurade (see p.112) dust off their finery for a procession through the town. They then announce the evaluation of the new vintage from the top of the Tour du Roi.

First weekend in July Monségur: 24 Heures du Swing Ⓣ05.56.61.89.40, Ⓦwww.swing-monsegur.com. Jazz festival featuring French and international artists. Concerts take place in the cafés, on the streets and under the market hall, many of them free, but tickets are required for the big-name events.

Early September Pauillac: Marathon des Châteaux du Médoc Ⓦwww.marathondumedoc.com. Some nine thousand runners descend on the Médoc, many in fancy dress, to be serenaded by musicians as they run through the vineyards. Followed by a party on the quay and more festivities the following day.

First weekend in September Langon: Foire du Vin et du Fromage. Over 150 wine and cheese producers from throughout France as well as displays of traditional crafts.

Third Sunday in September St-Émilion: Ban des Vendanges. Following their spring outing (see above), the Jurade once again parade through the town. This time they also induct new members of the Jurade and attend Mass in the Collegiate church before announcing the start of the harvest from the Tour du Roi.

December Bordeaux: Grand Marché de Noël. From early December stalls selling Christmas goodies set up along the allées de Tourny.

the stones were brought as ballast in ships returning home from the wine run. But the good times came to a grumbling halt as France and England battled it out during the Hundred Years' War. When the conflict ended in 1453 at Castillon-la-Bataille, not far east of Bordeaux, the city reluctantly surrendered to **French rule** under Charles VII. Their new overlords even felt it necessary to beef up their military presence by building a couple of smaller forts and the vast Château Trompette, on the site of what is now the esplanade des Quinconces.

Things began to take off again in the early 1700s as Bordeaux entered its second and most significant **golden age**, this time based on a rapid opening up of trade – including slaves – with Africa and the Caribbean. One of only thirteen ports permitted to trade with the Antilles, as the French West Indies were known, by the end of the century Bordeaux's crescent-shaped "port de la lune" had become the most important in France. Its ships carried manufactured goods, flour, salted beef and wine on the outward journey, returning home with cane sugar, cotton, coffee and cacao; for a long time sugar-refining was one of the city's major industries. This new-found prosperity led to another building boom. The Royal Intendants, most notably Claude Boucher (1720–43) and his successor the **marquis de Tourny** (1743–57), began knocking down the city's medieval walls, replacing them with the grand boulevards and triumphal arches you see today. The wealthy merchants quickly developed a taste for luxury, erecting fine mansions furnished with exotic woods. Strangely enough, despite all this construction, there was no attempt to bridge the Garonne – this wasn't achieved until Napoleon stopped here on his way to Spain in 1808 and ordered the construction of the elegant Pont de Pierre.

Even today, central Bordeaux boasts only two bridges, and the **modern city** remains concentrated on the river's left (west) bank, although a programme of regeneration has now begun in the Bastide district on the right bank, and there are even plans to build a new road bridge over the Garonne – a huge, raisable structure linking Bastide with the northern district of Bacalan. Such ambitious projects have become the hallmark of Bordeaux's energetic mayor, Alain Juppé who, during his first two terms in office from 1995 to 2004, succeeded in reinvigorating the once staid city. Under his mandate new public spaces were created and some of the more important landmarks given a much-needed spring-clean – the city's long-neglected riverfront in particular has benefited, now the scene for the hugely successful Fête du Vin and Fête du Fleuve (see box opposite) and just spectacular at night. Perhaps the most significant achievement of recent years is the state-of-the-art tram system linking central Bordeaux with its suburbs. Gliding quietly around the now largely pedestrianised centre, the trams juxtapose perfectly with the classical buildings, enhancing the electric, dynamic mood of the place.

Recognised by UNESCO in 2007 (and consequently the largest urban area on its World Heritage list), increasingly popular with visitors and enjoying continued enthusiasm for its twin draws of architecture and wine, Bordeaux is a city whose star looks set to keep on rising.

Arrival

Bordeaux's **airport** (Ⓦwww.bordeaux.aeroport.fr) lies 12km west of the city centre. Its facilities include **information desks** (daily 5.30am–11pm), a Travelex **bureau de change** (Mon–Fri & Sun 6am–9pm, Sat 6am–8pm) and several 24-hour ATMs; all the major **car rental** companies are also represented (see p.81). From the airport the Jet'bus shuttles into town (every 45min; €7), taking around 45 minutes. It terminates at the railway station, but will also stop by the tourist office or on place Gambetta if you ask the driver when you get on. Alternatively, a taxi will cost around €35.

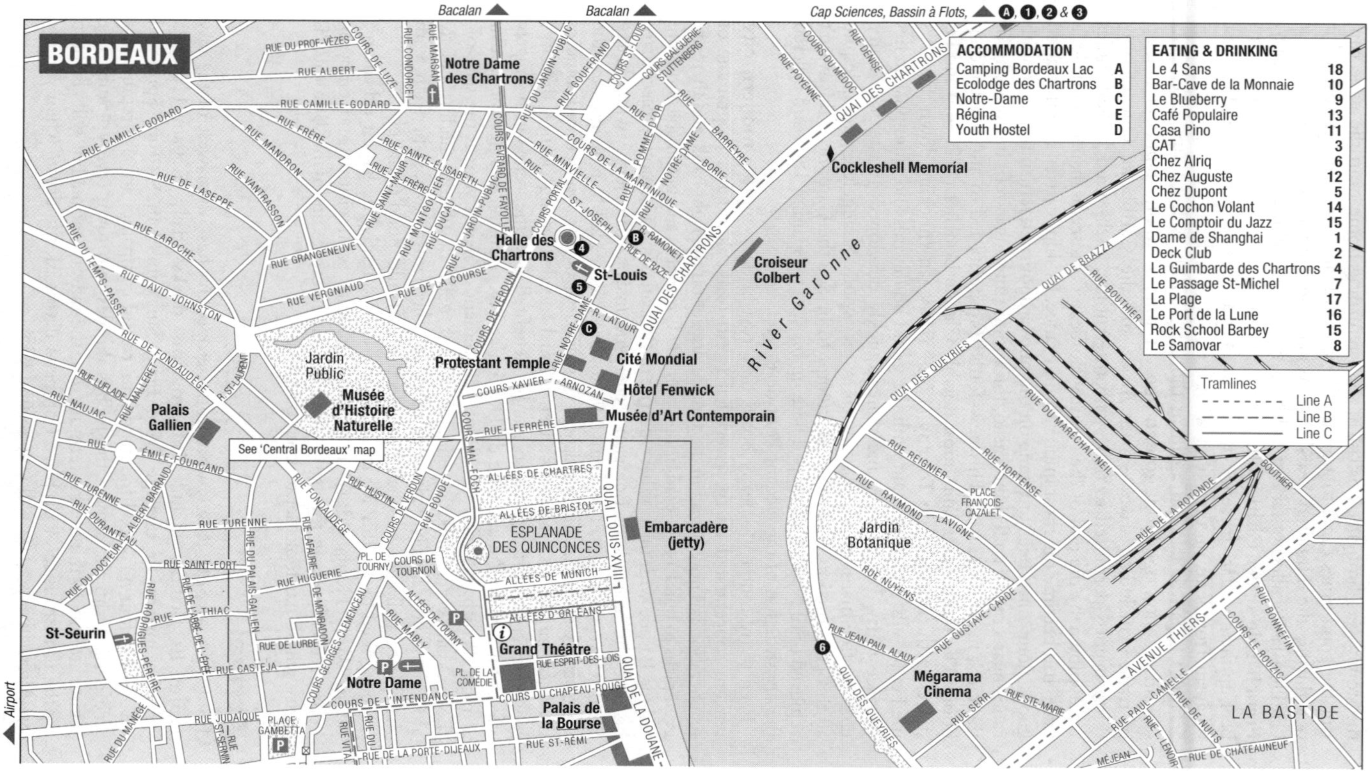
BORDEAUX
Bacalan
Bacalan
Cap Sciences, Bassin à Flots, A, 1, 2 & 3
Airport
ACCOMMODATION
Camping Bordeaux Lac A
Ecolodge des Chartrons B
Notre-Dame C
Régina E
Youth Hostel D
EATING & DRINKING
Le 4 Sans 18
Bar-Cave de la Monnaie 10
Le Blueberry 9
Café Populaire 13
Casa Pino 11
CAT 3
Chez Alriq 6
Chez Auguste 12
Chez Dupont 5
Le Cochon Volant 14
Le Comptoir du Jazz 15
Dame de Shanghai 1
Deck Club 2
La Guimbarde des Chartrons 4
Le Passage St-Michel 7
La Plage 17
Le Port de la Lune 16
Rock School Barbey 15
Le Samovar 8
Tramlines
Line A
Line B
Line C
Notre Dame des Chartrons
Halle des Chartrons
St-Louis
Cockleshell Memorial
Croiseur Colbert
River Garonne
Protestant Temple
Cité Mondial
Hôtel Fenwick
Musée d'Art Contemporain
Jardin Public
Musée d'Histoire Naturelle
Palais Gallien
See 'Central Bordeaux' map
ESPLANADE DES QUINCONCES
Embarcadère (jetty)
Grand Théâtre
Notre Dame
Palais de la Bourse
St-Seurin
Jardin Botanique
Mégarama Cinema
LA BASTIDE
QUAI DES CHARTRONS
QUAI LOUIS-XVIII
QUAI DE LA DOUANE
QUAI DES QUEYRIES
QUAI DE BRAZZA
AVENUE THIERS
COURS DE VERDUN
COURS MAL-FOCH
COURS DE L'INTENDANCE
COURS GEORGES-CLEMENCEAU
COURS DU CHAPEAU-ROUGE
COURS XAVIER-ARNOZAN
COURS EVRARD DE FAYOLLE
COURS DE LA MARTINIQUE
COURS PORTAL
RUE JUDAÏQUE
PLACE GAMBETTA
PL. DE TOURNY
PL. DE LA COMÉDIE
PLACE FRANÇOIS-CAZALET

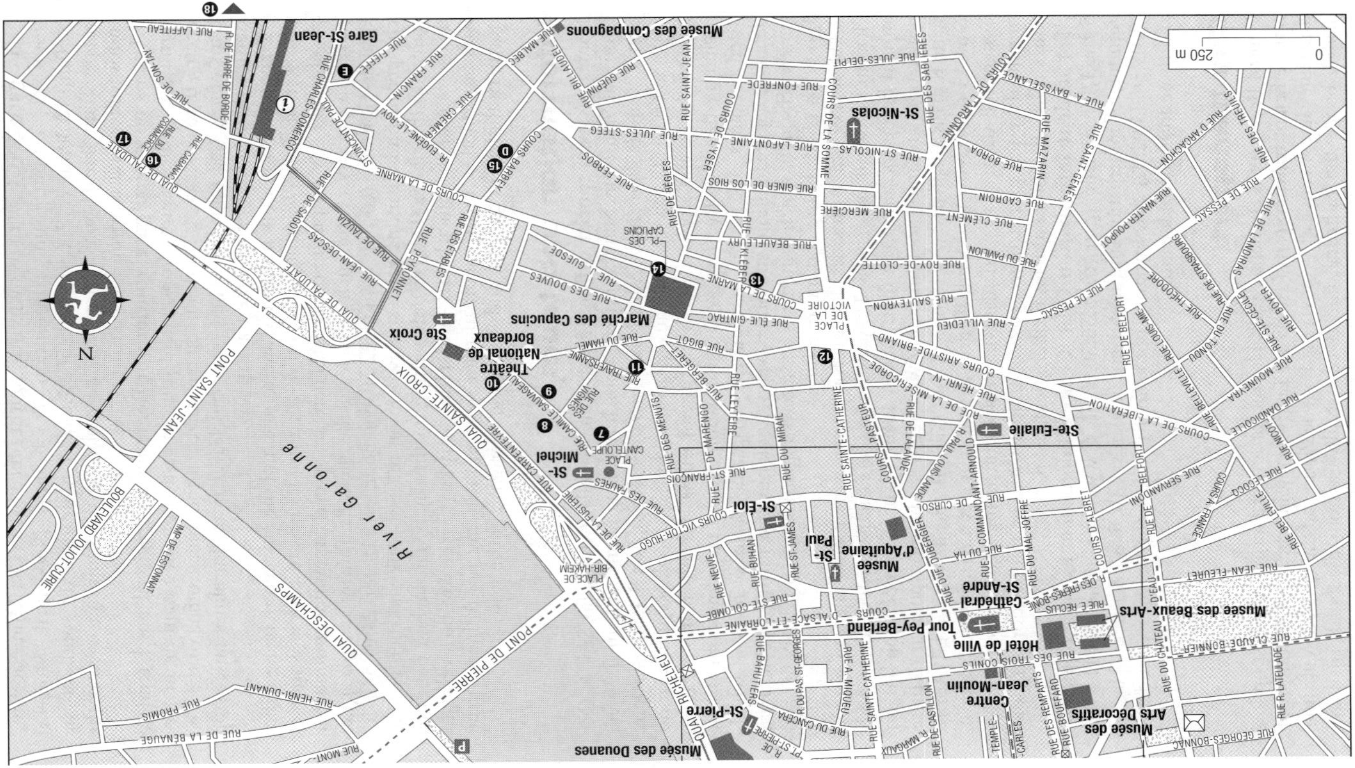
River Garonne
Musée des Douanes
St-Pierre
St-Michel
Théâtre National de Bordeaux
Ste Croix
Marché des Capucins
St-Eloi
St-Paul
Musée d'Aquitaine
Tour Pey-Berland
Cathédral St-André
Hôtel de Ville
Centre Jean-Moulin
Musée des Arts Décoratifs
Musée des Beaux-Arts
Ste-Eulalie
St-Nicolas
Musée des Compagnons
Gare St-Jean
PLACE DE LA VICTOIRE
PLACE DE BIR-HAKEIM
PLACE CANTELOUPE
QUAI RICHELIEU
QUAI SAINTE-CROIX
QUAI DE PALUDATE
QUAI DESCHAMPS
PONT DE PIERRE
PONT SAINT-JEAN
BOULEVARD JOLIOT-CURIE
COURS VICTOR-HUGO
COURS PASTEUR
COURS D'ALBRET
COURS D'ALSACE-ET-LORRAINE
COURS DE LA MARNE
COURS DE LA SOMME
COURS DE L'ARGONNE
COURS ARISTIDE-BRIAND
COURS DE LA LIBÉRATION
RUE SAINTE-CATHERINE
N
250 m

The **gare SNCF**, with its own small tourist office (May–Oct Mon–Sat 9am–noon & 1–6pm, Sun 10am–noon & 1–3pm; Nov–April Mon–Fri 9.30am–12.30pm & 2–6pm; Ⓣ05.56.91.64.70) is nearly 3km south of the centre. Tram line C, which stops on the esplanade des Quinconces near the tourist office, will save you the hike.

There's no central **gare routière** in Bordeaux and regional buses tend to terminate in the suburbs, from where you can easily hop on a tram to the city centre. If you're leaving Bordeaux by bus, check at the tourist office or the Tbc tram offices (see opposite) where your bus leaves from. Eurolines buses stop outside their office opposite the train station.

Driving in Bordeaux is difficult, due to much of the city centre being either one-way or closed to traffic, so if you've got a car, it's best to park it as soon as possible and rely on public transport. There are several large underground **car parks** in the city centre, such as beneath the allées de Tourny and place des Grands-Hommes (costing around €2.50 per hour, or €18 for 24hr), but it's cheaper to find a parking place somewhere on the east bank and then get the tram into the centre. If you're only visiting for the day, by far the best option is to use one of the official **park-and-ride** carparks (€3 per day, no overnight parking) found at many suburban tram stations, including Les Aubiers in the north, Buttinière in the east, and Pessac and Mérignac in the west.

Information and tours

Bordeaux's main **tourist office**, 12 cours du 30-juillet (May, June, Sept & Oct Mon–Sat 9am–7pm, Sun 9.30am–6.30pm; July & Aug Mon–Sat 9am–7.30pm, Sun 9.30am–6.30pm; Nov–April Mon–Sat 9am–6.30pm, Sun 9.45am–4.30pm; Ⓣ05.56.00.66.00, Ⓦwww.bordeaux-tourisme.com), can book accommodation free of charge and stocks a number of useful **maps** and information leaflets, including their *Heritage Tour*, with information on the city's most important listed buildings. Ask for the free quarterly magazine *Bordeaux Tourisme*, which details special exhibitions and other events. Look out, too, for the freebie *Spirit* (in French only), which sometimes has interesting articles on Bordeaux life and also offers good theatre and music listings.

The tourist office provides information on the wine region and can suggest château visits and *dégustations*. They also organise various **guided tours**, both around Bordeaux centre (on foot, daily at 10am, €8; or in an open-top bus, on reservation) and into the surrounding wine regions. The most popular of these wine tours is a half-day visit to one of the "Great Bordeaux Vineyards" (April–Nov 15 daily; Nov 16–March Wed & Sat; €29; usually departing at 1.30pm). Longer, full-day trips to particular wine regions, including a good lunch, are also organised by the tourist office, costing around €90. For information on **boat tours** of the harbour and trips further afield, see p.80.

For **student information** CIJA (Centre d'Information Jeunesse Aquitaine, 5 rue Duffour-Dubergier (Ⓣ05.56.56.00.56, Ⓦwww.info-jeune.net), has vast amounts of information and useful noticeboards. CROUS, 18 rue du Hamel (Ⓣ05.56.33.92.02, Ⓦwww.crous-bordeaux.fr), caters for university students and those in higher education.

City transport

Central Bordeaux is eminently walkable, but for longer journeys the best option is the efficient **tram system** (daily 5am–1am; Ⓦwww.infotbc.com). It consists of three lines: line A runs east–west via the Pont de Pierre and the Hôtel de Ville (the *mairie*), beside the cathedral; line B cuts southwest from the northern quays through the city centre, with stops at Quinconces, place Gambetta, the Hôtel de Ville and place de la Victoire; and line C heads north from the train station along the quays to Quinconces and the Jardin Publique. Transfers between the lines are possible at the Quinconces, Hôtel de Ville and Porte de Bourgogne (at the west end of the Pont de Pierre) stops. Trams run roughly every ten to twenty minutes depending on the line and the time of day. **Tickets** are available from machines at each stop (coins and cards only), from nearby *tabacs* listed on the machines or from one of the three Tbc trams at the train station, at 9 place Gambetta and on esplanade des Quinconces near the tourist office. A single-ride ticket costs €1.40, but it's cheaper to buy a "Tickarte", a carnet of five (€5.05) or ten (€10.10) tickets, each ticket being valid for unlimited changes within one hour. If you're going to be moving about a lot, it pays to buy a travelcard for unlimited use on one day (€4.10) or a whole week (€9.70). Whatever ticket you have, remember to stamp it in the machines on board each time you get on a bus or tram.

All tickets and passes are valid on the extensive **city bus** network, although in this case you can also buy single-ride tickets from the conductor. The most useful route is line #16 between the train station and Gambetta, stopping on cours de la Marne near the youth hostel.

Cycling is an increasingly popular and pleasant way to get around Bordeaux, with plenty of traffic-free lanes in the centre and particularly agreeable riverside routes. **Bike rental** is available from Pierre Qui Roule at 32 place Gambetta (Ⓣ05.57.85.80.87, Ⓔinfo@pierrequiroule.fr; Mon 2–7pm, Tues–Sat 10am–7pm; €10 per day), which also rents out in-line **skates** (€9 per day), and from the helpful chaps at Liberty Cycles, 104 cours de l'Yser (Mon–Fri 9am–7pm; €10 per day) which is also the place to go for repairs.

There are 24-hour **taxi** stands at the train station, on rue Esprit-des-Lois near the tourist office and at the top of cours Clemenceau near place Gambetta. Alternatively, call Taxi Télé (Ⓣ05.56.96.00.34).

Accommodation

The slightly insalubrious area around the train station – particularly rue Charles-Domercq and cours de la Marne – has many one- and two-star **hotels**. Better to head for the city centre, where you'll find a good choice, from the basic to the luxurious. Rooms are not difficult to come by, with the notable exception of the busy week of the Fête du Vin (even-numbered years) and Fête du Fleuve (odd-numbered years) in June. All the hotels listed below are marked on the map on p.67, except where indicated below.

Hotels

Acanthe 12–14 rue St-Rémi Ⓣ05.56.81.66.58, Ⓦwww.acanthe-hotel-bordeaux.com. See map, p.69. Professionally run, spick-and-span hotel with tasteful, comfortable en-suite rooms in a great location just behind place de la Bourse. Rooms on higher floors are marginally more expensive, but have a/c and, in some cases, good views. Great value for the city centre, so book ahead. ❹

Ariane 5 rue de Lurbe Ⓣ05.56.52.27.72, Ⓦwww.hotel-ariane33.com. Welcoming and attractive little hotel with well-kept rooms offering good-value accommodation just outside the Golden Triangle. Private garage available (€8). ❷

Une Chambre en Ville 35 rue Bouffard Ⓣ05.56.81.34.53, Ⓦwww.bandb-bx.com. This stylish *chambre d'hôte* in the old city makes a good option if you're looking for somewhere with character. The five rooms, blending modern with traditional touches, are unusually spacious and all en suite. ❺

Ecolodge des Chartrons 23 rue Raze Ⓣ06.98.39.50.15, Ⓦwww.ecolodgedeschartrons.com. See map, p.62–63. On a quiet road in the northerly Chartrons district, these five *chambres d'hôtes* have been renovated to be as environmentally sustainable as possible – from using sheep's wool as insulation to heating water with solar panels. The rooms are also very attractive, combining antique furniture and original beams, stone and hearths with brand-new bathrooms and wi-fi. ❻

De France 7 rue Franklin ⓣ05.56.48.24.11, ⓦwww.hotel-france-bordeaux.fr. Under friendly ownership, this small hotel is a real find, in the heart of the Golden Triangle. Rooms are quiet and well-kept, with clean bathrooms. The breakfast is good value and served in a charming little dining room. ❸

La Maison du Lierre 57 rue Huguerie ⓣ05.56.51.92.71, ⓦwww.maisondulierre.com. Stylish hotel with the atmosphere of a *chambre d'hôte* near place de Tourny. It has just twelve rooms – not huge but attractively decorated, with wooden floorboards and cheerful fabrics – and a lovely courtyard garden. Private garage available (€10). ❺

Notre-Dame 36–38 rue Notre-Dame ⓣ05.56.52.88.24, ⓦwww.hotelnotredame33.com. See map, pp.62–63. Quiet, refined establishment offering good value for money in an area of old streets just north of esplanade des Quinconces. Air conditioning and generous bathrooms come as standard, though the decor is unexciting. Free breakfast for children. ❸

The Regent (Grand Hotel) 2–5 place de la Comédie ⓣ05.57.30.44.44, ⓦwww.regenthotels.com. See map, p.69. In pride of place opposite the Grand Théâtre is Bordeaux's most luxurious hotel. No expense is spared in the 150 rooms, each a masterpiece of interior design, with marble bathrooms, subtle lighting, stucco ceilings and beautifully embroidered upholstery and wallpaper. Prices start at €260, but if nothing but the best will do, this is the place to head. ❾

Régina 34 rue Charles-Domercq ⓣ05.56.91.66.07, ⓦwww.hotelreginabordeaux.com. See map, pp.62-63. The best value for money near the train station, the *Régina* is open 24hr, offering clean, neat rooms at an excellent price, though you have to pay a little extra for en-suite facilities or a TV. Left-luggage and kitchen available for guests. ❶

Studio 26 rue Huguerie ⓣ05.56.48.00.14, ⓔhotelstudio@free.fr. Popular with backpackers as an alternative to the youth hostel (see below), in a more convenient and pleasant area – and it works out cheaper if you share a room (€33 for two people; €70 for five). Rooms are well equipped – all have TV, shower and phone – but there's not much soundproofing. ❶

La Tour Intendance 14 rue de la Vieille-Tour ⓣ05.56.44.56.56, ⓦwww.hotel-tour-intendance.com. This pleasant hotel tucked into a quiet corner off place Gambetta boasts a cheerful little lobby and somewhat expensive en-suite rooms. Situated in one of the towers of the old city wall, the views make it worth asking for a room at the top. Garage available for €12 per night. Closed Christmas and New Year. ❻

Hostel and campsite

Camping de Bordeaux Lac bd du Parc des Expositions ⓣ05.57.87.70.60, ⓦwww.camping-bordeauxlac.com. This campsite located north of the centre by Bordeaux's lake (tramline C to Les Aubiers) opened in summer 2009. As well as space for tents, there are also chalets and bungalows available for rent. A swimming pool is expected for summer 2010.

Youth Hostel 22 cours Barbey ⓣ05.56.33.00.70, ⓦwww.auberge-jeunesse-bordeaux.eu. See map, pp.62–63. Situated off cours de la Marne, this modern hostel is a 10min walk – or a short bus ride (line #16) – northeast of the train station. It's in a bit of a seedy area, but they've tightened up on security. All rooms (for two, four or six people) are equipped with showers (toilets are in the corridor), and there's a kitchen, plus free internet access. €21.50 per night per person, including sheets and breakfast.

The City

Bordeaux is spread out along the west bank of the Garonne River, with the eighteenth-century old town lying between the place de la Comédie to the north, cours d'Albret to the west and cours Victor-Hugo to the south. Cutting north–south through this district, the old Roman road, the die-straight **rue Ste-Catherine**, forms the city's spine and its principal shopping street. To the east of this you'll find the imposing buildings of the riverfront and **quartier St-Pierre**, its narrow streets lined with grand mansions from Bordeaux's glory days, while westwards the triple spires of the cathedral provide a focal point for the city's museum district. There are a couple of sights further south of rue Ste-Catherine, namely the churches of St-Michel and Sainte Croix, before heading north again across the vast, open square of the esplanade des Quinconces to the **quartier des Chartrons**, where Bordeaux's wine merchants once lived and worked. West of centre, there are some very scant remains of the city's Roman past beyond the welcome greenery of the Jardin Public and one last church, St-Seurin, which is worth a detour for its delicate alabaster carvings and collection of sarcophagi. Finally, the **east bank** of the Garonne merits a quick jaunt, if only for the views back across the river and a stroll along the quays to see a very contemporary botanical garden.

The Grand Théâtre

The social hub of eighteenth-century Bordeaux was place de la Comédie and the impeccably classical **Grand Théâtre**, built on the site of a Roman temple, at the northern end of rue Ste-Catherine. Completed in 1780 by the architect

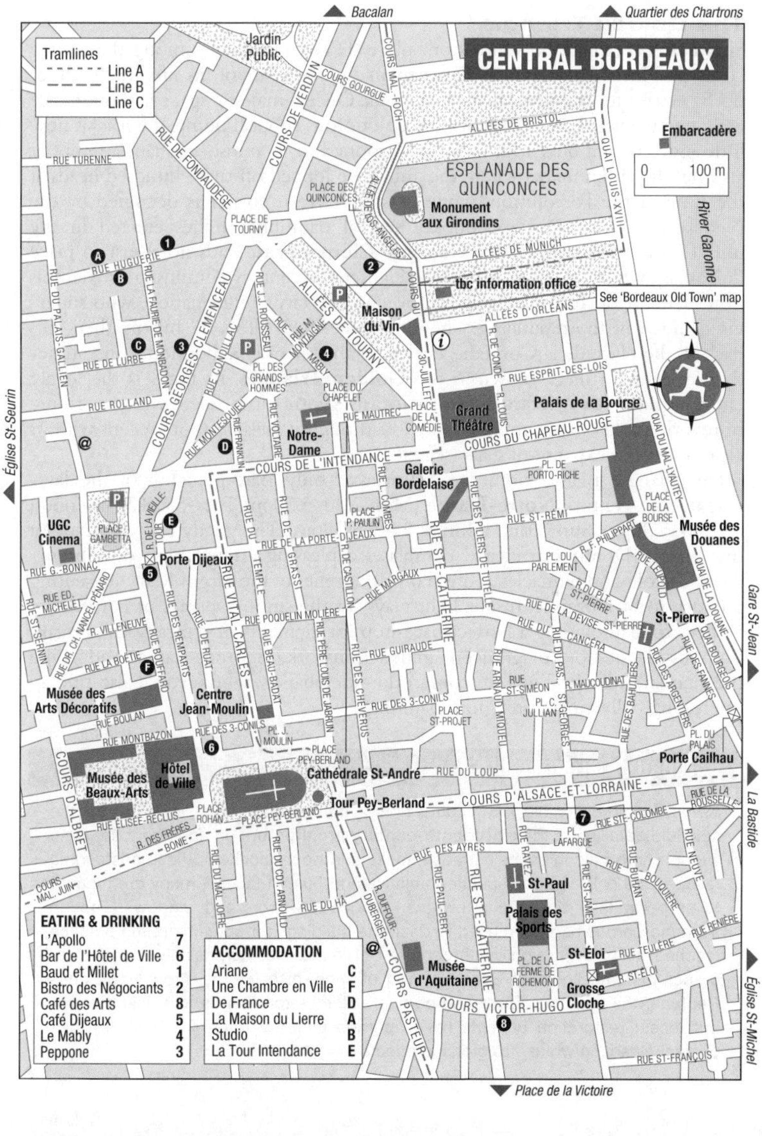

Victor Louis, this lofty building is decorated with an immense colonnaded portico topped by statues of the nine Muses and three Graces. Inside, a monumental stone staircase – the inspiration for Paris's Opéra Garnier and using natural light to great effect – leads to the theatre itself, now restored to its original blue, grey and gold colour scheme. Its walls are covered in sumptuous trompe l'oeil and the dome in allegorical scenes, lit by a massive crystal chandelier. The best way to see it is to attend one of the operas, concerts or ballets staged throughout the year (see p.79) – alternatively, sign up at the tourist office (see p.64) for one of their informative **guided tours** (1hr; €6.50), though note that these take place on a rather irregular basis, particularly in winter.

The Golden Triangle

Smart streets radiate outwards from place de la Comédie – among them ritzy cours de l'Intendance, where **Goya** spent the last years of his life (1824–28) at no. 57 – west to café-lined place Gambetta. Once a majestic space laid out in the early eighteenth century to replace a malodorous rubbish dump, the *place* is now little more than a busy roundabout. Marooned in its midst, a valiant attempt at an English garden marks where the guillotine lopped off three hundred heads at the time of the Revolution, while its southeastern corner is occupied by the Neoclassical Porte Dijeaux, one of several triumphal arches erected in the mid-1700s. From here **cours Georges Clemenceau** leads northeast to place de Tourny, which commemorates the eighteenth-century administrator Marquis Louis Aubert de Tourny, a prime mover in the city's rejuvenation, who supervised much of the rebuilding. The sandy, tree-lined allées de Tourny then cuts back to the place de la Comédie, enclosing an area of chic boutiques and attractive residential streets known as the **Golden Triangle**. Its focus is the lovely, circular **place des Grands-Hommes**, its centre now filled with a striking ironwork market hall completed in 1900, though it feels far more recent with its clean lines and expanse of glass (see p.81).

The triangle is also home to Bordeaux's only Baroque church, the late-seventeenth-century **Notre-Dame** (Mon 2.30–5.30pm, Tues–Sat 8.30am–noon & 2.30–5.30pm, Sun 10am–noon & 2.30–5.30pm). The gently curved facade of this former Dominican chapel comprises a pleasing arrangement of columns, friezes, scrolls and pinnacles centred on a bas-relief of the Virgin Mary presenting a rosary to St Dominic. Inside, light plays off the smooth planes of curved and arched stone, providing a perfect backdrop for elements of typically extravagant Baroque decoration: magnificent gilded ironwork, vigorous statuary adorning the altar and trompe-l'oeil frescoes in the side chapels, where you'll also find an interesting collection of religious paintings.

Bordeaux's architecture

As you explore the old city centre, now a conservation area, look out for the splendid detailing of the **eighteenth-century architecture**. In addition to intricate wrought-iron balconies, balustrades, locks and door-knockers, these aristocratic facades are enlivened by sculpted animals and human faces – many are thought to be portraits of the original owners – above the doors and windows. Though such *mascarons* had been used to decorate buildings for some time, the practice reached its peak in eighteenth-century Bordeaux. Not surprisingly, bunches of grapes and the figure of Bacchus, god of wine, also feature strongly, as does Neptune, the sea god. The local, porous building-stone tends to blacken easily, but recent restoration projects have returned many of these frontages to their original gleaming white – to glorious effect.

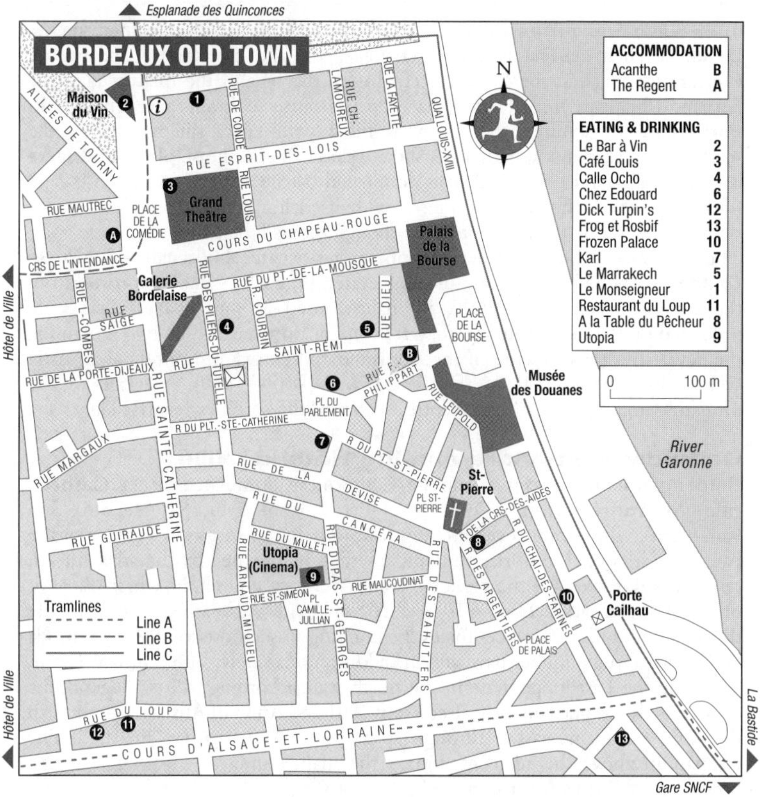

Place de la Bourse and the Quartier St-Pierre

East of place de la Comédie, cours du Chapeau-Rouge (the Red Hat), named after a venerable *auberge* once located here, leads to the banks of the Garonne and the imposing **place de la Bourse**. This superb, semi-circular classical ensemble is centred on the Grand Pavilion, in fact a relatively small building topped with a pinnacled grey-slate lantern; to either side stretch the Palais de la Bourse, the former stock exchange, to the north and the Hôtel des Douanes, the old customs house, balancing it to the south. When the square was first laid out in the early eighteenth century, it was known as the place Royale in honour of Louis XV, and its focal point was an equestrian statue of the king. Come the Revolution, however, the statue was melted down for cannon and wasn't replaced until the 1860s when the present Three Graces fountain was installed. The impressive bulk of the Hôtel des Douanes contains the **Musée des Douanes** (Tues–Sun 10am–6pm; €3), detailing the history of the French customs service, which for centuries stood at the front line of the conflict between protectionism and free trade.

Inland from place de la Bourse, **quartier St-Pierre** encompasses the area from cours du Chapeau-Rouge to cours d'Alsace-Lorraine in the south and west to rue Ste-Catherine. This is the heart of Bordeaux's old town and the most rewarding area for an aimless stroll, through narrow streets lined with typical Bordelais mansions (see box opposite). Its residents were a mixed bunch, from merchants and members of parliament – the old parliament house once stood on place du Palais to the south – to artisans whose trades are recorded in the street names: rue des Bahutiers (chest-makers); rue des Argentiers (gold and silversmiths); and rue du Cancéra (coopers, in the local dialect). To see the best of the quarter, take rue Fernand-Philippart from behind place de la Bourse to lovely, paved **place du Parlement**. In summer the square is filled with tables spilling out of the surrounding cafés and restaurants. A short walk to the southeast, **place St-Pierre** is even smaller and less formal. It is dominated by the attractive fourteenth- and fifteenth-century church of St-Pierre, with its delicate arched windows and a symmetry offset by the adjacent belfry, though there's little to see inside.

Further south, down rue des Argentiers, the ornate, almost fairy-tale **Porte Cailhau** – topped by an array of exaggerated pinnacles – takes its name from the stones (*cailloux*, or *cailhaux* in dialect) used as ships' ballast that were unloaded on the neighbouring quay. It is one of Bordeaux's only two remaining medieval city gates, erected in the late fifteenth century in honour of an early victory by Charles VIII in the Italian Wars (1494–1559). A statue of the monarch, holding an orb and sceptre, decorates the gate's eastern facade.

Cathédrale St-André and the Hôtel de Ville

Bordeaux's old town west of rue Ste-Catherine is dominated by the **Cathédrale St-André** (Mon 2–7pm, Tues–Fri 7.30am–6pm, Sat 9–7pm, Sun 9am–6pm), whose most eye-catching feature is the great upward sweep of the twin steeples over the north transept, an effect heightened by the adjacent but separate bell tower. Of the earlier eleventh-century church, in which Eleanor of Aquitaine married Louis VII in 1137, only the west wall remains. In the thirteenth and fourteenth centuries the building was almost completely remodelled, with a much higher nave and the addition of a finely carved **Royal Door**, depicting the Last Judgement, in the north wall; according to local legend, the door was closed permanently after Louis XIII and Anne of Austria, daughter of the king of Spain, passed through it on their wedding day in 1615. The tympanum above the adjacent door – the main entrance – features the Last Supper and Christ's Ascension.

▲ Carvings on Cathédrale St-André

The cathedral's interior holds no great interest, apart from the **choir**, which provides one of the few complete examples of the florid late-Gothic style known as *Rayonnant*. Some of the **carvings** are also worth closer inspection: in the ambulatory around the choir look out for an expressive statue of the Virgin with St Anne as a child, and a small and very gaunt St Martial, the legendary founder of the church, fashioned out of alabaster in the fifteenth century; the capitals on the far side of the Sacrament Chapel, behind the altar, tell the story of the birth of Christ and the flight into Egypt in superb detail; finally, flanking the cathedral's west door, under the organ loft, are two powerful Renaissance-era bas-reliefs of the descent into hell and the Resurrection.

In 1440 Archbishop Pey-Berland, who also founded Bordeaux University, laid the corner stone of the cathedral bell tower, built on a separate site as was the custom at the time. It's worth climbing the fifty-metre-high **Tour Pey-Berland** (Tues–Sun: June–Sept 10am–1.15pm & 2–6pm; Oct–May 10am–12.30pm & 2–5.30pm; €5) – topped by a gilded statue of Notre-Dame d'Aquitaine – for fine views over the cathedral and the city's red-tiled roofs to the river beyond.

West of the cathedral the **Hôtel de Ville** (45min guided tour; Wed 2.30pm; €3), formerly Archbishop Rohan's palace, was completed in 1784, marking the arrival of Neoclassical architecture in Bordeaux. The downstairs reception rooms are decorated with beautifully crafted carved wooden panelling and trompe l'oeil, while the grand stone staircase is a masterpiece of stonemasonry. Since 1837 the city council has met here in suitably sombre surroundings laden with Republican motifs reminding them of their civic duties.

The museum district

The cream of Bordeaux's museums lie scattered in the streets around the cathedral. Directly behind the Hôtel de Ville, with its entrance on cours d'Albret, the **Musée des Beaux-Arts** (daily except Tues 11am–6pm; free) offers a small but worthy selection of European painting mainly from the fifteenth to eighteenth centuries, as well as temporary exhibitions (€5). Although only a fraction of the three-thousand-strong collection is on view at any time, there are a few big names to look out for, including Titian, Delacroix and Rubens.

More engaging, however, is the **Musée des Arts Décoratifs** (daily except Tues 2–6pm; free), two blocks further north in rue Bouffard. It occupies the handsome Hôtel de Lalande, built in the 1770s as the home of a local wine merchant and member of parliament; today it is in remarkably good repair, with its high-ceilinged rooms, parquet floors and plasterwork mostly intact. It contains a collection of period furniture, miniatures, portraits, clocks and glassware relocated from fine houses across the city. The most remarkable items are the beautiful displays of mainly French porcelain and faïence, including some Oriental-inspired designs. There's also an attractive *salon de thé*-cum-restaurant in the museum's courtyard (closed Sun).

Continuing clockwise around the cathedral brings you to the **Centre Jean-Moulin** (Tues–Sun 2–6pm; free), a moderately interesting museum dedicated to the Resistance, on place Jean-Moulin. The ground floor is devoted to examples of German and Vichy propaganda and to documentation of resistance activity in the south. Look out also for a pint-size, collapsible motorbike that was dropped by parachute from British planes towards the end of the war and a replica of a cockle canoe (see box, p.74). The upstairs is decidedly more sombre, hosting a haunting collection of Holocaust-inspired paintings and some rare and extremely distressing archive film of the immediate aftermath of the discovery of the Nazi death camps. Finally, there is a mock-up of Jean Moulin's office in Nice, where he worked as an art dealer as cover for his resistance activities, before his arrest and death at the hands of Gestapo torturers in 1943.

A short walk or tram-ride south past the Tour Pey-Berland, down rue Duffour-Dubergier, the excellent **Musée d'Aquitaine** (Tues–Sun 11am–6pm; free) is perhaps the best of the city's museums. There isn't much labelling in English, so the English-language audioguide is worth the extra €2.20. The museum charts the history of Bordeaux and its region from prehistoric times to the present day, with a section devoted to artefacts brought back from around the world by local merchants, missionaries and colonial administrators. Best, though, are the ground-floor rooms covering the prehistoric and Gallo-Roman eras and containing a number of important finds; look out for the 20,000-year-old bas-relief of Venus carrying a crescent-shaped horn (known as the "Vénus à la Corne") with her pendulous breasts and stout hips, which was found at Marquay near Les Eyzies (see p.203). Moving into the Gallo-Roman rooms, the startling change in scale and level of sophistication of the exhibits amply illustrates the explosion of art that occurred at this time. There are some superb mosaic floors, goldware and statues but the piece that stands out most amongst all the gods and goddesses is the poignant funerary statue of a young girl erected by her father. She stands clutching her cat to her chest while a cockerel pecks at its tail. The medieval collection, upstairs, reveals some glorious religious sculpture, including the tomb of Curton, a thirteenth-century knight, and an impressive rose window. Later, look out for the elaborate funeral monument of the Renaissance essayist Michel de Montaigne (see box, p.179), who served as mayor of Bordeaux from 1581 to 1585.

A couple of minutes' walk east of the museum along cours Victor-Hugo, a heavy Gothic tower, the fifteenth-century **Grosse Cloche**, straddles rue St-James. A remnant of the city walls, the gate also doubled as a bell tower for the medieval city hall. Until 1945 the start of the grape harvest and all other major events in the city were marked by peals of the big, single bell hanging between the gate's sturdy towers.

The Quartier St-Michel

Bordeaux's **southern districts** were developed outside the medieval walls after the twelfth century as an artisans' quarter of coopers, carpenters and ships' chandlers, and as home to the sailors and stevedores who worked the boats and unloaded their cargoes at the nearby quays. Still very much a working-class area, the **quartier St-Michel** is also where the city's immigrant populations have settled, arriving particularly from North Africa and Portugal. The main sights – a pair of historic churches of considerable artistic interest – justify the foray out of the centre in their own right, but it's also worth dawdling a little on place Canteloupe and the surrounding back streets to experience a completely different side of Bordeaux.

The social centre of this area is the broad open space of **place Canteloupe**. Worlds away from the ordered sophistication and boutique opulence of the Golden Triangle, the square is lined with tiny cafés, spilling out onto the road in summer. It's at its most bustling and atmospheric on Sunday mornings, when the city's main **flea market** takes place here (see p.81). The whole square is dwarfed by the huge Gothic **Église St-Michel**, started in the mid-fourteenth century and not completed for another two hundred years. One of Bordeaux's most famous landmarks is its soaring **bell tower** (June–Sept daily 2–7pm; €3), which stands detached from the main body of the church. The second tallest steeple in France, after Strasbourg, it was commissioned in 1462 by Louis XI, keen to erect a symbol of royal authority in Bordeaux. This original spire was destroyed in a storm in 1760 and not restored until Paul Abadie (1812–84), the architect of Paris's Sacré-Coeur, got to work on it in 1861.

The main point of interest in the church of **St-Michel** itself (Mon–Sat 9am–6pm, Sun 9–11.15am) is its stained-glass windows. These striking examples of postwar religious art were commissioned in the 1960s to replace those destroyed by World War II bomb damage. Four craftsmen designed the windows, including Gérard Lardeur, whose St Michael weighing the souls presides over the south door, and Pierre Gaudin, who chose the massacre of the innocents for his theme in the second chapel on the left as you enter via the west door.

South of St-Michel

Rue Camille Sauvageau leads further south to the district's older and more attractive, honey-coloured **Église Sainte-Croix** (Mon 2.30–5.30pm, Thurs 9.30am–noon). This Benedictine abbey-church is said to have been founded by Clovis, the first Merovingian king (481–511) and a Christian convert, in 510 AD. It was heavily restored in the twelfth and thirteenth centuries, by which time it had become one of the region's most important religious foundations. In fact, old engravings show that the church was even better-looking before the ubiquitous Paul Abadie added the north tower and remodelled its Romanesque facade in the 1860s. Nevertheless, the irregular assembly of arches and columns provide a pleasing frame for the deep-set west door with its rhythmic carvings. By contrast the interior boasts very little decoration save a few carved capitals and faded murals. As you enter, note the sarcophagus in the first chapel on the left which holds the body of the abbot (later St Mommolin) who was buried here in 643 AD. Further on, to the left of the altar, there's also an unusual bald-headed representation of Christ on the Cross. It's believed that the fifteenth-century, lime-wood statue might originally have sported a wig for extra realism, as some Spanish figures do.

Further south, towards the railway station, is one final sight of interest, a museum devoted to the history of France's apprentice craftsmen. The **Musée des Compagnons du Tour de France** (Wed–Fri 2–5.30pm, Sat 10am–5pm; €3) has nothing to do with cycling, but refers to the tradition, established in the eighteenth century, if not earlier, of young apprentices undertaking a five-year odyssey around France, working a few months in each town to learn their trade. The museum contains some history of the practice and exhibits fine examples of nineteenth- and twentieth-century craftsmanship.

The Esplanade des Quinconces

Back in the centre of town, cours du 30 Juillet leads north from place de la Comédie into the bare, gravelly – and frankly unattractive – expanse of the **esplanade des Quinconces**. Said to be Europe's largest municipal square, it was laid out in the early nineteenth century on the site of the Château Trompette. At its eastern end stand two tall columns, erected in 1829 and topped by allegorical statues of Commerce and Navigation; at the opposite end is the **Monument aux Girondins**, a glorious late-nineteenth-century fantasy of statues and fountains built in honour of the influential local deputies to the 1789 Revolutionary Assembly, later purged by Robespierre as moderates and counter-revolutionaries (see p.362). During the last war, the occupying Germans made plans to melt the bronze statues down, only to be foiled by the local Resistance, who got there first and, under cover of darkness, dismantled them piece by piece and hid them in a barn in the Médoc for the duration of the war. It was only in 1983 that the monument was reassembled. It is, again, highly allegorical: at the top of the

The Cockleshell Heroes

On the night of December 7, 1942, in the midst of World War II, a British naval submarine dropped ten Royal Marine commandos in their two-man "cockle" canoes at the mouth of the Gironde estuary. Their mission, code-named **Operation Frankton**, was to paddle 120km up the Garonne to Bordeaux and block the harbour by scuttling as many ships as possible; with the British navy blockading the Channel ports, Bordeaux was a vital German supply route. The mission got off to a bad start: one canoe was swept away and another overturned when it hit the tide race at the mouth of the estuary; a third sank soon after. The six crew either drowned or were captured and shot. Undeterred, the remaining four commandos continued upriver, paddling under cover of darkness and lying up during the day. They finally reached Bordeaux harbour on the night of December 11 and attached their limpet mines, seriously damaging at least five ships and blocking the harbour for several months. They then set off to walk 160km northwards to link up with the French Resistance. Two were betrayed along the way and executed, leaving just two of the original team to make it back to London via Spain and Gibraltar in April 1943. Major "Blondie" Hasler, the leader of the mission, died in 1987 and Marine Billy Sparks in 2002. If you head up the Quai des Chartrons, you'll find a plaque in the pavement commemorating the "Cockleshell Heroes" just before the first of the converted warehouses (*les hangars*).

column Liberty breaks free from her chains; beneath her, facing the river, the French cockerel stands over three empty pedestals representing the Girondin deputies; on the opposite, west side, a trio of voluptuous nudes symbolize Bordeaux flanked by the rivers Garonne and Dordogne. The best statues by far, though, are the rescued bronze compositions in the fountains, particularly the powerful, semi-mythical horses with their webbed and clawed feet.

The Quartier des Chartrons

The district north of the esplanade is known as the **quartier des Chartrons** after the Carthusian monks who settled here in the fourteenth century and began draining the marshy land. They were followed in the next century by Dutch and other European wine merchants who avoided taxes by loading their boats outside the city walls. As business prospered in the seventeenth and eighteenth centuries, they built themselves offices, as well as comfortable houses complete with stone-lined cellars, for ageing the wine. Though most of the merchants, or *négociants*, have moved on, the Chartrons district still has a gentrified feel and its quiet streets make it a pleasant area to wander.

Starting on the quayside, the first sight you come to is the Neoclassical **Hôtel Fenwick** overlooking shady cours Xavier Arnozan. Built in 1795 to house America's first French consulate, it is a grand affair, topped with two viewing towers, presumably to enable the consul to keep an eye on happenings in the port. Across cours Xavier Arnozan, with its entrance on rue Ferrère, the **Musée d'Art Contemporain** (Tues–Sun 11am–6pm; free; temporary exhibitions €4) occupies a converted early-nineteenth-century warehouse for colonial imports. The vast, arcaded hall provides a magnificent setting for the mostly post-1960 works by artists such as Daniel Buren, Richard Long, Sol LeWitt and Christian Boltanski. Few pieces from the permanent collection are on display at any one time, the main space being filled by temporary exhibitions, so it's hit-and-miss as to what will be on offer. There's a suitably arty – and highly rated – café-restaurant on the roof (Tues–Sun 11.30am–6pm).

Rue Notre-Dame, which runs north from cours Xavier Arnozan, has become a centre for **antique shops**, while the **quayside** north of Quinconces is possibly the part of Bordeaux that has seen the greatest transformation in recent years. Once derelict and abandoned, it is now a smooth, traffic-free zone for joggers, skaters and cyclists – not to mention afternoon strollers. Heading northwards along the river, you follow a promenade lined with modern shops, restaurants and cafés.

The Jardin Public south to St-Seurin

West of the Chartrons district, across cours de Verdun, the formal **Jardin Public** (daily 7am to sunset; free) represents one of the city's rare open green spaces. It began life in the mid-1700s as a tree-filled park, another of Intendant Tourny's improvements, but later had to be redesigned after serving as a parade ground in the Revolution. This second, smaller garden follows English styling in its landscaped lake and lawns – for a change, you're allowed to walk and sit on the grass.

Behind the garden to the southwest stretches a quiet, provincial quarter of two-storey stone houses. Concealed among the narrow streets, next to rue du Dr Albert Barraud, a large chunk of brick and stone masonry, rather grandly titled the **Palais Gallien**, is all that remains of Roman Burdigala's arena, whose terraces could hold an estimated fifteen thousand spectators.

Further south again, **Église St-Seurin** (Tues–Fri 8.30–11.30am & 2–6.30pm, Sat 8.30–11.30am & 2.30–5.30pm), on place des Martyrs de la Résistance, was built on the site of a Gallo-Roman burial ground. Though the church's exterior reflects numerous remodellings since it was founded in the sixth century, it is of interest more for its fourth-century crypt (Sat 2.30–5.30pm; free) and collection of intricate alabaster carvings. The first group you come to, just before the altar opposite the equally ornate Gothic bishop's throne, comprises fourteen bas-relief panels portraying the lives of St Seurin, a fifth-century bishop, and St Martial, a third-century evangelist from Limoges, in superb detail.

Across the Pont de Pierre

The **Bastide district**, on the east bank of the Garonne, is the scene for various urban renewal projects tied in with the new tram system. To get here take tram

▲ A tram crossing Pont de Pierre

line A to Stalingrad or walk over the long, low **Pont de Pierre** – Bordeaux's first bridge, constructed after Napoleon struggled to ferry his troops across en route to the Spanish campaigns; its seventeen arches are said to commemorate each of his victories.

Immediately over the bridge, head north along the riverbank where Bordelais come at weekends to picnic in the shady gardens. The views from here, looking across to the place de la Bourse, are without doubt the finest in Bordeaux, particularly at night when the buildings along the quays are floodlit.

If you want something to aim for, continue north for about five minutes and you'll come to the **Jardin Botanique** (Tues–Sun 11am–6pm; free). Inaugurated in 2003, the garden is not quite the finished article yet, but it does house some interesting species, particularly in the Mediterranean greenhouses. The layout also follows the latest trends in garden design – almost Zen in its pure lines and division of space.

Venturing any further from the riverbank, the idyllic greenery gives way to run-down industrial estates where graffiti and smashed windows suggest there is much work still to be done to push Bordeaux's revival east of the Garonne.

Eating and drinking

Bordeaux is packed with a bewildering choice of **restaurants**, many of them top-notch, and because of its position close to the Atlantic coast fresh seafood features prominently on many a menu. You can pick up picnic fare at the **supermarket** in the basement of the Grands-Hommes building, and at the many **gourmet food shops** around: on rue Montesquieu, just off the square, Jean d'Alos runs the city's best fromagerie, with dozens of farm-produced cheeses. In summer, *guinguettes* – open-air **riverside stalls** selling shrimps, king prawns and other seafood – set up along the quai des Chartrons and on Sunday morning locals come here to feast on oysters and white wine after browsing the market. For locations of the following establishments see the maps on pp.62–63, p.67 and p.69.

Cafés and ice-cream parlours

Café Dijeaux 14ter place Gambetta. With outside seating just beneath the Porte Dijeaux, a classical arch once one of the gates in the city wall, this is a pleasant spot to watch the world go by over breakfast or a morning coffee in the sunshine. They also do omelettes and pizzas for lunch.

Chez Auguste 3 place de la Victoire. On the sunny side of a studenty square, this establishment serves as a café all day, with decent beer, wine and cocktails, and a good range of meaty snacks. It's lively in the evenings too, particularly on Thursdays, as a pre-club meeting point, and on Wednesdays, when it hosts an open-mic night (9.30pm). Closed Sun.

Frozen Palace 28 rue du Chai-des-Farines. Fabulous home-made ices and sorbets (one scoop for €2, three for €4) in inspired flavours that might include organic lavender or raspberry and verveine. Tues–Sun: April, May & Sept 3–7pm; July & Aug 3–10pm depending on the weather.

Le Samovar 18 rue Camille Sauvageau. Its walls lined with well-thumbed classic novels

Two little goodies

In the market building on place des Grands-Hommes is **Baillardran**, a confectioner specializing in soft and succulent little **canelé cakes**, which were once made by the Bordeaux nuns – surprising, since they are laced with rum. In a similar vein, little cubes of praline and wine-soaked raisins dipped in chocolate and cinnamon known as **pavés de Bordeaux** (Bordeaux cobblestones) are available at Darricau, 7 place Gambetta. For more specialist food and wine shops, see p.81.

and volumes of existentialist philosophy, this friendly tearoom is the place to go to meet Bordeaux's beret-wearing arts students. As well as the books, attractions include occasional concerts, plays and readings, and tasty vegetarian tarts and quiches.
Utopia 5 place Camille Jullian. Even if you're not going to see a film, the *Utopia*'s café-restaurant, either side of the entrance to the former church, makes an atmospheric place for a drink or light meal (salads and open sandwiches from €6 up) – or you can sit out on the square in fine weather. Daily 11.30am–10.30pm.

Restaurants

Bar-Cave de la Monnaie 34 rue de la Porte de la Monnaie ☎05.56.31.12.33. The best place to sample wines from around the Bordeaux region, accompanied by rich cheese and cold meat-based dishes. There are only a few tables, so reserve or get here early.
Baud et Millet 19 rue Huguerie ☎05.56.79.05.77. An excellent choice for a cheese-and-wine feast, with dishes such as a flaky-pastry starter filled with goat's cheese or braised Camembert with apples flambéed in calvados, consumed around a few tables at the back of a wine shop – choose your own bottle from the shelves. Prices start at €12.50 for a taster menu of cheese, charcuterie and wine. Closed Sun.
Bistro des Négociants 4 place des Quinconces ☎05.56.52.84.56. One of a growing number of smart, top-end brasseries in Bordeaux, catering for well-heeled, discerning locals in a position facing the fountains of the Monument aux Girondins. Meat and cheeses are top quality, and it's excellent value on weekday lunchtimes, with a menu for €19. Otherwise, reckon on at least €35 à la carte. Closed Sun.
Café des Arts 138 cours Victor-Hugo. A Bordeaux institution and one of the city's few old-style cafés, its ambience created from 1930s faded relics. It offers typical brasserie fare, with a good-value lunchtime *formule* at €11 and a *plat du jour* at €9, and has the advantage of serving till late. Daily 8am–2am.
Café Louis place de la Comédie. It's worth paying a little extra to experience the sumptuous surroundings – all trompe l'oeil, gilded mirrors and chandeliers – in this Belle Epoque café-restaurant in the Grand Théâtre. The short, uncomplicated menu includes salads, seafood and grills, but you should count on at least €30 for three courses. Closed Sun eve & Mon.
Casa Pino 40 rue Traversanne. This Portuguese restaurant combines a cheerful decor and atmosphere with hearty portions to attract a mixed crowd of artisans, market-goers, tourists and business people. It specialises in grilled meat and fish, with stuffed cod a particular house favourite. There's a menu for €12, except on Friday and Saturday evening when you pay double that. Closed Sun.
Chez Dupont 45 rue de Notre-Dame ☎05.56.81.49.59. Bustling, old-fashioned brasserie-restaurant in the Chartrons district with wooden floors and retro styling. Their fresh-from-the-market menus include toothsome dishes such as grilled aubergine with goat's cheese and artichoke carpaccio with foie gras, followed perhaps by grapefruit *gratin* with gingerbread ice cream. Prices are very reasonable, with a *plat du jour* for €9, and full menus from €15. Reservations are recommended in the evening. Closed Sun & Mon.
Chez Édouard 16 place du Parlement. Understandably popular with tourists due to its moderate prices and position on this lovely square, with outdoor seating in summer. There are good-value, three-course menus (from €13.50) offering a wide choice of regional dishes as well as salads and other standard brasserie fare. Open daily.
Le Cochon Volant 22 place des Capucins ☎05.57.59.10.00. A wonderful, bustling, no-frills restaurant in a former butcher's shop, now decorated with suitably surrealist murals based on the establishment's name (The Flying Pig). There are plenty of dishes on offer for under €10, such as pig's trotters with parsley or gizzard salad, while the more substantial dishes, using the very best cuts of meat, start at around €20. Serving until 4am, it makes for a lively place to end a night out as well. Opening hours: Tues–Fri 6pm–4am, Sat & Sun 8am–4am. Reservations advised in the evening.
La Guimbarde des Chartrons 10 place du Marché des Chartrons. Regulars and tourists rub elbows in this friendly little café-restaurant with perfectly placed seating on the pretty Chartrons market square. Dishes are marked on the slate boards: €8 for a main dish or at lunchtime have a set menu for €10. It's all fresh and well cooked. Closed Sat & Sun.
Karl 6 place du Parlement. From coffee and croissants with freshly squeezed orange to vast cooked platters, this is *the* place to come for breakfast (8.30am–3pm). It has a good range of cakes, pastries and ice creams to eat in or take away, and serves excellent, generous salads (€12) and light quiches (€6) all day. Daily 8.30am–8.30pm.
Restaurant du Loup 66 rue du Loup ☎05.56.48.20.21. Quite formal but

nonetheless friendly, this is one of the city's highest quality restaurants, serving traditional food with a strong southwestern feel – duck and *foie gras* feature heavily on the menus (€13 at lunchtime; €25 eves & Sat). Closed Sun & Mon.

Le Mably 12 rue Mably ⓣ05.56.44.30.10. Informal, friendly and unsurprisingly popular restaurant offering good value and a warm atmosphere among its mirrors, candles and sepia shots. The food is plentiful and of excellent quality, using classic, local country produce, with dishes such as rabbit and hazelnut terrine followed by veal steak with asparagus. Menus at €23 and €33. Closed Sun & Mon.

Le Marrakech 15 rue St-Rémi ⓣ05.56.48.52.51. An excellent-value Moroccan restaurant, specialising in tagines, couscous and salads served in an appropriately decorated dining room. There are even North African wines on offer to compliment the food. Full menus with large portions cost €10 at lunchtime and €20 in the evening.

Passage St Michel 14-15 place Canteloupe ⓣ05.56.91.20.30. With the St-Michel flea market on its doorstep, this old-fashioned brasserie and restaurant is an atmospheric place to eat after a day or morning spent hunting for bargains. The food is tasty and varied, from tuna tartare to the classic Perigordian duck breast. Menus are very reasonably priced at €14 for lunch and €18 for dinner. Open daily.

Peppone 31 cours Georges Clemenceau. One of central Bordeaux's better Italian restaurants, popular for its tasty, thin-crust pizzas (€12) and fresh pasta dishes (€10). Closed Sun.

Le Port de La Lune 58–59 quai de Paludate ⓣ05.56.49.15.55. Big, noisy brasserie with a great atmosphere out on the southern quays next to the *Comptoir du Jazz* (see p.80); the photos, the sound system and their motto – "jazz-abuse is good for your health" – give you some idea of the priority here. The food is reasonable and varied, with a three-course menu including coffee and wine at €22. Daily noon–1am.

A La Table du Pêcheur 16 rue de la Cour-des-Aides ⓣ05.56.48.22.61. Opposite the chevet of St-Pierre, this is one of the quieter and better places to eat in the old centre. It serves excellent fresh fish, much of it grilled over the open fire, not to mention the friendly service and very reasonable prices: menus from €15 at lunch and €25 in the evening. Closed Sun & Mon.

Bars

Student action mostly focuses around place de la Victoire, where places offer cheap drinks, DJ nights, live sport and theme evenings; all are packed on Thursday nights. Bordeaux's well-established **gay** scene is concentrated near the Hôtel de Ville.

L'Apollo 19 place Fernand Lafargue. On the corner of a quiet square, this rather dilapidated-looking bar attracts a Bohemian crowd in the early evening, chatting around a ramshackle collection of tables and chairs, playing pool and enjoying the funky soundtrack.

Le Bar à Vin Maison du Vin, 3 cours du 30 Juillet. Not much in the way of ambience, but the wine bar of the CIVB (see p.81) offers the best value in Bordeaux (€3–5 per glass) and expert advice from the trained sommeliers who serve as bar staff. Cheese or ham platters cost around €5. Mon–Sat 11am–10pm.

Bar de l'Hôtel de Ville (BHV) 4 rue de l'Hôtel-de-Ville. Friendly little gay and lesbian café-bar which stages a variety of free events every other Sunday between May and September as well as impromptu theme nights in summer. Daily 6pm–2am.

Café Populaire 1 rue Kléber. Bordeaux's clubbers gather at *Café Pop* for a drink or a meal – the food is good value and plentiful – or a warm-up bop before heading down to the quai de Paludate (see opposite). Things really get going after midnight, when the volume goes up a notch or three and everyone hits the dance floor. Tues–Sat 8pm–2am.

Calle Ocho 24 rue des Piliers-de-Tutelle. Bordeaux's best-known and liveliest salsa bar is bursting at the seams on Friday and Saturday nights. They serve real Cuban rum and *mojitos*, and the latino rhythms and party atmosphere are infectious. Mon–Sat 5pm–2am.

Dick Turpin's 72 rue du Loup. Opposite a wisteria-filled courtyard, this is a pretty good rendition of an English town pub, with a relaxed, friendly atmosphere and a mixed clientele. Happy hour 5–8.30pm. Mon–Sat 3pm–2am, Sun 5.30pm–midnight.

Frog et Rosbif 23 rue Ausone. A big pub-restaurant and microbrewery with a convivial, beer-hall atmosphere, this is the best and most active of Bordeaux's "English-style" pubs. The six creative house beers include an excellent, creamy stout (Darkitaine) and Ginger Twist, a great refresher in summer. There's also classic pub grub (main dishes around €11), darts, quiz nights, theme nights and live sports screenings, as well as a happy hour (5.30–8pm) and cheap drinks on Thursdays (student night). Open Mon–Fri 5.30pm–2am, Sat & Sun noon–2am.

Entertainment and nightlife

Bordeaux's cultural life runs the gamut from classical theatre to avant-garde performance art and big-name rock concerts. A vibrant late-night scene focuses among the clubs and discos lining the southern quays, though some of the scene has now shifted to the northern docks. To find out what's happening in and around Bordeaux, ask at the tourist office for the two free monthly **listings magazines**: *Spirit* gives good coverage of theatre and classical concerts, while the revered *Clubs et Concerts* is an excellent compilation of live music events and the biggest club nights in the city. *Sortir*, a free fortnightly publication, lists the most prestigious events across the whole of the Aquitaine region. To buy **tickets** for city and regional events, contact the venue direct or head for the Box Office (Ⓣ05.56.48.26.26, Ⓦwww.box.fr) in the nineteenth-century Galerie Bordelaise arcade wedged between rue Ste-Catherine and rue des Piliers-de-Tutelle. Both FNAC, 50 rue St-Catherine (Ⓣ08.25.02.00.20, Ⓦwww.fnacspectacles.com), and Virgin Megastore (Ⓣ05.56.56.05.51, Ⓦwww.virginmega.fr) on place Gambetta also have ticket outlets.

Theatre and classical music

The city's most prestigious **theatrical events** take place in the sumptuous Grand Théâtre, which hosts a huge varied programme of opera, ballet, contemporary dance and classical music. So much so, in fact, that performances often spill over into the Théâtre National de Bordeaux on square Jean-Vauthier near Eglise Sainte-Croix, and the unlovely Palais des Sport on place de la Ferme-de-Richemont, near cours Victor-Hugo; tickets and information are available from the Grand Théâtre (Ⓣ05.56.00.85.95, Ⓦwww.opera-bordeaux.com) or from the ticket outlets mentioned above. Théâtre Fémina, 10 rue Grassi (Ⓣ05.56.48.45.19, Ⓦwww.theatrefemina.fr), is another lovely old theatre putting on operetta, song recitals and comedy, often featuring big French names. Occasional **classical concerts** also take place in Bordeaux's churches, notably the cathedral, but also Notre-Dame, Sainte-Croix and St-Seurin. More informal **café-théâtre** and modern performance arts get a strong showing in venues throughout the city; particularly worth checking out is the Café Théâtre des Beaux Arts at 2 rue des Beaux-Arts near Sainte-Croix (Ⓣ05.56.94.31.31, Ⓦwww.theatre-beauxarts.fr).

Cinema

The best venue, where you're also most likely to find *Version Originale* (VO) films is the Utopia on place Camille Jullian (Ⓣ05.56.52.00.03, Ⓦwww.cinemas-utopia.org/bordeaux), housed in a converted church complete with frescoes and Gothic arches, not to mention five screens and a popular café-restaurant (see p.76). UGC Ciné Cité, 7 rue Castelnau d'Auros (Ⓣ08.92.70.00.00, Ⓦwww.ugc.fr), off place Gambetta, serves up more standard, Hollywood fare, some of it in VO, while films at the vast, new seventeen-screen Mégarama (Ⓦwww.megarama.fr), across the Pont de Pierre in the old Gare d'Orléans, are mostly dubbed into French.

Live music

Jazz and blues fans are well catered for in Bordeaux and there's no shortage of more **contemporary music** either. Ticket prices generally start at around €5, while opening hours and days vary – it's a good idea to phone ahead to be on the safe side.

Le Blueberry 61 rue Camille Sauvageau ⓦwww.le-blueberry.com. A cosy bar with an outstanding list of tasty house cocktails and an excellent programme of jazz and blues concerts, starting most days at 10pm. Entry is usually €3–5, except on Monday and Wednesday which are free improvisation nights. Closed Sun.

Cercle des Arts Traditionnels (Le CAT) 24 rue de la Faïencerie ⓣ05.56.39.14.74. A good venue for world music out in the northern, industrial Bacalan district. Take tramline B towards Bassins à Flots.

Chez Alriq quais de Queyres ⓣ05.56.86.58.49. This *guinguette* (open-air eatery) offers a lovely riverside setting and concerts focusing on blues, jazz and world music. Find it over on the east side of the river at the north end of quais des Queyries. April, May & Sept: Thurs–Sat, June–Aug Tues–Sat: 5pm–2am. Food from 8pm, concerts (€5) from 9pm.

Comptoir du Jazz 58 quai de Paludate ⓣ05.56.49.15.55, ⓦwww.leportdelune.com. This cosy club attached to the *Port de la Lune* restaurant (see p.78) on the southern quays is Bordeaux's premier jazz venue, with almost legendary status amongst the city's music lovers. Entry is usually €5 and concerts take place Tues–Sat. Open daily 7pm–2am.

Rock School Barbey 18 cours Barbey ⓣ05.56.33.66.00, ⓦwww.rockschool-barbey.com. Rock is alive and kicking at Bordeaux's very own rock music school and concert hall – not much in the way of decor but brilliant acoustics. This is the venue most likely to host internationally recognised acts on tour in Bordeaux.

Night clubs

The majority of Bordeaux's **night clubs** are spread out along southerly quai de Paludate. There are also a couple of river barges in the northern docks that have converted into discothèques, though drink prices tend to be slightly higher. Since venues are constantly changing – places often come and go within six months – it's best to ask around for the latest hot spots. Wherever you opt for, things don't really get going until midnight and continue till 4am. Entry usually costs around €8, which often includes one free drink

Le 4 Sans 40 rue Armagnac ⓣ05.56.49.40.05, ⓦwww.le4sans.com. This huge club-cum-disco behind the station pulls the crowds with its big-name DJ nights, normally featuring strong electro or techno playlists. Usually Fri & Sat 11pm–4.30am, entry €5–10.

Dame de Shanghai Bassin à Flot No. 1, quai Armand-Lalande ⓦwww.damedeshanghai.com. The bigger of two wooden barges moored in Bordeaux's northern docks, this one with Chinese-themed decor and regular theme nights, including salsa lessons and casino areas. Check the website for the programme. Wed–Sat 11pm–4am.

Deck Club Bassin à Flot No. 2, rue Lucien Faure ⓣ05.56.43.02.54. Smaller and more select than the neighbouring *Dame de Shanghai*, the *Deck Club* is best in summer when you can get outside for a breath of air. The DJs usually focus predominantly on techno.

Le Monseigneur 42 allées d'Orléans ⓣ05.56.44.29.91. Conveniently located by the tourist office, this fixture of Bordeaux nightlife has a mixed music policy, and tends to attract a crowd of varying ages. Wed–Sat 11pm–5am.

La Plage 40 quai du Paludate ⓣ05.56.49.02.46. One of the longer-standing clubs on the southerly quays, "The Beach" has a tongue-in-cheek tropical decor and is popular with a young, studenty crowd. Wed–Sat 11pm–4am.

Listings

Airlines Air France ⓣ36.54; British Airways ⓣ08.25.82.54.00; easyJet ⓣ08.99.70.00.41; Iberia ⓣ08.25.80.09.65.

Airport Bordeaux-Mérignac ⓣ05.56.34.50.50, ⓦwww.bordeaux.aeroport.fr.

Banks and exchange There are 24hr ATMs throughout the city, with major banks on cours de l'Intendance and allées de Tourny. For changing money, there's a bureau de change at the airport and American Express in the city centre at 11 cours de l'Intendance (Mon–Fri 9.30am–6pm). Both handle the major foreign currencies and brands of traveller's cheques.

Boat trips Several pleasure boats offer river trips along the quays of Bordeaux or further downriver towards Blaye. The *Burdigala* provides 90-minute commentated cruises around the quays (€15) and longer trips in the estuary (€30). Another vessel, the *Aliénor*, offers longer evening cruises with dinner (€55). For exact schedules, ask at the tourist office or check www.evolutiongaronne.com. The departure point is usually the quai de Queyries on the east bank – but it's safest to check and reserve beforehand (05.56.49.36.88).

Books and newspapers The best place for English-language papers is the Relay Livres newsagent in the basement of the gare SNCF, under the main ticket desks. Otherwise, try the Maison de Presse on place Gambetta or the news stand on place de la Victoire. France's largest independent bookstore, Mollat, 15 rue Vital Carles (www.mollat.com; closed Sun), has a good selection of local guides and maps, and stocks the city's widest range of English-language titles. Also worth a look is Bradley's Bookshop, 8 cours d'Albret (www.bradleys-bookshop.com; closed Sun & Mon morn).

Bus departures Bus services for the Gironde region, including many of the wine towns covered later in the Guide, leave from the outskirts of Bordeaux, so you have to take a tram to connect with them. If you're unsure, check at the Tbc bus office on esplanade des Quinconces, or with the main bus company Citram (05.56.43.68.43, www.cg33.fr). Some useful routes to be aware of are the #705 to Margaux and Pauillac, which leaves from Ravezies (take tramline C northbound); the #201 to Blaye, which leaves from Buttinière (tramline A eastbound); and the #403 to Sauveterre, via la Sauve Majeure, which leaves from Stalingrad (tramline A). Eurolines buses leave from outside their office opposite the train station at 32 rue Charles Domercq (08.92.90.90.91, www.eurolines.fr; office closed Sun).

Car rental All the main car rental firms have offices in or around the train station and at the airport (numbers given in that order): Avis 08.20.61.16.74, 08.20.05.05.05 www.avis.fr; Europcar 05.56.33.87.40, 05.56.34.89.72 www.europcar.fr; Hertz 05.57.59.05.95, 08.25.00.24.00 www.hertz.fr; National/Citer 05.56.92.19.62, 05.56.34.20.68 www.national.fr and Sixt 05.56.92.08.35, 08.90.71.20.35 www.sixt.fr.

Consulates UK, 353 bd du Président-Wilson 05.57.22.21.10, www.amb-grandebretagne.fr; USA, 10 place de la Bourse 05.56.48.63.80, www.amb-usa.fr. The nearest Canadian consulate is in Toulouse 05.61.52.19.06, consulat.Canada.toulouse@wanadoo.fr. In Paris there are embassies for Australia 01.40.59.33.00, www.france.embassy.gov.au; Ireland 01.44.17.67.00, paris@dfa.ie; New Zealand 01.45.01.43.43, www.nzembassy.com/france; South Africa 01.53.59.23.23, www.afriquesud.net.

Hospital Centre Hospitalier Pellegrin, place Amélie Raba-Léon (05.56.79.56.79), to the west of central Bordeaux, on tram line A. In an emergency, dial 112.

Internet access Two with fast connections and reliable opening hours are L@ Cyb, 23 cours Pasteur (Mon–Sat 10am–midnight, Sun noon–midnight; €2 per hr) and I-phone, 24 rue du Palais Gallien (Mon–Sat 10am–10.30pm, Sun noon–10.30pm; €2 per hr).

Police Commissariat Central, 23 rue François de Sourdis (05.57.85.77.77), west of centre on tram line A. In an emergency, dial 112.

Post office The central post office is located at 52 rue Georges Bonnac, 33000 Bordeaux. You'll find useful sub-post offices at 27 allées de Tourny and beside the junction of rue des Pilliers-de-Tutelle and rue St-Rémi.

Shopping and markets The main fresh-food **market** is the vast marché des Capucins (Tues–Sun 6am–1pm), while on Sunday mornings there's a lively food market towards the south end of the quais des Chartrons (7am–2pm). The square in front of St-Michel is the venue for flea markets (Tues–Fri and, the biggest, Sun morning) with more general fare on offer on Mondays and Saturdays (7am–4pm). Bordeaux's principal **shopping** streets are rue Ste-Catherine and rue de la Porte-Dijeaux. You'll find lipsmacking luxury food shops in and around place des Grands-Hommes, while antiques sellers gather at the south end of rue Notre-Dame in the Chartrons district. The main **wine shops** are all concentrated near the tourist office. La Vinothèque, right next door at 8 cours du 30 Juillet, stocks a broad range, mostly from the Bordeaux region, and is friendly and helpful in offering tastings. L'Intendant, 2 allées de Tourny (www.chateauprimeur.com), specializes in Premiers Grands Crus Classés (see p.59) and holds over 15,000 bottles in a specially designed circular tower with the oldest vintages at the top, while Badie, 62 allées de Tourny, also offers a good range of wine and local liqueurs.

Wine-tasting courses In summer (May–Oct) the Conseil Interprofessionnel du Vin de Bordeaux (CIVB) at La Maison du Vin, 3 cours du 30 Juillet (05.56.00.22.85, ecole.vins-bordeaux.fr), opposite the tourist office, holds introductory two-hour wine-tasting courses in English (Mon–Sat; €25). Reservations and further information available from the tourist office. For more serious study, their Wine School offers longer courses in various languages; a two-day course in English would cost €350 upwards, depending on the level and the wines studied.

The Médoc

The landscape of the **Médoc**, a long, thin slice of land northwest of Bordeaux wedged between the forests bordering the Atlantic coast and the Gironde estuary, is in itself rather monotonous. But the soils here sustain Bordeaux's best vineyards, producing some of the world's finest **wines**. Until Dutch civil engineers were employed to drain the Médoc in the early seventeenth century, the area was largely marshland, good only for sheep, corn or wheat, and most transport was by water. A century later the sand and pebble ridges had been planted with vines and the area never looked back.

The D2 **wine route**, forking off the N215 just north of Bordeaux, passes through a string of small, prosperous towns sitting in an island of vines. While none is particularly interesting in itself, each is surrounded by an incredible concentration of top-name châteaux, many of which are open to visitors by appointment. First stop for most people is **Margaux**, home to the great

The wines of the Médoc

The Médoc is Bordeaux's most iconic wine area, home to the majority of the highest-rated châteaux and the most renowned appellations: Margaux, Pauillac, St-Julien and St-Estèphe. The area produces almost exclusively **red wines**, from the grape varieties of Cabernet Sauvignon, Merlot, Cabernet Franc and, to a lesser degree, Malbec, Petit Verdot and Carmenère. Tannin-rich Cabernet Sauvignon is the quintessential Médoc grape. It gives body, bouquet, colour and maturing potential to the wine, while Merlot makes it rounder and softer. In **Margaux**, where the soils are more sandy, wines contain a larger proportion of Merlot. Consequently these are the most supple and feminine of the Médoc wines and can be drunk younger, though they also age extremely well. Further north a higher clay content makes for darker, fuller-bodied wines around **St-Julien**, though they still mature relatively quickly, while the very gravelly soils of **Pauillac** favour Cabernet Sauvignon – hence a high concentration of top-rank vineyards producing very individual wines which benefit from ageing. The region's fruitiest, most full-bodied wines, often compared to St-Émilion, come from **St-Estèphe**, on the northern border of Haut-Médoc.

The majority of Médoc vineyards date from the late seventeenth and early eighteenth centuries. In 1855 the most prestigious wines were ranked into five **Crus Classés** ("Classified Growths") by a committee of Bordeaux brokers in order that only the best should be represented at the Great Exhibition in Paris. The classified wines are still the area's most sought-after, but there has been little adjustment in 150 years, so the distinctions between the five classes should not be taken too seriously. In 2003, wines from vineyards further down the scale were classified as **Crus Bourgeois**, some of which are considered superior to a number of Crus Classés and equal in price, or the lowly but rapidly improving **Crus Artisans**, which often offer the best value for money. As a general price guide, you can get a good bottle of a Cru Bourgeois or Artisan for around €10–15, while the classified wines start at around €30 and go up to €500 for the most sought-after names, though these top prices are now starting to come down.

It's worth stopping at the brand new **Winery** (Tues–Sun 11am–7pm; ⓦwww.winery.fr), a large wine shop with a restaurant and bar attached, just off the D1 near the village of Arsac, which offers an introduction to the wines of the region and further afield, and to the art of tasting them. A *dégustation* of three wines, complete with advice and explanations, costs €10.

Château Margaux and within easy reach of Château Palmer and many other Grands Crus Classés. From here it's a hop northwards across remnants of marsh and lesser vineyards before reaching **St-Julien** and the biggest of the wine towns, **Pauillac**. Again the châteaux come thick and fast on the waves of higher ground, led by the Rothschilds' estates and Château Latour, until the wine route reaches its end at **St-Estèphe**.

Even before its value as a wine-producing area was discovered, the Médoc was seen as strategically important in military terms, as the estuary and flat land offered an easy approach to Bordeaux. Today you can see an impressive trio of seventeenth-century **fortifications** planned by the prolific military architect Vauban. Together, they form an imposing defence network, spanning the estuary between **Fort Médoc**, just north of Margaux, and the attractive citadelle of **Blaye** on the east bank.

Considering the number of visitors it attracts, the Médoc is surprisingly short of affordable or attractive places to stay, perhaps because many people come on a day-trip from Bordeaux. It's worth taking a little more time, however, and spending at least one night in the region; a sprinkling of pleasant *chambres d'hôtes* represent the best-value accommodation options. While it's easier to explore with your own car or bike (see p.81 & p.65 for rental outfits), there are regular **bus services** from Bordeaux to Margaux, Pauillac and Blaye and also a country **train** line which roughly tracks the D2 as far as Pauillac and then continues on to Lesparre, Soulac-sur-Mer and the Pointe-de-Grave. To cross the Gironde, meanwhile, there is a convenient **car ferry** between Lamarque and Blaye (see p.86)

Margaux and around

The small village of **MARGAUX**, some 20km north of Bordeaux on the D2, basks in the reflected glory of the surrounding châteaux, and not without reason. Château Margaux itself, arguably the prettiest in the Bordeaux region, sits right on the doorstep, while the renowned Château Palmer is within striking distance. With its helpful Maison du Vin, a couple of restaurants and places to stay, the village makes a natural place to start exploring the Médoc.

Unless you've already picked up the relevant information, first stop should be the **Maison du Vin** (May–Sept daily 10am–1pm & 2–7pm; Oct–April Mon–Sat 10am–noon & 2–6pm; Ⓣ05.57.88.70.82, Ⓔsyndicat.margaux@wanadoo.fr), on the main road through the village. They don't offer tastings, but sell a selection of local wines at châteaux prices and can advise on vineyard visits. It's necessary to book at least two weeks in advance (longer in summer) to visit the impeccable *chais* of **Château Margaux** (Ⓣ05.57.88.83.83, Ⓦwww.chateau-margaux.com; by appointment only Mon–Fri 10am–noon & 2–4pm; closed Aug & during harvest; free), beyond the church on the east side of the village. The château's wine, a classified Premier Cru and world-famous in the 1940s and 1950s, went through a rough patch in the two succeeding decades but has improved markedly since the estate was bought by a Greek family in 1977, and is now back as one of Bordeaux's premier wines. As well as its famous reds, Margaux also produces a small quantity of the well-regarded *Pavillon Blanc de Margaux*, a powerful white wine made exclusively from Sauvignon grapes.

Just to prove the area isn't exclusively about wine, Margaux village is also home to an artisan **chocolate maker**, Mademoiselle de Margaux (Ⓦwww.mademoiselledemargaux.fr; April–Sept Mon–Sat 10am–1pm & 2–6.30pm; Oct–March Mon–Fri same hours), across the road from the Maison du Vin.

Here, too, they offer tastings of their produce, such as *sarments du Médoc*, shaped appropriately like vine clippings, and the luscious *guinette*, a bitter cherry soaked in armagnac and dipped in dark chocolate.

Just south on the D2, with its owners' French, English and Dutch flags clearly visible across the vines, **Château Palmer** (Ⓣ05.57.88.72.72, Ⓦwww.chateau-palmer.com; visit and tasting by appointment only at 10am & 2pm Mon–Fri; €5) is Neoclassical in style, but unlike Margaux has a strong hint of the Loire in its steep, grey-tiled roof and corner turrets. The very English name derives from a General Charles Palmer, from Bath, who bought the estate in 1814 only to mismanage it completely and go bankrupt. The wines were nevertheless classified in 1855 and now rank among Margaux's best.

A couple of kilometres along the D2 south out of Margaux, you come to the village of **CANTENAC**, with several more notable châteaux. A good one to visit is **Château Kirwan**, signposted from the main road (visit and tasting at 4pm Mon–Fri, €6; or by appointment, €10), a pretty, moated castle with attractive gardens which produces complex wines, usually combining four different grape varieties. Less than a kilometre further south, on the D209, **Château Siran** (Ⓣ05.57.88.34.04, Ⓦwww.chateausiran.com; daily 10.15am–6pm; free, tasting €5) has been owned by the same family for 150 years. They produce a range of wines including an excellent Cru Bourgeois Exceptionnel, recognised in the 2003 classification.

Practicalities

The #705 **bus** between Bordeaux and Pauillac stops in the centre of Margaux village, while the **gare SNCF** lies less than a kilometre to the southwest. The Maison du Vin (see p.83), which also doubles as a **tourist office**, can provide information about the rather limited **accommodation** in the area, including the moderately expensive but very comfortable *Le Pavillon de Margaux* (Ⓣ05.57.88.77.54, Ⓦwww.pavillonmargaux.com; ❺), with a high-quality restaurant (lunch *plat du jour* at €14, menus from €34). Alternatively, book ahead for one of the two beautiful rooms at the *Maison de Soussans,* 3km north in the village of Soussans at 4 rue des Tastes (Ⓣ05.57.88.00.91, Ⓦwww.lamaisondesoussans.com; ❹). The English-speaking owner also offers *tables d'hôte* (€20) and has bikes available to hire out. You can **eat** at Margaux's *Auberge de Savoie* (Ⓣ05.57.88.31.76; closed Sun eve & Mon in winter), next to the Maison du Vin, with a lovely interior courtyard and good traditional food and menus from €28. Better still, head 4km south to the village of Labarde, to join the vineyard workers in the welcoming *Auberge des Grands Vins* (weekday lunch menu €13 including wine, otherwise from €20; closed Sun–Tues eves), a country inn specializing in meats, fish and even cheese grilled on the open fire. Or, in spring and summer (April–Oct), there's nothing to beat the two *guinguettes* – casual, open-air restaurants – beside the river at **MACAU** port, 6km south of Margaux, where they serve platters of prawns, winkles, crabs and other delicacies straight from the Gironde (dishes €10–15).

Moulis-en-Médoc, Listrac and around

Northwest of Margaux lie the two less-well-known Haut-Médoc *appellations*, **Moulis-en-Médoc** and **Listrac**. The **wines** are full-bodied and, while there are no classified châteaux in the district, there are some notable Crus Bourgeois and Crus Artisans. Although the area lacks the big names of Margaux and

Pauillac, the châteaux here are in many cases more interesting to visit: a couple have set up their own museums, while that of Lamarque is of historic interest and will appeal to those who like a castle to look fortified. The area also boasts some of the more appealing and affordable places to stay in the Médoc.

To sample some of the wine that **MOULIS** has to offer, head north on the D2 from Margaux for about 8km before turning left on the D5 to **Château Maucaillou** (daily: May–Sept 10am–5pm; Oct–April 10–11am & 2–4pm; €7 including tasting, *chai* and museum or museum only €5; ⓣ05.56.58.02.58, ⓦwww.maucaillou.com). The château, constructed in 1875 in a fanciful mix of architectural styles, produces an elegant, fruity Cru Bourgeois Supérieur as well as Haut-Médoc and Bordeaux AOC wines. The guided tour introduces you to the mysteries of modern wine production by visiting the vinification room and the *chai*, while the museum exhibits – mostly labelled in English – take you from planting via pruning and harvest to bottling, covering corks and cooperage on the way.

Turning right after Maucaillou onto the D5 extension and continuing for about 5km, you come to the village of **Listrac**, surrounded by more vineyards, again belonging to less prestigious but often very good-value châteaux. An excellent one to visit is the small but dynamic family-run Cru Bourgeois **Château Liouner** in the hamlet of Libardac just west of Listrac itself (Mon–Fri 9am–12.30pm & 2.30–6.30pm, weekends by appointment; visit and tasting free; ⓣ05.56.58.05.62, ⓦwww.chateauliouner.fr) which produces three good-value reds (the cheapest costs around €10).

LAMARQUE village, just east of the D2, boasts two interesting landmarks: a highly distinctive nineteenth-century church with an almost minaret-like domed tower, and a fourteenth-century castle with turrets, ramparts and stone mullion windows. **Château de Lamarque** (Mon–Fri 9am–noon & 2–5pm; free; ⓣ05.56.58.90.03, ⓦwww.chateaudelamarque.com), signed down a long alley in the middle of the village, is also a wine domaine, producing a Cru Bourgeois Supérieur and a rosé wine, unusual in this area. Unfortunately the guided tour doesn't take you inside the castle, but the vinification plant still has the traditional wooden vats, though they're only for show – inside each wooden casing is a modern vat.

Like Château Maucaillou above, **Château Lanessan** (daily 9.30am–noon & 2–6pm; €8; ⓣ05.56.58.94.80, ⓦwww.lanessan.com) distinguishes itself with a small museum, in this case showing off horse-drawn carriages, along with its two highly rated but reasonably priced Haut-Médoc Crus Bourgeois Supérieurs. It's signed west off the D2 down a dirt track about 5km north of Lamarque. As with so many Médoc châteaux, Lanessan was rebuilt in the late nineteenth century, in this case by someone with a taste for neo-Tudor gables, mullions and tall skinny chimneys, and also with a passion for horses. The stable block, where the museum is housed, was the last word in luxury: wood-lined stalls, marble water-troughs, even a tap for running water installed long before the château boasted such amenities. Not surprisingly, the carriages some of these pampered beasts pulled are also in immaculate condition. There are only ten in all, dating from 1884 to 1903, but the guide will explain what they were used for and point out their special features, such as their particular braking, lighting or suspension systems.

Practicalities

Lamarque and Cussac are both stops on the Bordeaux-Pauillac **bus** route while **trains** stop at the less convenient Listrac-Moulis **gare SNCF**, midway between Moulis and Lamarque.

As for **accommodation** in the area, one of the wings of *Château Maucaillou* (see p.85) has been converted into five rather grand *chambres d'hôtes* (Ⓣ05.56.58.01.23; ❺). More modest options are available in Listrac, at *Auberge des Vignerons* (Ⓣ05.56.58.08.68, Ⓕ05.56.58.08.99; ❷; closed Sun) on the main road with pleasant, modern rooms and a fine restaurant (closed Sat lunch, Sun eve & Mon; menus from €28) – they offer an excellent-value *soirée d'étape* of room, dinner and breakfast for €56 during the week. An alternative with more charm is the *chambre d'hôte* at *Château Cap Léon Veyrin* (Ⓣ05.56.58.07.28, Ⓦwww.vignobles-meyre.com; ❸), a working vineyard 3km east of Listrac, on the edge of **DONISSAN** village.

When it comes to **eating**, by far the best restaurant in the area is the *Lion d'Or* (Ⓣ05.56.58.96.79; closed Sun & July) in **Arcins** on the D2 a couple of kilometres south of Lamarque. Not only is the cooking excellent – from home-made pheasant terrine to local lamb or rabbit stew – and good value with a menu at €14 (Sat eve à la *carte* only, from around €30), but you can even take your own wine – local reds only. If they're full or closed, head to **Lamarque** and the very agreeable *L'Escale* (closed Tues; lunch menu €12, eves around €25), down by the port, which is also strong on local produce and home cooking: in season look out for elvers or young eels (*pibales*), shad (*alose*) and lamprey (*lamproie;* see box, p.111).

Fort Médoc and Blaye

A couple of kilometres north of Lamarque, a UNESCO-listed trio of fortifications forms an imposing barrier across the Gironde estuary. These were the work of the seventeenth-century architect, **Vauban**, whose impregnable military strongholds pepper France's borders. On the west bank stands the now ruined **Fort Médoc** (April–Sept daily 10am–7pm; Oct–March Sat & Sun 1–5pm; €2.50), where Vauban's signature is still apparent in the moats, grassy ramparts and in the star-shaped ground-plan. In summer the ruins have a leafy charm, marred only by a view of the nuclear power station across the river.

A **car ferry** (4–10 crossings daily in each direction; €3.10 per person, plus €13.30 per car; Ⓣ05.57.42.04.49, Ⓦwww.tourisme-gironde.fr) crosses the estuary between Lamarque and **BLAYE**, an attractive citadelle that's been impeccably restored to convey the full extent of its strength as conceived by Vauban. The higher ground on this side of the estuary gives Blaye a strategic importance that was recognised as long ago as the third century AD, when the Roman occupiers stationed a garrison here to protect the approach to Bordeaux. A castle was built in the twelfth century by the **Counts of Blaye**, one of whom was a famous *troubadour* (see box, p.357). It survived being captured three times by the Protestants during the Wars of Religion but later fell into ruin, rendered obsolete by Vauban's formidable series of curtain walls, each over 10m thick, still visible today.

A wander around the **citadelle** (free), which is still inhabited, is rewarded by stunning views out over the estuary, particularly from the place des Armes, where it's easy to imagine the French artillery surveying the waterway below. Halfway across, between Blaye and Fort Médoc, you can see the circular **Fort Paté**, marooned on an artificial island, cementing the military stranglehold on the estuary. After savouring the view, it's also worth having a look around the **museum** on rue de la Manutention (daily 1–7pm; €5.10), housed in a former prison where priests were held in the aftermath of the 1789 revolution. As well as the illicit religious carvings they created on the cell walls, the museum also contains archeological finds from the town's various military eras and a display on maritime trade in the Aquitaine region.

Blaye is also a notable **wine** area, the *côtes de Blaye* appellation producing reds plummier than those on the far bank, made predominantly from Merlot grapes. The best place to taste and buy is the Maison du Vin, on the main road below the citadelle (Mon–Sat 8.45am–12.30pm & 2–6.30pm) where you can pick up excellent bottles at château prices, starting as ridiculously cheap as €5.

Practicalities

Considering the lack of **accommodation** in the Médoc, it isn't a bad idea to stay in Blaye instead. The pick of the town's hotels is the outstanding *Auberge du Porche* at 5 rue Ernest-Régnier (Ⓣ05.57.42.22.69, Ⓦwww.auberge-du-porche.com; ❸), which has eight comfortable rooms, as well as a top-notch restaurant (closed Wed) serving regional cuisine on menus from €23.50. If you want to stay within the citadelle itself, choose between the luxury hotel *La Citadelle* (Ⓣ05.57.42.17.10, Ⓦwww.hotellacitadelle.com; ❺; restaurant from €30) with good views and a swimming pool, and the simple municipal **campsite** (Ⓣ05.57.42.00.20; closed Oct–April).

St-Julien

Back on the Médoc side of the estuary, the D2 wine route crosses some low, marshy land given over to poplars and pasture before being met by the vines of **St-Julien**. Here you're back among the big-name estates – including Talbot, Branaire and Léoville-Barton, the latter graced by a beautiful eighteenth-century *chartreuse* still owned by the Irish Barton family. Here on the undulating higher ground the estuary is more in evidence and **Château Beychevelle** (Ⓣ05.56.73.20.70, Ⓦwww.beychevelle.com; May–Sept Mon–Sat 10am–noon & 1.30–5pm; Oct–April Mon–Fri same hours; free; visit with tasting by appointment only; €8) in particular takes full advantage of this, with its long prospect down sloping lawns to the river over a kilometre away. Its name recalls that the duc d'Épernon, Grand Admiral of France, lived here in the seventeenth century; as ships passed by the command was issued to *baisse-voile* ("strike sail") in salute. The château itself is a classic, long, low, white-stone Médoc mansion surrounded by immaculate lawns and iron railings.

Two kilometres further on you pass through **ST-JULIEN** village, where the **restaurant** *Le St-Julien* (Ⓣ05.56.59.63.87; menus at €25 and €40; closed Sun) – not to be confused with the *Relais St-Julien* in the same village – is known for its excellent local dishes.

Pauillac and around

Pressing on northwards, you enter the neighbouring **Pauillac** district, home to the most important of the Bordeaux vineyards: no fewer than three of the five Premiers Crus come from these stony soils. Vineyards here occupy larger single tracts of land than elsewhere in the Médoc, and consequently neighbouring wines can differ markedly: a good vintage Lafite is perfumed and refined, whereas a Mouton-Rothschild is strong and dark and requires lengthy ageing to reach its best. As the surrounding vineyards developed in the eighteenth century, so the town of **PAUILLAC** grew into a bustling port; it then faded somewhat after the arrival of steamships, which sailed on up to Bordeaux, before undergoing a revival in recent years fuelled largely by wine and tourism.

Arrival and information

Pauillac itself is the terminus for the #705 **bus** from Bordeaux, which stops on the riverfront near the *mairie* and at the **gare SNCF** on the northern edge of town, about five minutes' walk from the centre. The big and helpful **Maison du Tourisme et du Vin** (July & Aug Mon–Sat 9.30am–7pm, Sun 10am–1pm & 2–6pm; Sept–June Mon–Sat 9.30am–12.30pm & 2–6pm, Sun 10.30am–12.30pm & 3.30–6pm; Ⓣ05.56.59.03.08, Ⓦwww.pauillac-medoc.com) lies south along the waterfront. They can help book accommodation (€3) and make appointments to visit the surrounding châteaux (€3.90 per château). They also run their own vineyard tours (€9; no children under 8 years old) as well as various other activities, including river cruises (mid-July to late Aug five departures each Sunday; €10), and sell a broad range of Médoc wines at châteaux prices.

Wine also features strongly at **festivals** in Pauillac, one of the most active towns in the Médoc. Events include the Fête de l'Agneau in May (see box, p.60), summer night markets and organized walks – even a marathon through the vines. Walking and biking are good ways to explore this area. The tourist office can provide route maps and **bike rental** is available from the Avia petrol station at the south end of the riverfront.

There's **internet** access at its Espace Multimédia, 20 route de la Rivière (Mon 2–6.15pm, Tues–Fri 10am–12.30pm & 2–6.15pm; €3 per hour), a short walk south of the tourist office.

Accommodation

Camping Les Gabarreys rte de la Rivière Ⓣ05.56.59.10.03, Ⓦwww.pauillac-medoc.com. A spruce, welcoming riverside campsite a kilometre south of the tourist office on route de la Rivière. Closed Oct to Easter.

Château Cordeillan-Bages rte des Châteaux Ⓣ05.56.59.24.24, Ⓦwww.cordeillanbages.com. If money is no object, treat yourself to a night in this plush seventeenth-century manor house. Located back from the main road on Pauillac's southern outskirts, it boasts 28 immaculate rooms. The Michelin-starred restaurant (closed Tues & Sat lunch and all day Mon), run by highly regarded chef Thierry Marx makes inventive use of local ingredients on its sophisticated menus (€90 at lunchtime, from €175 eves). Closed Dec to mid-Feb. ❽

Hôtel France-Angleterre 3 Quai Albert Pichon Ⓣ05.56.59.01.20, Ⓦwww.hoteldefrance-angleterre.com. A grand, long-established hotel facing the little harbour, which includes some three-star (❻) and some two-star rooms, all with the level of comfort you'd expect, but slightly expensive for what they are. ❹

Lou Bercail 26 Grande rue St-Lambert Ⓣ05.57.75.28.04, Ⓦwww.lou-bercail.com. 2km south of Pauillac, opposite Château Pichon-Longueville, this well-priced *chambre d'hôte* offers three light, spacious rooms, and a small swimming pool. ❸

La Rivière 8 Quai Jean Fleuret Ⓣ05.56.59.19.62, Ⓦwww.chambres-dhotes-pauillac.com. This *chambre d'hôte* at the quieter, north end of the quays is unquestionably the best place to stay in Pauillac itself. It offers good-value, pretty rooms and has a private garden. ❸

The Town

Pauillac is now easily the largest town in the Médoc but, while the little fishing harbour and riverfront are pretty enough, they can't counteract the looming presence of the nuclear power plant across the Gironde; to add to

Giant of the skies

Components of the **Airbus A380**, the world's largest aeroplane capable of carrying some 550 passengers, are made in factories in Germany, Spain, Britain and France. They are then assembled in Toulouse, 250 kilometres west of Bordeaux. Smaller pieces, such as the cockpit, are moved in a special cargo plane, but the wings and body sections are too big. Instead they have to go on an extraordinary – and costly – journey by boat, barge and road through southwest France. Specially adapted cargo boats bring the pieces up the Gironde as far as Pauillac, where they're offloaded onto a huge tailor-made barge. The barge chugs upstream to Bordeaux, where it has to get under the low-slung Pont de Pierre. This delicate operation involves partially submerging the barge and waiting for low tide when it can squeeze under the bridge with just centimetres to spare. It's then plain sailing down to Langon. Here the pieces are put on lorries 50m long, 8m wide and with no less than 96 tyres – yes, also built specially – for the last leg of the journey on a specially modified road. It takes the convoys three nights to cover the 240km from Langon to Toulouse travelling at an average speed of 25kph. It's all very impressive, and worth seeing if you're in the area when a cargo is passing through; ask at the tourist offices in Pauillac, Bordeaux and Langon. It does make you wonder, however, if it wouldn't just have been so much simpler to build the assembly plant in Bordeaux.

this, immediately east is the dock where components of the Airbus A380 planes are offloaded onto barges (see box above). Nevertheless, it serves as a reasonable base, with transport services, banks, a post office and a few accommodation options in the area. It is also home to an endearing, child-friendly museum, **Le Petit Musée d'Automates** (April–June & Sept Tues–Sat 10am–12.30pm & 2.30–7pm; July & Aug Tues–Sat 10am–1pm & 2–7pm; Oct–April Thurs–Sat 10am–12.30pm & 2.30–7pm; €3); turn up rue Aristide Briand from the quay near the jetty and it's a few doors along on the right. Behind the Aladdin's cave of a shop the owners have created several anthropomorphic scenes of animals' lives, of which the highlight is a chaotic classroom.

Eating and drinking

Most **restaurants** in Pauillac are conveniently located on the riverfront across the road from the harbour, while the village of **BAGES**, on the town's southern edge, boasts an excellent alternative and a fine traditional bakery, *Au Baba d'Andréa* (closed Sun & Mon), where you can buy wonderful breads, pastries and – of course – *rhum baba* baked in an open oven.

Café Lavinal place Desquet ☎05.57.75.00.09. Standing on a quaint cobbled square opposite the bakery in Bages, this café-brasserie belongs to the same group as the *Château Cordeillan-Bages* hotel (see opposite), so the cooking is pretty top-notch but at more affordable prices: weekday lunch menus cost €14. Closed Sun Sept–June.

Le Pauillac 2 quai Albert Pichon ☎05.56.59.19.20. Offers lots of seafood and a varied list of Bordeaux wines, and its menu prices are a real steal (lunch menus from €13.50, eves & weekends from €18.50).

Le St-Martin 5 quai Léon Périer. ☎05.56.59.19.82. Overlooking the river, this is the best restaurant in Pauillac, offering skate in red-pepper vinaigrette and snails with Roquefort among other local specialities, plus some vegetarian dishes. Weekday lunch menus from €12.50, eves & weekends from €29; closed Mon & Christmas hols.

Le Salamandre 15-16, quai Léon Périer. ☎05.56.59.24.87. Lively, riverfront place that's good for drinks and snacks, served all day.

Pauillac's vineyards

Though not one of the big three, **Château Pichon-Longueville** (Ⓣ05.56.73.17.17, Ⓦwww.pichonlongueville.com; by appointment only daily 9am–12.30pm & 2–6.30pm; €6), 2km south of the town of Pauillac and one of the first châteaux you come to approaching on the road from the south, is not only a striking building, its state-of-the-art facilities also provide one of the area's most interesting visits. The romantic castle you see today was built in the 1850s, after the original estate had been divided up by the Baron de Pichon-Longueville. He left the land over the road, where the **Château Pichon-Longueville Comtesse de Lalande** (visits Mon–Fri at 5pm; €5) now stands, to his daughters. Not to be upstaged, his son Raoul, who inherited the other half, set about building the turreted mansion now on show. Since it acquired the estate in 1987, the French insurance group AXA has invested enormous sums in restoring the château, completely rebuilding the vinification plant and constructing a vast new underground cellar. Their year-round visit is good value compared to other châteaux, as the tasting features three different wines, including the prestigious *grand cru*.

A visit to **Château Mouton-Rothschild** (Ⓣ05.56.73.20.20, Ⓦwww.bpdr.com; by appointment only Mon–Thurs 9.15am–12.30pm & 2–5.30pm, Fri 9.15am–12.30pm & 2–4.30pm; €6.50, or €15 with one tasting), 2km northwest of Pauillac, is more about the mystique of the place. Though it is now one of the area's three Premiers Crus – the others being Lafite-Rothschild and Latour, with its distinctive round tower – Mouton-Rothschild was ranked only as a Second Growth until the classification was revised in 1973. That this happened was largely thanks to the efforts of Baron Philippe de Rothschild (1902–88), a great publicist and innovator who built up the estate after 1922 and the first producer to bottle all his wines at the château to ensure quality. The *mouton*, by the way, does not refer to a sheep, but is believed to derive from the little hill (*monton* in local dialect) on which the best vines grow; the two rams on the family crest made their appearance later, as a visual pun.

The château itself (not open to the public) is pretty but surprisingly unassuming. The old underground *chais*, however, are suitably atmospheric, the tunnel walls thick with a purple-black deposit accumulated over decades of condensing wine vapour. Two of the tunnels contain the family's private cellar of some ninety thousand bottles of the world's top wines and there is also a priceless archive of every vintage produced on the estate over more than a century. Since 1955 international artists – Braque, Henry Moore and Warhol amongst others – have been invited to design the labels for each vintage, while even greater art treasures are in store, from Mesopotamian wine jugs to French tapestries, in the next-door museum of "wine in art" created by the baron in 1926, where the tour ends.

St-Estèphe

North of Pauillac, the wine commune of **St-Estèphe** is Médoc's largest *appellation*, consisting predominantly of Crus Bourgeois vineyards and producers belonging to the local *cave coopérative*, **Marquis de St-Estèphe**, on the D2 (Jan–March Mon–Fri 8.30am–12.15pm & 2–6pm; April–Dec Mon–Fri 8.30am–12.15pm & 2–6pm, Sat 10am–noon & 2–5pm). One of the *appellation*'s five Crus Classés is produced at the unmistakable **Château Cos d'Estournel**, also on the D2 about 4km north of Pauillac. Less château and more over-the-top nineteenth-century French pagoda, its crenellated walls are a striking sight from the road. The door supposedly once adorned the sultan of Zanzibar's palace while other exotic touches are the work of Louis-Gaspard d'Estornel, who founded the vineyard in 1811. He made such a success exporting his wines to India that he earned the nickname the Maharajah of St-Estèphe. When one of his consignments arrived in India the sale fell through, so he shipped it back again. He discovered the wine had improved markedly during the long sea voyage, presumably due to the warm temperatures and rocking motion. So began a bizarre but highly profitable practice where wines were shipped to India and back and then sold at a premium, marked "Retour des Indes".

While Cos d'Estournel is currently closed to the public for major renovations, visits and tastings are on offer directly opposite at the **Château Cos Labory** (ⓣ05.56.59.30.22; Mon–Fri by appointment; free), another of St-Estèphe's five classified vineyards.

The village of **ST-ESTÈPHE** itself is a sleepy affair dominated by its landmark, the eighteenth-century church of St-Étienne, every inch of its interior painted, gilded and sculpted; the choir is particularly beautiful. The small **Maison du Vin** (June & Sept Mon–Fri 10am–5.30pm, Sat 1.30–5.30pm; July & Aug Mon–Sat 10am–7pm; Oct–May Mon–Fri 10am–12.30pm & 1.30–5pm; ⓣ05.56.59.30.59, ⓦwww.vins-saint-estephe.com), is hidden in the church square.

St-Estèphe marks the end of the wine-route, although it's worth making a brief excursion to visit the pretty, rose-coloured **Château Loudenne** (April–Oct daily visits at 9.30am, 11am, 2.30pm & 5.30pm; Nov–March by appointment only; €5; ⓣ05.56.73.17.97, ⓦwww.lafragette.com), some eight kilometres north of St-Estèphe. Loudenne produces a very drinkable Cru Bourgeois Supérieur under the Médoc AOC as well as white and rosé Bordeaux wines, all of which form part of the tasting.

Instead of retracing your steps, lovers of Romanesque architecture should loop back inland via the village of **VERTHEUIL-EN-MÉDOC** to visit the eleventh-century **Église St-Pierre**. Inside the abbey church, located on the central square, you'll find some fine carved capitals, echoed by the carved wooden choir stalls of a later date.

Practicalities

The nearest **public transport** is in Pauillac. For an elegant place to **stay**, head south two kilometres to the village of **LEYSSAC**, where *Château Pomys* (ⓣ05.56.59.73.44, ⓦwww.chateaupomys.com; ❺) offers ten comfortable rooms and an elegant restaurant (menus €18 & €37; closed Sun eve & Mon) in a mansion set in its own park; it's also a working vineyard producing a Cru Bourgeois St-Estèphe. There are also several welcoming *chambres d'hôtes* in the area, including *Le Clos de Puyzac*, 3km west in **PEZ** village (ⓣ05.56.59.35.28, ⓔstephmetzger@wanadoo.fr; ❷) and, in **VERTHEUIL**, the very comfortable *Château le Souley* (ⓣ05.56.41.98.76, ⓦwww.lesouley.com; ❸) which also offers *table d'hôte* on request.

As for places to **eat**, your best bet is *Le Peyrat* (May–Sept closed Sun eve; Oct–April closed Sun; ⓣ05.56.59.71.43), on the banks of the Gironde one kilometre east of St-Estèphe. Unfortunately, the views are again dominated by the nuclear power station opposite, but it's the food you've come for: honest country cooking, such as eels in parsley and *magret* laced in local honey, or scallops with cèpes in season. The cheapest menu costs €18, but this is also a good place to splash out: the five-course *menu gastronomique* at €52 is excellent and varied.

Graves

The **Graves** region, encompassing a crescent of vineyards hugging the left bank of the Garonne southeast of Bordeaux, is the oldest of the city's wine-producing areas, originally planted during Roman times. Though now largely eclipsed by the Médoc, red Graves wines once provided the bulk of Bordeaux's wine exports, notably from the Pessac-Léognan *appellation* on the city's southern outskirts, where Château Haut-Brion still maintains a toehold amongst the suburban sprawl. The Graves heartland contains a series of wine towns, which were once bustling river ports and are now linked by the main Bordeaux–Toulouse train line and busy N113. This isn't an area in which you'll want to linger, but it's worth ducking off the main roads to visit fourteenth-century **Château de la Brède**, home to the philosopher Montesquieu, and at least some of the Graves' myriad wine producers. A good starting point is **Portets**,

Graves wines

The name **Graves** derives from *grabas*, the local term for the bed of sand and river pebbles, over three metres thick in places, deposited over the centuries by the Garonne. Though hostile to most other crops, these harsh, gravelly soils provide the perfect conditions for vines – not only are they well drained but the stones' reflected heat also ensures good, all-round ripening. The region contains three main *appellations*: **Graves** and **Pessac-Léognan**, both producing red and dry white wines, and the medium-sweet **Graves Supérieures**. Within this area the Sauternes enclave merits its own *appellation* (see box, p.96).

Graves' golden age was between the fifteenth and eighteenth centuries when many of today's great vineyards developed. Most notable among these was **Château Haut-Brion** where modern techniques introduced by the Pontac family revolutionized the production process. The Pontacs were also the first to market their wine under its château name, an event recorded by the London diarist Samuel Pepys in 1663: "Drank a sort of French wine, called Ho Bryan, that hath a good and most particular taste that I ever met with."

As the Médoc's star rose in the eighteenth century, so Graves' began to wane. Outbreaks of oïdium and then the deadly **phylloxera** in the late 1800s led many growers to turn their land over to pine trees, the only other crop able to tolerate such stony soils, and by 1935 the area under vines had decreased from 50 square kilometres to a mere 15 square kilometres. In the postwar period, however, Graves wines have enjoyed a **renaissance** and previously neglected vineyards are once again producing quality wines. In recognition of this fact a **classification** system was introduced in the 1950s establishing sixteen Crus Classés, all of which fall within the Pessac-Léognan area. (Previously, only Château Haut-Brion was deemed worthy, being granted Premier Cru Classé status when Bordeaux wines were classified in 1855.)

Red wines comprise around seventy percent of Graves output. In general they have more body than the Médoc reds and age well over five to ten years to yield a fine, aromatic wine. Their distinctive flavour results from the balance of Cabernet Sauvignon, Merlot and Cabernet Franc grape varieties. Dry white Graves – a blend of Sémillon, Sauvignon and Muscadelle grapes – have evolved considerably over recent years to rank among the region's finest. The best, now often aged in oak barrels, peak at three to four years of age. Though Graves Crus Classés fetch up to €50 a bottle, the majority of Graves wines sell for well under €15.

▲ Château de la Brède

one of the more appealing riverside towns with a clutch of châteaux noted for their gardens or architecture as well as their wines. For other ideas, call in at **Podensac**'s well-run information centre, the Maison des Graves, which showcases a broad selection of local producers.

The places mentioned below are relatively well served by **public transport**, in particular the TER railway line which calls at Portets and Podensac on its way from Bordeaux to Agen. La Brède, meanwhile, is accessible from Bordeaux by bus.

La Brède

One of the first villages you come to on leaving Bordeaux is surprisingly free of vines. Instead, sleepy **LA BRÈDE** is famous as the home of the philosopher Baron de La Brède et de Montesquieu who was born in nearby **Château de la Brède** in 1689. The **château** (45min guided tour: April & May Sat, Sun & public hols 2–6pm; June–Sept daily except Tues 2–6pm; Oct–11 Nov Sat, Sun & public hols 2–5.30pm; €7; park only €2.50; Ⓦwww.chateaulabrede.com), is located just west of the village and is now owned by a private foundation. It's encircled by a picturesque moat and a vast park, created by Montesquieu, which help soften the building's somewhat austere edges.

Though he spent his winters in Paris hobnobbing with fellow philosophers, Montesquieu revelled in the peace and quiet of his country retreat. This is where he wrote some of his best-known essays, among them the highly influential political treatise *L'Esprit des Lois* ("*The Spirit of Laws*"), and where he amassed a fabulous library of five thousand books, which was so weighty that the ceiling of the entrance hall below had to be strengthened with six stout, oak pillars. Sadly, they are no longer required: in 1926 Montesquieu's cash-strapped descendants were forced to sell 1500 volumes, followed in 1939 by his manuscripts; the remaining books were donated to Bordeaux library for safekeeping in 1995.

Other Montesquieu possessions have survived, including several sturdy travelling trunks and furniture he brought back from his travels. His writing table occupies pride of place in the wood-panelled bedroom downstairs, which he used towards the end of his life. Here, too, is a rare likeness – a profile in bas-relief sculpted just before he died in 1755. In his old age, his sight failing but his mind as sharp as ever, Montesquieu obliged his secretary to sleep in a small, adjoining bedroom, ready to take notes whenever inspiration struck. Records show that few secretaries sustained the onslaught for long.

Several buses per day (Mon–Sat, line #502) run from Bordeaux Talence to the centre of La Brède, where you'll also find a well-organised **tourist information** office (Mon–Sat: June 15–Sept 15 10am–1pm & 2–6pm; Sept 16–June 14 9am–noon & 2–6pm; ⓣ05.56.78.47.72, ⓦwww.otmontesquieu.com) , which offers wine tours (mid-June to mid-Sept daily; €10 per person) amongst other activities.

Portets to Podensac

PORTETS, set slightly off the N113 east of La Brède, is one of the Graves' more promising riverside towns with its neat church square and a quiet picnic spot down by the *halte nautique*. The main reason for coming here is to visit the delightful **Château de Mongenan** (mid-Feb to May, Nov & Dec Sat, Sun & public hols 2–6pm; June, Sept & Oct daily 2–6pm; July & Aug daily 10am–noon & 2–7pm; closed Jan to mid-Feb; €6; ⓦwww.chateaudemongenan.com) on Portets' western outskirts. This pretty little château contains a museum of eighteenth-century life commemorating one of its former owners, Antoine de Valdec de Lessart, who served as foreign minister under Louis XVI before being

Riding the wave

If you're exploring the lower stretches of the Garonne and Dordogne rivers in spring or autumn, don't be surprised to see dozens of surfers, kayakers and jet-skiers surfing *up* the river on a **tidal bore** – a series of half a dozen waves up to two metres high which race upstream for 150km at between 15 and 30kph. These waves form when exceptionally high tides funnelled up a narrow and gently sloping estuary push up and over the water flowing downstream. Though hardly the most thrilling ride in the world, surfing the *mascaret*, as it is known locally, first became popular in the late 1970s on the Garonne between Cambes and Cadillac. Then the action moved north to the Dordogne River, focusing around St-Pardon, just downstream from Libourne. It's now become something of a tradition, helped by the fact that this is the last tidal bore still running in France; the rest have fallen victim to flood-protection schemes and other forms of river management.

Apart from St-Pardon, the best spots to witness the *mascaret* are the Gironde estuary near Margaux and the Garonne between Portets and Podensac. The waves occur throughout the year for a few days each month, but are most spectacular at the time of the spring and autumn equinox (around March 21 and Sept 23) – autumn is generally better because the level of the river is lower and the effect is therefore more pronounced. Tourist offices can give you an accurate timetable detailing when the arrival of the Mascaret at each point of the river is predicted. Spectators need to get in position shortly after low tide, and make sure to stand on a bridge or somewhere well above the water to avoid getting swamped, if not washed away.

executed during the Revolution. Rare original documents, period costumes, faïence and fabrics fill every corner.

In 1741 de Lessart's predecessor, Baron de Gasq, created a beautiful, walled botanical garden inspired by Jean-Jacques Rousseau. It still exists today in front of the house, heavy with the perfume of old-fashioned roses, herbs, aromatic and medicinal plants alongside almost-forgotten varieties of vegetables. The family also continues traditional methods of wine production and you can end the visit by sampling their oak-aged red and white Graves.

For information about other local vineyards, head south another 8km to **PODENSAC**. While the village itself is instantly forgettable, the helpful **Maison des Graves** (May–Oct Mon–Fri 9.30am–6.30pm, Sat, Sun & public hols 10.30am–6.30pm; Nov–April Mon–Fri 9am–6pm; Ⓣ05.56.27.09.25, Ⓦwww.vins-graves.com) is on the town's western edge. Their cellars represent over three hundred wines from 150 properties in the Graves and Pessac-Léognan regions; prices are only a few cents above châteaux rates. Though staff can't arrange châteaux visits for you, they provide a list of those that accept visitors together with a useful map.

One of the larger, more welcoming vineyards in the area is **Château de Chantegrive** (Mon–Sat 9.15am–12.30pm & 1.30–5pm; free; Ⓣ05.56.27.17.38, Ⓦwww.chantegrive.com) on the southwest edge of Podensac. It's of interest mainly for its ultra-modern vinification techniques and superb red-wine *chais* of over six hundred oak barrels. They produce a range of well-rated Graves red wines in addition to a prestigious, oak-aged dry white and a sweet wine under the Cérons *appellation*.

Sauternes, Barsac and Langon

The little River Ciron forms the western boundary of a region famous for a sweet white wine justly described as "bottled sunshine". Compared with the Graves, the **Sauternes** hills are slightly higher, the landscape more rolling and every inch of space is covered with neat rows of vines presided over by noble châteaux. The foremost of these, **Château d'Yquem**, requires a bit of organizing to visit, but plenty of others are more than happy to offer tastings and tours of their *chais*. **Château de Malle** also provides a rare opportunity to peek inside a lived-in château and stroll around its elegant Italianate garden. The region boasts a number of recommended restaurants, both in Sauternes village itself and across the Ciron in **Barsac**, which has its own sweet white *appellation*. The main service town here is **Langon**, just outside the Sauternes region to the east, which also provides a convenient jumping-off point for the extravagantly decorated **Château Roquetaillade**, one of several local "Clémentine" fortresses built by relatives of Pope Clément V.

You can reach both Barsac and Langon via **public transport**, either by local trains on the Bordeaux–Agen line or by regional bus services operating out of

Bordeaux (see p.81). If you want to explore slightly further inland, though, particularly around Sauternes, you really need your own transport.

Sauternes village and around

SAUTERNES itself is a trim but sedate village dominated by a pretty church at one end, and the *mairie* and **Maison du Sauternes** (Mon–Fri 9am–7pm, Sat & Sun 10am–7pm; ⓣ05.56.76.69.83, ⓦwww.maisondusauternes.com) at the other. The *maison* is a treasure trove of golden bottles with white-and-gold labels sold at château prices. Cheapest is their own, blended *Duc de Sauternes* at just over €11 a bottle; free tastings available.

You can pick up information about visiting Sauternes châteaux, among other things, at the **tourist office** (May–Oct Tues–Sat 2–6pm; ⓣ05.56.76.69.13, ⓦwww.sauternais-graves-langon.com) halfway down the hill towards the church. The office offers half-day vineyard tours by minibus (€10 per person

Sauternes wines

The distinctive golden wine of **Sauternes** is certainly sweet, but also round, full-bodied and spicy, with a long aftertaste. It's not necessarily a dessert wine, either: the balance of sugar and acidity marries well with Roquefort and other strong cheeses, delicately flavoured fish and foie gras. Sauternes should be drunk chilled but not icy, somewhere around 8–10°C.

The main grape variety is Sémillon, blended with Sauvignon and usually a tiny amount of Muscadelle for its musky aroma. Gravelly terraces with a limestone sub-soil help create the smooth, subtle Sauternes taste, but mostly it's due to a peculiar microclimate of morning autumn mists and hot, sunny afternoons which causes the *Botrytis cinerea* fungus, or "**noble rot**", to flourish on the grapes. By penetrating the skin, the mould allows water to evaporate, thus concentrating the sugars and pectins and intensifying the flavours.

Harvest time is a nerve-racking period for Sauternes producers. The climate has to be just right for *Botrytis* to work its magic: too much rain and the grapes soak up water again like a sponge; leave it too late and there's a risk of frost damage. As a result, harvests are both unpredictable and time-consuming. Each grape is individually picked only when it's reached the exact point of shrivelled, rotting maturity, a process that can take up to two months with pickers passing over the same vine again and again. Many grapes are rejected, giving an average yield of perhaps only one glass per vine – as opposed to one to three bottles elsewhere in the region. Though they can be drunk young and fruity, Sauternes develop their full body only at around ten years and are not truly at their best until at least twenty, even thirty years old, and if properly preserved can be kept even longer than that. Not surprisingly, this is a luxury drink, with prices at the classified châteaux starting at around €25, even if you buy on site. Château d'Yquem has a particular allure and its wines are correspondingly pricey – in 2006, a 1787 Château d'Yquem became the most expensive bottle of wine in the world when it was sold at auction to an American for around €80,000.

Sauternes wines first came to the fore in the seventeenth century, when they were much prized in Holland. Such was their importance, in fact, that the wines were included in the **classification** at the Paris exhibition in 1855, when Château d'Yquem was the only vineyard to be awarded Premier Cru Supérieur status. At the same time 21 other producers – now 26 as a result of land subdivision – were designated Crus Classés, sub-divided into "premiers" and "seconds" crus.

and **bike rental** (€12 per day) should you wish to cycle around the vineyards. When the Sauternes office is closed, these services are offered by the branch in Langon (see p.99).

The closest **accommodation** is the sumptuous *Relais du Château d'Arche* (ⓣ05.56.76.67.67, ⓦwww.chateaudarche-sauternes.com; ❼), about 1km north of the village, a wine château offering elegant rooms in a lovely seventeenth-century chartreuse. Many rooms look directly out over the vines, the best views being from those in the towers. If your budget won't quite stretch to that, there are some excellent *chambres d'hôtes* nearby, including the good-value *Domaine du Ciron* (ⓣ05.56.76.60.17, ⓔmc_lav @hotmail.fr; ❸; meals on request €20), about 1km southeast of Sauternes in the hamlet of **PARROPIS**. More charming is *Peyraguey Maison Rouge* a couple of kilometres north of Sauternes in **BOMME**, which has three pretty rooms with new bathrooms. The location is also idyllic, in the midst of vines and with views from the garden onto the illustrious Château d'Yquem. Both *chambres d'hôte* have small swimming pools.

For **food**, head to *Auberge Les Vignes* (ⓣ05.56.76.60.06; closed Sun eve, Mon & Jan), a cosy little restaurant beside the church, with regional specialities such as *grillades aux Sarments* (meats grilled over vine clippings). Their weekday lunch menu for €13 is excellent value. For something a bit more refined, try *Le Saprien* (ⓣ05.56.76.60.87; closed Sun eve & Mon; menus from €25), opposite the tourist office, with the added bonus of a shady summer terrace with an uninterrupted view over the vineyards. They also serve *grillades aux Sarments* and modern variations of local dishes such as calves' sweetbreads in a curry and Sauternes sauce and *lamproie au Sauternes* – the latter definitely an acquired taste.

The châteaux

The Sauternes *appellation* covers some 240 producers tending over twenty square kilometres of vines. The landscape is peppered with handsome châteaux, the majority of which offer tastings, in most cases for free. Below are a few recommendations.

South of Sauternes

Right on the southern edge of Sauternes village, **Château Filhot** (ⓣ05.56.76.61.09, ⓦwww.filhot.com; Mon–Fri 9am–6pm, Sat & Sun by appointment; free) was one of the Crus Classés designated in 1855 and is arguably the best to visit today. Heading up the long drive through the castle's enormous park, complete with pond, you see the elegant Neoclassical edifice looking out over its balustrades and terraces. You can't see inside the château, but you do get a friendly and informative tour of the cellars where the prestigious first wine spends two to three years maturing in barrels, and then a generous tasting. If you're buying, prices start at around €25 per bottle.

Next to Filhot, a little to the north, is **Château Guiraud** (daily by appointment; €7; ⓣ05.56.76.61.01, ⓦwww.chateauguiraud.com), a member of the even more exclusive club of top-ranked Premiers Grands Crus vineyards. You have to pay for this tasting, but it's worth it for the real enthusiast: €18 to try three vintages, and €28 to taste six (note that these fees will almost certainly be waived if you make a significant purchase).

North of Sauternes

On the north side of Sauternes, near the village of Bommes, another Premier Cru Classé vineyard is at the **Château La Tour Blanche** (Mon–Fri 9am–noon & 2–5pm; free; ⓣ05.57.98.02.73, ⓦwww.tour-blanche.com). This domaine is now a wine school and the visits are particularly good for those wanting to delve into the more technical aspects of wine making. Alternatively, head for the family-run **Château Clos Haut-Peyraguey** (daily 9am–noon & 2–6pm; free; Ⓣ05.56.76.61.53, Ⓦwww.closhautpeyraguey.com), on the road north from Sauternes to Preignac, where you're guaranteed a warm welcome and a tour round the *chai*. Unfortunately, the same can't be said for **Château d'Yquem** further east along the same ridge of hills (Ⓦwww.chateau-yquem.fr) which only wine professionals are allowed to visit. You can, though, walk right up to the outside and wander around the castle's grounds (Mon–Sat; free). There's no sign at the entrance, but it's easy enough to spot, a honey-coloured sixteenth-century manor house with pepper-pot towers looking down over Château Lafon. The wines of Château d'Yquem were already highly valued in the sixteenth century but really came to prominence in the mid-1800s when the Lur-Saluces family perfected the technique of selecting the overripe grapes. In 1999, the domaine was taken over by the Louis Vuitton Moët Hennessy group after a bitter row among the inheritors, ending over four hundred years of Lur-Saluces history.

Château de Malle (April–Oct daily 9am–noon, also 2–5.30pm by appointment; €7; Ⓣ05.56.62.36.86, Ⓦwww.chateau-de-malle.fr), in the lowlands just beyond the motorway, straddles the Graves and Sauternes *appellations*. Alongside a Cru Classé, it produces not only a cheaper AOC Sauternes but also Graves reds and dry whites. This is one of the few local châteaux you can actually see inside, albeit only four rooms, heavy with wood panelling and period furniture under the watchful gaze of ancestral portraits. More engaging is the manicured Italian park complete with fountains, statues, terraces and an open-air theatre. The château was built in the early seventeenth century by Jacques de Malle, a member of the Bordeaux parliament, before passing into the ubiquitous Lur-Saluces family by marriage.

▲ The elegant Château de Malle

Barsac

BARSAC, immediately west of the River Ciron, is a potentially attractive village ruined by the main road cutting through its centre. Although they fall within the Sauternes region and were classified along with the Sauternes châteaux in 1855, Barsac's sweet white **wines** are permitted their own *appellation*. In general they choose to use it to describe wines which are lighter and slightly less sweet than the Sauternes, but it's not a significant distinction and the grape varieties, harvesting and production process (see box, p.96), as well as the quality and prices, are pretty much identical. To find out more about the area, call in at the **Maison du Vin** (daily 10am–12.30pm & 2.30–6.30pm; Ⓣ05.56.27.15.44, Ⓦwww.maisondebarsac.fr) which doubles as a tourist office and showcase for Barsac wines; find it on the main road, opposite the church.

There are two Premiers Crus châteaux in the Barsac area – Climens and Coutet – but if you want to visit one of the vineyards in the area, the best option is the less distinguished **Château Gravas** (daily 9am–noon & 2–6pm; free; Ⓣ05.56.27.06.91, Ⓦwww.chateau-gravas.fr), situated about a kilometre south of Barsac, which is a friendly, family-run place, producing high-quality but reasonably priced bottles from €15.

Overnight stays are catered for a by a handful of **chambres d'hôtes**. Closest are the three large, fully-equipped rooms at *Les Vignes de Camperos* (Ⓣ05.56.27.15.47, Ⓦwww.lesvignesdecamperos.com; ❸) signed off the D114 just south of Barsac on the far side of the railway line.

Langon and around

LANGON, 8km east of Sauternes village, is the most substantial town in the area and handily located between the Sauternes region and the southern reaches of Entre-Deux-Mers just across the Garonne (see p.101). Though it's not an especially attractive or interesting place to stay, its shops and range of practical services make it worth considering as a base.

Two hundred years ago the town was an important river-port, linked to Bordeaux by passenger-steamer in 1818. And now the river has come back into its own, with barges transporting the giant components of the Airbus A380 passenger plane from Bordeaux to Langon (see box, p.89). That apart, Langon has nothing particular in the way of sights beyond **St-Gervais church**, whose Chartres-like steeple dominates the old town centre. There's a very active cultural centre here, though: **Les Carmes**, 8 place des Carmes (Ⓣ05.56.63.14.45, Ⓦwww.lescarmes.fr), which puts on a varied programme of theatre, dance, music and circus arts between September and June.

The heart of Langon is place du Général-de-Gaulle. From here cours du Général-Leclerc leads west to the **train station**. You can pick up regional **buses** (most significantly the #501 to Cadillac and Bordeaux) on cours du Général-Leclerc or at the station. The **tourist office** is located just off the central square at 11 allées Jean-Jaurès (Mon 2–6pm, Tues–Fri 9.30am–1pm & 2–6pm, Sat 9.30am–12.30pm; Ⓣ05.56.63.68.00, Ⓦwww.sauternais-graves-langon.com). They organize various excursions, including a half-day mini-bus tour of the Graves and Sauternes vineyards (€10 per person) and can help arrange châteaux visits if you'd rather do it independently. They also offer **bike rental** and have detailed maps of the cycle tracks and footpaths crisscrossing the area. There's **internet** access at CyberLangon, 68 Cours des Fossés (Tues–Sat 10am–8pm,

Sun 3–8pm). Langon has only one central **hotel:** the three-star *Claude Darroze*, 95 cours du Général-Leclerc (Ⓣ05.56.63.00.48, Ⓦwww.darroze.com; closed two weeks in Jan & mid-Oct to mid-Nov; ❹–❺), whose spacious and stylish rooms play second fiddle to one of the region's top restaurants, offering imaginative cuisine – in summer, on a quiet shady terrace (menus €40–78).

For somewhere cheaper to **eat**, the *Cercle des Amis Réunis* (Tues–Sun, lunch only), opposite the tourist office on allées Jean-Jaurès, is a bustling brasserie serving a standard range of salads, main courses and menus (from €13).

Château de Roquetaillade

The **Château de Roquetaillade** (guided visits: April–June, Sept & Oct daily 3pm & 4pm; July & Aug daily 10am–5pm; Nov–April Sun, public hols & school hols 3pm & 4pm; €8, or €9 including farm museum; Ⓦchateauroquetaillade.free.fr) sits in a large park about 7km south of Langon. With its solid central keep, crenellations and massive walls, it bears a strong resemblance to an English fortress – not so surprising given that it dates from the early 1300s when Aquitaine belonged to the English Crown and new ideas of military architecture were being introduced. The castle was built by Cardinal Gaillard de la Mothe, nephew of Pope Clément V, and has been in the same family ever since, which partly explains why it is so well preserved. Another reason is the spunky character of former owner Marie Henriette de Lansac, who reputedly saved Roquetaillade from destruction in the Revolution. When the labourers arrived to demolish the castle she is said to have doubled their pay, asking them in return not to touch anything except the "good wine of Roquetaillade".

Even so, the castle you see today is not entirely genuine – the interiors in particular underwent extensive renovations in the late nineteenth century under the creative hands of **Viollet-le-Duc**, a restorer much in vogue at the time, but who has since been widely criticized for his fairy-tale conception of medieval architecture. At Roquetaillade, one of his colleagues went to work on the twelfth-century chapel with a colourful hotchpotch of Oriental, North African and European motifs. Viollet-le-Duc saved his own energies for the main castle where he added an extra gateway, decorative windows and machicolations around the parapet to create what he considered a medieval look.

Contemporary engravings show that, in fact, Viollet-le-Duc didn't tamper too much with the original facade, but **interiors** are another matter. The work was commissioned in 1886 by the then owner, Mauvesin, who wanted nothing but the best and could afford it thanks to his highly profitable Médoc vineyards. Viollet-le-Duc set about the task with gusto. He filled the entrance hall with a monumental white-stone staircase, painted every inch of wall – including two charming tricolour-winged angels in the Pink Room – and even designed a complete dining-room suite. So long did all this take, however, that Mauvesin ran out of money in the mid-1870s when the architect was only halfway through the Great Hall. A small engraving shows what he had in mind, but it's still an impressive room, dominated by a suitably exuberant Renaissance chimneypiece remarkably similar in style to those at Cadillac (see p.102). As you leave the castle's inner courtyard, look back at the carvings over the door: the two middle faces depict Mauvesin and his wife; that on the left, with the smile, is said to be Viollet-le-Duc. The castle also hosts concerts during the exceptional *Festes Baroques* **festival** in June and July (see box, p.60).

Stay nearby at the five plush and elegant rooms in a stately home only marginally less impressive than La Roquetaillade itself, the *Manoir de Belle Fontaine* (Ⓦwww.manoirdebellefontaine.com; ❺), a kilometre or so down the road from the château in the village of Roaillan.

Entre-Deux-Mers

The landscape of **Entre-Deux-Mers** (literally "between two seas") – so called because it is sandwiched between the tidal waters of the Dordogne and Garonne – is the prettiest of the Bordeaux wine regions. It's an area of gentle hills and scattered medieval villages, many of them *bastides* (see box, p.306) founded by the English during the Hundred Years' War, the most typical examples of which are **Sauveterre-de-Guyenne** and **Monségur**. Earlier builders and craftsmen left a legacy of Romanesque churches decorated with splendid carvings, which reached their apogee in the ruined abbeys of **La Sauve-Majeure**, **Blasimon** and **St-Ferme**. Moving on a few centuries, the artist Toulouse-Lautrec spent much of his life at Château Malromé near **Verdelais**, while François Mauriac wrote some of his greatest novels at Malagar, just outside **St-Macaire**. Further along the Garonne, **La Réole** boasts the oldest town hall in France. In **Rauzan**, in the far north of Entre-Deux-Mers, you can ring the changes with a visit to an underground river system.

Entre-Deux-Mers produces a wide variety of **wines**, but is best known for the dry whites, which are regarded as good but inferior to the super-dry Graves (see box, p.92). The vineyards of Cadillac, Loupiac and Sainte-Croix-du-Mont, three *appellations* overlooking the Garonne, also produce a sweet white wine comparable with many Sauternes, but at lower prices. Several Maisons du Vin scattered throughout the area provide tastings and advice on vineyard visits, as well as the opportunity to buy.

While most of the sights of Entre-Deux-Mers are widely scattered, a surprising number are still just about accessible by **public transport**. Trains on the Bordeaux–Agen line stop at Langon (see p.99), St-Macaire and La Réole, while infrequent buses then take you from Langon to Cadillac or from La Réole to Sauveterre and Monségur. From Sauveterre buses also head west to La Sauve-Majeure, en route to Bordeaux, and northwards via Blasimon and Rauzan to Libourne, where they connect with trains on the Bordeaux–Paris mainline. Note that many of these bus routes only run on demand. A disused railway line has been transformed into a dedicated surfaced **cycle route** from Latresne train station, on the outskirts of Bordeaux, to Sauveterre. Another eight circular routes have also been marked out; local tourist offices stock maps and brochures.

La Sauve-Majeure

The one place you should really try to see is the ruined Benedictine abbey in the centre of Entre-Deux-Mers, about 23km east of Bordeaux and accessible from there by bus, at **LA SAUVE-MAJEURE** (June–Sept daily 10am–6pm; Oct–May Tues–Sun 10.30am–1pm & 2–5.30pm; €7; Ⓦwww.monum.fr). Set in a tranquil valley of small vineyards and cornfields, it was once all forest here, the abbey's name being a corruption of the Latin *silva major* ("big wood"). It was founded in 1079 by a hermit later known as St Gérard and became an important stop for pilgrims en route to Spain's Santiago de Compostela. Thanks to royal and papal backing, at its height La Sauve boasted over seventy dependent priories stretching from England to Spain, but then fell into slow decay. Only the apse and stumps of wall topped by a defiant octagonal bell tower (worth the climb) still remain.

Despite such neglect, a series of outstanding **sculpted capitals** – big, bold and several unusually low on the walls – has survived from the twelfth century. The finest are those around the transepts and choir, some illustrating stories from the Old and New Testaments, others showing fabulous beasts and vegetal motifs. In the little chapels either side of the apse, look out for Adam's anguished face as Eve hands him the apple, and Daniel upside down in the lions' den. But the most remarkable scene occurs on a capital on the southern wall, near the entrance to the tower, where the story of John the Baptist is depicted in astonishing detail. On one side Salome dances as Herod twirls his moustache in appreciation; on the other you see John's head being removed from the prison.

There's a small museum at the abbey entrance, containing keystones from the fallen roof and fragments of painted wall, and the nearby grange now houses the **Maison du Vin** (June–Sept Mon–Sat 10.30am–12.30pm & 2–5.30pm; Oct–May Mon–Fri 10am–noon & 2–5pm; ⓣ05.57.34.32.12, ⓦwww.vins-entre-deux-mers.com) showcasing the dry white wines of the Entre-Deux-Mers.

If you have the time, stroll over to the parish church of **St-Pierre**, visible on the neighbouring hill, where St Gérard is buried (ask at the *mairie* if the church is locked). Though built around the same time as the abbey, the church has survived intact, including its thirteenth-century frescoes (all bar one retouched in the nineteenth century) showing St James and pilgrims on their way to Compostela.

There's nothing else to stay for apart from the excellent **restaurant**, *Restaurant de l'Abbaye*, just below the ruins (closed Mon), which offers an interesting selection of country classics and modern dishes (lunch Tues–Fri from €11.50, otherwise menus start at €22).

Cadillac

Twenty kilometres south of La Sauve-Majeure, on the banks of the Garonne, **CADILLAC** is as famous for its name as for the dour Renaissance **château** that dominates it. According to local legend, Antoine Laumet, the founder of Detroit, Michigan – home city of General Motors – originally came from Cadillac. Sadly, this is just too good to be true. He was born in St-Nicolas-de-la-Grave (see p.328), and on emigrating to Canada simply took the name of Lamothe de Cadillac, even though he had no connections with the town. Today, the tenuous link is celebrated every year in the last weekend of August, when a well-attended **rally** of the emblematic American vehicles is held here. An undisputed fact, however, is that Cadillac was founded by the English in 1280; a surprisingly long stretch of original wall still exists, punctuated by two gates: Porte de l'Horloge to the south and westerly Porte de la Mer. A pleasant, if not extraordinary town, Cadillac's range of accommodation and eating options, coupled with good transport connections, makes it one of the better bases in the area.

The château

In the late sixteenth century the newly named duc d'Épernon, a favourite of Henri III, was given permission to reconstruct a medieval castle at the confluence of the rivers Œuille and Garonne. His **Château de Cadillac**, on the north side of town (June–Sept daily 10am–1.15pm & 2–6pm; Oct–May Tues–Sun 10am–12.30pm & 2–5.30pm; €5; ⓦwww.cadillac.monuments-nationaux.fr), took nearly thirty years to build and was so luxurious – with sixty bedrooms, twenty fireplaces, tapestries and richly painted woodwork – that it was said to rival the king's own palaces. No doubt it yielded rich pickings to the revolutionaries who sacked the place in the 1790s, after which its echoing halls were turned into a notoriously harsh **women's prison**, the Maison Centrale de Force et de Correction, and it's this last usage which seems most fitting as you cross the uninspiring, wide, bare courtyard. Inside, although little remains of the original decoration, some of the Italianate painted ceilings and the magnificent Renaissance **fireplaces** with their over-exuberant plasterwork have now been restored on the ground floor. The real draw, though, is a superb collection of tapestries from various eras. Look out in particular for that depicting the 1573 siege of La Rochelle, which was part of a longer series depicting the life of Henri III and was made here in the castle by craftsmen brought in from Paris in the 1630s. In the Queen's apartments hangs an unusual series of tapestries from Aubusson, depicting six illustrious women, including Artemesia, Lucretia and Cleopatra, the latter dressed in incongruous seventeenth-century ruffles as she tempts her lover, Antony, with a pearl.

Upstairs is contrastingly sober, and houses displays about the history of the château and its occupants, including photos and documents relating to the prison, the majority of whose inmates were guilty of infanticide – often committed in the place of abortion. Conditions were extremely strict: absolute silence, a bread-and-water diet and no privacy. The great halls were converted into overcrowded dormitories and even the fireplaces were pressed into service as makeshift latrines.

While building his château, the duc d'Épernon was also planning a grand mausoleum for himself in the nearby **church of St-Blaise**. Though his funeral monument was largely destroyed during the Revolution, the celebrated bronze statue of *Renommée* – a winged trumpeter – somehow survived (the original is in the Louvre). The church's ornate altarpiece dates from the same period. It features two statues of the duke and duchess's patron saints, Ste Marguerite and St John, to either side of a crucifixion scene.

Practicalities

Cadillac's nearest **gare SNCF** lies a short walk across the Garonne at Cerons, while **buses** between Bordeaux and Langon stop outside the ramparts on place de Lattre-de-Tassigny. The **tourist office** (April–June Tues–Sun 9.30am–noon & 2–6pm; July–Sept daily 9.30am–12.30pm & 2–7pm; Oct–March Tues–Sat 9.30am–12.30pm & 2–6pm, Sun 9.30am–12.30pm; ⓣ05.56.62.12.92, ⓦwww.entredeuxmers.com) is located in front of the château on place de la Libération and offers a good walking guide to the town; **internet** access (€2 for 30min) is also available.

There are two good **hotels** in Cadillac, each catering for a different budget. At the top end is the luxurious *Château de la Tour* (ⓣ05.56.76.92.00, ⓦwww.hotel-restaurant-chateaudelatour.com; ❼), with a garden, swimming pool, wi-fi and a classy restaurant (menus €28–55; March–Nov daily; Dec–Feb closed Sat lunch & Sun eve), beside the D10 just north of town. The alternative is *Chez Détrée* (ⓣ05.56.62.65.38; ❶–❷), a smart two-star, whose cheapest rooms have shared facilities. The tourist office can also give you a list of **chambres d'hôtes** in the area, the best of which is the *Château de Grand Branet* (ⓣ05.56.72.17.30, ⓦchateaugrandbranet.free.fr; ❹; closed Jan), a wine château 11km north near **CAPIAN** village offering splendid en-suite rooms, with *table d'hôte* on request (€20). Cadillac is also a good destination for **campers**, with a small, cheap municipal site (ⓣ05.56.62.72.98; closed mid-Sept to mid-June) on the banks of the Garonne. If you've got transport though, head for the welcoming and peaceful *Domaine de Chicoye* (Ⓣ05.56.62.01.79; closed mid-Sept to Easter), 4km away near Loupiac on the road to Sainte-Croix-du-Mont (see below).

When it comes to **eating**, there's a clutch of cafés and brasseries, as well as a boulangerie, on the partly arcaded central place de la République, also the venue for a Saturday-morning market. The town's top restaurant, *L'Entrée Jardin*, is beside the bridge at 27 av du Pont (Ⓣ05.56.76.96.96; closed Sun eve, Mon & Wed eve in winter; weekday lunch menus from €13, Sun & eves €27–56), where rich dishes such as stuffed guinea fowl or foie gras and asparagus in a truffle sauce are served in a riverside setting. Another good option is *Les Artistes* (closed Mon, Tues eve & Wed eve) by the medieval Porte-de-la-Mer, just inside the city walls, an informal restaurant offering healthy cooking with fresh products (menus €12–27) and occasional art exhibitions.

Upstream to Verdelais

Either side of Cadillac the Entre-Deux-Mers plateau edges closer to the Garonne. There are good **viewpoints** all along the escarpment, but one of the finest is from the village of **SAINTE-CROIX-DU-MONT** about 6km to the southwest. Aim for the terrace running in front of the church and the medieval Château de Tastes, now the *mairie*, perched on the cliff edge. The **cliff** itself is also of interest. Its top layer, ranging in thickness from three to eight metres and extending back under the village, is composed of fossilized oyster shells deposited some 25 million years ago. If you wander down to the terrace below the church and castle, you can see a series of shallow caves (good fun for children), where the oyster shells are clearly visible. Ste-Croix's other draw is the sweet white **wine** produced within the small area which falls under its appellation. The wines are similar to those of Barsac across the river, and compare very favourably with Sauternes in terms of value for money. There are a couple of wine shops in the village where you can taste and buy.

A few kilometres east of here, **VERDELAIS** offers more views and an ornate Baroque **church**, every inch covered with votive plaques dedicated to a miracle-performing statue made of chestnut wood of the Virgin and Child. Although the statue, which is on display in the church, dates from the fourteenth century, Verdelais' first recorded miracle took place in 1185 and pilgrims have been flocking here ever since. Many of them left gifts of paintings, silver hearts and bejewelled cloaks for the statue in thanks, and a fraction of the collection is on display at the nearby **Musée d'Art Religieux** on Verdelais' main road, at no. 3 (Ⓣ05.56.62.02.04; July & Aug daily 3–6.30pm; Sept–June phone for opening times; €3).

Verdelais' main claim to fame these days, however, is the **tomb of Toulouse-Lautrec** (see box opposite), which lies across the road in the church cemetery; go straight ahead from the entrance gate to find it last on the left. Henri Toulouse-Lautrec spent his summers a couple of kilometres northeast of Verdelais in the enchanting **Château Malromé** (Ⓣ05.56.76.44.92, Ⓦwww.malrome.com). His mother, the Countess Adèle de Toulouse-Lautrec, bought the château in 1883 and had it renovated in neo-medieval style according to the then-fashionable ideas of Viollet-le-Duc (see p.100). She also rescued its neglected vineyard, which now produces eminently palatable red and white wines and a "clairet", a light red wine drunk chilled in summer. The house is sadly closed to the public, but if you make an appointment (Mon–Fri) you can visit the vineyard and have a tasting.

Toulouse-Lautrec

Known for his provocative portraits of Parisian low-life, **Henri Toulouse-Lautrec** was born in Albi, northeast of Toulouse, in 1864. His father, Count Alphonse de Toulouse-Lautrec, was a highly eccentric man with a passion for hunting, illicit affairs and bizarre outfits, who married his first cousin. This genetic mismatch is blamed for Henri's stunted growth and delicate constitution, exacerbated by two childhood accidents, which left him permanently crippled. Nevertheless, encouraged by an uncle and two family friends who spotted his artistic talent, Henri went to study in Paris under Bonnat and Cormon before setting up his own studio in **Montmartre** in 1884.

Henri was in his element here. He produced hundreds of paintings and sketches portraying the unglamorous reality of life in the cabarets, theatres, bars and brothels of *fin-de-siècle* Paris. Among his most famous works are those associated with the **Moulin Rouge**, which Henri began to frequent in 1890, recording events offstage as well as the great music-hall artists of the day: Yvette Guilbert, Jane Avril and May Belfort, among others. The portraits are often grotesque, with a strong element of caricature, but his affection for his subjects shines through. This is particularly true of his works in the *maisons closes*, when the prostitutes – if not their clients – are treated with great sympathy and sensitivity.

The bohemian life and excess of alcohol gradually took its toll. In 1900 Henri returned to southwest France to set up a studio in Bordeaux where the café and theatre world provided ample subject matter. But the following year, as his health began to deteriorate, he was taken back to Château Malromé, where he died on September 9, aged 37 years. Though originally buried in the nearby cemetery of St-André-du-Bois, in 1908 Henri's body was moved to **Verdelais**, where his mother eventually joined him.

Thanks to the uncompromising nature of much of his work, Toulouse-Lautrec met with very little critical success during his lifetime. His portraits were far too shocking for mainstream contemporary tastes and even in the 1920s both the Louvre and Toulouse city refused the family's gift of six hundred paintings, posters and sketches. The magnificent collection went instead to Albi. Since then Toulouse-Lautrec has been recognized as one of the founders of modern advertising, while his dynamic, almost calligraphic lines and bold swathes of colour have won worldwide acclaim.

St-Macaire and around

Just across the Garonne from Langon (see p.99), and some 12km southeast of Cadillac, **ST-MACAIRE** provides a more attractive alternative base, though it's a bit dead out of season. The town was founded in the first century AD by an itinerant Greek monk called Makarios. Later it grew wealthy on the wine trade, so that by the mid-fourteenth century the population had reached six thousand, only to decline from the early 1600s onwards as the river shifted and the port silted up. These days St-Macaire musters a mere 1600 souls but still retains several of its original gates and battlements as well as a beautiful medieval church.

St-Macaire's glory days are also still evident in the number of dignified edifices, the homes of wealthy merchants, many of which are now being renovated. Some of the most handsome lie just inside **Porte Benauge**, the main north gate, and around the old market square, **place Mercadiou**, to the east. The **church of St Sauveur**, on the other hand, occupies an abandoned river cliff on the south side of town. Nothing remains of the original Benedictine priory beyond a fragment of cloister-wall, but the fourteenth-century murals inside the church are what everybody comes to see. They were somewhat crudely restored – and embellished – in 1825, but even so present a fine spectacle. While the scenes behind the altar are based on St John the Evangelist's Revelation, his miracles and martyrdom in a vat of boiling oil are depicted over the transept.

Admirers of the Nobel-prize-winning novelist **François Mauriac** (1885–1970) should pay a visit to his bolt-hole and source of inspiration, **Malagar** (June–Sept daily 10am–12.30pm & 2–6pm; Oct–May Wed–Fri 2–5pm, Sat, Sun & public hols 10am–12.30pm & 2–5pm; €5.50; Ⓣ05.57.98.17.17, Ⓦwww.malagar.asso.fr), on the hills about 3km north of St-Macaire. The little château has been preserved largely as he left it, including the desk where he wrote one of his most famous novels, *Nœud de Vipères* (*Vipers' Tangle*), published in 1932. In the adjacent François Mauriac Centre you can see many original documents, alongside photos and videos of the great man. The centre also puts on a varied programme of cultural events throughout the year.

Practicalities

At least one **train** a day stops at the **gare SNCF**, less than half a kilometre north of town, or there are more frequent services to Langon (see p.99), 2km across the river. St-Macaire's **tourist office** (April & May Tues–Sun 10am–1pm & 3–7pm; June–Sept daily 10am–1pm & 3–7pm; Oct–March Wed–Fri 2–6pm, Sat & Sun 10am–noon & 2–6pm; Ⓣ05.56.63.32.14 Ⓦwww.entredeuxmers.com) occupies a handsome, sixteenth-century merchant's house just inside the gate. The office doubles as a showroom promoting regional produce, which here means honey and wine. Staff can help arrange visits to the *chais* and in July and August local wine-makers offer tastings in the tourist office.

The best **hotel** in town is stylish *Les Feuilles d'Acanthe* (Ⓣ05.56.62.33.75, Ⓦwww.feuilles-dacanthe.com; ❺) occupying another beautifully restored building opposite the tourist office. The decor features exposed stone walls and terracotta tiles, in addition to gleaming en-suite bathrooms. It even boasts a jacuzzi-solarium, while their *Le Pampaillet* restaurant serves traditional and regional dishes – menus start at €21. *Les Tilleuls* (Ⓣ05.56.62.28.38, Ⓦwww.tilleul-medieval.com; ❷–❸), meanwhile, just outside Porte Benauge, offers exceptionally good-value studio apartments, which come fully furnished with living space, kitchen and extra sofa beds to accommodate up to four people. Or you can eat in their cheerful restaurant, *Le Mediéval* (daily for lunch & for dinner Fri & Sat; menus from €14.50), which is popular for its hot-stone grills and attractive summer terrace, not to mention very reasonable prices.

St-Macaire's top **restaurant** is *L'Abricotier* (Ⓣ05.56.76.83.63; closed Mon all day & Tues eve; menus €20–40) west of town on the busy N113. It may not look much from the outside but this is one of the region's eminent addresses. It's best in summer when tables spread out into the pretty, walled garden, but the food remains excellent all year, featuring shad, lamprey and other local fish as well as game in season. They also have three very comfortable rooms, again with kitchenettes (❸); advance booking is essential.

La Réole and around

LA RÉOLE, 20km east of St-Macaire along the same escarpment, hides some good medieval architecture among its narrow, hilly streets, but somehow feels cramped and dowdy as opposed to quaintly aged. That said, it's worth visiting to see France's oldest town hall and the well-preserved Benedictine abbey, along with a quirky museum.

In medieval times La Réole was the region's second largest town after Bordeaux. To ensure their loyalty, Richard the Lionheart granted its townspeople a certain degree of self-government and ordered the building of a town hall. Even today, La Réole is fiercely proud of what is France's oldest surviving Hôtel de Ville, overlooking place Georges Chaigne on the north side of the old town. Not that there's much to see. The big, open hall downstairs has a few carved capitals, while proclamations were presumably made from the modest balcony on the north side; the first-floor meeting hall is open occasionally for exhibitions.

From here, walk south down rue Peysseguin, La Réole's prettiest and most atmospheric street, with one or two handsome townhouses and a smattering of half-timbered facades, then turn right along semi-pedestrianized rue Armand Caduc to find the **church of St-Pierre**, with its impressive interior lit by stained-glass windows and an unusually grandiose oak and marble pulpit, crowned by a sculpture of St George spearing a dragon. Next door is the entrance to the former cloister of the Benedictine abbey, which now houses municipal offices. Pride of the eighteenth-century building is some good wrought ironwork by local master-craftsman Blaise Charlut, who was also responsible for the screens in Bordeaux Cathedral (see p.70). You can admire the best of his craftsmanship in the gates of the southern door from where a pretty double staircase leads down onto a wide terrace overlooking the Garonne. On a clear winter's day it's even possible to see the Pyrenees from here.

The town of La Réole looks at its best from a distance, so it's worth crossing over to the far side of the Garonne for the best views. Here you can also follow the peaceful **towpath** by the Canal des Deux-Mers, leading to the village of **FONTET**, home to the delightfully wacky **Musée d'Artisanat Monuments en Allumettes** (Ⓣ05.56.71.21.17; Feb–Sept daily 2–6pm; Oct–Nov Sun & public hols 2–6pm; closed Dec & Jan; €5) dedicated to scale models made of matchsticks. The models include an awe-inspiring reproduction of Reims cathedral which consumed no fewer than 350,000 matchsticks, a magnificent rendition of the Château de Versailles, complete with goldfish swimming in its fountains, and the pretty Romanesque church of Fontet itself, which you can see a short walk from the museum. Needless to say, sparking up is strictly forbidden.

Also worth a visit on your way north to Sauveterre (see p.108) is the **Château de Lavison** (Ⓣ05.56.71.48.82; May to mid-Sept daily 2.30–6pm; mid-Sept to April by appointment only; free), north of St-Sève on the D129. This thirteenth-century fortress once belonged to Edward 1 of England and was later used by the Black Prince as a hunting lodge. In the fifteenth and sixteenth centuries, the castle was enlarged and made into a more comfortable residence, which it remains to this day, furnished with some splendid family heirlooms. The guided tour ends with a visit to the *chais* to sample the domaine's very palatable AOC wines.

Practicalities

La Réole is blessed with relatively good transport connections. Its regularly served **gare SNCF** is located a little way east of town, from where it's a steep ten-minute walk to the centre, while **buses** (mainly running only on demand) from Sauveterre-de-Guyenne and Monségur stop on central place de la Libération. The **tourist office**, on place Richard-Coeur-de-Lion (June–Sept Mon 2.30–6.30pm, Tues–Sat 9.30am–12.30pm & 2.30–6.30pm, Sun 9.30am–12.30pm; Oct–May Mon 3–6pm, Tues–Sat 9.30am–12.30pm & 3–6pm; Ⓣ05.56.61.13.55, Ⓦwww.lareole.fr) occupies one of the half-timbered buildings beside the former Hôtel de Ville.

While there's no **accommodation** in La Réole itself, there's a good choice of **chambres d'hôtes** nearby. Three kilometres north on the D21 to St-Sève you'll find *Au Canton* (ⓣ05.56.61.04.88, ⓔmoniquebauge@aol.com; ❸), with two rooms in a rustic eighteenth-century house with a pleasant park. They also offer evening meals for €20. Slightly further north, just off the main D670 to Sauveterre, *La Camiranaise* (ⓣ05.56.71.11.26, ⓦwww.lacamiranaise.free.fr; ❹), is also good, with five spacious rooms and a swimming pool. La Réole itself does offer a well-run, two-star **campsite**, *Le Rouergue* (ⓣ05.56.61.13.55, ⓔlareole@entredeuxmers.com; closed Nov–May), just across the old suspension bridge, with great views back to the abbey.

La Réole's finest **restaurant** is the light and airy *Les Fontaines* on rue de Verdun (ⓣ05.56.61.15.25; closed Sun eve, Mon & also Wed eve Sept–June), with a terrace looking across to the old Hôtel de Ville. The food consists of classic French cuisine and you can eat very well for €21. For a less formal lunch, head to *Les Quat' Sauces* on Avenue du Général Leclerc (ⓣ05.56.71.22.99; open for lunch Tues–Sat; €11), a restaurant-*traiteur* offering hearty, authentic meals served in a simple dining room.

La Réole's main **market** takes place on Saturday mornings on the esplanade des Quais along the Garonne – a good place to stock up on picnic provisions. On Sunday mornings a smaller, farmers' market sets up on place de la Libération.

Sauveterre-de-Guyenne and around

The majority of *bastides* (see box, p.306) in Entre-Deux-Mers were founded by the English. Of these, perhaps one of the most typical, with its large, arcaded central square, gate towers and gridiron street plan, is **Sauveterre-de-Guyenne**, 14km north of La Réole, and established under Edward I in 1281. The ramparts were demolished in 1814, replaced by what is now a ring-road, but they must have been a bit battered – Sauveterre changed hands ten times during the Hundred Years' War before finally falling to the French in 1451. The town boasts no real sights of its own, but is big enough to merit cafés, restaurants and other services grouped round place de la République, the venue for a lively Tuesday-morning **market**.

Sauveterre has bus connections to Libourne and La Réole; **buses** stop on place de la République and/or the ring road. You can find out more about these services and get other local information at the **tourist office** (June & Sept Tues–Sat 9am–noon & 2–6pm; July & Aug Tues–Sun 9.30am–12.30pm & 2–6pm; Oct–May Tues–Sat 9am–noon & 2–5.30pm; ⓣ05.56.71.53.45, ⓦwww.entredeuxmers.com) in the southeast corner of the central square. It also offers bike rental and has maps of the region's marked cycling routes. The building is also home to the **Maison des Vins** (same hours), which sells local wines at producers' prices.

As there's nowhere particularly attractive to **stay** in Sauveterre, it's better instead to head for one of the nearby *chambres d'hôtes*. Try the *Moulin de St-Léger* (ⓣ05.56.71.59.94, ⓦwww.moulindestleger.com; ❸), 3km away in the hamlet of St-Léger-de-Vignague, with three well-priced rooms in a good spot next to the church. For **food**, there's no need to stray from Sauveterre's central square, where the best option is *Les Arcades* (weekday lunch menus from €11, eves & weekends from €17; closed Mon) on the northwest corner. This café-restaurant-bar attracts a mix of locals and tourist traffic with its simple but well-cooked dishes and good-value menus. Opposite is *La Tosca*, a popular pizzeria (pizzas from €11), while the square also has a small supermarket and a boulangerie.

Around Sauveterre-de-Guyenne

Seven kilometres southwest of Sauveterre, through a rolling landscape of vines and windmills, lies the tiny, flowery village of **CASTELVIEL**, worth a visit for the carved south portal of its twelfth-century church. Though they're a bit worn in places, it's still possible to make out a wealth of detail on the portal's five tiers. The outer arch depicts scenes from rural life; on the second the Vices confront the Virtues; the third, which resembles a tug-of-war, represents the faithful united by their common bond. Monsters, biblical characters and layers of interlocking vegetation overspill from the remaining tiers to two small, flanking arches.

The same distance east of Sauveterre on the D230, the main claim to fame of **CASTELMORON-D'ALBRET** is as the smallest commune in France. The village comprises just 3.5 hectares and owns none of the surrounding agricultural land. With its wash-house, former seneschal's house and tiled market hall, and, of course, the inevitable potter, it's a picturesque spot almost verging on the twee.

Seven kilometres north of Sauveterre, **BLASIMON**, founded by the English in 1322, was one of the very last *bastides* constructed in the region. The town occupies a rocky promontory looking north over the Gamage valley and a ruined **abbey** established by Benedictine monks in the seventh century. The cloister and abbey buildings, which were obviously fortified at some time, were abandoned in the thirteenth century, but the church itself has survived. Again, it's the twelfth-century Romanesque carvings round the west door that are most absorbing. The elongated, sinuous figures of the Vices and Virtues are so incredibly delicate it's hard to believe their age. In other places the soft stone has weathered badly, though not so much that you can't identify the angels adoring the Lamb of God on the inner tier, hunting scenes on the outer edge, and at least get the gist of the exuberant motifs around. The interior is contrastingly unadorned save for the captivating faces on the capitals to either side of the entrance door. If you want to see inside, make an appointment on Ⓣ05.56.71.52.12.

RAUZAN, 6km northwest of Blasimon, is dominated by its **castle** (July & Aug daily 10am–noon & 2–6pm; Sept–June Tues–Sat 10am–noon & 2–5pm, Sun 2–5pm; €3; Ⓦwww.tourisme-rauzan.fr.fm), founded by English forces in the run up to the Hundred Years' War. No period furniture or fancy adornments here, just good authentic ruins and a great view from the top of the keep. In 1845 an underground river was discovered running beneath Rauzan and has since been made good use of by the townspeople for everything from lovers' trysts to shelter for Resistance fighters during World War II. Now known as the **Grotte Célestine** (Ⓣ05.57.84.08.69, Ⓦwww.rauzan.fr; same hours as castle; by appointment; €6.50) it now provides an enjoyable excursion as you splosh along the river bed equipped with helmet and waders to admire the limestone concretions and learn about their formation. Note that there's a minimum height restriction of 1.2m (4ft) tall to enter.

Both Blasimon and Rauzan lie on the **bus** route between Sauveterre and Libourne (Mon–Fri two daily on demand). To **stay** in Rauzan, make for *Le Manoir de Marie-Lou* at 34 rue du Petit Versailles (Ⓣ05.57.84.07.48; Ⓦwww.lemanoirdemarielou.fr; ❹–❺), a lovely *chambre d'hôte* with somewhat expensive but very attractive rooms, all parquet floors and bare stone walls, fully-equipped with large bathrooms and mod-cons. Rauzan also has an excellent, shady **campsite** with a pool, *Camping du Vieux Château* (Ⓣ05.57.84.15.38,

Ⓦwww.vieux-chateau.com; closed Nov–March), in the valley beneath the castle ramparts.

If you're looking for somewhere simple to **eat** in the area, a good choice would be the *Auberge Gasconne* (Ⓣ05.57.40.52.08; open Tues–Sun for lunch and Fri & Sat eves) in **ST-PEY-DE-CASTETS**, 6km northwest of Rauzan. It's a typical village inn, with an excellent €12 weekday lunch menu and other menus from €23.50.

Monségur

On the eastern fringes of the Entre-Deux-Mers region, some 20km northeast of La Réole, **MONSÉGUR** is rather lifeless these days, but does still represent another good example of a *bastide*. Founded by the English in 1265, its arcaded central square rivals that of Sauveterre-de-Guyenne, and has the added interest of a wrought-iron **market hall** in the centre, where there's a traditional market on Friday mornings. You could also glance inside the **church of Notre-Dame**, which dates from the original building of the *bastide*, though its steeple was added in the nineteenth century, and then wander around the grassy walkway outside the town's old **ramparts**, a good stretch of which have survived in healthy condition. The town does burst into action for its annual **jazz festival**, the 24 Heures Du Swing in early July, when concerts take place on the central square and in surrounding bars over three days – in spite of the festival's name.

Monségur is accessible by **bus** from La Réole and Sauveterre and is also in a decent location to serve as a base for visiting Ste-Ferme (see below) or moving on to Duras and the other bastides (see p.305). If you decide to stay here, by far the best bet is the *chambre d'hôte Sous le Cep d'Antan* (Ⓣ05.56.61.60.28, Ⓦwww.souslecep-dantan.com; ❸) on the market square, which has pleasant rooms and a restaurant serving excellent gastronomic menus (from €26), including imaginative country delights like hare pie, set around a leafy interior courtyard. Alternatively, you can't go wrong at the no-frills diner, *Les Tilleuls* (lunch only, closed Sat & Sun), on place des Tilleuls, where the *menu du jour* costs just €11 including wine.

St-Ferme and around

The last stop in Entre-Deux-Mers is **ST-FERME**, 11km north of Monségur. The village clusters round the solid, grey **abbey** – founded by Benedictine monks sometime before the eleventh century – from which it takes its name. The fortifications added to the abbey buildings during the Hundred Years' War came in handy again during the Wars of Religion when Protestant forces attacked on at least two occasions. Happily, the **church** (daily 8am–7pm) withstood the onslaught. There's no grand portal, but instead the twelfth-century craftsmen went to work on the **capitals** in the three bays around the altar. Best of the lot is the first pillar on the far wall of the north bay, depicting Daniel being saved from lions with two angels above, while on the opposite wall of the same bay, David aims his sling at Goliath.

A couple of kilometres east of St-Ferme on the D127 to Duras, the welcoming **chambre d'hôte** *Manoir de James* (Ⓣ05.56.61.69.75, Ⓦwww.manoir-de-james.com; closed mid-Dec to mid-Jan, July & Aug; ❹) occupies a quiet spot among fields. The rooms are a touch expensive, but big and airy, with sizeable

Bloodsucking delicacy

The **lamprey** (*lamproie*) is one of those gastronomic delicacies not everyone has the stomach for. This primitive eel-like fish never developed jaws but is equipped instead with a powerful tooth-lined sucker for a mouth. With this it attaches itself to passing prey – generally larger fish – and proceeds to suck their blood. That doesn't really justify slitting it open alive to drain the blood, but that's what happens to hundreds of lampreys caught each spring in the Garonne and Dordogne rivers when, like salmon, they swim upstream to breed. Local chefs then slice them up and cook them for several hours with leeks in red wine, mixing in the blood just before serving. Garlic croutons add texture.

In 1990, Ste-Terre, a former fishing village on the Dordogne near St-Émilion, declared itself the world's lamprey capital and instigated a lamprey festival (late April), when members of the lamprey brotherhood parade in their finery and drink a toast to the unfortunate fish before everyone tucks into tureens of *lamproie à la Bordelaise*.

If you're curious to see what they look like, head to the **Jardin de la Lamproie** (April–Sept Tues–Sat 10am–12.30pm & 2–6.30pm, Sun 2–6.30pm; Oct–March Tues–Sat 10am–noon & 2–5pm; free) in Lavagnac, on the river just west of Ste-Terre. There's a tank of them in the exhibition hall and a video presentation and you can also buy ready-prepared jars of lamprey, should you be so inclined. Lamprey appears on restaurant menus throughout the region at around €20.

bathrooms, plus there's a swimming pool and the English-speaking owners can help arrange visits to local wine producers.

The countryside north of St-Ferme is attractive, too. Take the D16 towards St-Foy-la-Grande, then turn left just before Pellegrue on the D126 to find a succession of castles between **AURIOLLES** and **LISTRAC-DE-DURÈZE**. Cutting back southwest, signs indicating "Butte de Launay" lead you to a grassy hillock outside **SOUSSAC** with 360-degree views.

St-Émilion

Roughly 40km east of Bordeaux, or directly north of Sauveterre along the D670, is the oldest wine town in France. It lies at the heart of one of the world's most densely cultivated wine regions, located on the north bank of the River Dordogne shortly before it flows into the Gironde. The **vineyards** alone justify a visit, but there's a lot more to St-Émilion than first meets the eye. The town has hardly grown in size beyond its original twelfth-century ramparts, an appealing collection of old grey houses nestled in a south-facing amphitheatre of low hills, with the green froth of the summer's vines crawling over its walls. Underneath its pretty, cobbled streets, the hillside has been hollowed out to create Europe's largest **underground church** and is riddled with catacombs and quarries that provide ideal conditions for storing the precious wine. Some of St-Émilion's most famous **wine châteaux**, notably Ausone and Belair, sit right on its doorstep, while the limestone plateau to the north is scattered with countless châteaux, country houses and Romanesque churches hemmed in by the rows of pampered vines.

Some history

While the Romans had introduced vines to the area before the third century, the history of St-Émilion really starts some five hundred years later when the **monk Émilion** (or Émilian), arrived here from Brittany and decided to stay. Making his hermitage in an enlarged natural cave he soon gathered a sizeable following, drawn as much by tales of miracle cures as by his piety. After Émilion's death in 767, the religious community continued to grow until the town boasted a population of around 10,000 (as opposed to under three thousand today) when it passed into the hands of the English Crown in 1152 as part of the duchy of Aquitaine. Richard the Lionheart considered the town sufficiently important to grant it the status of a self-governing commune, later ratified in a charter dated 1199 by his successor and brother King John. Thus was born the **Jurade**, an assembly presiding over local justice, taxes, defence, and, of course, the town's economic lifeblood, wine. Indeed, so sought-after was St-Émilion wine that when King Edward II of England reconfirmed the Jurade in 1312, following a brief period when the town was under French rule, he did so in exchange for "fifty barrels of clear, pure and good wine, to be delivered by Easter". Despite such strong English affiliations, St-Émilion retained its privileges after the Hundred Years' War and right up until the Revolution. The Jurade resurfaced again in 1948, but is limited strictly to promoting and maintaining the quality of the wine.

The worldwide fame of St-Émilion was sealed when it was added to UNESCO's World Heritage list in 1999 and now over a million visitors descend on the town each year, the majority during the summer months of July and August. To avoid the worst of the crowds it's best to come in the early morning or late afternoon, and better still to stay overnight here, though accommodation tends to be expensive. St-Émilion is also a feasible day-trip

The wines of St-Emilion

Louis XIV described **St-Émilion wines** as the "nectar of the gods". The best – notably the wines of Château Ausone and Château Cheval-Blanc – certainly rate on a par with the top Médocs (see box, p.82). They are the heartiest of the Bordeaux reds, though within the region there is considerable variety due to its complex geology and the fact that many producers are still small, family-run businesses – the average vineyard is a mere 70,000 square metres.

St-Émilion wines were not included in the 1855 **classification** (see box, p.58), partly for local political reasons (the Bordeaux-based merchants who selected the wines tended to look down on St-Émilion), but won great acclaim in the Paris Exhibition of 1867 and again in 1889, when sixty producers collectively won the Grand Prix. It wasn't until 1954, however, that the wines were fully classified. They were subdivided into two *appellations* – St-Émilion and St-Émilion Grand Cru – and then the latter category organized in three tiers, Grands Crus, Grands Crus Classés and Premiers Grands Crus Classés, of which the top is further subdivided into "A" and "B" wines. Only Ausone and Cheval-Blanc are ranked in the highest "A" category.

Whereas in the other major Bordeaux wine areas there has been little change in the classifications since the nineteenth century, St-Émilion has developed a more rigorous system, whereby the wines of the top producers are tasted and reclassified every ten years. It has run into trouble recently, however, as the last major overhaul (carried out in 2006) had to be abandoned after a handful of châteaux were demoted from *classé* to mere Grand Cru status, but appealed and had the whole classification annulled. Technically, the 1996 classifications now remain valid, but chaos has ensued as the producers attempt to negotiate a new system of evaluating wines from Bordeaux, either by yourself, or with one of the vineyard tours organized by the Bordeaux tourist office (see p.64).

Arrival and information

St-Émilion's **gare SNCF** lies down in the valley 2km to the south. Since only four trains a day stop here at best, you could also alight at more frequently served Libourne, 7km further west on the Bordeaux–Paris line, and call a taxi from there (Ⓣ06.09.35.78.39 or 06.09.33.37.77; around €15 during the day and €20 after 7pm). The less-than-satisfactory alternative is a sporadic **bus** service from Libourne station (Mon–Fri 2–3 daily, but note that most of these only run on demand: call the operators Citram Ⓣ05.56.43.68.43, or Prévost Ⓣ05.57.94.12.12). These drop you on place Bourgeoise, at the top end of the main street, rue Guadet. If you're driving, note that the town centre is closed to traffic during the day, but that there's limited free **parking** behind the gendarmerie just north of place Bourgeoise.

The super-efficient **tourist office** is on place des Créneaux beside the belfry (daily: June & Sept 9.30am–7pm; July & Aug 9am–8pm; Oct–May 9.30am–12.30pm & 1.30–6pm; Ⓣ05.57.55.28.28, Ⓦwww.saint-emilion-tourisme.com), and is where you need to sign up for tours of the Église Monolithe (see p.116). In summer they also organise tours of the vines by minibus (June–Sept daily at 2pm; €18 including one château visit and tasting) and rent out **bikes**. For **internet access**, head down the main street to the *Chai Pascal*, 37 rue Guadet (Tues–Sun 11am–11pm), a relaxed wine bar with wi-fi access and one PC in the corner for customers to use. For helpful advice on purchasing wine or visiting vineyards, call in at the town's **Maison du Vin**, round the corner from the tourist office on place Pierre Meyrat (daily: Aug

which will satisfy all parties. The vested interests of the *vignerons*, however, mean that nobody is banking on a solution being found any time soon.

The two St-Émilion *appellations* cover the eight villages of the medieval jurisdiction, the Jurade (see p.112), with a total of 5400 square kilometres under vines and an average annual production of around 250,000 hectolitres (well over thirty million bottles). More than half of this is exported. In addition, wines produced in the four "satellite" communes to the north – St-Georges, Montagne, Puisseguin and Lussac – are entitled to the St-Émilion name, but preceded by that of the commune: Montagne St-Émilion, for example.

The region's **soils** range from sand-gravel on the Dordogne valley floor to the limestone plateau around the town, in places capped with layers of clay, and the coarse gravel plains of the north and east. Merlot is the predominant **grape variety**, followed by Cabernet Franc (here called Cabernet Bouchet) and with smaller quantities of Cabernet Sauvignon and, occasionally, Malbec. The end result is a smooth, round wine which ages well, though some are ready to drink after only five years. But even a brief tasting session will reveal the tremendous variety among these wines which, combined with the relatively small output from some vineyards, adds to the prestige, and price, of the best ones. A bottle of Château Ausone, for example, will set you back at least €200, but among the Grands Crus you should be able to find some very fine wines, good enough for laying down, for between €15 and €20 a bottle.

For more information on these wines, call in at St-Émilion's **Maison du Vin** (see above). For general tips on visiting vineyards see p.59.

9.30am–7pm; Sept–July 9.30am–12.30pm & 2–6.30pm; ⓣ05.57.55.50.55, ⓦwww.vins-saint-emilion.com). They sell a large selection of wines at châteaux prices and run a **wine school** (mid-July to mid-Sept daily 11am–12.30pm; €20)

As you would expect, the most important of St-Émilion's annual **events** revolve around wine. In June members of the Jurade dust off their finery for the Fête de Printemps, and again in September to announce the harvest (see box, p.60). Over

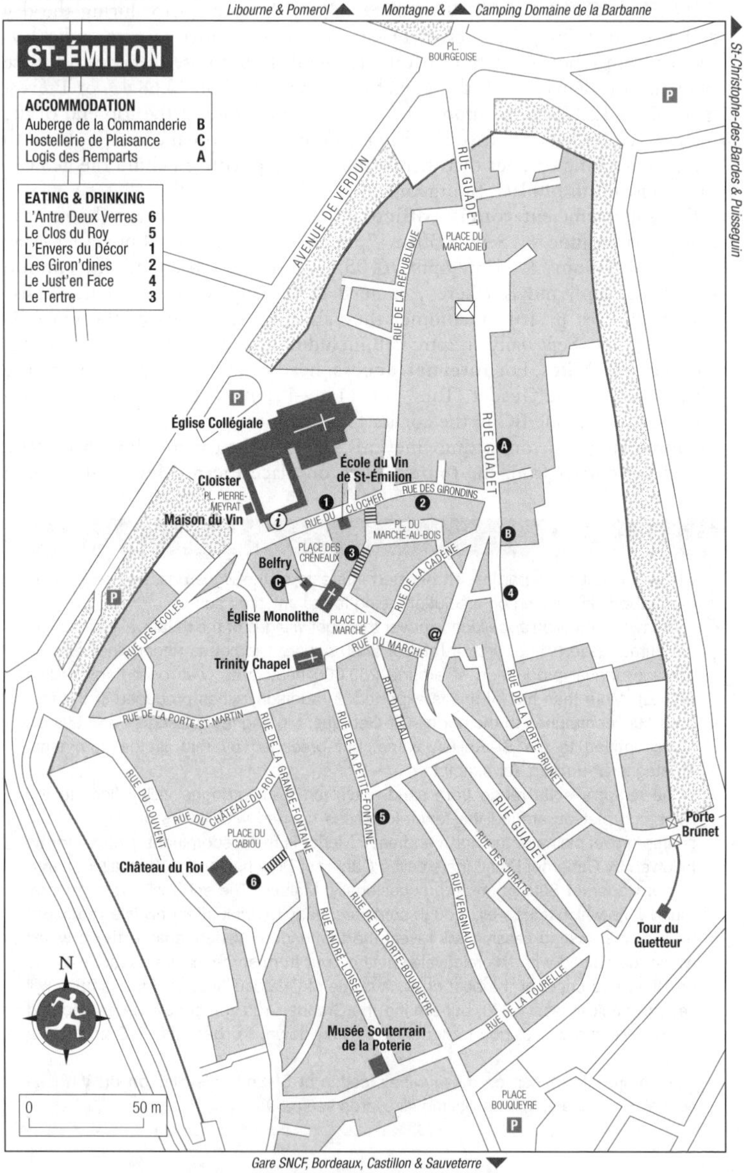

a long weekend in late April or early May (Sat–Mon) some eighty châteaux throw their doors open to the public, while throughout the year keep an eye out for concerts held in the châteaux – accompanied by a tasting of course.

Accommodation

St-Émilion offers a number of good but expensive **hotels**, while for those on a stricter budget there are some very reasonably priced **chambres d'hôtes** and a **campsite** in the surrounding area. Note that most hotels close in December and January, while in summer (notably July & Aug) and during the two main festivals (see above), everywhere gets booked up weeks in advance, with some places hiking their prices by as much as a third. The tourist office won't make reservations for you, but they will be able to advise on where rooms might still be available.

In St-Émilion

Auberge de la Commanderie 2 rue de la Porte-Brunet ⓣ05.57.24.70.19, ⓦwww.aubergedelacommanderie.com. Certainly the best value in St-Émilion, with comfortable rooms boasting a/c, flat-screen televisions and sparkling ensuite bathrooms. The bold colour scheme, with old postcard shots of St-Émilion superimposed on the walls, and daringly modernist furniture won't be to everyone's taste, but at least it's original. Some of the most attractive rooms are in an annexe on rue Guadet, just opposite the main reception. Closed mid-Dec to mid-Feb. ❹

Hostellerie de Plaisance place du Clocher ⓣ05.57.55.07.55, ⓦwww.hostelleriedeplaisance.com. This is St-Émilion's top hotel, with a prime location next to the belfry and stunning views from its terraced garden. There are only eighteen rooms and three suites, some verging on the Baroque, split between the main building and two annexes. It has all the four-star comforts you'd expect – and prices to match, rooms starting at around €350. The restaurant offers equally high-class cuisine and a lengthy wine list (menus from €95). Closed mid-Dec to mid-Feb. ❾

Logis des Remparts 18 rue Guadet ⓣ05.57.24.70.43, ⓦwww.logisdesremparts.com. Very presentable three-star hotel with classically decorated rooms, and an enticing outdoor pool in its pretty, walled garden on top of the town's old ramparts. Closed mid-Dec to Jan. ❺

Around St-Émilion

Balladins rte de Castillon ⓣ05.57.25.25.07, ⓦwww.balladins.com. 3km along the D670 to Libourne, this modern, business-like hotel is the cheapest around. It has unexciting but fully equipped rooms and a swimming pool. For those who are so inclined, there's even a nightclub opposite – not something you'll find in the town itself. ❹

Camping Domaine de la Barbanne rte de Montagne ⓣ05.57.24.75.80, ⓦwww.camping-saint-emilion.com. Excellent, very reasonably priced three-star campsite 3km north of St-Émilion signed off the D122 Montagne road. In the midst of vines and next to a large lake, with two swimming pools (one heated), canoes, bike hire and tennis courts amongst other facilities. Closed Oct to mid-April.

Château Meylet La Gomerie, rte de Libourne ⓣ05.57.24.68.85, ⓦchateau.meylet.free.fr. An exceptionally welcoming and well-kept *chambre d'hôte* among the vines less than 2km outside St-Émilion on the D243 to Libourne. The rooms are charming, with plenty of rustic touches and solid antique furniture, while the ensuite bathrooms are modern. No meals, but there's a kitchenette. Bikes available. ❸

Château Millaud Montlabert rte de Pomerol ⓣ05.57.24.71.85, ⓦpagesperso-orange.fr/millaud.montlabert/. 4km northwest of St-Émilion on the D245 to Pomerol, this attractive, typical eighteenth-century Girondin farm houses five good-value rooms, two of which have the added allure of nestling beneath the gables of the roof. There's a kitchenette but no meals, and you can sample the owners' Grand Cru wines. ❸

Château de Roques Puisseguin ⓣ05.57.74.55.69, ⓦwww.chateau-de-roques.com. Another vineyard location for this hotel in a rambling château about 10km northeast of St-Émilion on the D17. There are seventeen light and elegant rooms with modern comforts including internet access. Ancient grain stores beneath the château now serve as the *chais*, which you can visit and there's also a great restaurant situated in the vaulted former kitchens of the château (menus €27–34). Closed Christmas & New Year hols. ❹

Le Relais de Franc Mayne La Gomerie, rte de Libourne ⓣ05.57.24.62.61, ⓦwww.chateau-francmayne.com. Set well back from the busy D243 to Libourne just outside St-Émilion, this château hotel offers luxurious accommodation. Each of the eleven rooms is decorated in a different exotic style, from oriental splendour to the African Lodge, complete with pictures of zebra and elephants. There's also a billiard room, salon and private garden and tours of the *chais* available on request (see p.119). ❽

The Town

St-Émilion is built on a steep south-facing hill (flat shoes strongly recommended), with its belfry providing a convenient landmark in the town centre above the rock-hewn church with its entrance on place du Marché.

A good place to get your bearings is beside the belfry on **place des Créneaux**, from the terrace of which you get a marvellous view over the huddled roofs. Better still, if you have the energy, climb the **tower** itself (same hours as the tourist office; €1) for a panorama that sweeps beyond the town walls over the vines' serried ranks. Starting here, you can sign up for a tour of the underground church (see below) at the tourist office on place des Créneaux.

While in the tourist office, pop through the side door into the peaceful fourteenth-century cloister (same hours; free). Though it belongs to the Collegiate church (daily 9.30am–12.30pm & 2–7pm; free), the connecting door is sealed up; instead, to reach the church turn right outside the tourist office and keep going to enter via its north door. Inside, look out for the twelfth-century frescoes of St Catherine's martyrdom on the south wall of the nave, and next to it a lovely slender Virgin squeezed onto the protruding wall.

The rock on which this upper part of St-Émilion is built is a veritable honeycomb. It's estimated that 120,000 square metres have been excavated from under the town alone, including the vast subterranean **Église Monolithe** (guided tours daily from 10.30am according to demand; 45min; available in English April–Oct; €6.50 from the tourist office). Before you get to the church itself, the tour takes you to a dark hole beside the place du Marché, supposedly the **cave** where St Émilion lived a hermit's life in the eighth century, then back outside to the simple thirteenth-century **Trinity Chapel**, built in honour of St Émilion and converted into a cooperage during the Revolution; fragments of frescoes are still visible, including the benediction of a kneeling figure which some say is Émilion. On the other side of the yard, a passage tunnels beneath the belfry to the **catacombs**, where three chambers dug out of the soft limestone were used as a cemetery and then later, through lack of space, as an ossuary from the eighth to the eleventh century.

The **church** itself is an incredible place. Simple and huge, the entire structure – barrel-vaulting, great square piers and all – was hacked out of the rock by Benedictine monks between the ninth and twelfth centuries. It is nearly forty metres long, twenty wide and eleven metres at its maximum height. The whole interior was painted at one time, but only faint traces have survived the damp and the Revolution, when saltpetre was collected from the walls to make gunpowder. But you can still see various bas-relief carvings around the altar: a pair of four-winged angels, two zodiacal signs and a strange and badly damaged scene of a man with a spear standing between a horned monster and an angel musician.

In the lower part of town, a couple of minutes' walk from place des Créneaux down rue de la Grande-Fontaine, a warren of underground galleries makes an unusual home for the ever-expanding **Musée Souterrain de la Poterie**, 21 rue André Loiseau (daily 10am–6pm; €5); ask to borrow their excellent English-language guide. This private collection covering two thousand years of pottery and ironwork from southwest France is a treasure-trove of all sorts of interesting and unusual pieces, from earthenware fire-dogs sporting human faces to glazed roof finials (*épi de faîtage*) in the form of birds or humans, including a smartly turned-out gentleman in a top hat. Also on display are works by well-known contemporary potters such as local artist Michel Jouhanneau and Consuelo de Mont Marin.

Some of the rock dug from the museum's galleries undoubtedly went into building the massive square keep of the **Château du Roi** (daily: April–June, Sept & Oct 9.30am–12.30pm & 1.45–6.30pm; July & Aug 9.30am–8pm; Nov–March 9.30am–12.30pm & 1.45–6pm; €1) presiding over St-Émilion from the west, and constructed in the thirteenth century as a forceful reminder of the king's power in this otherwise independent town. Nowadays it comes into its own in June and September when the members of the Jurade, in their red and white robes, proclaim from its summit the judging of the new wines and the start of the grape harvest.

Eating and drinking

For picnic fodder, there's a Sunday-morning **market** on place Bouqueyre, where you'll also find a boulangerie and a small supermarket right at the north end of town beyond the roundabout. For buying wine, the Maison du Vin (see p.113) offers the best prices, while the countless wine *caves* in town also have good selections and all offer tastings to help you decide. While you're in St-Émilion you should try the local **macaroons** (*macarons*) – for three generations the Blanchez family (situated at 9 rue Guadet near the post office) has been baking these tiny melt-in-the-mouth biscuits to the original recipe devised by Ursuline sisters in 1620.

L'Antre Deux Verres place du Cabiou. Though they do offer full menus, this place is primarily a wine bar, serving some interesting and less well-known names by the glass, to enjoy in the rock-hewn *cave* or on the terrace near the Château du Roi. To accompany the wine, go for one of their *tartines* (open sandwiches, €9) or the tempting cheese or charcuterie platters (€10). A glass of wine starts at €3–4, or €7 for a St-Émilion Grand Cru. Closed Wed.

Le Clos du Roy 12 rue de la Petite-Fontaine ⓣ05.57.74.41.55. Reservations are recommended at St-Émilion's most appealing and most gastronomic restaurant, where the subtle,

▲ Eating out in St-Émilion

inventive cuisine makes use of a range of enticing produce. The menu changes frequently, but you might find, for example, cannelloni stuffed with crab followed by whole roast wood pigeon. It need not break the bank, either, with a two-course weekday lunch *formule* at €20 and menus from €28 to €49. Closed Mon, Tues & Jan.

L'Envers du Décor 11 rue du Clocher. Very popular bar-bistro just along from the tourist office, with a good range of local wines by the glass (from €5) and serving light brasserie fare designed to complement the wine (menus from €19). Closed two weeks at Christmas & New Year.

Les Giron'dines rue des Girondins. *Les Giron'dines* boasts a quiet back terrace, which is one of the most peaceful places to eat in the town. They offer a full menu for €19.50, which is fairly standard fare, but they really stand out for their lunches, with salads, savoury tarts and quiches (from €10) marked up on the blackboard daily. Closed Sun eve & Mon, and for dinner mid-Oct to April.

Le Just'en Face rue de la Porte-Brunet. Tapas, hot pies, crêpes and other simple meals in a garden setting on the far side of rue Guadet. Prices start at around €7, with full menus for €18. Closed Wed.

Le Tertre 5 rue du Tertre-de-la-Tente ⓣ05.57.74.46.33. For a splurge, try this romantic little restaurant on the cobbled street leading down to the market square. You're in for well-prepared classic cuisine plus a few surprises, such as a hot foie gras and Sauternes soup served with poached oysters. Menus start at €20 for weekday lunches, and €25 at dinner and on weekends. Closed Wed & mid-Nov to mid-Feb.

Around St-Émilion

Auberge du Village St-Christophe-des-Bardes. This country inn on the D243 just outside St-Christophe is worlds away from chic St-Émilion. It's starting to look a bit run-down now, but the weekday lunch menu for €13 including wine is still justifiably popular with the locals. Open daily for lunch and for dinner Fri & Sat.

Les Marronniers Montagne ⓣ05.57.74.60.42. An excellent-value restaurant in bright and breezy surroundings on the east edge of Montignac village, with a terrace looking out onto acres of vines. The weekday lunch for €13 is an absolute steal, but other menus for around €20 are well worth it as well. Strong on steaks in wine-based sauces, but the varied *carte* also includes fish dishes and galettes. Good choice of local wines, too. Closed Sun eve & Mon.

Le Vieux Presbytère Montagne ⓣ05.57.74.65.33. Smart but still affordable restaurant tucked behind Montagne church which serves imaginative variations on the classics, such as roast pigeon with pepper and courgette risotto or hake with quinoa and asparagus. The *menu du marché* (€20 for three courses including a glass of wine) represents excellent value. Closed Sun eve & Mon.

St-Émilion's vineyards

The **vineyards** of St-Émilion are the first ever classified by UNESCO as being – in combination with the town – of sufficient cultural, historical and scenic importance to merit inclusion on the World Heritage list. Every spare inch of ground is covered with vines. Their trellised rows march from the valley floor up over the lip of the plateau, accentuating its gentle undulations, and nestle round the pale-grey limestone walls of the myriad **châteaux**. On the whole these are more modest buildings than you'll find in the Médoc or Sauternes wine regions, though St-Émilion does have its share of handsome seventeenth- and eighteenth-century piles. Most are still family homes, and therefore not open to the public, the one exception being a weekend in late April/early May when about eighty châteaux accept visitors under the *portes ouvertes* initiative organized by St-Émilion tourist office; some also host the occasional concert. But the real reason to visit is the wine, and from that point of view owners are more than happy to receive visitors provided you phone ahead. English language tours are usually available on request. Below is a representative selection of the region's tremendous variety; you can pick up a map locating all these vineyards at the Maison du Vin.

One of the easiest vineyards to visit (and a particularly welcoming one) is **Château Monlot**, 3km southeast of St-Émilion off the D243 (daily, no appointment needed; ⓦwww.chateaumonlot.com), a small-scale operation producing some fine Grand Cru wines. The visit shows you the vines and

Illustrious Ausone

One of St-Émilion's most prestigious vineyards, Château Ausone claims a long and distinguished past. Its name recalls **Decimus Magnus Ausonius**, a renowned Gallo-Roman poet whose domains here produced highly prized wines as early as the fourth century. "My wine," Ausonius wrote, "is as celebrated in Rome as the town of Burdigala (Bordeaux) itself." Ausonius was born in Burdigala in 309. The son of an eminent doctor, he practised law for a while before becoming a respected teacher and tutor to the emperor's son, Gratian. After Gratian became emperor in 367, Ausone's star rose even further and in 379 he was appointed consul of Gaul. Four years later, however, Gratian was murdered. Ausone retired to his estates to pen his verses and tend his vines. He died around 394, at the ripe old age of 85.

the cellars where the wine ferments in vats and then ripens in oak barrels, before you get to sample a selection of three different vintages produced by the château.

A kilometre or so northwest of St-Émilion on the Libourne road, **Château Franc-Mayne** (daily by appointment; €6 including tasting; ⓣ05.57.24.62.61, ⓦwww.relaisfrancmayne.com) provides another interesting excursion through a warren of tunnels, seeing how the blocks of stone were cut and how the vine roots seek out the tiniest crevices. The visit ends in the rock-hewn tasting room sampling the château's Grand Cru. Neighbouring **Château Franc-Pourret** (daily by appointment; free if you buy; ⓣ05.57.24.72.29, ⓦwww.ouzoulias-vins.com) is a more modest, family-run vineyard and has the distinction of being one of only a handful producing organic wines – including a Grand Cru – in St-Émilion.

Three kilometres east along the same scarp on the D243, just beyond the village of **ST-CHRISTOPHE-DES-BARDES**, **Château Laroque** (ⓣ05.57.24.77.28, ⓦwww.chateau-laroque.com; by appointment Mon–Fri; tastings €4) is one of the area's largest and oldest vineyards. You approach through elaborate wrought-iron gates, then down a long alley of cedars towards the eighteenth-century château overlooking immaculate lawns and Italianate statues in one direction and the River Dordogne to the south. The round tower standing slightly apart is all that remains of the original feudal château while the *chais* occupy the outbuildings across the courtyard. Château Laroque attained Grand Cru Classé status in 1996 following two decades of investment and technical innovation.

Another Grand Cru Classé, though they produce a much smaller volume than at Château Laroque, is **Château Laniote** (ⓣ05.57.24.70.80, ⓦwww.laniote.com; daily by appointment; free) a kilometre northwest of town, signed off the D243 Libourne road. The visit is of particular interest for those wishing to go into the technical intricacies of wine-making in more detail, as a short video presentation allows you to see the whole process from start to finish. They also offer an introductory wine-tasting course (by appointment, €20).

When you've visited enough châteaux, it's worth heading to the hilltop village of **MONTAGNE**, some 5km north of St-Émilion. As well as being a far quieter and more authentic example of a wine village than St-Émilion itself, it also has a beautifully symmetrical Romanesque church, its perfect Latin-cross structure crowned by a dome, as well as two excellent restaurants (see opposite) and the **Ecomusée du Libournais** (April–Nov 11 daily 10am–noon & 2–6pm; closed Nov 12–March; €6), which combines replica artisans' workshops with displays concerning the life of the vine and the process of vinification, though none of the documents is translated. Afterwards you can follow a four-kilometre nature trail through the vines – ask at the museum for the map and explanatory leaflet. The museum doubles as a **tourist office** (same times; ⓣ05.57.24.95.62) which in summer and at weekends offers tastings of the local wines, produced under the Montagne, Lussac and St-Georges appellations.

Travel details

Trains

Bordeaux to: Agen (at least 1 hourly; 1hr–1hr 40min); Angoulême (at least 1 hourly; 1hr); Barsac (1–6 daily; 35min); Bergerac (4–6 daily; 1hr 30min); Brive (1–2 daily; 2hr 20min); Cérons, near Cadillac (5–10 daily; 20–30min); Langon (6–12 daily; 20–45min); Lesparre (4–9 daily; 1hr 40min); Libourne (at least 1 hourly; 25min); Margaux (4–9 daily; 1hr); Moulis-Listrac (4–9 daily; 1hr 10min); Paris (at least 1 hourly; 3hr–3hr 30min); Pauillac (4–9 daily; 1hr 25 min); Périgueux (6–10 daily; 1hr 10min–1hr 50min); Podensac (2–10 daily; 20–35min); Portets (2–10 daily; 20–25min); La Réole (6–10 daily; 30–55min); St-Émilion (4–10 daily; 30min–1hr); St-Macaire (1–3 daily; 25–45min); Sarlat (5–6 daily; 2hr 30min–3hr); Toulouse (at least 1 hourly; 2hr–2hr 40min).

Buses

Bordeaux to: La Brède (Mon–Sat 3–4 daily; 1hr); Blaye (4–16 daily; 1hr 15min); Cadillac (2–13 daily; 50min); Castelnau-de-Médoc (3–6 daily; 50min); Langon (2–9 daily; 1hr 20min); Libourne (1–12 daily; 50min); Listrac (3–5 daily; 1hr); Margaux (2–10 daily; 50min); Pauillac (2–10 daily; 1hr 15min); St-Julien (2–10 daily; 1hr); Lamarque (2–10 daily; 1hr); La Sauve-Majeure (Mon–Sat 2–4 daily; 40min); Sauveterre-de-Guyenne (Mon–Fri 1 daily; 1hr 20min); Verdelais (2–6 daily; 1hr 15min).

Langon to: Bordeaux (2–6 daily; 1hr 30min–1hr 45min); Cadillac (2–6 daily; 30min).

La Réole to: Monségur (Mon–Sat 1–4 daily; 10–15min; some on demand only; Cars Arts ⓣ05.56.61.17.12); Sauveterre-de-Guyenne (Mon–Sat 2–6 daily; 25min; some on demand only; Cars Arts ⓣ05.56.61.17.12).

St-Émilion to: Libourne (July–Sept 2–5 daily; Oct–June Mon–Fri 3 daily; 7min; on demand; phone Citram ⓣ05.56.43.68.43).

Sauveterre-de-Guyenne to: Blasimon (Mon–Fri 3 daily; 10min; on demand; phone Citram ⓣ05.56.43.68.43); Bordeaux (Mon–Fri 1 daily; 1hr 45min); Libourne (as for Blasimon; 1hr); Rauzan (as for Blasimon; 20min); La Réole (Mon–Sat 2–6 daily; 35min; on demand; Cars Arts ⓣ05.56.61.17.12); La Sauve-Majeure (Mon–Fri 1 daily; 45min).

Ferries

Lamarque to: Blaye (4–10 daily in each direction; 30min).

Planes

Bordeaux to: Lille (1–6 daily; 1hr 20min); Lyon (2–7 daily; 1hr 10min); Marseille (3–5 daily; 1hr 5min); Nantes (1–7 daily; 45min); Nice (1–2 daily; 1hr 15min); Paris CDG (5 daily; 1hr 20min); Paris Orly (1–4 hourly; 1hr 10min); Strasbourg (2–10 daily; 1hr 25min).

2

Périgueux and the north

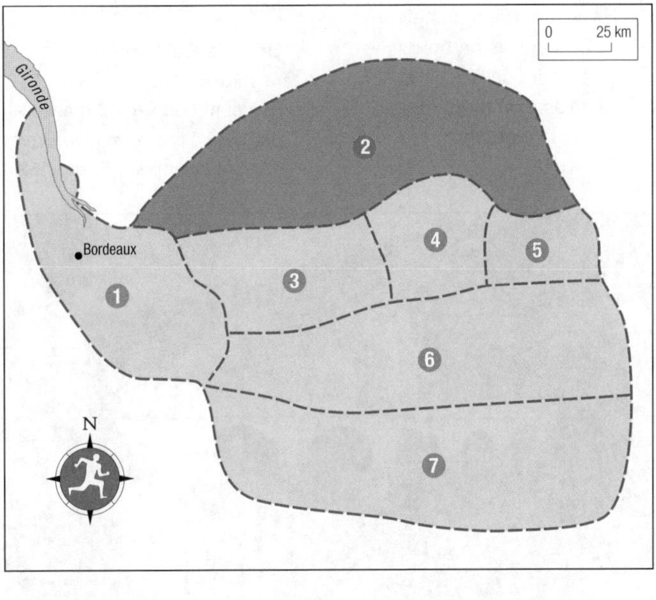

CHAPTER 2

Highlights

✱ **Périgueux** From prehistoric and Gallo-Roman remains via Renaissance-era mansions to the cathedral's Byzantine extravagance, Périgueux has something for everyone. **See p.124**

✱ **Brantôme** Stroll the willow-fringed waterways of this attractive town, then settle down to some serious eating. **See p.136**

✱ **Bourdeilles** Perched precariously over the River Dronne, the château of Bourdeilles harbours a splendid collection of Renaissance furniture and religious statuary. **See p.137**

✱ **Aubeterre-sur-Dronne** Though not the largest in the region, Aubeterre's subterranean church is both mysterious and awe-inspiring. **See p.142**

✱ **Château de Puyguilhem** A perfect example of early French Renaissance architecture. **See p.145**

✱ **Château de Hautefort** Built to rival the châteaux of the Loire, Hautefort stands out for its elegance and architectural harmony. **See p.151**

✱ **Brive-la-Gaillarde** A rewarding local history museum coupled with a well-restored city centre give Brive its special appeal. **See p.152**

▲ Brantôme

2

Périgueux and the north

The north of the Dordogne *département* is its least known and most rural corner, a land with few people and large tracts of pasture and woodland, its intimate green valleys lending it the name of the **Périgord Vert**. The region is bounded to the south by the **Périgord Blanc**, defined by its limestone plateaux and wide, gentle valleys that cut a broad swathe across the heart of the Dordogne, following the course of the River Isle. On its way the river flows through just one major city, **Périgueux**, capital of both Périgord Blanc and the whole *département*. It is easy to spend a day or two exploring the old city centre with its pineapple-capped cathedral, Roman remains and archeological museum – a first taste of the wealth of prehistoric art to come – but it's in the countryside around that the region's best attractions lie.

One of the loveliest stretches is the **Dronne valley**, which shadows the Isle to the north. At **Brantôme** the Dronne's still, water-lilied surface mirrors the limes and weeping willows along its banks, before flowing on past the twin fortresses of **Bourdeilles** to **Ribérac**, a market town beloved by the British, and **Aubeterre** on the Charente border. As at Brantôme, the river-carved cliffs at Aubeterre were hollowed out into primitive churches by twelfth-century monks. Others built dozens of little Romanesque churches on the sunny hills around, while south of the Dronne their successors helped tame the marshy, insalubrious plateau of the **Double**. In doing so they created the pine and chestnut forests that blanket the area today.

Upstream from Brantôme, two tributaries of the Dronne lead northeast to the tiny village of **St-Jean-de-Côle** and the decorative, Renaissance pile of **Château de Puyguilhem**. Further northeast, there's no mistaking the warlike nature of **Jumilhac** castle's granite hulk. As a break from the châteaux trail, connoisseurs of foie gras should head south to the little museum in **Thiviers**, while truffle-lovers might like to press on to **Sorges**, where there's a marked path through truffle country and another small museum to explain it all. These two towns are close to the southeast border of the Périgord Vert, where the scenery becomes softer towards the lovely Auvézère valley. Here, in a spectacular spot high over the river, the **Château de Hautefort** marks a return to the Périgord Blanc.

East of Hautefort, across the border in the Corrèze *département*, **Brive-la-Gaillarde** lies on an important crossroads and provides an alternative to Périgueux as a gateway to the region. For such a large city, Brive has a

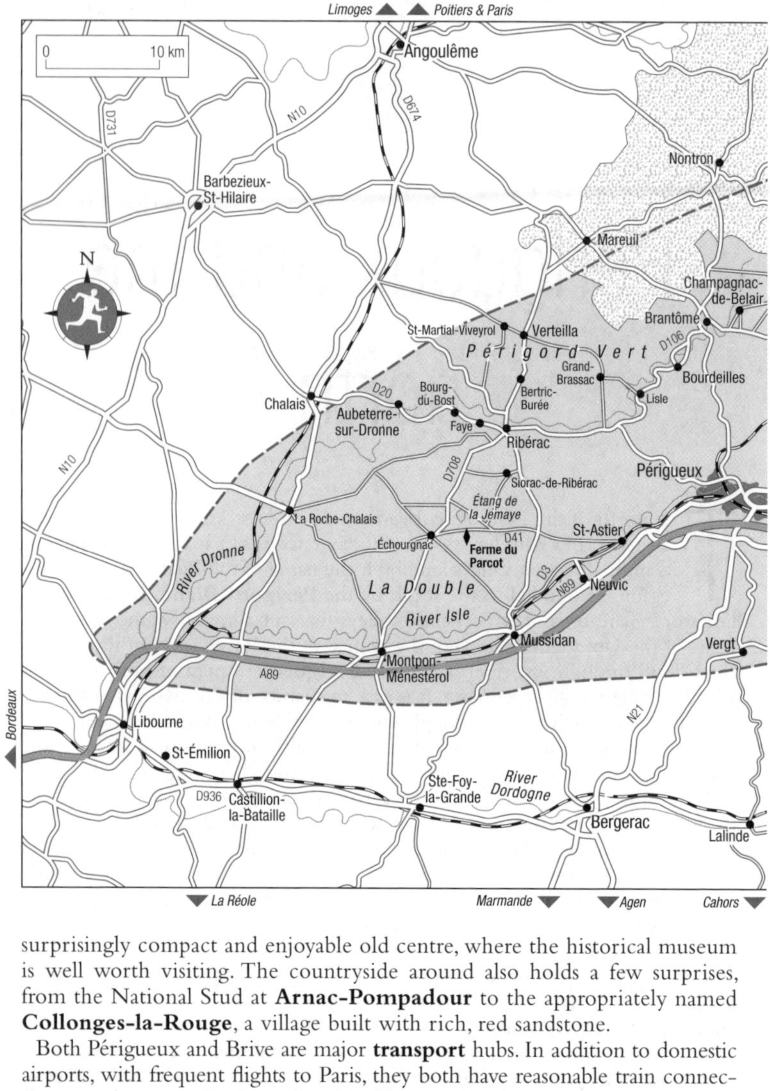

surprisingly compact and enjoyable old centre, where the historical museum is well worth visiting. The countryside around also holds a few surprises, from the National Stud at **Arnac-Pompadour** to the appropriately named **Collonges-la-Rouge**, a village built with rich, red sandstone.

Both Périgueux and Brive are major **transport** hubs. In addition to domestic airports, with frequent flights to Paris, they both have reasonable train connections to other towns in the region. Local bus services, however, are very sporadic.

Périgueux

PÉRIGUEUX, capital of the Dordogne, is a small, busy market town for a province made rich by tourism and specialized farming. Its name derives from the Petrocorii, the local Gaulish tribe, but it was the Romans who transformed it into an important settlement. While a few **Roman remains** survive, it is the city's **medieval and Renaissance core** that gives Périgueux its particular

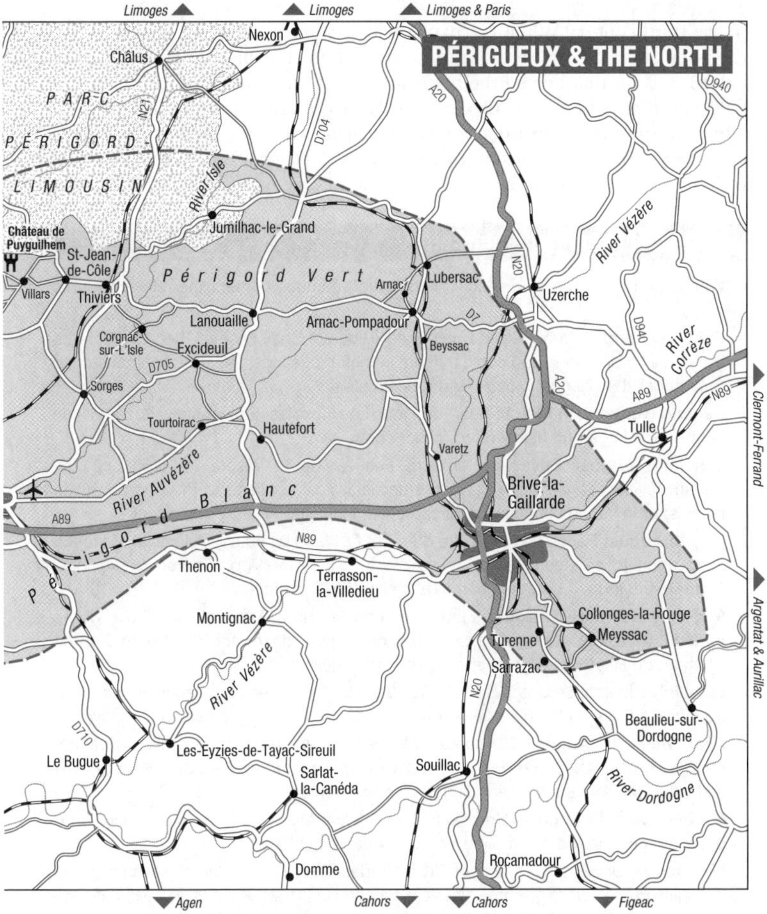

appeal. Pretty, stone-flagged squares and a maze of narrow alleys harbour richly ornamented merchants' houses, while above it all rises the startlingly white spire of **St-Front Cathedral**, flanked by its cluster of pinnacled, Byzantine domes. It looks best at night – particularly from across the river – when floodlights soften the sharper edges and accentuate its exotic silhouette. The city is also home to the interesting **Vesunna Gallo-Roman Museum** and the **Musée d'Art et d'Archéologie du Périgord**.

Some history

Périgueux began life some time after the fourth century BC as a fortified settlement inhabited by the **Petrocorii** ("Four Tribes"), whose craftsmen were noted for their ironwork. After 51 BC, however, the area came under Roman rule and a thriving town known as **Vesunna** (Vésone in French) began to develop, complete with amphitheatre, temples and luxurious villas. By the first century AD its population had reached an estimated twenty thousand, but the glory was shortlived. Vesunna, like many other towns, had neglected its defences under the *pax romana* and was caught unprepared by a succession of **barbarian invasions** in the third century. When Germanic tribes swept through the area in 275 AD, the population used stone from the surrounding civic monuments to construct defensive walls that helped the town survive, but in a much reduced state. As it faded it became known as La Cité des Pétrocores, then simply **La Cité**.

In the meantime, **St Front** arrived on the scene some time in the fourth century to convert the local population to Christianity. After giving La Cité a new breath of life by founding what eventually became St-Étienne Cathedral, St Front was

Festivals, events and markets

Where we haven't given a specific information number, contact the relevant tourist office.

First weekend in May Bertric Burée, near Ribérac: Snail Festival. Locals celebrate the snails by preparing and cooking them in their thousands; they are then consumed throughout the village by locals and tourists alike.

Second weekend in May St-Jean-de-Côle: Les Floralies. Flower stalls fill the village centre for a large and highly rated flower show.

July and August Brive and around: Festival de la Vézère (ⓣ05.55.23.25.09, ⓔfestival.vezere@wanadoo.fr). Operas and classical concerts in the open air (with picnics) or in various châteaux and churches, including Arnac-Pompadour.

July to August Périgueux: La Truffe d'Argent (ⓣ05.53.08.69.81). A festival of French song open to amateurs, which takes place in the streets on Thursday evenings. Entrants are judged and take part in a final on the last night.

Mid-July to early August Hautefort and around: Festival du Pays d'Ans (ⓣ05.53.51.13.63). A mix of classical concerts, jazz, opera and theatre held in the Château de Hautefort and other châteaux and churches hereabouts.

Late July Ribérac: Le Grand Souk (ⓣ05.53.92.52.30). Aimed at fostering young talent from around the world, this international music festival takes place over five days.

First week in August Périgueux: Mimos, the International Festival of Mime (ⓣ05.53.53.18.71). One of France's most exciting and innovative contemporary art festivals, with street artists and some ticketed events.

Second week in August Périgueux: New Orleans Music Festival. Jazz, gospel and blues concerts in a different area of the city each night.

Mid-August Brive-la-Gaillarde: Les Orchestrades. Over ten days, some seven hundred young instrumentalists give free classical concerts in the streets of Brive culminating in a grand open-air concert when they all play a specially commissioned piece.

Last week of August Périgueux and around: Sinfonia en Périgord (ⓣ05.53.09.51.30, ⓦwww.sinfonia-en-perigord.com). A ten-day celebration of Baroque and Renaissance music, with concerts in various venues in Périgueux, as well as in the nearby abbeys of Chancelade and Brantôme and the Château de Bourdeilles.

First weekend in November Brive: La Foire du Livre. A book fair held in Brive's market hall. It attracts some three hundred authors and artists presenting their new works, and around ten thousand book-lovers keen to snap up signed editions.

Early November Périgueux: Salon International du Livre Gourmand (ⓣ05.53.53.18.71). **Biennial** (2010, 2012 etc) book fair dedicated to wine and gastronomy. Events take place over four days in the theatre (1 allée d'Aquitaine), and include book exhibitions, cooking demonstrations and opportunities to sample the results.

Markets

The most important **weekly markets** in this region are: Brântome (Fri); Brive (Tues & Sat); Excideuil (Thurs); Périgueux (Wed & Sat); Ribérac (Fri); and Thiviers (Sat). In winter many local towns hold **foie gras**, **truffle** and **walnut markets**, generally on the same day as their weekly market.

later buried on a neighbouring hilltop, or *puy*, where his tomb became a pilgrimage centre. By the thirteenth century it had spawned a small but prosperous town of merchants and artisans known as **Le Puy-St-Front**, which began to rival La Cité, now the seat of the counts of Périgord. Though the two communities were joined by an act of union in 1240, they continued to glare at each other over their encircling walls – indeed, at the start of the **Hundred Years' War** La Cité sided with the English and Le Puy with France. For a while following the Treaty of Brétigny in 1360, Périgueux, as it was now known, fell under English rule, but the loyal burghers of Le Puy soon rallied to Charles V, and by 1369 Périgueux had been liberated by Bertrand du Guesclin, who then chased the English back towards the coast. Even so, by the early fifteenth century the city was in ruins, its population decimated by war, plague and famine and its buildings crumbling through neglect.

With peace, however, came renewed prosperity and a building boom that left Périgueux its wonderful legacy of **Renaissance** architecture, though much was lost or damaged during the **Wars of Religion**: despite being predominantly Catholic, Périgueux was held by the Protestants for six years after 1575, during which time they vandalized many religious buildings, amongst them St-Étienne. This proved to be the final blow for La Cité, which fell into slow decline, culminating in the transfer of cathedral status to St-Front in 1669.

Up to this time La Cité and Le Puy-St-Front remained firmly inside their respective walls, separated by open space, but in the eighteenth century Périgueux began to expand into today's **modern city**. In the process the medieval walls gave way to wide boulevards, while in the nineteenth century the canal and railway brought further development to what was by then the capital of Périgord. The old city centre was left largely untouched, so that in 1979 some twenty hectares were designated a preservation district. Nevertheless, Périgueux is still the *département*'s most industrialized town: its biggest current claim to fame – a result of 1970s decentralization policies – is the printing works where all French postage stamps are produced.

Arrival and information

Périgueux has a small domestic **airport** at Bassilac, 7km east of the city, with daily weekday flights to and from Paris. There are no facilities – though rented cars can be picked up here if booked in advance – and no convenient bus links, but a taxi into town will take less than twenty minutes (around €15). On the opposite side of the city, the **gare SNCF** lies roughly ten minutes' walk from the centre, or you can take bus #1 (direction Boulazac) to place Bugeaud or St-Front (€1.50). If you're **driving** you can park for free along the river below St-Front Cathedral, or there's plenty of pay-parking along allées de Tourny, to the north of the centre, in place Montaigne to the east and underneath place Francheville. **Long-distance buses** pull in beside Place Francheville on rue de La Cité (see p.136 for more details). The *place* is also where you'll find the **tourist office** (June–Sept Mon–Sat 9am–7pm, Sun 10am–1pm & 2–6pm; Oct–May Mon–Sat 9am–12.30pm & 2–6pm; ⓣ05.53.53.10.63, ⓦwww.tourisme-perigueux.fr), where you can book for their excellent themed **city tours** covering medieval and Renaissance Périgueux, the Gallo-Roman city (July–Sept) or with a focus on music or food and drink. Though the tours are predominantly in French, some guides also speak English; ask in advance.

Accommodation

Surprisingly, central Périgueux doesn't offer a particularly good range of **hotels**. There are only a couple of reasonable options in the old city

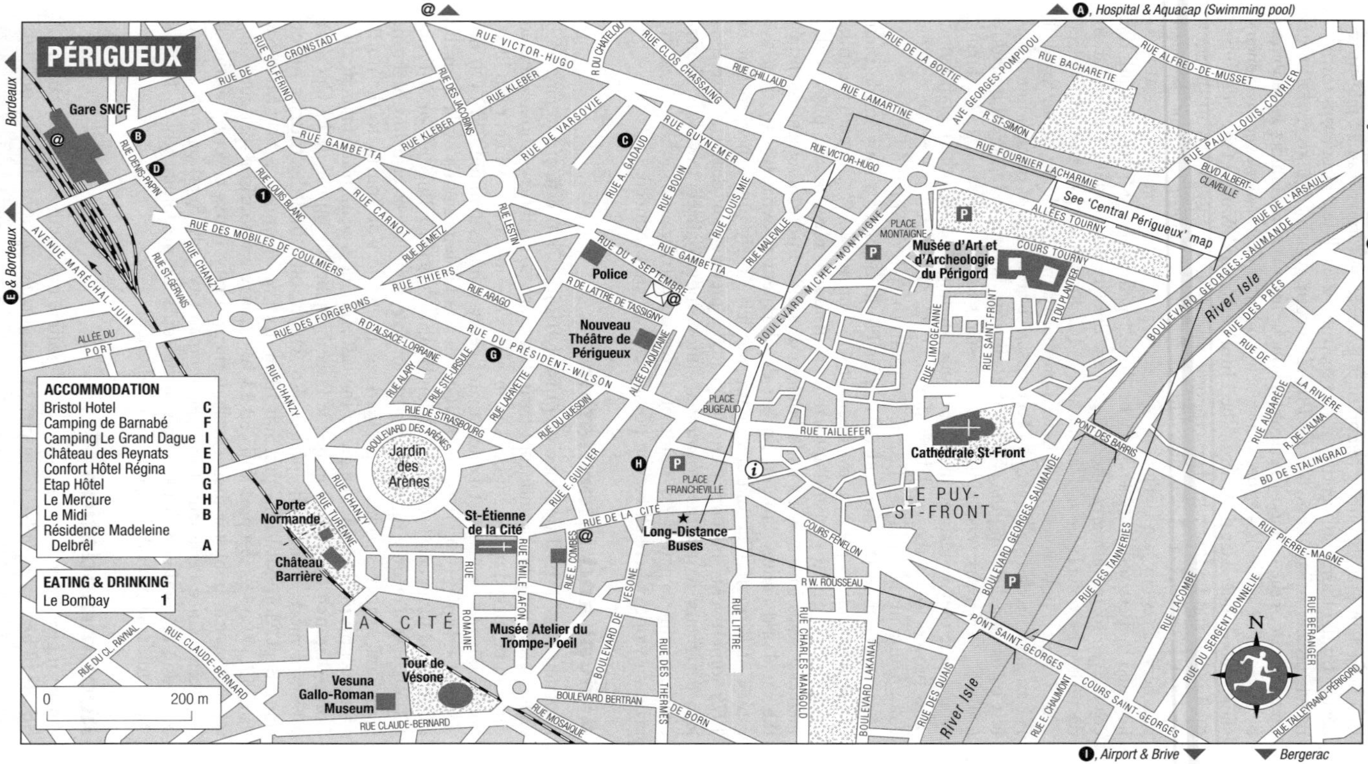
PÉRIGUEUX
ACCOMMODATION
Bristol Hotel C
Camping de Barnabé F
Camping Le Grand Dague I
Château des Reynats E
Confort Hôtel Régina D
Etap Hôtel G
Le Mercure H
Le Midi B
Résidence Madeleine Delbrêl A
EATING & DRINKING
Le Bombay 1
0 200 m
A, Hospital & Aquacap (Swimming pool)
Limoges
F
I, Airport & Brive
Bergerac
E & Bordeaux
Bordeaux
@
See 'Central Périgueux' map
Gare SNCF
Police
Nouveau Théâtre de Périgueux
Musée d'Art et d'Archeologie du Périgord
Cathédrale St-Front
LE PUY-ST-FRONT
Long-Distance Buses
St-Étienne de la Cité
Musée Atelier du Trompe-l'oeil
Jardin des Arènes
Porte Normande
Château Barrière
LA CITÉ
Tour de Vésone
Vesuna Gallo-Roman Museum
River Isle
PLACE MONTAIGNE
PLACE BUGEAUD
PLACE FRANCHEVILLE
ALLÉES TOURNY
COURS TOURNY
BOULEVARD MICHEL-MONTAIGNE
BOULEVARD GEORGES-SAUMANDE
PONT DES BARRIS
PONT SAINT-GEORGES
COURS SAINT-GEORGES
COURS FENELON
RUE GAMBETTA
RUE VICTOR-HUGO
RUE DU PRÉSIDENT-WILSON
RUE DU 4 SEPTEMBRE
AVENUE MARÉCHAL-JUIN
RUE DES MOBILES DE COULMIERS
RUE CHANZY
RUE DE LA CITÉ
RUE TAILLEFER
RUE LIMOGEANNE
RUE SAINT-FRONT
BOULEVARD LAKANAL
RUE CHARLES-MANGOLD
RUE LITTRE
RUE DES THERMES
BOULEVARD BERTRAN
RUE CLAUDE-BERNARD
N

itself, while the other alternatives are located within walking distance of the centre, with the best value for money to be found near the train station. All the accommodation listed is marked on the main Périgueux map opposite except where otherwise indicated.

Hotels

Les Barris 2 rue Pierre Magne ⓣ05.53.53.04.05, ⓦwww.hoteldesbarris.com. See map, p.130. Just across the river, this two-star Logis hotel has simple, fairly small but reasonably priced rooms, two with views of the cathedral. There's also a bar and restaurant, *Aux Berges de l'Isle* (see p.135). ❸–❹

Bristol Hotel 37 rue A. Gadaud ⓣ05.53.08.75.90, ⓦwww.bristolfrance.com. This place looks pretty bland from the outside, but inside it's perfectly comfortable with airy, cool rooms, free internet access and friendly, knowledgeable owners. ❸–❹

Confort Hôtel Régina 14 rue Denis-Papin ⓣ05.53.08.40.44, ⓔcomfort.perigueux@wanadoo.fr. Pleasant two-star hotel opposite the station offering cheerful rooms with high ceilings and windows to match (double-glazed on the front). All rooms are en suite and have satellite TV. ❹

Château des Reynats av des Reynats ⓣ05.53.03.53.59, ⓦwww.chateau-hotel-perigord.com. In the village of Chancelade, roughly 5km northwest of central Périgueux; the plush rooms (some in the Orangerie annexe) and excellent restaurant in this little nineteenth-century château make it one of the city's top hotels. Restaurant closed for lunch on Sat, Sun & Mon; in winter also for dinner Sun & Mon (menus from €30). Closed Jan. ❺–❾

Etap Hôtel 33 rue du Président Wilson ⓣ08.92.68.32.37, ⓦwww.etaphotel.com. *Etap* chain staple located in the city centre. The spacious rooms have a large double bed with single bunk above, an en-suite shower and toilet, and satellite TV. ❷

Le Mercure 7 place Francheville ⓣ05.53.06.65.00, ⓦwww.mercure.com. The most central hotel, just across the square from the tourist office. The old facade conceals a brand new three-star hotel with en-suite rooms offering free internet access and a/c. ❺–❼

Le Midi 18 rue Denis Papin ⓣ05.53.53.41.06, ⓦhotel-du-midi.fr/. Spruce hotel opposite the station. The cheapest rooms (with a washbasin but no shower or toilet) are rather small for two people, but there's a good-value restaurant offering regional cuisine (menus from €12.50; Nov–May closed Sat & Sun eve). ❶–❷

Hostel and campsites

Camping de Barnabé Barnabé-Plage ⓣ05.53.53.41.45, ⓦwww.barnabe-perigord.com. Charming two-star campsite fifteen minutes' walk northeast of the city along the Isle. It has a lovely riverside location, with an overspill site on the other bank, linked by boat. Bar with snack meals available in summer (April–Oct). March–Oct.

Camping Le Grand Dague Atur ⓣ05.53.04.21.01, ⓦwww.legranddague.fr. Lost in the hills 7km southeast of Périgueux, this spacious and immaculate four-star site is worth seeking out if you've got your own transport. May–Sept.

Résidence Hôtelière Madeleine Delbrêl 38 av Georges Pompidou ⓣ05.53.35.70.70, ⓦwww.prh-perigueux.com. This conveniently situated hostel/conference centre offers simple accommodation and good meals for those on a limited budget. All the rooms have twin beds and either a washbasin (€21 for one person, €25 for two sharing) or washbasin and toilet (€25 for one, €28 for two). There is free parking and an attractive garden, which is a haven of peace five minutes' walk from the city centre. Breakfast is €5, and half-board and full board are also available for stays of four days or more. ❶

The City

Périgueux's compact **historic centre** – much of it pedestrianized – sits on the west bank of the River Isle, occupying a rough square formed by the river, the tree-shaded cours Tourny to the north, boulevard Michel Montaigne to the west and cours Fénelon to the south. Though the hilltop **Cathédrale St-Front** provides a natural magnet, the surrounding streets hide some particularly fine Renaissance architecture as well as the **Musée d'Art et d'Archéologie du Périgord**, with its collection of Paleolithic tools, and a remnant of **medieval wall**. The main commercial hub is concentrated around rue Taillefer, running from the cathedral west to place Bugeaud, and along pedestrianized rue Limogeanne to the north. At the southwest corner of the old town lies the wide,

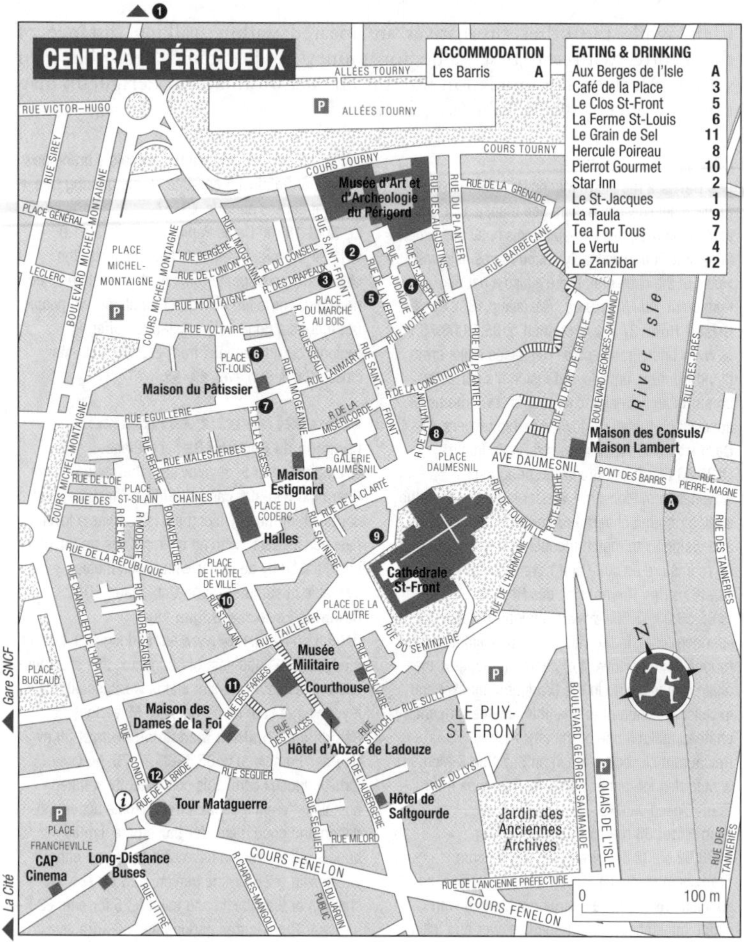

place Francheville, from where rue de la Cité leads westwards towards Périgueux's other principal area of interest, **La Cité**, centred around a rather mutilated church. This is where you'll find the smart Gallo-Roman Museum, **Vesunna**, featuring the foundations of a Roman villa, and an engaging **Musée Atelier du Trompe-L'oeil**. Everything is within easy walking distance, making it possible to explore the city comfortably in a day.

Le Puy-St-Front

There's still a slight medieval air to **Le Puy-St-Front**, the district tumbling downhill from the cathedral west to place Francheville and to cours Fénelon in the south. Its confined and cobbled alleys harbour Périgueux's oldest buildings – the former homes of wealthy merchants – as well as the last remaining fragment of the medieval fortifications; Le Puy was originally surrounded by 28 defensive towers, of which only stout, circular **Tour Mataguerre**, protecting the southwest corner, remains. According to legend, it was named after an

English captain imprisoned here during the Hundred Years' War, but the present structure dates from the late fifteenth century, when it was rebuilt using leper labourers. It's only accessible on guided tours organized by the tourist office (see p.127); there's little to see inside – just the prison and a simple guardroom above – but views from the roof are good.

From beside Tour Mataguerre, rue de la Bride runs into rue des Farges, where, at no. 6, you'll find Périgueux's most venerable building, **Maison des Dames de la Foi**, dating from the late twelfth century. The name, "House of the Ladies of Faith", refers to a convent established in the seventeenth century for young Protestant women wishing to convert to Catholicism. Two hundred years earlier, during the Hundred Years' War, it's said that du Guesclin stayed here while preparing to liberate nearby Chancelade Abbey from the English. Nowadays, you'd be forgiven for walking straight past, as the only evidence of its more illustrious history is the blocked-in window arches on the second floor.

At the top of rue des Farges, the **Musée Militaire** (Jan–March Wed & Sat 2–6pm; April–Dec Mon–Sat 2–6pm; €4) contains a vast and rather chaotic array of military memorabilia, one of the foremost such collections in France. Covering everything from the Franco-Prussian War to the Gulf War and today's UN peacekeeping missions, the exhibits are of rather specialized interest, but there are some noteworthy pieces including some poignant sketches of trench life in World War I and memorabilia dating back to the French colonial wars in Indochina (today's Vietnam, Laos and Cambodia), among them a couple of tattered Viet Minh flags.

Turning right outside the museum brings you into rue de l'Aubergerie with its two fortified fifteenth-century houses, of which **Hôtel d'Abzac de Ladouze** at no. 16, a typically dour building with an octagonal defensive tower, is the more interesting. The massive blind arch on the wall is evidence of much older foundations, while the incongruous ornamental balustrade above is a Renaissance addition. Note also the cockleshell carving on the side of the tower, indicating that the house once received pilgrims en route to Santiago de Compostela. Further down the street, at no.6, **Hôtel de Saltgourde** sports an impressive tower complete with a machicolated parapet.

Rue St-Roch leads east from below Hôtel d'Abzac past several interesting houses, one retaining its wood-timbered upper storey, others their overhanging latrines or decorative arcaded windows, to **rue du Calvaire**. This was the road that criminals in the Middle Ages climbed on their way to the courthouse, identifiable by its studded Renaissance door. The condemned would then continue to the gallows on **place de la Clautre**, which also served as an execution ground during the Revolution. Nowadays it provides a more peaceful setting for a twice-weekly fresh-produce **market** (Wed & Sat mornings) against the backdrop of the cathedral.

Cathédrale St-Front

The domed and coned **Cathédrale St-Front** (daily 8am–7pm; free) began life in the sixth century as a simple chapel over the tomb of St Front. Seven hundred years later – by then an important abbey – it was rebuilt after a fire and in the process the architects created one of the most distinctive Byzantine churches in France, modelled on St Mark's in Venice and on Constantinople's Church of the Holy Apostles.

Unfortunately, the cathedral of today is no beauty, thanks to the zealous attentions of the nineteenth-century restorer **Paul Abadie**, who went on to build Paris's Sacré-Coeur. The result is too regular, and the roof is spiked all over with ill-proportioned nipple-like projections; "a supreme example of how not to

▲ Périgueux's Cathédrale St-Front at night

restore", Freda White tartly observed in her travelogue, *Three Rivers of France*. Nevertheless, the Byzantine influence is still evident in the interior's Greek-cross plan – unusual in France – and in the massive clean curves of the domes. The bell tower also survived largely intact and is one of the few vestiges of the twelfth-century reconstruction.

North of the cathedral

North of the cathedral crowd the renovated buildings of the **Renaissance** city. The longest and finest street in this part of town is narrow **rue Limogeanne**, leading north from place de la Clautre via rue Salinière. Among the proliferating souvenir shops stand elegant mansions, now turned into swish boutiques and delicatessens; its most notable facade belongs to **Maison Estignard** at no. 5, whose elaborate architecture – mullions, dormer windows and ornamental columns – is typical of the Renaissance. It's also worth popping into the more sober courtyard of no. 3 to see a salamander carved above the inner door; this was the insignia of Francis I (1515–47), who brought Italian Renaissance style to France. Opposite, impasse Limogeanne leads into a series of courtyards and passageways known as **galerie Daumesnil** after the famous general born at 7 rue de la Clarté in 1776 (see box opposite).

Though nearby place du Coderc and place de l'Hôtel-de-Ville are both strong contenders, **Place St-Louis**, to the west of rue Limogeanne, is probably the prettiest of Périgueux's squares. In its southeast corner stands the handsome, turreted **Maison du Pâtissier** – built by a man who made his fortune from *pâté en croûte* (pâté in a pastry crust) – with a lovely Renaissance door bearing a fearsome warning on its lintel. There are more fine houses over to the east of rue Limogeanne on rue de la Constitution; from here the lanes begin to drop steeply to the river, where you'll find the semi-fortified fifteenth-century **Maison des Consuls** with the sixteenth-century **Maison Lambert** next door.

The last sight in this area is the **Musée d'Art et d'Archéologie du Périgord** (April–Sept Mon & Wed–Fri 10.30am–5.30pm, Sat & Sun 1–6pm; Oct–March Mon & Wed–Fri 10am–5pm, Sat & Sun 1–6pm; €4, free Oct to

May Mon–Fri noon–2pm; Ⓦmusee-perigord.museum.com), set in a grand, nineteenth-century building at the top of rue St-Front, overlooking the broad, tree-lined allées de Tourny. The museum houses an extensive prehistoric collection and some beautiful Gallo-Roman mosaics. Exhibits include a 70,000-year-old human skeleton, the oldest yet found in France, and a delicate engraving of a bison's head. However, these and many of the more fragile items on display are copies, and the museum's old-fashioned layout makes it hard to appreciate what's on offer.

La Cité

Remnants of the Roman town of Vesunna, now known as **La Cité**, lie southwest along rue de la Cité from place Francheville. Named after a local divinity, Vesunna was an important and prosperous town: by the first century AD it extended over some seventy hectares, complete with a forum, basilica, thermal baths and a seven-kilometre-long aqueduct. Today the most visible vestiges – a ruined amphitheatre, the remains of a temple complex and an excavated villa – lie scattered around the hulk of Périgueux's first cathedral, St-Étienne-de-la-Cité.

Approaching from the east, **St-Étienne**'s domes dominate La Cité. It was founded by St Front in the fourth century, then rebuilt in its present form, with a Romanesque nave comprising big square bays, some six hundred years later. The original building comprised four bays but two were destroyed, along with the bell tower, by Huguenots in 1577, leaving the church's west facade roughly truncated. The first bay you enter is the older of the two, dating from the eleventh century: the dome is more massive, the windows smaller and fewer and the stone less regular. The second bay was added a century later, then restored as an exact copy in the 1600s. Apart from being lighter and higher, its main feature is the line of decorative columns along the walls which stand out in the otherwise unornamented church.

The pretty **Jardin des Arènes** (daily: April–Sept 7.30am–9pm; Oct–March 7.30am–6.30pm; free), a circular garden northwest of St-Étienne, conceals a few remnants – comprising an entrance arch and traces of the foundations – of an enormous **amphitheatre** capable of holding twenty thousand people or more. Built in the first century AD, it was dismantled two hundred years later to

Daumesnil: the peg-leg general

A devoted follower of Napoleon Bonaparte, **Baron Pierre Daumesnil** (1777–1832) was fiery, impetuous, loyal, patriotic and, above all, brave. He first distinguished himself during the Italian campaign (1796–97) when he rescued the drowning Napoleon from a river during the Battle of Arcole. Then at Acre in 1799 Daumesnil threw himself in front of his hero when a bomb landed at Napoleon's feet. It failed to explode, but Daumesnil, by now a major, was less lucky at the **Battle of Wagram** in Poland in 1809, when his left leg was so badly mutilated that it had to be amputated. Three years later he was promoted to general and made **governor of the Château de Vincennes** – the country's largest arsenal – which he twice refused to hand over to the allied European armies fighting Napoleon. The second time, in 1815, he declared: "I will give up Vincennes when you give me back my leg". Nevertheless, Daumesnil was forced to retire a few months later following Napoleon's defeat at Waterloo, and he eventually died of cholera in 1832, though his wooden leg was preserved and is now on display in Paris's Musée de l'Armée. In Périgueux you'll find a statue of him towards the south end of boulevard Michel Montaigne, proudly pointing at his peg-leg.

construct defensive walls (see p.126), of which you can see a fragment, the **Porte Normande**, along nearby rue de Turenne. In the panic, the walls were cobbled together with whatever came to hand: a column, some capitals, a carved lintel, all pilfered from neighbouring monuments.

Heading southeast from here, past the empty carcass of twelfth-century Château Barrière and across the train lines, you reach Périgueux's most imposing Roman monument, the **Tour de Vésone**, in another public garden (same times as des Arènes; free). This high, circular tower was once the sanctuary of a temple dedicated to Vesunna's eponymous guardian goddess. The gaping breach on the north side is said to have been created when St Front exorcized the pagan gods; more prosaically, the bricks and stones probably went into local building works.

Just behind the tower on rue Claude Bernard is **Vesunna** (April–June & Sept Tues–Fri 9.30am–5.30pm, Sat & Sun 10am–12.30pm & 2.30–6pm; July & Aug daily 10am–7pm; Oct–March Tues–Fri 9.30am–12.30pm & 1.30–5pm, Sat & Sun 10am–12.30pm & 2.30–6pm; €5.50, audio guides available in English; ⓣ05.53.53.00.92, ⓦwww.vesunna.fr), a Gallo-Roman museum housed in a striking modern glass building and built around the well-preserved remains of a grand Roman villa, which were discovered by chance in 1959.

The villa was no humble abode. It was complete with at least sixty rooms, an under floor central heating hypocaust, thermal baths and colonnaded walkways around the central garden with its cooling pond and fountain. Around the walls you can see the remains of first-century murals of river and marine life, the colours still amazingly vibrant, and here and there, graffiti of hunting scenes, gladiatorial combat and even an ostrich – no doubt the work of some bored Roman teenager.

With time to spare, it's worth dropping by the **Musée Atelier du Trompe-L'oeil**, 5 rue Émile Combes (May–Sept Tues–Sat 10.30am–12.30pm & 2.30–6.30pm, Sun 3–6pm; Oct–April Tues–Sat 2–5.30pm, Sun 3–5.30pm; €5; ⓦwww.museedutrompeloeil.com), as you head back into central Périgueux. This small, privately owned museum traces the history of trompe-l'oeil from prehistoric cave-paintings to the present day, and doubles as a showroom and workshop for one of France's leading practitioners. She also runs occasional courses of between two to five days.

Eating, drinking and entertainment

There are several good places to **eat and drink** in Périgueux, particularly in the old city, while several **cafés** line boulevard Michel Montaigne. On place Francheville you'll find the multiscreen **CAP Cinema** (ⓣ08.92.68.01.21, ⓦwww.cap-cine.fr/perigueux), and the Nouveau Théâtre de Périgueux (NTP) at 1 allée d'Aquitaine (ⓣ05.53.53.18.71) puts on a varied programme of **theatre**, dance, concerts and variety shows.

Follow the river: La Voie Verte and La Voie Bleue

Fed up of tramping the streets, you might like to explore Perigueux's greener side. If you're on a bicycle, or on foot, take to **La Voie Verte**, a 15km path winding from Marsac in the west of the city to Trélissac in the east. With car parks, picnic areas and information points along the way, it's popular with both locals and tourists. **La Voie Bleue** is the water-based alternative – a 21km paddle down the river Isle by canoe. For more details ask at the tourist office, or for canoe hire contact the clubs at Trélissac (ⓣ05.53.08.63.95), Périgueux (ⓣ05.53.04.24.08) or Marsac (ⓣ05.53.04.11.57).

Restaurants

Aux Berges de l'Isle 2 rue Pierre Magne ⓣ05.53.09.51.50. Pretty little restaurant at the east end of Pont des Barris (entrance through the *Hôtel des Barris*), offering unrivalled views of the cathedral and traditional cuisine at reasonable prices. Specialities include lamprey, soufflé of foie gras and Limousin beef. There's a wide choice of menus, starting at €15 for two courses at lunchtime, €21 in the evening. Closed Sun eve & Mon.

Le Bombay 5 rue Louis-Blanc ⓣ05.53.09.69.92. See map, p.128. One of the few Indian and Pakistani restaurants in the region, this place serves up good-value, tasty vindaloos and tandooris with menus from €9 at lunchtime and €25 in the evenings. Closed Sun lunch & Mon eve.

Le Café de la Place 2 place du Marché au Bois ⓣ05.53.08.21.11. Just off the busy rue Saint-Front, which runs down to the cathedral, this popular café-restaurant with a sunny terrace is a convenient place to eat if you're visiting the Musée d'Art et d'Archéologie. The menus are fairly standard but good value, starting at €10.50 for two courses.

Le Clos St-Front 5 rue de la Vertu ⓣ05.53.46.78.58. This elegant restaurant has a well-earned reputation for its inventive and well-priced menus, starting at €27. The dishes are beautifully presented, the menu changes every six weeks and includes delights such as a trio of foie gras and chocolate pudding with szechuan pepper. In summer you can dine in the shady courtyard. Closed Sun eve & Mon Oct–May.

La Ferme St-Louis 2 place St-Louis ⓣ05.53.53.82.77. The most appealing of the many restaurants on the square, with its small terrace and homely, stone-walled interior. It serves a limited but well-priced menu, with a starter and main course at €24 (lunchtime only), or €27 for three courses. The food is all freshly prepared, portions are generous and the service impeccable. Closed Sun & Mon.

Le Grain de Sel 7 rue des Farges ⓣ05.53.53.45.22. Tucked away in a narrow street just along from the tourist office, this impeccable little restaurant uses fresh produce from the market to create original dishes. Menus from €18 for two courses at lunchtime to €40 for four courses, or let the chef choose for you with his surprise menu of five courses, for €48. Closed Sun & Mon.

Hercule Poireau 2 rue de la Nation ⓣ05.53.08.90.76. One of Périgueux's best-known restaurants, in a stone-vaulted room with cheerful red-check fabrics, offering top-quality local cuisine at surprisingly affordable prices. This is rich fare: house speciality is the luxurious *rossini de canard* (duck with a slice of foie gras in a truffle sauce). Menus €21–42. Closed Wed.

Pierrot Gourmet 6 rue L'Hôtel de Ville ⓣ05.53.53.35.32. Principally a gourmet deli and rotisserie, there are also a few tables for diners and table service from 10am–5pm daily. The food is fresh and includes a range of wonderful yet simple dishes such as mushroom pâté and pears poached in red wine.

Le St-Jacques 38 av Georges Pompidou ⓣ05.53.35.70.70. Situated in the hostel/conference centre (see p.129) but open to non-residents. Don't be put off by the slightly institutional atmosphere – this is one of Périgueux's best-kept secrets. As well as the spacious restaurant there is a terrace overlooking the peaceful garden. Tasty food is of outstanding value (lunchtime menu of three courses including coffee for €12) and the service efficient and friendly. If you fancy straying from the French wines, there are New world wines worth trying at €17. Closed Wed eve.

La Taula 3 rue Denfert Rochereau ⓣ05.53.35.40.02. Just opposite the cathedral, with cosy decor and welcome air-conditioning in the summer. House specialities include calves, kidneys with mustard, and spiced foie gras served with dried fruits. Menus from €17.90 for two courses (lunchtime only) to €35.50. Closed Mon Oct to mid-July.

Bars and cafés

Star Inn 17 rue des Drapeaux. Snug Anglo-Irish pub behind the Musée d'Art et d'Archéologie du Périgord, patronized by a mixed crowd of local expats and Anglophiles. Happy hour Mon–Thurs 8–9pm, book exchange, board games and – of course – darts and quiz nights. Mon–Sat 8pm–1am.

Tea For Tous 28 rue Eguillerie. Tea shop featuring over seventy types of teas from all over the world, from English breakfast to Moroccan mint. Also serves delicious home-made savoury snacks and cakes and desserts such as apple and cinnamon crumble with red fruits, and crème brulée flavoured with Earl Grey. Tea with scones or cake costs €5.80.

La Vertu 11 rue Notre-Dame. Appealingly eccentric bar where, in summer, you can lounge in wooden deck chairs outside in the quiet square. As well as a good choice of wines and beer, *La Vertu* serves cocktails, tapas and ice creams. Opening times are erratic.

Le Zanzibar 2 rue Condé. Bar with a tropical feel, a long list of exotic cocktails and imported island beers as well as a good selection of tapas. Salsa every Wednesday. Tues–Sat 6.30pm–1am.

Listings

Airlines Twin Jet (Ⓣ08.92.70.73.37, Ⓦwww.twinjet.net) operates twice-daily weekday flights from Bassilac airport to Paris Orly.
Bike rental Cycles Cum's, across the river at 37 route de Bergerac, Ⓣ05.53.53.31.56 or Patrick Duteil, at 15 cours Fénelon Ⓣ05.53.53.44.62.
Books and newspapers Maison de la Presse, 11 place Bugeaud, stocks the widest selection of English-language newspapers and magazines and has a decent selection of local guidebooks. Otherwise, try Librairie Marbot at 17 bd Montaigne, which also stocks a few English-language novels.
Bus departures Long-distance buses leave from the bus stop on rue de la Cité, behind place Francheville. Most routes are operated by CFTA, which has an information office on site (Ⓣ05.53.08.43.13). Tickets are available on board, €2 all routes.
Car rental Near the train station, try: Ada-Autoloc 24, 4 bis avenue Henri Barbusse Ⓣ05.53.05.40.28; Ⓣ05.53.53.39.02; Europcar, 7 rue Denis Papin Ⓣ05.53.58.97.97; Avis, 18 rue Président Wilson is in the city centre. You can also arrange to pick up cars at the airport.
Hospital Central Hospitalier, 80 av Georges Pompidou (Ⓣ05.53.45.25.25, Ⓦwww.hopitalperigueux.com), to the north of centre off bd Michel Montaigne.
Internet access Net Runner, 17 rue de la Cité (Mon–Fri noon–midnight; Sat & Sun 2pm–midnight, €3 per hour); Espace Multimédia l'Arche, 68 rue Pierre de Brantôme (Mon–Fri 9am–noon & 2–4pm, free); free access also at the Hôtel de Ville, the station and the main post office. Most hotels also provide wi-fi.
Markets Périgueux's largest markets take place on Wednesday and Saturday mornings principally in place de la Clautre, place du Coderc and place de l'Hôtel de Ville (all fresh foods) and place Bugeaud (Wed only; clothes and household goods). There's also a small, daily fresh-food market in place du Coderc's covered hall (8am–1pm). In winter (mid-Nov to mid-March), stalls selling foie gras and truffles set up in place St-Louis for the annual *marchés au gras* (Wed & Sat morn).
Police Commissariat de Police, rue du 4 Septembre Ⓣ05.53.06.44.44; Police Municipale, 2A rue Charles Mangold Ⓣ05.53.08.49.33.
Post Office The central post office is at rue du 4 Septembre, 24000 Périgueux Ⓣ05.53.03.61.10
Shopping The best place to look for regional produce is along rue Taillefer, where Pierre Champion (no. 21) sells local wines and truffles as well as duck and goose in all its guises; browse also among the tempting specialist shops on rue Limogeanne. You can buy picnic food in the Monoprix supermarket on place Francheville.
Swimming pool Aquacap (Ⓣ05.53.02.90.29) at Champcevinel, northeast of the city centre, just after the main hospital, is Périgueux's watersports centre, with space for serious swimmers as well as slides, aquagym, swimming for babies, jacuzzi, sauna and hammam.
Taxis Call Allo Taxi Périgueux on Ⓣ05.53.09.09.09. Alternatively, there's a taxi stand outside the train station and another on place Bugeaud.

Brantôme

Thirty kilometres north of Périgueux, the beautiful town of **BRANTÔME** is often described as the "Venice of Périgord". While that's rather overdoing it, the river walks and waterside restaurants are what draw most people here, along with a Benedictine **abbey** and some **troglodyte caves**. Sitting prettily on an island, which was created around one thousand years ago when local monks dug a mill-stream across a tight meander of the Dronne, the town is surrounded by leafy gardens and parks. It has a good range of accommodation and some fantastic eating options.

Arrival and information

Buses on the Périgueux–Angoulême route, timed to connect with TGV trains in Angoulême, stop on the Champs de Foire, at the south end of rue Gambetta. The **tourist office** is located in the Hôtel de Ville (Feb, March & Oct–Dec Mon & Wed–Sun 10am–noon & 2–5pm; April–June & Sept Mon & Wed–Sun 10am–12.30pm & 2–6pm; July & Aug daily 10am–7pm; Ⓣ05.53.05.80.52, Ⓦwww.ville-brantome.fr). For more than 450 years the streets of central Brantôme have been filled with a Friday-morning **market**, its stalls augmented in winter

(Dec–Feb) with truffles, foie gras and local walnuts. Between May and September, you can rent **canoes** (reservations are recommended in high season) from Allo Canoës, on the road to Bourdeilles (Ⓣ05.53.06.31.85, Ⓦwww.allocanoes.com) or Brantôme Canoë, just out of the centre on the road east to Thiviers (Ⓣ05.53.05.77.24, Ⓦwww.brantome-canoe.com). The latter also run **rock climbing** classes for individuals or small groups, taught by a registered monitor. **Bikes** can be rented from Spad'Zone on ave des Martyrs (Ⓣ05.53.08.02.65, Ⓦwww.spadzone.com), north on the Angoulême road.

Accommodation

Camping Peyrelevade Av André Maurois Ⓣ05.53.05.75.24, Ⓦwww.camping-dordogne.net. Shady and sunny site beside the rive Dronne with private beach, fishing and swimming pool. Children's playground, shop and camper van emptying facilities. May–Oct.

Camping Puynadal Ⓣ05.53.06.19.66, Ⓦwww.camping-puynadal.com. Large site equipped with bar, restaurant, children's playground, sports facilities, swimming pool and weekly disco in the summer. April–Sept.

Hôtel Chabrol 57 rue Gambetta Ⓣ05.53.05.70.15, Ⓦwww.lesfrerescharbonnel.com. Comfortable, pretty rooms decked out in wood and florals overlooking the river, excellent service and a well-rated restaurant (see *Les Frères Charbonnel* on p.138) make this one of Brantôme's most popular hotels. Closed mid-Nov to mid-Dec & Feb. ❹–❺

Château de la Borie-Saulnier Champagnac-de-Belair Ⓣ05.53.54.22.99, Ⓦwww.chateau-de-la-borie-saulnier.com. Set in extensive grounds, and with a pool, this imposing château offers five rooms full of period furniture and family knick-knacks. It's signposted off the D82 4km northeast of Brantôme. Evening meals on request. ❹–❻

Hôtel Coligny 8 place Charles-de-Gaulle Ⓣ05.53.05.71.42, Ⓦwww.hotel-coligny.fr. This friendly hotel is the cheapest option in Brantôme, with just eight newly refurbished rooms, including one with access for the disabled, above a decent restaurant (lunchtime menus from €12; closed Mon July & Aug and Fri & Sat rest of year). Closed mid-Nov to mid-March. ❸–❹

Maison Fleurie 54 rue Gambetta Ⓣ05.53.35.17.04, Ⓦwww.maison-fleurie.net. Stylish, centrally located English-owned *chambre d'hôte* with a pool and a quiet courtyard garden. Closed two weeks in Feb. ❹

Moulin de l'Abbaye 1 rue de Bourdeilles Ⓣ05.53.05.80.22, Ⓦwww.moulinabbaye.com. If you're feeling self-indulgent, treat yourself to a night of luxury in this beautiful old mill to the west of the abbey. Restaurant menus from €60 (closed for lunch Mon–Fri). Hotel and restaurant closed Nov–April. ❾

The Town

Brantôme's **old centre** is packed onto an almost circular island, seemingly tethered to the surrounding bank by its bridges. A modern bypass takes the worst of the traffic, but in summer it's still a bottleneck along the main road, rue Gambetta, which cuts north across the island to place de Gaulle on the far bank of the Dronne.

The town owes its existence to some rock-shelters – where the first hermits set up home around the fifth century – and a spring now hidden behind the church and convent buildings of the former **Benedictine abbey** standing on the river's far north bank. The first church was built under the cliffs here sometime before 817 – according to local tradition, it was Charlemagne (742–814) who founded the abbey with the endowment of St Sicaire's relic, one of the infants massacred by Herod. It had a rocky start, but by its twelfth-century heyday the abbey supported 24 parishes and had spawned a thriving town. Nevertheless, things started going downhill again with the Hundred Years' War and, after being rebuilt on several occasions, the abbey was finally abandoned after the Revolution. The present buildings, which date from the seventeenth century but were heavily restored two hundred years later, house the **Hôtel de Ville**, whose staring, serried windows still hint at ascetic institutional life.

The abbey **church** recalls some of this history. The death of St Sicaire is the subject of a stained-glass window behind the altar, while bas-reliefs to either side depict the Massacre of the Innocents and Charlemagne offering Sicaire's relic to the church. After a quick look in the neighbouring chapterhouse, with its palm-frond vaulting, next stop is the **caves** (July & Aug daily 10am–7pm; April–June & Sept Mon & Wed–Sun 10am–12.30pm & 2–6pm; Feb, March & Oct–Dec Mon & Wed–Sun 10am–noon & 2–5pm; €4), accessed through this northeast corner of the Hôtel de Ville. Despite being used as a quarry over the years, there's still considerable evidence of the monks' earlier troglodytic existence. The most interesting of the caves contains a large, rather crude **sculpture** of the Last Judgement, believed to date from the fifteenth century, in the aftermath of the Hundred Years' War.

A later, more worldly generation of monks built themselves an Italianate walled garden, now a public **park**, to the south of the abbey and across the old stone bridge from the water mill. It's a pleasant picnic spot, and a walk along the balustraded **riverbanks** is a must. In summer you can also take a 45-minute **boat trip** around the island from beside the old bridge (Easter to early Oct; €7). In July and August (Fri & Sat eves; 9pm) watch the locals take part in a lively jousting competition – in boats.

The more modern bridge directly in front of the abbey leads into rue Puy-Joli, Brantôme's main shopping street, where you'll find a variety of attractive **shops**, while the **café-bars** on place du Marché are a popular spot for a drink.

Eating and drinking

Brantôme has an unusual number of top-quality **restaurants** for such a small town; there's also one particularly good option a short drive away, the *Moulin du Roc*, while the hotels listed above are also decent places for a meal.

Au Fil de l'Eau 21 quai Bertin ⓣ05.53.05.73.65, ⓦwww.fildeleau.com. Under the same management as the *Moulin de l'Abbaye* hotel, and specializing in well-prepared and not too expensive fish dishes. At its best in fine weather, when tables are set out on the riverbank to the west of the centre. Menus from €24. Closed mid-Oct to Easter, and Wed & Thurs all year except July & Aug.

Les Frères Charbonnel *Hôtel Chabrol*, 57 rue Gambetta ⓣ05.53.05.70.15. This hotel-restaurant is in the gourmet class, but is still good value with menus from €30. Specialities of the house include lemon sole with truffles (Oct–June closed Sun eve & Mon, also closed mid-Nov to mid-Dec & Feb).

Les Jardins de Brantôme 33–37 rue Pierre-de-Mareuil ⓣ05.53.05.88.16, ⓦwww.lesjardins-brantome.com. Though the restaurant doesn't look much from the outside, the food served here is consistently good and there's a delightful garden behind for summer dining. It's at the far end of rue Pierre-de-Mareuil, a small street running north from place de Gaulle. Menus range from €21 to €36. Closed Mon lunchtime, Wed & Thurs.

Moulin du Roc Champagnac-de-Belair ⓣ05.53.02.86.00, ⓦwww.moulinduroc.com. For a real splurge in an idyllic waterside setting, head 6km northeast of Brantôme to find this very gracious hotel-restaurant beside the bridge as you come into Champagnac-de-Belair from the west. Apart from Sundays, lunch costs €42 including a cocktail, two glasses of wine and coffee; Sunday and evening menus start at €45. Closed Nov–May; also closed Tues & Wed lunchtime.

The lower Dronne valley

The country west of Brantôme and along the **River Dronne** remains largely undisturbed. It is tranquil, very beautiful and restoring, best savoured at a gentle pace, perhaps by bike or even by canoe along the river. **Bourdeilles**, the first sizeable town downstream from Brantôme, was the seat of one of Périgord's four baronies (see p.355), as its great tower testifies, while the

Renaissance château next door contains a marvellous collection of furniture. From the foot of the castle, the Dronne meanders through water meadows to one of the Dordogne's most famous market towns, **Ribérac**. Though Ribérac itself holds little else of interest, it makes an agreeable base from which to visit a crop of Romanesque churches scattered in the countryside around. **Aubeterre-sur-Dronne**, with another, better-preserved troglodyte church and a splendid position, represents the final stop along the river.

Bourdeilles

BOURDEILLES, 16km down the Dronne from Brantôme by the beautiful D106 back road, is relatively hard to reach – perhaps the most appealing way is by canoe (see p.137 for rental from Brantôme). It's a sleepy backwater, an ancient village clustering round its **château** (Feb, March & mid-Nov to Dec Mon, Wed, Thurs & Sun 10am–12.30pm & 2–5.30pm; April–June & Sept to Oct daily except Tues 10am–12.30pm & 2–6pm; July & Aug daily 10am–7pm; €6; Ⓣ05.53.03.73.36, Ⓦwww.semitour.com) on a rocky spur above the river. The château consists of two buildings: one a thirteenth-century fortress, the other a subdued Renaissance residence begun by the lady of the house, Jacquette de Montbrun, wife of André de Bourdeilles, as a piece of unsuccessful favour-currying with Catherine de Medici – unsuccessful because, though she passed through the area, Catherine never came to stay and so the château remained unfinished. The Renaissance château is now home to an exceptional collection of **furniture** and **religious statuary**. Among the more notable pieces are some splendid Spanish dowry chests; the gilded bedroom suite of a former Yugoslav king; and a sixteenth-century Rhenish entombment whose life-sized statues embody the very image of the serious, self-satisfied medieval burgher. The overly elaborate *salon doré*, the room Catherine de Medici was supposed to sleep in, has also been preserved. To clear your head, climb the octagonal **keep** for lovely views over the town.

▲ Bourdeilles

Practicalities

There's a small **tourist office** just downhill from the château entrance (April–Nov daily 2.30–5.30 pm; ⓣ05.53.03.42.96, ⓦwww.bourdeilles.com). Simple, old-fashioned, *Les Tilleuls* (ⓣ&ⓕ05.53.03.76.40; ❷; menus from €15), right across the street, makes a reasonable place to **stay**, or try the more comfortable *Hôtel du Donjon* opposite (ⓣ05.53.04.82.81, ⓦwww.hostellerie-ledonjon.fr; ❸; closed Jan to Easter), which serves delicious regional cuisine in its leafy courtyard restaurant (menus from €20). More upmarket again is the very stylish *Hostellerie les Griffons* (ⓣ05.53.45.45.35, ⓦwww.griffons.fr; ❺; closed mid-Oct to Easter) in a sixteenth-century house beside the humpback bridge, with top-notch regional cuisine (menus from €35).

For a good **meal** you could also head to the *Moulin du Pont* (ⓣ05.53.04.51.75, menus from €14; closed mid-Nov to Feb, and Sun eve & Mon except in summer), 8km downstream near the village of **LISLE**. Get here early to sit on the terrace with the weir on one side and the restaurant's trout ponds on the other. You could even arrive by river; **canoe** rental is available by the bridge at Bourdeilles from Canoës Bourdeilles Loisirs (ⓣ05.53.04.56.94; open all year).

Ribérac and around

Surrounded by an intimate, hilly countryside of woods, hay meadows and drowsy hilltop villages, **RIBÉRAC**, 30km downstream from Bourdeilles, is a pleasant if unremarkable town whose greatest claim to fame is its Friday **market**, bringing in producers and wholesalers from all around. There's nothing really in the way of sights, but the country here is dotted with numerous **Romanesque churches** that provide a focus for leisurely wandering – before setting off, you might want to collect information on these from Ribérac's tourist office (see below). Nowadays many are kept locked, but the route described opposite takes in a representative sample of those that are more likely to be open.

Ribérac lies on the south bank of the Dronne. Its main street starts in the south as rue Jean Moulin, runs through the central **place Nationale** and then continues northwards as rue du 26 Mars 1944. From place Nationale, rue Gambetta heads east to **place Général de Gaulle** and the vast market square beyond.

Arrival and information

Buses for Périgueux and Angoulême stop on the other side of this square near the Palais de Justice, which is where you'll also find Ribérac's **tourist office** (July & Aug Mon–Fri 9am–7pm, Sat 10am–1pm & 2–7pm, Sun 10am–1pm; Sept–June Mon–Fri 9am–noon & 2–6pm, Sat 9am–noon & 2–5pm; ⓣ05.53.90.03.10, ⓦwww.riberac.fr). The office doubles as a ticket office for SNCF, and in July and August they organize guided walks and farm visits. You can rent **bikes** at the *Café du Palais* in place Debonnière (ⓣ05.53.90.90.35), at the *Terrasse de la Rivière* and at the campsite (see opposite), beside the entrance to which Canoës Ribérac (mid-June to mid-Sept; ⓣ05.53.90.54.42, ⓦwww.canoriberac.free.fr) rents out **canoes** and can arrange two-day trips along the Dronne.

Accommodation

Ribérac isn't blessed with an abundance of accommodation; apart from its one new hotel, your best bet is to try one of the several *chambres d'hotes* – the tourist office has a list.

Chambres Florence 5 place Général de Gaulle ⓣ05.53.90.93.38, ⓦchambresflorence.monsite .orange.fr. In the town centre just across the square from the tourist office, this *chambre d'hôte* is in a spacious and elegant townhouse with exposed stone walls, lovingly polished old parquet floors, and even a swimming pool. The house also functions as an art gallery, Galerie le 5. ❹–❺

Municipal campsite ⓣ05.53.90.50.08, ⓔot .riberac@wanadoo.fr. Two-star site just across the Dronne on the Angoulême road. June to mid-Sept.

La Petite Clavelie 4km southeast of Ribérac ⓣ05.53.91.25.21, ⓦwww.lapetiteclavelie.com. Friendly *chambre d'hôte* with very prettily decorated rooms surrounded by charming gardens. ❷

Rev'Hôtel route de Périgueux ⓣ05.53.91.62.62, ⓦwww.rev-hotel.fr. A kilometre east of town, this new, single-storey, two-star hotel offers 29 bland but comfortable rooms (2 for disabled) and helpful service. ❷–❸

The Romanesque churches

A couple of hundred metres from the centre on the hill to the east of town, Ribérac's own **Collégiale Notre-Dame** (mid-June to mid-Sept daily 2–7pm, for exhibitions only; free), now an exhibition and concert hall, makes a good place to start exploring. It's a pleasing building, with its squat tower and semicircular apse designed on a grander scale than its country cousins, but the west end and interior have been extensively altered; if it's open, it's worth popping in to see the recently restored seventeenth- and eighteenth-century frescoes. The **church of St-Pierre** in the village of **FAYE**, 1km west of Ribérac on the D20, on the other hand, has great charm even though it's no architectural beauty. Its diminutive single nave seems barely able to carry the fortress of a tower above. There's more reason to stop at **BOURG-DU-BOST**, 6km further downstream, where the **Notre-Dame** (daily 9am–7pm) harbours some very faded twelfth-century murals: the four Evangelists inside the dome, and the twelve Apostles around the choir.

From here the route cuts north and climbs to an undulating plateau with good views back over the Dronne's river meadows, then meanders through a string of villages. The first one to aim for is **ST-MARTIAL-VIVEYROL**, roughly 15km due north of Ribérac. Its church (daily 9am–6pm) more resembles a castle keep; the windows are reduced to narrow slits, there's just a single, simple door at ground level and the belfry doubles as a watchtower with, behind it, a guardroom along the length of the nave big enough to hold the whole village. Looping southeast around Ribérac, the **church of St-Pierre-et-St-Paul** (daily 9am–7pm) in **GRAND-BRASSAC** is unusual in that sculptures were added over its north door. They show Christ in majesty flanked by St Peter and St Paul above a frieze of the Adoration with traces of earlier paintwork.

The last of the Romanesque churches, **St-Pierre-ès-Liens** (daily 9am–7pm), is also one of the most prettily sited. It lies in wooded country 6km south of Ribérac and is best approached from the west with the roofs of **SIORAC-DE-RIBÉRAC** clustered behind. From the hastily erected rubble walls it's easy to see where, in the fourteenth century, the nave was raised a couple of metres and a guard tower added at the west end. Again, there are almost no windows and the walls are up to three metres thick – which explains why the nave is so surprisingly narrow.

Eating and drinking

Café des Colonnes place de Gaulle. You can't beat this old-style place for a drink, with its shady terrace in the summer.

Le Citronnier 3 place Nationale ⓣ05.53.90.22.72. This refined, Swiss-owned restaurant, tucked away in what is probably the oldest house in Ribérac, specialises in fish (sea bass baked Provençal-style, bream, John Dory, turbot) and game (wild boar, pheasant and guinea fowl) and well as catering for vegetarians. Everything is seasonal and home-made and there is an extensive wine list of over 50 wines, including an impressive two pages of Bergeracs. You can eat in the quiet rear garden in summer. Closed Sun & Mon except in summer, lunch menus from €14, evenings from €22.90.

Le Commensal Rue du 26 mars ⓣ05.53.90.46.28. Here you'll find a warm welcome, simple decor and creative menus that change regularly. Quirky dishes include eggs baked in a ramekin with foie gras, filet mignon of pork with bananas, and terrine of foie gras with figs. Rear terrace and private parking. Closed Sat lunchtime, Sun eve & Mon; menus range from €11 for two courses at lunchtime to €26 for three courses in the evening.

Le Commerce 8 rue Gambetta ⓣ05.53.91.28.59. Generous portions at this good-value, friendly restaurant, which offers mainly traditional fare as well as more unusual dishes, such as a goats' cheese *clafoutis* or *coquilles St Jacques* in whisky. There's also a good range of fresh and healthy salads. Closed Tues eve & Wed; menus from €15.

La Terrasse de la Rivière ⓣ05.53.91.09.74. Locals tend to patronise this place for its riverside setting immediately across the Dronne beside the bridge on the Angoulême road. It's a simple, rustic place where you can still get a weekday lunch for €11; other menus start at €18. Closed Mon.

Aubeterre-sur-Dronne

Touristy but very beautiful, with its ancient galleried and turreted houses, **AUBETERRE-SUR-DRONNE** hangs on a steep hillside above the river, some 30km west of Ribérac. Its principal curiosity is the cavernous subterranean **church of St-Jean** (daily: June to Sept 9.30am–12.30pm & 2–7pm; Oct to May 9.30am–noon & 2–6pm; €4.50), in the lower town northeast of Aubeterre's lime-shaded central square, **place Trarieux**. Carved out of the soft rock by twelfth-century Benedictine monks, it took at least a century to excavate the twenty-metre-high chamber and gallery above. It's from up here that you get the best views over the capacious baptismal font, designed for total immersion, and the two-tiered, hexagonal structure, possibly a reliquary, cut from a single piece of rock – its precise arches seem strangely out of place against the rough walls. The side-chapels are riddled with rock-hewn tombs, while a now blocked-off tunnel connects the gallery with the château on the bluff overhead.

On the opposite, southwestern hillside, the upper town consists of a single street of houses culminating in the **church of St-Jacques**, where only the beautiful, sculpted west facade remains of the original twelfth-century church. The great tiered and decorated arch around the main door is lovely, but don't overlook the frieze of zodiacal signs on the smaller arch to the left: Taurus, Aries and Pisces are easy enough to recognize, then come Capricorn, Aquarius and Sagittarius. The other half of the frieze is missing.

Practicalities

Aubeterre's **tourist office** (April–June & Sept–Oct Tues–Fri 10am–noon & 2–6pm, Mon & Sat 2–6pm; July & Aug Tues–Sun 10am–noon & 2–7pm, Mon 2–7pm; Nov–March Mon–Sat 2–6pm; ⓣ05.45.98.57.18, ⓦwww.aubeterresurdronne.com) faces onto the town's main car park to the northwest of place Traricux. If you're **staying**, try the *Hostellerie du Périgord* (ⓣ05.45.98.50.46, ⓦwww.hostellerie-perigord.com; ❸–❹), down by the bridge on the Ribérac road. The latter offers bright en-suite rooms, a small pool and a recommended **restaurant** (menus €15.50–36; closed Sun eve & Mon). There's also a three-star municipal **campsite** (ⓣ05.45.98.60.17; May to mid-Sept) just across the bridge, with a small beach nearby and the possibility of **canoe** rental (ⓣ05.45.98.51.72) in summer. On weekdays there is a daily **bus** to Angoulême, which departs from near the Gendarmerie on the main road to the south of the bridge, while Chalais, which is on the Angoulême–Bordeaux train line, is only 12km away; call ⓣ05.45.98.28.11 if you need a **taxi**.

The Double region

South of the Dronne valley the landscape and atmosphere change dramatically as you enter the region known as the **Double**. This high, undulating plateau is strewn with lakes and brooding **forests** of oak, chestnut and pine, interspersed with pockets of vines, scattered farmhouses and an abbey at **Échourgnac**. The larger lakes, such as the **étang de la Jemaye**, have been developed for tourism and in summer the Double is a popular destination for walkers, cyclists and nature-lovers; the best place to pick up information is Ribérac tourist office (see p.140). While there is no **public transport** in the Double, both **St-Astier** and **Neuvic** are on the Périgueux to Bordeaux train line from where there are several services a day; they are also on the bus route (school term-time only) to Mussidan, though services are few and far between.

Échourgnac and the Ferme du Parcot

Until the late nineteenth century the Double was largely uninhabited thanks to its poor soils and malarial marshes. Then Napoléon III decreed that it should be drained and planted with maritime pines in similar fashion to the great Landes forest further south. This work was partly carried out by Trappist monks who arrived from Port-Salut in 1868. They settled near the only village of any size, **ÉCHOURGNAC**, plumb in the middle of the plateau nearly 20km southwest of Ribérac, where they founded the **Abbaye de Notre-Dame de Bonne-Espérance**. Since 1923 the walled abbey has sheltered a small community of Cistercian sisters – these days numbering about thirty, some under a vow of silence – who not only continued in the monks' spiritual footsteps but also in their role as local cheese-makers. But the enterprising and energetic sisters didn't stop there. In their well-stocked **shop** opposite the church entrance (daily 2.30–5.30pm; Ⓣ05.53.80.82.50, Ⓦwww.abbaye-echourgnac.org) you'll find the original Le Trappe Échourgnac, a firm, orange-crusted cheese with a smoky flavour, and a newer version laced with walnut liqueur, as well as jams, pâté, jellied sweets and handicrafts from missions around the world. You can also watch a video about the convent; the church is open during the same opening hours, except for when there are services.

Five kilometres east of the abbey, on the D41 from Échourgnac, the **Ferme du Parcot** (May, June & Sept Sun, visits at 2.30, 4 & 5.30pm; July & Aug daily same times) has been preserved as a more typical example of local architecture. With walls of mud and straw on latticed timber frames, protected by a limestone plaster, these farm buildings are quite unlike the sturdy stone houses found elsewhere in the Dordogne. They date from 1841 and, from the grandeur of the barn, it seems the farmer was relatively affluent. In true rural style, however, the house itself, which was inhabited up to 1990, consists of just two very spartan rooms containing a few bits and pieces of furniture and old implements. The farm also marks the start of a gentle **nature trail** (2.5km; accessible all year) through the fields and forest to a fishing lake. To fortify yourself before setting off on the trail, you can **eat** at the *Auberge de la Double* (Ⓣ05.53.80.06.65; closed Sun–Thurs eves & Dec) in Échourgnac, a little village inn which serves weekday lunches at €12 and a menu at €21 (Fri & Sat eves & Sun lunchtime).

Neuvic and St-Astier

It's worth dropping down to the **Isle valley**, which marks the edge of the Double to the south and east, to visit an imposing Renaissance château with a botanical garden on the outskirts of **NEUVIC**, roughly 15km east of Échourgnac. As you head east across the valley floor, a great bank of red-tiled roofs pinpoints the largely sixteenth-century **Château de Neuvic** (daily tours except Thurs: July & Aug 3pm & 5pm; €5.50 including garden; Ⓣ05.53.80.86.60, Ⓦwww.chateau-parc-neuvic.com), which now makes an unusually grand school for deprived children. Since the interiors have been extensively modified, there's not a lot to see beyond some badly damaged frescoes and an elegant eighteenth-century salon furbished with pastoral scenes. But it's the scale of the building, and particularly its handsome western facade, that grabs the attention. The best vantage point is from the **botanical garden** to the west of the château, which is also classed as a bird reserve (April–June, Sept & Oct 10am–noon & 1.30–6.30pm; July & Aug 10am–7pm, closed Thurs; €3.80), though you'll find your attention diverted by a wonderful collection of sculptures created by the pupils.

Cross back over the Isle and head upstream on the D3 for another 10km to find good eating options in the attractive town of **ST-ASTIER**. The smartest is *La Palombière* (Ⓣ05.53.04.40.61, Ⓦwww.restaurant-la-palombiere.com; menus from €14 to €42; closed Sun & Tues eve and Mon & Wed all day), with its pretty terrace beside the towering abbey church. *Le Calzone* opposite the tourist information office serves excellent pizzas and large salads from €6, while the *Auberge du Chapeau Rouge* (Ⓣ05.53.04.97.32; menus from €12; closed Sat lunchtime, Sun eve & Mon) is one of those glorious, no-nonsense locals' places where you can have a *plat du jour* for €7. To find it walk west from the church through place Gambetta and fork right in front of the post office along rue Montaigne.

St-Jean-de-Côle and around

Twenty kilometres northeast of Brantôme, **ST-JEAN-DE-CÔLE** ranks as one of the loveliest villages in the Périgord Vert. An ancient church and château constitute its major sights and, with a couple of restaurants, it makes a good lunchtime stop. From here the splendid **Château de Puyguilhem** lies within easy striking distance, and on the return journey you could loop north via the **Grotte de Villars**, notable for its formations rather than the smattering of prehistoric artwork.

Tiny and very picturesque without being twee, St-Jean's unusually open, sandy square is dominated by the charmingly ill-proportioned late-eleventh-century **church of St-Jean-Baptiste**. The view as you approach is harmonious enough – layers of tiled roofs from the low, square market-hall to the steeply pitched belfry – but on entering the single, lofty bay it becomes apparent that the nave was never completed, due to a lack of funds. Beside the church stands the rugged-looking **Château de la Marthonie** (not open to the public), which dates from the twelfth century, but has since acquired various additions in a pleasingly organic fashion. Apart from a huddle of houses round the square, the rest of the village consists of a line of pastel-plastered cottages stretching west to a humpbacked bridge over the River Côle and the inevitable water mill. The whole ensemble makes a perfect backdrop for the Floralies **flower festival**, held on the second weekend in May.

St-Jean's **tourist office** (mid-June to mid-Sept daily 10am–12.30pm & 2–6.30pm; mid-Sept to mid-June Thurs–Sun 10am–1pm & 2–6pm; Ⓣ05.53.62.14.15, Ⓦwww.ville-saint-jean-de-cole.fr) is on the square, as is the attractive **restaurant** *La Perla*, serving salads and light lunches (daily July–Aug, otherwise closed Mon & Oct–March). Though it doesn't have the same views,

▲ St-Jean-de-Côle

you'll also eat well at the wisteria-covered *St-Jean* (Ⓣ05.53.52.23.20, menus from €15, closed Sun & Mon eve) on the main road near the entrance to the square. It's an old-fashioned country place, nothing fancy but welcoming and well maintained.

Around St-Jean-de-Côle

About 10km west of St-Jean, just outside the village of **VILLARS**, the **Château de Puyguilhem** (Sept–April Wed–Sun 10am–12.30pm & 2–5.30pm; May–Aug daily 10am–12.30pm & 2–6.30pm; €5; Ⓣ05.53.54.82.18, Ⓦwww.puyguilhem.monuments-nationaux.fr) is a perfect example of early French Renaissance architecture. It was erected at the beginning of the sixteenth century by the La Marthonie family of St-Jean-de-Côle on the site of an earlier and more military fortress. The lake that once filled the foreground has long gone, but the château still makes an enchanting prospect, with its steep roofs, stone balustrades, mullion windows, carved chimney stacks and an assortment of round and octagonal towers reminiscent of contemporaneous Loire châteaux.

Though the **interior** suffered more from neglect and pillaging, it too has been beautifully restored and contains some noteworthy pieces of furniture and Aubusson tapestries. Its most remarkable features, however, are two magnificent fireplaces: the first, in the guardroom, depicts three Greek soldiers, while upstairs in the banqueting hall the theme is continued with six of the twelve Labours of Hercules. Both are heavily restored, but no less remarkable for that. The sculptors also went to work on the entrance hall and main staircase, leaving a wealth of oak, vine and acanthus leaves, thistles, fleur-de-lis and a few salamanders for good measure. Right at the top, it was the turn of the master carpenters, whose superb hull-shaped roof timbers have lasted five hundred years.

The ruined Cistercian **abbey of Boschaud**, 3km away in the next valley south, merits a quick visit while you're in the area. Standing in the middle of a field, it's reached by a lane not much bigger than a farm track. Though the pure, stark lines of the twelfth-century architecture hold a certain appeal, the abbey's real charm rests in the fact that it is – for once – unfenced, unpampered and free.

In 1953 speleologists discovered an extensive cave system in the hills 3km north of Villars, part of which has been opened to the public. While the **Grotte de Villars** (daily: April–June & Sept 10am–noon & 2–7pm; July & Aug 10am–7.30pm; Oct & Nov 2–6.30pm; €7.50; ⓣ05.53.54.82.36, ⓦwww.grotte-villars.com) boasts a few prehistoric paintings – notably of horses and a still unexplained scene of a man and bison – the main reason for coming here is the variety of **stalagmites** and, in particular, **stalactites**. Some are almost pure white and as fine as needles, others ochre yellow, and there are also cascades, semicircular basins and hanging curtains of semi-translucent calcium carbonate. The final cave you come to contains the **paintings**, dating from 17,000 years ago, the same age as those at Lascaux (see p.216). And look out, too, for the claw marks further back from the entrance, where generations of tiny bear cubs have left their imprints.

Thiviers

Not far east of St-Jean-de-Côle, and linked by a pleasant cycle ride along a disused train line, the small market town of **THIVIERS** sits on the main road and rail links between Périgueux, 40km to the south, and Limoges. The N21 bypasses the town these days, leaving its old centre – comprising a clutch of pretty, old houses round the church and along pedestrianized rue de la Tour – relatively peaceful. The one exception is during the Saturday **market**, when the streets present a lesson in local agriculture: walnuts, apples, Limousin beef, pork, duck and goose and all manner of associated foodstuffs. From mid-November to mid-March the *foies* come out in force at the *marché au gras*, some of them destined to go into the local speciality, *L'autre fois de Thiviers*, consisting of duck or goose liver robed in pâté (see box opposite). Thiviers' accommodation options make it a good base should you wish to make a detour to visit the **Château de Jumilhac** (see p.148) to the north.

Up until the 1920s Thiviers was an important centre for faience, a hundred or so pieces of which are displayed in the town hall (Sat 10am–noon & 3–5.30pm, free). But the pretty blue-and-white faience plays second fiddle to the town's prime concern – the history and production of **foie gras**, the subject of a small **museum** (€1.50) accessed via the tourist office (see below).

Practicalities

The **gare SNCF**, with services to Bordeaux, Périgueux and Limoges, is located just a few minutes' walk north of Thiviers' centre. The **tourist office**, on central place Foch (Mon–Fri 10am–1pm & 2–6pm; Sat 9am–1pm & 3–6pm; July & Aug also open Sun 10am–1pm; ⓣ05.53.55.12.50), can provide information on farm visits and walks in the local area, such as the **Voie Verte**, a 17km footpath and cycle-way that follows a disused railway line from Thiviers into the heart of the Périgord Vert. One of the nicest places to stay is the attractive and well-priced *Hôtel de France et de Russie*, 51 rue du Général Lamy (ⓣ05.53.55.17.80, ⓦwww.thiviers-hotel.com; ❸–❹), on the road north from the tourist office. At the other end of the scale, there's a well-run, three-star **campsite**, *Le Repaire* (ⓣ05.53.52.69.75, ⓦwww.camping-thiviers-perigord.com; open all year), beside an artificial lake on the eastern outskirts of Thiviers. In addition to the

Foie gras

It is generally agreed that it was the Egyptians who first discovered the delights of eating the **enlarged livers** of migratory geese and ducks gorging themselves in the Nile delta, and that it was the Romans who popularized the practice of force-feeding domesticated birds, generally with figs. For many the name (literally, "fat liver") is off-putting enough, let alone the idea of force-feeding the birds, while for others a slice of the succulent, pale rose-coloured liver is a pleasure not to be missed.

Duck or goose?

Foie gras is produced throughout southwest France and also in Alsace, Brittany and the Vendée. However, the yellowish-hued livers from the Périgord, where the birds are traditionally fed on local yellow – as opposed to white – maize, and where producers jealously guard their methods of preparation, are particularly sought after. Périgord farmers now favour hybrid Mulard or Barbary **ducks** over the more traditional **geese** for a variety of reasons: they fatten more quickly, are easier to raise and force-feed, and the liver is easier to cook with. The softer goose livers, on the other hand, have a more delicate flavour and smoother texture. They are also larger – 600g to 700g for an average goose liver (*foie gras d'oie*) as opposed to 500g for duck (*de canard*).

Production

The young birds are raised outside to the age of four months, after which they are kept in the dark and fed over one kilo per day of partly cooked maize for between two and three weeks. During this time the livers can quadruple in size. This **gavage**, or force-feeding, was traditionally carried out using a funnel to introduce the grain into the bird's throat and then stroking it down the neck by hand. Modern techniques follow the same principle but use a mechanized feeder. When done carefully, it's not nearly as terrible as it sounds and most small producers go to a lot of trouble not to harm their birds, if for no other reason than that a stressed bird will produce a rancid liver.

Where and what to buy?

All round, it's best to **buy** foie gras from small family concerns, either direct from the farm – local tourist offices can advise – or at the region's many *marchés aux gras* that take place from November to March. If you're buying fresh liver, choose one which is not too big, is uniform in colour and firm but gives slightly to the touch; the market price averages around €30–40 per kilo for foie gras of duck and €50–60 for goose. The alternative is the ready-prepared preserved version, of which there is a bewildering variety. The majority is de-veined, seasoned (wherein the secret recipes) and then sterilized by cooking briefly (*mi-cuit*) before being vacuum-packed or sealed in jars, either of which is preferable to the canned varieties; the tin taints the flavour. When choosing, check that it is locally produced and then look for the label *foie gras entier*, in other words consisting of one or more whole lobes, or simply *foie gras,* which is composed of smaller pieces but is still top-quality liver. Next step down is a *bloc de foie gras* made up of reconstituted liver (sometimes *avec morceaux*, visible pieces of lobe) pressed together. Below that come all sorts of *mousses*, *parfaits*, pâtés and so forth, each of which has to contain a specified minimum percentage of foie gras and to indicate this on the label.

hotel **restaurant** mentioned above, the little *Pergola* (closed Sun) in rue Gabriel Peri is perfectly pleasant, offering pizzas, crêpes and salads, as is *L'air du Temps* at 2 rue Pierre Sémard (Ⓣ05.53.62.31.95), on the way into town from the *gare SNCF,* whose menu features locally produced ostrich steaks, as well as more traditional fare; menus from €17.50. Finally, there's **internet** access at *Le Thiber. lien*, 30 rue du Général Lamy (Ⓣ05.53.62.57.89, Mon 2–6.45pm; Tues–Sat 10.30am–12.30pm & 2.30–6.45pm; Sun 3–6pm; €2 for 30min).

Jumilhac

In its upper reaches the Isle valley narrows down between steep, wooded banks to become a mini-ravine. One of its rocky bluffs, some 20km northeast of Thiviers, is home to the vast **Château de Jumilhac** (March–May & Oct daily 2–6pm; Nov–Feb Sun 2–5pm; June–Sept daily 10am–7pm & Tues 9.30am–11.30 pm; €6, €8 including gardens; reservations ⓣ05.53.52.42.97). While elements of the original thirteenth-century château remain – such as the stone-paved ground-floor rooms and the family chapel – the present structure largely owes its existence to an ironmaster, Antoine Chapelle, later count of Jumilhac, who made his fortune manufacturing arms for the future Henry IV during the Wars of Religion.

The body of the château is suitably uncompromising: the hard, grey stone allowed for little decorative detail, and what windows there are mostly consist of narrow slits. But the roof is another matter, adorned with no fewer than eight different **towers**, from great grey-slate wedges to pinnacled turrets and a jaunty pepper pot, topped off with delicate lead statues depicting the angels of justice or more mundane pigeon-shaped weather-vanes.

Inside, however, austerity reigns once again. This is particularly so in the cramped, ground-floor rooms, which date back to the thirteenth century, but also extends to the medieval rooms above, of which the much-vaunted **spinner's room** provides the focus of the tour. Not so much for its architecture – it's a small vaulted chamber decorated with naive frescoes of animals and flowers – but for the story attached. The spinner in question was Louise de Hautefort, wife of the then count of Jumilhac, who was imprisoned here for thirty years (1618–48) for her alleged infidelity. Not one to mope, Louise took to painting the walls and spinning to occupy her time. Or so it seemed. The shepherd who regularly called under her window, and from whom she bought her wool, was of course her lover in disguise, and the spindles were used to carry secret messages between them. According to one legend, the story ended in the lover being killed in a duel, while another has him retiring to a monastery. To give you some idea what all the fuss was about, there's a portrait of Louise, supposedly painted at the time of her release but still beautiful, defiantly holding her spindle aloft.

The two wings enclosing the courtyard were added later in the seventeenth century and are gradually being restored by the château's present owners, descendants of Antoine Chapelle, who bought it back from the state in 1927.

For more than two centuries Jumilhac has been closely associated with **gold**. The nearby mines closed in 2001, but you can learn more about the history of gold here and further afield in the **Galerie de l'Or** (same hours as tourist office, see p.146; free), a succinct but well-presented museum overlooking the grassy square in front of the château. Visit in summer and you can even try your luck **panning for gold** in the Isle river (July & Aug, call the tourist office to reserve a half-day course; €16); it's not uncommon to find tiny specks, but don't expect to make your fortune.

Practicalities

Jumilhac's **tourist office** (April, May, Oct & Nov Tues–Sat 10am–12.30pm & 2–6pm; June & Sept Wed–Sun 10am–12.30pm & 2–6pm; July & Aug daily 10am–1pm & 2.30–6.30pm; Dec–March Tues–Fri 2–5pm; ⓣ05.53.52.55.43, ⓦwww.pays-jumilhac.fr), located just down from the Galerie de l'Or, is a mine of information on local activities and accommodation.

One of the most attractive **places to stay** is *Les Vignes de Chalusset* (ⓣ05.53.52.38.25; ❷; meals on request €14), a pretty and very welcoming

chambre d'hôte, 5km east of Jumilhac, signed off the St-Yrieix road, with a pool and extensive grounds. Another good option is the three-star *La Chatonnière* **campsite** (Ⓣ05.53.52.57.36, Ⓦwww.chatonniere.com; mid-May to mid-Sept), beside the river just over a kilometre from Jumilhac on the same road. If you're in Jumilhac around lunchtime, try the *Lou Boueïradour* **restaurant** (Sept–June closed Wed eve; Ⓣ05.53.52.50.47), named after an implement used for blanching chestnuts, across the square from the tourist office. Their good-value regional menus start at €12.

Sorges

A small town on the Périgueux road about 15km south of Thiviers, **SORGES** is worth visiting simply for its informative **Musée de la Truffe** (Feb to mid-June & Oct to Jan Tues–Sun 10am–noon & 2–5pm; mid-June to Sept daily 9.30am–12.30pm & 2.30–6.30pm; €5), located just off the main road near the old centre. The dry limestone plateau around Sorges is particularly prolific for **truffles** – in the early 1900s the commune averaged 6000kg per year, and the largest black truffle discovered so far, a monster weighing well over a kilo, was found near Excideuil (see below) in 1999. By way of comparison, most truffle-hounds would be happy with a mere couple of hundred grams. You'll unearth all manner of similar facts and figures in the museum, the brainchild of an enterprising local mayor – a former *trufficulteur* – from how the fungus forms to how to create your own truffle-oak orchard, all helpfully translated into English. The tips on choosing a good truffle and what to do with it afterwards will come in handy if you happen to be in Sorges for the annual **truffle market** (last Sun in Jan), or if you're tempted by one of the preserved specimens on sale in the museum. You can also pick up details of a three-kilometre nature trail that gives an idea of how and where truffles grow (see box, p.150).

The museum doubles as Sorges' **tourist office** (same hours; Ⓣ05.53.05.90.11), and the town also boasts a very comfortable, reasonably priced **hotel**, called what else but *Auberge de la Truffe* (Ⓣ05.53.05.02.05, Ⓦwww.auberge-de-la-truffe.com; ❸–❹). Though it's on the main road, the rooms are all double-glazed and most face onto the garden and pool behind, or there's a quieter annexe (*Hôtel de la Mairie*) by the church. Even if you're not staying, try their excellent **restaurant** – naturally, truffles feature strongly, particularly in the *menu truffe* at €100, otherwise there are menus from €23 (closed Mon lunchtime all year & Sun eve Oct–March).

Excideuil

The old route between Périgueux and Limoges used to run up the Isle and Loue rivers to **EXCIDEUIL**, 15km east of Sorges, where two huge medieval keeps still dominate the little market town. The **castle** was one of the region's most heavily fortified and for a while the viscounts of Limoges held court here. Following the Hundred Years' War, however, the fortress lay in ruins until relatively recently, when restoration was carried out. Now privately owned, you can enter only the precinct, but it's an impressive sight, particularly if you approach from the west. From the castle, rue des Cendres leads north into the tight knot of streets concentrated around place Bugeaud and the much-restored church, with its Gothic portal. This square and the nearby *halle* are the venue

The black diamonds of Périgord

The **black truffle** of Périgord, *tuber melanosporum*, is one of those expensive delicacies that many people find overrated. This is mainly because it's usually served in such minute quantities or is combined with such strong flavours that its own subtle earthy taste and aroma are completely overwhelmed. Really to appreciate the truffle, it should be eaten in a salad, omelette or simple pastry crust.

The truffle is a **fungus** that grows entirely underground, and a fussy one at that. It prefers shallow, free-draining limestone soils rich in organic matter, a sunny position and marked seasonal differences, and requires the presence of certain species of oak, or occasionally lime or hazelnut, around the roots of which it grows. It's greedy, too, absorbing so much of the nutrients and water available that the vegetation overhead often dies. This tell-tale ring of denuded earth is just one of the clues truffle-hunters are on the lookout for. Others include small, yellow truffle-flies hovering just above the soil, and the distinct smell – which is where the pig, or generally these days the more amenable dog – comes in.

Even now the **life cycle** of the Périgord truffle – the most prized out of more than forty different varieties – is not completely understood, and attempts to cultivate them artificially have so far proved elusive. What is clear is that the spores are released in the spring and mature truffles are ready for harvest between December and early March. When ripe, the skin of a Périgord truffle is a deep purple-brown or black, while the lighter-coloured flesh is flecked with fine white veins. It should be firm to the touch and give off a pleasantly earthy aroma; an overripe truffle stinks.

for a lively farmers' **market** on Thursday mornings, augmented in winter (Nov to early March) by an important *foire aux gras*.

Excideuil can be reached by **bus** from Périgueux (see p.136). There's a bus stop beneath the castle on place du Château, where you'll also find the **tourist office** booth (all year Mon–Sat 9.30am–12.30pm; ⓣ09.52.68.95.56, ⓦwww.hautperigord.fr) and a recently renovated **hotel**, the *Hostellerie du Fin Chapon* (ⓣ05.53.62.42.38, ⓦwww.lefinchapon.com; ❷–❸), with good comfortable modern rooms and a **restaurant** with an emphasis on regional dishes (lunchtime menus from €12.50 for two courses, evening €19.50–26.50). There's also a basic but prettily sited municipal **campsite** (ⓣ05.53.62.43.72, ⓦwww.excideuil.fr; July & Aug) by the river on the east side of town.

The principal truffle markets take place at Périgueux, Sarlat and Brantôme, and at Lalbenque near Cahors in the Quercy. Prices these days average around €800–1000 per kilo. In the past, however, truffles were so common that they were considered a pest by vine growers. Ironically, the fungus proved a life-saver for many local farmers when phylloxera (see p.364) hit in the late nineteenth century, ushering in the truffle's "golden age". Since the 1950s the harvest has declined dramatically for a number of reasons – deforestation and rural depopulation amongst others – although there are signs of a revival with up to 90 hectares of truffle trees being planted each year in the Dordogne since 2000.

Hautefort and around

Southeast of Excideuil you cross the pretty Auvézère valley, the route of the GR646 footpath, and enter the limestone plateaux of the Périgord Blanc. The views are magnificent, and nowhere more so than around **HAUTEFORT** and its eponymous **château**, standing on a south-facing promontory some 20km from Excideuil and 40km northeast of Périgueux.

The **Château de Hautefort** (daily: March & Oct to mid-Nov 2–6pm; April–May 10am–12.30pm & 2–6.30pm; June–Aug 9.30am–7pm; closed mid-Nov–Feb; €8.50; Ⓦwww.chateau-hautefort.com) is a stunning sight from whichever direction you approach, a magnificent example of good living on a grand scale, endowed with an elegance that's out of step with the usual rough stone fortresses of Périgord. Indeed, when the then marquis de Hautefort rebuilt it in the mid-seventeenth century, his ambition was to create a château worthy of the Loire.

The original fortress, which was built some time around 1000, in the twelfth century belonged jointly to the famous troubadour **Bertran de Born** (see box, p.357) and his brother Constantin, until Bertran persuaded his overlord, Henry II of England, to grant him sole ownership in 1185. The following year Constantin took his revenge and left the place in ruins – at which point Bertran went off to become a monk. The château's recent history has been no less troubled. After decades of neglect, in 1929 Hautefort was bought and meticulously restored by Baron Henri de Bastard and his wife. Then in August 1968, just three years after the work was completed, a **fire** gutted everything except the chapel in the southeast tower. A year later the indomitable baroness – her husband having died before the fire – set about the whole task again, and master craftsmen were called in to recreate everything from the staircases to the ornate chimneypieces. There's no disguising the fact that it's all brand-new, but the quality of work is superb.

The approach lies across a wide esplanade, flanked by immaculate topiary gardens, and over a drawbridge to enter a stylish Renaissance **courtyard** opening to the south. The two wings end in a pair of round towers, whose great bulk is offset by grey-slate domes topped with matching pepper-pot lanterns; the southwestern tower, nearest the entrance, is the only part of the medieval château still standing. While the main building is equally symmetrical, the overall impression is one of rhythm and harmony rather than severity.

About the only furnishings saved from the fire were four sixteenth-century tapestries, now on display inside, but the real highlight is the **great hall**. This monumental room provides the perfect setting for two huge chimneypieces. Exact copies of the originals and carved from local walnut, each took five thousand hours' work.

After you've finished in the château and its thirty-hectare park, it's also worth wandering through the village to visit the **Musée de la Médecine** (April–May & Oct daily 10am–noon & 2–6pm; June–Sept daily 10am–7pm; €5; Ⓦwww.musee-medecine-hautefort.fr) in the midst of an open square and accessed via the tourist office (see p.152). It occupies part of a hospice for the poor founded in 1669 by the same marquis who rebuilt the castle, as its architecture – particularly the domed central chapel – suggests. One of the ground-floor rooms presents an early-nineteenth-century ward under the ministration of the Sisters of Charity. As if this wasn't sobering enough, things get worse upstairs among the displays of medical implements through the ages, culminating in examples of dental surgeries up to 1970 – they even have that awful smell.

Some caves at **Tourtoirac**, 8km west of Hautefort, are due to open to the public in 2010 (Ⓣ05.53.51.12.17, Ⓦwww.tourtoirac.fr). These caves were never inhabited, but contain a rich array of stalactites and stalagmites, and have the advantage of being probably the only caves in France that offer access to the wheelchair-bound and elderly, via a lift. You can also visit the abbey at Tourtoirac, parts of which date from the tenth century, and which houses an archeological museum containing weapons and tools found during the course of excavations at the site (July–Aug daily 10am–12.30pm & 2.30–6pm).

Practicalities

The **tourist office** (June–Sept daily 10am–7pm; Oct to mid-Dec & mid-Jan to May Mon–Fri 10am–noon & 2–6pm; ⓣ05.53.50.40.27, ⓦwww.ot-hautefort.com) is located in the hospice's north wing, where you can pick up details of places to visit along the Auvézère valley. For an overnight stay in Hautefort, there's a very pleasant **hotel** right under the castle walls; the *Auberge du Parç* (ⓣ05.53.50.88.98, ⓦwww.aubergeduparc-hautefort.fr; ❷; closed mid-Dec to Feb) has five comfortable rooms and a good local **restaurant** serving Limousin beef and foie gras (menus from €10.50–22; closed Sun eve & Wed), and a lakeside campsite, *Le Camping du Coucou* (ⓣ06.12.77.26.62, ⓦwww.campingducoucou.com; Easter to Oct), less than 2km to the south. It is possible to reach Hautefort by public transport, but you'll have to stay two nights: a **bus** leaves Périgueux at 5.20pm (Mon–Fri), with the return service departing from Hautefort at 6.30am.

Brive-la-Gaillarde and around

A major road and rail junction, **Brive-la-Gaillarde** is the nearest thing to an industrial centre for miles around. Nevertheless, it makes an agreeable base for exploring the beautiful towns and villages around, and it's not that far to Lascaux and the upper reaches of the River Dordogne.

North of Brive, among the green fields and apple orchards of southern Limousin, **Arnac-Pompadour** is a must for anyone remotely interested in horses. Its château, from where Madame de Pompadour got her name, provides a stately backdrop to a national stud farm and a splendid racecourse. Heading south, first stop is the village of **Turenne**. Two sky-scraping towers and a number of noblemen's houses are all that remain of this once-powerful town, which enjoyed almost complete independence up to the eighteenth century. Nearby **Collonges-la-Rouge** also prospered under Turenne rule, but it is the unexpected shock of the red sandstone as much as the time-worn buildings that gives the village its special appeal.

All these places can be reached by public **transport**. Arnac-Pompadour lies on a minor train line between Brive and Limoges, while Brive is also the departure point for buses to Turenne and Collonges.

Brive-la-Gaillarde

The largely pedestrianized old centre of **BRIVE-LA-GAILLARDE** comes as a pleasant surprise after its sprawling suburbs. It is enclosed within a circular boulevard shaded by plane trees, from where all roads lead inwards to the much-restored **church of St-Martin**. Brive's other main sight, the wide-ranging **Musée Labenche**, lies on the ring road to the southeast, while across the other side of town the local Resistance museum, the **Musée Edmond Michelet**, is of more specialist interest.

It's thought that Brive earned its nickname *la Gaillarde* during the Hundred Years' War when, for much of the time, it was a lone French stronghold surrounded by English. Opinions are divided, but the name "la Galliarde" (meaning strong, sprightly or bawdy) refers either to its fortifications or – the generally preferred option – the spirited, valiant nature of its people. The ramparts disappeared after the Revolution to make way for today's gardens and ring road, but the "Brivistes" themselves haven't changed, as they will happily tell you, citing their prowess on the rugby field as the prime example: Brive won the European Cup in 1997, and in 2000 made it to the finals of the French Cup, though there have been no new achievements since.

Arrival and information

The brand-new Brive airport (Ⓦwww.aeroport-brive-souillac.com), 10km to the south, is due to open in June 2010. It will be served by regular flights to and from Paris, while at the time of writing the question of low-cost flights to the

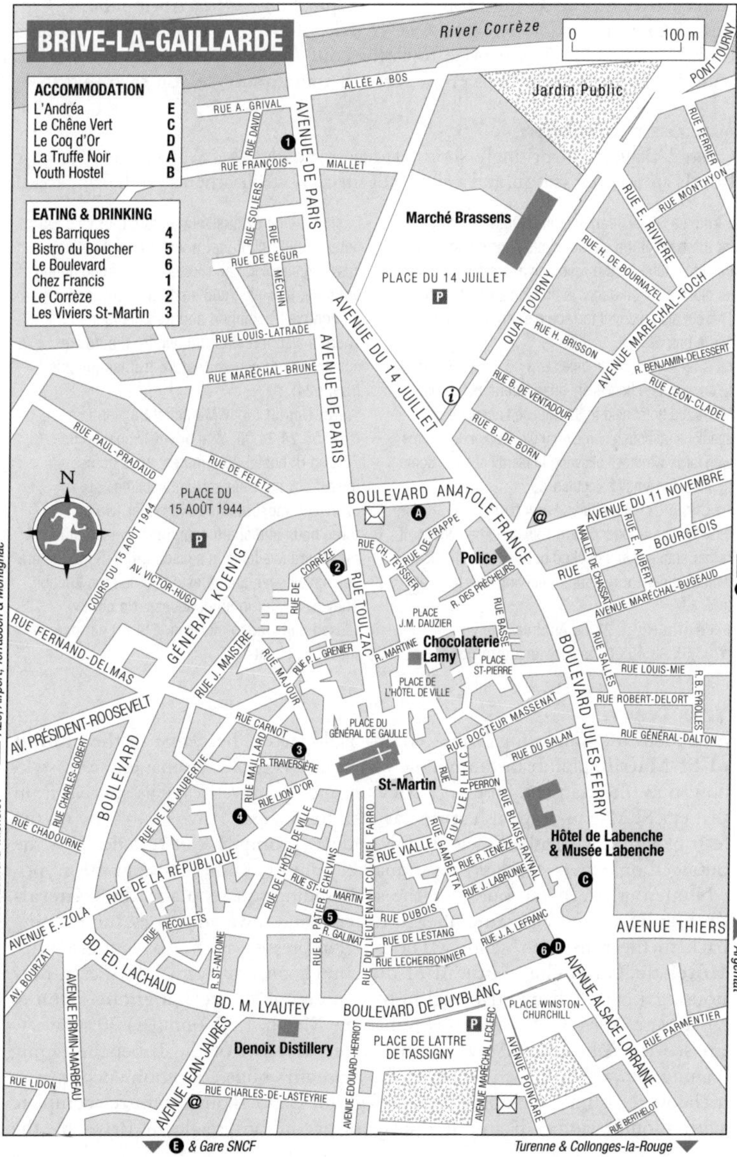

UK was still under discussion. A bus service to the town centre may be installed once the airport is open; at the time of writing no information was available. Taxis will certainly be an option (T05.55.24.24.24)

The **gare SNCF**, on the Paris–Toulouse and Bordeaux–Lyon main lines, is located on the south side of Brive, some ten minutes' walk along avenue Jean Jaurès from the centre. The regional **bus** service is unusually comprehensive. Buses depart from various spots round town, including the gare SNCF and place du 14 Juillet to the north of the old centre, which is also where you'll find the **tourist office** (July & Aug Mon–Sat 9am–7pm, Sun 3–7pm; April–June & Sept 9am–12.30pm & 1.30–6.30pm, Oct–March Mon–Sat 9am–noon & 2–6pm; T05.55.24.08.80, Wwww.brive-tourisme.com). It occupies an old pumping station and water tower built in the form of a lighthouse, so you can't miss it.

Accommodation

Central Brive is surprisingly short of decent hotels. There's a clutch of cheap **hotels** around the station, and a choice of smarter establishments on the ring road.

L'Andréa 39 av Jean Jaurès T05.55.74.11.84. By far the best of the cheap hotels near the station, this little hotel on the road down into town opts for an old-fashioned decor in its nine en-suite rooms. There's also a small terrace garden at the back, and a bar. ❷–❸

Le Chêne Vert 24 bd Jules Ferry T05.55.24.10.07, Wwww.hotel-chene-vert-brive.federal-hotel.com. Mid-sized hotel next to the Musée Labenche with spacious (although somewhat old-fashioned) rooms with large windows allowing in plenty of light. Some rooms have small balconies. ❸

Le Coq d'Or 18 bd Jules Ferry T05.55.17.12.92, Wwww.hotel-coqdor.com. This hotel has comfy, if rather small rooms decked out in pretty florals as well as a decent restaurant serving hearty local fare. ❸

La Truffe Noire 22 bd Anatole-France T05.55.92.45.00, Wwww.la-truffe-noire.com. Despite being extensively restored, Brive's top hotel is still full of warm wood panelling and cosy inglenooks. The rooms are disappointingly ordinary, however, and small at the cheaper end, though well-equipped and air conditioned. There's also a restaurant, where the house specialities of course feature truffles (menus from €24). ❻

Youth Hostel 56 av Maréchal Bugeaud T05.55.24.34.00, Eaj.brive@wanadoo.fr. 78-bed HI hostel 25 minutes' walk across town from the train station. Facilities are excellent: most rooms have either two or three beds and share communal washrooms, meals are available in season (April–Sept), as are snacks all year, and guests can use the kitchen. They also offer internet access. No curfew. Closed mid-Dec to mid-Jan. €11.50 per person including sheets.

The Town

As a focus for wandering Brive's compact old streets, head first to the **church of St-Martin**, plumb in the middle of town. Originally Romanesque in style, now only the transept, apse and a few comically carved capitals survive from that era. St Martin, a Spanish aristocrat, arrived in pagan Brive in 407 AD on the feast of Saturnus, smashed various idols, and was promptly stoned to death by the outraged onlookers; some say his unmarked tomb is among those in the crypt.

Numerous streets fan out from the surrounding square, **place du Général-de-Gaulle**, dotted with a number of turreted and towered houses, some dating back to the thirteenth century. The most impressive is the sixteenth-century **Hôtel de Labenche**, southeast of the church on boulevard Jules-Ferry, now housing a better-than-usual local history museum **Musée Labenche** (Mon & Wed–Sun: April–Oct 10am–6.30pm; Nov–March 1.30–6pm; €4.70; Wwww.musee-labenche.com). As you enter, note the busts of the Labenche family leaning forward over each window. The museum's huge collection encompasses archeological finds, including some delightful Gallo-Roman bronzes complete with moulds, and a beautiful display of accordions made in Brive by the

Dedenis factory prior to 1939. But the highlight is a rare collection of **Mortlake tapestries**. The Mortlake workshop, under the supervision of Dutch weavers, was founded by James I of England in 1620. Though they were only in business until the end of that century, they produced a number of important, highly prized works. The most interesting of the seven presented here are the three fox-hunting scenes – the colours are still exceptionally vibrant.

The tone changes considerably at Brive's other museum, the **Musée Edmond Michelet** at 4 rue Champanatier (Mon–Sat 10am–noon & 2–6pm; free; Ⓦwww.centremichelet.org; ask to borrow the audio guide in English), portraying the Resistance and deportations during World War II through photographs, posters and objects of the time, though little is explained in English. To get here take the main rue de la République west from St-Martin church as far as the ring road, from where the museum is signed straight ahead along avenue Émile Zola. It occupies the former home of Edmond Michelet, one of Brive's leading *résistants*, who was arrested here in 1943 and deported to Dachau, but survived to become a minister in de Gaulle's postwar government.

Returning to the centre, turn right along the ring road to find the **Denoix distillery**, founded in 1839, at 9 bd Maréchal Lyautey (Tues–Sat 9am–noon & 2.30–7pm; free; Ⓣ05.55.74.34.27, Ⓦwww.denoix.com). The liqueurs produced here are centred around walnuts, notably a very mellow tipple called Suprême Denoix, but they have also resurrected a local mustard. Made with grape must and spices, Moutarde Violette de Brive was first devised in the fourteenth century for Pope Clément VI, a native of Corrèze. Not surprisingly for this area, it goes very well with duck.

For something a little sweeter, pay a visit to **Chocolaterie Lamy** (Mon 2–7pm, Tues–Sat 9am–noon & 2–7pm) at 5 rue de l'Hôtel de Ville, where you can watch the delectable chocolates being made (Thurs mid-June to Aug, 3pm; €3) and even learn how to make them yourself on half-day courses (Ⓣ05.55.18.91.26 for details).

Those with children might like to head for the **Jardins de Colette** (April Wed–Sun 10am–12.30pm & 2–6.30pm; May, June & Sept Tues–Sun 10am–12.30pm & 2–6.30pm; July & Aug daily 10am–7pm; Oct to early Nov Wed–Sun 10am–12.30pm & 2–5pm; €6; guided tours in English; Ⓣ05.55.86.75.35, Ⓦwww.lesjardinsdecolette.com) ten minutes' drive west of Brive at **Varetz**. The controversial French writer, Colette, lived next door in Château de Castel Novel (now a hotel) between 1912 and 1923 with her second husband, Henry de Jouvenel and, through plants and landscaping, the gardens aim to represent the various places she lived – from Brittany to Paris via Provence. The highlight is an immense butterfly-shaped maze – dotted with educational signs outlining aspects of the writer's life – which will appeal particularly to kids. In the summer you can enjoy cool drinks at the *salon du the*.

Eating and drinking

In summer small **restaurants** and **bars** open in the gardens along the southern stretch of the ring road. Otherwise, avenue de Paris, leading north to the river, has a fair choice of places to eat as well as one of Brive's nicest cafés, the old-fashioned *L'Europe*, at no. 21.

Les Barriques 5 rue Maillard Ⓣ05.55.17.18.40. Lunchtime sees this modern bar-brasserie packed with office workers. It offers a limited range of dishes ranging from around €7 to €10, or you can make your own salad from the self-service hors-d'oeuvre buffet. Not the sort of place where you'll be able to linger over your meal.

Bistrot du Boucher 8 rue Galinat ⓣ05.55.17.67.73. This stylish bistro tempts customers with a bewildering array of *formules*, menus and daily specials. A main dish will set you back €12, while the three-course menu is priced at €24 including wine or mineral water. It also serves until relatively late, around 11pm. July & Aug closed Sun.

Le Boulevard 8 bd Jules Ferry ⓣ05.55.23.07.13. Though it doesn't look much from the outside, this is one of the nicest options along the southern boulevard. Beyond the chestnut-shaded terrace lurks a cosy dining room where locals come for delicacies such as eggs baked with cream and truffles, or *magret de canard* with local mustard, followed perhaps by a walnut and hazelnut soufflé. Menus €14–37. Closed Sun eve & Mon.

Chez Francis 61 av de Paris ⓣ05.55.74.41.72. You'll need to book ahead for this friendly, cluttered restaurant down towards the river. The imaginative seasonal menus feature the best of local ingredients. At lunch you can have two courses with a glass of wine for €16.50, while the fixed menus are priced at €16 and €25. A favourite haunt of writers, actors and artists during Brive's various festivals (see box, p.126), the walls, ceilings and lampshades are covered with messages of appreciation. Closed Sun & Mon.

Le Corrèze 3 rue de Corrèze ⓣ05.55.24.14.07. Cheap and cheerful locals' place to the north of St-Martin, with the choice of tiled floors and a handful of wooden tables packed together downstairs or a slightly smarter stone-walled room above. The food is nothing to write home about, but comes in hearty portions, with three-course menus starting at just €8.50. Closed Sun.

Les Viviers St-Martin 4 rue Traversière ⓣ05.55.92.14.15. It's worth seeking out this little restaurant in a backstreet just west of St-Martin church for its wide-ranging *carte* including salads, pasta and plenty of local delicacies; it's especially well known for fish (menus €13–26). Another attraction is the possibility of eating outside, and this is one of the few places open on a Sunday. Closed two weeks in both March & Oct.

Listings

Airlines Airlinair (ⓣ08.20.82.08.20, ⓦwww.airfrance.com) operates regular flights to Paris Orly.

Airport Brive-Vallée de la Dordogne ⓦwww.aeroport-brive-souillac.com.

Bus departures Buses around the *département* leave from just outside the tourist office (see p.154); for information on timetables contact CFTA buses ⓣ05.55.17.91.19. Eurolines buses (ⓣ05.56.92.50.42) en route from Toulouse to London depart from opposite Carrefour supermarket, located on the Rond Point du Teinchurier 5km west of Brive-la-Gaillarde, in the commercial zone. There are regular buses to the commercial zone.

Car rental Near the train station, try: Avis, 56 av Jean Jaurès ⓣ05.55.24.51.00; Europcar, 52 av Jean Jaurès ⓣ05.55.74.14.41; Hertz, 169 av Jean Jacques Rousseau ⓣ05.55.87.10.53; Ucar ⓣ05.55.88.11.11. All offer airport pick-ups.

Hospital Centre Hospitalier, bd Docteur Verlhac ⓣ05.55.92.60.00.

Internet access You can log on at BCM, 3 av du 11 novembre (Tues–Sat 10am–noon & 2–7pm) and at Centre Culturel, 31 av Jean Jaurès, (Mon, Tues, Thurs & Fri 9am–noon & 2–7pm, Sat 10am–noon & 2–7pm).

Markets The modern Marché Brassens, behind the tourist office, is the venue for a famous market three times a week (Tues, Thurs & Sat mornings) and the important *foires grasses* for foie gras, truffles and other local produce held on the first Sat of each month between December and March. During the first weekend in November each year the fruit and veg gives way to a book fair, La Foire du Livre, which attracts a number of well-known authors and artists.

Police Commissariat de Police, 4 bd Anatole-France ⓣ05.55.17.46.00.

Post office The central post office is at place Winston-Churchill, 19100 Brive-la-Gaillarde.

Taxis Call ⓣ05.55.24.24.24.

Arnac-Pompadour

Roughly 30km northeast of Brive, and also accessible by train from Brive, **ARNAC-POMPADOUR** is dominated by its grey, turreted château overlooking one of the most picturesque racecourses in France. It's consequently a very horsey place, although if you're in the area in mid-July, you might catch the annual donkey festival – **La Journée Nationale de l'Âne** – a one-day fête that takes place on July 14, in honour of all things donkey-related.

The present château largely dates from the fifteenth century. When the Pompadour line died out in 1745, it was ceded to Louis XV who promptly bestowed the title on his mistress, the **Marquise de Pompadour**. Though she never bothered to visit, the Marquise started breeding horses on her estate before being forced to sell for financial reasons in 1760; she nevertheless kept the title. On regaining possession of the castle the following year, Louis founded the Royal Stud, which became a **National Stud** in 1872. In between, the horses were sold off during the Revolution, but Napoleon I soon re-established the stud to keep his cavalry supplied. He sent four Arab stallions, booty from his Egyptian campaign, which were crossed with English thoroughbred mares to produce the first **Anglo-Arabs**.

The **château** was gutted by fire in 1834 and now houses the stud's headquarters. You can visit its terraces and interior on a **guided tour** (April–Oct & school hols daily; rest of year daily except Sunday; €5) organised by Trois Tours de Pompadour (see box below).

For those less enamoured of horses, the Romanesque **abbey church** of Arnac (part of the Pompadour *domaines*) 2km to the northwest, is of interest for its carved capitals. Though exceptionally high, enlarged photos beside each pillar help identify the striking images, including Daniel in the lions' den.

Also worth a visit is Pompadour's own parish church, the **Chapelle St Blaise**, in the town centre just behind the château (ask at the tourist office – see below – for information about opening hours). Since its restoration in 2008, the chapel is home to over three hundred square metres of paintings depicting Old and New Testament scenes by the contemporary artist, André Brasilier, worth seeing for the scale of the work alone.

Practicalities

Arnac-Pompadour lies on a minor **train** line between Brive and Limoges. It can also be reached from Brive by **buses**, which stop by the château before terminating at the **gare SNCF**, 500m southeast on the D7 to Vigeois. The **tourist office** (daily: April–Sept 9.30am–noon & 1–6pm; Oct–March 10am–noon & 1.30–4.30pm; ⓣ05.55.98.55.47, ⓔtourisme@pompadour.net), is situated in the gatehouse of the National Stud. There's even a reasonable place to **stay**: the *Hôtel du Parc* (ⓣ05.55.73.30.54; ③), behind the château. The hotel

Visiting the National Stud

The stallions are housed in the **Écurie des étalons**, across the chestnut-shaded esplanade from the château (April–Sept & school hols daily; rest of year daily except Sunday; €6). During the spring breeding season (March–June) there are fewer stallions in the *écurie*, but this is the best time to visit the mares (*juments*) at the **Jumenterie de la Rivière** (afternoons only: April–June daily; €6), 4km southeast near the village of Beyssac. In late spring (May–June) the fields around are full of mares and foals, the best being kept for breeding, the rest sold worldwide as two-year-olds. In each case you have to join a guided tour organized by Trois Tours de Pompadour, based at the entrance to the château (ⓣ05.55.98.51.10 or 06.78.62.97.00, ⓦwww.les3tours-pompadour.com). Times of the visits vary, so check first. They also sell tickets to the château and a "passport", with which you can visit two of the three sites for €9).

At any time of year, you will see horses being exercised round the magnificent track in front of the château. From May to October there are frequent **race meetings**, as well as dressage and driving events, shows and open days. Trois Tours de Pompadour can provide a calendar of events.

offers cheerful rooms and a small pool, as well as a good-value regional restaurant (menus from €12 at lunchtime, and from €15 in the evening). The other option in the area is the modern *Auberge de la Mandrie* (Ⓣ05.55.73.37.14, Ⓦwww.la-mandrie.com; ❸; closed Nov–March) 4km west on the D7, with chalet rooms around a pool, and more refined cuisine (menus from €12.50).

Turenne

TURENNE, just 16km south of Brive, is the first of two very picturesque villages in the vicinity. In this case slate-roofed, mellow stone houses crowd under the protective towers of a once-mighty fortress. At their peak during the fifteenth century, the viscounts of Turenne ruled over a vast feudal domain containing some 1200 villages. Virtually autonomous, it was one of the most powerful estates in France. The viscounts retained the right to raise taxes and mint their own coins, amongst other privileges, up until 1738 when Louis XV bought the viscountcy in the aftermath of the Fronde rebellion (see p.361).

Although Louis also ordered that the castle be demolished, two towers still sprout from the summit; to reach them, take the lane running northeast from the main road and keep climbing. One of the towers is occupied by the present owners of the château, but the round **Tour de César** can be visited (April–June, Sept & Oct daily 10am–noon & 2–6pm; July & Aug daily 10am–7pm; Nov–March Sun 2–5pm; €3.80) and is worth climbing for vertiginous views away over the ridges and valleys to the mountains of Cantal. On the way up to the castle you pass a number of elegant Renaissance houses and the all-important salt store, as well as a **church** hurriedly thrown up in 1662 during the Counter-Reformation to bring the local populace back to Catholicism; take a peek inside at the gilded altar and unusual mosaic ceiling.

Practicalities

Buses from Brive stop on the main road near the **tourist office** booth (May & Sept Tues–Sun 10am–12.30pm & 3–6pm; July & Aug daily 9.30am–12.30pm & 2.30–6.30pm; Ⓣ05.55.85.59.97, Ⓦwww.brive-tourisme.com), where you can rent **bikes** and pick up walking **maps** of the village (€1). The maps are also available at the nearby souvenir shop, from beside which the lane leads up to the castle. Follow it and you'll come to the old village square and a lovely small **hotel**, *La Maison des Chanoines* (Ⓣ05.55.85.93.43, Ⓦwww.maison-des-chanoines.com; ❹; closed mid-Oct to Easter). The rooms are decorated with the same flair and imagination that's apparent in their **restaurant**, where you'll eat extremely well for around €30 (closed lunchtime Mon–Sat & Wed eves in June; reservations essential). Across the square, you can't miss the jolly facade of *La Vicomté* (lunch only; closed Nov–Feb), which offers views up to the château from its terrace and main dishes at around €10 or a traditional regional menu for €19. Another delightful option, as either a place to stay or eat, is in the village of **Sarrazac**, in the depths of the country seven kilometres southeast of Turenne. *La Bonne Famille* (Ⓣ05.65.37.70.38, Ⓦwww.labonnefamille.fr; ❷) is exactly what its name suggests: a traditional country inn run by an exceptionally welcoming family. The rooms, in an annexe, are nothing fancy but perfectly comfortable, while the food is top-quality home cooking, all freshly prepared and served in hearty portions (lunch menus from €10, eve & weekends from €14; reservations recommended).

Collonges-la-Rouge

There's a great view back to Turenne as you head southeast on the D20 before cutting eastwards on pretty back lanes through meadows and walnut orchards to reach **COLLONGES-LA-ROUGE** some 10km later; alternatively, you can walk between the two on the GR446 footpath. The village is the epitome of bucolic charm, with its rust-red – even verging on mauve – sandstone houses, pepper-pot towers and pink-candled chestnut trees, although you need to time your visit carefully, as it is very much on the tourist route. Though small-scale, there is grandeur about the place. This is where the nobles who governed Turenne on behalf of the viscounts built their mini-châteaux, each boasting at least one tower – there's a wonderful view of the bristling roofs as you approach from the west.

On the main square the twelfth-century **church** is unusual in having two naves, of which the shorter, north nave – the one used today – was a later addition. They came in handy during the sixteenth century when Turenne supported the Huguenot cause; here at least, Protestants and Catholics conducted their services peacefully side by side. Outside, the covered **market hall** still retains its old-fashioned baker's oven. On your way back up the main street, look out for the sixteenth-century **Maison de la Sirène**, diagonally opposite the tourist office, which is named after the little mermaid sculpted above the entrance. Though battered, she's still charming as she preens herself, comb in one hand and mirror in the other. This is the only house in the village that you can visit; the small **museum** (July–Aug daily 10.30am–12.30pm & 3–6pm; €2; ⓣ05.55.84.08.03) contains archeological remains including a Merovingian sarcophagus, tools relating to local trades and rooms arranged with typical rural furniture from the eighteenth and nineteenth centuries. The curator is a mine of information on the village and also gives guided tours; book through the tourist office (see below).

Practicalities

Buses from Turenne and Brive pass Collonges on their way to the terminus at Meyssac (see below). They stop on the main road at the northern entrance to the village. Follow this street south into the village and you'll come to the *mairie* and **tourist office** (April–June & Sept daily 10am–noon & 2–6pm; July & Aug daily 10am–1pm & 2–7pm; Oct & March Mon–Sat 10am–noon & 2–5pm; Nov–Feb Mon–Sat 2–5pm; ⓣ05.55.25.47.57, ⓦwww.ot-collonges.fr). A little further down, there's an attractive **hotel**, the *Relais de St-Jacques de Compostelle* (ⓣ05.55.25.41.02, ⓦwww.restaurant-relaisstjacques.com; ❸; closed mid-Nov to mid-March), with lovely views from the bedrooms and a decent restaurant (menus €17–37). If you want somewhere quieter, head east 2km to **MEYSSAC**, a smaller town built in the same red sandstone with its tourist office in place de la Halle (July–Aug Mon–Sat 10am–noon & 4–7pm, Sun 10am–noon; Sept–June Mon–Sat 10am–noon; ⓣ05.55.25.32.25; ⓦwww.meyssac.fr). Here you'll find the very pleasant *Relais du Quercy* (ⓣ05.55.25.40.31, ⓦwww.logis-de-france.fr; ❸; closed three weeks in Nov), with a pool and pretty restaurant (menus start at €12.50). Alternatively, there's a three-star **campsite**, *Moulin de la Valanne* (ⓣ05.55.25.41.59; May–Sept), halfway between Collonges and Meyssac; contact the tourist office for further information.

Collonges has a number of crêperies and snack bars in summer. Outside the season the choice of **restaurants** is more restricted, although both the hotel (see above) and *Le Prieuré* (light meals up to €15.50, menu at €26.50; closed Wed & Thurs except in July & Aug), beside the church, are safe bets. *Le Cantou*, on the main street, serves more modest regional dishes as well as brasserie-type fare for €12 (July & Aug open daily for lunch & dinner; Sept–June closed eves & all day Mon).

Travel details

Trains

Brive-la-Gaillarde to: Arnac-Pompadour (3–4 daily; 40min); Bordeaux (3–4 daily; 2hr 30min); Cahors (5–8 daily; 1hr 10min); Paris Austerlitz (4–6 daily; 3–4hr); Périgueux (3–5 daily; 1hr); Souillac (5–8 daily; 25min); Toulouse (6–9 daily; 2hr–2hr 30min).
Périgueux to: Bordeaux (8–14 daily; 1hr–1hr 30min); Brive (4–6 daily; 1hr); Neuvic (3–5 daily; 20–30min); St-Astier (6–11 daily; 10–15min); Terrasson (4–6 daily; 45min–1hr); Thiviers (7–11 daily; 20–50min).

Buses

Aubeterre-sur-Dronne to: Angoulême (Mon–Sat 1–2 daily; 1–2hr).
Brantôme to: Angoulême (3 weekly; 1hr); Périgueux (Mon–Fri & Sun 1–3 daily; 40min).
Brive to: Argentat (Mon–Sat 2 daily; 1hr 15min–1hr 30min); Arnac-Pompadour (Mon–Sat 1 daily; 2hr); Beaulieu-sur-Dordogne (school term Mon–Sat 1–3 daily, school holidays Tues, Thurs & Sat 1–2 daily, July & Aug Mon, Tues & Thurs–Sat 1–2 daily; 1hr–1hr 30min); Collonges-la-Rouge (Mon–Sat 1–4 daily; 25min–1hr); Meyssac (Mon–Sat 1–4 daily; 30min–1hr 5min); Montignac (Mon–Fri 1 daily; 1hr 15min); Terrasson (Mon–Fri 2–3 daily; 1hr); Turenne (Mon–Sat 1–3 daily; 20–40min).
Périgueux to: Angoulême (1–3 daily; 1hr 45min); Bergerac (Mon–Fri 5 daily; school holidays 3 daily; 1hr); Bourdeilles (school term Mon–Fri 1 daily; 45min); Brantôme (Mon–Sat 2 daily, Sun 1 daily; 40min); Le Bugue (school term Mon–Fri 1 daily; 1hr); Excideuil (school term Mon–Fri 5 daily, school holidays Mon–Fri 3 daily; 1hr); Hautefort (Mon–Fri 1 daily; 40min); Montignac (school term Mon–Fri 2–3 daily, school holidays Wed 1–3 daily; 1hr); Neuvic (school term Mon–Fri 1–3 daily; 40min); Ribérac (Mon–Fri 4 daily; school holidays 3 daily; 1hr); Sarlat (school term Mon–Fri 1 daily, school holidays Wed 1 daily; 1hr 30min); St-Astier (school term Mon–Fri 1–3 daily; 30min); Thiviers (school term Wed 1 daily; 40min); Villars (school term Fri 1 daily; 1hr).
Ribérac to: Angoulême (Mon & Fri 1 daily; 1hr); Périgueux (Mon–Fri 4 daily; school holidays 3 daily; 1hr).
Turenne to: Brive (school term Mon–Fri 1–2 daily; 20min); Collonges-la-Rouge (school term Mon–Sat 1 daily; 15min); Meyssac (school term Mon–Sat 1 daily; 20min).

Planes

Brive-la-Gaillarde to: Paris Orly (1–2 daily; 1hr 20min).
Périgueux to: Paris Orly (1–3 daily; 1hr 20min).

3

Bergerac and around

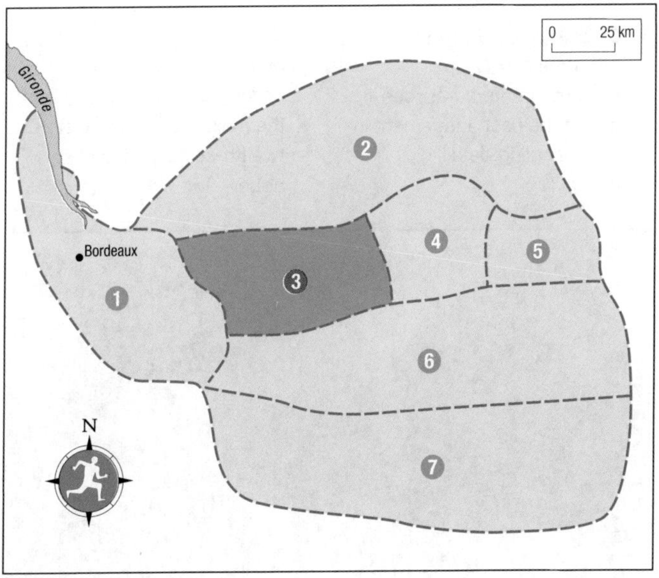

CHAPTER 3

Highlights

✱ **Bergerac** Surrounded by vineyards, this sleepy provincial town of cobbled squares and half-timbered facades makes for an atmospheric day's wander. See p.165

✱ **Bastides** The fortified towns of Eymet, Lalinde and Beaumont, with their arcaded central squares, retain a medieval atmosphere relatively untouched by tourism. See p.174, p.182 & p.186.

✱ **Church of St-Eutrope, Allemans-du-Dropt** Fifteenth-century frescoes depict the Last Judgement in spine-tingling detail. See p.175

✱ **Montcaret** The elaborate mosaics in a fourth-century villa unearthed here provide ample evidence of luxury living Roman-style. See p.179

✱ **Château de Montaigne** See where philosopher Michel de Montaigne wrote some of his most influential essays. See p.179

✱ **Cingle de Trémolat** A classic Dordogne meander, best viewed from the limestone cliffs to the north. See p.183

✱ **Cadouin** An exceptionally pretty village with unusual accommodation options and the main draw of an austere twelfth-century Cistercian abbey. See p.187

▲ The Cingle de Trémolat

3

Bergerac and around

In its lower reaches the Dordogne slides wide and slow through a landscape of vine-planted hills. This is the heart of the **Périgord Pourpre**, a major wine-growing area that blends seamlessly into the Bordelais vineyards to the west. For centuries the region's most important market town, port and commercial centre has been **Bergerac**, the second largest city in the Dordogne *département*, but still a pleasantly provincial place with a clutch of worthwhile sights amongst its twisting lanes. As for the wine region itself, its foremost sight is the Renaissance **Château de Monbazillac**, clearly visible on the ridge to the south and surrounded by its prestigious vineyards, originally planted by monks in the Middle Ages, which produce a very palatable sweet white wine. The high country further south of Bergerac, where the gentle River Dropt marks the border of the Dordogne and Lot-et-Garonne *départements*, wasn't always such a bucolic scene, as a glance at the remaining fortifications of **Issigeac** and particularly **Eymet** – the ramparts built in the run-up to the Hundred Years' War – goes to show. The prevailing sense of unease following more than a century of war, plague and famine is caught in the fifteenth-century frescoes of the Last Judgement in the little church of **Allemans-du-Dropt**, while further downstream at **Duras** another semi-ruined château dominates the valley.

To the west of Bergerac the Dordogne valley becomes wider, busier and less attractive. Nevertheless, there are one or two appealing sights, notably the Gallo-Roman remains at **Montcaret** and the nearby **Château de Montaigne**, where the eponymous philosopher wrote his original, wide-ranging *Essais*. North of here, the **Forêt du Landais** stretches north across the top of the Périgord Pourpre. It's a pretty region of wooded hills, meandering streams and sparse habitation, good for wandering, though without any particularly compelling sights.

Upstream of Bergerac, the pure waters of the River Couze, a tributary of the Dordogne, have spawned a paper-making industry at **Couze-et-St-Front**, where traditional, handmade paper is still produced to this day. Further east the Dordogne has carved two gigantic meanders at **Trémolat** and **Limeuil**. Here also the Périgord Pourpre gradually gives way to wooded hills on the western edge of the Périgord Noir. The change is perhaps most obvious in the landscapes south of the river, where the *bastide* town of **Beaumont** and the nearby abbey of **St-Avit-Sénieur** stand isolated on the edge of a high, open plateau. Just a few kilometres to the east, however, **Cadouin**'s abbey church sits in a hidden valley deep among the chestnut forests.

Overall, exploring this region by **public transport** is not easy. While the main towns along the Dordogne valley are well served by trains on

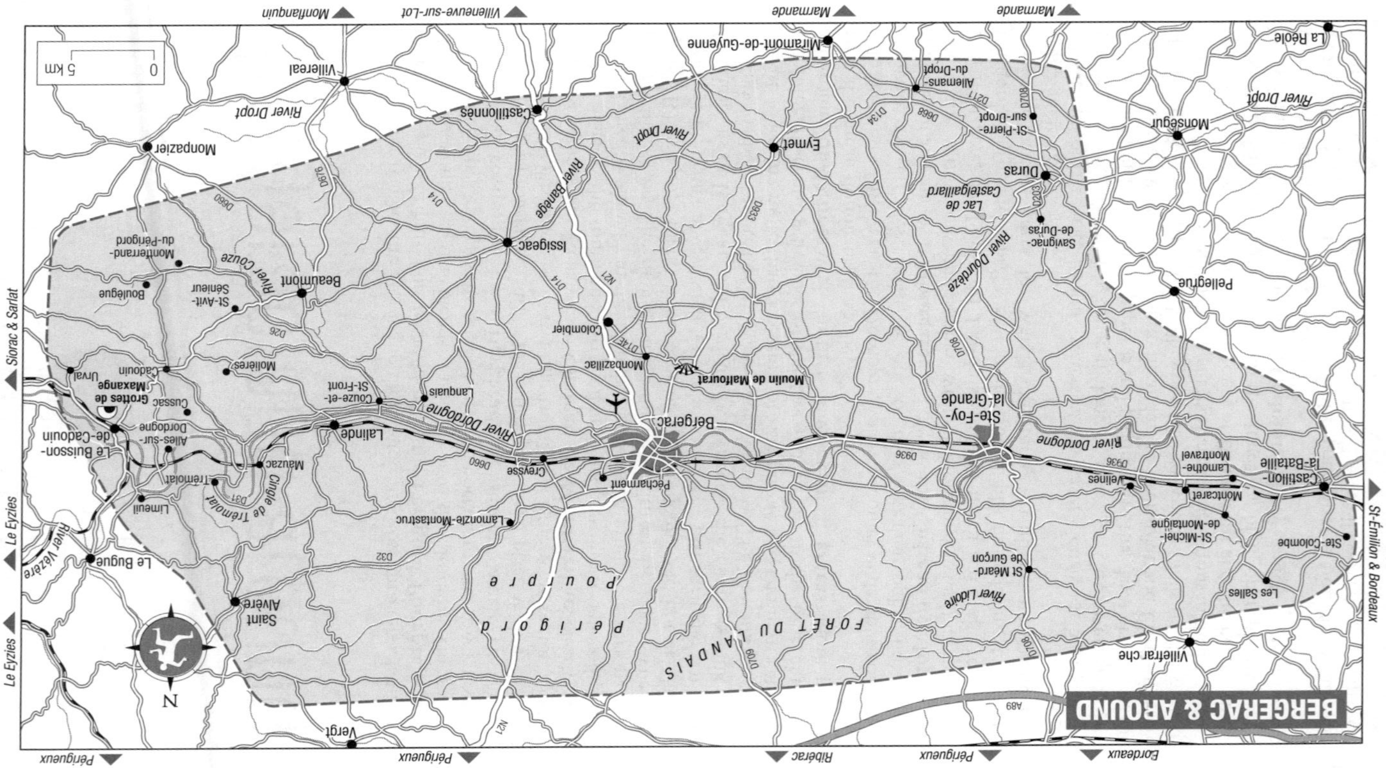
BERGERAC & AROUND
Bergerac
Ste-Foy-la-Grande
Castillon-la-Bataille
Lamothe-Montravel
Montcaret
St-Michel-de-Montaigne
Vélines
Ste-Colombe
Les Salles
Villefranche
St Méard-de Gurçon
River Lidoire
FORÊT DU LANDAIS
Périgord Pourpre
Pécharment
Creysse
Lamonzie-Montastruc
Saint Alvère
Le Bugue
Limeuil
Trémolat
Cingle de Trémolat
Mauzac
Lalinde
Alles-sur-Dordogne
Le Buisson-de-Cadouin
Cussac
Grottes de Maxange
Cadouin
Urval
Molières
Couze-et-St-Front
Lanquais
River Dordogne
Monbazillac
Moulin de Malfourat
Colombier
Issigeac
River Banège
Castillonnès
Beaumont
River Couze
St-Avit-Sénieur
Bouliègue
Montferrand-du-Périgord
Monpazier
Villeréal
River Dropt
Eymet
Miramont-de-Guyenne
Allemans-du-Dropt
St-Pierre-sur-Dropt
Duras
Lac de Castelgaillard
Savignac-de-Duras
River Dourdèze
Pellegrue
Monségur
La Réole
River Vézère
Vergt
Le Eyzies
Siorac & Sarlat
Monflanquin
Villeneuve-sur-Lot
Marmande
St-Émilion & Bordeaux
Bordeaux
Périgueux
Ribérac
N
0
5 km

the Sarlat-Bordeaux line, anywhere inland requires your own steam. What limited bus services do exist are planned around the needs of school children, not travellers.

Bergerac and around

Lying mostly on the Dordogne's north bank overlooking its wide flood plain, **BERGERAC** is a rather sleepy place for much of the year, but bursts into life for the summer tourist season, when cafés and restaurants spill out into the cobbled squares and alleyways. It suffered particularly badly during the Wars of Religion, but in recent years the old streets fanning out from the former port have been carefully restored to bring out the best in the rows of half-timbered cottages and more bourgeois, stone-built residences. Among several interesting and attractive reminders of the past, the main sights are a surprisingly rewarding **museum** devoted to tobacco and a former **monastery**, which now houses an information centre on the local wines. Two wine-growing areas within easy reach provide rewarding excursions: **Monbazillac**, which produces very sweet whites, and **Pécharmant**, whose reds – though smirked at by the Bordelais – are the best Bergerac has to offer.

Some history

The largest town in the Dordogne valley, Bergerac owes its existence and prosperity to the **river**. By the twelfth century it was already an important bridging point and port, controlling the trade between its Périgord hinterland and Bordeaux, particularly the burgeoning **wine trade**. Things began to take off after Henry III of England sought to keep the townspeople sweet by giving them certain privileges in 1254: they were exempted from local taxes, given the right of assembly and allowed to export their wines to Bordeaux unhindered. Local burghers took advantage of the new dispensations to ship their own wines first, while the less privileged were forced to sell later, at disadvantageous prices, and were also charged a tax of five *sous* per barrel. Bergerac's wine aristocracy were thus able to corner the lucrative foreign market until the seventeenth century, when the technique of ageing wines was discovered.

The town's heyday came in the decades preceding the Wars of Religion (1561–98) when Bergerac was among the foremost centres of **Protestantism** in southwest France. One of many truces between the warring factions was even signed here in 1577, but in 1620 the Catholic Louis XIII seized the town and ordered that the ramparts and fortress be demolished. Worse was to come when Catholic priests arrived to bring Bergerac back into the fold. They met with mixed success – the majority of the Protestant population fled, principally to Holland, where they soon established a long and mutually profitable business importing Bergerac wines.

Since then wine has continued to be the staple of the local economy. Up until the railway arrived in the 1870s, the bulk of it was transported by river, leading to a thriving **boat-building** industry all along the Dordogne. Though most have long disappeared, a few sturdy *gabares* (barges) are still being built to cater to the tourist trade.

Arrival and information

Ryanair and Flybe run regular flights from numerous regional airports in the UK to Bergerac's **airport**, 5km southeast of the city on the Agen road; from

Festivals, events and markets

Where we haven't given a specific information number, contact the relevant tourist office.

July and August Bergerac: Les Mercredis du Jazz (Ⓦwww.bergerac.fr). Free concerts by French jazz artists on Wednesday evenings on place de la Myrpe.

Mid-July Bergerac: La Table de Cyrano (Ⓣ05.53.74.66.66). The old town is transformed into a gigantic outdoor restaurant for this magnificent food festival, usually held the weekend before July 14 (Bastille Day). There are also free concerts every night.

Third weekend in July Duras: Fête de la Madeleine (Ⓦwww.paysdeduras.com). This traditionally Basque festival is marked in Duras by cheap or free concerts in the castle courtyard, a firework display on the Monday night, and plenty of wine-tasting.

Third Sunday in July Issigeac: Foire aux Paniers. Unique basket-weavers' fair held on the place du Château. Some sixty artisans from all regions of France demonstrate their different techniques and styles. Entry fee €2.

Late July to mid-August Bergerac and around: Été Musical en Bergerac (Ⓣ05.53.74.30.94). Performances of classical music, jazz and ballet in Bergerac, the Château de Biron, Monpazier, St-Avit and Cadouin.

Mid-July to mid-August Castillon-la-Bataille: La Bataille de Castillon (Ⓣ05.57.40.14.53, Ⓦwww.batailledecastillon.com). Local citizenry stage a spectacular floodlit re-enactment of the battle that ended the Hundred Years' War. Some five hundred actors and fifty cavaliers take part, performing every Sat and Sun evening for around six weeks; €20 per performance.

August Dropt valley: Itinérance Médiévale en Vallée du Dropt (Ⓣ05.53.27.11.46). This two-week festival sees all kinds of events – gastronomic markets, parades in medieval costumes, joustings and concerts by torchlight – laid on in towns and villages along the Dropt valley (including Duras, Eymet, Issigeac, and Cadouin).

Second weekend in August Duras: Fête du Vin (Ⓦwww.cotesdeduras.com). Two-day wine-fest held beside the château with free tastings (you have to buy a glass at the entrance for €5). The festival features some good music too, with live jazz/blues on the Sunday afternoon.

Late September to early October Bergerac: Fêtes des Vendanges (Ⓣ05.53.63.57.55, Ⓦwww.vins-bergerac.fr). Various festivities take place – starting with a procession of *gabares* – over one week to celebrate the end of the grape harvest.

Markets

The main **markets** in this region are at Bergerac (Wed & Sat); Le Buisson (Fri); Cadouin (Wed); Eymet (Thurs); Issigeac (Sun); Lalinde (Thurs); Ste-Foy-la-Grande (Sat); Trémolat (Tues).

here it's a ten to fifteen minute taxi ride to the centre (around €15) – taxis are often in short supply, so you may need to order one on Ⓣ05.53.23.32.32. The **gare SNCF** is located at the north end of cours Alsace Lorraine, ten minutes' walk from the old town. Most **bus** services also terminate at the station, though some stop on either place du Foirail or place de la République. Driving in, you'll find free **parking** in the cobbled area beside the old port and on place du Foirail, a short walk east of the town centre.

Bergerac's main **tourist office** is at 97 rue Neuve d'Argenson (July & Aug Mon–Sat 9.30am–7.30pm, Sun 10.30am–1pm & 2.30–7pm; Sept–June Mon–Sat 9.30am–1pm & 2–7pm; Ⓣ05.53.57.03.11, Ⓦwww.bergerac-tourisme.com). In summer they also open an annexe in the Cloître des Récollets (July

& Aug daily 10.30am–1pm & 2.30–7pm; same number as above), and organize **guided tours** of the old town several times a week (July & Aug; 1hr 30min; €4.50).

Accommodation

De Bordeaux 38 place Gambetta Ⓣ05.53.57.12.83, Ⓦwww.hotel-bordeaux-bergerac.com. In terms of facilities, if not character, this is probably Bergerac's top hotel, boasting a sizeable pool and plush bar. The rooms are bright and comfortably furnished – ask for one of those at the back, which are quieter and have a/c and views of the pool and small garden. ❹

Camping la Pélouse 8bis rue J-J Rousseau Ⓣ05.53.57.06.67, Ⓔcamping@ville-bergerac.fr. A very cheap and friendly municipal site with reasonable facilities. It's in a beautiful position on the peaceful south bank of the river, a short walk west from the bridge. Open all year.

Le Colombier de Cyrano et Roxane 17 place de la Myrpe Ⓣ05.53.57.96.70, Ⓔbluemoon2@club-internet.fr. This lovely little *chambre d'hote* in a flagstone sixteenth-century cottage is adorned with blue shutters, flower boxes and a tiny blue wooden door. There are two en-suite rooms, one of which – only a touch more expensive – has its own private terrace. ❹

Family 3 rue du Dragon Ⓣ05.53.57.80.90, Ⓕ05.53.57.08.00. A welcoming, family-run cheapie in a lively position just off the market square. Rooms are small, but all kitted-out with TV, shower and a/c. They're well-kept and brightly painted, making this

The wines of Bergerac

The **Bergerac wine region** extends along the north bank of the Dordogne from Lamothe-Montravel in the west to Lalinde in the east, and south as far as Eymet and Issigeac. It comprises no fewer than thirteen different *appellations*, of which over half the total output is red wine, although the region's most famous wine is the sweet white Monbazillac.

There is evidence of wine production around Bergerac since Roman times, but the vineyards really began to develop in the thirteenth century to supply the English market. Demand from Holland, for sweet white wines in particular, led to a second spurt in the sixteenth century and then again after the Wars of Religion, when Protestant émigré merchants virtually monopolized the market in Monbazillac wines. By the nineteenth century vines covered 100,000 hectares around Bergerac, only to be decimated by phylloxera in the 1870s; the area under AOC wines today covers a mere 12,000 hectares.

Pre-eminent among the Bergerac wines is **Monbazillac**. This pale golden, sweet white wine is blended from Semillon, Sauvignon and Muscadelle vines grown on the chalky clay soils of the valley's north-facing slopes. As with Sauternes, a key element is the cold, autumn-morning mists which lead to the development of *Botrytis cinerea*, or "noble rot", on the grapes (see p.364). The result is an intensely perfumed, concentrated wine best consumed chilled with foie gras, desserts or as an apéritif. Though they can't compare to the finesse of Sauternes, even a top-quality Monbazillac is eminently affordable at around €15 a bottle.

Pécharmant, the best of the local reds, is often compared unfavourably to Bordeaux wines (see box, pp.58–59), though some now rival a number of less prestigious St-Émilions. Pécharmant wines are produced from Cabernet Sauvignon, Cabernet Franc and small quantities of Malbec or Merlot grapes, grown on the most favourable pockets of sand and gravel soils found to the north and east of Bergerac. They are thus far more complex and full-bodied than other Bergerac reds, and some will age well up to seven years.

You can sample the range of local AOC wines at Bergerac's Maison des Vins (see p.169). Alternatively, many producers offer **tastings and visits** to their *chais* – for a full list see the brochure *Route des Vins de Bergerac* available at the Maison du Vin or Bergerac tourist office. For general tips on visiting the vineyards, see the box on p.59.

one of the best deals around. They also offer hearty meals at their simple, good-value restaurant. ❶–❷

De France 18 place Gambetta ⓣ05.53.57.11.61, ⓦwww.hoteldefrance-bergerac.com. This three-star has an unpromising modern exterior but comfortable, fully-equipped rooms inside, and an open-air pool at the back. ❹

Le Logis Plantagenet 5 rue du Grand Moulin ⓣ05.53.57.15.99, ⓦwww.lelogisplantagenet.com. This restored fourteenth-century house has three spacious and very elegant double rooms – all beams, wood floors, rugs and country-style furnishings – as well as attractive communal lounges and a courtyard garden for breakfast (included in price). ❺

Le Moderne av du 108e Régiment-d'Infantrie ⓣ05.53.57.19.62, ⓔhotelrestolemoderne@yahoo.fr. Eleven spruce and cheerful rooms at a good price right opposite the station. Phone, TV and a/c are standard, though the few cheaper rooms at the front share bathrooms and look directly onto the main road. Downstairs you'll find a popular, bustling restaurant (closed Fri eve & Sun eve; lunch €13, eves from €20). ❶–❷

The Town

Although Bergerac sits astride the Dordogne, nearly everything of interest is located on the north bank. The best place to start is beside the old port where, in season, replica *gabares* pick up passengers for leisurely **river trips** (1hr; €7) along the Dordogne to a nature reserve home to herons, cormorants and kingfishers, amongst other wildlife; commentary is bilingual. Departures are at least four times daily from Easter to October, and up to once an hour in July and August (10am–8pm). For more information, call ⓣ05.53.24.58.80.

A short hop east of the port lies the entertaining **Musée du Tabac**, in the narrow lanes of the **vieille ville** which spreads gently uphill. A calm and pleasant area to wander, with numerous late-medieval houses and perfect pavement cafés, its main artery is the Grand'Rue, which runs north from the central church of St-Jacques to join rue de la Résistance, the old town's northern perimeter; these two form Bergerac's principal shopping streets. Just beyond their junction, across the wide place de Lattre-de-Tassigny, stands another useful landmark, **Notre-Dame church**.

The Musée du Tabac

Rue de l'Ancien Pont leads northwards from portside rue Hippolyte Taine to the splendid seventeenth-century Maison Peyrarède, which houses the informative, three-storey **Musée du Tabac** (March 15–Nov 15 Tues–Fri 10am–noon & 2–6pm, Sat 10am–noon & 2–5pm, Sun 2.30–6.30pm; Nov 16–March 14 Tues–Fri 10am–noon & 2–6pm, Sat 10am–noon; €3.50), detailing the history of tobacco (which used to be a major crop in the Bergerac region; Europe's major tobacco research centre is also based here), though rather glossing over its more dire medical effects. Nevertheless, this is a stunning collection of pipes, snuffboxes, cigar holders, tobacco jars, graters and various tools of the trade. There are wooden graters etched with religious scenes, snuffboxes engraved with the busts of Napoleon and Marie Antoinette, blushing young beauties adorning porcelain pipe-bowls and hunting scenes fashioned out of meerschaum. Among many rare and beautiful pieces, the museum's prize possessions are an incredibly ornate Viennese meerschaum-and-amber cigar holder depicting a Sicilian wedding, and an intriguing machine, invented in the 1860s, for carving fourteen brier pipes at once. Look out, too, for the clay pipe in the ominous form of a skull with glittering glass eyes.

The rest of the old town

North of the museum, you cross the attractive place du Feu, one of many such well-restored squares in central Bergerac, to enter the **Cloître des Récollets**. This simple, galleried cloister dates from the seventeenth century when, in the aftermath of the Wars of Religion, Louis XIII dispatched five monks of the Franciscan Récollets order to bring Protestant Bergerac back to the faith. They were not warmly welcomed – it took a visit by Louis himself, in 1621, to assure their authority – but by the end of the decade the Récollets had succeeded in founding a new chapel and monastery. Not that they had the last word. After the Revolution, Bergerac's remaining Protestant congregation bought the chapel and re-established a temple on the site, which is still used for regular Sunday-morning worship.

The monks' vaulted grain and wine cellars now form an unusual setting for Bergerac's **Maison des Vins** (Feb to mid-June & mid-Sept to Dec Tues–Sat 10.30am–12.30pm & 2–6pm; mid-June to mid-Sept daily 10am–7pm; free; ⓦwww.vins-bergerac.fr), which can be entered either through the cloister, where there are interesting displays about the history of the Bergerac appellation, or at street level on the riverfront. As well as selling wine at excellent prices and offering free tastings, they provide wine-tasting lessons (July & Aug Tues & Thurs in English, Mon, Wed & Fri in French; €5; reservations required) and produce the *Route des Vins de Bergerac*, a handy guide to visiting the vineyards around the town.

On its north side the Cloître des Récollets opens onto one of Bergerac's most picturesque squares, the cobbled **place de la Myrpe** (also spelt Mirpe), lined with stone and half-timbered labourers' cottages looking onto a statue, erected in 1977, honouring Edmond Rostand's fictional hero **Cyrano de Bergerac** in typically haughty pose.

At the opposite end of place de la Myrpe, on the corner with rue des Conférences, the small **Musée du Vin et de la Batellerie** (Tues–Fri 10am–noon & 2–5.30pm, Sat 10am–noon; mid-March to mid-Nov also open Sun 2.30–6.30pm; €2.50) contains a rather motley collection of items related to viticulture, farming and the town's once bustling river trade. This latter section is the most interesting, with models of the *gabares* alongside some engaging text on the practicalities of navigating the Dordogne. If you'd been wondering how non-motorised vessels used to make any progress at all going upriver against the flow, the answer is that they did so with difficulty. The river was only navigable upstream on about 150 days per year, and for a long time this relied on men hauling the boats from the river bank – a practice banned in 1837 for humanitarian reasons.

Further uphill, along rue St-Jacques, stands the patchwork **church of St-Jacques** (Mon–Sat 2–7.30pm). The church, a stop on the route to Santiago de Compostela, has had a chequered past, founded in the twelfth century but plundered and destroyed in the Hundred Years' War and the Wars of Religion. Today's church is fairly modest, but has a certain grandeur in its narrow, high nave lit by stained-glass windows.

Rue St-James runs east from the church across the top end of pedestrianized **place Pelissière**, in the heart of the old town, which now boasts its own statue of Cyrano, one bearing an uncanny resemblance to Gérard Depardieu (see box below). From here pretty **rue des Fontaines** continues uphill past prosperous, fourteenth- and sixteenth-century houses – no. 29 on the corner with rue Gaudra is particularly noteworthy with its large, arched windows and carved capitals – to the **market square**. The covered *halle* is the focus of a vast market on Wednesday and Saturday mornings, with more stalls on the square outside the **church of Notre-Dame** (Mon–Sat 8.30am–5.30pm), north of rue de la Résistance, which was built in 1865 as the town's congregation grew too large for once church. Designed by Paul Abadie of Sacré-Coeur fame, it does impress for the resolutely Neo-Gothic style of its architecture, though the twee miniature columns and nativity-scene sculptures on its main facade border on greeting-card kitsch. It's worth peering inside to see two

Cyrano de Bergerac

In 1897, the poet and playwright Edmond Rostand penned his most successful play, **Cyrano de Bergerac**. It tells the story of a guardsman and poet, renowned for his bravery and intellect, who falls in love with his cousin Roxane, but feels unable to declare his feelings because of his unattractive looks – in particular his large, protruding nose. Instead, he writes letters to her on behalf of one of his cadets, the handsome but dim-witted Christian, who has also fallen for her charms. First attracted by Christian's looks, Roxane falls in love with the soul revealed in the letters — not discovering until it is too late that it is in fact Cyrano's soul. Rostand's play has since been the subject of numerous adaptations, perhaps most famously the 1990 French film version staring Gérard Depardieu.

The lead character was inspired by a seventeenth-century soldier, playwright and free-thinking philosopher called Savinien de Cyrano, who was born in Paris and only decided to embellish his name while serving in a Gascon company. It seems Cyrano was well able to match the Gascon reputation for swaggering boastfulness and impetuosity. Not only was he a famous duellist, but many of his works were so outspoken that they had to be withheld from publication until after his death.

large oil paintings in the east chapel: *The Adoration of the Shepherds*, attributed to a pupil of Leonardo de Vinci, and *The Adoration of the Magi* from the Venetian School.

Eating and drinking

When it comes to **places to eat**, the streets of old Bergerac present a promising hunting ground. A good **bar** in the evening is the pub-style *Plus que parfait*, which sometimes has live music on Saturday evenings. Find it at 12 rue des Fontaines – just next door to the *Imparfait* restaurant.

La Blanche Hermine place du Marché-Couvert ⓣ05.53.57.63.42. An excellent rendition of a Breton crêperie offering an imaginative range of savoury buckwheat *galettes* (€6–9) to be followed by sweet crêpe desserts (€3–5). Try one of their *galettes spéciales*, like the *Périgordine* – stuffed with duck breast and peaches. Closed Sun and Mon.

La Cocotte des Halles 14 place du Marché Couvert ⓣ05.53.24.10.00. A locals' favourite on one corner of the market hall, serving filling meals based around regional classics, with plenty of authentic patés, duck & rabbit, but also a fresh fish dish every day. The no-frills menu costs €11. Open daily for lunch.

L'Imparfait 8 rue des Fontaines ⓣ05.53.57.47.92. Bergerac's longest-standing and most refined traditional restaurant with an attractive high-ceilinged, stone dining room and a spacious summer terrace (reservations recommended for dinner in season). The menu changes daily, but revolves around fresh fish and meat, subtly flavoured by a talented chef. Closed Sun, Mon & Jan.

Le St Jacques 30 rue St-James ⓣ05.53.23.38.08. This place has a charming shaded garden at the back complete with outdoor fireplace and stone walls strewn with lanterns and candles. The sophisticated menu is small but quite varied, from the local duck breast in a sweet Bordeaux sauce or lightly fried foie gras with stewed apples and nuts, to Scottish salmon with guacamole. Reckon on €30 à la *carte*.

Le Sud 19 rue de l'Ancien Pont ⓣ05.53.27.26.81. Feast on *couscous Royale*, exotic salads and, if you still have room, home-made desserts or eye-boggling ice creams at this good-value, welcoming Moroccan restaurant. The decor is equally seductive with mosaic-tiled walls, carved wooden screens and flickering table lanterns. There's a good choice of North African wines alongside one or two well-priced Bergeracs. Main courses are around €15, count on €25 for a full meal. Closed Mon.

Listings

Airlines Air France ⓣ36.54, ⓦwww.airfrance.com; Flybe ⓣ0044/13922 68513 (in UK), ⓦwww.flybe.com; Ryanair ⓣ08.92.55.56.66, ⓦwww.ryanair.com; Transavia ⓦwww.transavia.com.

Airport Roumanière ⓣ05.53.22.25.25, ⓦwww.bergerac.aeroport.fr.

Bike rental First choice should be the friendly and helpful Apolo Cycles, 31 bd Victor-Hugo ⓣ06.20.64.59.25 – call ahead to make an appointment. Otherwise, there's Périgord Cycles, 11 place Gambetta ⓣ05.53.57.07.19, which also does repairs (Tues–Sat 9am–noon & 2–7pm).

Books and newspapers A number of English-language newspapers are sold at the Presse-Tabac on place de la Résistance, which also has a good collection of maps. Bergerac's fantastic independent bookshop, the Colline Aux Livres on place du Marché Couvert, has a small selection of books in English.

Bus departures Most buses around the region depart from outside the gare SNCF, with the exception of those for Lalinde (Les Cars Boullet; ⓣ05.53.61.00.46) which leave from place du Foirail, a five-minute walk east of the old town. The other routes out of Bergerac are: Périgueux (CFTA; ⓣ05.53.08.43.13) and Eymet via Issigeac (Les Cars Bleus; ⓣ05.53.23.81.92). Timetables can be found at ⓦwww.cg24.fr.

Car rental Near the train station, try: Avis, 26 cours Alsace Lorraine ⓣ05.53.57.69.83; Budget, 32 Avenue du 108e Régiment-d'Infantrie ⓣ05.53.74.20.00; Europcar, 3 av du 108e Régiment-d'Infantrie ⓣ05.53.58.97.97; Ucar, 31 bd Victor Hugo ⓣ05.53.61.08.16, ⓦwww.apolo-cars.com. All offer airport pick-ups on demand.

Hospital Central Hospitalier Samuel Pozzi, 9 bd du Professeur Albert Calmette, the eastern extension of rue du Professeur Pozzi ⓣ05.53.63.88.88.

Internet access Available at Central Net, 51 rue Bourbarraud (Mon–Sat 10am–10pm, Sun 2–8pm; €2 per hr).
Markets There's a fresh-food market from Monday to Saturday in the central *halle*, while Bergerac's main market takes place on Wednesday and Saturday mornings in the *halle* and the roads and squares around it. Place de la Myrpe is the venue for a flea market on the first Sunday of the month.
Police Commissariat de Police, 37 bd Chanzy ⓣ05.53.74.74.17.
Post Office The main post office is at 36 rue de la Résistance, 24000 Bergerac.
Taxis There's a taxi stand outside the station. Otherwise, call ⓣ05.53.23.32.32.
Tourist train In July and August a tourist train, the Autorail Espérance, runs along the Dordogne valley from Bergerac to Sarlat, via Lalinde and Le Buisson; en route they serve various local products, including paté, goat's cheese and a glass of wine. The train leaves Bergerac around midday (Mon–Sat), and takes an hour and a half to reach Sarlat; you then return on a regular SNCF service. Tickets cost €13 return (there are no one-way fares) and reservations are required: phone ⓣ05.53.59.55.39 to make a booking.

Around Bergerac

The area **around Bergerac** provides a couple of enjoyable excursions geared primarily around wine. On the hills to the south, **Monbazillac** is most famous for its sweet white wines, though the village is also home to an imposing château housing a local history museum. East along the Dordogne the vineyards of **Pécharmant** produce wines a cut above the surrounding Côtes de Bergerac and Bergerac *appellations*.

Monbazillac and around

Six kilometres south of Bergerac, **MONBAZILLAC** is the name not only of a village but also, more famously, of a château and a sweet white wine similar to those of the Sauternes (see p.96). Visible from across the valley floor, the handsome sixteenth-century **Château de Monbazillac** (daily: April 10am–noon & 2–6pm; May & Oct 10am–12.30pm & 2–6pm; June–Sept 10am–7pm; Nov–March by appointment; €5.20; ⓣ05.53.61.52.52, ⓦwww.chateau-monbazillac.com) looks down over the gentle slopes of its long-favoured vineyards. An eye-catching blend of Renaissance residence and mock-medieval fortress, its corners reinforced by four sturdy towers, the château was a Protestant stronghold during the Wars of Religion. Surprisingly, it has survived virtually intact and now contains a moderately interesting **museum**. Best are the wine-related displays in the cellar, including antique bottles specially labelled for the Dutch market (see p.187), and the ground-floor grand salon with its richly decorated ceiling and a parquet floor of oak, pine and cherry wood.

The Château de Monbazillac now belongs to the local wine producers' co-operative, the **Cave de Monbazillac**, which produces the velvety sweet white wine. You can taste – and buy – the wines at the château or at the main **showroom** (Mon–Sat: Jan & Feb 10am–12.30pm & 2–6pm; March–June 10am–12.30pm & 1.30–7pm; July & Aug 9am–7pm; Sept–Dec 10am–12.30pm & 1.30–7pm; ⓣ05.53.63.65.00) located 2km west on the D933 Bergerac–Marmande road. Three kilometres further west again, you'll find a well-rated **restaurant**, the *Tour des Vents* (ⓣ05.53.58.30.10; closed Sun eve, Mon & Wed lunch, also closed Jan), beside the Moulin de Malfourat, a ruined windmill perched on the highest point for miles around. Though it's not an attractive building, the views from the restaurant's picture windows and terrace are superb – and the food is excellent value; menus start at €25, or fans of *foie gras* can try a selection of four kinds for €23.

After whetting your appetite at Monbazillac, investigate some of the area's private **vineyards**. There are two good options to the east of Monbazillac near the village of **COLOMBIER**. The first you come to on the D14E, after about

4km, is the sixteenth-century **Château de la Jaubertie** (July & Aug Mon–Sat 10am–5pm; Sept–June Mon–Fri 10am–5pm; free; ⓣ05.53.58.32.11, ⓔjaubertie@wanadoo.fr), which was supposedly built by Henry IV for his mistress, Gabrielle d'Estrée, and later belonged to a doctor of Marie Antoinette. Now owned by an English family – the Rymans – the estate produces a variety of very reasonable wines under the Bergerac *appellation*. In Colombier itself, the **Domaine de l'Ancienne Cure** has won any number of awards for its high-quality Monbazillac, Bergerac and Pécharmant wines – their Cuvée Abbaye and the highly concentrated L'Extase are fantastic. You can visit the *chais* by appointment (ⓣ05.53.58.27.90, ⓦwww.domaine-anciennecure.fr), but tastings are available at any time at their shop just below the village on the main N21 Bergerac–Agen road (April–Oct Mon–Sat 9am–7pm; Nov–March Mon–Sat 9am–6pm).

Pécharmant

East of Bergerac, if you leave the river valley at Creysse and head north, you're soon back among vine-covered hills. Some of this region's best red wines are produced around the village of **PÉCHARMANT**, 6km northeast of Bergerac. The family-run **Domaine du Haut-Pécharmant** (daily 9am–noon & 3–7pm; ⓣ05.53.57.29.50, ⓦwww.haut-pecharmant.com) is a good place to aim for. It stands in the thick of the vines with views across to Monbazillac, and produces a typically full-bodied, aromatic wine, which ages well. The domaine is signed north off the D32 between Bergerac and Ste-Alvère. Opposite the turning, at the end of a long alley, the much grander **Château de Tiregand** (April–Oct Mon–Sat 9am–noon & 2–6pm; Nov–March Mon–Fri 9am–noon & 2–5.30pm; ⓣ05.53.23.21.08, ⓦwww.chateau-de-tiregand.com) also offers tastings and, if you phone ahead, visits to its extensive park and seventeenth-century *chais* (€3).

South of Bergerac

South of Bergerac, you gradually leave the vines behind as you cross an area of high, rolling country, featuring several small towns, which are well off the beaten tourist track but all the more appealing for that. First stop is **Issigeac**, with its picturesque medieval centre situated on a tributary of the Dropt. From here you can follow quieter back roads southwest along the **Dropt valley** to **Eymet**, a particularly satisfying *bastide* with a well-preserved central square and an abandoned castle, and on to **Allemans-du-Dropt**, where the focus of interest is a remarkable series of frescoes in its otherwise unassuming church. Last but not least comes **Duras**, the town from which the twentieth-century novelist Margaret Duras took her pen-name after spending part of her childhood in the region. Duras's semi-ruined but still forbidding castle holds a commanding position on Périgord's southwestern border.

Public transport is almost non-existent. **Buses** do link Bergerac with Eymet and Issigeac, and Eymet with Allemans, but there are only one or two in each direction daily, none of which allows for a day-trip from Bergerac.

Issigeac

An almost perfectly circular huddle of houses in the midst of pastureland and orchards 8km southeast of Colombier along the D14, **ISSIGEAC** owes its prosperity to the bishops of Sarlat who established a residence here in 1317. Only fragments of the outer walls remain, and in recent years the village has been considerably tarted up, but otherwise its core of half-timbered medieval buildings is largely unspoiled and the narrow streets mercifully traffic-free.

The seventeenth-century **bishop's palace**, now containing various administrative offices, and the **Maison des Dîmes**, the former tax office, with its immense roof, command the village's north entrance. Behind the palace, and not much larger, the Gothic **church of St-Félicien** contains little of interest beyond some polychrome statues. Better instead to wander the old streets, starting with the **Grand'Rue**, leading south to Issigeac's most famous building known as the **Maison des Têtes** for its roughly carved, almost grotesque crowned and grimacing heads. It stands on the corner with rue Cardénal, at the east end of which a house with a half-timbered upper storey on a narrow stone pedestal – allowing carts to pass on either side – resembles nothing so much as a toadstool. From here, take rue Sauveterre circling southwest past more medieval houses and then cross over the southern end of the Grand'Rue to find the rue de l'Ancienne Poste, which meanders generally back northwards to the Maison des Dîmes.

Buses from Bergerac stop on the main road on the southwest side of Issigeac. The **tourist office** is located in a vaulted cellar beneath the bishop's palace (June–Sept Tues–Fri 10am–12.30pm & 2–6pm, Sat 2–6pm, Sun 10am–1pm; Oct–May Tues–Fri 10am–noon & 2–5pm; ⓣ05.53.58.79.62, ⓦwww.issigeac.fr). As well as holding temporary exhibitions, which allow you to explore a few rooms of the palace, the office can provide you with a walking guide to the village. On Sunday mornings, the village fills with **market** stalls. As for **restaurants**, make sure you book ahead at *Chez Alain* (closed Mon, plus Sun eve & Tues Sept–June, and closed completely mid-Jan to mid-Feb; ⓣ05.53.58.06.03, ⓦwww.chez-alain.fr), a classy **restaurant** just across the ring road from the bishop's palace. It boasts a log fire in winter and a very pretty courtyard with a fountain for alfresco dining in summer. The menus (starting at €19) contain a number of seafood delights, such as tuna and shrimp carpaccio, and a heavy presence of crayfish and lobster, but for lunch on Sunday you should go for the delicious *grand buffet* (€25).

Eymet

In contrast to Issigeac's meandering medieval streets, **EYMET**, 15km to the southwest, is laid out on a typical *bastide* chequerboard plan around a well-preserved arcaded central square, **place Gambetta**, one side of which is still lined with timbered medieval houses. Founded in 1270 by Alphonse de Poitiers (see p.357), Eymet changed hands on several occasions – not always by force – during the Hundred Years' War and later joined Bergerac as a bastion of Protestantism. Indeed, locals are still proud of the fact that in 1588 Henry of Navarre, the then leader of the Protestant armies and future King Henry IV, wrote a letter from Eymet to his mistress, Diane d'Andouins. With its corner tower and trefoil windows, the house in which he supposedly set pen to paper is the grandest on place Gambetta; it is naturally called the **Maison d'Amour**.

Once you've soaked up the atmosphere on the main square – which will take longer if you chance to be here for the Thursday-morning **market** – head to Eymet's ruined castle, just north of the centre. The castle hasn't been developed as a tourist sight at all, so you're free to wander inside the curtain wall and right up to the largely intact thirteenth-century keep, built shortly before the *bastide* itself.

There's a **tourist office** under place Gambetta's arcades (May–Sept Mon–Sat 10am–12.30pm & 2–6.30pm; July & Aug also Sun 10am–12.30pm; Oct–June Tues–Sat 10am–12.30pm & 2–5.30pm; ⓣ05.53.23.74.95, ⓦwww.eymet-perigord.fr), which can provide various maps of the town, including one with children's games. **Buses** from Bergerac and Issigeac stop on the main boulevard east of the central square. If you need to **stay**, a good place to do so is the small, comfortable **hotel**, *Les Vieilles Pierres* (ⓣ05.53.23.75.99, ⓦwww.lesvieillespierres.fr; ❸), which has a pool, garden and restaurant (from €11.50), and is just off the D933 to the south of town. Alternatively, there's a well-run two-star municipal **campsite** between the château and the river (ⓣ05.53.23.80.28; open May–Sept).

Place Gambetta has plenty of places to **eat**, the best of which is the *Maison d'Amour*, a crêperie and *salon de thé* (closed Mon–Wed in winter; ⓣ05.53.22.34.64), which is popular for its weekday breakfast *formules* (from €5), and well-stuffed *galettes* and salad platters. Alternatively there's a pizzeria or a traditional French option, *Daudine d'Aymet*, serving menus from €16.

Allemans-du-Dropt

A good place to head is downstream 10km from Eymet to the tiny village of **ALLEMANS-DU-DROPT**, not much more than a homely little central square and the **church of St-Eutrope** (daily 9am–6pm; free). The church's top-heavy lantern tower and grand west door – both nineteenth-century additions to the much-altered tenth-century building – are rather misleading; inside, the walls are covered with recently restored fifteenth-century **frescoes** depicting the Crucifixion and Last Judgement. A number of scenes have been lost or damaged over the years, but on the whole the paintings, which were only rediscovered in 1935, are unusually complete. They read from left to right as you enter, starting with the Last Supper and ending with a particularly graphic view of Hell. Despite the best efforts of St Michael, clad in medieval armour, a mere two souls seem bound for heaven while the damned are being carried off by the basket-load, or skewered on a spit, to be thrust into a boiling cauldron.

Once you've had enough of that, take a stroll to Allemans' western outskirts. As you set off on the D211 out of the village towards Duras, you pass first an old *lavoir*, then a splendid **pigeonnier** standing in somebody's back garden. Such pigeon-houses, which only noblemen had the right to build, are fairly common throughout southwest France, but this elegant hexagonal brick and oak-framed structure, raised up on seven pillars, each capped to prevent rats climbing up, is a particularly fine example.

Though Allemans is easy enough to find your way around, it's still worth picking up an English-language walking guide from the **tourist office** (May, June, Sept & Oct Tues–Sat 1–6pm; July & Aug Tues–Sat 10am–noon & 1–6pm; Nov–April Tues & Thurs 10am–noon; ⓣ05.53.20.25.59) opposite the church. **Buses** stop on place de la Mairie, southwest of the church, which is where you'll also find a peaceful and good-value **hotel**, *L'Étape Gasconne* (ⓣ05.53.20.23.55, ⓦwww.letapegasconne-hotel.com; ❷), whose comfortable rooms rather belie the dowdy, old-fashioned bar downstairs. Some of the rooms have balconies looking onto the hotel's outdoor pool, and there's a decent **restaurant** (Oct–April closed Fri eve & Sun eve) serving traditional cuisine; menus start at €15. There's also a tiny, low-key municipal **campsite** (ⓣ05.53.20.23.37; April–Sept) beside the river, north across the old stone bridge from the village. In July and August you can also rent **canoes** here (ⓣ06.33.65.42.24).

Duras and around

From Allemans, the Dropt winds its way northwest for 10km to where the castle-town of **DURAS** lords it over the valley from its rocky outcrop. The château towers were truncated during the Revolution, but they still afford fine views beyond the Dropt to the country around, an enchanting region of rolling hills topped with windmills, of pasture, orchards, woods and, particularly to the north, of vines.

The chequered history of Duras is evident in the mix-and-match architecture of the **Château des Ducs de Duras**, which dominates the town (Feb, March, Nov & Dec daily 2–6pm; April–June, Sept & Oct daily 10.30am–1pm & 2–6pm; July & Aug daily 10am–7pm; €6; Ⓦwww.chateau-de-duras.com). The château was founded in 1137, but then rebuilt after 1308 by Bertrand de Goth, nephew of Pope Clément V; it is said he used money confiscated from the Templars. Rebuilt again after the Hundred Years' War, it was then extensively remodelled during the more peaceful and prosperous late sixteenth and seventeenth centuries. The finishing touches were added in 1741, just in time to be thoroughly ransacked during the Revolution, after which the château was left to crumble until the commune bought it in 1969. Since then, it has been thoroughly restored, allowing you to visit almost the whole building, from the basements, where the bakery is still recognisable, to the panoramic ramparts at the top. On your way round, look out for wells cut straight through the bedrock and freshwater tanks in case of siege, and a monstrous kitchen fireplace big enough to roast a whole ox. The dukes obviously liked to build on a grand scale – across a wide, open courtyard the entrance hall is impressive enough, and the ceremonial hall above is heated by no fewer than eleven chimneys.

The town of Duras sits at the heart of an interesting **wine region**, worthy of its own appellation. Sandwiched between Bergerac and the Entre-Deux-Mers region, Duras wines come in all shades: reds, dry whites, and some increasingly well-regarded sweet whites, lighter than those of Monbazillac. The best place to find out more is the tremendously innovative **Maison des Vins** on the D668 just downhill from Duras to the south. As well as the standard opportunity to taste and buy, this showcase also has interactive displays and quizzes on the history of the appellation, and its own small sample vineyard, planted with different types of vine.

Three kilometres southeast of Duras, back on the banks of the river Dropt just north of the town of St-Pierre, the **Moulin de Cocusotte** (May–Sept Wed–Sun 2–6pm; €4) and its surrounding garden are a haven of bucolic calm. As well

▲ The Château de Duras

as the ivy-covered thirteenth-century mill and its slowly turning waterwheel, the garden has a wide variety of trees and plants and a shop-cum-café selling some rustic local produce including wine and honey.

Practicalities

Sadly, Duras is pretty much inaccessible without your own **transport** – the closest station is at Ste-Foy-la-Grande, but from there a taxi costs €30. The **tourist office** is at 14 boulevard Jean Brisseau (July & Aug Mon–Sat 9am–12.30pm & 2–5.30pm, Sun 10am–1pm; Sept–June Mon–Fri 9am–noon & 2–5.30pm; Ⓣ05.53.83.63.06, Ⓦwww.paysdeduras.com). Also on boulevard Jean Brisseau, near the tourist office, the *Hostellerie des Ducs* (Ⓣ05.53.83.74.58, Ⓦwww.hostellerieducs-duras.com; ❹) makes a very comfortable place to **stay**. In addition to a pool and flower-filled terrace, there's also an excellent **restaurant** serving upmarket regional cuisine, with menus from €15 (closed Sat lunch, Sun eve & Mon lunch). Duras also has a choice of **campsites:** closest is the basic municipal site right under the château's north wall (Ⓣ05.53.83.70.18, Ⓔmairie-de-duras@wanadoo.fr; July & Aug only), but continue on this road, the D203 to Savignac, another 600m and you'll come to *Le Cabri*, a well-equipped site located on a former farm (Ⓣ05.53.83.81.03, Ⓦwww.lecabri.eu.com; June–Sept).

West to Castillon-la-Bataille

Downstream from Bergerac, the steep north slopes of the Dordogne valley are once again clothed in vines all the way along to the more illustrious vineyards of St-Émilion (see p.118). The valley here is flat and uninteresting, dominated by a major road and rail line, but there are a few diversions en route. First is **Ste-Foy-la-Grande**, which – with its excellent Saturday market and medieval traces – is by far the most rewarding town on this stretch, and certainly the best base, offering good transport links, hotels and restaurants. From here, you could make a couple of worthwhile excursions to see the well-preserved mosaics at Montcaret's Gallo-Roman villa, and the **Château de Montaigne**, where the influential Renaissance thinker and confirmed sceptic, Michel de Montaigne, wrote most of his famous *Essais*. **Castillon-la-Bataille**, the other main town on the river here, is where the Hundred Years' War came to a spectacularly bloody end in 1453; today the battle is commemorated in a monumental summer spectacle. Other than that, the town seems rather down on its luck compared to Ste-Foy, and you won't want to linger except to sample the area's good-value red wines, produced on the border with St-Émilion.

Public transport along this stretch of the Dordogne is limited to **trains** on the Sarlat–Bordeaux line. With just a couple of trains per day between some of these towns, it requires careful planning and a fair bit of walking to reach the area's more interesting sites.

Ste-Foy-la-Grande

Heading west from Bergerac along the River Dordogne, the first place you come to of any size is the prosperous town of **STE-FOY-LA-GRANDE**. The central **place Gambetta** retains some of its original arcades, now shading lively café terraces, while **rue de la République** also boasts several fine, timbered medieval houses, the most grandiose of which, with its corner tower, now houses the tourist office (see p.178). Also worth a wander is the riverside esplanade a short walk to the north, from where you can cross the river via the pont Michel

Montaigne to visit Ste-Foy's modest museum, the **Maison du Fleuve et du Vin** (June–Sept daily 1.30–5.30pm; Oct–May Mon, Tues, Thurs & Fri 9.30am–12.30pm & 2.30–4.30pm; €2.50), covering the role played by river trade in the town's history and providing information on the wine produced around Ste-Foy. Even if that doesn't tempt you, it's definitely worth timing your visit to Ste-Foy to catch the Saturday-morning **market**, one of the region's biggest and most important, when the whole town centre is closed to traffic.

Practicalities

As well as being a pleasant place in its own right, Ste-Foy is the obvious base if you're planning to visit Montcaret (see opposite) and Montaigne (see below). The **gare SNCF** lies five minutes' walk south of town; from the station, turn left along avenue de la Gare then walk north along avenue Paul Broca and then rue Victor Hugo, Ste-Foy's major shopping street. The **tourist office** stands at no. 102 rue de la République (June & Sept Mon–Sat 9.30am–12.30pm & 2.30–6pm; July & Aug Mon–Sat 9.30am–6.30pm Sun 10am–1pm; Sept–May Mon–Sat 9.30am–12.30pm & 2.30–5.30pm; ⓣ05.57.46.03.00, ⓦwww.tourisme-dordogne-paysfoyen.com).

For **accommodation** in central Ste-Foy, you can't do better than the *Grand Hôtel*, with its airy, old-fashioned rooms. The hotel is handily located opposite the tourist office at 117 rue de la République (ⓣ05.57.46.00.08, ⓦwww.grandhotelstefoy.com; ❷; closed two weeks in both Dec & Feb) and also has a restaurant in its magnolia-shaded courtyard (menus from €21; eves only; closed Sun). With your own transport, however, there's also the option of the *Escapade* (ⓣ05.53.24.22.79, ⓦwww.escapade-dordogne.com; ❷; closed Nov–Jan). Four kilometres west of Ste-Foy, just south of the D936, this country hotel offers twelve unfussy rooms in a converted tobacco-drying barn as well as sports facilities and a restaurant serving generous Périgord cooking (menus from €20; eve and Sun lunch only, reservations recommended).

As for **restaurants** back in Ste-Foy, *Au Fil de l'Eau* (ⓣ05.53.24.72.60; closed Sun eve & Mon), at 3 rue de la Rouquette on the north side of Pont Michel Montaigne, is a cracking fish restaurant serving dishes like monkfish fried in red wine and cod served in a creamy asparagus sauce; menus start at €21, though you need to pay at least €27 for the best fish dishes; reservations strongly recommended. For something more relaxed, *Les Sarments*, one block down from the tourist office at 36 rue J-J Rousseau (ⓣ05.57.46.00.22; closed Tues & Wed), is a homely place serving grilled meats and traditional cooking on menus from €20.

Anyone with a tent should head about 500m east along the river's south bank on avenue Georges Clemenceau – the extension of rue de la République – to the three-star **Camping de la Bastide** (ⓣ05.57.46.13.84, ⓦwww.camping-bastide.com; April to mid-Oct), which has its own pool. In season you can rent **canoes** from the *base nautique* (ⓣ05.53.24.86.12; June–Sept) on the north side of the river opposite the campsite. Alternatively, **bike rental** is available all year from Tendance Cyclo, 9 place Broca (ⓣ05.57.41.28.14; closed Sun & Mon pm).

Downstream to St-Michel-de-Montaigne

Travelling west on the D936 from Ste-Foy, garden-lovers might like to make a brief detour after about ten kilometres up into the hills north of the river to visit the **Jardins de Sardy** in Vélines (April–Oct daily 10am–6pm; €6). Though not huge, the gardens – a combination of English and Italian style – occupy a pretty, sheltered spot overlooking the Dordogne. The centrepiece is an informal pond-garden set against the wisteria-covered farmhouse, where it's tempting to linger on the terrace over a cold drink or a light lunch (salad platters €8–12; July & Aug only, reservations required ⓣ05.53.27.51.45), surrounded by the heady scents of aromatic plants.

Three kilometres further along the main road, another right turn brings you to the village of **MONTCARET** and the remains of a fourth-century **Gallo-Roman villa** (June–Sept daily 9.45am–12.30pm & 2–6.30pm; Oct–May daily except Sat 10am–noon & 2–5.30pm; €3) with superb mosaics and an adjoining museum displaying some of the many objects found on the site. Only about one-tenth of the villa has been fully excavated, but it's more than enough to demonstrate the occupants' affluent lifestyle, from underfloor heating and a variety of hot and cold baths to a grand reception room measuring 350 square metres. The floors, baths and covered walkways were laid with elaborate mosaics, of which large areas have survived relatively intact, notably in the cold bath decorated with shellfish, dolphins and octopuses, and the more abstract pattern of shields and fish scales in the "dining room". This latter is the villa's best-preserved room and has been incorporated into the museum building; note, however, that from mid-November to mid-April those mosaics outdoors are covered to protect them from frosts and are therefore not on view.

Back lanes lead another three kilometres northwest to the sleepy village of **ST-MICHEL-DE-MONTAIGNE**, where Montaigne (1533–92) wrote many of his chatty, digressive and influential essays on the nature of life and humankind. Even if you haven't read any of his works, it's worth making the pilgrimage to the **Château de Montaigne** (Feb–April Wed–Sun 10am–noon & 2–5.30pm; May–June, Sept & Oct Wed–Sun 10am–noon & 2–6.30pm; July & Aug daily 10am–6.30pm; closed Nov, Dec & Jan; €6; ⓦwww.chateau-montaigne.com), just beyond the village to the north, to learn more about this engaging, if somewhat quirky and complex, character (see box below).

Montaigne's castle residence burned down in 1885, and its modern reconstruction is now closed to the public. You can, however, go on a guided tour

Montaigne

The third son of a Catholic father and a mother from a wealthy Spanish-Portuguese Jewish family, Michel Eyquem, **Lord of Montaigne**, had an unusual education which involved everyone, including the servants, speaking to him in Latin, and being woken by a musician to ensure "his brain not be damaged". It certainly seems to have caused no harm, since Montaigne went on to become a councillor and later mayor of Bordeaux and was highly respected for his tolerance, wisdom and diplomacy. There is evidence that he also possessed a mischievous sense of humour – throughout the bitter Religious Wars, the Catholic Montaigne apparently took pleasure in ringing his chapel bell as loudly and as often as possible to annoy his Protestant neighbours. On the other hand, it must also be said that Montaigne, who held the Protestant leader Henry of Navarre in great esteem, played an important role in resolving the conflict, though he didn't live to see peace restored in 1598.

Though he attended Mass regularly before his death, and received the last sacrament, Montaigne's writings are renowned for their scepticism; in a typical outburst he declares, "Man is insane. He wouldn't know how to create a maggot, and he creates Gods by the dozen." His philosophical standpoint was essentially an argument for introspection – "if man does not know himself, then what can he know?" While it is criticized as being inconclusive, his legacy is rather his great originality of thought and his essays' wide-ranging questioning of generally accepted truths.

(45min; in French only) of the fourteenth-century **tower** where Montaigne closeted himself away after 1571 to work on his three volumes of essays. On the ground floor was his private chapel, the first floor is the room where he died, and the final storey held the library. Unfortunately his priceless collection of more than a thousand books, all carefully annotated, was dispersed immediately after his death, but some traces of his thought can still be found in the Greek and Latin maxims he inscribed on the beams. Two or three **trains** per day in each direction serve the station of Lamothe-Montravel, on the line between Bordeaux and Bergerac, which lies 5km west of Montcaret and 5km south of the Château de Montaigne. A better option would be to rent bikes in Ste-Foy (see p.178) and then follow the flat, quiet side roads running parallel to the D936.

Castillon-la-Bataille

As you travel the final five kilometres west from Lamothe-Montravel to **CASTILLON-LA-BATAILLE** you'd be forgiven for not noticing as you cross the Lidoire valley. In 1453 this is where the French routed the English in the last major **battle** of the Hundred Years' War (see box below). There's nothing to mark the site, save an uninspiring monument to the English General Talbot on the spot where he supposedly died close to the River Dordogne, two kilometres east of Castillon, but every summer the local citizenry stage a spectacular floodlit re-enactment (see box below).

The **town** itself is run-down and instantly forgettable. If you've got time to kill here, you could wander down to the river east of town, where there are a few blades of grass and some picnic tables, taking in on your way the Porte de Fer – all that remains of the medieval walls – and the eighteenth-century church of St-Symphorien, a rare example of Baroque architecture in the region, though it has the feel of a municipal building rather than a church. Another option is to call in at the **Maison du Vin** facing the church across the central place de Gaulle (Ⓣ05.57.40.00.88, Ⓦwww.cotes-de-castillon.com). They stock a representative sample of wines and can advise on visiting vineyards in the area. One of the more prestigious names is **Château Cap**

The Battle of Castillon

What is now known as the **Hundred Years' War** had been rumbling back and forth through southwest France from 1337, but in the 1440s the French, led by the great military commander Bertrand du Guesclin, began to push the English armies back. In reply, the English despatched the equally renowned **Sir John Talbot**, Earl of Shrewsbury, with orders to regain the lost territory. He took Bordeaux in 1452 and had swept through to Castillon by July 1453.

Here a large French force, camped beyond the town, was waiting for him, but when the Castillon garrison withdrew without much of a fight, Talbot believed it would be an easy battle. Instead he was walking straight into a trap. The French had gathered three hundred pieces of artillery – a relatively new development – and ranged them in the hills either side of the valley. On **July 17**, after Talbot had heard Mass, a messenger reported mistakenly that the French were breaking camp and retreating when all they were doing was moving the baggage to the rear. Talbot hastily rallied his men and led them in pursuit straight into the mouth of the valley and a murderous crossfire. Talbot and four thousand of his men were killed – if not immediately, then by the pursuing archers or simply drowning as they attempted to flee across the Dordogne. As news of the carnage spread, other English-held towns quickly capitulated, until more than a century of warfare finally came to an end.

de Faugères (ⓣ05.57.40.34.99, ⓦwww.chateau-faugeres.com; visits and tastings by appointment), a couple of kilometres northwest from Castillon outside the village of Ste-Colombe. The red wines of the area are of lower quality, but similar in spirit to those of neighbouring St-Émilion – but they come in a lot cheaper, usually at under €10 per bottle. One of the taller stories told hereabouts is that the English defeat (see box opposite) was partly due to their troops discovering a stash of the local hooch one evening and developing such a taste for it that it affected their performance on the battlefield the next day.

Practicalities

Castillon's **gare SNCF** is located on the northeast side of town about five minutes' walk along rue Gambetta, while its **tourist office** is on place Marcel Paul (Mon–Sat 9.30am–noon & 2–6pm; ⓣ05.57.40.27.58, ⓔotcastillonpujols@wanadoo.fr); to find it, take rue Victor-Hugo heading west from the north end of place de Gaulle. If you decide to **stay** here, go for the good-value and attractive rooms above the bar-restaurant *Le Phénix* at 24 place Pierre Orus (ⓣ05.57.40.00.14; ❸) – all have bathrooms, televisions and air-conditioning. Alternatively, the tourist office keeps lists of *chambres d'hôtes* in the vicinity. A small two-star municipal **campsite**, *La Pelouse* (ⓣ05.57.40.04.22; May to mid-Oct), sits by the river to the east of Castillon.

The best **restaurant** in town is *La Fontaine de Manon* at 57 rue Victor Hugo (ⓣ05.57.40.24.48; closed Sun eve & Wed), which doesn't quite qualify as *haute cuisine*, but offers an agreeable atmosphere to enjoy some French classics, like duck paté or *moules-frites* (menus €12 at lunchtime, €17 eves).

East to Le Buisson

The Dordogne River begins to get more interesting upstream from Bergerac, thanks largely to the two great meanders it makes near **Trémolat** and **Limeuil** before the hills begin to close in. The castles, abbeys and villages south of the river are also worth exploring, giving the option of two routes: along the Dordogne itself, or looping inland up the heavily wooded Couze valley to the village of **Cadouin**, with its austere abbey church and elaborately carved cloister.

Transport along the Dordogne valley is provided by **trains** on the Bergerac–Sarlat line, with the stations at Lalinde, Trémolat and Le Buisson served fairly regularly. To get to the towns and churches on the inland route, you need your own car or bike – though it's hilly country for cycling.

Along the Dordogne

Following the Dordogne east from Bergerac, the first sight of any interest is the half-completed **Château de Lanquais**, as much for the story behind its architecture as for its somewhat dilapidated interiors. The working paper mills at **Couze-et-St-Front** also merit a quick stop, while **Lalinde** provides hotels, transport and other tourist facilities, before you meet the first of the Dordogne's great loops, the **Cingle de Trémolat**. At the top of the second meander, the feudal village of **Limeuil** marks where the River Vézère flows into the Dordogne and where you pass into the Périgord Noir, while the final destination, **Le Buisson-de-Cadouin**, sits on an important rail junction on the Bergerac–Sarlat and Agen–Périgueux lines.

Lanquais and Couze-et-St-Front

The **Château de Lanquais** (April & Oct daily except Tues 2.30–6pm; May, June & Sept daily except Tues 10.30am–noon & 2.30–6.30pm; July & Aug daily 10am–7pm; €8), 15km east of Bergerac on the south side of the river, is described in tourist literature as "Périgord's unfinished Louvre". The story goes that in the mid-sixteenth century, when Bergerac and much of the surrounding country was under Protestant sway, Lanquais was owned by a Catholic, Isabeau de Limeuil, cousin to Catherine de Medici. In a brave – or foolhardy – move, Isabeau commissioned the architects of the Louvre in Catholic Paris to add a wing in similar style to her castle. Before the work could be completed, however, the Protestant armies besieged the château in 1577 and left the facade pitted by cannonballs.

They didn't destroy it, though, and you can still discern the change in styles where the Renaissance wing, with its dormer windows and ornamentation, was grafted on to the medieval fortress. It's an imposing rather than an attractive building and some of the interiors are in need of restoration, but there are one or two rooms worth a peep. As in many Périgord châteaux, it's the fireplaces that steal the show, notably that occupying one whole wall of the "blue salon" with its two enigmatic bulls'-skull carvings.

The present owners of the château have set aside two immense rooms with period furniture and en-suite bathrooms as **chambres d'hôtes** (Ⓣ05.53.61.24.24, Ⓔchateaudelanquais@yahoo.fr; ❻; closed Nov–March). For cheaper accommodation options, head on to Lalinde (see below). Below the castle is a small **lake**, offering children-focused activities including supervised swimming (July & Aug daily 1.30–7.30pm; €2.50) and the hiring out of miniature novelty motorboats – including a trawler, cruise liner, and police boat – on which to chug slowly around the lake (April–Oct daily; €4 for 15min). One kilometre north along the D22 you come to **LANQUAIS** village, which boasts an endearingly asymmetrical Romanesque church and an authentic **restaurant**, the *Auberge des Marronniers* (Ⓣ05.53.24.93.78; closed Tues eve & Wed) with country menus from €15.50.

Two kilometres from Lanquais you drop down to the Dordogne again at what was once an important paper-making centre, **COUZE-ET-ST-FRONT**. Head down a side street in the northwest corner of the town to see a series of beautiful old mill buildings, some cut into the cliff face itself, all profiting from the source of power provided by the Couze river. The only water-wheel still turning is that of the fifteenth-century **Moulin de la Rouzique** (April–June & Sept daily except Sat 2–6.30pm; July & Aug Mon–Fri 10am–7pm, Sun 2–6.30pm; €6), where you can see paper being made in time-honoured fashion and examine a collection of antique watermark paper in the drying rooms upstairs. At the equally venerable **Moulin de Larroque**, on the main road through the town centre, they make traditional cotton- and linen-rag paper by hand (Mon–Fri 9am–noon & 2–5pm; free); there's also an array of paper products on sale.

Departing from Couze-et-St-Front, you have the choice either to continue east along the river to Lalinde or delve inland along the Couze valley to Beaumont (see p.186).

Lalinde

The only town of any size along this stretch of the Dordogne, **LALINDE** guards an important river-crossing 3km upstream from Couze and 23km from Bergerac. In 1267 Henry III of England chose the little settlement on the river's north bank to become the first English *bastide*. The central market square, grid plan and fragments of wall remain, but Lalinde's most attractive aspects are the church and gardens on its balustraded riverfront and a large canal basin immediately to the north. The canal was built in the nineteenth century to bypass a dangerous set of rapids, made more hazardous in legendary times by the presence of a dragon, La Coloubre, which lurked in a cave on the opposite bank. According to legend, St Front (see p.126) got rid of the monster in the fourth century by burning it on an enormous bonfire on the hill above its lair – grateful citizens later erected the tiny cliff-top **Chapelle de St-Front** in his honour. You can get to the chapel in ten minutes on foot by crossing the bridge and then scrambling up the steep marked path in the hillside.

Nowadays Lalinde is a bustling market town (Thurs is the main market day, and there's also a smaller farmers' market on Sat) and prosperous commercial centre. Its **gare SNCF** lies three minutes' walk across the canal, while **buses** to Bergerac depart from the central place de la Halle. The **tourist office** (June & Sept Mon–Sat 10am–1pm & 2–6pm; July & Aug Mon–Sat 10am–1pm & 2–7pm, Sun 10am–1pm; Oct–May Mon–Fri 10am–1pm & 2–6pm; ⓣ05.53.61.08.55, ⓦwww.pays-des-bastides.com) is on the riverbank near the old bridge. You can rent **bikes** from the Centre VTT de Lalinde, Maison de l'Écluse (closed Nov–March; ⓣ05.53.24.12.31), beside the canal bridge.

There are two good **hotels** in Lalinde. *Le Forêt*, 2 place Victor Hugo (ⓣ05.53.27.98.30, ⓦwww.leforet-hotel-dordogne.com; ❷–❺) boasts the greater charm, with paintings and antiques dotted around and a tearoom and cake shop downstairs. It offers a range of rooms, even the cheapest of which are well-equipped with three-star comforts. *Le Périgord*, closer to the station at 1 place du 14-Juillet (ⓣ05.53.61.19.86, ⓦwww.hotelduperigord.com; ❸) also has extremely comfortable rooms for the price and runs the best **restaurant** in the town centre, which specialises in traditional duck dishes, with plenty of *foie gras* on menus from €22. Campers should head east along the river 1500 metres to the *Moulin de la Guillou*, a relaxed two-star **campsite** (ⓣ05.53.61.02.91, ⓔla-guillou@wanadoo.fr; mid-April to Sept), which offers canoeing, archery and a swimming pool.

Trémolat

Some 8km upstream from Lalinde the Dordogne snakes its way through two huge meanders, of which the first you come to, the **Cingle de Trémolat**, is the tighter and therefore more impressive. The best views are from the limestone cliffs to the north – follow signs to the Panorama de Trémolat, or on upwards to the Bélvèdere de Rocamadour – from where the whole meander is visible. Over to the east, a heavily fortified church tower pinpoints the picturesque village of **TRÉMOLAT**, where the *Bistrot d'en Face* makes a good pit stop (menus from €14.50). The **restaurant** belongs to the nearby *Vieux Logis* (ⓣ05.53.22.80.06, ⓦwww.vieux-logis.com; ❾), a beautiful luxury **hotel** in a former priory with a large pool, formal gardens – with a lovely terrace for summer dining at the hotel's second, more gastronomic restaurant (menus from €40) – and all sorts of cosy nooks and crannies. The restaurant also runs short cookery classes in the summer under the guidance of its top chef. There's a **campsite**, with pool and sports facilities, on the bank of the Dordogne (ⓣ05.53.22.81.18; closed Oct–April). The **gare SNCF** is located just over a kilometre to the south of the village, and Trémolat also has a boulangerie and small supermarket for stocking up on picnic supplies.

Limeuil

The D31 east from Trémolat takes you over the ridge for a bird's-eye view of the second meander in the Dordogne. The road then drops down to the

▲ Limeuil

honey-stoned village of **LIMEUIL**, on the confluence of the Vézère and Dordogne rivers and an attractive sight, straggling down the steep hillside. Limeuil reached its first peak in the Middle Ages, thanks to its strategic location, and then another in the nineteenth century when local craftsmen built boats for the booming river trade. Today, the village retains its medieval character, as you'll soon discover if you wander under the old gate and up narrow, central rue du Port on the way to the hilltop **park** (Easter–June, Sept & Oct daily except Sat 10am–12.30pm & 2–6pm; July & Aug daily 10am–8pm; €6), where the feudal château once stood. The park is pleasantly leafy, with some pretty water features, and does monopolize the best views from here, but since the entry fee is about as steep as the hill it's on, you might prefer to head for the classic viewpoint near Trémolat (see p.183).

Back at the bottom of the hill, the willow-shaded riverbank makes a good picnic spot, and also has a pebbly **beach** from which you can go for a dip in the river, though it's too shallow and fast-flowing to allow serious swimming. There are a couple of prettily located cafés here, but for a proper meal head up rue du Port to the small, friendly **hôtel-restaurant** *Au Bon Accueil* (ⓣ05.53.63.30.97, ⓦwww.au-bon-accueil-limeuil.com; ❶–❷; closed mid-Nov to mid-March). The hotel has five clean and bright, if a little sparsely furnished rooms, and the restaurant is outstanding, serving tasty, filling meals, like rabbit in a rich mustard sauce, and super home-made desserts, with the bonus of a vine-covered terrace with views along the valley. Menus start at just €11 at lunch and €18 in the evening (closed Mon except July & Aug). **Campers** are catered for at the three-star *Port de Limeuil* just across the river (ⓣ05.53.63.29.76, ⓦwww.leportdelimeuil.com; May–Sept). You can rent **canoes** and **bikes** from Canoës Rivières Loisirs (ⓣ05.53.63.38.73, ⓦwww.canoes-rivieres-loisirs.com) based on Limeuil's beach, and there's also an excellent **riding centre**, La Haute Yerle, in Alles-sur-Dordogne (ⓣ05.53.63.35.85, ⓦwww.rando-equestre-hauteyerle.com), which offers treks from half a day up to a week's circuit of the Périgord Noir. One kilometre northeast of Limeuil on the Le Bugue road is the **Chapelle St-Martin** (daily 9am–7pm; free); if it's locked, you can get the key from the house opposite. A Latin inscription inside this dumpy little Romanesque chapel records that it was dedicated to St Thomas à Becket, the archbishop of Canterbury murdered by Henry II's courtiers in 1170 after the king famously asked who would rid him of "this turbulent priest". The inscription goes on to relate that the chapel was founded in 1194 by Henry's son and successor, Richard the Lionheart, together with Philippe II (Philippe Auguste) of France on their return from the Third Crusade, "to beseech the pardon of God". There are also the remnants of fifteenth-century frescoes in the choir: to the right a Crucifixion scene and the Descent from the Cross; to the left the Flight from Egypt. Note also the *pisé* floor – giving the appearance of pebbles, but actually made of long, narrow stones placed upright – and the roof of stone slates, *lauzes*, over the choir. You'll meet these architectural features again and again as you penetrate deeper into the Périgord Noir.

Le Buisson-de-Cadouin

LE BUISSON-DE-CADOUIN, 5km south of Limeuil, is the last stop on this stretch of river. The town has nothing in the way of sights, but 1km southeast, the **Grottes de Maxange** (April–June, Sept & Oct daily 10am–noon & 2–5pm; July & Aug daily 9am–7pm; closed Nov–March; €7.20) hide unusually extensive displays of *excentriques*. These delicate limestone formations, some looping round on themselves, others suddenly veering off in a different direction, are believed to occur where water evaporates from extremely fine fissures in the rock. Here and there the walls glitter with star-like formations known as *aragonites*. The caves were first discovered in 2000 in a working quarry and originally opened in 2003, while a newly discovered and equally impressive gallery was revealed to the public in 2009. Maxange is also one of the more accessible caves in the region, with no stairs or narrow passages to negotiate.

Le Buisson is a junction on the Bordeaux–Sarlat and Agen–Périgueux train lines, and its **gare SNCF**, to the north of the town centre, is also the closest station to Cadouin (see p.187); for a **taxi** call Taxi Morante on

Cussac Cave

In September 2000, great excitement broke out among art historians and archeologists when a speleologist nosing around Cussac, near Le Buisson-de-Cadouin, stumbled on a previously unknown decorated cave containing more than one hundred **prehistoric engravings**. So important is Marc Delluc's discovery that it's been dubbed the "Lascaux of engraving", in reference to the famous Vézère-valley cavern (see p.216).

Cussac cave is particularly significant because of the number and size of the engravings. The biggest is a four-metre-long bison, while some scenes comprise as many as forty figures. They are also unusually well preserved, the outlines etched deep into the clay by artists sometime between 25,000 and 30,000 years ago. **Horses**, **bison**, **mammoths**, **rhinoceros** and **deer** all feature strongly, but there are also very rare representations of **birds**, as well as **female silhouettes**, **fertility symbols** and a strange long-snouted animal that has yet to be identified.

Because of the vulnerability of these caves (see p.216), it is unlikely that Cussac will ever be opened to the public. The local authorities, however, are keen to capitalize on the tourist potential. There's talk of creating a replica as at Lascaux, but in the meantime you can get a glimpse of what all the fuss is about at ⓦwww.culture.fr/culture/arcnat/cussac/en.

Ⓣ05.53.22.06.51. There's a well-run **tourist office** opposite the station on place André Boissière (July & Aug Mon–Fri 10am–1pm & 2–5.30pm, Sat 10am–1pm; Sept–June Mon–Fri 10am–1pm & 2–5.30pm; Ⓣ05.53.22.06.09, Ⓦwww.dordogne-vezere.com).

Less than two kilometres east on the road to Siorac, the *Manoir de Bellerive* (Ⓣ05.53.22.16.16, Ⓦwww.bellerivehotel.com; ❽; closed Dec & Jan), an elegant little château built on the orders of Louis-Napoleon in 1830, now contains a charming luxury **hotel** set in an English-style park on the banks of the Dordogne. Some of the rooms in the original manor house have river views, while those in the quieter *orangerie* annexe, have private terraces. Its refined **restaurant**, *Les Délices d'Hortensee*, won its first Michelin star in 2000 and now serves delicacies such as sturgeon with foie gras followed by roast veal with a mushroom and artichoke sauce (menus €48–90; open eves only). There's also a tennis court, pool and a perfect breakfast spot on the terrace overlooking the Dordogne. For something cheaper, there's a three-star **campsite** by the river just north of Le Buisson called *Le Pont de Vicq* (Ⓣ05.53.22.01.73, Ⓦwww.campinglepontdevicq.com; April to mid-Oct). As well as a long beach for bathing and canoe hire on site, there's a *guinguette* bar in summer where you can drink and eat barbecued food till late.

The Couze valley

The **Couze valley**, striking southeast of the paper-making town of Couze-et-St-Front, has provided an important thoroughfare since Gallo-Roman times, and part of Edward's I's motivation for founding **BEAUMONT** in 1272, on a dominant spur 10km upstream, was to guard the route. As in many such *bastides*, the church, **St-Front**, was built for military as well as religious reasons – a final outpost of defence in times of attack – hence the bulky tower at each of the four corners and the well inside. Nearby, the central square retains some of its arcades, and off to the west you'll find Porte de Luzier, one of the original sixteen town gates, but otherwise there's little to detain you. The **tourist office** is on the central square (June–Sept Mon–Sat 10am–1pm & 2–7pm, Sun 10am–1pm; Oct–June Mon–Fri 10am–noon & 2–5pm; Ⓣ05.53.22.39.12, Ⓦwww.pays-des-bastides.com), which stocks impressive English-language history and architecture leaflets on Beaumont, St-Avit and Montferrand. To **eat**, make for the *Hostellerie de St-Front*, a stone's throw from the church and colonnaded square at 3 rue Romieu (Ⓣ05.53.22.30.11; restaurant closed Sat lunch & Tues), whose restaurant excels with traditional recipes and home-made products. The *Hostellerie* also has ten pleasant **rooms** (❷), most with shared facilities; those at the back have private terraces with good views over the countryside.

On the other side of the valley, roughly 4km by road, the semi-ruined abbey of **ST-AVIT-SÉNIEUR** stares across at Beaumont from another rocky knoll. It grew up around the burial place of a fifth-century hermit, Avitus, who was born at Lanquais and later served in the Visigoth army until taken prisoner in 507 by the Frankish king Clovis, a recent convert to Christianity. At some point during his fourteen years' captivity in Paris, Avitus followed suit, and was then instructed in a vision to return to Périgord, where he lived as a hermit until his death in 570. Tales of his miracles soon attracted pilgrims and the simple chapel grew into a monastery, then the present **church** (daily 10am–noon & 2–6pm; free) was founded in the early twelfth century; an inscription records that the saint's bones were brought here in 1117. Next door to the simple church is a quiet, pleasant **café-restaurant** *Au Relais de Compostelle*, a great spot for a refresher in summer.

The D26 continues southeast up the narrowing valley for another 8km to the seemingly forgotten village of **MONTFERRAND-DU-PÉRIGORD**, where a clutch of typical Périgord houses shelters beneath the semi-ruined château. A single street leads up past a sixteenth-century market hall – bigger than some of the surrounding houses – to where a path takes off west through the woods. Roughly a kilometre later it comes out near the hilltop **church of St-Christophe**, standing on its own in a cemetery. It used to be the parish church but has gradually been diminished over the years to little more than a stocky bell tower – it's surprising to find that the twelfth- and fifteenth-century frescoes have survived. The oldest painting is that on the north wall of the choir, portraying St Leonard releasing prisoners.

You'll find a good **accommodation** option back down on the main road: owned by a young, friendly English–French couple, the *Lou Peyrol* (Ⓣ05.53.63.24.45, Ⓦwww.hotel-loupeyrol-dordogne.com; ❷; closed Oct–Easter) is a small, creeper-covered country hotel with five rustic rooms and a restaurant serving traditional Perigordian cooking (menus from €19).

Cadouin

At the same time that Augustinian monks were busy building their church in honour of St Avit (see opposite), the Cistercians founded a typically austere **abbey** in what is now the village of **CADOUIN**, 8km to the northeast of Montferrand-du-Perigord, up the D25. Their efforts were given a boost when, in 1117, Crusaders returning from the Holy Land brought them a piece of cloth believed to have been part of Christ's shroud. For eight hundred years it drew flocks of pilgrims – including Eleanor of Aquitaine, Richard the Lionheart and King Louis IX – until in 1935 the two bands of embroidery at either end were shown to contain an Arabic text from the early eleventh century. The cloth is usually displayed in the flamboyant Gothic **cloister**, accessed via a separate entrance to the north of the church door (April–June, Sept & Oct daily except Tues 10am–12.30pm & 2–6pm; July & Aug daily 9am–7pm; Nov–March Mon, Wed, Thurs & Sun 10am–12.30pm & 2–5.30pm; €6; Ⓦwww.semitour.com), though at the time of writing it was removed for restoration work. In any case, it plays second fiddle to the finely sculpted but badly damaged capitals around the cloister: look out for two merchants squabbling over a goose and the parable of Lazarus. There are some more good carvings on the cloister's north wall, either side of the abbot's seat, showing Jesus carrying the cross while two soldiers dice for his tunic, and a procession of monks alongside a prostrate Mary Magdalene – the remains of a Crucifixion scene.

Adjacent to the cloister stands the contrastingly austere Romanesque **church** (free), with its stark, monumental west wall and unusual double-tier belfry roofed with chestnut shingles. Inside, the triple nave is equally spartan and so high that the pillars appear to bulge outwards. You can still see the chains above the altar where the shroud was suspended in its casket, but the main point of interest is the stained glass in the north aisle, installed around a century ago, which recounts the story of the shroud's journey from Jerusalem.

Practicalities

The only way to get here by public transport is to take the **train** to Le Buisson (see p.185) and then a taxi for the final 6km (count on around €10) otherwise it's a long hike up the steep hill. The village has its own summer-only **tourist office** (May–Sept Mon–Fri 9am–1pm & 2–6pm, Sun 2–6pm, closed Sat; Ⓣ05.53.57.52.64, Ⓦwww.dordogne-vezere.com), which doubles as a boutique selling local produce.

There's a good range of **accommodation** and restaurants, mainly set around the attractive, open square dominated by the church. Adjacent to the cloister, the monks' dormitories have been turned into an excellent and very friendly HI **youth hostel** (Ⓣ05.53.73.28.78, Ⓦwww.fuaj.org/Cadouin; dorm beds €17.10; closed mid-Dec to end Jan) with a well-equipped kitchen, bikes on loan and fantastic private rooms with shower, desks and mezzanine floor sleeping area (❶). There are more comfortable lodgings in another unusual location, namely the town's erstwhile police station just off the main square, where the *chambre d'hôte L'Ancienne Gendarmerie* (Ⓣ05.53.58.39.84, Ⓦwww.anciennegendarmerie.com; ❸) offers four lovely en-suite rooms, with warm stone walls and exposed beams. Two of the rooms have balconies, and there's an elegant communal sitting room with an open hearth. The price includes an excellent Dutch-French breakfast. Just over the road from the church, Cadouin's best **restaurant** is the *Restaurant de l'Abbaye* (Ⓣ05.53.63.40.93, Ⓔdelpech@wanadoo.fr; Nov–March open daily for lunch and Sat eve, April–Oct open daily except Mon for lunch and dinner), a very friendly place offering tasty, traditional menus from €12. Upstairs are four rooms (❷), with high ceilings and views of the church, which make yet another appealing place to stay in the village. If you've had enough duck and foie gras, *Chez Cathy et Paulo,* with tables set out on the square, serves generous salads, pizzas and omelettes for around €8.

Good **campsites** are not in short supply either. Closest is *Les Jardins de l'Abbaye* (Ⓣ05.53.61.89.30, Ⓦwww.jardinsabbaye.com; April–Sept), a calm, shady site just above the village on the Montferrand road. With your own transport, however, you can reach the better-equipped three-star *La Grande Veyière* (Ⓣ05.53.63.25.84, Ⓦwww.lagrandeveyiere.com; mid-June to mid-Sept), 3km southwest on the road to Molières.

Leaving Cadouin, most people drop straight down to the Dordogne at Le Buisson, from where the caves around Les Eyzies (see p.203) are within easy striking distance.

Travel details

Trains

Bergerac to: Bordeaux (6–12 daily; 1hr 15min–1hr 30min); Le Buisson (4–8 daily; 40min); Castillon-la-Bataille (6–12 daily; 40–50min); Couze (1–2 daily; 15min); Lalinde (4–8 daily; 15–20min); Lamothe-Montravel (1–3 daily; 35–40min); Libourne (6–12 daily; 45min–1hr); St-Émilion (3–7 daily; 40min); Ste-Foy-La-Grande (6–12 daily; 20min); Sarlat (4–8 daily; 1hr 20min–1hr 30min); Trémolat (3–7 daily; 30min).

Le Buisson to: Agen (2–5 daily; 1hr 30min); Bergerac (6 daily; 30–40min); Le Bugue (4–6 daily; 8min); Couze (2–3 daily; 25min); Les Eyzies (4–6 daily; 15min); Lalinde (6 daily; 20min); Périgueux (4–6 daily; 50min); Sarlat (5–7 daily; 40min); Trémolat (5 daily; 10min).

Castillon-la-Bataille to: Bergerac (5–12 daily; 40min); Bordeaux (6–12 daily; 30–40min); Lamothe-Montravel (Mon–Sat 1–4 daily; 5min); St-Émilion (4–7 daily; 8min); Ste-Foy-La-Grande (5–12 daily; 15–20min).

Ste-Foy-La-Grande to: Bergerac (5–12 daily; 20min); Bordeaux (6–12 daily; 1hr); Castillon-la-Bataille (6–12 daily; 15–20min); Lamothe-Montravel (1–3 daily; 15–20min); St-Émilion (4–7 daily; 35min).

Buses

Bergerac to: Eymet (Mon–Fri 1–2 daily; 50min–1hr 20min); Issigeac (Mon–Fri 1–2 daily; 45min); Lalinde (school term Mon–Sat 1–3 daily, school holidays Tues–Thurs & Sat 1–2 daily; 40min); Périgueux (Mon–Fri 3 daily; 1hr); Port de Couze (as for Lalinde; 30min).

Eymet to: Allemans-du-Dropt (school term Mon–Fri 1 daily; 15min); Bergerac (Mon–Fri 1–2 daily; 40min); Issigeac (Mon–Fri 1–2 daily; 30min).

Lalinde to: Bergerac (school term Mon–Sat 1–3 daily, school holidays Tues–Thurs & Sat 1–2 daily; 40min); Port de Couze (as for Bergerac; 15min).

4

Sarlat and the Périgord Noir

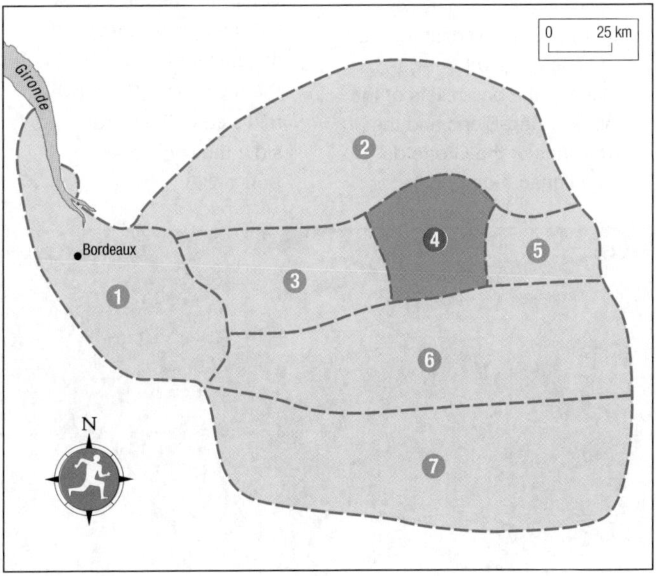

CHAPTER 4

Highlights

* **Sarlat** Wander the cobbled lanes of this beautifully preserved medieval town, which hosts one of the region's best markets. See p.193

* **Manoir d'Eyrignac** These formal gardens, with their manicured hornbeam hedges and trompe-l'oeil parterre, are as much a work of art as of nature. See p.199

* **Vézère valley** Prehistoric artists left moving testimony of their skill in myriad decorated caves here, among them the magnificent friezes of Lascaux and Font-de-Gaume, the bas-reliefs of the Abri du Cap-Blanc and the drawings of the Grotte de Rouffignac. See p.201

* **La Roque-St-Christophe** Multi-storey living medieval-style in these dozens of rock-shelters cut into the limestone cliffs. See p.212

* **Château de Castelnaud** This archetypal feudal fortress lording it over the Dordogne valley contains a superb museum of medieval warfare. See p.224

* **La Roque-Gageac** Very touristy, but nevertheless one of the region's most picturesque villages, with its jumble of roofs and the towering cliffs above mirrored in the Dordogne's slow-moving waters. See p.226

▲ Swimming at the Vézère valley

4

Sarlat and the Périgord Noir

The central part of the Dordogne valley and its tributary, the valley of the Vézère, form the heart of the **Périgord Noir**. This is distinctive Dordogne country: deep-cut valleys enclosed within limestone cliffs; fields of maize; dense, dark oak woods; orchards of walnut trees (cultivated for their oil); flocks of ducks and low-slung grey geese; and primitive-looking stone huts called *bories* – these are all hallmarks of the region. You'll also find mottled-grey roofs made of limestone slabs (*lauzes*), although the cost of maintaining these – the stones weigh on average 500kg per square metre – means that they are gradually being replaced with terracotta tiles. A floor made out of *lauzes* is called *pisé*, and is commonly found in châteaux and chapels, the stones inserted upright into a bed of clay and lime. None of these features is unique to the Périgord Noir, of course, but their prevalence here adds a defining stamp to the region – no more so than in the well-preserved medieval town of **Sarlat-la-Canéda**, the capital of the Périgord Noir. Though it boasts no great monuments, the warren of old lanes, hidden courtyards and fine architecture, the background for many a period drama, not to mention its excellent weekly markets, are not to be missed. Sarlat is within spitting distance of the two iconic river valleys, which have come to define the whole region. First up is the **Vézère valley**, cutting diagonally across the region from the northeast. The valley's immense, slightly overhanging cliffs have been worn away by frost action over the millennia to create natural rock-shelters where humans have sought refuge for thousands of years, leaving an incredible wealth of archeological and artistic evidence from the late Paleolithic era. The two unmissable highlights are the outstandingly preserved polychrome paintings of the **Grotte de Font-de-Gaume**, which you can still visit in the original, and the reproduction at **Lascaux**, near Montignac. The valley has more than cave paintings to offer, however: several sites show how cliff shelters were lived in throughout the middle ages up until relatively recently, while some breathtaking chasms like the **Gouffre de Proumeyssac** are the work of nature alone. In the **Dordogne Valley**, meanwhile, it's the region's medieval, feudal history that's most palpable in this sublime, château-studded stretch. **Beynac** and **Castelnaud**, two semi-ruined fortresses on either side of the river, are without doubt the most spectacular. Closer to river-level, **La Roque-Gageac** presents a more

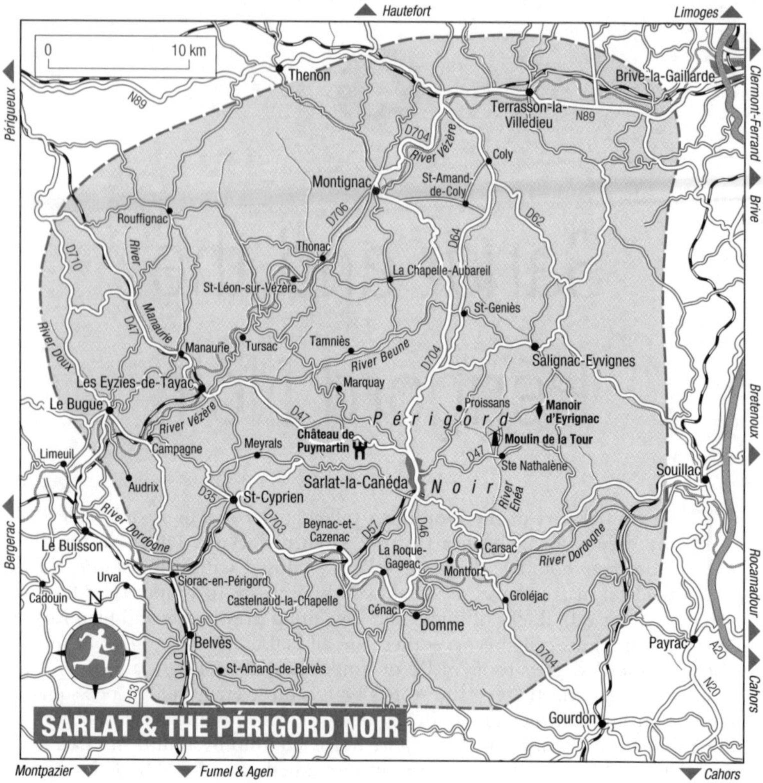

homely scene. From a distance, save for its red-tile roofs, the village is barely distinguishable from the vertical cliff into which it nestles. This is also one of the best spots in the whole country to hop on a **canoe** and take a leisurely trip downstream.

With so many first-class sights in such a compact area, it's not surprising that this is one of the most heavily visited inland areas of France, and as a result has all the concomitant problems of crowds, high prices and tack. It is really worth coming out of season, but if you can't, seek accommodation away from the main centres, try to visit places first thing in the morning and always drive along the back roads – the smaller the better – even when there is a more direct route available.

Though you'll need your own transport for exploring much of the Périgord Noir, two **train** lines cut through the area. Sarlat is the terminus of a line from Bordeaux via Bergerac, while trains between Agen and Périgueux stop at Le Bugue and Les Eyzies; the best place to change between the two lines is Le Buisson (see p.185). In addition, the northern Vézère valley can be accessed from Terrasson, on the Brive–Bordeaux main line. There is also a minimal smattering of **bus** routes, though even these early-morning school services fizzle out entirely during July and August.

Sarlat-la-Canéda and around

Very picturesque and very touristy, **SARLAT-LA-CANÉDA** (usually known just as Sarlat) sits in a green hollow between hills 10km or so north of the River Dordogne. You hardly notice the modern suburbs, as it is the mainly fifteenth- and sixteenth-century houses of the old town in mellow, pale ochre-coloured stone that draw the attention. Unless you are here for the Saturday market, it won't take more than half a day to explore. There's a large range of **accommodation**, both in and just outside the town, making it the most natural base for exploring the Périgord Noir.

The hills above Sarlat contain a good range of sights, from the **Moulin de la Tour**, a water mill making walnut oil by traditional methods, to the topiary gardens of the **Manoir d'Eyrignac**, with perhaps a detour to the picturesque village of **St-Geniès**. Heading westwards, the still-occupied **Château de Puymartin** tends to be overshadowed by the more famous castles along the Dordogne, but contains some unusual interior decorations, while the nearby

Festivals, events and markets

Where we haven't given a specific information number contact the relevant tourist office.

Late May or early June Sarlat: La Ringueta (Ⓣ05.53.31.53.31). At Pentecôte (Whit Sunday) in even-numbered years, place de la Grande-Rigaudie is the venue for traditional games and sports of the Périgord.

Mid-July to early August Sarlat: Festival des Jeux du Théâtre (Ⓣ05.53.31.10.83, Ⓦwww.festival-theatre-sarlat.com). One of France's most important theatre fests, covering a wide range of material from Shakespeare to the avant-garde Theatre of the Absurd, as well as several productions for children. It's staged over three weeks, including many open-air performances (tickets required) and theatre workshops.

Mid- to late July Montignac: Festival de Montignac (Ⓣ05.53.50.14.00, Ⓦwww.festivaldemontignac.assoo.org). Major arts festival featuring local and international folk groups from as far afield as South America and China. As well as ticket-only events, there are street performances, food stalls, exhibitions and crafts demonstrations during the week.

August St-Léon-sur-Vézère and around: Festival du Périgord Noir (Ⓣ05.53.51.95.17). Baroque and classical music concerts in the atmospheric churches of St-Léon, St-Amand-de-Coly and others throughout the region.

Early August Les Eyzies and around: Festival Musique en Périgord (Ⓣ05.53.07.23.77). Interesting mix of medieval and classical works alongside traditional music from around the world. Concerts take place over ten days in the Romanesque churches of Les Eyzies, Campagne and Audrix, among other venues.

First fortnight in August Belvès and Cadouin: Festival Bach (Ⓦwww.festivalbach.fr). Dedicated to the composer and comprising a handful of concerts in Belvès church and Cadouin's abbey.

Early November Sarlat: Festival du Film (Ⓣ05.53.29.18.13). One-week festival previewing films from around the world, including special screenings of student productions.

Markets

The main **markets** in this region are at Belvès (Sat); Le Bugue (Tues & Sat); Domme (Thurs); Les Eyzies (Mon; April–Oct only); Montignac (Wed & Sat); St-Cyprien (Sun); St-Geniès (Sun); Sarlat (Wed & Sat); and Terrasson (Thurs).

Cabanes de Breuil, a harmonious group of what were probably shepherds' huts, represent a completely different architectural tradition. With the exception of St-Geniès, which, with an early start, is accessible on the Sarlat–Périgueux bus route, you'll need your own **transport** to reach any of these places.

Some history

Though it started life as a Gallo-Roman settlement, Sarlat really came to prominence in the late eighth century when Benedictine monks established an **abbey** here, later dedicated to a former bishop of Limoges, St Sacerdos. In 1147 **Bernard of Clairvaux** also left his mark when he preached to the Second

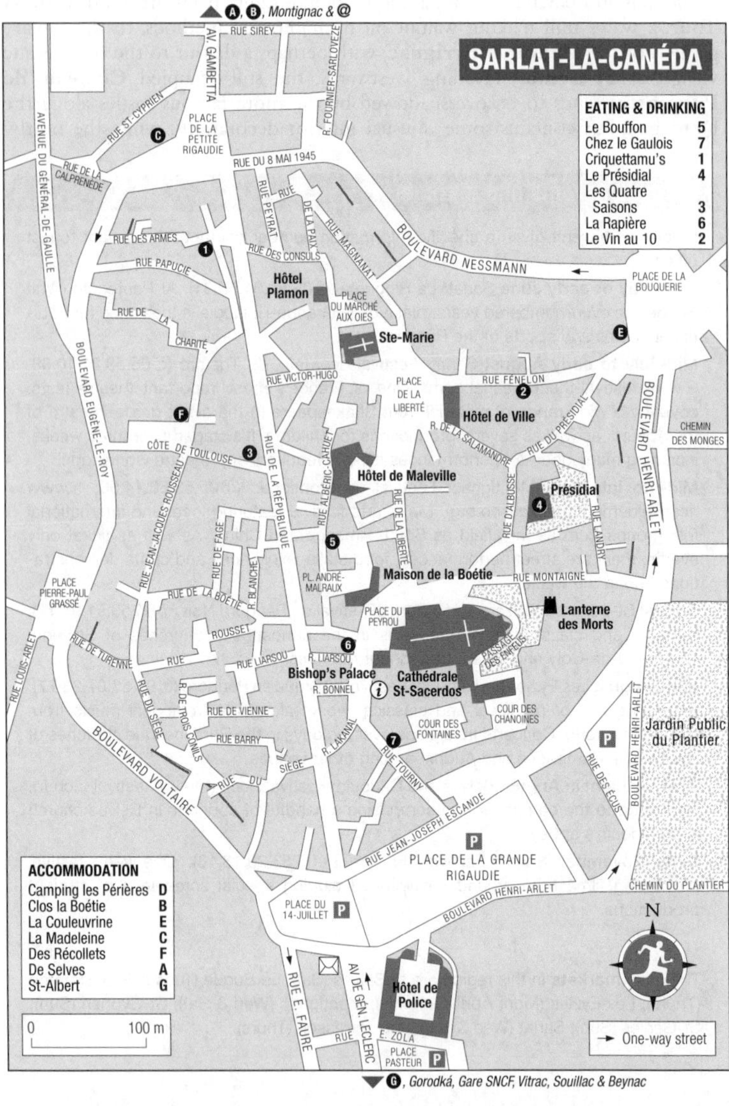

Crusade – according to legend he miraculously cured the sick by offering them bread he had blessed. In spite of this, the townspeople were keen to gain independence from church rule, and in 1298 were eventually granted the right to elect their own consuls by Louis VIII. In return, they remained loyal to the French Crown during the Hundred Years' War and staunchly Catholic in the Wars of Religion, when the town suffered considerably at the hands of the Protestants. The fine **Renaissance** facades visible today date from a period of prosperity in between these two wars. That they are so well preserved is largely due to the fact that the town went into slow decline after the late 1700s and for the most part escaped the ravages of modernization. Indeed, by the early twentieth century the centre was in a pretty poor state, but was saved from further decay by the vision of **André Malraux**, the novelist, Resistance hero and politician who invented the concept of the *secteur sauvegardé* ("protected area") in 1962. Sarlat's town centre was a pilot for this "Malraux Act" and was saved from excessive postwar renovation and received funds for a huge restoration project. Today, the sixty-five protected monuments in the medieval centre make it the most popular tourist destination in the whole of Dordogne, packed to the gunwales in summer, though still relatively undisturbed during the winter months.

Arrival and information

Sarlat's **gare SNCF** is just over 1km south of the old town on the road to Souillac. **Buses** from Périgueux and Souillac pull in to place Pasteur, immediately south of the centre. Most people **drive** to Sarlat; it's normally easy to find a parking space, but these are at a premium on market day and in July and August. Paid **parking** is available all around Sarlat's ring road, the most convenient being on place de la Grande-Rigaudie. Prices and the length of time you can park for vary by season, so check the instructions on the meter. The **tourist office** is in the heart of the old centre on place du Peyrou (April–Sept Mon–Sat 9am–6pm, Sun 10am–noon & 2–5pm; Oct & Nov Mon–Sat 9am–noon & 2–5pm, Sun 10am–1pm; Dec–March Mon–Sat 9am–noon & 2–5pm; ⓣ05.53.31.45.45, ⓦwww.sarlat-tourisme.com). From April to September you can join one of their **guided tours** round the town (2–3 daily; 1hr 30min; €5). They also sell maps of hiking and bike trails around the Périgord Noir (€1.50 per map; €13 for all 29 maps). While here, pick up the leaflet *Sortir à Sarlat*, a comprehensive run-down of the town's cultural calendar, including its excellent theatre and film festivals (see box, p.193).

Accommodation

Note that during the peak holiday season (June–Sept) it's advisable to book several weeks in advance and to consider the quieter places outside the town centre. If you arrive without a reservation, the tourist office will do what they can to assist, but they can't guarantee to find anything; they charge a nominal fee of €2 to €3.

Accommodation in Sarlat

Camping Les Périères route de Ste-Nathalène ⓣ05.53.59.05.84, ⓦwww.campings-dordogne.com/les-perieres. Sarlat's closest campsite is on the hillside 1km northeast of the centre up rue Jean Jaurès. It's spacious and extremely well equipped – facilities include heated indoor pool, outdoor pool, washing machines, tennis courts and grocery shop – but it costs almost as much as a cheap hotel. Daily rates for two people start at around €30 in July and August, though it's a good deal if you're alone without a car (€12). Closed Oct–March.

Clos la Boétie av Gambetta ⓣ05.53.29.44.18, ⓦwww.closlaboetie-sarlat.com. Central Sarlat's most luxurious hotel by a distance, this nineteenth-century mansion has just eleven rooms, each exquisitely decorated, some with four-poster beds, hanging tapestries and Versailles-style furnishings, others with a more modern look. The most appealing of all are those on the top floor tucked under the wooden eaves. With the additional draws of a gym, sauna and heated pool, the rates (starting at €200 in summer) are not expensive for the quality of the establishment. Closed mid-Nov to March. ❾

La Couleuvrine 1 place de la Bouquerie ⓣ05.53.59.27.80, ⓦwww.la-couleuvrine.com. Offering the best value around after *Des Récollets* (see below), *La Couleuvrine*, which occupies a part-medieval castle with exposed stone walls and big fireplaces downstairs, contains 28 comfortable rooms, though the cheapest are quite small – best is the tower room with views across town. One of the few hotels in Sarlat to have a good restaurant: menus from €21; closed three weeks in Jan. ❸

La Madeleine 1 place de la Petite Rigaudie ⓣ05.53.59.10.41, ⓦwww.hoteldelamadeleine-sarlat.com. Newly reopened, Sarlat's oldest and once grandest hotel, located just outside the medieval centre, offers excellent value. The rooms are fully equipped and you can take advantage of an elegant bar and salon downstairs, plus the reasonably priced restaurant (from €19). A pool and other facilities should be ready by 2010. ❹

Des Récollets 4 rue Jean-Jacques Rousseau ⓣ05.53.31.36.00, ⓦwww.hotel-recollets-sarlat.com. This small hotel, in the former Récollets' cloister on a quiet street to the west of rue de la République, is one of the nicest places to stay in Sarlat, and certainly offers the best value; a warm welcome, and a range of comfortable rooms in bright modern colours with gleaming en-suite bathrooms, all set around a quiet leafy interior courtyard where breakfast is served in summer. ❷

De Selves av Gambetta ⓣ05.53.31.50.00, ⓦwww.selves-sarlat.com. The sister hotel to the *Clos la Boétie* (see p.195) does not have the same charm, but is considerably cheaper and gives access to the same pool and other facilities. The rooms here have modern decor, a/c, flat-screen televisions and a wi-fi connection. Closed Jan to mid-Feb. ❺

St-Albert place Pasteur ⓣ05.53.31.55.55, ⓦwww.hotelsaintalbert.com. This well-run two-star on the main road a two-minute walk south of the centre is not the most characterful place to stay, but the rooms are comfortable and there's a good restaurant, serving traditional Périgord cuisine (menus from €21). ❹

Accommodation around Sarlat

Camping La Palombière Ste-Nathalène ⓣ05.53.59.42.34, ⓦwww.lapalombiere.fr. A four-star job, this is one of the region's best campsites, roughly 10km east of Sarlat on the D47. It's in a lovely, peaceful location in six hectares of woodland, is very well equipped – including restaurant, bar, grocery store, pools and tennis courts – and puts on all sorts of kids' events in summer. Closed Oct–April.

Camping Les Terrasses du Périgord Pech d'Orance ⓣ05.53.59.02.25, ⓦwww.terrasses-du-perigord.com. Welcoming, well-tended campsite in a superb hilltop position 2.5km north of Sarlat on the Proissans road. Plenty of flowers and spacious plots make this one of the nicest sites around. Closed mid-Sept to mid-April.

La Ferme de la Croix d'Allon La Croix d'Allon ⓣ05.53.59.08.44, ⓦwww.lacroixdallon-sarlat.com. Five *chambres d'hôtes* on a working cattle farm 2km from Sarlat on the road to Proissans. The rooms all have private bathrooms and a kitchen and barbecue are also available for guests. ❸

Gorodka 4km south off the D704 in the direction of Gourdon ⓣ05.53.31.02.00, ⓦwww.gorodka.com. Simple *chambre d'hôte* housed in an eclectic art gallery – see p.198. ❶

La Hoirie rue Marcel Cerdan, La Giragne ⓣ05.53.59.05.62, ⓦwww.lahoirie.com. This vine-covered thirteenth-century hunting lodge with a pool and small park lies 2km south of Sarlat, signed off the Souillac road. Though a touch on the expensive side, the rooms are large and comfortable, with solid rustic furniture. There's also a sophisticated restaurant (dinner only; closed Tues) with menus from €35. Closed Jan & Feb. Breakfast included. ❺–❼

Le Relais de Moussidière Moussidière-Basse ⓣ05.53.28.28.74, ⓦwww.hotel-moussidiere.com. Coming from Sarlat, turn left off the busy D57 Bergerac road beside the Citroën garage to find this luxury hotel nestled among trees in a peaceful seven-hectare park with a pond, ducks, swans and swimming pool. The hotel occupies a very attractive Périgordin manor house, which retains plenty of original stone floors and wooden beams. The rooms themselves, many of which have private balconies, are all furnished in original fashion, some modern and others in period style, with countless African touches around the place. Breakfast included. Closed Nov–April. ❼

La Treille Vitrac ⓣ05.53.28.33.19, ⓦwww.latreille-perigord.com. On the banks of the Dordogne some 7km south of Sarlat, this friendly, family-run hotel has just eight pretty rooms, which are large for the price, and an excellent restaurant (menus €20–40; closed Mon & Tues in winter). ❷–❸

Aux Trois Sources Pech-Lafaille ⓣ05.53.59.08.19, ⓦwww.hebergement-sarlat.com. A very well-priced *chambre d'hôte* in a handsome seventeenth-century manor house 3km east of Sarlat on the road to Ste-Nathalène. The five charming, rustic, en-suite rooms, with wooden floors, rugs and original hearths, are squeezed into a converted barn surrounded by an attractive park, with chestnut trees and pond. ❷

The Town

The ramparts surrounding old Sarlat were torn down in the late 1800s, at about the same time that the north–south **rue de la République** was cut through the centre to create its main thoroughfare. The streets to the west remain relatively quiet; the east side is where you'll find the majority of sights. Note that from June to September (daily 11am–midnight), Sarlat's medieval core is closed to traffic, while rue de la République is pedestrianized in July and August.

Sarlat's labyrinthine lanes fan out from **place de la Liberté**, the central square where the big Saturday **market** spreads its stands of geese, flowers, foie gras, truffles, walnuts and mushrooms according to the season; it's mostly foodstuffs in the morning and general goods after lunch. The square's finest building is the **Hôtel de Maleville**, tucked into its southwest corner. The facade facing onto the square consists of a tall, narrow building in French Renaissance style with ornate window surrounds; turn down the lane beside it to see its more classical Italianate frontage, with a balustraded terrace and two medallions above the door representing Henry IV and, according to popular belief, his mistress Gabrielle d'Estrée. The lane continues through a series of passages and geranium-filled courtyards to emerge beneath Sarlat's most famous house, the **Maison de La Boétie**. Though its prominent gables and tiers of mullion windows, each within a sculpted frame, are certainly eye-catching, much of the building's fame derives from the fact that the poet and humanist Étienne de La Boétie, a close friend of Michel de Montaigne (see p.179), was born here in 1530. He went on to study law in Orléans, where he wrote his most famous work, *Discourse on Voluntary Servitude*, though it wasn't published until after his premature death at the age of 33. A treatise on the tyranny of power, and thus a very early expression of anarchism, the *Discourse* later struck a cord with Rousseau and other radical thinkers in the run-up to the Revolution.

Opposite the Maison de La Boétie, the former bishop's palace also sports a Renaissance gallery and windows, while the large and unexciting **Cathédrale St-Sacerdos** to which it is attached mostly dates from a seventeenth-century renovation. More interesting are the two pretty courtyards to the south of the cathedral – **cour des Fontaines**, filled with the sound of playing water, and **cour des Chanoines**, surrounded by a pleasing assembly of buildings – and the passage around the chevet where Sarlat's nobles were laid to rest in arched niches, *enfeux*, let into the wall. Less illustrious mortals were buried in the cemetery above, presided over by a curious bullet-shaped tower, the **Lanterne des Morts**, built in the twelfth century. Its exact purpose is unknown. Local tradition maintains that it commemorates St Bernard's visit in 1147 (see p.194).

Further north along the same slope you come to the **Présidial**, the former seat of royal justice, now a restaurant (see p.198). From here, drop back down to place de la Liberté and pass behind the back of the badly mutilated church of Ste-Marie to find the place du Marché-aux-Oies – a delightful corner decorated by three bronze geese – and the **rue des Consuls**. Of several handsome houses along here, the most remarkable is the **Hôtel Plamon**: built by wealthy drapers in the fourteenth century, it was then added to over the next three hundred years, starting with a lovely row of flamboyant Gothic windows on the first floor.

It's worth crossing over rue de la République to wander the western sector, particularly rue Jean-Jacques Rousseau. There's nothing in particular to see, beyond more cobbled lanes and ornate doorways or the odd defensive tower, but this side of Sarlat is less touristy and quieter.

Just outside Sarlat, 4km south off the D704 in the direction of Gourdon, **Gorodka** (July & Aug daily 10am–midnight, Sept–June daily 2–6pm; €8; ⓣ05.53.31.02.00, ⓦwww.gorodka.com), the home and gallery of conceptual artist Pierre Shasmoukine, is well worth a visit. This is a rambling place with four different galleries crammed full of inventive pieces of art. The extensive grounds serve as an offbeat gallery of the weird and wonderful including a giant dragonfly made from the body of a helicopter, and bizarre, sinister-faced plastic totems that glow in the dark. A coatstand by the entrance asks you to leave your preconceptions here on your way in. They also have a *chambre d'hôte*, see p.196.

Eating and drinking

During the main tourist season Sarlat is chock-a-block with **restaurants**. In winter pickings are thinner, but those that do stay open tend to be the better quality places patronized by locals. You'll find foie gras, duck and walnuts in various guises everywhere, but look out, too, for *pommes sarladaises*, potatoes crispy-fried in duck fat with lashings of garlic, parsley and, sometimes, mushrooms.

Restaurants

Le Bouffon 11 rue Albéric Cahuet ⓣ05.53.31.03.36. Reliable regional restaurant behind the Hôtel de Maleville, with outside seating in one of Sarlat's most medieval-looking courtyards. Menus cost between €15 and €25, the latter featuring some less ubiquitous dishes like pikeperch in a lemon sauce.

Chez Le Gaulois 1 rue Tourny ⓣ05.53.59.50.64. Charcuterie addicts will love this authentic little restaurant where cured Savoy, Corsican and Spanish hams and sausages hang from the ceiling. They're served, along with Savoy cheeses, in salads and open sandwiches (around €10–13) or you can buy to take away. Sept–May closed Sun & Mon.

Criquettamu's 5 rue des Armes ⓣ05.53.59.48.10. For something a bit different, give this quirky restaurant a go, where Perigordian staples are joined on the menus (from €19) by Middle Eastern flavours. Choose between duck breast with Sarladais potatoes and Lebanese lamb curry. Closed Oct–March.

Le Présidial 6 rue Landry ⓣ05.53.28.92.47. Consistently reliable and classy restaurant to the east of the centre in the former tribunal with a walled garden and airy, elegant rooms. This is one of the few places where it's worth spending more than the cheapest menu, with dishes like delicately spiced salmon tartare followed by veal kidneys in a mushroom sauce. Menus cost €19–39. Closed Sun, Mon lunchtime & mid-Nov to March.

Les Quatre Saisons 2 Côte de Toulouse ⓣ05.53.29.48.59. Along with the *Présidial*, this small restaurant is a cut above most of the competition. The cooking is refined and the dishes beautifully presented: try foie gras fried with apples and spices followed by tuna Rossini. The location is great too, off the main drag up a steep flight of steps into a quiet courtyard. Menus €20–49. Closed Tues & Wed in winter.

La Rapière place du Peyrou ⓣ05.53.59.03.13. Popular restaurant opposite the cathedral, known for its good choice of fresh fish dishes in addition to standard Périgord fare. You can eat on their terrace while examining the engaging facade of the Maison de La Boétie. Menus from €15. Reservations recommended at any time of year. Closed Jan.

Le Vin au 10 10 rue Fénelon ⓣ05.53.29.47.80. A stylish wine bar with a handful of tables outside. They serve a carefully selected range of wines from the region and further afield, with good meaty dishes (around €13) to accompany them. Alternatively there's a full, duck-heavy menu for €15.

Listings

Bike and scooter rental Bikes are available from Cycleo, 44 rue des Cordeliers (ⓣ05.53.31.90.05, ⓦwww.cycleo.fr), while MC Moto, 4 av de Selves (ⓣ05.53.59.06.11, ⓦwww.mcmoto24.com) rents out scooters (from €38 per day) and motorbikes (from €100 per day).
Bus departures Regional buses for Périgueux (Perigord Voyages; ⓣ05.53.59.01.48) and Souillac (SNCF; ⓣ05.53.59.00.21) depart from place Pasteur on the south side of town; Souillac-bound buses also call at the train station.
Canoe rental For canoe rental, head to Vitrac, 7km south of Sarlat, where two of the river's major canoe companies set up either side of the bridge: Copeyre Canoë (ⓣ05.53.28.23.82, ⓦwww.canoe-copeyre.com) and Canoë Loisirs (ⓣ05.53.28.23.43, ⓦwww.canoes-loisirs.com).
Car rental Europcar (ⓣ05.53.30.30.40) is on place de Lattre-de-Tassigny near the train station.
Hospital The Centre Hospitalier is on rue Jean Leclaire (ⓣ05.53.31.75.75) to the northeast of the centre.
Newspapers You'll find several English papers and the *International Herald Tribune* on sale around Sarlat. Try the Maison de la Presse at 34 rue de la République and 45 rue Gambetta.
Internet access Easy Planet, 16 av Gambetta (Mon–Sat 10am–7pm; €5 per hr).
Police Sarlat's Gendarmerie is at 1 bd Henri-Arlet ⓣ05.53.31.71.10.
Post office The main post office is at place du 14 Juillet, 24200 Sarlat.
Shopping While the markets are the best place to buy foie gras, walnuts, walnut oil, prunes and other local foods straight from the farmer, place de la Liberté, rue de la Liberté and rue des Consuls are full of speciality shops. On the former, the Distillerie du Périgord (ⓦwww.distillerie-perigord.com) makes delectable liqueurs from walnut and plum, amongst other things, and fruits in alcohol – try their Guinettes, containing local morello cherries. Ordinary groceries are available from the mini supermarket on rue de la République.
Taxis Allo Philippe Taxi ⓣ05.53.59.39.65; Brajot ⓣ05.53.59.41.13.

East and north of Sarlat

On the banks of the River Enéa, 9km east of Sarlat and 2km north of **STE-NATHALÈNE** on the Proissans road, a sixteenth-century water mill still grinds out walnut oil in time-honoured fashion. The pressing room of the **Moulin de la Tour** (30min guided tours: April & May Wed & Fri 9am–noon & 2–7pm; June & Sept also open Sat 2–7pm; July & Aug Mon, Wed, Fri 9am–noon & 2–6pm, Sat 2–6pm; Oct–March Fri 9am–noon & 2–6pm; €4.40; ⓦwww.moulindelatour.com), where creaking cog-wheels drive a cylindrical grinding stone set at right angles to the flat base, is dark, cosy and full of the most delicious aromas. Here the nuts – ready-shelled by local pensioners – are ground to a paste, heated gently over a wood fire and then pressed to extract the oil; an average pressing gives roughly fifteen litres of oil from thirty kilos of nuts. At the end of the guided visit, you get the opportunity to taste some of the produce. If you come on a day when the grinding room is not operating, only the shop (Mon–Sat 9am–noon & 2–7pm) will be open, selling the mill's own walnut, hazelnut and almond oils.

The River Enéa rises among oak woods on a plateau to the north of Ste-Nathalène. Though the hills appear scrubby and dry, one of the Enéa's tributaries is fed by seven springs, the same springs that prompted a seventeenth-century noble, Antoine de Costes de la Calprenède, to build a manor house here, the **Manoir d'Eyrignac**, and which now sustain his descendants' glorious **gardens**, signed to the northeast along back roads from Ste-Nathalène (daily: April 10am–7pm; May–Sept 9.30am–7pm; Oct–March 10.30am–12.30pm & 2.30pm–dusk; €9.50; house not open to the public; ⓦwww.eyrignac.com). The gardens aren't huge, but, consisting of lush evergreens – mainly hornbeam, box, cypress and yew – clipped and arranged in formal patterns of alleys and borders, achieve remarkable effects with almost no colour, the regimented lines softened by the occasional pavilion or fountain and by informal stands of trees framing the countryside around. The original formal garden was laid out by an eighteenth-century Italian landscaper, and later converted to an English romantic garden according to the fashion of the times. What you see today is the work of the last forty years, the creation of the present owner's father in a combination of Italian and French styles.

The complex also contains a small **exhibition hall** next to the ticket office, where you can watch a video about the garden and its history, and a snack bar. You can also bring your own food and take advantage of their picnic tables.

With time to spare, cut across country northwestwards to the cluster of buildings some 14km north of Sarlat known as **ST-GENIÈS**. It's a typical Périgord Noir village, with its partly ruined château and fortress-like church all constructed from the same warm-yellow stone under heavy *lauze* roofs. Unless it's market day (Sunday morning), it won't take long to explore, the only sight being the **Chapelle de Cheylard**, standing on its own on a small knoll to the east. The fourteenth-century frescoes inside have suffered over the years – at one time the chapel served as a dance hall – but a number remain visible, including St Michael weighing souls in a balance and a particularly manic bunch pelting St Stephen with stones.

West of Sarlat

Eight kilometres northwest of Sarlat on the D47, the **Château de Puymartin** (50min guided tours: April–June & Sept 10am–noon & 2–6pm; July 10am–noon & 2–6.30pm; Aug 10am–6.30pm; Oct to mid-Nov 2–5.30pm; €7; Ⓦwww.chateau-de-puymartin.com) stands guard over the headwaters of the Petite Beune river, which flows down to join the Vézère at Les Eyzies (see p.203). The castle, which underwent extensive remodelling in the seventeenth and nineteenth centuries, has been in the same family since 1450 and is remarkably well preserved. Among a large collection of family heirlooms, most noteworthy are the **tapestries**, particularly those in the grand hall, depicting the Siege of Troy. The Classical theme continues in the seventeenth-century trompe-l'oeil paintings on the chimneypiece here and in the guest bedroom, where Zeus visits Danaë in a shower of gold – presumably he would have been surprised to find her clothed and holding a cross, a liberty taken in the more puritanical 1800s. The same sensibilities demanded that a number of naked figures in the **mythological room** also be dressed. This is an extraordinary room, not large, but completely covered in monochrome scenes from mythology: snake-haired Medusa, Argus with his hundred eyes and Althaea murdering her son Maleagra by means of a burning brand. The general consensus is that the room was a place of meditation, though surprisingly it also served as a children's nursery for some time. Like all good castles, Puymartin also has its ghost, in this case La Dame Blanche, who supposedly haunts the north tower. In real life she was Thérèse de St-Clar, the lady of the

Autorail Espérance

In July and August a **tourist train**, the *Autorail Espérance*, runs along the Dordogne valley from Sarlat to Bergerac, via Lalinde and Le Buisson; various local products are served en route, including a glass of wine. The train departs from Sarlat mid-morning for the hour and a half-long journey (Mon–Sat), after which you return on a regular SNCF service. Tickets cost €13 return (there are no one-way fares) and reservations are required: phone Ⓣ05.53.59.55.39 to make a booking, or the Association l'Autorail Espérance on Ⓣ05.53.31.53.46 for further information.

Périgord walnuts

According to archeological evidence, **walnuts** have formed part of the Périgordin diet for more than 17,000 years. In medieval times, walnut oil was so valuable that it was sometimes used as a form of currency, and in the seventeenth century it was exported by river (via Bordeaux) to Britain, Holland and Germany. Walnuts are still central to the local economy today: rich in polyunsaturated fats, potassium, magnesium and vitamin E, both nuts and oil are marketed for their health-giving properties – they're said to help reduce cholesterol, stimulate the memory and protect against the effects of ageing. The nuts are also incorporated into bread, cakes, tarts and ice cream, or served whole with salads and the local *Cabécou* cheese. Green walnuts are often pickled in vinegar, but can also be made into jam or used to flavour wines and liqueurs. Not even the leaves are wasted: picked young, they give a distinctive tang to walnut apéritif.

In recognition of the walnut's importance to the economy – and indeed culture – of the region, four varieties (Grandjean, Marbot, Corne and Franquette) were granted an **Appellation d'Origine Contrôlée** (AOC) in 2002, to guarantee that you're buying only premium quality, locally grown produce. Walnuts are grown in the Lot, Corrèze and Charente *départements*, but the heart of the industry is the Dordogne, with more than 4000 hectares (40 square kilometres) of orchards. To capitalize on the AOC label, the local authorities have put together a **Route de la Noix**, along the Dordogne valley from Argentat to Beynac and north to Hautefort. Free leaflets outlining the four suggested itineraries are available from tourist offices, indicating producers and traditional oil mills open for visits as well as specialist patisseries and restaurants serving dishes with a nutty theme.

household during the sixteenth century, who, on being surprised in the arms of a lover, was walled up in the tower until she died fifteen years later. More prosaically, it's worth climbing up into the roof here to admire the elaborate timber framework supporting the *lauzes*.

At the opposite end of the architectural scale are the **Cabanes du Breuil** (April–Oct daily 10am–7pm; Nov–March Sat & Sun 2–6pm; €5; ⓦwww.cabanes-du-breuil.com), a couple of kilometres up in the hills to the northwest of Puymartin. You'll find these dry-stone circular huts under conical *lauze* roofs scattered throughout the region, but none so picturesque as this group belonging to a small, working farm. Known locally as *bories*, the huts were originally used for human habitation, then for animals or storage. In season (June–Sept) there's a video presentation explaining how the huts are made, but really these beautiful structures speak for themselves.

The Vézère valley and around

Billed as the "Vallée de l'Homme", the **Vézère valley** is home to the greatest concentration of **prehistoric sites** in Europe. They are by no means the oldest, but the sheer wealth and variety are quite stunning. It was here also that many important discoveries were made in the nineteenth and early twentieth centuries.

The valley, now listed by UNESCO as a World Heritage site, draws more than 300,000 visitors a year. The epicentre of all this activity is **Les Eyzies-de-Tayac**, where the National Museum of Prehistory contains many important finds and gives a good overview of what's on offer. The choice of sites nearby is bewildering, but at the very least you should visit the **Grotte de Font-de-Gaume** and the **Abri du Cap Blanc**, both in the Beune valley to the east of Les Eyzies and harbouring the best cave paintings and bas-relief sculptures still open to the public. Also within striking distance of Les Eyzies, this time to the north, are the **Grotte de Rouffignac**, one of the area's largest caves, with a breathtaking array of animal engravings accessible only by an underground electric train, and the **Château de l'Herm**, an evocative ruined castle with literary associations.

Back on the river Vézère, the market town of **Le Bugue** is a good place to base yourself, less dominated by tourism than Les Eyzies. It also gives access to the **Grotte du Sorcier**, with its highly significant human image, and to a different kind of cave, the stunning chasm of the **Gouffre de Proumeyssac**.

Alternatively, you can head north along the river from Les Eyzies to reach a more diverse collection of sights, ranging from the semi-troglodytic settlements at **La Madeleine** and **La Roque St-Christophe** – where a whole town was built into the cliff-face – to prehistoric theme parks and the appealing Renaissance castle, the **Château de Losse**. Finally you come to the pretty town of **Montignac**, just a couple of kilometres from the valley's biggest name, the cave of **Lascaux**. Lascaux itself has been closed to the public for nearly half a century, but its legendary paintings – with all their exceptional detail, colour and realism – have been faithfully reproduced in nearby **Lascaux II**.

Most of the Vézère sites can be visited only on **guided tours**. Some are offered in English, while others provide a translated text, but they are tiring – and the talks get repetitive – so select just a few of those covered below. At several caves, notably Font-de-Gaume and Lascaux II, visitor numbers are limited so you need to buy **tickets** in advance. And in high season it's best to go early in the morning or later in the day – or concentrate on the less well-known ones, some of which are every bit as enjoyable.

As far as **transport** is concerned, Le Bugue, Les Eyzies and Terrasson, the northern gateway to the valley, are accessible by train, while you can get to Montignac by bus from Sarlat if you plan carefully and don't mind an early start.

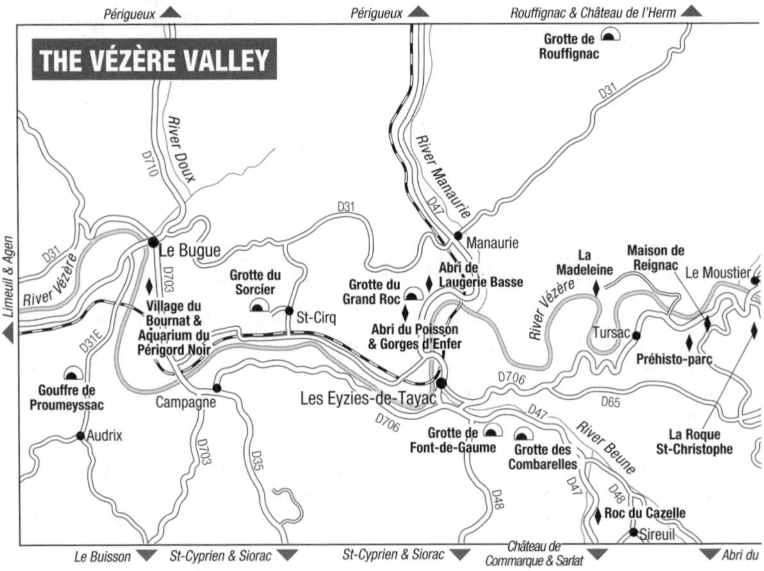

Most sights are at least a couple of kilometres away from these centres, though, so without your own vehicle you'll rely heavily on walking or taxis.

Les Eyzies-de-Tayac and around

The principal base for visiting the Vézère valley is **LES EYZIES-DE-TAYAC**, 20km northwest of Sarlat. Its location, between the river and a towering cliff, is dramatic, but the town consists of only one street and boasts nothing of interest apart from its national museum, home to the largest collection of Paleolithic art in France. While out of season it offers a good choice of hotels and restaurants, Les Eyzies gets completely overrun in summer.

Arrival and information

A stop on the Périgueux–Agen train line, Les Eyzies' **gare SNCF** lies about half a kilometre northwest of the centre just off the main road before you cross the river. The **tourist office** is right in the town centre (April–June Mon–Sat 9am–noon & 2–6pm, Sun 10am–noon & 2–5pm; July & Aug Mon–Sat 9am–7pm, Sun 10am–noon & 2–6pm; Sept & Oct Mon–Sat 9am–noon & 2–6pm; Nov–March Mon–Fri 9am–noon & 2–6pm, Sat 10am–noon & 2–5pm; Ⓣ05.53.06.97.05, Ⓦwww.tourisme-terredecromagnon.com). In addition to plentiful information on local sights, *chambres d'hôtes* and hiking trails, they also **exchange** cash (or there's a 24hr ATM outside) and have **internet** access (€6 per hour). You can also rent **bikes** and **cars** here (the latter through Avis, see p.28). If you need a **taxi**, call Taxi Tardieu (Ⓣ05.53.06.93.06). Les Eyzies is also the main base for **canoeing trips** on the Vézère. Several companies are clustered around the bridge just north of the town centre, including Canoës Vallée Vézère (Ⓣ05.53.05.10.11, Ⓦwww.canoesvalleevezere.com; mid-April to Sept) and AVCK (Ⓣ05.53.06.92.92, Ⓦwww.vezere-canoe.com; Easter to Sept); all operate by driving you upstream to Tursac (10km) or St-Léon (20km) before you canoe back down to finish where you started in Les Eyzies. The Vézère is narrower and quieter than the Dordogne, cutting a thin channel between high

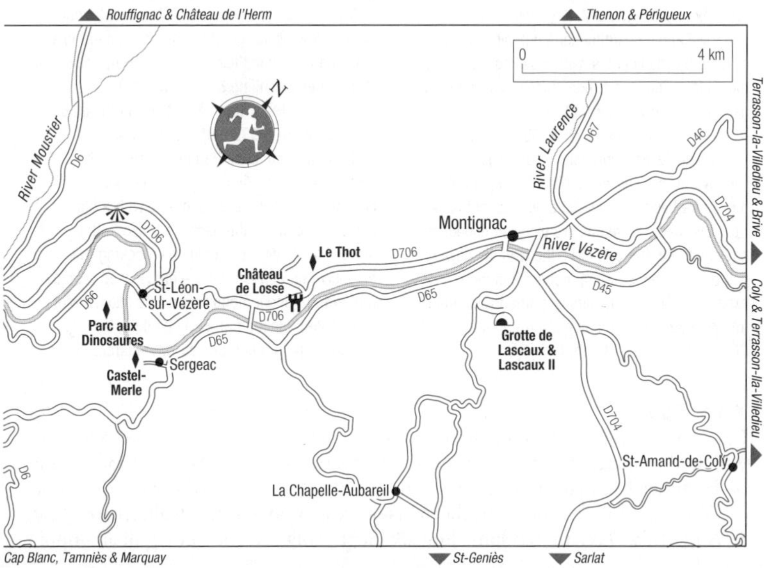

cliffs and wooded banks. The scenery is perhaps less dramatic than the château-studded stretch of the Dordogne around Beynac (see p.222), but you do pass beneath several of the troglodytic forts and dwellings covered below.

Accommodation

Most hotels in Les Eyzies are pricey and may require *demi-pension* in high season, when it's better to stay in one of the villages around. Note that most places close in winter, so it's essential to have a reservation if you're visiting between October and April.

In Les Eyzies

Le Cro-Magnon ⓣ05.53.06.97.06, ⓦwww.hostellerie-cro-magnon.com. Just down the road from the station, the *Cro-Magnon* is a sunny, inviting building with yellow shutters and ivy-covered walls. Rooms are bright with all the necessary comforts and there are good communal areas, with open hearths, armchairs and a small library. The restaurant (€13 lunch, €23–42 eves) serves hearty regional food, including good lamb dishes in season. Closed mid-Nov to mid-March. ⑤

Hotel des Falaises ⓣ05.53.06.97.35, ⓔhotel-d-falaises@wanadoo.fr. The best-value rooms in Les Eyzies are located behind a central café run by a friendly owner. They're bright and cheerful, clean and well-kept. All are en-suite (though there's no TV) and the marginally more expensive ones (②) have their own balconies. Free private parking available; open all year on reservation. ②

Les Glycines ⓣ05.53.06.97.07, ⓦwww.les-glycines-dordogne.com. Les Eyzies' most beguiling hotel by some distance stands just north of the centre, back from the main road. It's a romantic place, with light, airy rooms, full of drapes and frills, and a beautiful garden behind, criss-crossed by shady paths, with a swimming pool in the middle. The nicest rooms open directly onto the garden. Closed Nov–Feb. ⑥–⑦

Hostellerie du Passeur ⓣ05.53.06.97.13, ⓦwww.hostellerie-du-passeur.com. The ivy-covered *du Passeur* is in a prime spot right in the centre beside the tourist office, but set back from the road. The rooms are pleasant enough and have all three-star comforts; those in the newer half of the hotel are more modern and more expensive (⑦). Downstairs is a smart restaurant (menus €32–49) with a super terrace by the river. Closed early Nov to March. ⑤

Le Moulin de la Beune ⓣ05.53.06.94.33, ⓦwww.moulindelabeune.com. A pretty, converted mill building on the southern edge of Les Eyzies, this old-fashioned hotel has simple, spacious rooms, some looking out onto its peaceful garden and the rushing stream. There is also a lovely restaurant, *Au Vieux Moulin* (see opposite), so it's well worth considering the half-board option. Closed Nov–March. ③

La Rivière 3 route du Sorcier ⓣ05.53.06.97.14, ⓦwww.lariviereleseyzies.com. A good, inexpensive choice about 1km from Les Eyzies on the Périgueux road. There are just six unfussy rooms, all en suite, in a typical Périgord farmhouse with access to a pool, bar, laundry and a simple restaurant. There's also a well-tended, three-star campsite, which shares the same facilities as the hotel. Closed Nov to early April. ②

Around Les Eyzies-de-Tayac

La Grange du Mas 5km east of Les Eyzies ⓣ05.53.29.66.07, ⓦwww.grange-du-mas.com. Welcoming *ferme-auberge* with five simple rooms just outside the village of Sireuil. You can eat foie gras and truffles in their rustic hall. Menus €18–32; closed Tues lunchtime & Oct–March. ②

Hôtel Laborderie Tamniès, 13km northeast of Les Eyzies ⓣ05.53.29.68.59, ⓦwww.hotel-laborderie.com. Perched north up the Beune valley, this geranium-decked hotel occupies four separate buildings, with a big choice of rooms – the best are those in the newer blocks with balconies overlooking the extensive garden and pool – and a good restaurant with regional menus from €22 (closed Mon, Tues & Wed lunchtime). Early booking is advisable in summer. Closed Nov–March. ③–⑤

The Town

Les Eyzies' single, unnamed street runs parallel to the jutting limestone cliff which dominates the town. Beneath its overhang, Paul Dardé's 1930 statue of Neanderthal man, portrayed as an ape-like hunk, stands staring out over the Vézère, while beside him, the **Musée National de la Préhistoire** (July & Aug daily 9.30am–6.30pm; June & Sept daily except Tues 9.30am–6pm;

Oct–May daily except Tues 9.30am–12.30pm & 2–5.30pm; €5; Ⓦwww.musee-prehistoire-eyzies.fr) occupies the remains of a castle built into the rock as well as a striking new building built around it. The museum contains a vast array of increasingly sophisticated stone tools of the Paleolithic era (two million to 10,000 years ago). The first floor is devoted to blades found at various archeological sites, accompanied by some rather more engaging short films showing how these blades were made and then used. Upstairs are some good recreations (and the odd original) of engravings and sculptures from the era.

In the late nineteenth century local farmer Martial Pataud discovered prehistoric remains when he was cutting a new road beside what is now the National Museum. The rock-shelter (*abri*), which had been occupied for over 15,000 years before the roof collapsed around 20,000 years ago, yielded a rich hoard of finds, a selection of which are now on display in the next-door **Musée de l'Abri Pataud** (1hr guided visit: Feb–March & mid-Nov to Dec Mon–Thurs 10am–12.30pm & 2–5.30pm; April–June & Sept to mid-Nov daily except Sat 10am–noon & 2–6pm; July & Aug daily 10am–7pm; closed Jan; €6), occupying what was previously the Patauds' wine cellar. Much of the excavation was carried out in the late 1950s and early 1960s, one of the first "modern" digs which enabled unusually precise analysis of the successive human occupations – unless you're an archeology buff this may not seem hugely exciting, but the guide's explanations help sort out all the different eras mentioned at other sites. The most famous find is the female figurine known as the **Vénus à la Corne** ("Venus with a Horn"). The exaggerated bas-relief, with her pendulous breasts and stout hips, now resides in Bordeaux's Musée d'Aquitaine (see p.72). Archeologists also found eleven skeletons, including a young mother with her newborn baby wearing a necklace; she is now closer at hand in the National Museum, though there's a copy here alongside a bronze statue modelled from her bone structure. Look out, too, for the enchanting little ibex (*bouquetin*) carved on the museum's rock ceiling.

If you're here in summer and feel the need to get a bit of space from the crowds on the main street, head down to the riverbank, where there's a nice picnic area and riverside path, or 500m past the railway station to the twelfth-century **fortified church** of Tayac. Nobody ever went to much effort to prettify it, but it's a forbidding defensive structure, with no steeples, but two broad parapets to give archers a proper shot at any attackers.

Eating

The finest **restaurants** in Les Eyzies belong to the town's hotels. One of the best is the *Au Vieux Moulin* (Ⓣ05.53.06.94.33; closed lunchtimes Tues, Wed & Sat), attached to the *Moulin de la Beune* hotel, where you can enjoy great dishes like truffle risotto or lightly smoked salmon with spinach sitting either in the old-fashioned, stone-walled dining room, or outside in the garden where the tiny river Beune rushes past. The prices are great too, with full menus costing €18–32. If you want the very best cooking, try the restaurant at *Les Glycines* (see opposite), where the lunch menu is €28 and dinner €49 – or splash out on the tremendous truffle menu at €95. For cheaper meals, stick to the hotel restaurants, or the clutch of cheap-and-cheerful brasseries around the tourist office. There is also a pair of perfectly respectable pizzerias on the main street, both with pleasant terraces.

Grotte de Font-de-Gaume

Since they were first discovered in 1901, over two hundred Magdalenian-era (18,000–10,000 years old) polychrome paintings and engravings have been found in the narrow tunnel of the **Grotte de Font-de-Gaume** (45min guided tours daily except Sat: May 15–Sept 15 9.30am–5.30pm; Sept 16–May 14 9.30am–12.30pm & 2–5.30pm; €7; ⓣ05.53.06.86.00), just over a kilometre east of Les Eyzies along the D47 to Sarlat. In order to preserve them, only 180 people are allowed to enter the cave each day, in groups of twelve. It is essential to book ahead by phone at least a week in advance in July and August (or further ahead for larger groups), and you may be required to pay by credit card when you make your booking. If you haven't done so, it's still worth enquiring on site first thing in the morning as some tickets may be held back to be sold on the day.

The cave mouth is no more than a fissure concealed by rocks and trees above a small, lush valley. Inside is a narrow twisting passage of irregular height over 100m long, where you quickly lose your bearings in the dark. The majority of the **paintings** depict bison, but also horses, mammoths, reindeer and wild cats, and many unexplained signs such as the so-called "**tectiforms**", comprising a very gently inclined, upside down "V" with vertical lines beneath. The first you come to is a frieze of bison at about eye level: reddish-brown in colour, massive, full of movement and an almost palpable force. Further on a horse stands with one hoof slightly raised, resting, another appears to be galloping or jumping, and, in a breathtakingly tender depiction, one reindeer gently licks another's nose. But the most miraculous painting of all is a frieze of five bison discovered in 1966. The colour, remarkably sharp and vivid, is preserved by a protective layer of calcite. Shading under the belly and down the thighs is used to add volume with a sophistication that seems utterly modern. Another panel consists of **superimposed drawings**, a fairly common phenomenon in cave-painting, sometimes the result of work by successive generations, but here an obviously deliberate technique: a reindeer in the foreground shares legs with a large bison to indicate perspective.

Grotte des Combarelles and Roc de Cazelle

The myriad engravings of the **Grotte des Combarelles** (1hr guided tours same hours as Font-de-Gaume; €7), a short distance further along the D47, were discovered a few days before Font-de-Gaume in 1901. Only five decorated caves had been discovered prior to this, and with the jury still out on primitive man's artistic abilities, they were an incredibly significant find. As with Font-de-Gaume, visitor numbers are restricted (there's a maximum of six people per tour) and pre-booking is recommended, especially in peak season; apply to the Font-de-Gaume booking office (see above).

Again, you make your way down a long, claustrophobic tunnel, stopping every now and then while the guide picks out a tiny selection of the six-hundred-plus **engravings** identified so far. It is a veritable Magdalenian menagerie: mostly horses, but also bison, reindeer, mammoths, rhinos, bears, ibex, aurochs and wild cats; stylized human figures and geometric symbols also feature. A good deal of imagination is required to recognize some of the fainter outlines, often superimposed one upon another, while others are astounding in their simplicity and realistic treatment – among the finest are the heads of a horse and a lioness, where the dips and projections in the rock provide eyes, nostrils and even bone structure.

Continue along the D47 for another couple of kilometres and you'll be greeted by mammoths roaring and the sound of people chipping flints at **Roc de Cazelle** (daily: March, April, Oct & Nov 10am–6pm; May, June & Sept 10am–7pm; July & Aug 10am–8pm; Dec–Feb 11am–5pm; €6.80; ⓦwww.rocdecazelle.com), a theme park that reconstructs life 12,000 years ago. It's really best for children, but the imaginative design helps bring the surrounding caves to life. Various scenes – from hunting and gathering to painting and sculpting – are scattered around a wooded valley once occupied by prehistoric man, culminating in a real troglodyte fortress and a troglodyte farm that was inhabited up to the 1960s.

Abri du Cap Blanc and beyond

Not a cave but a natural rock-shelter, the **Abri du Cap Blanc** (45min guided tours daily except Sat: mid-May to mid-Sept 9.30am–6.30pm; mid-Sept to mid-May 9.30am–12.30pm & 2–5.30pm; €7) lies on a steep wooded hillside above the River Beune about 7km east of Les Eyzies; it's signed left off the D47 shortly after the Grotte des Combarelles. The shelter contains a superb **sculpted frieze** of horses and bison dating from the middle Magdalenian period (16,000–13,000 years ago), discovered in 1909 behind thick layers of sediment. Unfortunately, the excavation was carried out in such a hurry that the frieze had been badly damaged before anyone realized it was there. Even so, it is quite remarkable, mainly for its scale – the middle horse, which closely resembles the wild Przewalski horse of Central Asia, is virtually life-size – but also the depth of some of the sculptures. The bodies were obviously polished to set them off against the rough background, while traces of ochre and manganese pigments indicate that they were also painted at one time.

Continuing up the Beune valley from Cap Blanc you come to the elegant sixteenth-century Château de Laussel (closed to the public) and, on the opposite side, the romantic ruins of the **Château de Commarque** (daily: April 10am–6pm; May, June & Sept 10am–7pm; July & Aug 10am–8pm; €6.40; Ⓦwww.commarque.com). Dating from the twelfth century, Commarque was a **castrum** – a fortified village made up of six separate fortresses, each belonging to a different noble family, of which the best preserved is that built by the powerful Beynac clan in the fourteenth century. The site was abandoned some two hundred years later, then left to moulder until the late 1960s when the present owner, Henri de Commarque, came to the rescue. The ruins have now been made structurally sound and it's possible once again to climb the Beynac's thirty-metre-high tower for views over the surrounding countryside. The easiest way to reach the château is by a footpath starting below Cap Blanc. Cars have to approach it from the south, following signs from the D47 Sarlat road; note that it's about six hundred metres' walk from the car park to the entrance.

Grotte du Grand Roc and around

Two kilometres north of Les Eyzies on the D47 to Périgueux, the entrance to the **Grotte du Grand Roc** (35min guided tours daily: Easter–June, Sept & Oct 10am–6pm; July & Aug 9.30am–7pm; €7.50; Ⓦwww.grandroc.com) lies under the cliffs that line much of the Vézère valley. There's a great view from the mouth of the cave and, inside, along some 80m of tunnel, a fantastic array of **rock formations**. Most unusual are the still-unexplained *excentriques* growing in all directions and triangles formed by calcite crystallizing in still, shallow pools.

The cave was discovered in 1924 in the continuing search for prehistoric art; sixty years earlier Edouard Lartet and Henry Christy had discovered a rock-shelter further along the same cliff. The **Abri de Laugerie Basse** (same hours as Grotte du Grand Roc; €6) was inhabited almost constantly over the last 15,000 years – most recently in the form of farmhouses built against the rock – and yielded hundreds of **engravings** and **sculptures**, not on the rock face but on pieces of bone or fashioned out of individual stones. The majority date from the late Magdalenian period (13,000–10,000 years ago) when prehistoric art reached its peak. They include a mysterious engraving of a very pregnant woman lying under a reindeer, and a sculpted female torso, the first so-called "Venus figure" – obviously symbols of fertility, though it's not known whether they relate to fertility rites – discovered in France. These and other important finds are presented in a slide-show before visiting the shelter; there's little to see otherwise, though during the visit you learn a lot about the history of the excavations and what conditions were like during the Magdalenian era.

More interesting, though, is the **Abri du Poisson** (1hr guided tours daily except Sat, by appointment only, ⓣ05.53.06.86.00; €3), which lies on the road from Les Eyzies just before the Grotte du Grand Roc. The rock-shelter – one of many along a side valley – contains one of the very few sculpted fish in prehistoric art. It's a real beauty too, a metre-long male salmon, complete with gills and beak, probably carved about 25,000 years ago. The deep-cut rectangular outline is not a prehistoric picture-frame, however, but the remains of an abortive attempt by a Berlin museum to acquire the salmon soon after it was discovered in 1912. Since then the shelter has been kept sealed up and can now be visited by a maximum of forty people per day.

Rouffignac and the Château de l'Herm

Soon after Grand Roc, the D47 turns northwest to follow the Manaurie valley. Seven kilometres beyond the village of **MANAURIE**, you'll pass a right turn signed to the **Grotte de Rouffignac** (1hr guided tours daily: April–June, Sept & Oct 10–11.30am & 2–5pm; July & Aug 9–11.30am & 2–6pm; €6.30; ⓦwww.grottederouffignac.fr), another 7km uphill among dense woods; unfortunately the tour is in French only and there's no English-language leaflet. It starts with a one-kilometre ride on a little electric train along the bed of an underground river that dried up about three million years ago. On the way the guide points out where hibernating bears scratched their nests and human visitors left their mark in the form of graffiti – including a priest, Abbé de la Tour, in 1808. In fact records show that the cave was known about in the sixteenth century, but it took until 1956 before the 13,000-year-old monochromatic drawings and engravings were recognized. Around 270 animal figures have been identified so far, the vast majority of which are mammoths, including a superb patriarch, his great tusks arcing under a piercing eye. Most dramatic is the final chamber, when you descend from the train to wander around beneath a ceiling covered with mammoths, woolly rhino, horses, bison and ibex. When these drawings were done, the cave here was less than a meter high – proof that the authors were prepared to suffer for their art, and of their mysterious obsession with penetrating as deep into these caves as possible.

The cave is located about 5km south of **ROUFFIGNAC** town, which was destroyed by German troops in 1944 and subsequently rebuilt. They drove everyone out before torching it; the only buildings to survive were the church, with its carved portal and unusual, twisted columns inside, and the adjacent house. Four kilometres further north, the **Château de l'Herm** (April to mid-Nov daily 10am–7pm; €6; ⓣ05.53.05.46.61, ⓦwww.chateaudelherm.com) also has an unhappy history, in this case a complicated tale of murders, forced marriages and disputed inheritance rights. In the end the castle was abandoned and has been crumbling away for more than three centuries to leave an atmospheric ruin engulfed by trees. Two big round towers and some decorative touches from the fifteenth and sixteenth centuries remain: a late Gothic doorway opens onto a spiral stone staircase, at the top of which is a beautifully worked palm-tree vault, while three sculpted fireplaces cling one above the other to the wall of an otherwise empty shell. At the bottom of the keep, you

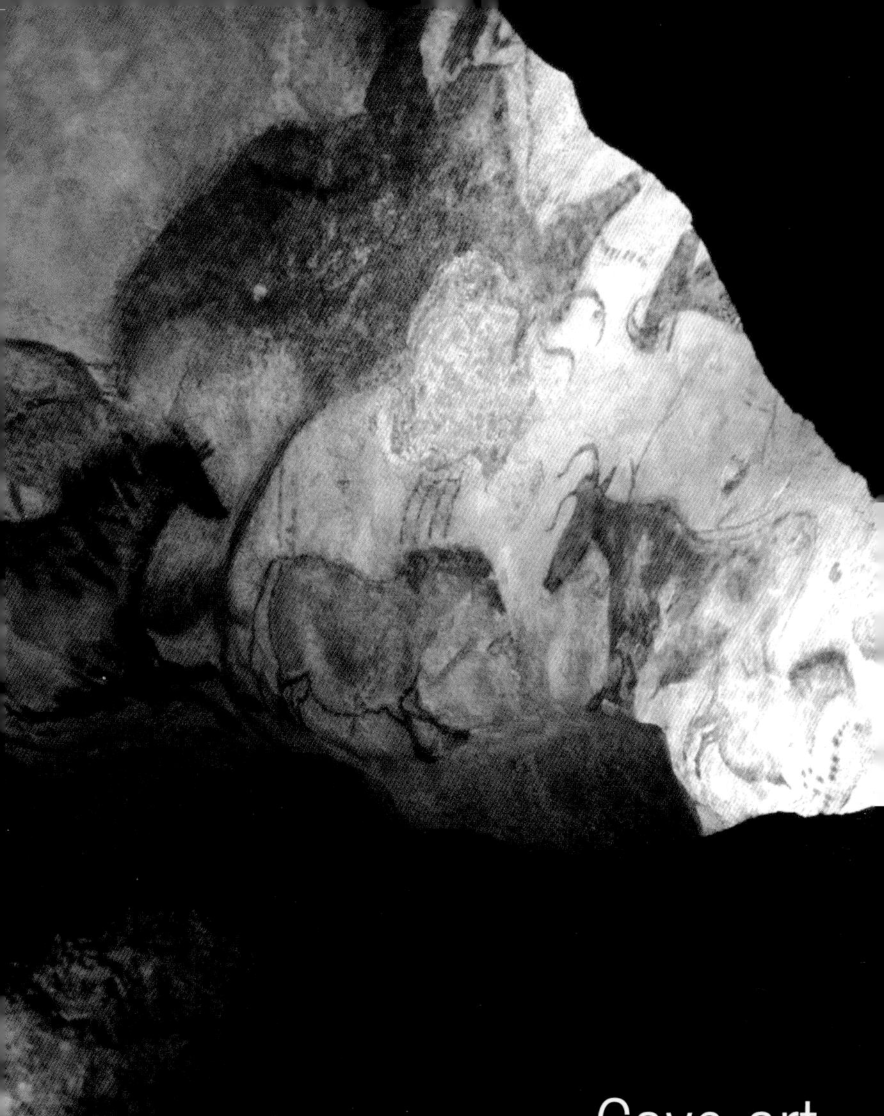

Cave art

Thousands of years ago early inhabitants of the Dordogne and Lot region created some of the most expressive and moving prehistoric paintings, engravings and reliefs ever seen anywhere in the world. While these stunning works of art lie scattered throughout the area, hidden deep within limestone caves and on cliff walls, by far the greatest concentration is in the Vézère valley in the heart of the Dordogne.

Early man, hunting ▲

A Magdalenian-era horse ▼

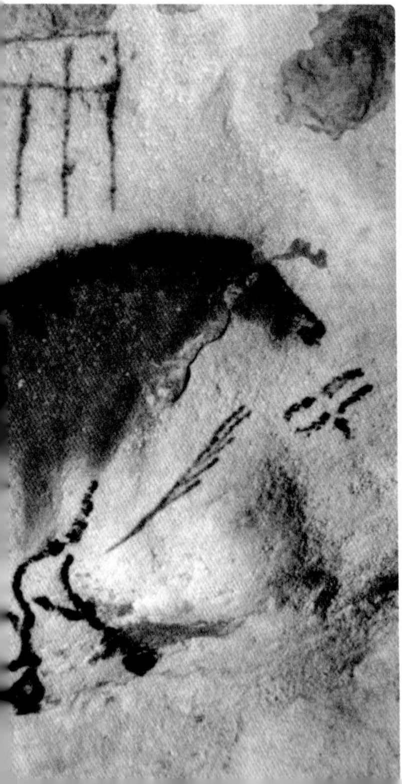

The first artists

The **Cro-Magnon** people swept across Europe 40,000 or so years ago, and are responsible for the earliest cave art in the region. Named after a rock-shelter near Les Eyzies, where the first skeletons were discovered, they were a nomadic people, who tracked herds of reindeer across what was then steppe, occasionally settling in riverside rock-shelters under overhanging cliffs. They developed increasingly sophisticated tools using bone, ivory and antlers and later crafted ornaments such as necklaces. Some 20,000 years ago, the Cro-Magnon had honed their artistic skills sufficiently to depict supremely **realistic animals** on the walls of their rock-shelters, by means of engraving and sculpting with flints or painting with dyes made from charcoal, manganese dioxide and red ochre.

Magdalenian era

So-called after another archeological site in the Vézère valley, the **Magdalenian** era specifies approximately 17,000 years ago, when there was a real explosion in the quantity and level of sophistication of prehistoric art. It was prompted by the use of the **tallow lamp**, fuelled with reindeer fat, which allowed artists to penetrate deep within the limestone caves. Here they covered the walls of passages and cavern ceilings with hundreds of drawings, paintings and engravings. In some places artists used the natural contours of the rock to produce supremely realistic, almost 3-D representations of horses, bison and other animals. There are even drawings almost like caricatures, in which mammoths are portrayed with just a couple of lines. The occasional **human** figures also appear, most spectacularly in the Grotte du Sorcier (see p.211).

Top 6 caves for art

▸▸ **Lascaux II** Superb replica of the summit of Cro-Magnon art. See p.216

▸▸ **Grotte de Font-de-Gaume** Beautifully preserved paintings and engravings in a narrow tunnel. See p.205

▸▸ **Abri du Cap Blanc** Sculpted frieze of life-size horses and bisons. See p.207

▸▸ **Grotte de Pech-Merle** "The chapel of mammoths" stands out among more than five hundred drawings. See p.282

▸▸ **Grotte de Rouffignac** Hop on an electric train to view drawings of mammoths and woolly rhino in a kilometre-long cave. See p.208

▸▸ **Grotte de Sorcier** Mystifying engraving of a human – the "Sorcier" – among many animals. See p.211

Magic, ritual or art?

Why exactly did these cave-dwellers dedicate such skill and time to the art? It's a question that evokes endless debate and varying opinion. Some scholars believe that the cave engravings were some form of **ritual** practice or **magic** to evoke a successful hunt, while others think they have a **shamanistic** role, with the animals advancing into the caves as into the afterlife. It's likely that the significance of the caves was in some way **spiritual**, but the exact nature of the relationship between Cro-Magnon people and their art remains opaque. You'll often hear guides at the sites lament the fact that we know so little, but perhaps the desire for categorical meaning misses the point – that the paintings and engravings reveal a desire to capture elusive, transcendant beauty – or in other words, "art for art's sake". Whatever the truth, not knowing certainly adds to the wonder and magic of these caves.

▲ Lascaux II

The Grotte de Rouffignac ▲

National Museum of Prehistory ▼

Guide to the caves

- Visitor numbers to most caves are severely restricted, either for conservation reasons or, in the case of Lascaux II (see p.216), simply because the site can only hold up to forty people at a time.
- At all of the caves you have to join a guided tour, which usually lasts 30–40min.
- At the most popular caves – Lascaux II (see p.216), Grotte de Font-de-Gaume (see p.205) Grottes de Cambarelles (see p.206), among others – you have to buy tickets in advance by phoning the ticket office or visiting in person. It's best to buy your tickets at least a week in advance, sometimes longer during peak periods.
- Unless you're a real prehistory buff, limit yourself to just two or three sites, rather than risk losing that sense of magic.
- The remote location of the caves makes them hard to access for travellers with disabilities. As a reconstruction, Lascaux II is one of the more accessible but if you're in doubt, it's best to ask.

Learn more

▸▸ **Musée National de la Préhistoire** This museum's vast collection of archeological finds crowns Les Eyzies as the "capital of prehistory". See p.204

▸▸ **Roc de Cazelle** An interactive and dramatic introduction to the people behind the art – particularly suitable for children. See p.206

▸▸ **Castel-Merle** A very under-rated site with passionate staff, it's also the only place in the region where you can still see excavations in progress. See p.214

▸▸ **Prehistoric Art in Europe by N K Sanders (Yale)** The foremost study on prehistoric art, placing the French examples in an international context. Academic but readable, with illustrations.

can still distinguish the castle's grim-looking dungeons. It was these evocative ruins, looking out over the thickly wooded country where rural rebels thrived, which inspired Eugène Le Roy for his novel *Jacquou le Croquant* (see p.369), in which a nineteenth-century rebellion culminates in the Château de l'Herm being burned to the ground.

Le Bugue and around

LE BUGUE lies on the north bank of a meander in the Vézère 11km downstream from Les Eyzies, and is a good alternative base. It's not only less crowded in season but is also a more attractive town, with a riverfront setting and scattering of old houses along the River Doux, which flows into the Vézère here. On Tuesdays and Saturdays, the town comes alive with one of the better markets in the area.

Arrival and information

Trains on the Périgueux–Agen line pull into Le Bugue's **gare SNCF**, roughly 2km southeast on the D703; call Taxis Sourbier (ⓣ05.53.07.41.35) if you need a taxi. Note that the station is unstaffed and you can't buy tickets here. There is an **SNCF ticket office** in the town centre next to the tourist office (ⓣ05.53.07.20.05; Mon–Fri 9.30am–12.30pm & 2–6pm) or you can buy a ticket on the train. The **tourist office** (April–June Mon–Sat 9.30am–12.30pm & 2–6pm, Sun 10am–noon & 2–5pm; July & Aug Mon–Sat 9.30am–6.30pm, Sun 10am–1pm & 2–5pm; Sept & Oct Mon–Sat 9.30am–12.30pm & 2–6pm; Nov–March Tues–Sat 9.30am–12.30pm & 2–6pm; ⓣ05.53.07.20.48, ⓦwww.tourisme-terredecromagnon.com) is on the river bank a short walk west of place de la Mairie. **Canoe rental** is available from Canoëric (ⓣ05.53.03.51.99, ⓦwww.canoe-perigord.com), beside the Village du Bournat. For **internet**, head to the tourist office or the *Hôtel de Paris* (see below).

Accommodation

In Le Bugue

Le Cygne 2 rue du Cingle ⓣ05.53.06.01.16, ⓦwww.lecygne-perigord.com. The best hotel in Le Bugue is this friendly, good-value place opposite the tourist office with very comfortable, bright rooms and an excellent traditional restaurant offering menus from €22 (closed Fri eve, Sun eve & Mon). ❸

Hôtel de Paris 14 rue de Paris ⓣ05.53.07.28.16, ⓦwww.hotel-bugue-perigord.com. This old-fashioned budget hotel has cheap rooms above a bar, all with en-suite showers and television. ❶–❷

Les Trois Caupain Le Port ⓣ05.53.07.24.60, ⓦwww.camping-des-trois-caupain.com. A three-star campsite with pool and other facilities located on the riverbank on the eastern edge of the town. Closed Nov–March.

Around Le Bugue

Camping Brin d'Amour St-Cirq ⓣ05.53.07.23.73, ⓦwww.brindamourcamping.com. Up in the hills north of St-Cirq, midway between Le Bugue and Les Eyzies, this three-star campsite is an excellent choice if you've got your own transport: small, friendly, well-run and lacking the regimented feel of so many sites. Closed Nov–March.

Hôtel du Château Le Bourg, Campagne ⓣ05.53.07.23.50, ⓔhotduchateau@aol.com. A traditional sort of place with big, bright rooms and a good regional restaurant (menus €20–45). It's located in Campagne, a pretty village gathered round a château and diminutive church, well-positioned between Le Bugue and Les Eyzies. Closed mid-Oct to Easter. ❸

Hôtel Les Fontenilles 10 route de Campagne ⓣ05.53.07.24.97, ⓦwww.hotel-lesfontenilles.com. Set back from the D703 on a hilltop between Le Bugue and Campagne, this is a friendly, country option with just six simple rooms, a pool and a decent restaurant (menus from €16). ❸

La Maison Oléa La Combe de Leygue ⓣ05.53.08.48.93, ⓦwww.olea-dordogne.com. Two kilometres out of town in the direction of Sarlat, this *chambre d'hôte* has three pretty rooms and two suites for families. All five have private balconies with good views of the surrounding countryside, and there's a heated swimming pool. ❹

The Town

The heart of Le Bugue is place de la Mairie, the town centre and market square, from where there are good views in both directions along the river. From here, rue de Paris, the main shopping street, heads north towards Le Bugue's old quarter around the generously named Grande Rue, while the D703, heading southeast along the river, takes you out past the town's two rather second-tier sights.

The more interesting, particularly for younger children, is the **Village du Bournat** (daily: March, April, Oct & Nov 10am–5pm; May, June & Sept 10am–6pm; July & Aug 10am–7pm; July & Aug €12, rest of year €10; Ⓦwww.lebournat.fr), a fair recreation of a Périgord village in the early 1900s complete with *lauze*-roofed cottages, chapel, schoolhouse, baker, café and so forth. The entry price seems expensive, but there's a lot to see, including demonstrations of local crafts, such as clog- and barrel-making, potting and basketry, and you can come and go as you please within a day. Next door, the **Aquarium du Périgord Noir** (daily: Feb, March, Oct & Nov 1–5pm; April, May & Sept 10am–6pm; June 10am–7pm; July & Aug 9am–7pm; €9.90; Ⓦwww.parc-aquarium.com) has a large collection of freshwater fish – kept for the most part in open tanks, some of which you can walk under. At set times each day you can watch – and children can assist with – the feeding of the more benign species. The aquarium has also recently expanded to include an indoor reptile zone, full of coils of snakes and bored-looking iguanas.

Eating

Le Bugue's best **restaurant** is *L'Abreuvoir*, tucked away at 31 Grande Rue, off rue de Paris (Ⓣ05.53.03.45.45; closed Sat lunch and Sun eve). There's a cosy, romantic dining room, and a shady wooden terrace for summer. Main courses cost around €12, with some particularly good fish dishes on offer. Alternatively, try the restaurant at the *Royal Vézère* hotel, in the town centre by the river (Ⓣ05.53.07.20.01), which serves decent traditional cuisine (menus €18–38) and is in prime position with a terrace jutting out over the river.

The Gouffre de Proumeyssac

High-tech has hit the Vézère in a big way at the **Gouffre de Proumeyssac** (45min guided tours daily: Feb, Nov & Dec 2–5pm; March, April, Sept & Oct 9.30am–noon & 2–5.30pm; May & June 9.30am–6.30pm; July & Aug 9am–7pm; €8.40), a vast and spectacular limestone cavern 5km south of Le Bugue on the D31E. Its forty-metre-high vault dripping with multicoloured stalactites, ranging from fine needles to massive petrified waterfalls, is dubbed the "crystal cathedral". To heighten the sense of atmosphere you enter in the dark, then the music builds as lights pick out various formations before revealing the whole chamber in a grand finale. It's cleverly done, though some will find it too commercialized, even down to stacks of calcite-coated pottery souvenirs, and a far cry from when the cave was first opened in 1907. At that time the only way in was via a basket lowered through a hole in the roof under flickering torchlight – you can still make the descent by two-person basket for €16.50 per person including the entry fee. Even before the chasm was fully explored and its size and beauty discovered, it had a gruesome notoriety in local folklore: it gets a mention in Eugène Le Roy's 1899 work *Jacquou le Croquant* as the "*Trou de Pomeissac* near Le Bugue, into which so many people had been thrown after being murdered on the neighbouring highway, that the hole had to be blocked up..."

Audrix

Two kilometres further on up the hill from the chasm, you reach the tiny, picturesque hamlet of **AUDRIX**, with a few houses clustered around a simple twelfth-century Romanesque church and superb views out over the surrounding countryside. Audrix is also home to a hidden gem of a **hotel-restaurant**, *L'Auberge Médiévale* (Ⓣ05.53.07.24.02, Ⓦwww.auberge-medievale.fr; closed Nov to mid-March; ❷), with eight pretty rooms, all with en-suite facilities and views either of the church or the valley below. The restaurant serves delicious regional cuisine (menus €14.50–30) and in summer you can sit out in the shade of a rose-draped trellis; it really is one of the most peaceful and idyllic spots in the region.

The Grotte du Sorcier

If you take the D703 south from Le Bugue and turn left down a quiet back road just before crossing the railway line, you come to the village of **ST-CIRQ**, halfway to Les Eyzies. St-Cirq is known above all for the **Grotte du Sorcier** (daily: March, April & Sept–Nov 10am–6pm; May & June 10am–6.30pm; July & Aug 10am–7.30pm; Dec–Feb 11am–5pm; €6.50; Ⓦwww.grottedusorcier.com), a shallow cave with some thirty engravings dating from between seventeen and nineteen thousand years ago. Most are animals (look at the tremendous depiction of the horse turning its head back towards the entrance), but the most significant is the "Sorcerer" himself, a rare image of a human being in Magdalenian cave art. The enigmatic figure has been interpreted in countless ways: as a fertility symbol, half man and half pregnant woman; as a shaman or spiritual leader, with his musical instrument and dancing legs; or indeed as a man's head with the body of a horse. However you choose to see him, he's fascinating as a counterpoint to the supremely realistic animals you see elsewhere: the Sorcerer is not a naturalist image, and so is compelling evidence of ancient cave art's figurative or metaphorical purpose. After the guided tour of the cave, have a quick look around the site's **museum**, a collection of blades and fossils dating from different eras in which it was occupied.

The Vézère between Les Eyzies and Montignac

To the northeast of Les Eyzies, the D706 follows the river all the way to **Montignac**, taking you past a range of sights appealing to all ages, and the prettiest village in the whole valley – **St-Léon-sur-Vézère**. The village of **Tursac**, 5km upstream from Les Eyzies, is a good place to base yourself as an alternative to Les Eyzies.

La Madeleine

First stop northeast along the Vézère is a semi-troglodytic medieval settlement on the north bank of the river 7km upstream from Les Eyzies. **La Madeleine** (daily: July & Aug 10am–8pm; Sept–June 10am–6pm; €5.50; Ⓦwww.village-la-madeleine.com) lies near the neck of a huge meander, where the Vézère takes a 3km loop to cover less than 100m as the crow flies. The cliffs here have been inhabited on and off for the last fifteen thousand years. Indeed, the prehistoric rock-shelter down by the water's edge yielded such a wealth of late-Paleolithic tools and engravings that archeologists named the era Magdalenian; one of the more intriguing finds was a carving of a man with a bestial head, believed to be a mask, now on display at Les Eyzies' museum (see p.205). Further up the cliff subsequent settlers constructed a whole village complete with fortress, drawbridge, village square and chapel, all dating back to the tenth century. La Madeleine was inhabited until 1920 and the Resistance (see p.365) used it as a hideout, but now the chapel is the only building completely intact. Nevertheless, enough remains to give a good sense of what such cliff-dwellings were like.

Préhisto-parc and Reignac

Plastic Neanderthals hunting mock mammoths to an accompanying soundtrack won't be everyone's cup of tea, but the **Préhisto-parc** (daily: Feb, March, Oct & Nov 10am–5.30pm; April–June & Sept 10am–6.30pm; July & Aug 10am–7.30pm; €6.50; Ⓦwww.prehistoparc.fr), upriver from La Madeleine along the D706, is another attempt to recreate the daily life of prehistoric man. If you've already visited the more varied Roc de Cazelle (see p.206), you can give this a miss, but otherwise it's fun to take in, especially if you've got children in tow. A woodland walk takes you past tableaux of encampments, people making flints, painting, sculpting and generally being busy in a prehistoric sort of way.

Next door to the Préhisto-parc, the cliffs were occupied throughout the middle ages at the **Maison Forte de Reignac** (daily: March, April & Oct to mid-Nov 10am–6pm; May, June & Sept 10am–7pm; July & Aug 10am–8pm; €6.80; Ⓦwww.maison-forte-reignac.com), a fortified feudal residence whose knights owed allegiance to the superior lord at St-Christophe (see below). Though it's not as extensive as La Madeleine (see p.211), Reignac is arguably the more rewarding visit, an intriguing combination of primitive cave-dwelling (the back wall of the house is the cliff face) and medieval opulence. The three storeys of the house are all furnished with items from different periods of its occupation and contain interesting displays on the feudal system (pick up the English leaflet at the entrance for full translations). The most interesting rooms are the "Great Room" on the ground floor, with its authentic *pisé* floor, monolithic washbasin and smoking wood fire, and the last room you see, the former bedroom of the Countess of Reignac, which is very elegantly furnished. Above the house, you can climb onto a parapet in the cliff-face for good views along the valley.

Tursac

Tursac's central square is home to a well-regarded **restaurant**, *La Source* (Ⓣ05.53.06.98.00; closed Tues & Wed; reservations recommended), with a pleasant garden and imaginative daily specials on menus from €22.50. It's also one of the best bets around for vegetarians, with a menu for €24.50, which is a cut above the ordinary. On the edge of the village, the *Auberge du Pêche-Lune* (Ⓣ05.53.06.85.85, Ⓦwww.peche-lune.com; ④) is a **hotel** whose rooms, with eclectic, original decors, are set in a complex of wooden, chalet-style buildings with views of the river valley. There's also a heated indoor pool, a bar and a restaurant (menus from €15). There are two good **campsites** in the area: first is the more basic but spectacularly located *La Ferme du Pelou* (Ⓣ05.53.06.98.17, Ⓦwww.lafermedupelou.com; mid-March to mid-Nov), a two-star site perched on the hilltop overlooking La Madeleine and its meander from the east; it's signed off the D706 to the south of Tursac. North of the village, *Le Vézère Périgord* (Ⓣ05.53.06.96.31, Ⓦwww.levezereperigord.com; Easter to Sept) is a well-run, spacious and good-value three-star site set back from the main road among trees.

La Roque St-Christophe

The enormous natural refuge of **La Roque St-Christophe** (daily: Feb–March & Oct 10am–6pm; April–June & Sept 10am–6.30pm; July & Aug 10am–8pm;

Nov–Jan 2–5pm; €7; Ⓦwww.roque-st-christophe.com), 3km upriver from Tursac, is made up of about one hundred **rock-shelters** on five levels hollowed out of the limestone cliffs. The whole complex is nearly a kilometre long and up to 80m above ground-level, where the River Vézère once flowed. The earliest traces of occupation go back over fifty thousand years, although permanent settlement dates from around the ninth century when the site's natural defences really came into their own. At its peak during the Middle Ages it had grown into a veritable town clinging to the rock face – with its own marketplace, church, prison, abattoir, baker and artisans' workshops – and was able to shelter over one thousand people in times of trouble. And there was no shortage of those, culminating in the Wars of Religion when Protestant sympathizers took refuge here. After they were kicked out in 1588, Henri III ordered the town and fortress demolished – which means you need a good imagination to recreate the scene from the various nooks and crannies hacked into the rock. In summer, there are frequent **guided visits**, but though instructive they can get a bit tedious – better to take one of their English-language leaflets and wander at your own pace.

St-Léon-sur-Vézère and around

ST-LÉON-SUR-VÉZÈRE, 6km above Tursac, is by far the most attractive village along the whole Vézère valley. It sits in a quiet bend of the river guarded by two châteaux – one topped by a fairy-tale array of turrets – and boasts one of the region's most harmonious Romanesque churches. In summer the church serves as one of the principal venues, along with St-Amand-de-Coly (see p.217), for classical music concerts during the **Festival du Périgord Noir** (see box, p.193). For the best views of the whole ensemble, walk over the iron-girder bridge and turn left along a footpath on the opposite bank.

If you head up the hill on the far side of the bridge, you come to the **Parc aux Dinosaures** (daily: April–June 10am–6pm; July & Aug 10am–7.30pm; Sept & Oct 2–5pm; €7.50; Ⓦwww.parc-aux-dinosaures.com), an attraction aimed at families. It includes a series of shallow troglodytic shelters known as

▲ St-Léon-sur-Vézère

Le Conquil, the most interesting of which contains dozens of niches in the rock, used for housing pigeons in the Middle Ages. Otherwise the caves don't have much to see, but children might enjoy wandering through the woods trying to spot the full-size model dinosaurs lurking in the trees, before you get up to the clifftop belvedere. The park also features a nicely situated tree-top obstacle course, with **zip-wires** running along the bank of the Vézère (€18 per person). Overall the park can't really compare to some of the others in the valley, but it's a good bet if you're after something of interest to various ages.

Southeast across the Vézère from St-Léon, the rock-shelters of **Castel-Merle** (April–Sept daily 2–6pm; €5; ⓣ05.53.50.79.70) are unusual in that excavation activities are still going on here, carried out by a joint Franco-American project. There are a total of ten shelters, of which you can visit five, either on a guided tour or with a thorough booklet in English. Only one still contains any **cave art**, including three rather poorly preserved bison sculptures from the same era as Cap Blanc (see p.207). However, the site has yielded a terrific number of **flints, bones** and **beads**. A good number of these are on show in a small private **museum** (same opening hours; free) in the village of **SERGEAC**, 500m below Castel-Merle. The owner takes great delight in explaining the objects, many of them unearthed by his archeologist father, of which the highlight is a collection of six necklaces strung together about thirty thousand years ago. One is made up of shells from the Atlantic, presumably obtained by trade, and another of various animal teeth including wolf's.

Practicalities

You can rent **canoes** at *Le Paradis* and also through Aventure Plein Air (ⓣ05.53.50.67.71, ⓦwww.canoevezere.com), who set up by the bridge in St-Léon from May through September depending on the weather.

The closest **hotel** to **St-Léon** is *Le Relais de la Côte de Jor* (ⓣ05.53.50.74.47, ⓦwww.lerelaisdejor.com; ❷; closed Dec–March), in the pine-forested hills 2.5km north, whose good-value rooms have private balconies with views down the valley to La Roque St-Christophe. There's also a great panoramic terrace with a swimming pool. As for **campsites**, there's a choice between St-Léon's small municipal site beside the bridge (ⓣ05.53.50.73.16; May–Sept), and the luxurious *Le Paradis* (ⓣ05.53.50.72.64, ⓦwww.le-paradis.fr; April–Oct) complete with heated pools, 3km down the road to Les Eyzies. St-Léon's *Auberge du Pont* (closed Tues eve, Wed & Nov–Feb) is a lovely wisteria-covered **restaurant** beside the bridge, which offers a wide choice of dishes on menus starting at €15, and also serves fire-grilled pizzas and a wicked array of home-made ice creams. Tucked down beside the church you'll also find the *Déjeuner sur l'Herbe* (closed Mon & Jan). This tiny **shop** sells top-notch local produce and also does takeaways: a platter of cheese or charcuterie, for example, with a hunk of country bread, costs €12, while a sandwich comes in at €4.50. You can then decamp to the picnic tables along the riverbank.

The same family who run the museum in Sergeac (see above) also own a **hotel**, the *Auberge de Castel-Merle* (ⓣ05.53.50.70.08, ⓦwww.hotelcastelmerle.com; ❸; closed Oct–March) on the hill above the prehistoric shelters. It's a handsome Périgord building and the rooms are cheerful, but its main attribute is its clifftop terrace where on fine days you can **eat** lunch overlooking the Vézère (menus from €14; closed Mon & for lunch on Tues).

Château de Losse and Le Thot

Of several castles along the Vézère valley, the Renaissance **Château de Losse** (May–Sept daily except Sat noon–6pm; €7.50; ⓦwww.chateaudelosse.com)

stands out as the most striking. It occupies a rocky bluff 4km upstream from St-Léon on the main D706, though the best views are from the opposite bank, where the D65 provides a quiet and picturesque back road from St-Léon to Montignac (see below). The present castle was constructed in the 1570s by Jean II de Losse, royal tutor and the governor of Guyenne, on medieval foundations. It has changed little since then, a well-proportioned L-shaped building surrounded by dry moats and watchtowers. Inside, the château's present owners have established an impressive collection of sixteenth- and seventeenth-century **furniture** and **tapestries**. Among the latter, the Florentine *Return of the Courtesan* is particularly successful in its use of perspective, while the colours of this and the Flemish rendition of knights preparing for a tournament remain exceptionally vibrant. There's also a rare, tulip-decorated tapestry dating from around the time of the Dutch Tulipomania in 1634, when tulips cost more than gold. On your way out, note the inscription over the unusually imposing gatehouse which quotes one of Jean II's favourite maxims: "When I thought the end was in sight, I was only beginning." His perhaps jaundiced view is forgivable – of his five sons, four were killed in war and the fifth had no heirs to inherit the family estates.

It's back to prehistory at the next stop, **Le Thot** (Feb, March, Oct & Nov Tues–Sun 10am–12.30pm & 2–5.30pm; April–June & Sept daily 10am–6.30pm; July & Aug daily 10am–7.30pm; €6), 1km into the hills west of the château. Somewhat whimsically described as an "Espace Cro-Magnon" (loosely translated as "space of the Cro-Magnon"), the combined museum and animal park focuses on prehistoric art, not only the technical aspects but also some of the **wildlife** that provided inspiration: reindeer, Przewalski horses with their erect manes, ibex, deer and European bison are all resident here. You'll also see **aurochs**, though these primitive wild cattle really died out in the 1600s – the beasts here are a close approximation achieved through selective breeding in the early twentieth century. The **museum** explains the different techniques and styles of cave art, but the most interesting part is a video showing the painstaking recreation of the Lascaux caves (see p.216). For once, it's subtitled in English and the majority of displays here have English-language explanations.

Montignac and around

Some 26km upstream from Les Eyzies, **MONTIGNAC** is an attractive town, with a vibrant annual **arts festival** in July (see box, p.193). The town serves as the main base for exploring the Vézère valley's northern sights, foremost of which is **Lascaux**'s painted cave, though the Romanesque abbey church of **St-Amand-de-Coly** is also worth a visit.

Arrival and information

Buses from Périgueux, Sarlat and Terrasson stop on place Carnot and on place Tourny. Also on this road, the **tourist office** is tucked away beneath the arcades on place Bertran-de-Born (March–June, Sept & Oct Mon–Sat 9am–noon & 2–5pm; July & Aug daily 9am–7pm; Nov, Dec & Feb Mon–Sat 10am–noon & 2–5pm; closed Jan; ⓣ05.53.51.82.60, ⓦwww.tourisme-montignac.com). Below it you'll find the summer **ticket office for Lascaux II** (see p.216; April–Sept daily 9am–6pm). For **internet access** go to the bar *Le Comptoir* further down rue de 4 Septembre towards the river. **Bikes** are available to rent from Les Briconautes (ⓣ05.53.51.75.50) out in the industrial zone of Franqueville, just off the road to Brive, and there are two **canoe rental** outlets: Les 7 Rives (ⓣ05.53.50.19.26; June–Sept) beside the more northerly Pont de la Paix; and Kanoak (ⓣ06.75.48.60.47; June to mid-Sept) below the old bridge.

Accommodation

Montignac has several **hotels** but, as usual in these parts, it's sensible to book ahead in high season.

Hostellerie la Roseraie place d'Armes Ⓣ05.53.50.53.92, Ⓦwww.laroseraie-hotel.com. In a characterful ivy- and wisteria-clad building on a quiet square, this is the nicest place to stay in Montignac. The rooms are prettily decorated with period furniture, while the garden has a landscaped pool and the terrace of Montignac's best restaurant, whose menus (from €23–49) include some opulent dishes featuring woodpigeon, lobster, truffles and other rich regional cuisine – if you're staying in the hotel, it's well worth considering the *demi-pension* option. Closed Nov to Easter. ❺

Hôtel de la Grotte 63 rue du 4 Septembre Ⓣ05.53.51.80.48, Ⓦwww.hoteldelagrotte.fr. An old-fashioned place with a fair amount of charm and spacious rooms. It also has an excellent traditional restaurant (menus from €17) and hires out bikes. ❸

Le Moulin du Bleufond Ⓣ05.53.51.83.95, Ⓦwww.bleufond.com. A well-tended three-star campsite on the riverbank 500m downstream from Montignac. Closed mid-Oct to March.

Le Petit Monde 54 rue du 4 Septembre Ⓣ05.53.51.32.76, Ⓦwww.hotellepetitmonde.com. A short walk from the centre, this is the cheapest option in town, offering simple rooms with television and either shared or en-suite facilities. ❷

Relais du Soleil d'Or 16 rue du 4 Septembre Ⓣ05.53.51.80.22, Ⓦwww.le-soleil-dor.com. A three-star hotel with comfortable, fully-equipped rooms, most of which are situated in a modern annexe at the back, in one corner of the hotel's pretty park with a small pool. Closed Jan. ❹

The Town

Montignac straddles the Vézère, with the tourist office and most hotels south of the river along rue du 4 Septembre and the old town, with its numerous timbered fourteenth- to sixteenth-century houses north of the river. The **old town** centres on pretty place d'Armes, a harmonious square of warm, sun-bathed stone, adorned by hanging creepers and smart blue shutters. Nearby is place Carnot, where a **market** is held on Wednesday and Saturday mornings, beneath the dominant spire of the square's somewhat unexciting twentieth-century church. To the west of the two squares, a narrow alleyway called rue des Jardins leads you uphill to give a view of the town's abandoned feudal castle (not open to the public), which was home to the once powerful Counts of Périgord (see p.355). South of the river is the Faubourg, with more elegant buildings, including the galleried former hospice where the town's municipal offices are now housed, and a number of older timbered structures on rue de la Pegerie.

Eating

For quality, you can't beat the hotel restaurants at *La Grotte* (see above) and *La Roseraie* (see above), but if your priority is the setting, head to the northern river bank where a number of **places to eat** have outside seating right on the river, beneath medieval timbered supports. In pride of place is *Pilotis* (Ⓣ05.53.50.88.15), which serves pizzas and salads (around €8 each) on its justifiably popular terrace. Another option is *La Chaumière* at 53 rue 4 Septembre (Ⓣ05.53.50.14.24), a cosy place serving meaty dishes and *tartiflette* from the Savoie. Reckon on €15 for a hearty meal.

Grotte de Lascaux and Lascaux II

The **Grotte de Lascaux** was discovered in 1940 by four teenagers in search of their dog, which had fallen into a deep cavern near Montignac. The cave was found to be decorated with marvellously preserved animal paintings, executed by Cro-Magnon people some seventeen thousand years ago, which are among the finest examples of prehistoric art in existence. Lascaux was opened to the public in 1948 and over the next fifteen years the humidity created by more than a million visitors caused algae and then an opaque layer of calcite to form over the paintings. The algae can be cured by disinfection, but the "white disease" is a more serious problem, and in 1963 the authorities decided to close the cave and build a replica.

Opened in 1983, some 200m from the original cave, **Lascaux II**, signed 2km south from central Montignac (40min guided tours in French or English: April–June & Sept daily 9.30am–6.30pm; July & Aug daily 9am–8pm; Oct to mid-Nov daily 10am–12.30pm & 2–6pm; mid-Nov to Dec & Feb–March Tues–Sun 10am–12.30pm & 2–5.30pm; closed Jan; €8.50; Ⓦwww.lascaux.culture.fr), was the result of ten years' painstaking work by twenty artists and sculptors using the same methods and materials as the original cave painters. The almost perfect facsimile comprises ninety percent of the Lascaux paintings concentrated in the Hall of Bulls and the Axial (or Painted) Gallery, a distance of less than 100m. While it can't offer the excitement of the real thing, the reproduction is still breathtaking. In the **Hall of Bulls** five huge aurochs – one 5.5 metres long with an astonishingly expressive head and face – dominate the ceiling, while the **Axial (Painted) Gallery** is covered with more cattle surrounded by deer, bison and horses rendered in distinctive Lascaux style with pot-bellies and narrow heads. Some are shaded or spotted with different coloured pigments, while others, like the bulls, are drawn in black outline. One particularly dynamic series is of three horses appearing to be in the different phases of breaking into a gallop. You don't have to be an expert to appreciate the incredible skill employed by the prehistoric artists, who would have painted these animals from memory by the light of flickering oil lamps, nor to appreciate their sense of perspective and movement, and the sheer energy they manage to convey.

Two thousand **tickets** are on sale each day, but these go fast during the peak holiday periods, when it's best to buy in advance either by going to the ticket office in person or making a credit-card booking over the phone (Ⓣ05.53.51.95.03); bookings can be made up to seven days in advance. Note also that in winter (Oct to Easter) tickets are normally on sale at the site, while in season (Easter to Sept) they are available only from an office beneath Montignac tourist office – the system varies from year to year, so check in Montignac first before heading up to the cave.

Even at Lascaux II, the volume of visitors has been causing trouble, with threats to the original cave posed simply by the proximity of the replica. Another Lascaux revolution is therefore planned, and the authorities hope to open **Lascaux III** around 2012; this one is to cover more of the original cave and include some of the engravings with which the other chambers were adorned. The new replica will be located a safe distance from the original, down in the valley below.

St-Amand-de-Coly

Nine kilometres east of Montignac, the village of **ST-AMAND-DE-COLY** boasts a superb fortified Romanesque **church** (daily 9.30am–7pm; free). Despite its size and bristling military architecture, the twelfth-century abbey church manages to combine great delicacy and spirituality. It is supposedly built over the burial place of the sixth-century St Amand, who gave up soldiering to become a hermit. Despite a promising start, however, the abbey never really prospered and had largely been abandoned by the late 1400s. In 1575 a Protestant garrison withstood a heavy siege here for six days, after which the building continued to crumble until 1868, when it was classified as a historic monument; since then it has been entirely restored. With its purity of line and simple decoration, the church is at its most evocative in the low sun of late afternoon or early evening. Its **defences**, added in the fourteenth century, left nothing to chance: the church is encircled by ramparts, its walls are 4m thick, and a passage once skirted the eaves, with numerous positions for archers to rain down arrows and blind stairways to mislead attackers. If you're lucky enough to be here in July or August you might catch a classical music concert in the church during the **Festival du Périgord Noir** (late July to late Aug).

Near the church, clean and simple **accommodation** offered by the small *Hôtel Gardette* (Ⓣ05.53.51.68.50, Ⓦwww.hotel-gardette.fr; ❷; menus from €18; closed Oct–March) makes it possible to stay overnight in this tiny, idyllic place. There's also a very grand – but not sniffy – creeper-clad manor house, the *Manoir d'Hautegente* (Ⓣ05.53.51.68.03, Ⓦwww.manoir-hautegente.com; ❻; closed Nov–March), some 3km north, beyond the village of Coly. Set in its own grounds well back from the road, the hotel has a pool, sumptuous rooms overlooking the grounds to the river and one of the region's best **restaurants** (menus €48–100; closed lunchtimes Mon–Thurs).

Terrasson-la-Villedieu

Beyond Montignac the prehistoric sites die out and the Vézère valley becomes busier and more industrialized as it opens out towards Brive (see p.152) and **TERRASSON-LA-VILLEDIEU**, 15km upstream. The old part of Terrasson, a knot of lanes on the river's south bank leading up from the arched stone bridge to the church, merits a quick wander, but the main reason for coming here is to visit its resolutely contemporary garden, **Les Jardins de l'Imaginaire** (1hr 15min guided tours only: April–June, Sept & Oct daily except Tues 10–11.30am & 2–5pm; July & Aug daily 10am–1pm & 2–6.20pm; €7) on a terraced hillside to the west of the church. Opened in 1996, the **gardens** were designed by American landscaper Kathryn Gustafson. In them she explores common themes found in gardens throughout history and among different

▲ Les Jardins de l'Imaginaire, Terrasson

cultures, from the Romans' sacred groves and the Hanging Gardens of Babylon to moss, water and rose gardens, the last a magnificent display of nearly two thousand varieties. In this respect it is much more than "just" a garden, which is why they insist you go with a guide to explain the complicated symbolism; English-language texts are available. Afterwards, however, you can wander at leisure to enjoy the garden on its own terms. It's full of imaginative touches: a forest of wind chimes, a stark line of weather-vanes and, above all, the use of water to splendid effect.

If you're travelling by public transport, you might find yourself passing through Terrasson since it lies on the Brive–Bordeaux train line and has occasional buses to Montignac. The **gare SNCF** lies on the north side of town at the far end of avenue Jean Jaurès. **Buses** stop at the station and place de la Libération, on the main west–east Brive road, near the old bridge. Place de la Libération is also where you'll find the **tourist office** (July & Aug daily 9.30am–12.30pm & 2.30–6.30pm; Sept–June Mon–Sat 9am–noon & 2–6pm; ⓣ05.53.50.37.56, ⓦwww.ot-terrasson.com). If you're looking for somewhere to **eat** near the gardens, *Les Saveurs des Jardins* (closed Mon eve & Tues, & Nov–March), just outside the entrance, does a range of soups, salads and sandwiches, followed by home-made ice creams garnished with edible flowers and flower-based syrups; in fine weather you can eat on their terrace – flower-decked of course. There's also a good and rather classy **restaurant**, *L'Imaginaire*, nearby on place du Foirail (ⓣ05.53.51.37.27, ⓦwww.l-imaginaire.com; closed Sun eve & Mon lunchtime & three weeks in Nov), in two elegant stone-vaulted rooms. Three-course lunch menus start at €25, while in the evening they're from €43, though they also do slightly cheaper *formules*. It also offers seven large, plush **hotel rooms** (❻), boasting wi-fi, flat screen televisions, wooden floors and minimalist bathrooms with roomy showers and baths.

The middle Dordogne

The stretch of river to the south of Sarlat sees the Dordogne at its most appealing, forming great loops between rich fields, wooded hills and craggy outcrops. This is also castle country, where great medieval fortresses eyeball each other across the valley. Most date from the Hundred Years' War, when the river marked a frontier of sorts between French-held land to the north and English territory to the south.

For the visitor today, things start slowly in the west with the service town of **St-Cyprien** and nearby **Belvès**, now a sleepy little place where people once lived in troglodyte houses beneath its streets, but châteaux come thick and fast thereafter. The first you reach on the river's north bank is **Beynac**, a stunning village of russet-hued, stone-roofed cottages cascading to the river. A short distance further upstream, the **Château de Marqueyssac** provides respite among its Italian-style terraced gardens and woodland promenades, with views of both Beynac and its archrival over on the south bank, the **Château de Castelnaud**. Castelnaud is all that a medieval castle should be: barbicans, curtain walls, inner courtyards, fluttering pennants and watchtowers surrounding a seemingly indomitable keep. It also contains an excellent museum of medieval warfare. Then a brief diversion westwards brings you to the far-from-militaristic castle of **Les Milandes**, once owned by the cabaret artist Josephine Baker and now set up as a museum in her honour.

Heading back upstream, the next stop is **La Roque-Gageac**. This lovely village caught between the river and the rock-face is up there with Beynac and Castelnaud as one of the Dordogne's most photographed – and visited – sights.

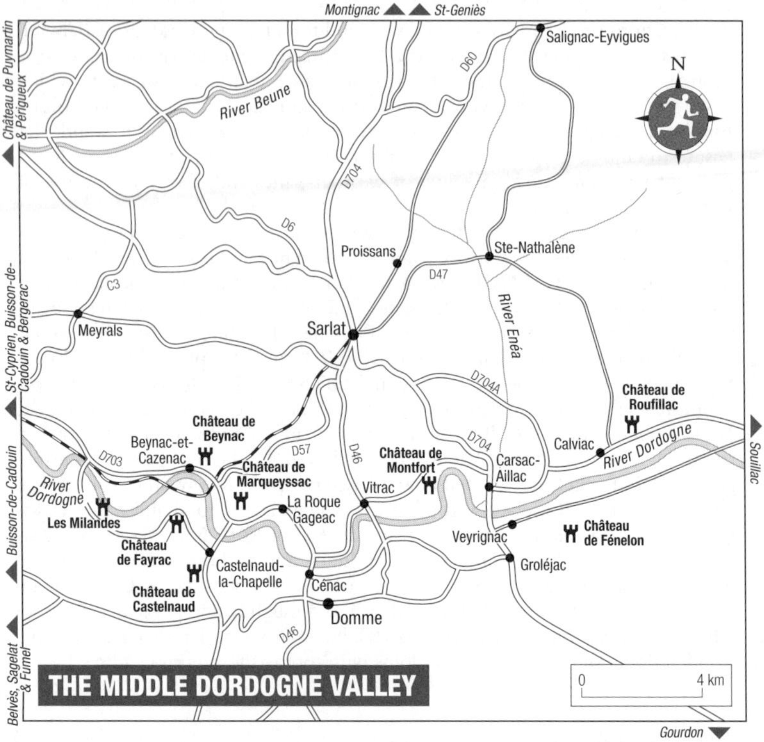

THE MIDDLE DORDOGNE VALLEY

Across on the south bank, **Domme**, a fortified *bastide* town perched on the cliff edge, is no pushover on either the tourist stakes or as regards its views. From up here you can take in a ten-kilometre sweep of the river, giving you a foretaste of the **Cingle de Montfort**, a particularly picturesque meander set off by yet another glorious château to the east. Before you cross from the Dordogne *département* into the Lot, there's just one more castle to go, the **Château de Fénelon**, an attractive blend of medieval and Renaissance architecture with good collections of furniture and weaponry.

You can just about forget about public transport in this area. St-Cyprien, Siorac-en-Périgord and Belvès are accessible by **train**, but the picturesque Sarlat line runs past all the prime sights around Beynac without stopping. The only place accessible by **bus** is Carsac, a village with a pretty church just east of Montfort, which is a stop on the Sarlat–Souillac bus route.

St-Cyprien

Despite its location, just 20km west of Sarlat and 10km south from Les Eyzies, **ST-CYPRIEN** remains a refreshingly workaday place set back from the busy D703. Admittedly, it hasn't got much in the way of sights, but the whole place really comes to life on Sunday mornings for one of the area's best **markets**. The hillside setting is also attractive and, although the town itself has few accommodation options, hotels and inns in neighbouring villages make it a possible base. The old centre's narrow lanes of medieval houses and labourers' cottages, a good number still unprettified, hold the greatest interest. They zigzag up from the modern, lower town towards the austere **abbey church** founded by twelfth-century Augustinian monks. You certainly can't accuse the church of being pretty either, though there's a certain robust grandeur about its Romanesque tower and the echoing nave. The interior is worth a look for some fine, eighteenth-century sculpted wooden statues on its retables, and is an evocative setting for classical music concerts in summer.

Practicalities

St-Cyprien's **train station**, on the Bordeaux-Sarlat line, is located about 1km south of the centre, while the helpful **tourist office**, on place Charles-de-Gaulle in the centre of the lower town (Mon–Sat 9.30am–12.30pm & 3–6pm, Sun 10am–12.30pm; Ⓣ05.53.30.36.09, Ⓦwww.stcyprien-perigord.com), produces a good walking map of St-Cyprien and coordinates an active programme of concerts, events and activities in summer.

There are a couple of fine, rustic **accommodation** options in the hills 5km to the north of St-Cyprien near the typical Périgord village of **MEYRALS**. You'll need to book early to get one of the twelve stylish **rooms** at *La Ferme Lamy* (Ⓣ05.53.29.62.46, Ⓦwww.ferme-lamy.com; ❼) on the C3 north of the village. The whole place is immaculate, from the en-suite bathrooms to the big, landscaped pool and flower-filled garden, not to mention the breakfast-spread of home-made jams and breads. There are cheaper rooms at the beguiling country inn, the *Ferme-Auberge de la Rhonie* (Ⓣ05.53.29.29.07, Ⓦwww.chambres-larhonie.com; ❹; Nov–March), which has pretty rooms and an excellent **restaurant** focusing on traditional Périgord dishes that make use of the geese bred on the farm itself. Menus start at €22.

The other option is to head 8km downstream to **SIORAC-EN-PÉRIGORD** – a junction, albeit infrequently served, on the Sarlat–Bordeaux and Agen–Périgueux train lines – where you'll find the *Auberge du Trèfle à Quatre Feuilles* (Ⓣ05.53.31.60.26, Ⓦwww.letrefle4feuilles.com; ❷; closed Nov), which has seven comfortable en-suite rooms in pastel shades located in two old stone cottages in the centre of the village; it also boasts a popular **restaurant** (closed Wed except July & Aug; menus from €19). On the north side of the river from Siorac, the *Petit Chaperon Rouge* (Ⓣ05.53.29.37.79, Ⓔle-petit-chaperon-rouge@wanadoo.fr; ❶; closed Nov) is another good-value, peaceful country inn, with a handful of newly renovated rooms, a shady terrace with good views across the valley, and an authentic restaurant (menus from €12; closed Tues & Wed lunch off-season). **Campers** are provided for by the *Camping du Port* (Ⓣ05.53.31.63.81, Ⓦwww.campingduport.net; mid-May to Sept), a cheap and relaxed site back down by the riverbank.

Belvès

Accessible by public transport, and another possible base before you reach the most touristy stretch of the Dordogne valley, is the rather more picturesque hilltop town of **BELVÈS**, 12km south of St-Cyprien. There's no mistaking the town's strategic importance, encircled by ramparts on a promontory above the Nauze valley and bristling with seven towers – even the central square is called place d'Armes. These days, however, the only battles likely to take place here involve haggling over prices at the Saturday-morning **market** under the old *halle*, or a hotly disputed game of *boules*.

In 1907 the wheel of a cart crossing place d'Armes broke through the roof of a warren of **troglodyte houses** (35min guided tours: Mon–Sat 11am & 4pm; €4); note that it's best to confirm opening hours with the tourist office, which is where tickets are sold in any case. Hollowed into the rampart wall, these damp, dark and insalubrious dwellings were inhabited from the twelfth century up to the mid-1700s, after which they were blocked up and forgotten. So far eight "houses" have been opened, consisting of single rooms averaging a mere twenty square metres apiece for a family plus animals. It's hard to imagine what they must have been like to live in, even if the more sophisticated dwellings boast chimneys, raised sleeping areas and shelves cut into the soft rock.

Several fine streets, lined with handsome houses from various eras, lead off place d'Armes: **rue Rubigan**, reached under the old stone gateway, is a narrow, winding medieval street, while on rue des Filhols you can see the imposing tower of the Maison des Consuls and further up a battered ornate Renaissance facade. **Rue Jacques Manchotte**, on the other side of the square, leads past shops and cafés towards the imposing thirteenth-century **church of Notre-Dame**, an interesting example of early, undecorative Gothic architecture. The church now contains some interesting displays on the town's history. If it's open, you could also pop into the **Organistrum** at 14 rue Jacques Manchotte (no fixed hours; free; ⓣ05.53.29.10.93), a combined museum and workshop producing medieval instruments. Music-lovers might also be interested in Belvès' principal annual event, the **Festival Bach**, dedicated to the composer, with a couple of concerts in the church largely during the first fortnight of August (see box on p.193).

Practicalities

Like Siorac, Belvès lies on the Agen–Périgueux railway line, with the **gare SNCF** down on the main road below the town. Its **tourist office**, 1 rue des Filhols (June 15–Sept 15 daily 10am–1pm & 3–7pm; Sept 16–June 14 Mon–Sat 10am–12.30pm & 3–6.30pm; ⓣ05.53.29.10.20, ⓦwww.perigord.com/belves), occupies the ground floor of the fifteenth-century Maison des Consuls, just off the market square, while the town's two **hotels** stand next to each other on place de la Croix-des-Frères, at the far west end of rue Jacques Manchotte. First choice should be *Le Home* (ⓣ05.53.29.01.65, ⓦwww.lehomedebelves.fr; ❶), for its excellent-value rooms, friendly service and popular restaurant, serving dishes varying from classic French to curry or lasagne (menus from €12). The next-door *Belvédère* (ⓣ05.53.31.51.41, ⓦwww.belvedere-perigord.com; ❸; closed Jan, & Oct–May closed Mon) is slightly more upmarket, offering modern rooms complete with wi-fi access as well as a decent restaurant (from €21). Belvès' nearest **campsite** is the three-star *Les Nauves* (ⓣ05.53.29.12.64, ⓦwww.lesnauves.com; April–Sept), in a quiet spot 4km southwest off the D53 Monpazier road.

Beynac-et-Cazenac and around

Clearly visible on an impregnable cliff edge on the Dordogne's north bank, its clifftop castle soaring above the valley, the eye-catching village of **BEYNAC-ET-CAZENAC** was built in the days when the river was the only route open to traders and invaders. Now the busy main road squeezes between the cliffs and the water, creating a horrible bottleneck from July to mid-September. At this time you're best advised to arrive first thing in the morning to escape the worst of the crowds.

You need your own vehicle to get to Beynac, and **parking** is available either down by the river or up beside the castle. Once you've bought a permit from the machines in the riverside car park (€2 for two hours, €4 for a day), you're free to use either or both. The tourist office (ⓣ05.53.29.43.08; April–June, Sept & Oct daily 10am–12.30pm & 2–5.30pm; July & Aug daily 9.30am–12.30pm & 2–6pm; Nov–March Mon–Sat 10am–12.30pm & 2–5pm) is at the bottom of the road up to the château.

Alternative ways to enjoy Beynac

Particularly in summer, the tiny village of Beynac, cramped between road and cliff-face, can get oppressively crowded. Thankfully there are a number of ways to escape and enjoy a more peaceful perspective on the countless castles in the area.

River trips Gabarres de Beynac (April–Oct 10am–12.30pm & 2–6pm; €7.50; ⓣ05.53.28.51.15, ⓦwww.gabarre-beynac.com), based by the river on a jetty opposite Beynac's tourist office, offer 50-minute river cruises on their replica *gabarres*, the traditional wooden river-craft, affording excellent views of castle and village.

Canoeing The stretch of the Dordogne between Vitrac and Beynac, taking you past a breathtaking parade of castles, is the most stunning canoe-trip in the region. If you hire a canoe in Beynac, the company will drive you upriver before you canoe back down to your vehicle. In town, you'll find Copeyre Canoë (ⓣ05.53.28.23.82, ⓦwww.canoe-copeyre.com; May–Sept), while Canoës Rougeoffre (ⓣ05.53.29.54.20, ⓦwww.canoe-rougeoffre.com), based a few kilometres downstream near St-Vincent-de-Cosse, offers the best value around and is open all year.

Hot-air ballooning The ultimate slow-paced activity is also a possibility here: visit the office of Montgolfière et Châteaux by the port in Beynac (ⓣ06.71.14.34.96, ⓦwww.montgolfiere-chateaux.com; from €180 per adult).

Walking The cheapest way to get away from the crowds around Beynac's port and castle is to walk inland away from the river; the tourist office sells maps of suggested routes for €1.50. One of their walks takes you 3km above Beynac to the beautifully unspoilt fifteenth-century church of Cazenac, with some unusual modern stained-glass windows depicting scenes from daily life in this area in the nineteenth century.

Beynac's two **hotels** are *Hostellerie Maleville* (ⓣ05.53.29.50.06, ⓦwww.hostellerie-maleville.com; ④), which has a restaurant (menus €15–26) and a cheaper café serving pizzas, salads and drinks all day right on the river. Its rooms are situated off the main drag in its annexe, the *Hôtel Pontet*, on the road up to the castle. They're all comfortable, if slightly uniform, with a/c, en-suite and television. The rooms at the *Hôtel du Château* (ⓣ05.53.29.19.20, ⓦwww.hotelduchateau-dordogne.com; ③–④), on a bit of a busy corner opposite the tourist office, are more varied in decor, though this borders on the bizarre in places. The most expensive rooms have private balconies with river views, and there's also internet access, a tiny pool, and a decent restaurant (menus €23–36). The riverside *Le Capeyrou* **campsite** (ⓣ05.53.29.54.95, ⓦwww.campinglecapeyrou.com; April–Sept) lies immediately east of town.

When it comes to **eating**, the restaurant at the *Hôtel du Château* (directions as above) probably offers the highest quality in town, but you could also head for the popular *Café de la Rivière* (ⓣ05.53.28.35.49, ⓦwww.cafedelariviere.com) on the riverbank, which serves full menus from €11 on its wonderful terrace, taking in a view of no fewer than four castles.

Château de Beynac

It's three kilometres by road from the waterfront to the **Château de Beynac** (1hr guided tours daily: March–May 10am–6pm; June–Sept 10am–6.30pm; Oct & Nov 10am–dusk; Dec–Feb 11am–dusk; €7) or, alternatively, it takes fifteen minutes to walk up the steep lane among the *lauze*-roofed cottages. The lichenous-grey castle is protected on the landward side by double walls and ditches; elsewhere the sheer drop of almost 150m does the job. The redoubtable Richard the Lionheart nevertheless took and held Beynac for a decade, until a gangrenous wound ended his term of blood-letting in 1189; apparently the heart-shaped keys and keyholes were fashioned in his memory. Though the English regained the castle briefly – thanks to the Treaty of Brétigny rather than any military prowess – in essence Beynac remained loyal to the French Crown during the Hundred Years' War.

The buildings are in surprisingly good condition thanks to a mammoth restoration project over the last forty years, which is scheduled to continue until at least 2030. You enter into a **guardroom** lit by flickering oil lamps, one of the castle's more atmospheric rooms along with the **great hall**, where the nobles of Beynac, Biron, Mareuil and Bourdeilles – the four baronies of Périgord (see p.355) – met; note the unusual ox-skull motif over the fireplace, previously found at the Château de Lanquais (see p.182). Also good are the twelfth-century **kitchens**, complete with a cobbled ramp allowing horses access to the central courtyard, and kitted out with no-nonsense tables, vats, meat-hooks and great pulleys. If it looks familiar, that's because it featured in Luc Besson's epic, *Jeanne d'Arc*. For most people, however, it's the **views** that steal the show, notably from the top of the keep, where you get a stupendous – and vertiginous – sweep over the surrounding châteaux: Marqueyssac, Fayrac and Castelnaud (see below).

Château de Marqueyssac

Three kilometres east of Beynac, the Dordogne loops south round a long and narrow wooded promontory, at the tip of which the **Château de Marqueyssac** (daily: Feb, March & Oct to mid-Nov 10am–6pm; April–June & Sept 10am–7pm; July & Aug 9am–8pm; mid-Nov to Jan 10am–5pm; €7.20, or €13.40 with Château de Castelnaud; Ⓦwww.marqueyssac.com) presides over its terraced gardens. The château itself, a typically mellow Périgord mansion of the late eighteenth century, is rarely open to the public, but the **view**, encompassing the châteaux of Beynac, Fayrac and Castelnaud, is magnificent. The **gardens** were first laid out in the 1600s by the then owner, Bertrand Vernet de Marqueyssac, under the inspiration of Le Nôtre, the landscaper responsible for Versailles. However, most of the features you see today were added two centuries later when the half-kilometre long Grande Allée was established, thousands of box trees clipped into plump cushions, and six kilometres of woodland walks opened up along the ridge to the east. All paths lead to a 130m-high **belvedere** from where you can see La Roque-Gageac nestling under its cliff (see p.226). Between Easter and mid-November, the **salon de thé** serves light refreshments, and on Thursday evenings in July and August fairy lights give the gardens a magical touch (on these days, the gardens are open until midnight; entry €9).

Castelnaud-la-Chapelle

Rivals for centuries, the feudal fortresses of Beynac and **CASTELNAUD-LA-CHAPELLE**, on the Dordogne's south bank, now vie over visitor numbers. There's no question that Beynac has the edge with its more dramatic location and arguably the better views, but the **Château de Castelnaud** (daily: Feb–March & Oct to mid-Nov 10am–6pm; April–June & Sept 10am–7pm; July & Aug 9am–8pm; mid-Nov to Jan 2–5pm; Christmas hols 10am–5pm; €7.60, or €13.40 with Château de Marqueyssac; Ⓦwww.castelnaud.com) provides the more entertaining visit – and more informative, thanks to the excellent English-language guidebook you can borrow; allow at least a couple of hours.

Like Beynac, Castelnaud was founded in the twelfth century and bitterly fought over on many occasions, starting with the bellicose Simon de Montfort, who seized it as early as 1214 during his Cathar Crusades (see p.356). Then during the Hundred Years' War the lords of Castelnaud sided with the English, slugging it out for nearly four decades with the French at Beynac until Charles VII besieged Castelnaud in 1442. After holding out for three weeks, a treacherous English captain handed over the keys in return for his life and the princely sum of four hundred crowns.

Heavily restored in the last decades, the château now houses a great **museum of medieval warfare**. Its core is an extensive collection of original weaponry, including all sorts of bizarre contraptions, such as an "organ" which sprayed lead balls from its multiple barrels, and a fine assortment of armour. The displays are interspersed with interesting video presentations (in French only) on the history of warfare. In summer (July & Aug), staff give demonstrations of the various siege engines dotted around the ramparts, and evening visits led by guides in period costume are also on offer (Mon–Fri at 8.15pm; €8; in French only).

On the road down to the village, where it joins the D57, it's worth stopping off briefly at the **Eco-musée de la Noix du Périgord** (April to mid-Nov daily 10am–7pm; €5), for everything you ever wanted to know about nuts – **walnuts**, specifically. As well as detailing oil pressing, the exhibition reveals historical gems such as the fact that Louis XI's beard was trimmed using heated walnut shells, and that walnuts are used in the insulation of American spaceships. It also points out the nuts' many health benefits, before you're shepherded through to the well-stocked shop. If you're lucky the mill itself will be working, but otherwise there's a self-explanatory video featuring Ste-Nathalène's more authentic Moulin de la Tour (see p.199). The adjacent orchard, spattered with giant cement walnuts and picnic tables, is particularly good for young children.

Back on the riverfront, you'll find free **parking**, as well as a couple of cafés and a place to rent **canoes**: the Base Municipal Canoë-Kayak (Ⓣ05.53.29.40.07; open all year). While there are no hotels in Castelnaud, there's a lively three-star **campsite**, *Lou Castel* (Ⓣ05.53.29.89.24, Ⓦwww.loucastel.com; May–Oct), among oak woods on the plateau a couple of kilometres to the south. It has several pools, water slides, a bar and a restaurant.

Les Milandes

From Castelnaud it's a scenic drive 5km west along the river past **Château de Fayrac** (not open to the public) with its slated pepper-pot towers – an English forward position in the Hundred Years' War, built to watch over Beynac – to **Les Milandes** (April & May daily except Sat 10am–6.30pm; June & Sept daily except Sat 10am–7pm; July & Aug daily 9.30am–7.30pm; Oct daily except Sat 10am–6.15pm; €8; Ⓦwww.milandes.com). Built in the late 1400s, the ivy-clad château was the property of the Caumont family (the lords of Castelnaud) until the Revolution, but its most famous owner was the Folies Bergère star, **Josephine Baker** (see box, p.226), who fell in love with it while visiting friends in the area in 1937.

It's easy to see why. The Renaissance château, sitting high above the Dordogne, has all the necessary romantic ingredients: towers, machicolations, balustrades, gargoyles, ornate dormer windows and terraced gardens shaded by great, glossy-leafed magnolias. After she bought Les Milandes in 1947, Josephine set about modernizing it, adding creature comforts such as the en-suite bathrooms, whose decor was inspired by her favourite perfumes – Arpège-style black tiles with gold taps and ceiling in one, Dioresque pink marble with silver-leaf in another. But it's really the stories surrounding Josephine and Les Milandes that are more intriguing than the château itself. Her roller-coaster life story is enough to fill a book, but you can trace the broad outlines from the collection of photos and posters. The few costumes that escaped the auctioneer's hammer in 1968 are

Josephine Baker and the Rainbow Tribe

Born on June 3, 1906, in the black ghetto of East St Louis, Illinois, **Josephine Baker** was one of the most remarkable women of the twentieth century. Her mother washed clothes for a living and her father was a drummer who soon deserted his family, yet by the late 1920s Baker was the most celebrated cabaret star in France, primarily due to her role in the legendary **Folies Bergère** show in Paris. On her first night, de Gaulle, Hemingway, Piaf and Stravinsky were among the audience, and her notoriety was further enhanced by her long line of illustrious husbands and lovers, which included the crown prince of Sweden and the crime novelist Georges Simenon. She also mixed with the likes of Le Corbusier and Adolf Loos, and kept a pet cheetah, with whom she used to walk around Paris. During the war, she was active in the **Resistance**, for which she was awarded the Croix de Guerre. Later on, she became involved in the civil rights movement in North America, where she insisted on playing to non-segregated audiences, a stance which got her arrested in Canada and tailed by the FBI in the US.

By far her most bizarre and expensive project was the château of **Les Milandes**, which she rented from 1938 and then bought in 1947, including 300 hectares of land, after her marriage to the French orchestra leader Jo Bouillon. Having equipped the place with two hotels, three restaurants, a mini-golf course, tennis court and an autobiographical wax museum, Baker opened the château to the general public as a model multicultural community, popularly dubbed the "village du monde". Unable to have children of her own, in the course of the 1950s she adopted babies (mostly orphans) of different ethnic and religious backgrounds from around the world. By the end of the decade, she had brought twelve children to Les Milandes, including a black Catholic Colombian and a Buddhist Korean, along with her own mother, brother and sister from East St Louis.

Over 300,000 people a year visited the château in the 1950s, but her more conservative neighbours were never very happy about Les Milandes and the "Rainbow Tribe". In the 1960s, Baker's financial problems, divorce and two heart attacks spelled the end for the project, and despite a sit-in protest by Baker herself (by then in her sixties), the château and its contents were auctioned off in 1968. Still performing and as glamorous as ever, Josephine died of a stroke in 1975 and was given a grand state funeral at La Madeleine in Paris, mourned by thousands of her adopted countryfolk.

also on display, though these are somewhat moth-eaten after mouldering in the cellar for 25 years.

From the terrace in front of the château, where they hold **falconry demonstrations** every afternoon, you can look down on the J-shaped swimming pool belonging to one of the many fun-parks Josephine established in the area.

La Roque-Gageac

The village of **LA ROQUE-GAGEAC**, on the river's north bank 5km east of Beynac, is almost too perfect, its ochre-coloured houses sheltering under dramatically overhanging cliffs. Regular winner of France's prettiest village contest, it inevitably pulls in the tourist buses, and since here again the main road separates the village from the river, the noise and fumes of the traffic can become oppressive. The best way to escape is to slip away through the lanes and alleyways that wind up through the terraced houses. The other option is to rent a canoe and paddle over to the opposite bank, where you can picnic and enjoy a much better view of La Roque than from among the crowds milling around beneath the village, at its best in the burnt-orange glow of the evening sun.

Look carefully at the cliff above the village and you'll see guardposts, ramparts and other remnants of a **troglodyte fort** (Easter to Oct daily 10am–6pm; €5). At one time belonging to the bishops of Sarlat, who built themselves a château within the ramparts, the fort provided the villagers with a virtually impregnable refuge from the Vikings' ninth-century invasions right up until the early 1800s when it was largely dismantled; only once was it taken by force: during the wars of religion by the Protestant army of the famous Geoffroy de Vivans (see p.360). The remaining defence-works are of only moderate interest, but it's worth tackling the vertigo-inducing ladder for the views.

A less athletic option is to take a **boat ride** down to Castelnaud. From April to October two companies offer these one-hour round-trips in a *gabarre*: Gabares Norbert (ⓣ05.53.29.40.44, ⓦwww.norbert.fr; €8.50) and Gabarres Caminades (ⓣ05.53.29.40.95; same price). There's nothing to choose between the two companies; both offer live commentary in French, or a pre-recorded English version on a headset. If you'd rather go under your own steam, you can rent **canoes** from Canoë Dordogne (ⓣ05.53.29.58.50, ⓦwww.canoe-dordogne.fr) and Canoë Vacances (ⓣ05.53.28.17.07, ⓦwww.canoevacances.com), both east of La Roque towards Vitrac and Sarlat.

Practicalities

For more information about activities in the area, contact La Roque's **tourist office** (Easter to June, Sept & Oct daily 10am–12.30pm & 2–5.30pm; July & Aug daily 10am–6pm; ⓣ05.53.29.17.01), in a hut by the main car park on the Sarlat side of town. Since most people just come here for a day-trip, there's usually space if you want to **stay** the night outside the summer peak. Nicest of the town's hotels is *La Belle Étoile* (ⓣ05.53.29.51.44, ⓦwww.belleetoile.fr; ❸; closed Nov–March), on the main road below the fort, whose airy, rustic rooms almost all have river views. The hotel also boasts a restaurant serving classic cuisine on a terrace (menus from €26; closed Mon & Wed lunchtime). More luxurious is the *Manoir de la Malartrie* (ⓣ05.53.29.03.51, ⓦwww.chambresdhotes-lamalartrie.com; ❻), which

▲ La Roque-Gageac

has four romantic *chambres d'hôtes* in a Belle-Epoque château off the D703 just east of La Roque. Even if the faux-medieval exterior isn't quite your cup of tea, the interiors are sumptuous and it's in a perfect setting, with a pool, garden and terraces overlooking the river. There's also a *gîte d'étape* called *la Ferme Fleurie,* 1km along the road to Sarlat (Ⓣ05.53.28.33.39; €14 per person; closed Nov–March), which offers basic accommodation in shared dorms.

Of the many **campsites** in the vicinity, the two-star *La Plage*, 1km west of La Roque (Ⓣ05.53.29.50.83, Ⓦwww.camping-laplage.fr; closed Oct–March) is relatively cheap and has great views up to the castle of Castelnaud. Alternatively, *La Butte* (Ⓣ05.53.28.30.28, Ⓦwww.campinglabutte.com; closed Nov–March), off the D703 in a top location to the west, is better equipped, with a bar and small shop, as well as various activities on site.

Domme and around

High on the scarp on the south bank of the river, 5km southeast from La Roque-Gageac and 10km due south of Sarlat (see p.193), **DOMME** is an exceptionally well-preserved, terribly pretty *bastide*, now wholly given over to tourism. Its foremost attraction, however, is its position. From the chestnut-shaded **Esplanade du Belvédère** at the town's northern edge, you look out over a wide sweep of river country encompassing everything from Beynac to the Cingle de Montfort (see opposite). The drop here is so precipitous that fortifications were deemed unnecessary when the *bastide* was founded in 1281. They lived to regret it: in 1588 a small band of Protestants scaled the cliffs at dawn to take the town completely by surprise. The intruders stayed four years, during which time they destroyed the church amongst other buildings, before they were forced to abandon the town again to Catholic control.

Much of Domme's thirteenth-century walls and three of the gateways they skirted remain. Of the latter, the best-preserved and most interesting is easterly **Porte des Tours**, flanked by two round bastions. In 1307 a group of Templar knights was imprisoned here for eleven years; if you peer through the openings you can just make out the graffiti – Crucifixion scenes, the Virgin Mary, angels and various secret signs – they carved on the walls. Alternatively, you can visit it on a guided tour run by the tourist office (May–Sept; by appointment only; €6.50), or there are photos of the carvings in the **Musée des Arts et Traditions Populaires** (same hours as tourist office, see below; €4) on central place de la Halle. Its displays of local life are nicely done, though not wildly interesting, whereas the **caves** (daily: Feb to mid-Nov; contact tourist office for hours & tickets; €8 including museum), which extend hundreds of metres under the village from beneath the timbered market hall, can definitely be given a miss. The concretions are badly discoloured with algae and can't compare with any of the area's other limestone caverns; the only good point is the exit onto the cliff-face with a panoramic lift up to the top and a pleasant stroll back along the promenade de la Falaise.

On the way to – or from – Domme, it's worth making a brief stop in **CÉNAC**, down by the river, to admire its Romanesque **church**, located a short distance along the D50 to St-Cybranet. Apart from a lovely *lauze* roof, its main draw is the remarkably distinct carving on the capitals, featuring various animals and demons, including Daniel taming the lions.

Practicalities

Domme's **tourist office** (Feb–June & Sept to mid-Nov daily 10am–noon & 2–6pm; July & Aug daily 10am–7pm; mid-Nov to Jan Mon–Fri 10am–noon & 2–6pm; Ⓣ05.53.31.71.00, Ⓦwww.ot-domme.com) is located on place de la

Halle. On **market** days (Thursday mornings) stalls spill out of the square south down the main commercial street, the Grande-Rue, itself lined with souvenir shops. At the top of this road, *Le Nouvel Hôtel* (ⓣ05.53.28.38.67, ⓦwww.domme-nouvel-hotel.com; ❷; closed Sun eve & Mon except in July & Aug, also closed Jan–March) offers simple, reasonably priced **rooms** above a restaurant serving regional fare (menus from €15). For those on a more generous budget, the smartest place to stay is *L'Esplanade*, right on the cliff edge (ⓣ05.53.28.31.41, ⓦwww.esplanade-perigord.com; ❺; closed Nov–Feb except Christmas holidays); be sure to ask for a room with a view over the cliff, as these are not necessarily more expensive. *L'Esplanade* also has a great **restaurant** (closed Mon & Wed), with menus from €36 and – for the true enthusiast – a sublime *menu de truffes* costing €98.

The nearest **campsite** is Cénac's one-star municipal site (ⓣ05.53.28.31.91, ⓕ05.53.31.41.32; closed mid-Sept to mid-June) beside the bridge. In summer several **canoe rental** places set up here, including Le Sioux (ⓣ05.53.28.30.81, ⓦwww.canoes-le-sioux.com) and Cénac Périgord Loisirs (ⓣ05.53.29.99.69).

Upstream towards Souillac

If you're taking the prettier north bank of the Dordogne from Domme, the spectacular, white-walled **Château de Montfort** (not open to the public) soon hoves into view atop its well-defended promontory. The distinctive, Disney-esque turrets date from its nineteenth-century reconstruction. To complete the picture it overlooks the almost perfect curve of the **Cingle de Montfort**, not the biggest but certainly the tightest of the Dordogne's many meanders.

Two kilometres further on another inviting little Romanesque **church** below the village of **CARSAC-AILLAC** makes a good place to pause. Though the meadow setting is delightful, the church's **carvings** are the main point of interest: in this case Arabic-influenced capitals around the choir and some later keystones. Note, too, the Stations of the Cross made by Russian abstract artist Léon Zack, who was a refugee here during World War II. Carsac also has a couple of good **hotels**, which could be used as a base for Sarlat, only 10km to the northwest and accessible by bus. In the village itself, the family-run *Hôtel Delpeyrat* (ⓣ05.53.28.10.43, ⓔhotel.rest.delpeyrat@wanadoo.fr; ❶; closed Oct & Nov) is a charmingly old-fashioned place offering well-priced rooms, most of them set back from the road overlooking a small garden, and equally homely cooking (menus from €13; restaurant closed Sun eve & Sat midday). The more upmarket option is *Le Relais du Touron* (ⓣ05.53.28.16.70, ⓦwww.lerelaisdutouron.com; ❸; closed mid-Nov to March; menus €14.50–32), set in extensive grounds a short distance along the Sarlat road. Its bright and cheery rooms occupy a modern block, beside an outdoor pool.

From Carsac you need to cross back over the Dordogne and continue along its south bank for some 5km to find the **Château de Fénelon** (Feb & Nov weekends 2–5pm; March & Oct daily except Tues 2–5pm; April–June & Sept daily except Tues 10.30am–12.30pm & 2.30–6pm; July & Aug daily 10am–7pm; closed Dec & Jan; €7.50), clamped to its own rocky outcrop. With its triple walls and great round towers topped with *lauzes*, the castle exudes all the might of the original medieval fortress. As you get closer, however, the Renaissance-era additions and other, later embellishments become more apparent – the large mullion windows and the gallery closing the interior courtyard, for example. The castle's most illustrious occupant was **François de Salignac de la Mothe-Fénelon**, who was born here in 1651. Private tutor to the heir to the throne and later archbishop of Cambrai, he fell from grace when King Louis XIV interpreted his work *Télémaque* – which recounts the adventures of Ulysses' son – as a thinly veiled attack on the Crown. His intention had been to teach the young prince the finer points of kinghood, but for his pains Fénelon was banished to Cambrai where he died in 1715. He is remembered with much pride at Fénelon today. There's a mock-up of his study and numerous portraits, but the present owners have also amassed a worthwhile collection of period furniture, tapestries and medieval weaponry. The ornate walnut chimneypieces are also eye-catching.

From the Château de Fénelon the route continues east along the Dordogne, past one of its main rivals, the Château de Rouffillac (not open to the public), on the opposite bank, before finally reaching Souillac (see p.235) 17km later.

Travel details

Trains

Belvès to: Agen (3–4 daily; 1hr–1hr 15min); Le Bugue (5–6 daily; 20–35min); Le Buisson (5–6 daily; 15–30min); Les Eyzies (5–6 daily; 30–40min); Périgueux (5–6 daily; 1hr–1hr 15min); Siorac-en-Périgord (2–3 daily; 6min).
Le Bugue to: Agen (3–4 daily; 1hr 30min); Belvès (3–4 daily; 20–35min); Le Buisson (3–4 daily; 15min); Les Eyzies (5–6 daily; 7min); Limoges (1 daily; 2hr); Périgueux (5–6 daily; 50min); Siorac-en-Périgord (3–4 daily; 20min).
Les Eyzies to: Agen (3–4 daily; 1hr 40min); Belvès (3–4 daily; 30min); Le Bugue (3–4 daily; 7min); Le Buisson (3–4 daily; 15–20min); Limoges (1 daily; 1hr 50min); Périgueux (5–6 daily; 40min); Siorac-en-Périgord (3–4 daily; 30min).
Sarlat to: Bergerac (5–6 daily; 1hr–1hr 30min); Bordeaux (5–6 daily; 2hr 20min–2hr 45min); Le Buisson (5–6 daily; 30–45min); Castillon-la-Bataille (5–6 daily; 1hr 40min–2hr); Lalinde (5–6 daily; 40min–1hr); Ste-Foy-la-Grande (5–6 daily; 1hr 30min–1hr 50min); Siorac-en-Périgord (2–3 daily; 20min); Trémolat (4–5 daily; 35–50min).
Siorac-en-Périgord to: Agen (3–4 daily; 1hr 10min–1hr 20min); Belvès (3–4 daily; 6min); Bergerac (2–3 daily; 45min–1hr 15min); Bordeaux (2–3 daily; 2hr 20min); Le Buisson (4–6 daily; 7min); Le Bugue (2–3 daily; 15–30min); Les Eyzies (2–3 daily; 25–40min); Périgueux (2–3 daily; 50min–1hr 10min); Sarlat (1–2 daily; 35min).
St-Cyprien to: Sarlat (5–6 daily; 25min); Bergerac (5–6 daily; 1hr); Le Buisson (5–6 daily; 25min).
Terrasson-la-Villedieu to: Brive (4–7 daily; 15min); Périgueux (3–7 daily; 35–50min).

Buses

Le Bugue to: Périgueux (school term Mon–Fri 1–2 daily, school hols Wed only; 1hr).
Carsac to: Sarlat (1–4 daily; 20min); Souillac (2–5 daily; 40min).
Montignac to: Brive (Mon–Fri 1 daily during school term only; 1hr 15min); Périgueux (school term Mon–Fri 1–2 daily, July & Aug & school hols Wed only; 1hr); St-Geniès (as for Périgueux; 15min); Sarlat (as for Périgueux; 30min); Terrasson (as for Brive; 25min).
Sarlat to: Carsac (2–5 daily; 20min); Montignac (July & Aug & school hols Wed only, rest of year Mon–Fri 1–2 daily; 30min); Périgueux (as for Montignac; 1hr 40min); St-Geniès (as for Montignac; 20min); Souillac (2–5 daily; 50min).

5

The Upper Dordogne valley and Rocamadour

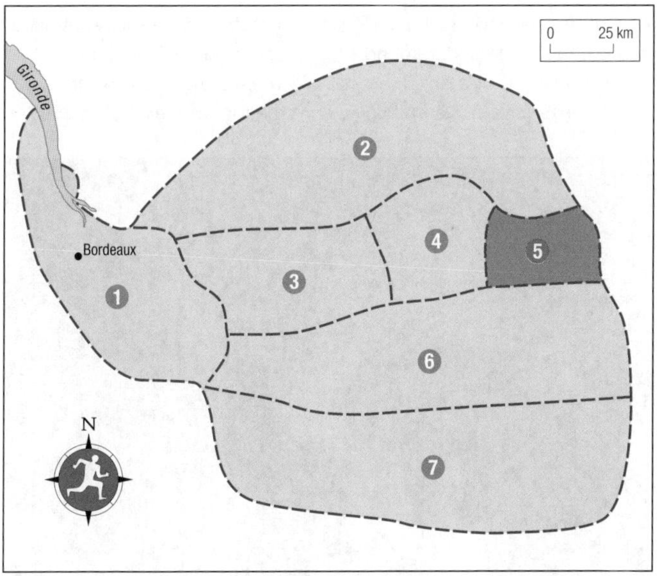

CHAPTER 5

Highlights

* **Souillac** In the abbey church of Ste-Marie the image of the prophet Isaiah is a masterpiece of Romanesque art. See p.235
* **Rocamadour** One of France's top pilgrimage sites defies gravity in its spectacular cliff-edge location. See p.239
* **Carennac** Wander the lanes of this typical Quercy village and then peek inside its quiet cloister. See p.249
* **Gouffre de Padirac** Take a boat trip on an underground river accessed via an immense cavern. See p.250
* **Château de Castelnau** Fans of military architecture shouldn't miss this brooding fortress. See p.252
* **Beaulieu-sur-Dordogne** Laid-back market town on the banks of the Dordogne that sees fewer tourists than it deserves. See p.252
* **Château de Montal** Admire some of the region's finest Renaissance carvings on the facade and staircase of this stately home. See p.258
* **Autoire** Picture-perfect village encircled by limestone cliffs. There are good views from the top, as well. See p.259

▲ Admiring the Gouffre de Padirac

5

The Upper Dordogne valley and Rocamadour

In its upper reaches the River Dordogne cuts a green swathe through the rocky limestone plateau of **Haut-Quercy**, as the northern sector of the Lot *département* is traditionally known. Though the cliffs rise to considerable heights in places, the valley here lacks the drama of the perched castles and towns immediately downstream. Instead, away from the main towns, it offers quieter lanes, more modest castles and a succession of unspoilt riverside villages.

The main gateway to the Upper Dordogne valley is **Souillac**, a busy little town whose major attraction is its domed abbey church, containing the finest of several examples of Romanesque carving scattered along the valley. A short distance upstream from Souillac, an attractive back road strikes off along the River Ouysse, a minor tributary of the Dordogne, heading southeast to the spectacular pilgrimage town of **Rocamadour**, whose seven religious sanctuaries are built almost vertically into a rocky backdrop.

Back on the Dordogne, near the little village of **Lacave**, the river meanders in a northeasterly direction through walnut orchards and dozing villages to the dramatic crags around **Gluges**, where it has carved the **Cirque de Montvalent** out of the plateau. North across the river from here, the market town of **Martel** sees surprisingly few tourists, given its medieval centre full of turreted mansions, while to the east **Carennac** merits a stop for its picturesque lanes and the twelfth-century carved portal adorning its church. Carennac also lies within striking distance of the **Gouffre de Padirac**, several kilometres to the south, where a collapsed cavern has left a gaping hole in the limestone plateau. Down below, a river heads deep underground through passages festooned with giant stalactites.

Upstream of Carennac the Dordogne valley begins to open out to form a broad plain around its confluence with the Cère. **Bretenoux**, the main town guarding the Cère valley, isn't itself a particularly engaging place, but it's more than compensated for by the nearby **Château de Castelnau**, an impregnable

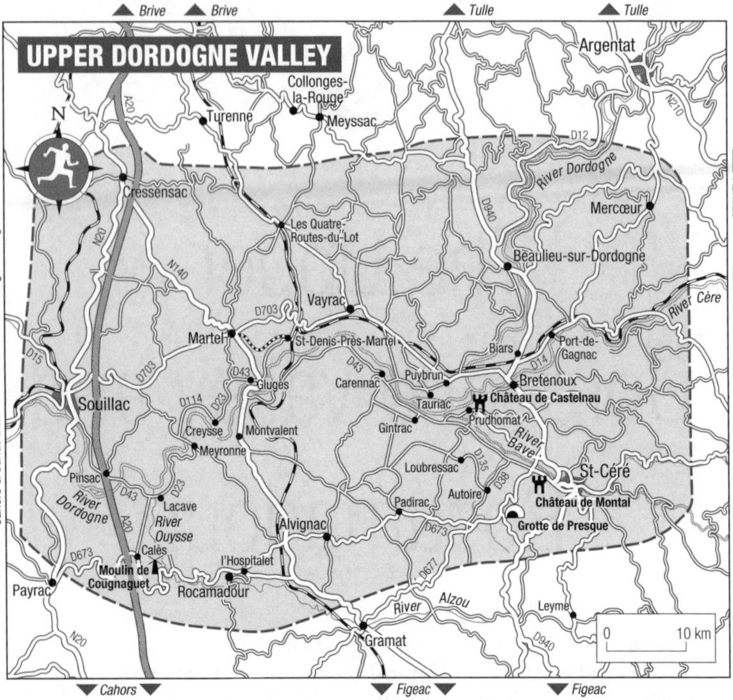

fortress standing on the frontier between the old provinces of Quercy and the Limousin, which still dominates the country for miles around. To the north of Bretenoux, **Beaulieu-sur-Dordogne** is a pleasing town, featuring an abbey church with another magnificent tympanum carved in the same style as those at Souillac and Carennac.

To the south of Bretenoux, **St-Céré**, like Beaulieu, provides another good base for exploring the region, and beneath the brooding towers of its ruined château, a scattering of stone and half-timbered townhouses attest to the town's fifteenth- and sixteenth-century heyday. There's more Renaissance architecture on show on the facade and in the superb stone staircase of the **Château de Montal**, a few kilometres to the west. The nearby villages of **Autoire** and **Loubressac**, meanwhile, are rooted firmly in the Quercy soil, their houses sporting little pigeon-lofts and the red-tile roofs splayed gently above the eaves which are typical of the region. From beside Loubressac's encircling walls or, better still, from the *cirque* above Autoire, there are sweeping views across the Dordogne valley and eastwards towards the river's source among the green foothills of the Massif Central.

Public transport in this region is patchy. You can reach Souillac, Rocamadour, St-Denis-lès-Martel (for Martel) and Bretenoux by train and, except for Rocamadour, by bus too. There are also buses to Martel, Carennac, Beaulieu and St-Céré, but services are fairly infrequent and the connections between the smaller towns are not particularly good. If you plan to do a lot of bus journeys, it would be worth getting hold of the comprehensive timetable, *Les Bus du Lot*; tourist offices in larger towns such as Souillac and Bretenoux should have copies.

Souillac and around

Traffic-ridden **Souillac** suffers from being the major gateway to both Sarlat and the Périgord Noir to the west and to the upper reaches of the Dordogne valley to the east, and though the nearby A20 autoroute brings some relief, it will never be a particularly pretty place. The town's main attraction is the **Église Ste-Marie**, with its exquisite carvings, but it also has a small enclave of old streets, which are worth a quick wander, and an engaging museum containing a large collection of automated dolls.

Immediately upstream from Souillac, the valley is dominated by the A20 road-bridge, but a few meanders of the river later and you're back among quiet lanes and unspoilt scenery. One place to head for is **Lacave**, a village on the south

Festivals, events and markets

Second Sunday in May Beaulieu-sur-Dordogne: Fête de la Fraise. France's strawberry capital gets down to some serious baking with an 800-kilo strawberry tart. There's a great strawberry market, too.

Late May or early June Rocamadour: Fête des Fromages Fermiers. At Pentecôte (Whit Sunday) artisan cheese producers gather above the town at L'Hospitalet to show off their wares. In addition to the cheeses, there are folk concerts.

Mid-July Rocamadour: Les Éclectiques de Rocamadour. This week-long music festival ranges from classical ballet to Eastern European folk groups. Ticket-only concerts take place in the Basilique St-Sauveur and the château.

Mid-July to mid-August St-Céré and around: Festival de St-Céré et du Haut-Quercy (Ⓣ05.65.38.28.08, Ⓦwww.festival-saint-cere.com). Three weeks of opera, recitals, orchestral works and chamber music in St-Céré (including the châteaux of Montal and Castelnau), Beaulieu, Martel, Cahors and Souillac. Tickets required.

Third week in August Rocamadour: Cantica Sacra (Ⓦwww.cantica-sacra.fr). One-week sacred singing course open to members of the public wishing to improve their singing technique in an exceptional setting.

Third weekend in July Souillac: Souillac en Jazz (Ⓣ05.65.37.81.56, Ⓦwww.souillacenjazz.net). International jazz acts let rip in the streets of Souillac for six days of concerts, films, exhibitions and a feast on the final night. The big-name, ticket-only events take place outdoors next to the abbey church.

July 23 Martel: Foire à la Laine. A wool fair, in which the best fleeces are judged under the market hall.

Second weekend in August Souillac: Festival du Mime Automate (Ⓣ05.65.37.07.07). About fifteen groups of mime artists give performances (mostly free) in the streets of Souillac on the Friday and Saturday.

Early September Rocamadour: Semaine Mariale. The week dedicated to the Virgin Mary is celebrated with pilgrimages, prayers and Masses, including torchlight processions to the Chapelle Notre-Dame.

Last weekend in September Rocamadour: Rassemblement Européen de Montgolfières. Hot-air balloons take off from the valley below Rocamadour; for the best views, take up position early on the Belvédère in L'Hospitalet.

Markets

The main **markets** in this region are at: Beaulieu-sur-Dordogne (Wed & Sat); Bretenoux (Tues & Sat); Martel (Wed & Sat); St-Céré (Sat & first and third Wed of month); and Souillac (Fri). In addition to the weekly market, an annual truffle market takes place in Martel between mid-December and the end of January.

bank with some passably interesting limestone caves. From Lacave you can take an attractive detour south along a tributary river, the Ouysse, as it cuts its way through a mini-gorge in the limestone plateau, to visit a 600-year-old working flour mill. Continue on this route and you will eventually find yourself in Rocamadour (see p.239).

Arrival and information

Getting to Souillac by public transport is not a problem since it lies on the main Paris–Toulouse **train** line. The gare SNCF lies just over a kilometre northwest of town; take avenue Jean Jaurès and then avenue Martin-Malvy, which will bring you out at the west end of avenue Gambetta, the old quarter's main east–west artery. **Buses** from Sarlat, Brive, Gourdon and St-Denis-lès-Martel (on the Brive–Figeac train line) mostly stop at the train station or the Sarlat road, while Eurolines buses (tickets from Voyages Belmon, av de Sarlat; ⓣ05.65.37.81.15, ⓦwww.eurolines.fr), en route between Toulouse and London, Brussels, Hanover and Amsterdam, stop in central Souillac on the place du Foirail, a large square to the east of the main N20. This square also provides the most convenient **car parking** for the centre.

The **tourist office** (July & Aug Mon–Sat 9.30am–12.30pm & 2–7pm, Sun 10am–noon & 3–6pm; rest of year Mon–Sat 10am–noon & 2–6pm; ⓣ05.65.37.81.56, ⓦwww.tourisme-souillac.com) is located in the town centre on boulevard Louis-Jean Malvy, just across the road from place du Foirail; from inside the office a window gives a view down into the nave of the disused church of St Martin.

You can **rent cars** from the Renault garage on the road to Martel (Ets Sanfourche; ⓣ05.65.32.73.03, ⓕ05.65.32.77.15), or from A.C. Loc'46, 22 avenue du Général de Gaulle (ⓣ05.65.32.68.74, ⓦhttp://acloc46.fr) and **bicycles** from Carrefour du Cycle, 23 av de Gaulle (ⓣ05.65.37.07.52), the northern extension of boulevard Louis-Jean Malvy. Bikes and **canoes** are also available from Copeyre Canoë (ⓣ05.65.32.72.61, ⓦwww.copeyre.com), next to *Les Ondines* campsite (see below). **Internet** access is available at the Point Information Jeunes (Cyberbase), avenue de Sarlat (ⓣ05.65.37.89.58; Tues–Fri 10am–noon & 3–6pm, Sat 10am–noon). Souillac's main **market** takes place on Friday mornings.

Accommodation

Hôtel Chastrusse 10km southwest of Souillac in Nadaillac-de-Rouge ⓣ05.65.37.60.08, ⓦwww.hotel-restaurant-chastrusse.com. Delightfully unpretentious place with rooms either in the old block – the nicer option – or modern bungalows around the pool, with an excellent restaurant serving regional fare including home-made *confit*, foie gras and other meat preserves – they expect you to have a hearty appetite (closed Sat & eves in winter, menus from €12). Closed Nov. ❷

Domaine de la Paille Basse 9km northwest of Souillac ⓣ05.65.37.85.48, ⓦwww.lapaillebasse.com. Four-star campsite that's the place to head for if you've got your own transport. It's set on a lovely, high spot, signed off the D15 to Salvignac.

Grand Hotel 1 allée de Verninac ⓣ05.65.32.78.30, ⓦwww.grandhotel-souillac.com. Friendly hotel decked out in a contemporary style, located next to the tourist office. Some rooms have private balconies while their shady terrace on the main street is ideal for a quick snack, and their elegant restaurant, *L'Imprévu*, offers menus from €15.50–29.50. Closed Jan–Feb. ❷–❸

Les Ondines ⓣ05.65.37.86.44. Large, three-star campsite down by the river to the south of town. Closed Oct–April.

Le Pavillon Saint-Martin 5 Place Saint-Martin ⓣ05.65.32.63.45, ⓦwww.hotel-saint-martin-souillac.com. Housed in a sixteenth-century notary's mansion, *Le Pavillon Saint-Martin* has a lovely stone-flagged entrance hall and a spectacular staircase, and is furnished with a variety of bright, comfortable rooms, ranging from old-fashioned floral to eye-assaulting reds and oranges. Breakfast includes fresh strawberries in season and is served in a vaulted cellar. ❸–❺

La Vieille Auberge 1 rue de la Recège ⓣ05.65.32.79.43, ⓦwww.la-vieille-auberge.com. Across the old quarter at the west end of avenue Gambetta, this is Souillac's most upmarket hotel. The rooms in the main building are well equipped but rather functional. The pricey restaurant offers menus from €32 (closed Mon–Sat lunchtime all year & all day Sun Jan–March). Hotel closed mid-Nov to Christmas. ❹

The Town

Souillac's two major sights are located in the compact old quarter to the west of boulevard Louis-Jean Malvy. A handy landmark to aim for is the semi-ruined **belfry** of St-Martin church, partially destroyed in the Wars of Religion, on the southeast corner of the old centre.

Walk one block west of the belfry and you come to a wide, open space dominated by the beautiful Romanesque **abbey church of Ste-Marie**. Its Byzantine domes are reminiscent of the cathedrals of Périgueux and Cahors, though on a smaller scale, while its largely unadorned interior conveys a far greater sense of antiquity. The first church on this site belonged to a priory founded in the tenth century, which became an abbey five hundred years later. Badly damaged during both the Hundred Years' War and Wars of Religion, the church was restored in the seventeenth century before being abandoned during the Revolution. Sadly, only fragments of the **Romanesque sculptures** that once graced the main, west portal have survived, but those that do remain – now reassembled inside the west door – are superb. Those on the tympanum tell the story of a local monk, Théophile, who was dismissed from the treasury for corruption. Desperate to regain his position, he is said to have made a pact with the Devil, but then fell seriously ill and, full of remorse, beseeched the Virgin Mary for forgiveness. His luck was in – the final scene depicts Théophile's dream of the Virgin accompanied by St Michael driving the Devil away. The greatest piece of craftsmanship is the bas-relief of the prophet Isaiah to the right of the door. Fluid and supple, it appears that the elongated, bearded figure clutching his parchment and with one leg extended is dancing for joy as he proclaims news of the coming of the Messiah.

Behind the church to the west, the **Musée de l'Automate** (Jan–March, Nov & Dec Wed–Sun 2.30–5.30pm; April, May & Oct Tues–Sun 10am–noon & 3–6pm; June & Sept daily 10am–noon & 3–6pm; July & Aug daily 10am–7pm; €5.50) contains an impressive collection of nineteenth- and twentieth-century mechanical dolls and animals that dance, juggle and perform magical tricks. Most come from the once-famous Rouillet-Decamps workshops in Paris and include such pieces as a life-sized 1920s jazz band, Charlie Chaplin and a woman doing the twist.

Eating

Along with those listed below, don't forget the hotel **restaurants** mentioned opposite, which are all worth trying.

Le Beffroi 6 place St-Martin. Serves up simple *plats du jour* at €6.50 and menus (€10–25) beneath the old bell tower – it's particularly lovely in summer, when it's warm enough to eat out on the terrace under the wisteria. Closed Sun & Mon Nov–March.

Lycée d'Hôtellerie av Roger Couderc ⓣ05.65.27.03.00. If you fancy a more novel eating experience, head for the *Lycée*, situated on a hill to the west of the old quarter, where you can act as guinea-pigs for trainee chefs and waiters/waitresses. Don't be put off, though – the food is generally excellent and you'll need to reserve several days in advance. Menus are under €20 at lunchtime for four courses, and €30 in the evening for a five-course meal.

Closed weekends and during school hols, & June–Sept.

Le Redouillé 28 av de Toulouse ⓣ05.65.37.87.25. Despite its inconvenient location about 1km south of the centre along boulevard Louis-Jean Malvy, this is the best place to eat in Souillac. Menus range from €17 and make innovative use of local produce to create such mouthwatering dishes as calves' sweetbreads with *sauce aux morilles*, duck wings in kumquat sauce or *charlotte de confit de canard*. Closed Sun eve & Mon, also Jan to mid-Feb.

Lacave

Following the Dordogne upstream along the D43 you soon leave the autoroute behind as you crest the hill and drop down to **LACAVE**, on the river's south bank 14km southeast of Souillac. A cavernous hole in the limestone cliffs overshadowing the village marks the entrance to a series of underground lakes, together making up the **Grottes de Lacave**, which can be visited on 1hr 15min guided **tours** (daily: mid- to end March & Oct 10am–noon & 2–5pm; April–June 9.30am–noon & 2–6pm; July–Aug 25 9.30am–6pm; Aug 26 to Sept 30 9.30am–noon & 2–5.30pm; €8; ⓦwww.grottes-de-lacave.com). You travel the first few hundred metres by electric train, after which there's a lift up to the kilometre-long gallery resplendent with all manner of stalactites and stalagmites, from petrified "waterfalls" to great organ pipes. But the highlight here are the magical reflections in the lakes' mirrored surfaces – at one point they also use ultraviolet light to reveal the glittering fluorescence of the "living" water-filled formations while the older, dry deposits remain lost in the darkness.

There's a **hotel-restaurant** right opposite the cave entrance, but it's overpriced and very basic. With extra cash, treat yourself instead to a meal at the Michelin-starred *Le Pont de l'Ouysse* (ⓣ05.65.37.87.04, ⓦwww.lepontdelouysse.fr; ❽; closed mid-Nov to mid-March), which also has fourteen immaculate rooms. It's in an idyllic spot about a kilometre west of Lacave on the Souillac road (restaurant closed for lunch on Mon & Tues; menus from €30). Heading 2km out of Lacave in the opposite direction, on the D23 northeast to Meyronne, more rustic fare is available at the friendly *Ferme-Auberge Calvel* (ⓣ05.65.37.87.20; reservations required; July to mid-Sept daily except Mon; rest of year weekends only; menus €15 and €16), which also offers basic *camping à la ferme* with space for a handful of tents (closed mid-Sept to April). Alternatively, in a peaceful setting right next to the river Ouysse off the D23 between Lacave and Calès, is the *camping à la ferme de l'Ouysse* (ⓣ05.65.32.63.01).

South to Rocamadour

From where the River Ouysse empties into the Dordogne just west of Lacave, a minor road heads south along the Ouysse, winding its way up the valley side to the plateau near the village of **CALÈS**, 5km later. The village is a neat and tidy place with little more than a couple of decent **hotels** in its centre. The more appealing of the two is *Le Petit Relais* (ⓣ05.65.37.96.09, ⓦwww.hotel-petitrelais.fr; ❸; closed Jan to mid-Feb; restaurant closed Sat lunch), with a rustic atmosphere, spick-and-span rooms and a pretty, flowery terrace where you can enjoy a good-value lunchtime menu at €13 for four courses.

At Calès the road from Lacave joins the D673 and turns east before dropping back down to the Ouysse, which has here carved out a mini-gorge. For an interesting diversion, turn left just after crossing the river and about a kilometre later you'll reach the **Moulin de Cougnaguet**, a fourteenth-century fortified mill, which ceased working commercially only in 1959. During thirty-minute guided tours (daily: April–Sept 10am–noon & 2–6pm; Oct 1–15 until 5pm; €4; ⓣ05.65.38.73.56, ⓦwww.cougnaguet.com), the enthusiastic owner points out its many defensive features – including arrow slits and sluice gates which, when opened from inside the mill, unleashed a torrent of water to sweep away anyone attempting to ford the millrace – and also puts the mill through its paces. Standing close to 1.5 tonnes of stone spinning at eighty revolutions per minute you get a real feel for the pent-up power of the water waiting calmly upstream.

From the mill it's only another 12km to Rocamadour. The D673 takes you back up onto the plateau and into Rocamadour from the north, but for a more dramatic approach follow the footpath (the GR6) along the valley. It runs alongside the River Ouysse past another mill – this was once big wheat country and even in high summer the Ouysse, part of which flows underground, never dries up – before turning eastwards along the River Alzou. Gradually the valley closes in until you round a bend and see the pilgrimage town of Rocamadour clinging to the cliff like a lost city.

Rocamadour and around

Halfway up the northern cliff-face of the deep and abrupt canyon of the River Alzou, the spectacular setting of **ROCAMADOUR** is hard to beat, with the turrets and spires of the **Cité Religieuse** at its heart, sandwiched between the jumbled roofs of the medieval town and the château's crenellated walls above. However, as you draw closer the spell is broken by the constant stream of pilgrims and more secular-minded visitors, particularly in summer, who fill lanes lined with shops peddling incongruous souvenirs. The main reason for Rocamadour's popularity – going back centuries – is the supposed miraculous properties of the statue of the **Black Madonna**, enshrined in the Cité's smoke-blackened **Chapelle Notre-Dame**. Modern tourists are also courted with a number of secondary attractions, including two wildlife parks, scattered on the plateau to the north and east of town. Even if those don't appeal, it's worth venturing up to the hamlet of **L'Hospitalet**, on the cliff to the east of Rocamadour, for the finest views of the town.

The first mention of Rocamadour's Chapelle Notre-Dame dates from 1105, although evidence suggests pilgrims started coming here as early as the ninth century. However, things really got going when a perfectly preserved body was discovered in a rock-hewn tomb beside the chapel in 1166. It was promptly declared to be that of Zacchaeus, later **St Amadour**; according to one legend, Zacchaeus – a tax-collector in Jericho at the time of Christ – was advised by the Virgin Mary to come to France and lived out his years in Rocamadour as a hermit. As tales of the saint and associated miracles spread, the faithful began to arrive in droves from all over Europe. St Bernard, numerous kings – including Henry II of England and Louis IX of France (St Louis) – and thousands of ordinary mortals crawled up the **Grand Escalier** (the pilgrims' staircase) on their knees to pay their respects and to seek forgiveness or cures. Others came simply to plunder the shrine – among them the Young King Henry (see box, p.248) – but they were easily outclassed by the Huguenots, who, in 1562, tried in vain to burn St Amadour's corpse and finally resigned themselves to hacking it to bits instead. In the meantime, centuries of warfare and plague led to a decline in the number of pilgrims. The buildings gradually fell into ruin until the bishops of Cahors, hoping to revive the flagging pilgrimage, financed a massive reconstruction in the early nineteenth century and so gave us the Rocamadour we see today.

Arrival and information

Getting to Rocamadour by public transport is awkward. There are no buses, and Rocamadour-Padirac **gare SNCF**, on the Brive–Figeac line, lies 3km away to the northeast. If you don't want to trek into town alongside the main road, you can call a taxi (Taxi Herbert ⓣ06.73.44.79.98 or 06.81.60.14.60). Note that the station is rarely staffed, and there's no ticket machine, so check the times of return trains carefully on arrival and buy a return ticket beforehand. Since Rocamadour is pedestrianized, if you arrive **by car** you'll have to park in L'Hospitalet or else in the valley several hundred metres below the town. Rather than walking into town from the valley car park, you could take Le Petit Train (April–Sept departures every 15 min; €2.50 one way, €3.50 return); they also do two 30min evening tours with a commentary (9.30 or 10pm; €5).

In the village centre, a **lift** (daily: April & Oct 9am–6pm; May, June & Sept 9am–7pm; July & Aug 8am–8pm; Feb, March, Nov 1–15 & Christmas school hols, 9am–6pm; closed Nov 15 to Jan 31, except the school hols; every 3min; €2 one-way, €3 return) links the town's main street, rue de la Couronnerie, with the Cité Religieuse above, while a **cable car** (daily: April & Oct 9am–6pm; May, June & Sept 9am–7pm; July & Aug 8am–10pm; Nov–March 10am–12.30pm & 2–5.30pm; every 3min; €2.50 one-way, €4 return) departs from just east of the Cité to emerge on the cliff-top near the château and the upper car parks.

Rocamadour has two **tourist offices**: the main one is located on the western outskirts of L'Hospitalet (April daily 10am–12.30pm & 2–6pm; May, June & Sept daily 10am–12.30pm & 2–7pm; July & Aug daily 10am–7pm; Oct Mon–Fri 10am–noon & 2–5pm, Sat & Sun 2–5.30pm; Nov–March Mon–Fri 10am–noon & 2–5pm; ⓣ05.65.33.22.00, ⓦwww.rocamadour.com), and you'll find a second on rue de la Couronnerie next to the Hôtel de Ville (daily: April, June & Sept

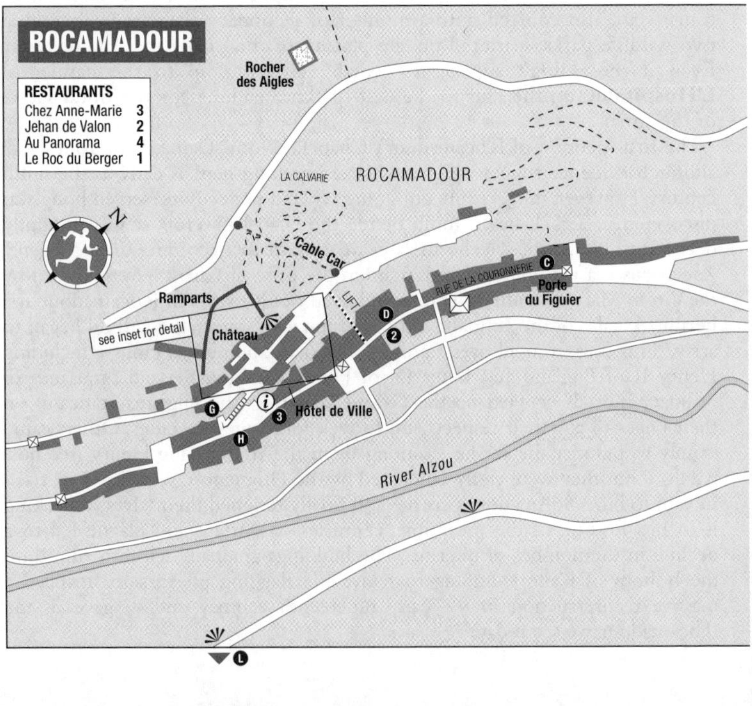

10am–12.30pm & 1.30–6pm; July & Aug 9.30am–7pm; Oct 10am–12.30pm & 2–5.30pm; Nov–March 2–5pm; same telephone number as above). There's a 24hr ATM outside the L'Hospitalet office.

The **mini-market** in l'Hospitalet sells basic provisions (see p.245), but otherwise the nearest food shops are in Alvignac, 7km northeast, which is also where you'll find the closest **pharmacy**.

Accommodation

One of the benefits of staying over in Rocamadour is that you can enjoy the town at its quietest in the early morning and late evening, and the **hotels** here are not too expensive. The downside is that everywhere is completely booked up in summer for miles around, and most places close during the winter months. Outside these periods, there are some good options, with a choice between central Rocamadour, the modern places in L'Hospitalet or somewhere in the surrounding countryside.

Hotels in the old town

Grand Hôtel Beau Site rue de la Couronnerie ⓣ05.65.33.63.08, ⓦwww.bestwestern-beausite.com. Rocamadour's top hotel occupies a lovely old mansion – its entrance all flagstone floors and oak beams – right in the centre, with more modern rooms in an annexe across the road. It has an excellent restaurant, the *Jehan de Valon* (see p.245), and a pool 2km away. Closed mid-Nov to early Feb. ④–⑦

Lion d'Or Porte Figuier ⓣ05.65.33.62.04, ⓦwww.liondor-rocamadour.com. Just inside the old city gate at the east end of rue de la Couronnerie, this old-fashioned, family-run hotel is the cheapest option in the old quarter, offering small but adequate en-suite rooms. Their restaurant is right across the street with good but equally no-nonsense food. Closed Nov–March. ②–③

Sainte-Marie place des Senhals ⓣ05.65.33.63.07, ⓦwww.hotel-sainte-marie.fr.

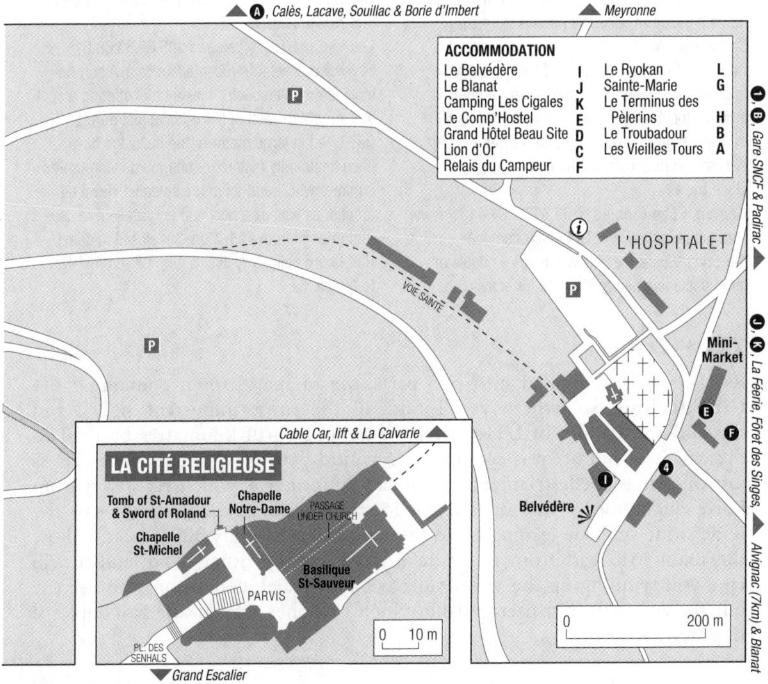

If the *Lion d'Or* is closed, try this friendly place halfway up the Grand Escalier. The rooms are simple and some quite small, but the location and restaurant with tasty food and superb views down into the valley make up for it (*plat du jour* at €10.50 and menus €14–28. The terrace also makes a nice spot for a pre-dinner drink. Closed Nov–March. ❸

Le Terminus des Pèlerins place de la Carreta ⓣ05.65.33.62.14, ⓦwww.terminus-des-pelerins.com. A good option on rue de la Couronnerie at the bottom of the Grand Escalier. Some rooms have terraces overlooking the valley, while all are painted fresh, modern colours and have spacious bathrooms. Their restaurant is popular for its traditional and regional cuisine, with a *plat du jour* at €10 and brasserie menus from €14.50 or €17 in the restaurant proper (closed Thurs eve & Fri April–June & Oct & Nov–March). ❸–❹

Accommodation in L'Hospitalet and around

Le Belvédère L'Hospitalet ⓣ05.65.33.63.25, ⓦwww.hotel-le-belvedere.fr. This is not the most beautiful hotel, but the rooms are decent and the location, on the cliff edge as you come into L'Hospitalet from Rocamadour, is superb. Note that only the more expensive rooms enjoy prime views, though you can also enjoy them from the restaurant's big picture windows (menus from €15). Closed Nov–March. ❸

Le Blanat Blanat ⓣ05.65.33.68.27, ⓦwww.gite-blanat-rocamadour.com. Four kilometres east of Rocamadour, just across the N140 and in a tiny hamlet, *Le Blanat* offers three simple *chambre d'hôte* rooms. The GR6 runs close by. ❷

Camping Les Cigales ⓣ05.65.33.64.44, ⓦwww.camping-cigales.com. Three-star campsite east of the *Comp'Hostel* (see below). It has a couple of large pools and plenty of space for activities including volleyball, mini-golf and table tennis. Closed Sept to Easter.

Le Comp'Hostel place de l'Europe ⓣ05.65.33.73.50, ⓦwww.hotelcompostelle.fr. No views from this modern hotel a hundred metres north of the *Belvédère*, but acceptable rooms – some with a small terrace – and a swimming pool. Closed mid-Oct to March. ❸

Relais du Campeur ⓣ05.65.33.63.28, ⓦwww.lerelaisducampeur.com. Leafy, two-star campsite situated next to the *Comp'Hostel* (see above). Closed Dec–Jan.

Le Ryokan Mages, just south of Rocamadour and signed off the D32 ⓣ05.65.11.63.67, ⓦwww.leryokan.com. Meaning "Japanese country inn", this *chambre d'hôte* occupies a converted stone barn decked out in a Japanese theme, furnished with objects collected during the hosts' travels in Asia. One room is decorated in warm red tones, the other in soothing pastel colours. They also use renewable energy sources to heat the barn. ❸–❹

Le Troubadour Belveyre ⓣ05.65.33.70.27, ⓦwww.hotel-troubadour.com. A small, spruce hotel, 1km north of L'Hospitalet on the D673, with flowery, en-suite rooms, where you can truly get away from the crowds. There's a pool and bikes, and a residents-only restaurant, open for dinner only (menus from €27; closed July & Aug). Closed mid-Nov to mid-Feb. ❹–❺

Les Vieilles Tours Lafage ⓣ05.65.33.68.01, ⓦwww.vieillestours-rocamadour.com. A surprisingly affordable country-house hotel offering a spot of luxury 3km west of L'Hospitalet just off the D673. Set in large grounds, the buildings have been beautifully restored – one room incorporates a mini-tower – and there are splendid views all around, as well as a pool and an excellent restaurant (menus from €25; Mon–Sat closed midday). Half-board obligatory July & Aug. Closed mid-Nov to March. ❹

The Town

Rocamadour is divided into two parts: the medieval town containing the **Cité Religieuse**, where you'll find all the most important sights, and the cliff-top hamlet of **L'Hospitalet**, one and a half kilometres by road to the east. The old town is easy enough to find your way around since there's just one street, pedestrianized rue de la Couronnerie, which runs west from Porte du Figuier – one of Rocamadour's four medieval gateways – to the wide stone staircase leading up to the sanctuaries roughly 300m later. Follow the main road east from Porte du Figuier, on the other hand, and it will take you winding up the valley side to L'Hospitalet; pedestrians can use the quieter Voie Sainte, a narrow lane which branches off left after a couple of hundred metres.

La Cité Religieuse

The steep hillside above rue de la Couronnerie supports no fewer than seven chapels, known collectively as "Les Sanctuaires", or the **Cité Religieuse**. There's a lift dug into the rock-face (see p.240), but it's far better to climb the 216 worn and pitted steps of the **Grand Escalier**, up which the devout once dragged themselves on their knees to the doors of the Cité. Inside lies a small square, the parvis, completely hemmed in by the various chapels. The largest of these, lying straight ahead of you, is the **Basilique St-Sauveur** (daily: July & Aug 8am–9pm; rest of year 8.30am–6.30pm, though these times can vary), which up until 1900 provided lodgings for pilgrims who couldn't afford anything better. There's nothing much to see inside, however, so turn left for the little **Chapelle Notre-Dame** (same hours), nestled against the rock and the basilica wall, where the miracle-working twelfth-century Black Madonna resides. The crudely carved statue, less than 70cm tall, still wears a faint smile despite her mutilated state, though the adult-featured Jesus balanced on her knee looks decidedly out of sorts. The rest of the chapel is unremarkable, but note the empty recess in the rock outside, where St Amadour's body was found, and a rusty sword protruding from the cliff above. According to local tradition this is Durandal, the trusty blade of the legendary Roland whose heroic exploits are recorded in the twelfth-century *Chanson de Roland* (*The Song of Roland*), though it's not revealed exactly how it got here from northern Spain, where Roland supposedly died in battle against the Moors in 778. Beside the chapel's ornately carved door there are also some faded fifteenth-century frescoes depicting a macabre fight between the Living and the Dead.

Opposite the Chapelle Notre-Dame two incredibly well-preserved twelfth-century polychrome paintings of the Annunciation and the Visitation adorn the **Chapelle St-Michel**, which, along with the other four chapels, is only accessible on guided tours of the Cité (1hr 30min: by arrangement with the tourist office, see p.240).

East of the Cité there's a sandy esplanade and the cable car (see p.240) that will take you to the top of the cliff. Alternatively, you can walk up the shady zig-zag path, *La Calvarie*, past tableaux depicting the Stations of the Cross, or take a more direct and steeper path to come out near the château, a full 150m above the river below. While the château itself, a mostly nineteenth-century reconstruction, is private, you can walk round the **ramparts** (daily 8am–8pm; €2) for vertiginous views.

Around Rocamadour

The road leading west from the château brings you almost immediately to the first of Rocamadour's two wildlife parks, the **Rocher des Aigles**

Walk with the animals

If you're a keen walker and happen to be in the area in the last week of April, you might like to join in the **Transhumance**, a five-day, seventy-kilometre walk spear-headed by a flock of sheep. Open to the public, the route starts off in Rocamadour and heads to Luzech (see p.296), via narrow country lanes and rolling fields. Unlike in mountainous regions in France, transhumance is not yet a tradition in the Lot, but local associations, as well as the Conseil Général (www.lot.fr), are actively promoting it in the hope that it will become so. There's a practical side to the idea, too: as the sheep traverse fields lent by local landowners, they will eat down the grass, in a demonstration of ecological land maintenance.

(Ⓣ05.65.33.65.45, Ⓦwww.rocherdesaigles.com; April, May & Sept Tues–Sun 2–5pm; June Tues–Sun 1–6pm; July & Aug daily 1–7pm; Oct Tues, Thurs, Fri & Sun 2.30–5pm; closed Nov–March; €8.50), a breeding centre for birds of prey. The cages seem uncomfortably small, but with a production rate of nearly a hundred chicks a year the birds can't be overly stressed about it. There's a film explaining the breeding programme, which aims to reintroduce a number of rare species to the wild, and you can also see the hatching room where scrawny chicks warm themselves under sun lamps. Best, though, are the thirty-minute flying demonstrations (April, May & Sept Tues–Sun 2.30pm & 4pm; June Tues–Fri 1.30, 3 & 4.30pm; July & Aug daily 1–5.30pm roughly every hour; Oct Tues, Thurs, Fri & Sun 3pm), in which a dozen or so condors, fish eagles and other such majestic birds are allowed to soar free over the valley.

Continuing east about 700m along the cliff edge you join the main road, the D673 from Calès (see p.238), and then after another 150m reach the modern, plate-glass **tourist office** (see p.240), which marks the western extent of L'Hospitalet. The name refers to a pilgrims' hospital founded on the cliff-top here in the thirteenth century, of which only a few ruined walls and a chapel containing a copy of the Black Madonna remain. A crossroads lying immediately to the northeast of the chapel represents the centre of modern L'Hospitalet, which consists of a scattering of hotels, cafés and shops.

A hundred metres east of this crossroads, along the D36 to Gramat and Figeac, is **La Féerie autour du Rail**, essentially a landscaped model railway, albeit an

▲ Rocamadour

amazingly detailed one, which took more than fifteen years to build. Forty-five-minute mini-son et lumière shows (daily: April to mid-June & Sept four shows 11am–4.45pm; mid-June to mid-July five shows 11am–5pm; mid-July to Aug eight shows 10.30am–6pm; Oct 3pm & 4.30pm; closed Nov–March; €8.50; Ⓦwww.la-feerie.com) highlight different scenes: not only do trains scuttle about, but there are also automated cars, boats, fairs and fire engines, and even skiers and hot-air balloonists. It may not be everyone's cup of tea, but the whole thing is full of imaginative touches, and it's a must for kids.

Another couple of hundred metres east along this same road is the second of the wildlife parks, the **Forêt des Singes** (April & Sept 1–15 daily 10am–noon & 1–5.30pm; May & June daily 10am–noon & 1–6pm; July & Aug daily 9.30am–6.30pm; Sept 16 to Oct 31 Mon–Fri 1–5pm, Sat & Sun 10am–noon & 1–5pm; Nov Sat & Sun 10am–noon & 1–5pm; €7; Ⓦwww.la-foret-des-singes.com); it's one of the better such parks, with some 130 Barbary apes roaming twenty hectares of oak and scrubland in relative freedom. Again, the aim is conservation – so far around six hundred young monkeys have been reintroduced to North Africa. The best time to visit is during the cool of the early morning or evening and in early summer when the youngsters are frisking about.

Another possibility, particularly for those with children, is **La Borie d'Imbert** (daily March 15 to Nov 1; 10am–6.30pm; Ⓦwww.rocamadourlaboriedimbert.com; €4, some parts free); situated on the D247 in the direction of Souillac. The old farmhouse, La Maison de Justine, has countrified rooms complete with traditional cookware and furniture, while the baby farm animals are a sure winner for the very young. The goats are milked every day from 5.30–7pm, and in the farm shop you can taste and buy the Rocamadour goats' cheese (see below) and home-produced charcuterie.

Even if none of the above sights appeals, it's still worth coming up to **L'Hospitalet** for the tremendous views of the medieval Cité from the cliff-edge *belvédère*, beside the eponymous hotel, just south of the central crossroads. It's stunning at any time, but particularly magical at night when the buildings are illuminated (March–Nov & Christmas hols).

Eating

Eating in Rocamadour is a mixed bag and there are a good few greasy fast-food joints and tourist traps. In general, the best of Rocamadour's **restaurants** are those attached to the hotels (see p.241) along with a few more everyday recommendations; note that most places are closed in winter. The local speciality, which you'll find on most menus, is *Rocamadour*, a round disc of goat's cheese, often served on toast or with a walnut salad, or occasionally flambéed in brandy or drizzled with honey. Elsewhere in the region it is known as *Cabécou*, but cheeses produced around Rocamadour warrant their own special *appellation* – and even their own festival (see box, p.235). You can buy it at shops selling the inevitable foie gras and other regional produce, but for other **picnic fare** the only proper food shop hereabouts is the mini-market (April to mid-Oct) beside the *Comp'Hostel* (see p.242) in L'Hospitalet.

Chez Anne-Marie rue de la Couronnerie Ⓣ05.65.33.65.81. A jolly little place just west of the *Hôtel Beau Site* that's popular for its cheap-and-cheerful mix of grills, omelettes and salads in addition to regional dishes. They also serve a vegetarian menu (€14.50). *Plat du jour* at €9 and menus from €11.50 with lots of choice.

Jehan de Valon rue de la Couronnerie Ⓣ05.65.33.63.08. You need to book ahead for a table in this elegant restaurant, with panoramic views over the Alzou valley. Their seasonal menus include a good variety of fresh fish as well as local specialities, with prices starting at €21; count on at least €40 for the à la *carte* menu. Simpler fare is on offer in their adjoining brasserie where a *plat du jour* will set you back around €9 and a three-course menu €14. Closed mid-Nov to early Feb.

Au Panorama L'Hospitalet. If you're looking for somewhere to eat in L'Hospitalet, try this unpretentious café-restaurant across from the *Belvédère* hotel (see p.242). They serve an eclectic mix of regional dishes, salads and snacks. Salads cost €7–14, while full-blown menus start at €17. Closed mid-Nov to March.

Le Roc du Berger Bois de Belvyre ⓣ05.65.33.19.99, ⓦwww.rocduberger.fr. A wooden country inn, situated 1.5km from the town, in the direction of Pauillac, in the middle of a truffle orchard, where traditional dishes such as *confit de canard* and lamb steaks are given extra flavour by being cooked over an open fire. Menus €18–23.50. Reservation advisable. Open daily end-March to Sept 30 and weekends only in Oct.

Meyronne, Creysse and Gluges

Moving eastwards from Souillac via Lacave, the D23 takes a leisurely route alongside the meandering Dordogne. Seven kilometres upstream you come to the sleepy hilltop village of **MEYRONNE**, where the road crosses from the south bank to the north. In the eleventh century the bishops of Tulle, northeast of Brive, built a château here to defend what was then an important bridging point. Their residence is now a splendid **hotel**, *La Terrasse* (ⓣ05.65.32.21.60, ⓦwww.hotel-la-terrasse.com; ❹; closed Nov to early March), complete with spiral stairs, old chimneys and an excellent restaurant (menus from €20).

On the north side of the bridge turn right onto the tiny D114, which hugs the river for the next 4km east to **CREYSSE**. This idyllic hamlet, with its dinky market hall and fast-running stream, sits in the lee of a knuckle of rock where a fortified gate and scraps of wall are all that remain of a château once owned by the viscounts of Turenne (see p.158). Their twelfth-century **chapel**, standing immediately above the village (ask for the key at the *mairie*), has fared rather better, and is worth a look for its *pisé* floor and unique arrangement of two apsidal chapels. There's a simple but very appealing **hotel**, the *Auberge de L'Île* (ⓣ05.65.32.22.01, ⓦwww.auberge-de-lile.com; ❸; closed Nov to mid-March), straddling the stream in the village centre, whose plane-tree-shaded terrace is hard to resist; they offer a brasserie menu in addition to full meals (menus from €13.50). Campers, meanwhile, should head for the excellent two-star **campsite**, the *Camping du Port* (ⓣ05.65.32.20.82, ⓦwww.campingduport.com; closed Oct–April), down beside the Dordogne a hundred metres east of the village – **bikes** and **canoes** are available for rent on site from Port Loisirs (ⓣ05.65.32.20.82, ⓦwww.portloisirs.com).

The cliffs lining the Dordogne valley are more dramatic upstream from Creysse. For the most impressive scenery, follow the D23 northeast for a good two kilometres and then branch off right along the D43. The road quickly narrows down to a single track – with passing spaces – cut into the rock. You emerge two kilometres later at another huddle of houses, **GLUGES**, whose prime attraction is its location under the cliffs and its views south to the **Cirque de Montvalent**, where the meandering river has carved a great semicircle out of the cliffs; for a sweeping panorama, climb up to the hilltop Belvédère de Copeyre, signed off the main road one kilometre above Gluges to the east. Otherwise, apart from a quick wander around Gluges' medieval lanes, the only thing to do is relax on the terrace of the welcoming **hotel** *Les Falaises* (ⓣ05.65.27.18.44; ❸; closed Nov to Easter; restaurant for hotel guests from €25, eves only) at the western entrance to the village. There's a three-star riverside

campsite opposite, also called *Les Falaises* (ⓣ05.65.37.37.78; closed Oct–April), though it's not under the same management. You can also rent canoes and bikes from Copeyre Canoë (ⓣ05.65.37.33.51, ⓦwww.copeyre.com) down by the water.

Martel

Five kilometres north of Gluges, and fifteen east of Souillac, **MARTEL**'s medieval centre is built in a pale, almost white, stone, offset by warm reddish-brown roofs. Another Turenne-administered town (see p.158), its heyday came during the thirteenth and fourteenth centuries when the viscounts granted certain freedoms, including the right to mint money, and established a royal court of appeal here. The good times ceased, however, when the wars showed up: Martel was occupied briefly by English forces during the Hundred Years' War and suffered again at the hands of the Huguenots in the sixteenth century.

Arrival and information

Without your own transport, the best way to get to Martel is via one of two **bus services**, both of which stop on the ring road to the southwest of the centre. One route comes from Brive and the second from Souillac, passing through Martel on its way to the **gare SNCF** at **ST-DENIS-LÈS-MARTEL**, 7km to the east, on the Brive–Figeac and Brive-Aurillac train lines; if there's no convenient bus heading back from St-Denis to Martel, call Mme Daubet (ⓣ05.65.37.34.87) for a taxi. In season, a **tourist train** runs along a splendid stretch of decommissioned line from Martel towards St-Denis and back – but not as far as St-Denis station – along cliffs 80m above the Dordogne (departures by diesel train: April–June & Sept Tues & Thurs 2.30pm; July & Aug Mon, Tues, Thurs & Fri 11am, 2.30pm & 4pm, Sat 2.30pm; €7 return; departures by steam train: April–Sept Sun & hols 11am, 2.30pm & 4pm, also mid-July to end-Aug Mon–Thurs same times; €9.50 return; ⓣ05.65.37.35.81, ⓦwww.trainduhautquercy.info). It departs from the otherwise disused station two hundred metres south of town; reservations are recommended.

The small **tourist office** in the Palais de la Raymondie on place des Consuls (April–June, Sept & Oct Mon–Sat 9am–noon & 2–6pm; July & Aug daily 9am–7pm; Nov–March Mon–Fri 9am–noon & 2–5pm; ⓣ05.65.37.43.44, ⓦwww.martel.fr) can provide further information about the train and about Martel's **festivals**, including the annual wool fair (see box on p.235 for more).

Accommodation

Auberge des 7 Tours on Martel's northern outskirts on the road to Les Quatres-Routes ⓣ05.65.37.30.16, ⓦwww.auberge7tours.com. Rather small and simply furnished rooms are compensated for by the shaded terrace with views of the town, or over the countryside from the restaurant's picture windows; menus from €13.30; restaurant closed Sun eve & Mon. ❷

La Callopie ⓣ05.65.37.30.03. Decidedly spartan municipal campsite, with two stars, just north of town, opposite the *Auberge des 7 Tours*. Closed Oct–April.

Relais Ste-Anne rue du Pourtanel ⓣ05.65.37.40.56, ⓦwww.relais-sainte-anne.com. If you have money to spare, this expensive but absolutely gorgeous hotel occupies a former girls' boarding school and is set in immaculate gardens with its own chapel, pool and beautifully appointed rooms. Closed mid-Nov to mid-March. ❺–❼

The tale of Young King Henry

At the end of the twelfth century, Martel provided the stage for one of the tragic events in the internecine conflicts of the Plantagenet family. When Henry Plantagenet (King Henry II of England) imprisoned his estranged wife Eleanor of Aquitaine, his sons took up arms against their father. The eldest son, also **Henry** (nicknamed the Young King since he was crowned while his father was still on the throne), even went so far as to plunder the viscountcy of Turenne and Quercy. Furious, Henry II immediately stopped his allowance and handed over his lands to the third son, Richard the Lionheart. Financially insecure, and with a considerable army to maintain, Young King Henry began looting the treasures of every abbey and shrine in the region. Finally, he decided to sack the shrine at Rocamadour (see p.243). This last act was to mark his downfall, for shortly afterwards he fled to Martel and fell ill with a fever. Guilt-ridden and fearing for his life, he confessed his crimes and asked his father for forgiveness. Henry II was busy besieging Limoges, but sent a messenger to convey his pardon. On the messenger's arrival in Martel, Young Henry died, leaving Richard the Lionheart heir to the English throne.

The Town

Despite the town's rather turbulent past, on the whole the compact old centre has survived remarkably intact. The exception to this is the ramparts, which have been dismantled to make way for the wide boulevard that now rings Martel's pedestrianized centre. Take any of the lanes leading inwards and you will soon find yourself in the cobbled main square, **place des Consuls**. It is mostly taken up by the eighteenth-century *halle*, scene of a busy market on Wednesday and Saturday mornings, but on every side there are reminders of the town's illustrious past, most notably the grand Gothic **Palais de la Raymondie** on the square's east side, now occupied by the *mairie*. Begun in 1280, it served as both the Turenne law courts and fortress, hence the large square tower – one of seven that gave the town its epithet, *la ville aux sept tours*. On the square's south side is another of the towers – a circular five-storey turret belonging to the **Maison Fabri**. According to tradition, this striking building is where Young King Henry, son of Henry II, died in 1183 (see box above).

One block south of here, rue Droite leads east to the town's main church, **St-Maur**, built in a fiercely defensive, mostly Gothic style, with a finely carved Romanesque tympanum depicting the Last Judgement above the west door.

Eating and drinking

Ferme Auberge Moulin à Huile de Noix ⓣ05.65.37.40.69. Attached to a working walnut-oil mill 3km east off the D703 to St-Denis and Bretenoux. Don't be put off by the modern concrete exterior; the dining rooms upstairs have a bit of character and the food – all regional dishes with a strong preference for duck and walnuts – is both excellent and plentiful (menus from €15). Reservations essential. Closed Nov–March.

Au Hazard Balthazar rue Tournemire ⓣ05.65.37.42.01, ⓦwww.lesbouriettes.com. You can eat outside or upstairs in the cheerily rustic restaurant above the shop (Easter to Oct closed Mon) selling home-made local produce such as foie gras, wholesome lamb stew and walnut oil. Serving meat-heavy menus from €16.50, the restaurant is open Easter to Sept for lunch only Fri–Sun.

La Mère Michèle rue Senlis ⓣ05.65.37.35.66. Popular for its well-presented dishes at prices that won't break the bank; *plat du jour* €7.50; menus from €11. Closed Sun eve & Wed.

Plein Sud place des Consuls ⓣ05.65.37.37.77. Serves a decent pizza (€7–11) as well as regional specialities and a wide choice of salads (menus from €12). Closed mid-Oct to March.

Carennac and around

CARENNAC is without doubt one of the most beautiful villages along this part of the Dordogne valley. It sits on a terrace above the river's south bank 16km or so east of Martel; backtrack to Gluges and then head upstream on the D43 for the prettiest route. It is best known for its typical Quercy architecture and the richly carved tympanum of its Romanesque priory church. Founded in the eleventh century by Benedictine monks, the priory grew rich from pilgrims en route to Santiago de Compostela. Sacked during the Hundred Years' War (see p.357), it then enjoyed a second renaissance in the late fifteenth and sixteenth centuries, when the church was restored and a château built alongside. But by the 1700s the rot had set in as the monks became lazy and corrupt, and the priory was finally closed after the Revolution.

You get one of the best views of the village's towers and higgledy-piggledy russet-tiled roofs as you approach from the west. The houses cluster so tightly round the priory buildings that it's hard to tell them apart, but if you follow the road along the river bank, you'll soon find a gateway leading to a cobbled courtyard and the **Église St-Pierre**. Straight ahead of you the church's twelfth-century tympanum – in the style of Moissac and Cahors – dominates its recessed west door, with its carvings in exceptionally good condition.

South of the church, still inside the courtyard, you gain access to the **cloister and chapter house** (same hours as the tourist office, opposite; €2). The cloister's Romanesque and flamboyant Gothic galleries were somewhat mutilated during the Revolution, but they are in any case overshadowed by the late-fifteenth-century, life-size *Mise au Tombeau* (*Entombment of Christ*) on display in the chapterhouse. So supremely detailed is the sculpture that you can even see the veins in Christ's hands and legs. Joseph of Arimathea and Nicodemus, holding either end of the shroud, are richly attired as a fifteenth-century nobleman and pilgrim respectively, while behind them Mary Magdalene, her hair a mass of ringlets, ostentatiously wipes away a tear.

In the sixteenth century the *doyens* (deans) in charge of the priory and its dependent churches built themselves a grand residence, referred to nowadays as the **château**, abutting the church's north wall. A few stone chimney-pieces and the great hall's painted ceiling remain from this era, but little else, since the building has been partially modernized to serve as an **Espace Patrimoine** (Easter to June & Oct Tues–Fri 10am–noon & 2–6pm; July–Sept Tues–Sun same hours; closed Nov to Easter; free). Displays cover the geography, history, architecture and economy of the Dordogne valley from Bretenoux downstream to Souillac; it provides a good overview of what the region has to offer. Staff here also organize a broad range of guided visits (to Carennac, Martel and Souillac, for example, some in English) and workshops based on the art and history of the Dordogne valley; contact the Service Animation du Patrimoine (Ⓣ05.65.33.81.36, Ⓦwww.pays-vallee-dordogne.com) for further information.

Practicalities

Carennac's nearest **gare SNCF** is at Vayrac, 8km northwest on the other side of the river, on the Brive–Aurillac line; note that there are no ticket sales at this station but you can buy tickets from the conductor on board the train. Call Ⓣ05.65.32.40.32 if you need a **taxi**. However, services are more frequent to St-Denis-lès-Martel, 10km to the west (see p.247), on the Brive–Figeac line. **Buses** from Gramat, St-Céré and Vayrac (with connections to Brive,

St-Denis and Biars-Bretenoux) will drop you beside the *mairie* on the south side of town. Carennac's **tourist office** is located in the priory courtyard (Jan–March & Oct Mon–Sat 10am–noon & 2–5pm; April–June & Sept Mon–Sat 10am–noon & 2–6pm; July & Aug daily 10am–1pm & 2–7pm; Nov–Dec Mon–Fri 10am–noon & 2–5pm, Sat 2–5pm; ⓣ05.65.10.97.01, ⓦwww.tourisme-carennac.com).

The village has just one **hotel**, *Hostellerie Fénelon* (ⓣ05.65.10.96.46, ⓦwww.hotel-fenelon.com; ❸; closed Jan to mid-March, restaurant from €22.50, closed Fri & Sat lunch except in July & Aug) on the main street to the east of the château. Comfortable and reasonably priced, it has a pool and good restaurant specializing in traditional regional cuisine. There's also a municipal **campsite**, *L'Eau Vive*, beside the river 1km east of Carennac (ⓣ05.65.10.97.39, ⓕ05.55.28.12.12; closed mid-Oct to April), where you can also rent canoes in season from Saga Team (ⓣ05.55.28.84.84, ⓦwww.dordogne-soleil.com).

In addition to the above hotels, you can also **eat** well, if more simply, immediately west of the château at *Le Prieuré*. It's primarily a crêperie, but they also do good big salads and omelettes (*plat du jour* €10; menu at €17). There are also a few restaurants worth seeking out in the countryside around Carennac. For something special, try the *Côté Jardin* (ⓣ05.36.38.49.51; reservations required; weekday menu at €17, or €24.50 at weekends), just north of **TAURIAC**, a pretty village roughly 3km east of Carennac on the other side of the river. The well-prepared dishes using ultra-fresh ingredients taste their best on summer eves under the fairy lights. The *Relais de Gintrac* (ⓣ05.65.38.49.41; Oct–April closed evenings, also closed two to three weeks in Sept; menus from around €12), in the hamlet of **GINTRAC**, about 3km from Carennac southeast along the D30, is a popular if isolated place, at the opposite end of the spectrum, offering wholesome country cooking washed down with well-priced wines.

The Gouffre de Padirac

Local legend holds the Devil responsible for opening the gaping mouth of the **Gouffre de Padirac** (1hr 30min guided tours daily: April–June 9.30am–5pm; July 9.30am–6pm; Aug 8.30am–6.30pm; Sept & Oct 10am–5pm; ⓦwww.gouffre-de-padirac.com; €9) in the middle of the limestone plateau 10km south of Carennac. The hole is over 30m wide and 75m deep, its sides festooned with dripping ferns and creepers, though the sense of mystery is somewhat diminished these days by the presence of a lift-cage built against the side. Rather than the Devil, the chasm was probably formed by a cave roof collapsing centuries ago; locals took refuge here during the Hundred Years' War and probably long before. The cave system was not properly explored, however, until 1889 when spectacular stalactites – the biggest a staggering 75m tall – and lakes were discovered. Even today teams are still exploring the caves and passages.

The visit starts with a half-kilometre-long **boat trip** along an underground river, after which you walk on past barrages and massive cascades formed by calcite deposits over the millennia. The lakes are pretty, but the most notable feature here is the sheer scale of the formations and the height of the passages carved out of the rock, reaching nearly one hundred metres at their highest. Be warned, though: it is very, very touristy and best avoided at weekends and other peak periods, when you'll wait an age for tickets. And in wet weather you'll need a waterproof jacket.

The nearest **gare SNCF** is Rocamadour-Padirac, more than 10km to the west, from where you could take a **taxi** (Ⓣ05.65.33.63.10). There's a **tourist office** (July & Aug Mon–Sat 10am–12.30pm & 2–7pm; June 15–30 & Sept 1–18 Mon–Fri 2–6pm; Ⓣ05.65.33.47.17) in Padirac village, a couple of kilometres south of the *gouffre*, while the best **accommodation** hereabouts is the ivy-covered *Auberge de Mathieu* (Ⓣ05.65.33.64.68, Ⓦpagesperso-orange.fr/auberge.mathieu; ❷; closed mid-Nov to mid-March; menus from €15), 300m south of the *gouffre* on the D90, with plain rooms but a nice terrace and garden. Alternatively, *Les Chênes* (Ⓣ05.65.33.65.54, Ⓦwww.campingleschenes.com; closed Oct–March) is a very well-organized four-star **campsite** just south of the *Auberge*, with a bar, restaurant and pool.

Bretenoux and around

Some 10km east of Carennac, the *bastide* town of **BRETENOUX**, founded in 1277 by the barons of Castelnau, sits on the south bank of the River Cère just upstream from where it joins the Dordogne. It was obviously a pretty little place at one time – the cobbled and arcaded **place des Consuls** behind the tourist office is a delight, especially on **market** days (Tues & Sat mornings) – but these days the town suffers from a busy main road and modern development. With its transport connections, however, Bretenoux is a useful staging post for the nearby towns of St-Céré and Beaulieu-sur-Dordogne (see p.255 & p.252). And east of here, the journey to Aurillac takes you through a very picturesque and otherwise inaccessible landscape, popular with walkers and cyclists.

Bretenoux's **gare SNCF**, on the Brive–Aurillac line, is officially known as Bretenoux-Biars since it is located some 2km north of the River Cère in the town of Biars. **Taxis** wait outside the station (or call Ⓣ05.65.10.90.90) and there are **buses** (line 11, operated by Delbos; Ⓣ05.65.38.24.19) from here to Bretenoux and St-Céré, but only on Wednesday, Thursday and Saturday; in Bretenoux the bus stop is on the main road, avenue de la Libération, near the post office a couple of hundred metres south of the river.

On the way you'll pass the well-organized **tourist office** (July & Aug Mon–Sat 9.30am–7pm, Sun 10am–1pm; rest of year Mon–Sat 10am–noon & 2–6pm; Ⓣ05.65.38.59.53, Ⓦwww.ot-bretenoux.com) on avenue de la Libération just south of the bridge. Carry on a bit further south along this road and you'll find Cycles Bladier (Ⓣ05.65.38.41.56), where you can rent **bikes** for a trip out to the Château de Castelnau.

Bretenoux has just one small and very reasonable **hotel**, *Le Quercy* (Ⓣ05.65.38.40.27; ❶, menus from €13) with just five basic rooms, situated in the quiet central square, the place des Consuls. You can also eat outside, on the opposite side of the square at the **restaurant**, *Les Saveurs*, which offers menus from €10.50. There are a couple of excellent, family-run places 6km northeast on the D14 in the village of **PORT-DE-GAGNAC**, on the north bank of the Cère. The slightly homelier of the two is the *Auberge du Vieux Port* (Ⓣ05.65.38.50.05, Ⓦwww.auberge-vieuxport.com; ❷–❸), serving very good-value regional cuisine (menus from €14.50; closed Sun eve). Just beyond it, the *Hostellerie Belle Rive* (Ⓣ05.65.38.50.04, Ⓦwww.bellerive-dordogne-lot.com; ❸–❹; restaurant closed Nov–March Sat & Sun, also closed April–June, Sept

& Oct Fri eve, Sat lunch & Sun eve; menus €15–39) is a touch more upmarket. Local campsites include the three-star *La Bourgnatelle* (ⓣ05.65.10.89.04, ⓔcontact@dordogne-vacances.fr; closed Oct–April), located on an island just across the bridge from Bretenoux, and the quiet *camping à la ferme* (ⓣ05.65.38.52.31; closed Oct–May) on the river bank a couple of kilometres west along the D14 towards Prudhomat. **Canoe** rental is available in July and August at the *Bourgnatelle* campsite (ⓣ05.65.10.89.04).

Château de Castelnau

Brenetoux lies within striking distance of the **Château de Castelnau** (April & Sept daily 10am–12.30pm & 2–5.30pm; May–Aug daily 10am–12.30pm & 2–6.30pm; Oct–March Wed–Sun 10am–12.30pm & 2–5.30pm; €7), 2.5km to the southwest – one of this region's most outstanding examples of medieval military architecture. The great fortress dominates an abrupt knoll to the east of the village, its sturdy towers and machicolated red-brown walls visible for miles around. It dates from the mid-tenth century, but took on its present form – a triangular fort with a massive square keep and three round towers, the whole lot surrounded by ramparts and dry moats – during the Hundred Years' War under the ownership of the powerful barons of Castelnau. By the early eighteenth century, however, the Castelnau family had died out. Their abandoned château was sacked during the Revolution, sustained even greater damage in a fire in 1851 and was left to rot until it was salvaged, somewhat bizarrely, in 1896 by a celebrated tenor of the Parisian Comic Opera, Jean Mouliérat. He threw his fortune into its restoration and into amassing the valuable but rather dry collection of religious art and furniture from the fifteenth to eighteenth centuries, which populates the handful of rooms you see on the guided tour. The views from the ramparts, though, are extremely impressive; on a clear day you can just make out the towers of Turenne, nearly thirty kilometres to the north (see p.158).

As you exit the castle's inner enclosure, turn left along the walls to take a quick look in the **Collégiale St-Louis**. Built of the same red stone and with powerful buttresses, this little Gothic church contains a fine fifteenth-century polychrome statue of the Baptism of Christ – note the startled expression of the angel holding his clothes – and a macabre treasure in the form of a bone from the arm of St Louis (alias King Louis IX of France). In 1970 the relic was taken to St Louis in America to commemorate the founding of the city.

Beaulieu-sur-Dordogne and beyond

At Bretenoux the River Dordogne turns northwards; the valley here is wide and industrial – with factories such as Andros churning out enough jam to make this the "jam capital" of Europe – but things get better 8km north of Bretenoux to find **BEAULIEU-SUR-DORDOGNE** beautifully situated on a wide bend in the river. It's a perfectly proportioned town, with an abbey church that boasts another of the great masterpieces of Romanesque sculpture, and yet is refreshingly untouristy.

Arrival and information

It's just over 6km from Beaulieu to the Bretenoux-Biars **gare SNCF** (see p.251). Unfortunately there are no connecting **buses**, although you can get to

Beaulieu by bus from Brive; services stop on place du Champs-de-Mars, a large shady square just west of place Marbot, which marks the modern centre. If you need a **taxi** in Beaulieu, call ⓣ05.55.91.02.83. The **tourist office** – which has internet access – is located on the south side of place Marbot (April–June & Sept–Oct Mon–Sat 9.30am–12.30pm & 2.30–6pm, Sun 9.30am–12.30pm; July & Aug daily 9.30am–1pm & 2.30–7pm; Nov–March Mon–Sat 10am–12.30pm & 2.30–5pm; ⓣ05.55.91.09.94, ⓦwww.beaulieu-tourisme.com), while you can rent **bikes** at Aventures Dordogne Nature (ADN; ⓣ05.55.28.86.45, ⓦwww.adndordogne.org), at the *base nautique* on the other side of the river; you can drive round or get there via a footbridge to the north of the town centre.

Accommodation

Camping des Isles on the island to the north of the main road-bridge ⓣ05.55.91.02.65, ⓦwww.camping-des-iles.net. Well-kept, shady three-star site also offers mobile homes for rent. Swimming pools, bar and different activities for all ages in season. Closed Nov–March.

Camping du Pont on the island to the south of the main road bridge ⓣ05.55.91.00.57, ⓦwww.camping-beaulieu.com. Offers canoe rental (ⓣ05.55.28.84.84 or the campsite). Closed Oct–April.

Les Charmilles 20 bd St-Rodolphe-de-Turenne ⓣ05.55.91.29.29, ⓦwww.auberge-charmilles.com. The most appealing option in Beaulieu, this bright, clean, riverside hotel is on the northeast side of town. It has just eight rooms and a flowery terrace – you'll eat well here, too; menus start at €20 (restaurant closed Wed). ❺

HI hostel rue de la Chapelle ⓣ05.55.91.13.82, ⓔbeaulieu@fuaj.org. Welcoming hostel set in a magnificent half-timbered and turreted building, with surprisingly modern dorms inside and a well-equipped kitchen. Breakfast is available, as are meals on request for groups of four or more. Dorm bed €12; closed Nov–March.

Relais de Vellinus place du Champ-de-Mars ⓣ05.55.91.11.04, ⓦwww.vellinus.com. Comfortable hotel imaginatively decorated in warm, contemporary colours. It also has a good restaurant, where you can enjoy elegantly presented dishes that combine regional products with original flavourings – spiced scallops or walnut soufflé accompanied by walnut liqueur for example; restaurant closed Sat lunch & Sun eve from mid-Nov to mid-March; menus from €26. ❹

The Town

Arriving from Bretenoux, the main road skirts south of Beaulieu's compact and semi-pedestrianized core of old streets. On its way it passes through a large square, **place Marbot**, which represents the town's modern centre, off which rue de la République leads north to **place du Marché**. Here, you'll find some nicely jaded stone and half-timbered buildings, along with the twelfth-century **abbey church of St-Pierre**, a surprisingly large building, whose architecture reflects its position on the border between Limousin and Languedoc. The pairs of rounded arches piercing the belfry, for example, are typical Limousin styling, while the subject matter and style of carving on the magnificent **south portal** belongs firmly to the south. The tympanum is presided over by an Oriental-looking Christ with one arm extended to welcome the chosen on the Judgement Day. Around him a mass of angels and Apostles, even the dead rising from their graves below, seem ready to burst with vitality.

It won't take long to cover the rest of Beaulieu, but it's worth devoting half an hour or so to wandering its maze of lanes. In particular, there are a number of half-timbered houses along **rue Ste-Catherine**, running east from place du Marché, while if you head northwest along **rue de la République** and **rue de la Chapelle** you'll pass some handsome sculpted facades before emerging

▲ Carvings on the church of St-Pierre, Beaulieu

beside the **Chapelle des Pénitents** in an attractive spot on the river bank. This twelfth-century chapel now makes a splendid venue for the occasional art exhibition or concert; if it's open, it's worth popping in to see the collection of religious art. From May to October traditional wooden **gabares** depart from the river bank here for a one-hour jaunt upstream (contact the tourist office, see p.253).

Upstream from Beaulieu, the Dordogne valley becomes wilder as you enter the first forest-covered foothills of the Massif Central. It makes for a lovely drive along the D12 as far as **Argentat**, the last town of any size on the river, where it's easy to while away an hour or so sitting at one of the waterside cafés. Beyond Argentat, however, the Dordogne changes character entirely, due to a series of hydroelectric dams that turn the river into a succession of huge reservoirs.

Eating

The hotel **restaurants** are good places to eat, but for a change it's well worth seeking out *Velouté* (☎05.55.91.14.51; closed Mon; menus from €15) tucked away beside the church in rue de la Bridolle. Both the decor and cuisine are appealingly modern, the latter changing inventively according to season. Another great place for a light snack is *Café Douceur* (☎05.55.28.67.05; 9am–7pm, closed Wed from 2pm & Sat) on the main street, rue du Général-de-Gaulle, which serves a wide choice of teas and coffees as well as savoury snacks and desserts. The atmosphere is pleasant and relaxed, with armchairs for lounging in.

St-Céré and around

About 9km south of Bretenoux on the River Bave, a minor tributary of the Dordogne, you come to the medieval town of **St-Céré**, dominated by the brooding ruins of the **Château de St-Laurent-les-Tours**. The château is now home to an engaging museum dedicated to tapestry designer Jean Lurçat, who revitalized contemporary French tapestry, but the town's prime attraction is its old centre peppered with picturesque half-timbered houses.

St-Céré also makes a useful base for exploring the surrounding area. The town lies on the border between the empty but glorious wooded hills of the Ségala to the east and south, and the dry limestone *causse* to the west. However, the region's most impressive sight, and one not to be missed, is the Renaissance **Château de Montal**, 2km west of St-Céré, with its sculpted facade and grand staircase. From here you can loop south via the **Grottes de Presque** – a limestone cave with a tremendous variety of unusually colourful concretions – to arrive at the lip of the Cirque d'Autoire for dramatic views over the russet-red roofs of **Autoire** village, which provide a splash of colour in the valley far below. On the way back to St-Céré the route passes through another captivating little village, **Loubressac**, which can hardly have changed for centuries.

It's possible to reach St-Céré by bus from Bretenoux, Cahors and Figeac, but you'll need your own **transport** to explore the rest of the area. If you've got the energy to tackle some of these hills, you can always rent a bike in St-Céré (see below).

Arrival and information

The nearest **gare SNCF** to St-Céré is Bretenoux-Biars (see p.251), a good 10km to the north, from where there are **buses** on two days a week (Wed & Sat; Delbos ⓣ05.65.38.24.19) on to St-Céré. You can also reach St-Céré by bus from Cahors via Gramat, and from Figeac (both also operated by Delbos). All these services drop you on place de la République, on the north side of which you'll find the **tourist office** (July & Aug Mon–Sat 9am–7pm, Sun 10am–1pm; rest of year Mon–Sat 10am–noon & 2–6pm; ⓣ05.65.38.11.85, ⓦwww.tourisme-saint-cere.com). For exploring the countryside around St-Céré, you can rent **bikes** from Cycles St-Chamant, 45 rue Faidherbe (ⓣ05.65.38.03.23), to the west of place de la République.

Accommodation

Hôtel de France 139 av François-de-Maynard ⓣ05.65.38.02.16, ⓦwww.lefrance-hotel.com. Modern, upmarket place east off place de la République, with well-priced en-suite rooms, a pool and a flowery garden where you can eat out under a huge chestnut tree (Mon–Sat eves only, Sun open for lunch & dinner; menu at €21). Hotel closed late-Dec to Jan. ❸

Le Soulhol Quai Salesses ⓣ05.65.33.47.81, ⓦwww.campinglesoulhol.com. Three-star campsite beside the river a short walk east of the *Hôtel Victor-Hugo*. Closed Oct–April.

Hôtel du Touring place de la République ⓣ05.65.38.30.08, ⓦwww.hoteldutouring.com. Decent and reasonably priced hotel owned by a young couple. The hotel has a terrace on the square where you can enjoy light lunches (menus from €11–20). ❷

Hôtel Victor-Hugo 7 av des Maquis ⓣ05.65.38.16.15, ⓦwww.hotel-victor-hugo.fr. You'll get a warm welcome from the young owners at this hotel beside the old bridge in the southeast corner of place de la République. There are three family rooms with balconies, and four others that open directly onto a sunny terrace overlooking the river. The chef uses fresh local produce in the restaurant (closed Sun & Mon eve out of season; menus from €16.50–39). ❸

The Town

Arriving in St-Céré from the north, the first things you see are the two powerful keeps of the Château de St-Laurent-les-Tours, once part of a fortress belonging to the viscounts of Turenne (see p.158). The town itself sits in the valley to the southwest where the old houses cluster round place du Mercadial and place de l'Église. These two squares lie north and south respectively of rue de la République, the main shopping street cutting through the old centre which, at its southeast end, comes out into **place de la République**. This big, open square is where you'll find car parks, cafés and the town's main tourist facilities.

St-Céré owes its existence to the martyrdom of **Ste Spérie** in 780. Born the daughter of the then lord of St-Laurent, Sérenus, Spérie pledged her life to God at an early age, and when later she refused to marry a local nobleman, she was beheaded by her brother and buried on the river bank. Later a chapel was erected on the spot around which the town began to develop in the tenth century. It lay initially under the jurisdiction of the counts of Auvergne, but was transferred to the Turenne viscounts in 1178. They beefed up the fortress and, as usual, granted the town a certain degree of autonomy. Its heyday didn't arrive, however, until after the fifteenth century when St-Céré's wealthy merchants began investing in the noble houses that can still be seen today.

The best of these lie in the streets to the north of rue de la République, notably around **place du Mercadial**, which, with its fountain and cobbles, is particularly appealing; to find it, walk one block north from rue de la République and turn left along rue du Mazel. You come out opposite the town's most eye-catching building, the **Maison des Consuls**, where the administrative council used to meet – it now hosts various free art exhibitions in summer. Beneath a steeply pitched tile roof, the building's most striking feature is the slightly overhanging upper storey of neatly layered brick in a timber frame. The same design is echoed in the **Maison Arnoud**, on the north side of the square, whose ground floor is a mere three metres wide. Rue St-Cyr, the lane to the right of this house, takes you east and then

▲ Château de St-Laurent-les-Tours

south past several elegant Renaissance buildings and into a recently renovated area of courtyards and alleys.

There's less of interest on the south side of rue de la République, though the **church of Ste-Spérie**, largely rebuilt after the Wars of Religion, is worth a quick peek for its eighteenth-century altarpiece with a statue of Ste Spérie standing on the left. It was carved by a local monk who received 240 *livres* and, for some reason, four handkerchiefs for his pains.

St-Céré is rather prouder of another, more recent local artist, **Jean Lurçat** (1892–1966), who first came to the Lot to join the Resistance in 1941, then decided to settle in Château St-Laurent after the war. He is best known for his big, bold tapestries, of which the most famous is the eighty-metre-long *Chant du Monde* (*Song of the World*), which portrays the vagaries of human existence and our inherent power for both good and evil. The tapestry is now on display in Angers, but you can get an idea of Lurçat's distinctive style – typically incorporating animals and birds, both real and fantastic, against dark blue or black backgrounds – by visiting the **Galerie d'Art Le Casino**, avenue Jean Mouliérat (July–Sept daily 9.30am–noon & 2.30–6.30pm; Feb–June daily except Tues same hours; rest of year also closed Mon; ⓣ05.65.38.19.60; free), 100m northeast of the old town; from place de la République walk north on boulevard Lurçat a short distance before turning right down avenue Jean Mouliérat.

You can see more of his work in his former studio in the **Château de St-Laurent-les-Tours** a kilometre or so above St-Céré – take avenue du Docteur Roux heading northeast past the hospital and then follow the signs winding uphill. Of the Turenne fortress only the ramparts and two square towers remain, the smaller one dating from the late twelfth century and the taller, eastern tower from the 1300s. The rest of the castle was destroyed during the Wars of Religion, but around 1895 the then owner built himself a neo-Gothic mansion between the two towers. It is this building in which Jean Lurçat set up his studio in 1945 and which is now the **Atelier-Musée Jean Lurçat** (mid-July to Sept daily 9.30am–noon & 2.30–6.30pm; also two weeks at Easter same hours; ⓣ05.65.38.28.21; €2.50). Alongside his sketches and illustrations, a slide show of the *Chant du Monde* and a short biographical film, the museum's most interesting feature is the artist's unmistakable paintings covering the ceilings and doors.

Eating and drinking

The best places to **eat** in St-Céré are the restaurants at the *Hôtel de France* (see p.255) and *Hôtel Victor-Hugo* (see p.255). Otherwise, try the cafés and brasseries around place de la République and place du Mercadial. For picnic fodder, there's a small **market** on Sunday mornings on place de la République and a much larger affair spreading throughout the old town on the first and third Wednesdays of the month.

L'Entre-Pots rue Centrale ⓣ05.65.33.71.93. Friendly restaurant with a shady terrace that serves up traditional dishes such as *cassoulet*. Menus €11.50–20. Closed Sun.

L'Instant T 3 place du Mercadial ⓣ05.65.10.66.82. Serves delicious quiches and salads on its covered terrace and courtyard. In the afternoons from May–Sept it turns into a cosy tearoom. Menus from €19.50, closed Sun.

Pizzeria du Mercadial 4 place du Mercadial ⓣ05.65.38.35.77. Rustic setting with terrace in the square. Pizzas from €12, also pasta and grills. Closed Mon & Tues, also Nov.

Le Tama des Îles rue du Mazel ⓣ05.65.38.13.46. Exotic fare – think spring rolls, samosas and rum punch – are served up at this convivial place. Menus from €13–20. Closed Mon.

Les Trois Soleils Immediately west of Château de Montal ⓣ05.65.10.16.16, ⓦhttp://pagesperso-orange.fr/trois.soleils. It's worth combining a meal at this one-star Michelin restaurant with a trip to the Château de Montal (see below). Their lunchtime weekday menu at €26.50 is a bargain for such a perfect setting amongst immaculate gardens. Other menus (€39.50–75) feature fresh, locally produced ingredients with creative twist – try the pig's trotter stuffed with preserved duck meat served with a *galette* and sauce of *cèpes*, for instance. Hotel closed Dec & Jan; restaurant closed Oct–March Sun eve to Tues midday.

Château de Montal

Two kilometres west of St-Céré, the **Château de Montal** (April & Sept daily 10am–12.30pm & 2–5.30pm; May–Aug daily, as above but until 6.30pm; Oct–March as above but closed Mon & Tues; €7) is a superb example of French Renaissance architecture. Its interesting history started in 1523 when Jeanne Balzac d'Entraygues, the widow of Amaury de Montal, started transforming the medieval fortress into a Renaissance palace, as was all the rage. But then came news that her eldest son, Robert, had been killed in Italy and poor Jeanne lost the heart to continue. Nevertheless the de Montal family continued to own the château up to the Revolution, after which it was bought by a certain Monsieur Macaire who gradually sold off the chimneypieces, sculptures and even the carved window surrounds. Rescue was at hand, however, in the form of Maurice Fenaille, a rich industrialist and patron of the arts, who bought the château in 1908 and began to restore it to its former glory. In just five years he managed to track down nearly everything that had been sold, including some of the original wall-coverings, and also filled the rooms with a fine collection of Renaissance and Louis XIII furnishings, before giving the whole caboodle to the state in 1913. Later, during World War II, Montal was chosen as a hiding place for thousands of paintings from the Louvre, including the *Mona Lisa*, which were moved from Paris for safekeeping.

As you approach, the rear of the château still exudes a thoroughly medieval air with its small windows, steep *lauze* roof and pepper-pot towers, but turn the corner into the **inner courtyard** and you're immediately transported to sunny Italy. The lovely pale stone of the two facades is worked into delicate carvings, including a frieze of mermaid-like sibyls and, above, busts representing three generations of the de Montal family: Jeanne is flanked by her husband and son Robert on the west wing, while her parents take pride of place over the front door.

The craftsmen went to work inside, too, on a magnificent **staircase** made from the same local limestone. As you climb up, notice the carving on the panels above, each bearing a different design, which gets finer and more elaborate towards the top. The rest of the interior can't quite compare, but there are some massive old oak tables, a good, homely kitchen and an excellent collection of tapestries, including a rare example featuring a pastoral scene with descriptive boxes of text, like an early cartoon.

Grottes de Presque

About 3km southwest along the D673 from the Château de Montal the road cuts through a hillside as it climbs up onto the *causse*. When they were digging this road in 1825, engineers discovered the entrance to the **Grottes de Presque** (45min guided tours daily: mid-Feb to June & Sept–mid-Nov 9.30am–noon & 2–6pm; July & Aug 9.30am–6.30pm; Ⓦ www.grottesdepresque.com; €7). The cave system is not only unusually accessible, with a few stairs, but it also contains a marvellous variety of stalactites and stalagmites, some up to 10m high, as well as columns, semi-translucent curtains and glistening crystalline cascades. The other notable feature is the amount of colour, from pure white to grey, yellow and deep orange. This is the result of rainwater picking up iron, manganese and other minerals as it percolates through the 90m of rock above, minerals that are then deposited along with the calcite, drip by drip, inside the cave.

Autoire and Loubressac

Further west along the same line of hills, the River Autoire has carved an impressive canyon, the **Cirque d'Autoire**, into the limestone plateau; to get here from the Grottes de Presque, follow the D673 southwest for another 4km and then turn right on the D38. This brings you in above the *cirque* – for the best views, walk west from the car park for about five minutes, following the footpath across a bridge and up onto the opposite hillside. In the valley bottom, some 2km below you, lies the extremely pretty little village of **AUTOIRE** where the ochre-hued houses, including several rather grand piles built by nobles from St-Céré in the fifteenth and sixteenth centuries, snuggle round a very plain, solid Romanesque church.

The village also boasts a **hotel** – the *Auberge de la Fontaine* (ⓣ05.65.10.85.40, ⓦwww.auberge-de-la-fontaine.com; ❷; closed two weeks in Oct, also Sun eve & Mon except in July & Aug) on the main street opposite the church, a simple country inn offering basic but well-kept rooms and family cooking washed down with local Coteaux de Glanes wines (menus from €12). For food, try *La Cascade* across the road, serving crêpes, salads and regional dishes in a cheerful stone-walled room or on a terrace with views up to the *cirque* (closed Oct–April, also Mon eve & Tues except in July & Aug; menus from around €15).

It's only 8km back to St-Céré from Autoire, but it's worth taking a short diversion 6km northwest along the D135, little more than a country lane, to **LOUBRESSAC**. The narrow lanes of this fortified hilltop village are full of flowers and typical Quercy houses. You can't visit the château standing on the cliff edge, but there are grand views from the lookout point immediately to the east of the village, taking in the whole sweep of the Dordogne, Bave and Cère valleys across to St-Céré and the châteaux of Castelnau and Montal.

In season a **tourist office** (April Mon–Sat 2–6pm; May, June & Sept Mon 2.30–6.30pm, Tues–Sat 10am–12.30pm & 3–6.30pm; June–Aug Mon–Sat 9am–1pm & 3–7pm, Sun 4–7pm; ⓣ05.65.10.82.18, ⓦwww.tourisme-saint-cere.com) opens up just outside Loubressac's southern gateway. There are also a couple of decent **hotels**. The simpler of the two is the *Lou Cantou* (ⓣ05.65.38.20.58, ⓦwww.logis-de-france.fr; ❸; closed Mon & Sun eve mid-Nov to March) on the southwest side of the village, with good views from its front rooms and the picture windows of its restaurant (menus from €12). Moving up a few notches, the modern *Relais de Castelnau* (ⓣ05.65.10.80.90, ⓦwww.relaisdecastelnau.com; ❹–❺; closed Nov to Easter) sits just outside the village on the main road west to Padirac. Apart from more splendid views, it also boasts a pool and a highly rated restaurant (menus from €18) but it has rather bland rooms. There's also a very pleasant little three-star **campsite**, *La Garrigue* (ⓣ05.65.38.34.88, ⓦwww.camping-lagarrigue.com; closed Oct–March), with a pool and restaurant among fields a couple of hundred metres south of the village.

Travel details

Trains

Bretenoux-Biars to: Aurillac (3–4 daily; 45min–1hr); Brive (3–4 daily; 35–40min); St-Denis-lès-Martel (3–4 daily; 15min); Vayrac (1–2 daily; 10min).

St-Denis-lès-Martel to: Brive (4–5 daily; 25min); Figeac (5–6 daily; 1hr); Gramat (5–6 daily; 20–30min); Rocamadour-Padirac (4–5 daily; 15–20min); Vayrac (2 daily; 5min).

Souillac to: Brive (6–9 daily; 25min); Cahors (6–9 daily; 40min–1hr); Gourdon (6–9 daily; 15min); Montauban (6–8 daily; 1hr 30min); Paris (5–6 daily; 4hr 30min); Toulouse (6–8 daily; 1hr 55min).

Buses

Carennac to: Gramat (school term Wed 1 daily; 30min); St-Céré (school term Mon–Fri 1 daily, rest of year Wed 1 daily; 20min); Vayrac (school term Mon–Fri 1 daily, rest of year Wed 1 daily; 10min).
Beaulieu-sur-Dordogne to: Argentat (July & Aug Mon–Sat 3 daily; 40min); Brive (school term Mon–Sat 1–3 daily, July & Aug Mon–Sat 1–2 daily, rest of year Tues, Thurs & Sat 1 daily; 1hr).
Bretenoux-Biars to: Bretenoux (Wed, Thurs & Sat 1–3 daily; 5min); St-Céré (Wed & Sat 2 daily; 15min).
Martel to: Brive (school hols Tues & Sat 1 daily; rest of year Tues 1 daily; 1hr); St-Denis-lès-Martel (Mon–Sat 1–2 daily; 10–15min); Souillac (Mon–Sat 2 daily; 35min).
St-Céré to: Bretenoux (Wed & Sat 2 daily; 5min); Bretenoux-Biars (Wed & Sat 2 daily; 10min); Cahors (Mon & Wed–Sat 1 daily; 1hr 45min); Carennac (school term Mon–Fri 1 daily, rest of year Wed 1 daily; 20min); Figeac (3–4 weekly; 1hr); Gramat (school term Mon–Sat 1–2 daily, rest of year Mon & Wed–Sat 1 daily; 30–40min).
Souillac to: Brive (school term Mon–Sat 1–2 daily, rest of year Tues–Thurs & Sat 1–2 daily; 1hr–1hr 15min); Martel (Mon–Sat 1 daily; 20–30min); St-Denis-lès-Martel (Mon–Sat 1 daily; 35–45min); Sarlat (3–5 daily; 50min).

6

The Lot Valley and around

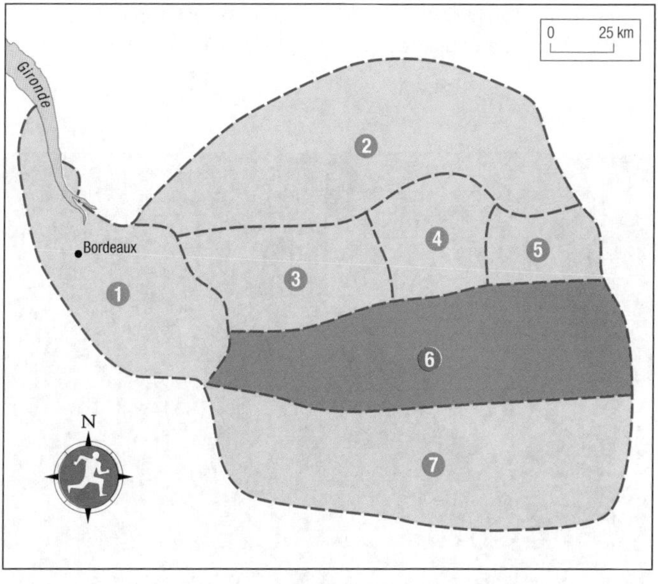

CHAPTER 6

Highlights

* **Pont Valentré** Cahors' signature sight is the fortified medieval bridge guarding the town's western approaches. See p.273

* **St-Cirq Lapopie** Perched high above the River Lot, this former feudal stronghold boasts stunning views and lovely, labyrinthine alleys to explore. See p.277

* **Grotte de Pech-Merle** The combination of dazzling limestone formations and more than five hundred prehistoric drawings make this cave unmissable. See p.282

* **Figeac** A laid-back riverside town with plenty of medieval architecture and a fascinating museum of writing. See p.284

* **Château de Bonaguil** One of the last medieval fortresses built in France, and now a magnificent ruin. See p.300

* **Bastides** Monpazier provides an almost perfect example of the region's myriad fortified towns. See p.308

▲ St-Cirq Lapopie

6

The Lot Valley and around

Like the Dordogne, the **River Lot** rises in the foothills of the Massif Central and is dammed in its upper reaches to form huge reservoirs. It begins to get more interesting, however, where it enters the Lot *département*, the boundaries of which roughly coincide with the old province of **Quercy**.

The largest town in the Lot valley, and capital of the *département*, is **Cahors**. It may lack the higgledy-piggledy charm of Sarlat or Bergerac, but compensates for this with a pleasingly workaday atmosphere and a wonderful location in the middle of a meander. It also boasts the best example of a fortified medieval bridge left in France, the **Pont Valentré**, while the country round about produces an extremely distinctive dark, almost peppery red **wine**.

The Lot valley is at its most picturesque upstream from Cahors. The scenery may not be as dramatic as the middle reaches of the Dordogne, but the sheer cliffs here host their fair share of perched fortresses and feudal villages. Foremost among these is spectacular **St-Cirq Lapopie**, while the nearby **Grotte de Pech-Merle**, with its glittering rock formations and prehistoric cave art, draws almost as many visitors. Pech-Merle lies in the hills above the wild and pretty **Célé valley**, which leads northeast to lovely, medieval **Figeac**, the Lot's second largest town.

North and west of Figeac stretches the **Causse de Gramat**, the biggest and wildest of the region's limestone *causses*. With its huge vistas, it makes a welcome change from the confining valleys and a great place for walking or cycling, though it has few notable sights beyond the village of **Assier**, in the far southeast, with its extraordinary church. On its western edge the Causse de Gramat suddenly gives way to a lovely area of gentle wooded hills known as the **Bouriane**. Again, there are no must-see sights, though its capital, **Gourdon**, a once-prosperous town built of butter-coloured stone, is worth a stop-off, and the nearby **Grottes de Cougnac**, with a smattering of prehistoric cave paintings and some exceptionally delicate limestone concretions, repay a visit.

Returning to the Lot valley, the river south of Cahors wriggles its way westwards through vineyards and past ancient towns and villages. By far the most striking of these is **Puy-l'Évêque**. An outpost of the bishops of Cahors, the town's medieval and Renaissance houses jostle for space on a steep incline, reaching upwards like trees for light, though none is equal to the bishop's

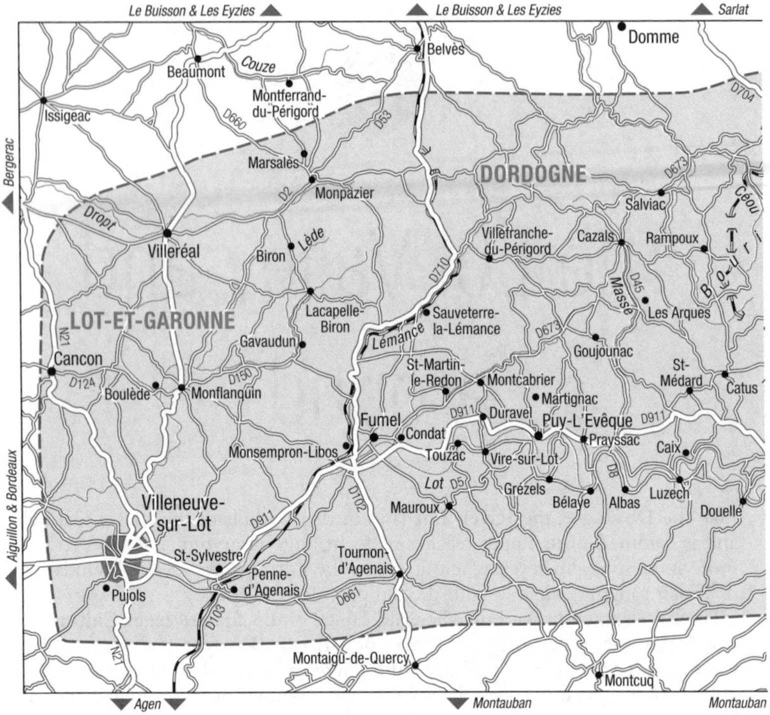

thirteenth-century keep towering above. An even more dramatic sight lies in store in the country northwest of Puy-l'Évêque where the **Château de Bonaguil** is an outstanding example of late-fifteenth-century military architecture, its great bulk silhouetted against the wooded hillside.

Further downstream things begin to quieten down again as the valley flattens out towards **Villeneuve-sur-Lot**. Despite unattractive modern suburbs, the town has a decent supply of hotels and restaurants, and with the river sliding through an old centre built of stone and warm red brick, it's a pleasant and convenient place to stay. Villeneuve – as its name indicates – was also one of the many "new towns", or *bastides*, founded in this area in the thirteenth and fourteenth centuries. You'll find the best examples of *bastide* architecture in the hills to the north, where the villages of **Monflanquin** and **Monpazier** seem hardly to have changed since the Middle Ages. The same can't be said for the **Château de Biron**, lying between the two, which was altered and expanded extensively during the Renaissance, but its superb hilltop location makes it hard to resist.

Travelling by **public transport** is not that easy, and many bus services to smaller towns only run at school times, if at all. There are however **bus services** running along the Lot valley from Cahors east to Figeac and west to Fumel. Other buses head north from Cahors and Figeac to Gramat, while Gramat and Gourdon are served by trains from Brive. Future cuts to the network are likely, so for any public transport it's wise to get information from the relevant tourist offices before you travel. All the buses to places listed in this chapter are covered in a useful booklet, *Les Bus du Lot*, available at tourist offices; otherwise contact the transport information desk of the Conseil Général du Lot (☎05.65.53.43.91,

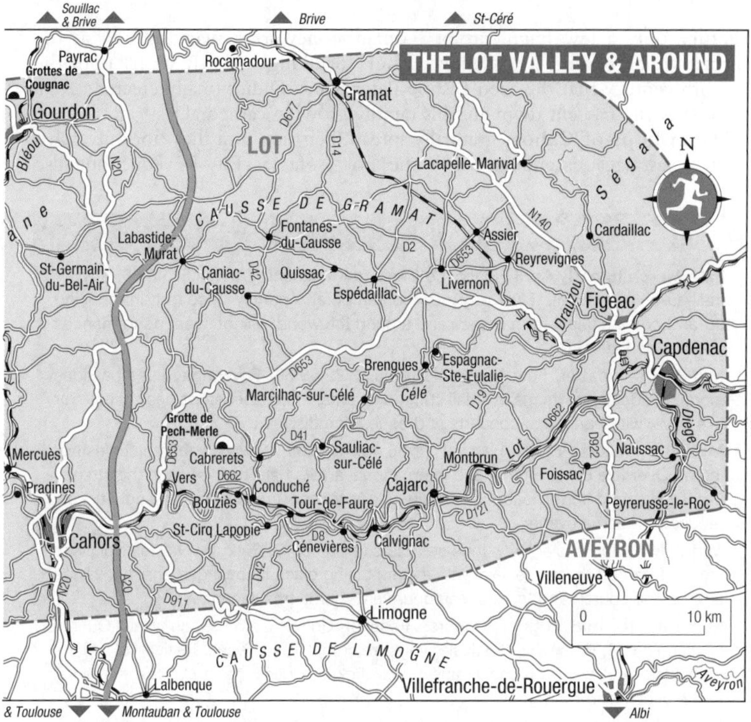

Ⓦwww.lot.fr). You'll need your own transport for exploring the Célé valley, the Bouriane and other places off the beaten track.

Look out for the free **walking** map, *Carte de la Randonnée*, and the series of booklets *Promenades et Randonnées* (€7) available from local tourist offices or from the departmental office (see p.48). Another more leisurely possibility is to rent a **houseboat** and pootle along the Lot (see p.29).

Cahors

A sunny southern backwater built in a tight meander of the River Lot, **CAHORS** was the chief town of the old province of Quercy and is now the modern capital of the Lot *département*. Its somewhat troubled history has left a warren of dark medieval lanes, a rather knocked about cathedral and impressive fortifications, among them Cahors' famous landmark, the turreted **Pont Valentré**. Another reason to come here is to sample the local **wines**, heady and black but dry to the taste (see box, p.269).

Some history

Both the names Quercy and Cahors derive from the area's first-known inhabitants, the local Gaulish tribe known as the **Cadurci**. During the first century BC they founded a settlement near a sacred spring, immediately across the river to the southwest of modern Cahors, which the Romans later called **Divona Cadurcorum**. Following successive Vandal and Frankish invasions after the fifth century, only a few fragments of Roman stonework remain, as well as the spring, which continues to supply Cahors' drinking water. It wasn't until the seventh century that the then Bishop (later Saint) Didier finally erected a wall to protect the nascent town and his rapidly growing cathedral.

The **bishops of Cahors** gradually spread their net until they not only ruled over a vast area extending down the Lot as far as Puy-l'Évêque but also

Festivals, events and markets

Late March to early April Figeac: Le Chaînon Manquant (ⓣ05.34.51.48.88, ⓦwww.reseau-chainon.com). Five days of contemporary performance art introducing up-and-coming talent from France and around the world. Mix of street performances and ticketed events.

Mid-July Monpazier: Fête Médiévale (ⓣ05.53.22.68.59, ⓦwww.pays-des-bastides.com). In addition to its many small summer events, Monpazier steps back in time for five days, with banquets, concerts and equestrian displays.

Mid-July Cahors: Blues Festival (ⓣ06.45.71.75.60, ⓦwww.cahorsbluesfestival.com). Over five days, French and international artists bare their souls in the streets, Les Docks and the Théâtre de Verdure, rue Wilson (mostly free, though tickets required for some events).

Mid-July Assier: Assier dans tous ses États (ⓣ05.65.40.42.42, ⓦwww.festivalassier.com). Jazz and theatre festival with events taking place in local gardens, the village square, the church and the château courtyard. Some free events.

Mid-July to mid-August Cahors: Festival de St-Céré et du Haut-Quercy (ⓣ05.65.38.28.08, ⓦwww.festival-saint-cere.com). Three-week festival of opera, orchestral works and chamber music, with ticketed concerts in Cahors' cathedral and Musée Henri-Martin.

Late July Cajarc: Africajarc (ⓦwww.africajarc.com). Cajarc moves to an African beat during three days of concerts, exhibitions, craft displays, markets and food stalls. Tickets required for the main concerts.

First weekend in August Gourdon: Grande Fête Médiévale. Gourdon lets rip with two days of junketing complete with jugglers, fire-eaters, musicians and the works. Entry €3.50.

Early August Puy-l'Évêque: Fête Votive. One of the area's most important local fêtes, lasting five days with a free dance every night, a funfair and a fireworks spectacular with music on the Sunday.

Early to mid-August Château de Bonaguil: Festival du Théâtre (ⓣ05.53.71.17.17, ⓦwww.bonaguil.org). The inner court and moats make a spectacular venue for this festival of French theatre held over eight or nine days. There's a play or musical event every night (tickets required), as well as workshops, street theatre and lectures.

Mid-August Monflanquin: Journées Médiévales. Two days of mead, minstrels and merry japes as Monflanquin goes medieval. Jousting, banquets, siege engines – you name it. You can even rent costumes.

First weekend in September Peyrusse-le-Roc: Spectacle Pyrosymphonique. The ruined towers of Peyrusse make a spectacular setting for a *son-et-lumière*-cum-fireworks display, complete with banquet (€15–20 including dinner).

Markets

The region's main **markets** take place at Cahors (Wed & Sat); Cajarc (Sat); Duravel (Sat); Figeac (Sat); Fumel (Sun); Gourdon (Tues & Sat, also Thurs in July & Aug); Gramat (Tues & Fri); Luzech (Wed); Monflanquin (Thurs); Monpazier (Thurs); Monsempron-Libos (Thurs); Puy L'Évêque (Tues); and Villeneuve-sur-Lot (Tues, Wed, Sat & Sun).

controlled the all-important river trade. By the early thirteenth century Cahors was entering its **golden age**, as powerful local merchants known as Caorsins, together with Lombard bankers fleeing the Cathar Crusades, turned the town into Europe's chief banking centre – a wealth that was reflected in the gentrification of various townhouses, bridges and cathedral. When the local Bishop Jacques Duèze was named **Pope John XXII** in 1316, Cahors had reached its apogee. His greatest legacy was a university, which remained one of the most important in France for the next four centuries.

By now, however, the English and French armies were at loggerheads. Cahors was never attacked during the Hundred Years' War, but the end result was the same: under the Treaty of Brétigny (1360) it succumbed reluctantly to **English occupation**. When French rule was eventually restored around 1440, the Cadurciens set about rebuilding their ravaged town, adding a few Italianate flourishes and developing a distinctive decorative style comprising carved or moulded rose blossoms, flaming suns and the so-called "*bâtons écotés*" ("pruned branches"), which is still in evidence today.

Unlike several of its neighbours, Cahors remained staunchly Catholic during the **Wars of Religion**. As a consequence it was sacked by the Protestant Henry of Navarre, the future King Henri IV of France, when he seized it after a brief battle in 1580. Later the same year, however, one of many peace treaties saw the town returned to the Catholic fold. By way of recompense, Henry later donated six thousand *livres*, half of which went towards restoring the cathedral.

Over the years Cahors gradually expanded to fill the entire peninsula, though it was not until the nineteenth century that Bishop Didier's ramparts were finally razed. They were replaced by a tree-lined boulevard that was later named after Cahors' most famous son, the politician **Léon Gambetta** (see box, p.271).

Arrival and information

The heart of present-day Cahors is place François Mitterrand, a wide, open square towards the middle of the main boulevard Gambetta. An underground car park has been built underneath it. East of here medieval houses cluster round the cathedral, while the post-seventeenth-century town spreads west towards the **gare SNCF**, 500m away along rue Joachim Murat. The station is also the terminus for some regional **buses**, while others stop on place de Charles-de-Gaulle at the north end of the main boulevard.

Cahors' **tourist office** (July & Aug Mon–Sat 9am–12.30pm & 1.30–6pm, Sun 10am–noon; rest of year same hours but closed Sun; ⓣ05.65.53.20.65, ⓦwww.mairie-cahors.fr) occupies a handsome building on the north side of place François Mitterrand. It provides detailed walking maps of the town, and also organizes **guided tours** (some in English) in season, covering a variety of themes (various dates throughout the year, €6.50; see tourist office for details).

Accommodation

Cahors has a broad range of **hotels**, though the choice, particularly in the middle price categories, is not particularly inspiring. Instead, there's better value for money in the **surrounding region**, though you'll need your own transport to get there. Note that unless otherwise stated, the accommodation listed below is marked on the main Cahors map (p.268).

Hotels in Cahors

Hôtel Jean XXII 5 bd Gambetta ⓣ05.65.35.07.66, ⓕ05.65.53.92.38. See map, p.270. This small hotel at the north end of the main boulevard is comfortable and good value; make sure you book well ahead in season. The rooms are cosy and well maintained. Closed occasionally mid-Oct to Easter. ③

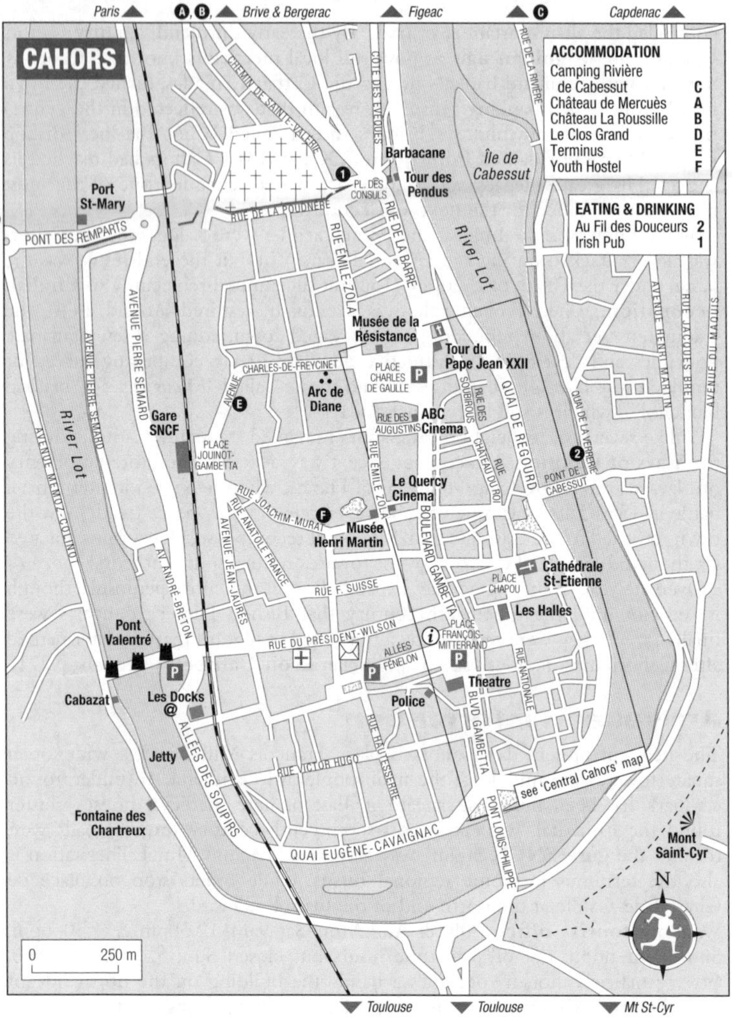

De La Paix 30 place Saint-Maurice ⓣ05.65.35.03.40, ⓦwww.hoteldelapaixcahors.com. See map, p.270. Right in the heart of the old town, this hotel, situated above a popular café, offers clean, bright rooms, though some are on the small side. Staff speak English. ❸

Terminus 5 av Charles de Freycinet ⓣ05.65.53.32.00, ⓦwww.balandre.com. Cahors' most opulent hotel occupies a nineteenth-century bourgeois residence near the station. The grandeur has faded somewhat, but quirky touches such as pianos on the landing help make it nostalgic rather than shabby. ❺

Hotels around Cahors

Château de Mercuès Mercuès ⓣ05.65.20.00.01, ⓦwww.chateaudemercues.com. High on its promontory 6km to the northwest of Cahors, for centuries this was the humble residence of the bishops of Cahors. It is now a luxury hotel with pool, tennis courts, excellent wine cellars (tastings available July & Aug; free) and a 1-star Michelin restaurant (closed Mon & for lunch Tues–Thurs; menus from €65). Closed Nov to Easter. ❾

Château La Roussille chemin du Moulin, Labéraudie ⓣ05.65.22.84.74, ⓦwww.chateauroussille.com. A welcoming *chambre* *d'hôte* five minutes drive from Cahors centre; take the D8 in the direction of Moulin de Labéraudie. It has one room and two suites, all with their own individual character, a lounge, a billiard room, and is set in a large park complete with swimming pool. Open end March to mid-Nov. ❺

Le Clos Grand 12 rue des Claux Grands, Labéraudie, Pradines ⓣ05.65.35.04.39. In Pradines, a suburb 5km northwest of Cahors, this welcoming hotel looks out over fields and has a pleasant, shady garden. Most rooms occupy a purpose-built annexe beside the pool, each with a little terrace or balcony and en-suite bathroom. Locals come here for the good-value cooking (menus €17–46). Closed Jan, one week end-May & one week end-Sept. ❷

Hostel and campsite

Camping Rivière de Cabessut rue de la Rivière ⓣ05.65.30.06.30, ⓦwww.cabessut.com. Three-star campsite in a quiet spot beside the river just over 1km from Cahors across Pont de Cabessut. Facilities include a shop, snack bar, small pool and canoe rental. Closed Oct–March.

Youth Hostel 222 rue Joachim Murat ⓣ05.65.35.64.71, ⓦwww.fuaj.org/cahors. Pleasantly situated in a quiet building behind a park, this hostel is not far from the train station. Breakfast (€4) and other meals available (from €9 for three courses), as well as a laundry and TV room. No curfew. €10 per person per night, extra to hire bedding.

The Town

Compact and easily walkable, Cahors is surrounded on three sides by the River Lot and protected to the north by a series of fourteenth-century fortifications. Most sights of interest lie within the cramped confines of the medieval streets on the peninsula's eastern edge, focused around the twin domes

The wines and vineyards of Cahors

So dark that they're often referred to as "black wines", the red **wines of Cahors** are by far the most distinctive of the southwestern wines, hard and full-bodied with lots of tannin, and they generally need long ageing to bring out their best. The dominant **grape variety** is Auxerrois (also known as Malbec or Cot), which gives the wine its rich tannin content, its colour and its ability to age. The other thirty percent is made up of Merlot and Tanat – Merlot for roundness and aroma, Tanat to help the ageing process. The distinctive bite of a young Cahors wine goes well with charcuterie and stews, while the more aromatic older wines usually accompany red meats, game and the local goat's cheese, *Cabécou*.

There are approximately 43 square kilometres under vines in the *appellation*, which stretches from Cahors west along the Lot for 30km to Soturac, producing on average 240,000 hectolitres (roughly 32 million bottles) per annum. Before **visiting the vineyards**, pick up a copy of the free *Le Vignoble de Cahors, Châteaux et Domaines*, which details the two hundred or so producers in the *appellation*; it's available from the tourist office (see p.267) and from wine merchants in Cahors (see p.275), or from the Maison du Vin de Cahors, 430 av Jean Jaurès (Mon–Fri; ⓣ05.65.23.22.24), opposite the station; note that the Maison du Vin does not otherwise cater to individuals.

For an introduction to what's on offer, head for the imposing **Château Lagrézette** (daily 10am–7pm; ⓣ05.65.20.07.42, ⓦwww.chateau-lagrezette.tm.fr), 10km northwest of Cahors on the D12 midway between Douelle and Mercuès. In addition to sampling their award-winning wines you can visit the magnificent, state-of-the-art *chais* dug into the hillside, though it's best to call in advance to arrange this. Also worth a visit for its reliably good wines – if not for its ambience – is the **Côtes d'Olt** co-operative (April–Oct Mon–Sat 8am–noon & 2–6pm, July & Aug also Sun 10am–12.30pm & 2–6pm; rest of year same hours but closed Sun; ⓣ05.65.30.71.86) on the river's south bank about 17km west of Cahors on the D8 in the commune of Parnac.

In general you can expect to pay between €10 and €20 for a very decent Cahors, although some of the region's prestige wines fetch €70 or more.

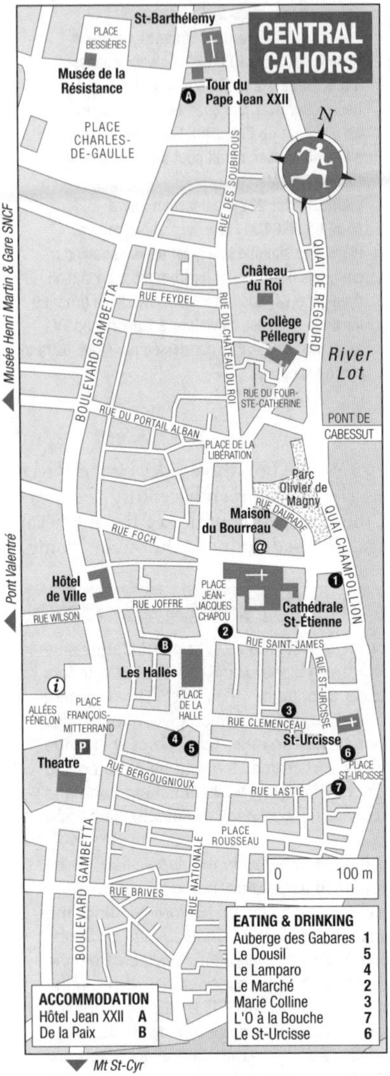

of the **Cathédrale St-Étienne**. From here, **rue Nationale** leads south past the former homes of wealthy merchants to the flood-prone artisans' quarter, while north of the cathedral the land continues to slope gently upwards along **rue du Château-du-Roi**, where bankers and aristocrats once lived, towards the old town gate with its guardhouse and tower. Of medieval Cahors' three fortified bridges, only westerly **Pont Valentré** remains – one of the finest surviving bridges of its time. More recent history is commemorated in a couple of passably interesting **museums** and, on a fine day, there are good views from the summit of **Mont St-Cyr**, which overlooks the town from the southeast.

The cathedral and around

The oldest and simplest in plan of the Périgord-style Romanesque churches, the **Cathédrale St-Étienne** dates largely from the early twelfth century, when Bishop Didier's original cathedral was rebuilt in part to house the relic of the Holy Coif. According to local legend, this cloth, said to have covered Christ's head in the tomb, was brought back from the Holy Land around this time by Bishop Géraud de Cardaillac.

Numerous reconstructions have been carried out over the centuries, meaning St-Étienne's exterior is unexciting, with the notable exception of the elaborately decorated portal above the **north door**. Carved around 1140, it depicts Christ's Ascension. Side panels show scenes from the life of St Stephen (St Étienne), the first Christian martyr who was stoned to death around 35 AD, while the outer arch portrays people being stabbed and hacked with axes.

Inside, the cathedral is much like Périgueux's St-Étienne (see p.133), with a nave lacking aisles and transepts, roofed with two monumental domes. High in the west dome, original fourteenth-century frescoes again depict the stoning of St Stephen, encircled by eight giant prophets. In 1988 further paintings from the same era were discovered behind layers of plaster just inside and above the

Léon Gambetta

Heralded as the "father of the Republic", **Léon Gambetta** was born in Cahors in 1838. After graduating as a lawyer, he specialized in defending republican sympathizers accused of political crimes against Emperor Napoléon III. The republicans soon rallied around Gambetta – a charismatic man and great orator – and, when Napoléon was forced to surrender to an invading Prussian army in 1870, he was among those who quickly proclaimed the **Third Republic**, the regime which continued to govern France until 1940. It had a rocky start, however. With the Prussians besieging Paris, Gambetta fled the capital by balloon to organize the war effort in the provinces. While he opposed the armistice signed in 1871, Gambetta and his band of moderate republicans, or "Opportunists", were able to keep the Republic afloat despite constant attacks from both the monarchist majority and the radical Left. He served as president of the National Assembly from 1879 to 1882, but later that year his career was cut short when he accidentally shot himself with a revolver, and died soon after.

west door. They consist of faded but beautiful Creation scenes, including Adam and Eve in the Garden of Eden and many finely observed birds and animals.

To the right of the choir, the aptly named **Deep Chapel** bears scars from the Wars of Religion, when Protestant armies hacked away at its carvings. They also caused irreparable damage to the **cloister**, accessed by a door next to the Deep Chapel, though the flamboyant Gothic colonnades still retain some intricate craftsmanship. The door surrounds are also beautifully carved, if rather battered; that on the northeast wall leads into **St-Gausbert's Chapel** (only accessible as part of the guided tours run by the tourist office, see above), which holds the **Holy Coif** – a decidedly unimpressive, rather grubby looking piece of padded cloth – among chalices, gilded statues and other treasures.

The square on which the cathedral stands, **place Jean-Jacques Chapou**, commemorates a local Resistance leader killed in a German ambush in July 1944. On its west side, look for a sign above what is now a bank announcing *Bazar Gênois: Gambetta Jeune et Cie.* This is where **Léon Gambetta** (see box above), the son of an Italian grocer, spent his childhood. At its southern end the square extends into place Galdemar, popularly known as place de la Halle. The covered **market hall** at its centre, built as a corn exchange in 1865, provides the focus for Cahors' lively markets. There's a fresh food **market** in the *halle* here (daily except Sun pm & Mon), and a more extensive market on Wednesday and Saturday mornings spreading north into the cathedral square; in winter (Nov to mid-March), the *halle* plays host to a Saturday morning *marché au gras*, selling all manner of duck and goose products. Nearby place François Mitterrand also hosts an antiques fair-cum-flea market on the first and third Saturdays of the month.

The medieval streets

A warren of narrow lanes and alleys fills the area between boulevard Gambetta and the eastern riverbank, where the majority of houses, turreted and built of flat, thin southern brick, have been handsomely restored during recent decades. From the market square, **rue Nationale** cuts almost due south through the heart of medieval Cahors to where the old Roman bridge once stood – the foundations are still just visible when the water level is low. Other roads worth exploring in the area are canyon-like rue Bergougnioux and its easterly extension rue Lastié, which comes out among a pretty group of brick and timber buildings around place St-Urcisse.

Les Jardins Secrets

A somewhat quirkier way to unearth Cahors' history is to find the **Jardins Secrets**, a series of around thirty gardens making use of otherwise vacant patches of land dotted around the old town and the river. Medicinal herbs, vines and fruit orchards all feature, laid out as they would have been by monks or local gardeners. Pick up a map of the garden locations from the tourist office (see p.267) or at the boat tour ticket booths near Pont Valentré; all the descriptions are in English.

One of Cahors' most attractive corners lies just north of the cathedral along **rue Daurade**, where a lovely row of buildings overlooks a little park named after the sixteenth-century poet Olivier de Magny, who lived at no. 12. His house is overshadowed, though, by the thirteenth-century **Maison du Bourreau**, the "executioner's house", with its big arched openings and line of double windows above. The name dates from the Revolution, when the public executioner lived here; naturally, the building is said to be haunted.

Continuing north along rue Daurade you reach the southern end of **rue Château-du-Roi** and its extension, **rue des Soubirous**. This is the "upper town", where the houses become distinctly grander. One of the most imposing is the fourteenth-century **Château du Roi** itself, built by cousins of Pope John XXII but later taken over by the king's emissary when the bishops lost their stranglehold on Cahors in the fifteenth century. Its massive, featureless walls now contain the local prison.

Wealthy Cadurciens were very fond of adding turrets to their homes and there are a number of examples scattered through the Soubirous quarter. To see them properly it's best to head down to the river – rue du Four-Ste-Catherine provides the most interesting route – to a vantage point across Pont de Cabessut. Cahors' skyline stretches in front of you from the cathedral domes in the south via Collège Pélegry, with its crenellated hexagonal turret, and the square, solid tower of the Château du Roi. In the far distance the **Tour du Pape Jean XXII** and the **Tour des Pendus** pinpoint Cahors' northern ramparts, which still stretch partway across the peninsula.

The museums

Back in the centre, Cahors' two museums deserve a brief stop. The first, in a small building on the north side of place Charles-de-Gaulle, is the **Musée de la Résistance** (daily 2–6pm; free), which documents the history of the local Resistance movement against the broader context of German occupation, deportations and, finally, Liberation in 1945. The most interesting section, on the ground floor, deals with local history, where you can read about Jean-Jacques Chapou, after whom the cathedral square is named (see p.271), and about the *Mona Lisa*'s sojourn in the area (see p.258).

Continuing south down rue Émile-Zola, you come to the **Musée Henri Martin** at no. 792 (Mon & Wed–Sat 11am–6pm, Sun 2–6pm; closed when changing temporary exhibitions; ⓣ05.65.20.88.66; €3), in the seventeenth-century former episcopal palace. Exhibits range from Gallo-Roman pots to works by nineteenth- and twentieth-century artists such as Dufy, Vlaminck and Utrillo. However, pride of place goes to seventeen oil paintings by local artist **Henri Martin** (1860–1943), whose mix of Impressionism and Pointillism perfectly evokes the lazy sun-filled landscapes of this part of France, and an important collection dedicated to **Léon Gambetta**. With over two thousand documents, photographs, sculptures and paintings, only a fraction is on show at any one time.

Pont Valentré

The top reason most people venture to Cahors is to see the dramatic **Pont Valentré**, which guards the western river crossing. Its three powerful towers, originally closed by portcullises and gates, made it an independent fortress, which was so imposing, in fact, that the bridge was never attacked. Building it was a problem, however: work started in 1308, but the bridge was not completed for another seventy years. According to legend, the Devil was to blame – at least in part. The story goes that the architect, exasperated at the slow progress, sold his soul in exchange for the Devil's assistance. As the bridge was nearing completion, he tried to wriggle out of the deal by giving the Devil a sieve with which to carry water for the masons. The Devil took revenge by creeping up the central tower every night to remove the last stone, thus ensuring that the bridge would never be finished. If you look carefully at the top of the tower's east face, you'll see a little devil, which was added when Pont Valentré was renovated in 1879. On the far side of the river, the old pumping station of **Cabazat** now houses a museum detailing the bridge's history (June–Aug daily 10am–1pm & 3–7pm; Sept–Dec Fri–Mon 11am–1pm & 3–6pm; Ⓣ05.65.53.04.99). Most of the information is in French, but you can pick up a leaflet that has the basics in English. Glass floors show off the pumping mechanism below, while the café makes for a pleasant, if a little pricey, riverside spot.

From April to October, Safaraid (Ⓣ05.65.35.98.88, Ⓔbateaux.safaraid@club-internet.fr) operates **boat tours** (with English commentary) round the Cahors meander from the jetty below Pont Valentré (1hr 15min; €8.50). In addition, Les Croisières Fénelon (Ⓣ05.65.30.16.55, Ⓔbateaufenelon@wanadoo.fr), also puts on a varied programme of excursions including day-trips upriver to St-Cirq Lapopie (€54); prices include a meal onboard. There are ticket booths for both companies beside the Pont Valentré jetty.

Mont St-Cyr

All around Cahors rise the dry, scrubby uplands of the *causse*. These valley sides were carpeted with vines from Roman times until the nineteenth century when phylloxera set in, after which the land was used for grazing sheep; now, however, only the lines of tumbled-down stone walls and abandoned farmhouses remain. One of the few landmarks around is the red-and-white TV

Quercy saffron

Saffron was originally introduced by returning Crusaders in the twelfth century, and quickly became a major source of income for the region. However, production of the spice declined drastically in the eighteenth century, largely due to the significant manpower requirements. Obtained from the dried stigmas of the saffron crocus, the spice can only be picked by hand early on autumn mornings. It takes 200,000 flowers and over forty hours' labour to obtain a kilogram of dried saffron, and pound for pound it's more expensive than gold. Historically the spice has been used in sweet and savoury dishes, particularly in central Asia, as well as for dyeing cloths, as a hangover remedy, and to cure tuberculosis and measles. It's also supposed to have cancer-suppressing properties.

Around seventy farms in the Lot valley area now produce saffron commercially, and many of them can be visited, particularly around harvest time in **October**. Their organisation's website, Ⓦwww.safran-du-quercy.com, details recipes using saffron, and they host two major **saffron fairs**, at Saint-Céré (see p.255) in mid-July to mark the planting season, and at Cajarc (see p.279) at the end of October to celebrate the harvest – the latter is larger and offers more opportunities for tasting and buying.

mast on the summit of **Mont St-Cyr**, overlooking Cahors to the southeast. At 264m, this is the place to head for bird's-eye views of the town: the division between medieval and seventeenth-century Cahors becomes very apparent from the summit, particularly in summer when tree-lined boulevard Gambetta picks out the former course of the ramparts.

It's a stiff but straightforward climb to the summit of Mont St-Cyr. From the southern end of boulevard Gambetta, cross Pont Louis-Philippe, then take the steps behind the Virgin's statue and keep going up for about twenty to thirty minutes. Though you can drive, it takes almost as long, as the road winds for about 5km among stunted oaks and pines across the plateau. Apart from the views, there are picnic tables at the top and a café-bar, which also serves food till 7pm from June (closed Mon & Tues) till the end of summer.

Eating and drinking

Cahors has no shortage of good **places to eat**, many of which make full use of the excellent local produce. Most are concentrated in the streets of the medieval town, though you'll also find brasseries, pizzerias and cafés along boulevard Gambetta. There are plenty of boulangeries and boucheries around the market square and the cathedral, and for excellent cakes head to *Patisserie du Valentré*, 334 rue du Président-Wilson. Unless otherwise stated, the places listed below are marked on the central Cahors map (p.270).

Auberge des Gabares 24 place Champollion ⓣ05.65.53.91.47. This sort of traditional, single-menu restaurant is usually found in the depths of the country rather than in the middle of a town, albeit on a wisteria-covered terrace overlooking the Lot. The food, like the decor, is simple and unfussy, and it's good value, too, with five courses for a mere €14 including wine. There's more choice on Saturday evenings, when they stretch to two menus (€21 and €22, excluding wine). Reservations recommended. Closed Sun & Mon.

Le Dousil 124 rue Nationale ⓣ05.65.53.19.67. This wine bar is a great place to sample local reds before setting off on the wine trail. They dish up good food, too, from cheese or charcuterie platters (€9–16.50) to open sandwiches (from €2.30) and more substantial fare such as *cassoulet* (around €11–15). Wine by the glass or bottle, from a wide selection. Closed Sun & Mon.

Au Fil des Douceurs 90 quai de la Verrerie ⓣ05.65.22.13.04. See map, p.268. A floating restaurant moored on the far side of Pont de Cabessut, with splendid views of the Cahors skyline. The food is haute cuisine, with typical local dishes. Three-course menus start at €14 for a weekday lunch and otherwise at €24–55. Reservations recommended Sat eve. Closed Sun & Mon.

Le Lamparo 76 rue Georges Clemenceau ⓣ05.65.35.25.93, ⓦwww.lelamparo.com. Large, bustling restaurant that spills out onto the square in summer. Decked out in sunny blues and yellows and with lots of greenery, it's justifiably popular for its enormous portions and very reasonable prices. Though the speciality is pizza (from €7.60), there's something for everyone, including salads and local dishes, plus enticing desserts to follow. Menus from €15.90, lunch and eve. Closed Sun.

Le Marché 27 place Chapou ⓣ05.65.35.27.27 ⓦwww.restaurantlemarche.com. This elegant restaurant just next to the market hall serves delicate dishes made from fresh local produce. Menus from €11 lunch, €20 eves. Closed Mon, plus Sun except Jul & Aug.

Marie Colline 173 rue Georges Clemenceau ⓣ05.65.35.59.96. You need to reserve or wait till around 1pm to find space at this bright, airy vegetarian restaurant run by two sisters. The choice is limited – two entrées and two main dishes which change daily – but it's all freshly made, using locally produced vegetables. Save room for one of their scrumptious desserts. *Plat du jour* €8.50, or three courses for €16. Open lunchtime only Tues–Fri. Closed Aug.

L'O à la Bouche 134 rue St-Urcisse ⓣ05.65.35.65.69. A tasty mix of traditional ingredients and contemporary cuisine, such as creamy lentil soup with foie gras, served in a simple but elegant red-bricked restaurant. Menus from €13 at lunch and €26 in the evening. Closed Sun & Mon, also two weeks beginning of April.

Le St-Urcisse place St-Urcisse ⓣ05.65.35.06.06. Stylish restaurant with a lovely big garden for alfresco eating. The menu consists largely of grilled meats with sauces, though there are other options. Menus from €12 at lunchtime, à la carte around €25–30 in the evening. Open daily.

Nightlife and entertainment

There's little in the way of **nightlife**, especially out of season, but one of the livelier spots is the *Irish Pub* (see map, p.268), tucked away to the northwest of place des Consuls, which hosts live bands on Saturdays. Down on the waterfront, *Les Docks* (Ⓣ06.65.22.36.38, Ⓦwww.myspace.com/lesdocks) serves as a youth venue and events space, with bands every Friday. For other **events**, ask at the tourist office, which publishes lists of the many festivals (see box on p.266 for more), exhibitions, concerts and plays taking place in Cahors. For plays, the principal venue is the Neoclassical – and very plush – **Municipal Theatre** on place François Mitterrand (Ⓣ05.65.20.88.60, Ⓦwww.mairie-cahors.fr/theatre/index.html), which puts on a varied programme of theatre, dance, concerts and opera. Classical concerts are also held in the cathedral.

Listings

Bike rental The nearest outlets are in Douelle, about 10km west of Cahors, where you'll find Antinéa Loisirs (Ⓣ05.65.30.95.79), who also rent kayaks, and Made in Douelle (Ⓣ05.65.30.78.20 Ⓦwww.madeindouelle.fr). The latter are open all year, the former only in July & Aug.

Books and newspapers The Maison de la Presse, 73 bd Gambetta, stocks the main English-language papers and magazines as well as local guides, while Librairie Calligramme, 75 rue du Maréchal Joffre, is a more serious bookshop carrying a few English-language titles.

Bus information The tourist office stocks bus timetables, or phone the Conseil Général's central information desk (Ⓣ05.65.53.43.91). Tickets for Eurolines buses are available from Voyages Belmon, 2 bd Gambetta (Ⓣ05.65.35.59.30), at the north end of bd Gambetta.

Car parks The most convenient place to park is in the Parking de l'Amphithéatre under the allées Fénelon.

Car rental The most convenient is Avis, opposite the train station on place Jouinot-Gambetta Ⓣ05.65.30.13.10.

Cinema Cahors has two cinemas, the three-screen ABC, 24 rue des Augustins (Ⓣ05.65.35.03.11, Ⓦwww.abc-cahors.fr), and Le Quercy, 871 rue Émile-Zola (Ⓣ05.65.22.20.05, Ⓦwww.lequercy.fr), near the Musée Henri-Martin.

Hospital Centre Hospitalier Jean Rougier, 449–335 rue du Président Wilson Ⓣ05.65.20.50.50. Emergencies should head round the back of the building.

Internet access There's an internet café (Mon–Sat 10am–8pm, Sun 2–8pm) opposite the north entrance to the cathedral. Alternatively, *Les Docks* by the Pont Valentré also has an internet cafe (Tues–Fri 9am–noon & 2–6pm) and offers free Wi-fi.

Police Commissariat de Police, 1 rue de l'Ancienne Gendarmerie Ⓣ05.65.23.17.17.

Post office The main post office is at 257 rue du Président Wilson, 46000 Cahors.

Taxis There are taxi stands outside the train station and on bd Gambetta, or call Allo Taxi on Ⓣ05.65.22.19.42.

Wine Try the huge Atrium showroom (Ⓦwww.g-vigouroux.fr), on the N20 as you come into town from the south, which sells wines from the châteaux de Mercuès, de Haute-Serre, Caïx and Leret Monpezat at close to château prices, offers tastings and advises on vineyard visits. In town, head for the smaller Le Cèdre Valentré, 32 av André Breton, which also sells local produce and souvenirs, at the east end of Pont Valentré (Ⓦwww.cedrevalentre.com). Château Lagrézette (see box, p.269) also has a boutique right beside the bridge.

East along the Lot

Upstream from Cahors the Lot valley becomes narrower and the cliffs higher. The river is confined to ever-tighter meanders and castles sprout from inaccessible knuckles of rock, often with red-tiled villages clinging to their flanks. Delightful **St-Cirq Lapopie**, 30km or so east of Cahors, perched precariously on the edge of a 100m drop, is the most dramatic sight in the whole valley. Further along the river's south bank on the D8, the Renaissance **Château de**

Cénevières boasts an interesting history, as well as some unusual frescoes and a good collection of period furniture. The only major settlement along this stretch of river is **Cajarc**, an important market town with an incongruous modern art gallery; the town is also a stop on the pilgrims' road to Santiago de Compostela. Upstream, the scenery takes over once again as the Lot winds its way past more medieval villages and castles, and beneath a 300-metre-high belvedere, the **Saut de la Mounine**, on the valley's southern lip. There's nothing particular to stop for along the last stretch of river heading northeast to **Capdenac**, near **Figeac** (see p.284). Instead, you could take a diversion south across the *causse* to where the **Grotte de Foissac** harbours some prehistoric remains alongside a varied and colourful array of stalactites and stalagmites, and then continue on across country to the atmospheric ruins of **Peyrusse-le-Roc**.

The Lot valley is unusually well served by **public transport**, with an SNCF **bus** running along the river's north bank from Cahors via Figeac to Capdenac. It stops at almost every village en route, though you'll have to walk across to those south of the river, and will need your own transport to explore the high country on either side.

Vers and Bouziès

Immediately east of Cahors, the Lot valley is taken up with a busy main road, train tracks and scattered modern developments, above which soars the bridge for the A20 *autoroute*. However, things improve dramatically after the village of **VERS**, some 15km upstream, where the main D653 to Figeac strikes off north-eastwards. Vers itself doesn't merit a stop, unless you are in search of overnight **accommodation**. The most attractive option is *La Truite Dorée* (Ⓣ05.65.31.41.51, Ⓦwww.latruitedoree.fr; ❷; closed mid-Nov to March), at the entrance to the village overlooking the River Vers where it flows into the Lot from the north; rooms in the modern annexe have balconies over the river. There's a good-value **restaurant** with menus from €19 (closed mid-Dec to Feb, also eves except Fri & Sat). **Buses** stop near the hotel. You can rent **bikes** at La Roue Libre, place du Communal (Ⓣ05.65.31.45.57, Ⓦwww.larouelibre.net), in the centre of the village near the church.

East of Vers, the D662 hugs the north bank of the Lot as it meanders back and forth beneath cliffs that loom ever higher as you near **BOUZIÈS**, located on the south bank across a narrow suspension bridge. The main reason for coming here is to walk along the **chemin de halage**, a towpath cut into the cliff just above water level on the river's south bank. In pre-railway days it was used by men hauling produce-laden *gabarres* boats upstream. It now forms part of the GR36 long-distance footpath, indicated by red and white markers, which you can join at the car park on the east side of Bouziès. The rock-hewn section starts after about 500m and extends for some 300m; if you're feeling energetic, you can then continue on to St-Cirq Lapopie (see opposite).

Another way of exploring the river bank is to take to the water. Bouziès is a **boating** and **canoeing** centre, with several companies setting up shop on the south side of the bridge in the summer. You can rent canoes by the river, while Lot Navigation (Ⓣ05.65.24.32.20, Ⓦwww.lot-navigation.fr; April–Nov) has "**picnic boats**" for rental by the hour (four-person boats at €29) and by the day (four-person boats €99, twelve-person €175); reservations are recommended at least one week in advance. If you don't want to pilot your own vessel, Bateaux Safaraid (Ⓣ06.65.35.98.88, Ⓦwww.safaraid-croisieres.com) runs **excursions** to St-Cirq Lapopie and back (April–Oct 3–5 trips daily; 1hr 30min; €9). Finally, you can rent **houseboats** here through Nicols (see p.29 for more).

SNCF **buses** stop on the main road near the bridge. There's no tourist office, but Bouziès has a decent **hotel**, *Les Falaises* (Ⓣ05.65.31.26.83, Ⓦwww.hotel-falaises-bouzies.federal-hotel.com; ❹; closed Nov–March; menus from €14), with its own restaurant, in the village centre. Note that the rooms in the main building overlooking the pool and gardens are preferable to those in the older block behind.

St-Cirq Lapopie

Next stop up the valley is the cliff-edge village of **ST-CIRQ LAPOPIE**, 5km east of Bouziès, sitting high above the south bank of the Lot. With its cobbled lanes, half-timbered houses and gardens virtually unspoilt by modern intrusions, the village is an irresistible draw for the tour buses, but it's still worth the trouble, especially if you visit early or late in the day.

Some history

There has been a **fortress** on this rocky protuberance, known as La Popie, since Gallo-Roman times, if not before. It was such a strategically important site that in the Middle Ages it was owned by not only the viscount of St-Cirq but with the other three viscounts of Quercy (Gourdon, Cardaillac and Castelnau). A feudal town soon grew up within the protection of its walls, although it wasn't a particularly safe haven: St-Cirq took a battering from the English during the Hundred Years' War, while in the Wars of Religion it was seized by the Protestant Henry of Navarre, who ordered the castle to be destroyed in 1580 to keep it from the Catholics. Undaunted by these events, local craftsmen built up a reputation for their skill in **wood turning**, specifically of boxwood, which they fashioned into goblets, furniture and taps for casks. They continued to ply their craft into the nineteenth century, but following industrialization St-Cirq went into steep decline until it was rediscovered in the early twentieth century by the artistic fraternity, most famously **Henri Martin** (see p.272), **Man Ray** and the surrealist poet **André Breton**, who came to live here in the 1950s.

Arrival and information

Buses on the Cahors–Figeac route drop you across the river in the hamlet of Tour-de-Faure; from here you can call a **taxi** (Philippe Merle; Ⓣ06.15.23.61.61) or leg it up the steep hill for the last 2km. If you're driving, there are three **car parks** for St-Cirq: the lowest, 800m below the village, is free, the one closest to the village centre charges €3, including entry to the two museums, and the third sits 300m above the village and costs €2. The **tourist office**, on place du Sombral (daily 10am–1pm & 2–6pm; Ⓣ05.65.31.29.06, Ⓦwww.saint-cirqlapopie.com), can furnish you with a handy English-language walking guide to St-Cirq.

Accommodation

There are various **accommodation** options, mostly *chambres d'hôtes*, all of which get booked up weeks ahead in summer.

Auberge du Sombral place du Sombral Ⓣ05.65.31.26.08, Ⓦwww.lesombral.com. Very pleasantly located in the heart of the village, though this does mean parking some distance away. Offers plain but perfectly adequate rooms. Closed mid-Nov to March. ❸

Camping de la Plage Down by the bridge Ⓣ05.65.30.29.51, Ⓦwww.campingplage.com. Well-run three-star campsite. Offers canoe and bike rental as well as all sorts of other activities, including guided walks, rock climbing and pot-holing, through Kalapca loisirs (Ⓣ05.65.30.29.51, Ⓦwww.kalapca.com). Open all year.

Gîte d'étape ⓣ&ⓕ05.65.31.21.51. In the same building as the Musée de la Mémoire (see below), a well-equipped stopover offering comfortable beds. €13 per person. Closed Nov 11 to Easter. ❶

La Truffière ⓣ05.65.30.20.22, ⓦwww.camping-truffiere.com. Spacious, well-managed campsite on the plateau 3km southeast of St-Cirq via the D42. Closed Oct–March.

The Town

St-Cirq today consists of one main street running steeply downhill for 500m from Porte de la Peyrolerie in the west to easterly Porte de Pélissaria; in between which it's variously known as rue de la Peyrolerie, **rue Droite** – between the central market square, place du Sombral, and the church – and rue de la Pélissaria. All along are stone and half-timbered houses, under steeply pitched and gabled Quercy roofs. Starting from Porte de la Peyrolerie, the first place to head for is the ruined **château** to the north of place du Sombral. Precious little remains of the castle, but the site is fantastic, plunging down to the river 100m below. Further east along the cliff edge, the fortified **church of St-Cirq** is now the village's dominant building. It's in a pretty sorry state itself, though you can still make out faint traces of thirteenth-century murals where the original Romanesque chapel was incorporated into a larger church three hundred years later.

Below the church to the east, the **Musée Rignault** (late March to end Sept daily except Tues 10am–12.30pm & 2.30–6pm; July & Aug open until 7pm; closed two weeks in May or June to change exhibitions; €1.50) occupies a lovely fortified mansion with a romantic little rock garden and various other embellishments added by an art dealer who came to live here in 1922. A few pieces of his wide-ranging art collection are on display, while the rest of the space is given over to temporary exhibitions. On the way back up the hill, St-Cirq's local history museum, the **Musée de la Mémoire du Village** (April to mid-Nov daily except Mon 2.30–7pm; €1.50), in a Renaissance mansion one block south of rue Droite, is worth a peek for its exhibition on wood-turning. **Maison Daura** (ⓣ05.65.40.78.19, ⓦwww.magp.fr), near the entrance to the village, was once the home of Catalan painter **Pierre Daura** and now serves as a residence for international artists, as well as putting on regular modern art exhibitions.

Eating and drinking

In July and August there's a small **market** on place du Sombral on Wednesday mornings, but note that the nearest **food shop** is a small grocer down in Tour-de-Faure.

Le Gourmet Quercynois Rue de la Peyrolerie ⓣ05.65.31.21.20, ⓦwww.restaurant-legourmetquercynois.com. Sit out on the shady terrace to enjoy dishes such as pork with honey and herbs and duck with truffles. Menus from €14.80. Closed Mon eve except in July & Aug.

L'Oustal ⓣ05.65.31.20.17. A tiny little place tucked into a corner at the top end of rue de la Pélissaria just south of the church, serving only organic food. Midday menus from €12. Closed Nov–March & Mon except in July & Aug.

Lou Bolat At the top of the village just inside Porte de la Peyrolerie ⓣ05.65.30.29.04 ⓦwww.quercy.net/com/lou_bolat. Serves a choice of crêpes, salads and regional dishes, with menus starting at €12. Closed mid-Nov to mid-Feb, also Mon eve & Tues except in July & Aug.

The Château de Cénevières

Travelling on eastwards from St-Cirq, rather than carry on along the main D662 it's best to take the smaller and quieter D8 along the river's south bank. Seven kilometres out of St-Cirq, you reach the **Château de Cénevières** (guided tours daily except Sun morning, April–Sept 10am–noon & 2–6pm, Oct & Nov daily 2pm–5pm; €6; Ⓦwww.chateau-cenevieres.com), perched on another rocky spur just beyond Cénevières village; the nearest **bus stop** is in St-Martin-Labouval, a good kilometre downstream and across on the north bank.

The château, which largely dates from the sixteenth century in its present form, belonged to the **de Gourdon** family for nine hundred years until the line petered out in 1616. The last in line, Antoine de Gourdon, was a fervent supporter of the Reformation, so much so that the Protestant leader Henry of Navarre stayed here before attacking Cahors in 1580. Antoine brought back a rich haul that included the cathedral's principal altar – the boat carrying it, however, capsized and the altar is now somewhere at the bottom of the Lot. The château was saved from being torched during the Revolution by a quick-thinking overseer who opened the wine cellars to the mob, though he couldn't save the library, nor the coat of arms and other carvings on the facade. Cénevières was sold only once during its long history, to the ancestors of the present owners in 1793. Over the years they have uncovered several unusual Renaissance-era **frescoes**: notably, a frieze of the Istanbul skyline in the grand salon, and scenes from Greek mythology alongside what is believed to be a representation of an alchemist's fire and the philosopher's stone adorning a little vaulted chamber.

Cajarc

CAJARC, which lies on the river's north bank 9km upstream from Calvignac, is the biggest town on the Lot between Cahors and Capdenac. It consists of a small core of old lanes encircled by the boulevard du Tour-de-Ville, where you'll find facilities such as banks, food shops and a post office as well as cafés and brasseries. The town's only sight as such is the **Maison des Arts Georges-Pompidou** (open during exhibitions daily except Mon 2–6pm; Ⓣ05.65.40.78.19, Ⓦwww.magp.fr; free) on the northeastern outskirts on the D19 Figeac road. The gallery is named in honour of the former French prime minister, who bought a holiday home near here in 1963, and hosts three or four major contemporary art exhibitions a year.

SNCF **buses** stop on the north side of town on place du Foirail, a big open square where you'll also find the **tourist office**, housed in a converted chapel (April–June & Sept Mon–Sat 3–6pm, Sun 10am–12.30pm; July & Aug daily 10am–12.30pm & 2.30–7pm; Ⓣ05.65.40.72.89, Ⓕ05.65.40.39.05). A **market** takes place on Saturday afternoons on place du Foirail, with larger *foires* (country fairs) on the 10th and 25th of each month.

Cajarc has three **hotels**, the smartest of which is *La Ségalière* (Ⓣ05.65.40.65.35, Ⓦwww.lasegaliere.com; ❺; closed Nov–Feb), around 400m east on the D662 to Capdenac. It's a modern, concrete building – not beautiful, but airy and with nicely decorated rooms, some with a small balcony overlooking the pool and spacious gardens. There's also a good restaurant with menus from €23 (closed lunchtimes except weekends plus July & Aug). Of the other two, you're better off at *La Promenade*, place du Foirail (Ⓣ05.65.40.61.21, Ⓕ05.65.40.79.12; closed Christmas and New Year, plus 3 weeks in June–July; ❷), with a handful of simple rooms above an equally unfussy but convivial restaurant (menus €15–30, closed eves Sun & Mon). There's also a *gîte d'étape* on Place du Foirail (Ⓣ06.14.66.54.89; €9, linen €5.50) and a two-star municipal **campsite**, *Le Terriol* (Ⓣ05.65.40.72.74, Ⓕ05.65.40.39.05; closed Oct–April), beside the river roughly 200m southwest of the centre.

In addition to the above hotel **restaurants**, it's worth trying *Cajarc Gourmand* (Ⓣ05.65.40.69.50; Oct–April closed Wed & Thurs lunch), on a quiet square beside the church. They serve inventive and well-presented cuisine such as foie gras ravioli with vegetables and have various *formules* and menus ranging from

€15 up to €26. The *Brasserie du Tour de Ville* (Ⓣ05.65.40.67.09; closed Thurs; menus from €14), on the eastern side of the town, is a good place to watch the world go by, though it can get busy in summer.

On to Capdenac

Upstream from Cajarc, the Lot twists through one more giant meander and then straightens out until you reach the next big loop at Capdenac. Buses follow the northerly route past a succession of picturesque villages and castles, but if you've got your own transport, the less-travelled roads along the river's south bank make for a more interesting journey through walnut orchards and past weathered farm buildings, then up on to the flat, empty *causse* with little sign of habitation, save for the occasional dolmen or *cabane*, the traditional, stone-built shepherds' huts.

Where the D127 first climbs up from the river, 7km from Cajarc, it skirts along the edge of a 300-metre high cliff formed by the meander. The spot is known as the **Saut de la Mounine** ("Monkey's Leap"), after a legend concerning a local lord who ordered his daughter thrown off the cliff when she fell in love with a boy he disapproved of. A hermit took pity on the girl and secretly dressed a monkey in her clothes instead. When the poor beast was chucked over the edge, the lord repented, of course, and was only too relieved to discover he'd been outwitted. He apparently forgave his daughter, but history doesn't relate whom she married. Whatever the outcome, it's a marvellous view from up here, taking in the meander filled with patchwork fields and the ruined Château de Montbrun on the far hillside – where the lord and his fortunate daughter once lived.

A few kilometres further on you drop back down to the river along tiny lanes that wend their way northeastwards for about 15km before hitting the main D922. Turn left here and you'll be in Figeac (see p.284) in about ten minutes. Alternatively, if you cross over and follow the D86 along the river, another 7km will bring you to **CAPDENAC**, a major railway town on the south bank of the River Lot. There's a great view from the high ridge above the town and river to the north, but otherwise Capdenac is of little interest.

The Grotte de Foissac

On reaching the D922, instead of heading immediately north to Figeac or carrying on to Capdenac, it's worth taking a detour south towards Villefranche to visit one of the less-frequented caves, the **Grotte de Foissac** (1hr guided tours: April, May & Oct daily except Sat 2–5pm; June & Sept daily 10–11.30am & 2–6pm; July & Aug daily 10am–6pm; €7.60; Ⓣ05.65.64.77.04, Ⓦwww.grotte-de-foissac.com); it's signposted about 6km down the D922 and lies another 3km west across the *causse* through Foissac village. The cave was discovered in 1959 by a local pot-holing club, who found not only a huge cavern of colourful and varied concretions, including delicate needles, some bulging out into onion shapes, but also evidence of human activity going back at least four thousand years. From the number of **skeletons** and their positions, it seems that, unusually, the cave was used as a cemetery. It was also a source of clay – you can still see where people dug it out with their hands, and they also left large and beautifully fashioned pots, probably for storing grain. But the most moving evidence is the lone footprint left by a child deep inside the cave.

Peyrusse-le-Roc

Twenty kilometres to the east of Foissac, via beautiful back lanes through Naussac and along the Roselle, the ruined towers of **PEYRUSSE-LE-ROC** are also well worth a look. The "modern" village, a tiny weatherworn huddle of half-timbered houses gathered round a seventeenth-century church, sits above a narrow valley. On the valley sides, hidden in the steep woods, lie the scattered remains of a fortified medieval town which once sheltered some 4500 people – a sizeable population in those days – who were seeking their fortunes in the local silver mines. But their luck ran out in the early sixteenth century, when silver from the recently discovered Americas began to flood the market, and the town was eventually abandoned around 1700. The site is gradually being tidied up and some of the buildings restored, but still remains a moving and atmospheric place.

A path leads from the northwest corner of the church square to a pinnacle of rock crowned by **twin towers**, all that's left of the medieval fortress that protected the town. If you've got a head for heights, you can scramble up the iron ladders for a vertiginous view of the gorge. From here a cobbled mule trail leads steeply down through the woods, where the stones of a Gothic church, synagogue and hospital stand roofless, to the river and a little thirteenth-century chapel, complete but not open to the public. To return to the modern village, follow the river downstream and pick up another path, which takes you past the old market hall to the village gate. It's possible to do shorter circuits simply by following the signs, or you can buy a guidebook and map (€3.50) from the **tourist office** beside the church (Mon–Sat 10am–noon; Ⓣ05.65.80.49.33, Ⓔpeyrusseinfo@wanadoo.fr), or from either of Peyrusse's two cafés.

The Célé valley

Instead of following the River Lot east from Cahors, you can take an alternative route to Figeac along the wilder and narrower **Célé valley**, which joins the Lot a kilometre or so upstream from Bouziès (see p.276). A single road winds through the luxuriant canyon-like valley, frequented mainly by canoeists and walkers on the GR651 footpath, which runs sometimes close to the river, sometimes on the edge of the *causse* on the north bank. The major settlement along here is **Cabrerets**, a village not far upstream from the Célé's confluence with the Lot, which serves as a base for the nearby cave system of **Grotte de Pech-Merle**. Continuing northeast, the valley is punctuated by a succession of villages and hamlets built against the cliff face. Of these, two in particular stand out: **Marcilhac-sur-Célé**, about halfway along the valley, for the atmospheric ruins of its abbey; and the tiny hamlet of **Espagnac-Ste-Eulalie** in the north, where another, more substantial church sports a delightfully whimsical belfry.

There's no **public transport** along the Célé, but you can rent **bicycles** at Conduché (on the bus route from Cahors to Figeac), where the Célé joins the Lot, at Bureau des Sports Nature (Ⓣ05.65.24.21.01, Ⓦperso.orange.fr/bureau-sports-nature). Another good option is to descend the Célé by **canoe**; rental outlets in St-Cirq, Figeac and near Cabrerets will organize the necessary transport.

Cabrerets

CABRERETS lies 4km up the Célé from its confluence with the Lot, the approach guarded by the sturdy **Château de Gontaut-Biron** (not open to the public), on a small flood plain where the River Sagne joins the Célé. It's a pretty enough spot, but the only real reason to linger here is to take advantage of its tourist amenities.

There's a small summer-only **tourist office** in the village centre on the road to Pech-Merle (June Wed–Sat 11am–1pm & 2–6pm, July Mon–Sat 10am–1pm

& 2–6pm, Aug Mon–Sat 10am–1pm & 3–7pm; ⓣ&ⓕ05.65.31.27.12), which sells handy guides detailing walks in the area. There's also a pair of two-star **hotel-restaurants**. In the village itself, overlooking the Célé, *Les Grottes* (ⓣ05.65.31.27.02, ⓦwww.hoteldesgrottes.com; ❷; closed Nov–March) is a welcoming place with functional rooms – the cheapest without an en-suite toilet – and a decent restaurant (menus from €15.50). The alternative is the slightly smarter and absolutely spotless *Auberge de la Sagne* (ⓣ05.65.31.26.62, ⓦwww.hotel-auberge-cabrerets.com; ❸; closed mid-Sept to May), 1km west of the village on the road to the caves; there's a pool, well-tended garden and a restaurant offering good-quality home cooking (occasionally closed lunchtimes out of season; reservations recommended). The last option is a small two-star **campsite**, *Le Cantal* (ⓣ05.65.31.26.61, ⓕ05.65.31.20.47; closed Nov–April), immediately north of Cabrerets on the other side of the Célé.

Grotte de Pech-Merle

Up in the hills 3km west of Cabrerets by road, or 1km via the footpath from beside the *mairie*, the **Grotte de Pech-Merle** (1hr guided visits, English written commentary available: April–Nov daily 9.30am–noon & 1.30–5pm; ⓣ05.65.31.27.05, ⓦwww.pechmerle.com; €7.50) takes some beating. Discovered in 1922 by two local boys, the galleries are not only full of the most spectacular limestone formations – structures tiered like wedding cakes, hanging like curtains, or shaped like discs or "cave pearls" – but also contain an equally dazzling display of more than five hundred **prehistoric drawings**. To protect the drawings, tickets are restricted to seven hundred per day (it's advisable to book four or five days ahead in July and August and at least one day ahead at other times; internet bookings must be made at least a week in advance), and the guides make sure you're processed through in the allotted time. If possible, it's worth allowing yourself time to visit the **museum**, located beside the ticket office (same hours; same ticket), before your scheduled tour. A twenty-minute film, subtitled in English, provides an excellent overview of Pech-Merle and its prehistoric art.

The drawings date mostly from the early Magdalenian era (around 10,000–17,000 years ago), contemporaneous with much of the cave art in the Vézère valley (see p.201), with which they share many similarities. The first drawings you come to are in the so-called **Chapelle des Mammouths**, executed on a white calcite panel that looks as if it's been specially prepared for the purpose; note how the artists used the contour and relief of the rock to do the work, producing utterly convincing mammoths with just two lines. In addition to the mammoths, there are horses, oxen and bison charging head down with tiny rumps and arched tails; the guide will point out where St-Cirq's André Breton (see p.277) added his own mammoth – he was fined but the damage was done. Next comes a vast chamber containing the glorious **horse frieze**, the oldest of the drawings (at around 25,000 years). Two large horses stand back to back, the head of one formed by a natural protuberance of rock, and their hindquarters superimposed to provide perspective. The surface is spattered with black dots of some unknown symbolic significance and silhouettes of hands, while the ceiling is covered with finger marks preserved in the soft clay. On the way you pass the skeletons of cave-hyena and bears that have been lying there for thousands of years, and, finally, the footprints of an adolescent preserved in a muddy pool some eight thousand years ago.

Upstream to Marcilhac-sur-Célé

Back on the D41 heading up the Célé from Cabrerets, you emerge from a tunnel after 3km to find old bikes, mannequins and even the shells of cars hanging from the rock face. They belong to the gloriously eccentric **Musée de l'Insolite** (Museum of the Quirky; April–Sept 9am–1pm & 2–8pm; rest of year by appointment; €2, €5 if you want to take photos; ⓣ05.65.30.21.01, ⓦwww.museedelinsolite.com), run by a sculptor with an engaging sense of humour, mostly based on wordplay and puns in French. Both his garden and gallery are full of bizarre montages fashioned out of tree stumps, old machines and other bits of scrap. Along the river here you'll also find two **canoe rental** outlets: Les Amis du Célé (open all year; ⓣ05.65.31.26.73, ⓦwww.amisducele.fr), and Nature et Loisirs (July & Aug; ⓣ05.65.30.25.69, ⓦwww.nature-et-loisirs.net; out of season ⓔmarie-helene.flaujac@wanadoo.fr for info). Both organize descents of the Célé, while the former also has **bikes** for rent and offers rock-climbing and pot-holing outings.

The next village of interest is **MARCILHAC**, 16km upstream from Cabrerets, with its partly ruined Benedictine **abbey** (call ⓣ05.65.40.65.52 for guided tours; July to mid-Sept 2–4.30pm; €3). Founded some time prior to the ninth century, the abbey had the good fortune to be in charge of the modest sanctuary at Rocamadour (see p.239), in which St Amadour's body was discovered in 1186. The subsequent revenue from pilgrims and benefactors led to a brief golden age, which came to a grinding halt when English troops laid waste to the building in the Hundred Years' War. It never really recovered and was abandoned after the Reformation. Entering the abbey from the south, a rather primitive and badly damaged ninth-century Christ in majesty decorates the tympanum over the ruined door. In the damp interior of the church itself are late-fifteenth-century frescoes of the Apostles and another Christ in majesty, with the local nobility's coats of arms below. The few religious treasures that survived – such as a seventeenth-century polychrome pietà and a nicely rendered statue of a pilgrim – are now on display in the small **Musée d'Art Sacré**, in a handsome half-timbered house immediately west of the abbey church, which also doubles as a **tourist office** (July to mid-Sept 10.30am–noon & 3–5.30pm; ⓣ05.65.40.68.44, ⓔmarcilhac@quercy.net).

There's a two-star municipal **campsite**, *Le Pré de Monsieur* (ⓣ05.65.40.77.88, ⓦwww.camping-marcilhac.com; closed mid-Oct to March), just north of the village.

Espagnac-Ste-Eulalie

The tiny and beautiful hamlet of **ESPAGNAC-STE-EULALIE** lies about 12km upriver from Marcilhac and is reached via an old stone bridge. Immediately across the bridge, an eye-catching octagonal lantern crowns the belfry of the priory **church of Notre-Dame-du-Val-Paradis** (1hr guided tours: daily 10.30am & 4.30pm, with extra visits at 6pm for walkers, by appointment, call Mme Bonzani on ⓣ05.65.40.06.17). The building itself is strangely ill-proportioned, a result of the nave being truncated in the Hundred Years' War, which somehow adds to its charm. Inside, apart from a typically over-the-top altarpiece of the Counter-Reformation, the most interesting features are the ornate tombs of the church's thirteenth-century benefactor, Aymeric d'Hébrard de St-Sulpice, a local man who became bishop of Coimbra in Portugal, and those of the duke of Cardaillac and his wife, who financed the rebuilding of the choir in the fourteenth century.

An ancient fortified gateway south of the church now houses a **gîte d'étape** (ⓣ05.65.11.42.66; closed early Nov to Feb) with a choice between a dormitory (€10 per person), and rooms with three beds (€12 per person, or €15 for sole occupancy). Simple but good-quality **food** is available at *L'Hôte Paysan* (reservations only, ⓣ05.65.11.41.50), in the row of houses next to the church. The only other accommodation around is under canvas: there are two good three-star **campsites** beside the river in **BRENGUES**, a hamlet 3km back downstream from Espagnac: *Le Moulin Vieux* (Ⓣ05.65.40.00.41, Ⓦwww.camping-lemoulinvieux.com; closed Oct–March), with a restaurant, pool and **canoe** rental, and the smaller municipal site (Ⓣ05.65.40.06.82, Ⓕ05.65.40.05.71; closed Oct–May).

Figeac

Situated on the River Célé some 70km east of Cahors, **FIGEAC** is a very appealing town with an unspoilt medieval centre that's, surprisingly, not encumbered by tourism. Its principal church, the **Église St-Sauveur**, contains a sumptuous rendition of the Passion of Christ in a side chapel, and there's an excellent **museum** devoted to famed locally-born Egyptologist Jean-François Champollion. Apart from these two sights, it's a pleasure just to wander the narrow lanes, lined with a delightful array of houses, both stone and half-timbered, adorned with carvings, ornate colonnaded windows and elaborate ironwork.

Some history

Like many other provincial towns hereabouts, Figeac owes its beginnings to the foundation of an **abbey** in the early days of Christianity, one which quickly became wealthy thanks to its position on the pilgrim roads to both Rocamadour (see p.239) and Compostela (see p.354). In the Middle Ages the town flourished as a trading centre exporting wine and woollen fabrics throughout Europe, so much so that the wealthy merchants began to challenge the abbey's authority. In 1302 King Philip IV (the Fair) resolved the issue by sending his representative, the Viguier, to bring Figeac directly under royal control. At the same time he granted the town the all-important right to mint money. Figeac's fortunes declined during the Hundred Years' War, then revived at the time of the Renaissance, but it was the Wars of Religion that pushed it into eclipse. The town threw in its lot with the Protestants in 1576, providing them with an important safe-haven, until it was brought forcefully back into line in 1622. Figeac later became an important centre for tanning hides, and received a further boost with the arrival of the railway in 1862.

During **World War II** the Germans converted Figeac's Ratier metal workshop into a factory churning out propellers for Luftwaffe bombers. When the Resistance destroyed the plant in 1944, more than five hundred local men were carted off to labour and concentration camps, from which at least 120 failed to return at the end of the war. By the 1960s the town's old quarter had declined to such an extent that the majority of buildings were declared uninhabitable. It was designated a preservation zone in 1986, since when the authorities have put a tremendous effort into restoring the medieval and Renaissance buildings.

Arrival and information

Figeac's **gare SNCF** – on the Toulouse–Clermont-Ferrand and Toulouse–Figeac–Brive lines – lies about 600m south of the town centre. SNCF **buses** from Cahors, Gramat and Villefranche-de-Rouergue stop at the train station. If you're arriving **by car**, note that the old quarter is largely pedestrianized. The most convenient parking is along the river bank, where it's free, or on

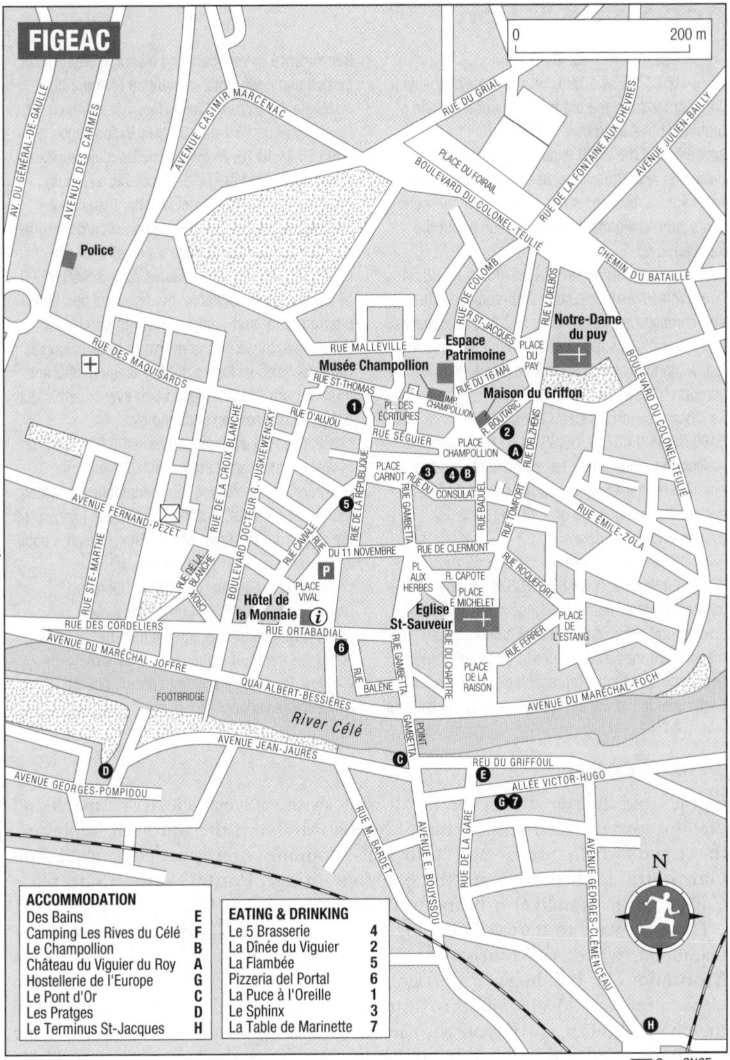

place Vival, where you'll also find the **tourist office** (May, June & Sept Mon–Sat 10am–12.30pm & 2.30–6pm, Sun 10am–1pm; July & Aug daily 10am–7pm; Oct–April Mon–Sat 10am–noon & 2.30–6pm; ⓣ 05.65.50.04.58, ⓦ www.tourisme-figeac.com or www.tourism-figeac.com in English), in the very striking Hôtel de la Monnaie building. They supply a useful do-it-yourself guide to Figeac (€0.20), and sell booklets outlining walks in the surrounding area, while in summer you can sign up for one of their excellent **guided tours** (in French only), of which "*À la découverte de Figeac*" provides the best general introduction (April, May & Sept Sat 4.30pm; July & Aug Tues–Thurs, Sat & Sun 4.30pm; 1hr 30min; €5.50).

Accommodation

Des Bains 1 rue du Griffoul ⓣ05.65.34.10.89, ⓦwww.hoteldesbains.fr. Just across from the old town, this hotel is one of the nicest places to stay in Figeac. Rooms are spotless and the more expensive have a/c, balconies and internet access. What makes the hotel special though, is the friendly and energetic hosts, who are a mine of information about the local area. ❷

Camping Les Rives du Célé ⓣ05.61.64.88.54, ⓦwww.lesrivesducele.com. Well-equipped three-star campsite that also has a restaurant, grocery and several pools. By the river 2km east of town – follow signs for the Domaine du Surgié leisure complex. Closed Oct–March.

Le Champollion 3 place Champollion ⓣ05.65.34.04.37, ⓕ05.65.34.61.69. This welcoming place offers ten surprisingly modern en-suite rooms above a popular café right in the centre. Try and get one of the two rooms overlooking the square. ❷

Château du Viguier du Roy 52 rue Émile-Zola ⓣ05.65.50.05.05, ⓦwww.chateau-viguier-figeac.fr. Figeac's one and only luxury hotel occupies a national monument, a magnificent medieval residence that was formerly the seat of the king's representative, the Viguier. Each room is individually designed in such styles as Renaissance or Venetian, and a pool, pretty cloister garden and a top-notch restaurant (see p.288), complete the picture. Closed late Oct to March. ❾

Hostellerie de l'Europe 51 allée Victor-Hugo ⓣ05.65.34.10.16, ⓦwww.hostelleriedeleurope.com. One block behind the *Hôtel des Bains*, on a busy main road, this 1930s hotel is better than it looks from the outside. The rooms come with a/c and other two-star comforts, and there's a small pool. ❸

Le Pont d'Or 2 av Jean Jaurès ⓣ05.65.50.95.00, ⓦwww.hotelpontdor.com. Modern riverside hotel offering spick-and-span rooms with good-sized bathrooms; those on the riverfront have balconies. Other facilities include a slightly dingy restaurant (menus from €11.50; closed Sun eve except in July & Aug), a bar, rooftop pool and gym. ❻

Les Pratges 6 av Jean Jaurès ⓣ05.65.50.01.42, ⓦwww.lesmaisonsdemarie.com. Lovely quiet *chambre d'hôte* offering four beautifully decorated rooms, all en-suite, in a large old house just across the river from the town centre. There's also a pool, and a small park on the doorstep. ❹

Le Terminus St-Jacques 27 av Georges Clemenceau ⓣ05.65.34.00.43, ⓦwww.hotel-terminus.fr. This small family-run hotel is handy for the train station and a favourite with walkers. Rooms are nothing special, but are comfortable enough. ❹

The Town

Figeac's old quarter sits on the north bank of the River Célé, its ramparts and ditches now replaced with a ring of boulevards. From the southern boulevard, the town's main artery and principal shopping street, pedestrianized **rue Gambetta**, leads north from the old stone bridge, **Pont Gambetta**, to place Carnot, with its market hall, and to neighbouring place Champollion.

The best place to start your explorations is on **place Vival** to the west of rue Gambetta, where the tourist office occupies the eye-catching **Hôtel de la Monnaie**. The building's origins go back to the thirteenth century when the city's mint was located in this district, and it's typical of Figeac's medieval merchants' houses, starting off with arcaded openings on the ground floor, while the colonnaded and sculpted windows above indicate the living quarters. These are now home to a none-too-exciting **museum** (same hours as the tourist office – see p.285; €2) of old coins and archeological bits and pieces found in the surrounding area.

On the eastern side of rue Gambetta you'll find the much-altered **Église St-Sauveur** on a big, gravelled square overlooking the river. Its lofty yet restrained nave provides a striking contrast to the intimate **Notre-Dame de la Pitié** chapel, to the south of the choir, decorated with heavily gilded but dramatically realistic seventeenth-century carved wood panels.

Continuing north along rue Gambetta, cafés spread their tables under the nineteenth-century *halle* in the middle of **place Carnot**, surrounded by a delightful range of stone and half-timbered houses. Some sport open wooden galleries at the top; another typical feature of this region, these *solelhos* were used for drying and storing foodstuffs. To the east, place Carnot opens into the grander but equally alluring **place Champollion**, named after **Jean-François Champollion**, who finally cracked Egyptian hieroglyphics by deciphering the Rosetta Stone (see box below). The square's south side is dominated by a stunning, white-stone Gothic mansion with a row of handsome ornamental windows, filled with lacy trefoil stonework. Opposite, the **Maison du Griffon** on the corner with rue de Colomb is far less ostentatious, but this is Figeac's oldest house, built in the twelfth century and named after a barely visible griffin carved on the left-hand window arch (now blocked up) on the third floor.

Champollion was born nearby in a house off place Champollion, to the northwest of the square, which now contains the fascinating **Musée Champollion**, dedicated not only to Champollion's life and work but also to the history of writing, with displays on Egyptian, Chinese, Mayan and Hebraic systems. In addition to many beautiful examples of hieroglyphic script, the museum houses an excellent collection of Egyptian funerary objects from the sixth and seventh centuries BC – sarcophagi, amulets and statues of the gods and goddesses, such as Bastet, a superb bronze cat, and an exquisitely crafted head of the god-king Osiris.

At the west end of impasse Champollion, a gigantic reproduction of the Rosetta Stone – the work of American artist Joseph Kossuth – forms the floor of the tiny **place des Écritures**, above which is a little garden with medicinal herbs and tufts of papyrus in pots. If it's open, you can cut through the **Espace Patrimoine** (April to early July & late Sept to end Oct Tues–Sun 2–6pm; early July to late Sept daily 10am–12.30pm & 3–7pm; free), a one-room exhibition illustrating Figeac's history and architecture, to rue de Colomb.

On the east side of place Champollion, it's worth walking along rue Émile Zola past the front of the **Hôtel du Viguier**, now a luxury hotel (see opposite).

Champollion and the Rosetta Stone

Jean-François Champollion was born in Figeac in 1790, the son of a bookseller who opened a shop on place Carnot, in what is now *Le Sphinx* café (see p.289). His interest in Egypt was first sparked by news coming back from Napoleon Bonaparte's 1798 Egyptian adventures, and when an acquaintance showed him the ancient Egyptians' so-far indecipherable script two years later, he became hooked. Declaring that he would solve the puzzle, Champollion set about studying ancient and Middle Eastern languages – he eventually mastered a mind-boggling total of twenty – and poring over hieroglyphs. One of the most important resources available was the **Rosetta Stone**. A slab of black basalt measuring around 120cm in height and 80cm wide, the stone was discovered in 1799 by French soldiers building fortifications around the town of Rosetta in the Nile delta; three years later it fell into British hands when they seized Egypt from the French, and it now resides in London's British Museum.

The crucial significance of the Rosetta Stone is that the same text – a decree issued in 196 BC recording the honours to be accorded to the young Pharaoh Ptolemy – is repeated in three different scripts: **hieroglyphics**, demotic (an abbreviated, cursive form of hieroglyphics used for everyday affairs), and Greek. By being able to translate the Greek, scholars then had fresh clues, but it took until 1822 before Champollion made the final breakthrough when he realized that hieroglyphs were, broadly, not pictograms but phonetic characters – within two years he had identified the majority of symbols. And all this without having set foot in Egypt. He made his one and only voyage to the country in 1828, but died of a stroke four years later at the age of 41.

As you go by, look out for three small sculptures on the facade: to the left a very fine portrait of the building's fifteenth-century owner; to the right an architect clutching his callipers; and in the middle the present owner, added during recent renovations. Round the corner on rue Delzhens, the large square tower looming over the street is the last vestige of the Viguier's fourteenth-century residence. You'll get a better view of it if you continue on up the hill to the **church of Notre-Dame du Puy**. Transformed into a veritable fortress by the Protestants in the late 1500s, then partially destroyed by Catholic reprisals, it now contains little of interest, but its cedar-shaded terrace is a peaceful spot from which to look down on the roofs of Figeac. When you're done, take cobbled rue St-Jacques twisting and turning down the hillside back to rue de Colomb and place Champollion.

Eating and drinking

Figeac's old centre is well provided with **restaurants**, offering everything from pizza to haute cuisine. For picnic food, there's a handy supermarket on the corner of rue Gambetta and rue de Clermont, and the charcuterie at 20 quai Bessières sells a wide range of salads as well as meats. The main weekly **food market** is on place Carnot on Saturdays, while dry goods are sold on place Vival.

Le 5 Brasserie 5 place Champollion. Stylish place with dark-brown leather furniture, vaulted ceilings, and huge windows. It serves up tasty French food with an Indian influence such as spicy frog's legs with sautéed rice and Goan *cassoulet*. Menus from €16.

La Dînée du Viguier 4 rue Boutaric ⓣ05.65.50.08.08. The restaurant of the *Château du Viguier du Roy* hotel (see p.286) isn't as expensive as one might expect for such rarefied cuisine: there's a good-value midday menu at €20 and three-course menus from €30, though you're looking at around €60 eating *à la carte*. There are only a handful of tables in its elegant stone-walled room, so reservations are essential. Closed Sat & Mon lunches, also Sun eve & Mon eve Oct–May and three weeks in Nov.

La Flambeé 28 rue Caviale ⓣ05.65.34.72.12. Join the locals in this excellent little restaurant specializing in chargrilled meats and pastas. Menus range from €10.50 to €16.50, but beware it gets very busy. Closed Sun.

▲ Place Champollion

Pizzeria del Portel 9 rue Ortabadial. Another good-value and convivial place serving tasty pizzas, big salad platters and no fewer than seven varieties of *moules frites* including pesto and Roquefort. It also has the benefit of an outside terrace. Most dishes come in at under €12. Closed Sun lunch & Mon except in high season.

La Puce à l'Oreille 5 rue St-Thomas ⊕05.65.34.33.08. Located north of place Carnot in a handsome fifteenth-century residence with an interior court for fine weather, and walls adorned with work by local artists, this place serves rich Quercy fare – make sure you leave room for one of their scrumptious desserts. Menus start at €19.80, and there's a fulsome regional wine list. Closed Mon, and Sun eve except in July & Aug; also closed one week in June & three weeks in Sept–Oct.

Le Sphinx 7 place Carnot ⊕05.65.14.05.81. Just around the corner from the Musée Champollion, on the market square, you'll find this swish cocktail bar, which also serves good traditional food. Menus from €13. Closed Sun, also Mon out of season.

La Table de Marinette 51 allée Victor-Hugo ⊕05.65.50.06.07. It's worth venturing south across the river for the well-priced menus in this stylish Art Deco restaurant. The choice isn't huge but it's all good, and they offer a wide range of pricing with menus starting at €16, while eating *à la carte* will set you back upwards of €35. Closed Sat lunch & Fri, also 3 weeks in Jan & mid-Nov-mid-Dec.

Listings

Bike rental Office Intercommunal du Sport du Pays de Figeac/Cajarc, 2 av du Général-de-Gaulle ⊕05.65.34.52.54, ⓦwww.ois-figeac-cajarc.com.

Books and newspapers For local guides and English newspapers, try Maison de la Presse, down by the river at 2 rue Gambetta.

Bus information For details of all bus routes, call the central information desk on ⊕05.65.53.43.91.

Car rental ADA, on the road west to Cahors ⊕05.65.11.62.92; Avis, 1 ave Georges-Pompidou ⊕05.65.34.10.28. Both offer station pick-ups on request.

Hospital Centre Hospitalier is to the west of the old quarter at 33 rue des Maquisards ⊕05.65.50.65.50.

Police Commissariat de Police, Cité Administrative, place des Carmes ⊕05.65.50.73.73.

Post office The central post office is at 6 av Fernand Pezet, 46100 Figeac.

Taxis Call Bernard Taxis on ⊕05.65.50.00.20, or Didier Escribano on ⊕05.65.50.01.73.

The Causse de Gramat

After the intimate beauty of the Lot and Célé valleys, the wide horizons of the **Causse de Gramat** to the north make a refreshing change. It's an empty land with few people or villages, filled only with the sound of sheep bells and the cicadas' persistent clamour during the tinder-box-dry summers. Across the gently undulating landscape of scrubby pines and oaks, and close-cropped grass spattered with orchids and aromatic plants, you'll come across dolmens, shepherds' dry-stone huts and strange *lacs de St-Namphaise* – water holes hacked out of the rock – but little else to make you want to stop. The exceptions are mostly along the *causse*'s southern boundary, starting off in the far southeast with **Assier**, a small village put on the map by a vainglorious military man who built a château and church here. From Assier the route tracks westward through a series of picturesque villages to the even more diminutive **Caniac-du-Causse**, last resting place of the hermit St Namphaise. At Caniac the route turns northwards into the wildest part of the *causse* towards the busy market town of **Gramat**, home to an above-average wildlife park.

The main towns in this area are well served by **public transport**. Assier and Gramat both lie on main **train** lines and are also accessible by **bus**. However, to do the *causse* justice you really do need your own means of getting about. With few roads and only a sprinkling of villages, this is a great area for **walking** or **mountain biking**; most tourist offices have maps of recommended routes.

▲ Pastoral land of the Causse de Gramat

Assier

If it weren't for the immoderate – and immodest – nature of Galiot de Genouillac, **ASSIER**, some 17km northwest of Figeac, would probably have remained an insignificant village. Chief of artillery under François I and an inspired tactician, de Genouillac earned his stripes during the decisive French victory at Marignano in 1515 during the Italian Wars, after which he returned to his native village bathed in glory to erect a **château** befitting his status (May–June & Sept daily except Tues 10am–12.30pm & 2–6.45pm; July & Aug daily 10am–12.30pm & 2–6.45pm; Sept to end-April daily except Tues 10am–12.30pm & 2–5.30pm; €3; Ⓦwww.assier.monuments-nationaux.fr). Built in the latest Renaissance style, it was said to rival the châteaux of the Loire, with its vast interior courtyard flanked by four round towers, its galleries, loggias and carved friezes – and liberal repetition of de Genouillac's motto: *J'aime fortune* ("In love with chance/success"). After 1768, however, the château and its contents were sold off lock, stock and barrel to raise money, leaving only part of the west wing – and even that is in a pretty poor state.

You can get a better idea of de Genouillac's decorative tastes from the **church** he also had built in the village square. It's an extraordinary edifice, not just because of its size and the feeling that it was built to the glory of de Genouillac rather than God, but mainly due to a frieze running round the exterior depicting Roman centurions, guns being hauled across the Alps, flame-spewing cannon and cities under siege – all beautifully realized but hardly normal church ornamentation. Less surprisingly, the most interesting feature inside is the great man's tomb in an intricately vaulted chapel near the west door. He appears twice: as a bearded man lying with his feet on powder sacks, and as a soldier leaning nonchalantly against a cannon.

Practicalities

Assier is a stop on the main Figeac–Brive train line. The **gare SNCF** lies nearly 1km west of the village. All **buses** running between Figeac and Gramat stop at the *gare*, and some also stop on the church square. There's a very helpful **tourist office** (mid-June to mid-Sept Mon–Sat 10am–12.30pm & 3–6.30pm; mid-Sept to mid-June hours unconfirmed at the time of writing, but approximately as above; ⓣ05.65.40.50.60, ⓦwww.otivalleecausse.com) on the square's northeast corner and, opposite the church, an equally accommodating **hotel-restaurant**, *L'Assiérois* (ⓣ05.65.40.56.27, ⓦwww.lassierois.com; closed Sun eve & Mon; €36–39), with six small but immaculate rooms, all en-suite. The restaurant offers traditional family cuisine (menus from €12 at lunch, €26 eves). On weekday evenings they only open for reservations.

The southern causse

With your own transport, you can take a circuitous route from Assier through **the southern causse** before cutting northeast to Gramat. There are a few scattered sights to aim for, but on the whole it's the scenery that takes precedence in this high, open country with its grand vistas.

Five kilometres southwest of Assier on the D653, **LIVERNON** is the first of a string of attractive villages, in this case distinguished by a particularly appealing Romanesque belfry, with its rhythmically spaced arches. The route then meanders further south via **ESPÉDAILLAC** – a cluster of crumbling towers and pigeon-lofts – to **QUISSAC**, roughly 10km from Livernon. The main claim to fame of this tiny village is that the ninth-century soldier-turned-hermit **St Namphaise** lived in a nearby grotto. He's a very important person on the *causse*, since it was he who, according to legend, dug the shallow ponds in the rock that are characteristic of this region, thus providing water for the flocks of sheep; ironically, he is said to have been killed by an irate bull. There's a statue of Namphaise dressed as a soldier in Quissac church, and you can see one of his famous *lacs* about 1km south of the village beside the Coursac road.

The dying Namphaise supposedly threw away his hammer – with which he presumably created the ponds – and declared that he would be buried wherever it came to rest; it landed 8km away in what is now the village of **CANIAC-DU-CAUSSE**. It's a sleepy, flowery place undisturbed by the trickle of visitors coming to view Namphaise's small, unadorned sarcophagus lying in a diminutive twelfth-century crypt beneath the village church.

From Caniac cut north across country on the D42, keeping a lookout on the right for signs down a dirt track to the Site de Planagrèze, a couple of kilometres later. At the end of the track various footpaths and biking trails strike out across the *causse*, while one of the more accessible dolmen stands a short walk south. On the way you pass a fenced-off area, in the middle of which is another typical feature of the *causse*, a limestone sinkhole, the **Igue de Planagrèze**; in this particular case pot-holers have so far explored 800m of tunnels.

From here the D42 continues north to Fontanes-du-Causse, where there's a choice of routes to Gramat: you can either stick to the back lanes, or cut west to the faster D677.

Gramat

The biggest town on the *causse*, and its capital, **GRAMAT** developed at the junction of two major Roman roads. Its fortunes increased further when pilgrims started passing through en route to Rocamadour (see p.239), and it received another boost when the railway came here in 1863. Even today it's an important market town, with two weekly **markets** (Tues & Fri morn) and bigger *foires* on the second and fourth Thursdays of each month. Though a few vestiges of the medieval town remain, Gramat is mostly of interest as somewhere to base yourself for a day or so; as well as being an ideal starting point for exploring the *causse*, it's within easy striking distance of Rocamadour, only 9km away to the northwest, and fairly convenient for sights in the upper Dordogne valley (see p.233).

Gramat would be more appealing if it weren't for the busy N140 and D677 funnelling through **place de la République**, a big square on the east side of town. If you walk west from here along the **Grande Rue**, though, you'll suddenly find yourself among the narrow lanes of the old quarter. There's not a lot to see here, but both the place de l'Hôtel de Ville, at the top of the Grande Rue, and the market square, south of the Grande Rue down rue Notre-Dame, are attractive corners.

South out of town, head to the flourishing **Jardins du Grand Couvent** (daily: June, Sept & Oct 2–6pm; July & Aug 10am–7pm; private visits available in May; €5; Ⓦwww.jardinsgrandcouvent.com), behind a convent complex, you can also see the lovely old wash house and bread ovens used by the nuns until fairly recently; they also run a small shop and tea room. Of more immediate interest, however, and the main reason for most people's visit, is the **Parc Animalier de Gramat** (daily: Easter to Sept 9.30am–7pm; Oct to Easter 2–6pm, Sun in Oct plus school hols 9.30am–6pm; €9; Ⓣ05.65.38.81.22 Ⓦwww.parcanimaliergramat.fr), a couple of kilometres further south on the D14. Encompassing half a square kilometre of the *causse*, the park is home to an unusually varied selection of animals: the 150 mostly European species include wolves, otters, bears, ibex – with their magnificent curved horns – and *mouflon*, a type of goat crowned with four horns. Allow at least two hours if you want to cover the whole park.

Practicalities

Arriving in Gramat by train, you'll pitch up at the **gare SNCF** 1km south of the centre; if no **taxis** are waiting, call Adgié on Ⓣ05.65.38.75.07 or 05.65.38.0.54. Some **buses** call at the station but most drop you on place de la République, which is also where you'll find the **tourist office** (April–July & Sept–Nov Mon–Sat 10am–12.30pm & 2–6pm, Nov–March Mon–Sat 10am–12.30pm & 2–5.30pm, Jul & Aug Mon–Sat 10am–12.30pm & 2–7pm, Sun 10am–12.30pm; Ⓣ05.65.38.73.60, Ⓦwww.rocamadour.com) on the east side of the square.

The most appealing place to **stay** in Gramat is the *Relais des Gourmands* opposite the train station (Ⓣ05.65.38.83.92, Ⓦwww.relais-des-gourmands.fr; ❸–❹; closed two weeks in Feb & New Year). It's a delightful, flowery spot, with airy rooms, a pool and an excellent restaurant serving all the classics as well as lighter versions of regional cuisine (menus from €18; closed Sun eve & Mon except in July & Aug). If it's full, try one of the two hotels on place de la République. The more refined *Lion d'Or* (Ⓣ05.65.10.46.10, Ⓦwww.liondorhotel.fr; ❹–❺) is on the north side of the square; its rooms are modern, smart and comfortable, while the restaurant offers top-quality cooking (menus from €18). On the square's east side, you can't miss the electric-green shades of *Le Centre* (Ⓣ05.65.38.73.37, Ⓦwww.lecentre.fr; ❷–❸; end Nov to early Feb closed weekends except Sun lunch), which is equally cheerful inside, with good-value, brightly decorated en-suite rooms and a restaurant (menus from €16.50).

In addition to the hotel **restaurants**, *La Cuisine d'Alain*, in the old town at 2 rue de la Liberté (Ⓣ05.65.38.87.87; closed Sun & eves on Mon & Tues), makes a good pit stop. You'll need to get here early – or reserve – at lunchtime, when locals fill the two small rooms and pavement tables between scurrying serving staff. There's a bewildering choice of *formules* and menus starting at €10.

Gourdon and the Bouriane

Thirty-five kilometres west of Gramat, **GOURDON** is an attractive town, its medieval centre of butter-coloured stone houses attached to a prominent hilltop, neatly ringed by shady modern boulevards, known collectively as the **Tour-de-Ville**. While it has no outstanding sights, Gourdon makes a quiet, pleasant base, not only for the nearby **Grottes de Cougnac**, with their prehistoric paintings, but also for the **Bouriane** to the south, a very pretty area of luxuriant woods and valleys merging into neighbouring Périgord. The Bouriane is primarily a place to wander with no particular destination in mind, but anyone interested in twentieth-century art should visit **Les Arques**, in the south of the region, where a number of powerful, sometimes disturbing, sculptures by Russian exile, Ossip Zadkine are on display.

Gourdon lies on the main Toulouse–Brive **train** line and is also accessible by **bus** from Souillac. However, to explore the Bouriane you'll need your own means of getting about.

Arrival and information

Gourdon's **gare SNCF** is located roughly 1km northeast of the old centre. From the station, walk south on avenue de la Gare, then turn right onto avenue Gambetta to come out on the south side of the Tour-de-Ville. If you want a **taxi**, call Taxi Brice (ⓣ06.99.52.56.16). Arriving by **bus**, services terminate on place de la Libération on the southwest side of the Tour-de-Ville. **Car rental** is available through Ada at 101 avenue Gambetta (ⓣ05.65.41.40.08).

The **tourist office** is in the old centre at 24 rue du Majou (March–May & Oct Mon–Sat 10am–noon & 2–6pm; June & Sept Mon–Sat 10am–noon & 2–6pm, Sun 10am–noon; July & Aug Mon–Sat 10am–7pm, Sun 10am–noon; Nov–Jan Mon–Sat 10am–noon & 2–5pm; ⓣ05.65.27.52.50, ⓦwww.tourisme-gourdon.com), and dispenses details of Gourdon's festivities (see box on p.266). They also offer guided tours at 5pm on Thursdays in July & August (€4). You can rent **bikes** from Nature Evasion, 73 av Cavignac (ⓣ05.65.37.65.12), out on the west side of town.

Accommodation

Domaine le Quercy Well-equipped, three-star campsite 1.5km north on the D704 Périgueux road beside a leisure lake ⓣ05.65.41.06.19, ⓦwww.domainequercy.com. Closed Oct–May.

Hostellerie de la Bouriane place du Foirail ⓣ05.65.41.16.37, ⓦwww.hotellabouriane.fr. The smartest option in town, with elegant decor and a good traditional restaurant (mid-Oct to end April closed lunchtime except Sun, rest of year also open Mon lunch) with menus from €26. ❺

Hôtel de la Promenade 48 bd Galiot-de-Genouillac ⓣ05.65.41.41.44, ⓦwww.lapromenadegourdon.fr. Basic, cheerful and very reasonably priced with immaculate rooms and a pub-style restaurant (closed Sun lunch; menus from €12). ❸

The Town

Where the ramparts once stood, Gourdon's medieval centre is now entirely surrounded by the **Tour-de-Ville**. The best-preserved gateway into the centre is southwesterly Porte du Majou, which stands guard over the old town's main street, **rue du Majou**, lined with mellow stone-built houses, some, like the **Maison d'Anglars** at no. 17, with its ogive arches and mullion windows, dating back as far as the thirteenth century; look out on the right, as you go up, for the delightfully – and accurately – named rue Zig-Zag.

At its upper end, rue du Majou opens onto a lovely cobbled square beneath the twin towers of the massive fourteenth-century **church of St-Pierre**. Note the traces of fortifications, in the form of machicolations, over the west door, but you'll find nothing of particular interest inside, beyond some seventeenth-century gilded bas-reliefs by a local sculptor depicting the life of the Virgin Mary. The **Hôtel de Ville** – a handsome if unpretentious building whose arcaded ground floor once served as the market hall – stands on the west side of the square, while east of the church in place des Marronniers an ornately carved door marks the home of the Cavaignac family, who supplied the nation with numerous prominent public figures in the eighteenth and nineteenth centuries.

From the north side of the church, a path leads to the top of the hill where Gourdon's castle stood until it was razed in the early seventeenth century in the wake of the Wars of Religion. At 264m in height, it affords superb views over the wooded country stretching north to the Dordogne valley.

Eating and drinking

In addition to the hotels (see p.293), you'll find cafés and **restaurants** scattered around Tour-de-Ville. For picnic fare, there are fresh-food **markets** on Tuesdays beside the church in place St-Pierre, and on Saturdays beside the post office. In July and August an important farmers' market takes place on Thursday mornings in place St-Pierre, while the Tour-de-Ville is closed off on the first and third Tuesdays of each month for a traditional country fair.

The Grottes de Cougnac

Signed off the Sarlat road a couple of kilometres north of Gourdon, the **Grottes de Cougnac** (1hr guided tours daily: April–June & Sept 10–11.30am & 2.30–5pm; July & Aug 10am–6pm; Oct 2–4pm; €6; in-depth 2hr-long tours Wed at 9am; €12; Ⓦ www.grottesdecougnac.com) were discovered in 1949 by a local water-diviner. To begin with all the subsequent explorers found were rock formations – notably ceilings festooned with ice-white needles like some glitzy ballroom decoration – but three years later they hit gold when they came across **prehistoric paintings**. These date from between 25,000 and 19,000 years ago, when Cro-Magnon people ventured deep inside the caves to paint panels of ibex, reindeer and mammoths in elegant outline, using the rock's undulating surface to provide a sense of form and movement. They also left hundreds of mysterious signs – mostly dots and pairs of short lines – in addition to two human figures seemingly pierced by spears, a motif also found in Pech-Merle (see p.282).

Southwest through the Bouriane

The country southwest of Gourdon is a delight. Lanes tunnel through chestnut and pine woods, twisting up the valley sides past the occasional patch of vines and then popping out obligingly on high ground for the views. The **Céou valley** to the south of Gourdon provides one particularly beguiling route, although what sights there are in the Bouriane lie further west and are most easily accessed via the D673.

The first place of any size you come to along this road is the fortified village of **SALVIAC**, 14km from Gourdon, whose Gothic church (known as the Abbaye Nouvelle) was built in the late thirteenth century by Jean Duèze of Cahors, the future Pope John XXII (see p.267), and still contains fine stained-glass windows from that era. It's worth a brief stop for the location as much as anything, but is sadly rarely open to the public; call ⓣ05.65.41.25.24 to arrange a visit.

Seven kilometres further on, the *bastide* town of **CAZALS** has seen better days: its feudal château and ramparts were largely destroyed during the Hundred Years' War, though its big central square remains. Part of the old ramparts now house a **chambre d'hôte**, *La Caminade* (ⓣ05.65.21.66.63, ⓦwww.lacaminade.com; ❺), signed off the main road out to Cahors and Cajuls. The beautiful rooms are peaceful, and there's a salt-water pool and barbecue terrace. From here, you can work your way 9km eastwards through enticing back lanes to **RAMPOUX**. This unusually scattered hamlet is home to a Romanesque priory church in which one of the original frescoes can still be seen – a very faded Christ in majesty in the apse. Better preserved are those from the fifteenth century in the south chapel, portraying the life of Jesus.

The next port of call, **LES ARQUES**, is equally buried in the countryside, 10km southwest of Rampoux and 6km south of Cazals. It's a higgledy-piggledy village on a hillock above the River Masse, but its main draw is the Romanesque **church** and the neighbouring **Musée Zadkine** (daily except Mon: April–Oct 10am–1pm & 3–7pm; Nov–March 2–6pm; €3). A Russian émigré and well-known sculptor, **Ossip Zadkine** set up a studio in Les Arques in 1934 and worked on and off in the village until his death in 1967, producing big, powerful statues full of restless energy. Many are on a mythological or musical theme, such as those of Orpheus and Diana, the latter metamorphosing from tree to woman, and there's a strong Cubist influence, although his works grew more abstract towards the end of his life. Some of his most compelling pieces are displayed inside the church opposite the museum, whose cool stone interior provides the perfect foil for a passionate rendering of Christ on the Cross and, in the crypt, the *Pietà*. During his time in Les Arques, Zadkine also discovered some twelfth-century frescoes in the nearby Eglise St André – you can get a key from the museum. In season, it's worth timing your visit to have lunch in the old schoolhouse at the entrance to the village, now home to an attractive **restaurant**, *La Récréation* (ⓣ05.65.22.88.08; reservations essential; closed Wed & Thurs, also Nov–Feb). There's a single seasonal *menu carte* at €33 for five courses.

Another possibility for eating, or for an overnight stay, would be to continue southwest for 5km to **GOUJOUNAC**, whose **church** has rather worn Romanesque carvings of Christ in majesty and the four Evangelists over the south door. Opposite the church, the Dutch-owned *Hostellerie de Goujounac* (ⓣ05.65.36.68.67, ⓦwww.goujounac.com; ❸; closed Jan) offers honest country cooking (menus from €15, Indonesian buffets on some Sun eves €24.50, otherwise closed Sun eve & Mon) in addition to five simple **rooms**; if you want to stay here, you'll need to book well ahead in the summer season. Otherwise, there's a three-star **campsite**, *Camping La Pinède* (ⓣ05.65.36.61.84, ⓦmonsite.orange.fr/camping-de-goujounac; closed mid-Sept to mid-June, though they rent mobile homes out year-round), immediately west of Goujounac on the D660 Villefranche road.

West along the Lot from Cahors

The Bouriane's southern boundary is marked by the River Lot, which follows a particularly convoluted course downstream of Cahors as it doubles back on itself again and again between cliffs that gradually diminish towards the west. Standing guard over one of the larger meanders is **Luzech**, whose main claim to fame is the scant remains of a Roman encampment on the hill above the town. Continuing downstream, the route winds through a series of villages perched above the river, culminating in one of the most beautiful along the entire Lot valley, **Puy-l'Évêque**. A castle-town built on a terraced cliff, it dominates the last of the river's meanders, and its wandering lanes, tunnels, staircases and fountains together compensate for the lack of any first-rate sights. The area around **Duravel** and **Touzac**, further west again, with its fine selection of hotels and restaurants, provides a good base for visiting the impressive **Château de Bonaguil** in the hills to the north of the Lot. The last of the medieval castles to be constructed in France, and now partially in ruins, it still bristles with sophisticated defensive devices. Back on the Lot, **Fumel** is a major transport hub and service centre, though otherwise contains nothing to make you dally – better to hurry on downriver to where **Penne-d'Agenais**, with its striking basilica, lords it over the valley.

Public transport along this stretch of the river consists of an SNCF **bus** that threads along the valley from Cahors via Luzech, Puy-l'Évêque and Fumel to Monsempron-Libos, on the Agen–Périgueux train line. On the way it also passes through or close by most of the smaller villages cited below, but you'll need your own transport to reach the Château de Bonaguil and the villages north of the valley.

Luzech

Twenty kilometres downriver from Cahors, **LUZECH** is situated on the narrow neck of a particularly large meander, overlooked by a twelfth-century **keep**. There's a small area of picturesque alleys to the north of **place du Canal**, the central square spanning the isthmus. Just off this, on Grande Rue de la Ville, you'll find the **Maison des Consuls**, built in 1270. The building is home to the tourist office, as well as two of Luzech's three museums.

The first houses a collection of ammonites (June–Sept Mon–Fri 10am–1pm & 3–7pm, Sat 3–7pm; €3, or €5 with Ichnospace), and you can continue in the prehistoric vein with a trip to the **Ichnospace** (June–Sept, Mon–Fri 10am–1pm & 3–7pm, Sat 10am–1pm & 2–6pm; €3, or €5 with the Musée Armand Viré) also on Grande rue de la Ville in the *médiathèque*. Inside you'll find 140-million-year-old dinosaur footprints from nearby Crayssac, displayed over an area of sixty square metres.

Back in the Maison des Consuls, the **Musée Armand Viré** (same hours as tourist office – see below), displays archeological finds from around Luzech. The majority of items come from a fortress on a hill above the town, which has been occupied since the early Iron Age; the Romans reinforced it and erected a temple on the site, which is now known as the Oppidum d'Impernal. Though there are some delicate Gaulish safety-pins and needles, the exhibits in the museum demonstrate the huge leap in craftsmanship ushered in by the Romans in the first century BC: look out for the unusual folding spoon and the coins chopped in half for small change.

Little remains of the fortress itself beyond a few foundation stones, but it's worth trekking up for a splendid view over the Luzech meander. It's 1.5km by road, or you can walk up in about ten minutes: from the north end of rue de la Ville, follow signs for the GR36 footpath, past the castle keep and then just keep climbing. For a less strenuous jaunt, head south for about 2km to visit a tiny chapel, **Notre-Dame de l'Isle**, surrounded by vines and walnut trees on the very tip of the meander.

Practicalities

Buses from Cahors pull in beside a roundabout at the east end of place du Canal, near which you'll find the **tourist office** in the Maison des Consuls

(May–Sept Mon–Sat 10am–1pm & 2pm–6pm; Feb–March & Oct Mon–Thurs 10am–1pm & 2–5pm, Fri 10am–noon; winter opening times restricted to three days a week, and variable; ⓣ05.65.20.17.27, ⓦwww.ville-luzech.fr). The best **accommodation** is a few hundred metres off the Cahors road at *Domaine le Peyrou* (ⓣ05.65.30.51.98, ⓦwww.surf.to/peyrou; ❸), a small estate with a beautiful park. The rooms are spacious, peaceful, and some have views of the keep. If this is full, try the welcoming *Zotier chambre d'hôte* (ⓣ05.65.30.54.22, ⓦwww.zotier.com; ❷) on the western edge of the village with five very prettily decorated bedrooms, a shady garden and delicious evening menus on request (from €20). Alternatively, there's a **gîte d'étape** (ⓣ05.65.30.72.32, from €10) just before the bridge on the west side, a two-star municipal **campsite**, *Camping de l'Alcade* (ⓣ05.65.30.72.32, ⓔmaire.luzech@wanadoo.fr; closed Oct–June), beside the river immediately west of town on the Albas road.

If you're looking for somewhere special to **eat** in the area, head north to St-Médard, where *Le Gindreau* (ⓣ05.65.36.22.27, ⓦpagesperso-orange.fr/le.gindreau; closed Mon & Tues, and two weeks end-Nov) rates as one of the Lot's best restaurants, serving up such delights as seafood bisque with a gratin of crustaceans or local lamb with Rocamadour cheese, potatoes and pickled pork rind; the desserts in particular are real works of art and include cherries soaked in Cahors wine. Menus start at an affordable €38, rising to a gastronomic €140. In summer tables are laid out under the chestnut trees.

Luzech marks the end of the navigable river descending from St-Cirq Lapopie. **Houseboats** are available through Nautic (see p.29), while pleasure **boats** can be rented by the day or half-day from Naviglot (ⓣ05.65.20.18.19; mid-May to mid-Sept), both based a couple of kilometres north of Luzech near the village of **CAIX**. Naviglot also rent out **canoes** and **bicycles**, and organise river-trips with wine-tasting (1hr 30min; €8).

Albas to Grézels

The prettiest route downstream from Luzech – and that followed by the bus – is the D8 along the river's south bank. It's especially beguiling in summer when the intense green of the vines and walnut trees in the valley bottom is offset against the dark grey cliffs. The river loops back and forth across the flood plain, with a village at the bottom of each meander. The first you come to, and the most attractive, is **ALBAS**, 5km from Luzech, instantly recognizable by its tall church spire. The church is nineteenth-century and otherwise uninteresting, but the steep lanes below retain a few noble fourteenth- and fifteenth-century facades, a reminder of when the bishops of Cahors maintained a residence here. Look out for the painted cobblestones at the top of the main street down to the river: some have been entertainingly turned into ladybirds and other bugs.

Two kilometres east, the *Auberge d'Imhotep* (ⓣ05.65.30.70.91; April–Oct; reservation essential) is a friendly little restaurant named after the ancient Egyptian who supposedly discovered the art of gavage – the process of force-feeding ducks for foie gras – in 2600 BC. Naturally, duck features strongly on the menu – as does background jazz – and they also offer an excellent Cahors wine list (menus from €15).

Two meanders and 18km west of Albas, **GRÉZELS** was another episcopal seat, though in this case its château – a very sober affair – has survived thanks to a seventeenth-century rebuild. But the prime attraction here, on the main road through the village, is another restaurant, the rustic *La Terrasse* (ⓣ05.65.21.34.03; lunch only; closed Mon & three weeks in Sept), renowned for its jovial host and no-nonsense cuisine. There's only one menu that changes daily (€27 on Sun, €17 at other times, including wine). Make sure you've got a healthy appetite, and note that reservations are strongly recommended.

Puy-l'Évêque and around

Five kilometres from Grézels and 30km from Cahors by the main D911, **PUY-L'ÉVÊQUE** contends with St-Cirq Lapopie (see p.277) as the Lot valley's prettiest village. After 1227 it marked the western extremity of the Cahors bishops' domains and it's the remains of their thirteenth-century **château**, a big square keep like that at Luzech, which provides the town's focal point. Puy-l'Évêque changed hands any number of times during the Hundred Years' War, but then withstood a prolonged Protestant siege in 1580 during the Wars of Religion. Ardent anti-clerics tried to change the name to Puy-Libre during the Revolution, then Puy-sur-Lot, but the locals weren't convinced and it soon reverted to Puy-l'Évêque.

Arrival and information

SNCF **buses** from Cahors stop in front of the church on place du Rampeau and down on rue des Platanes to the southeast of the old centre. The **tourist office** sits down towards the bottom of the old town at 12 Grand' Rue (July & Aug Mon–Sat 9.30am–6.30pm, Sun 9am–12.30pm; Sept–June Mon & Sat 9am–12.30pm, Tues, Thurs & Fri 9am–noon & 2–5.30pm, Wed 9am–12.30pm & 3–5.30pm; ⓣ05.65.21.37.63, ⓦwww.puy-leveque.fr).

You can hire **canoes and bikes** from Copeyre (ⓣ05.65.37.33.51, ⓦwww.copeyre.com), just across the river at the watersports centre Le Pigeonnier, and a wander up Grand' Rue will provide you with options for **picnic** supplies.

Accommodation and eating

Hôtel Bellevue place de la Truffière ⓣ05.65.36.06.60, ⓕ05.65.36.06.61. Perched on the edge of a cliff, this refurbished place has very stylish rooms, all with highly contemporary decor and fine views, and with a restaurant to match. For more laid-back dining they also have a brasserie (menus from €35, or €10–16 for a main dish in the brasserie; closed Sun & Mon). Closed 4 weeks Jan–Feb & 2 weeks end Nov. ❹

Camping Les Vignes ⓣ05.65.30.81.72, ⓦwww.camping-les-vignes.net. 3km south along the river on the D28; signed off the road to the bridge from town. Superb, spick-and-span three-star campsite, with exceptionally friendly owners. There's also a small shop, and activities for children such as sports and games in the summer, as well as a discount if you produce *The Rough Guide*.

Hôtel Henry 23 rue du Docteur Rouma ⓣ05.65.21.32.24, ⓕ05.65.30.85.18 . Has pleasant rooms, though you should try and get one at the back to avoid road noise. The restaurant is excellent, serving large quantities of local cuisine (menus from €17, closed Sun eve & occasionally Sat in winter). Closed 3 weeks in Jan & 2 weeks in Oct or Nov. ❸

Maison Rouma 2 rue du Docteur Rouma ⓣ05.65.36.59.39, ⓦwww.puyleveque-maisonrouma.com. English-owned *chambre d'hôte* with three immaculate rooms that ooze with character, but the highlight is the glorious view of Puy-l'Évêque from the garden. ❸

The Town

There are no great sights to speak of, just lanes of medieval and Renaissance houses built in honey-coloured stone. Beside the castle keep at the top of the town, the **place de la Truffière** is the venue for the main weekly **market** (Tues morning); in summer a small farmers' market also takes place on Saturdays in the lower town on place Georges Henry, at the west end of rue des Platanes. From place de la Truffière, **rue du Fort** leads steeply down then flattens out beneath an imposing fourteenth-century building distinguished by its Gothic windows, which served as the bishops' audience chamber. As it curves round the hill, rue du Fort becomes rue Bovila and then peters out beside a staircase descending to rue des Capucins. This road heads back east along the hillside to **place Guillaume-de-Cardaillac** and then **place de la Halle**, the town's two most picturesque corners. Downhill from place de la Halle again, you come to rue de la Cale, with the dark alleys of the artisans' quarter off to the left, and the old **port**. For the best **view** of the whole ensemble walk out onto the modern bridge which crosses the Lot here. Alternatively, head for the belvedere in front of the **church of St-Sauveur** that guards Puy-l'Évêque's northeast quarter – literally, since it once formed an integral part of the fortifications; look carefully and you can still see where cannonballs found their target during the siege of 1580.

Martignac

One of the best excursions in the vicinity is to the hamlet of **MARTIGNAC**, 2.5km north, where the much-altered Romanesque **church of St-Pierre-ès-Liens** contains some remarkable late-fifteenth- and early-sixteenth-century frescoes – hidden under plaster until 1938, they are reasonably well preserved. Characters on the north wall represent the Seven Deadly Sins being escorted to the mouth of Hell, each mounted on a different animal: Lust on a billy goat, Gluttony scoffing ham and wine and riding a pig, and scruffy Sloth on a donkey bringing up the tail. The Seven Virtues surround the apse, their grey robes tumbling about them, with Courage and Temperance being the easiest to recognize – the former holds a serpent, while Temperance carefully waters down her wine.

Duravel and around

Downstream of Puy-l'Évêque, the Lot valley begins to open out as the hills along the southern bank fade away. Those to the north continue a while longer, providing a green backdrop for the pretty eleventh-century **church** at **DURAVEL**, 6km from Puy-l'Évêque. Its crypt contains the remains of no fewer than three saints – Poémon, Agathon and Hilarion, their bodies having been brought back from the Holy Land in the eleventh century – but the village is unfortunately spoilt by the busy main road passing through its centre.

There are, however, a number of excellent **chambres d'hôtes** and **eating** options round about. It's worth making the effort to arrange a meal at the welcoming *Aux Dodus d'Audhuy* (Ⓣ06.71.72.03.24, Ⓦauxdodus.free.fr), signed just off the D911 3km northeast of Duravel. Although they have just one room (❺) to let, their excellent cooking is still available to all if booked in advance.

Five kilometres southwest across the Lot, you'll find an idyllic **hotel**, the *Hostellerie de la Source Bleue* (Ⓣ05.65.36.52.01, Ⓦwww.hotel-sourcebleue.com; ❼; closed Jan to mid-April; menus from around €30, closed Wed & all lunchtimes except Sun), just south of the village of **Touzac**, in an ancient, spring-fed water mill swamped by luxuriant vegetation. Rooms are spacious and housed either in the old mill or in the newer building next door. There's also a shady two-star **campsite**, *Le Clos Bouyssac* (Ⓣ05.65.36.52.21, Ⓦwww.leclosbouyssac.eu; closed Nov–March), a short distance south along the riverbank.

North to the Château de Bonaguil

With your own transport, you can cut northwest across country from Duravel to visit the magnificent ruined castle of Bonaguil. On the way it's worth taking a short detour to **MONTCABRIER**, just over 5km north of Duravel, if for no other reason than because this tiny *bastide* seems to have been forgotten by the renovators and tourist authorities. There's a clutch of once-noble residences around the chestnut-shaded main square, but the village is best known for a diminutive statue lodged in the north nave of its quietly crumbling **church of St-Louis**. It is one of the first stone representations of the saint, formerly King Louis IX, showing him as a bearded figure wearing a painted crown. It's also slightly macabre: when Louis died on a crusade in 1270, his body was immediately chopped into pieces and dispatched around Europe to meet the demand for relics. Apparently, one unspecified piece of the king now resides inside this little statue.

From Montcabrier take the D673 from below the village heading southwest, then turn west through the delightful hamlet of St-Martin-Le-Redon and start climbing. As the road crests the ridge you get a stunning view of the **Château de Bonaguil** (daily: March, April & Oct 10.30am–12.30pm & 2–5.30pm; June 10am–12.30pm & 2–6pm; July & Aug 10am–7pm; Sept 10.30am–12.30pm & 2–6.30pm; Nov Sun, bank hols & school hols 2–5pm; Dec & Feb school hols 2–5pm; €6; Ⓣ05.53.71.90.33, Ⓦwww.bonaguil.org), 7km from Montcabrier, perched at the end of a wooded spur. The castle dates largely from the fifteenth and sixteenth centuries when Bérenger de Roquefeuil, from a powerful Languedoc family and by all accounts a nasty piece of work, inherited the partially ruined castle. Fearing revolts by his vassals, he decided to transform it into an impregnable fortress, just as his contemporaries were abandoning such elaborate fortifications. It took him around forty years to do so, constructing a double ring of walls, six huge towers, a highly unusual, narrow boat-shaped keep, and sophisticated loopholes with overlapping lines of fire. Perhaps because of such elaborate precautions, Bonaguil was never attacked, and although some demolition occurred during the Revolution, the castle still stands, bloodied but unbowed.

The site attracts up to two thousand tourists per day in July and August. It's best to arrive first thing in the morning to avoid the worst of the crush, and

▲ Capturing the Château de Bonaguil

rather than joining the **guided tours** (1hr 30min; English tours available in July & Aug), which get tedious when it's very busy, it's preferable to buy a guidebook from the ticket gate and do it yourself. The château provides the backdrop for a **firework** extravaganza on the Friday following July 14, and then in early August makes a stunning venue for a **festival** of theatre (see p.266).

There are a couple of **eating** places below the castle, including the English-run *Auberge les Bons Enfants* (closed Wed lunch and eves except Thurs, Fri & Sat, except in July & Aug), which serves drinks and snacks all day in July & August, as well as more substantial regional menus from around €13.

Fumel and around

Eight kilometres southwest of Bonaguil and 12km west of Duravel, **FUMEL** – an important stronghold in medieval times – is now a busy industrial town, which holds little of interest beyond its transport facilities and a decent hotel. It lies on the north bank of the Lot, spilling along the main road from its old centre – focused around **place du Postel** – in the east, past a huge factory making car parts, and then merges 4km later with the western suburb of **MONSEMPRON-LIBOS** where you'll find the **gare SNCF**, set back from the river near the new road-bridge at the end of avenue de la Gare. This is where SNCF **buses** from Cahors terminate, having first called in Fumel at place du Postel.

Fumel's **tourist office** is on place Georges Escandes, immediately east of place du Postel (July & Aug Mon–Sat 9am–1pm & 2.30–6.30pm, Sun 9am–1pm; Sept–June Tues–Sat 10am–noon & 3–6pm; Ⓣ05.53.71.13.70, Ⓦwww.tourisme-fumelois.fr). **Bike rental** is available from AJF Cycles, 8 place du Postel (Ⓣ05.53.71.14.57), and for a **taxi**, call Taxi Fumélois (Ⓣ05.53.71.39.50).

The best bet for an overnight **stay** is the modern and welcoming, Dutch-run *Hôtel Kyriad*, place de l'Église (Ⓣ05.53.40.93.93, Ⓦwww.kyriad.fr; ❸), perched on the cliff to the south of place du Postel. Most rooms have valley views, and there's also a pool and a good-value **restaurant**, *La Soupière*, offering a choice of a self-service buffet at €11.50, menus from €12.50 and à la *carte* around €20. For a **campsite** nearby, head 3.5km east through the village of Condat to the friendly, two-star *Camping les Catalpas* (Ⓣ05.53.71.11.99, Ⓦwww.les-catalpas.com; open all year); SNCF buses stop 1.5km up the road in Condat itself.

With your own transport, a better option is to head 9km southeast of Fumel, on the D5 Puy-l'Évêque road, to the *Hostellerie Le Vert* (Ⓣ05.65.36.51.36, Ⓦwww.hotellevert.com; ❻; closed Nov to March), a lovely old farm set in fields just east of **Mauroux**, with a heated pool, a handful of nicely refurbished rooms and a good **restaurant** serving upmarket regional cuisine (eves only; menu at €45 or around €35 *à la carte*). In Mauroux itself, check out *Rouge Passion* (Ⓣ05.65.22.97.26, Ⓦwww.rouge-passion.eu; closed lunchtimes except Sun, Tues eve & Sun eve except in July & Aug; menus from €25), a modern bistro that makes use of simple ingredients flavoured with plenty of herbs.

Penne-d'Agenais

The last stop along the valley before Villeneuve-sur-Lot is the beautiful but touristy old fortress-town of **PENNE-D'AGENAIS**, 15km downstream from Fumel on the river's south bank, where a silver-domed **basilica** teeters on the cliff edge. **Notre-Dame-de-Peyragude** dates back to 1000, but had the misfortune to be built on a particularly strategic pinnacle of rock. After Richard the Lionheart erected a castle right next door in 1182, the chapel found itself in the crossfire on any number of occasions; in 1412 Penne changed hands no fewer than four times. The most recent construction was only completed in 1949; there's nothing particular to see inside, and the neighbouring castle was razed during the Wars of Religion, but the climb is rewarded with panoramic views.

From **place Gambetta**, the main square immediately south of the old town, **rue du 14-Juillet** ducks under a medieval gate. From here just follow your fancy uphill along narrow lanes lined with an alluring mix of brick and stone houses – all incredibly spick and span. A few twists and turns later you emerge beside the basilica.

Penne lies on the Agen–Paris main line, its **gare SNCF** a couple of kilometres southeast down the D103 to Agen. If you need a taxi, call Andrée Garcia (ⓣ06.15.27.05.91). The **tourist office**, just inside the medieval gate on rue du 14-Juillet (Mon–Sat 9am–12.30pm & 2–6pm, Sun 2–6pm; ⓣ05.53.41.37.80, ⓦwww.penne-tourisme.com), can supply comprehensive lists of *chambres d'hôtes* and *gîtes* in the area. As for **campsites**, there's a choice between the small, two-star riverside *Camping Municipal Les Berges du Lot* (ⓣ05.53.41.22.23; closed Oct to mid-May), near the bridge over the Lot in St-Sylvestre-sur-Lot, and the three-star *Camping Municipal Lac Férrié* (ⓣ05.53.41.30.97; open July & Aug) beside a lake just north of Penne's gare SNCF. For something to **eat**, try *La Maison sur la Place* (ⓣ05.53.01.29.18, ⓦwww.lamaisonsurlaplace.com; closed Sun eve & Mon, also Tues & Wed in winter), by the entrance to the village, for sophisticated country cooking in elegant surroundings. *Le Bombecul* (ⓣ05.53.71.11.76, ⓦbombecul.free.fr), on Place Paul Fromet, offers more casual dining with a Moroccan twist, as well as a wide selection of locally made ice cream.

Villeneuve-sur-Lot and around

Straddling the river 10km west of Penne-d'Agenais, **VILLENEUVE-SUR-LOT** is a pleasant, workaday sort of town. It has no terribly compelling sights, but the handful of attractive timbered houses in the old centre go some way to compensate, while the nearby hilltop village of **Pujols** makes for an enjoyable excursion. Founded in 1251 by Alphonse de Poitiers, Villeneuve was one of the region's earliest *bastide* towns (see box, p.306), and in no time it developed into an important commercial centre, which it remains to this day. As elsewhere, its ramparts have given way to encircling boulevards, but the distinctive chequerboard street plan survives, along with two medieval gates and the old, arched bridge.

Arrival, information and accommodation

SNCF runs regular **bus services** from Agen, which is on the Bordeaux–Toulouse and Agen–Périgueux lines. These buses call at Villeneuve's former *gare SNCF* (where there's an SNCF ticket office), five minutes' walk south of the centre, before terminating at the Hôtel de Ville on the opposite side of town. The only other buses likely to be of use are those to Pujols, but the timetables change frequently, so you should call for information (Société Beyris ⓣ05.53.41.74.85) or ask at the **tourist office**, at 3 place de la Libération (July & Aug Mon–Sat 9.30am–12.30pm & 2.30-6.30pm, Sept–June Mon–Sat 9am–noon & 2–6pm; ⓣ05.53.36.17.30, ⓦwww.tourisme-villeneuve-sur-lot.com). **Internet** is available at Cyberphone.com at the corner of rue Parmentier and rue du Collège.

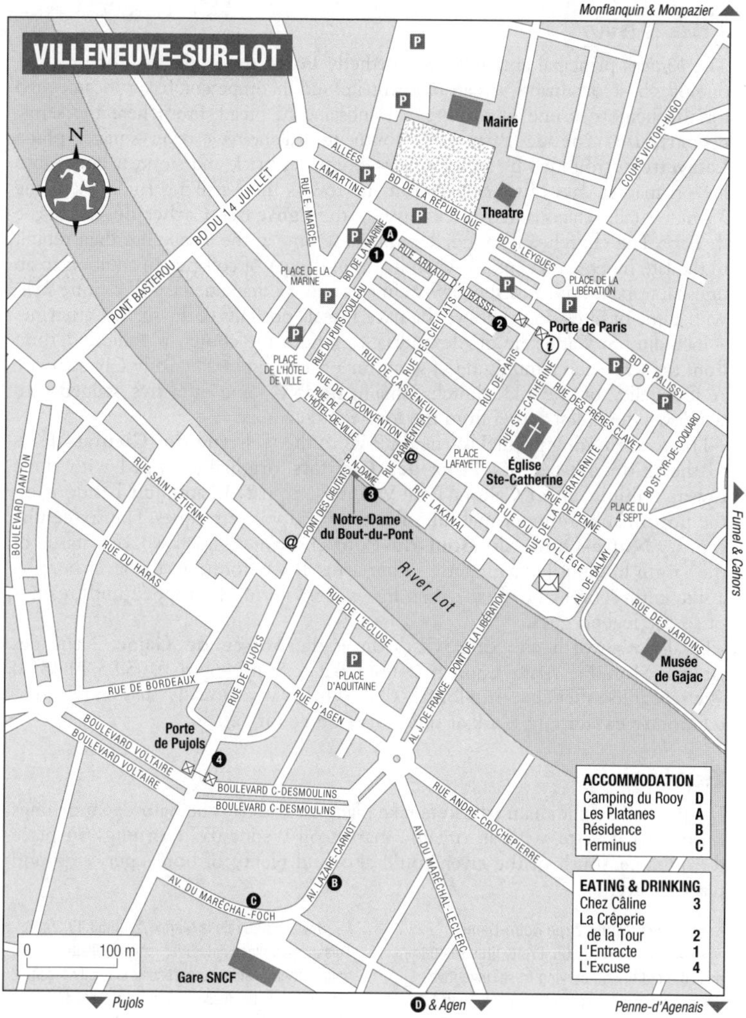

Accommodation

Camping du Rooy ⓣ05.53.70.24.18. Two-star campsite 2km away in the southern suburbs, signed off the Agen road. Closed Oct to mid-April.

Les Platanes 40 bd de la Marine ⓣ05.53.40.11.40, ⓕ05.53.70.71.95. Located on the old quarter's northwest corner, *Les Platanes* has old-fashioned rooms, the cheapest with bathroom facilities on a different floor, but it's all spotlessly clean. Closed two weeks at Christmas and last week in Aug. ❷

Résidence 17 av Lazare Carnot ⓣ05.53.40.17.03, ⓦwww.hotelaresidence47.com. This friendly place offers unbeatable value for money. Closed for Christmas & New Year. ❶

Terminus 2 av Maréchal Foch ⓣ05.53.70.94.36, ⓔleterminus@alicepro.fr. Modern rooms above a large bar and restaurant (menus from €13, closed weekends other than for reservations on Sat). ❷

The Town

The *bastide*'s principal entrance was northerly **Porte de Paris**, also the prison – one of whose occupants was an unfortunate, and incompetent, baker incarcerated for the heinous crime of turning out substandard bread. From here the semi-pedestrianized rue de Paris leads south to Villeneuve's main square, **place Lafayette**; surrounded by arcaded town houses in brick and stone, it bursts into life on market days (Tues & Sat). But the town's most striking landmark is the 55-metre-tall, octagonal red-brick tower of the **Église Ste-Catherine**, east of rue de Paris. The church was founded at the same time as the *bastide*, but then rebuilt in the late nineteenth century when it was in danger of collapse. In addition to an unusual north–south axis, the new architects chose a dramatic neo-Byzantine style, with a line of three domes above the nave, mosaic portraits of the six St Catherines – including St Catherine of Alexandria, to whom the church is dedicated, third from the left – and a multitude of saints on a frieze inspired by early Christian art. A few relics of the old church remain, notably some attractive stained-glass windows, the oldest dating from the fourteenth century.

The road running parallel to rue de Paris to the west, **rue des Cieutats**, leads to the thirteenth-century **Pont des Cieutats**, originally topped with three towers reminiscent of Cahors' Pont Valentré (see p.273), and, just beside it on the north bank, a tiny chapel full of candles and votive plaques. The sixteenth-century **Notre-Dame du Bout-du-Pont** enshrines a small wooden statue of the Virgin holding Jesus gingerly in her arms. It was found in the river here by a sixteenth-century boatman when his craft mysteriously stopped midstream – or so the legend goes.

Finally, it's worth checking what's on at the **Musée de Gajac**, 2 rue des Jardins (Mon–Fri 10am–noon & 2–6pm, Sat & Sun 2–6pm; ⓣ05.53.40.48.00 ⓦwww.ville-villeneuve-sur-lot.fr; €1), which occasionally has interesting temporary exhibitions – ask at the tourist office for details.

Eating

For picnic fare, the main **markets** take place on Tuesday and Saturday mornings on place Lafayette, with an organic market on Wednesday mornings on place d'Aquitaine, south of the river. You'll also find plenty of boulangeries around place Lafayette.

Chez Câline 2 rue Notre-Dame ⓣ05.53.70.42.08. Pretty little restaurant near the old bridge serving fresh, inventive dishes in a tiny brick-vaulted room. Their miniscule terrace, suspended over the river, is worth arriving early for, though it's not for vertigo-sufferers. Closed Tues & Weds eves & Sun. Menus from €12.

La Crêperie de la Tour 5 rue Arnaud d'Aubasse ⓣ05.53.70.97.86. Serves *galettes*, crêpes and salads with menus from around €7.50. Closed Mon & Sun except for reservations.

L'Entracte 30 bd de la Marine ⓣ05.53.49.25.50. This elegant place caters for more traditional tastes. Their seafood in particular is highly recommended, and the desserts excellent. Closed Wed. Menus from €13.90.

L'Excuse 86 rue Pujols ⓣ05.53.36.00.33. Pick a table near the bar, which is in fact the kitchen, and watch the chef prepare and cook your food from scratch. Even pancake batter is made to order. Add in a Gallic disregard for the smoking ban, and you'll feel like you're in *ancienne France*. Dishes €8–15. Closed Sun & Mon eve.

Pujols

Three kilometres south of Villeneuve, the two-street village of **PUJOLS** stands high above the plain behind its thirteenth-century ramparts. The town is a popular excursion destination, partly because it's a beguiling little place with its

A Taste of Périgord

The Périgord region, which encompasses the Dordogne *département*, boasts one of France's great culinary traditions. Here you'll taste country cooking at its best, robust fare in which the flavours and textures speak for themselves. The staple ingredients are duck and goose, both of which are served in all sorts of delectable guises, while walnuts, game and wild mushrooms also feature prominently on regional menus. And to wash it all down, there's no shortage of excellent wines to choose from.

An order of snails? ▲

Cassoulet ▼

Meat

No part of a **duck** or **goose** goes to waste in the Périgord – from the carcasses *(demoiselles)*, which are roasted over a wood fire and then picked over for their remaining morsels of meat, to the most famous dish, **foie gras** (see below and opposite). But it's not all fowl: you'll find many pork dishes, along with lamb that's been raised on the *causses* of Quercy or the Médoc's salt marshes. To the north and east of the region, excellent Limousin **beef** begins to feature more strongly. In summer, **snails** make an appearance on market stalls and at village *fêtes*, often cooked in a garlic or a spicy tomato sauce. Later in the year, more upmarket restaurants offer **pigeonneau** (young pigeon), and **lièvre** (hare) among other types of game.

Decoding the menu

▸▸ **Foie gras** Fattened livers (duck or goose).

▸▸ **Confit** Meat (often duck or goose) preserved in its own salted fat.

▸▸ **Cou farci** Goose neck stuffed with sausage meat, foie gras and truffles.

▸▸ **Magret** Grilled duck breast (sometimes served with a sauce of truffle, pepper or a seasonal fruit).

▸▸ **Rillettes** Coarse local paté made of duck or goose meat.

▸▸ **Tourin** (or *tourain*) Traditional Périgord soup, served with an egg over thick country bread.

▸▸ **Cassoulet** Hearty concoction of confit, Toulouse sausage and haricot beans.

▸▸ **Pommes sarladaise** A dish originating in Sarlat (see p.198) in which sliced potatoes are fried in duck or goose fat, with lashings of garlic and parsley.

▸▸ **Salade de gésiers** Confit of duck gizzards served warm on a bed of lettuce.

▸▸ **Enchaud périgourdin** Sliced slow-roasted pork loin stuffed with garlic.

Foie gras

One of this region's most celebrated food is **foie gras** (see p.147), whose rich and buttery taste is an experience not to be missed. Though best eaten on its own in succulent slabs, foie gras is equally irresistible pan-fried with a seasonal fruit compôte, and makes a gloriously over-the-top garnish for meat dishes.

▲ Tins of foie gras

Black diamonds

Foie gras is often combined with the region's other culinary star, **truffles** (*truffes*), aptly known as the "black diamonds of Périgord" (see p.150). These expensive black fungi crop up in all sorts of dishes, from rich Périgourdin sauces to the humble omelette. All too often, however, there's so little truffle or the other ingredients are so strong that it's impossible to detect its delicate flavour. Far better to splash out and order a simple, unadorned truffle you can really enjoy.

Another popular fungi is **cèpes**, plump brown mushrooms, which are prolific around Monpazier and Villefranche-du-Périgord. They come fried, grilled, stuffed and in omelettes.

▼ A "black diamond"

Fish and seafood

Around Bordeaux and along the banks of the Garonne, seafood holds sway. **Salmon**, **eel**, **whelks**, **prawns**, **smelt**, **oysters** and even farmed **sturgeon** can all be sampled in local restaurants. Young fried **elvers** (*pibales*) are expensive but popular along the estuary in January and February, while further inland **shad** (*alose*) is traditionally grilled over vine clippings. Another local delicacy is **lamprey** (*lamproie*), an eel-like creature poached in Sauternes wine, leeks, onions and its own blood.

▼ Oysters on sale

Pastis ▲

Market day in Sarlat ▼

Cheese and puddings

While you'll find good farm cheeses in the markets, the only local speciality cheese is **Cabécou**, a little flat medallion of goat's cheese from around Rocamadour. It's often served on a bed of lettuce with walnut oil. **Walnuts** (*noix*) provide another mainstay of Périgourdin cusine. In addition to the oil, you'll come across walnuts in breads, cakes and desserts or simply as a garnish.

The best-known local puddings are **pastis**, a thin apple tart topped with almost transparent crinkled pastry and a hint of alcohol, and **clafoutis**, a pudding-like cake made with cherries, pears or any other fruit. Walnut cakes and puddings are popular nowadays, as are strawberries from around Bretenoux and to the south of Périgueux. Agen, further south again, is famous for its **prunes** (see p.320) and all sorts of derived goodies.

Top 5 markets

▸▸ **Sarlat (Wed & Sat)** The region's most perfect town centre hosts one of its largest markets – the place to go for truffles and walnuts. See p.197

▸▸ **Ste-Foy (Sat)** Less touristy than Sarlat but just as vibrant, this market offers local foodstuffs, plus good wines from nearby Bergerac. See p.178

▸▸ **Marché des Capucins, Bordeaux** (daily) Bustling city market offering the best prices on fresh produce, especially seafood. The only place in town where you can reasonably drink a glass of wine at 9am. See p.81

▸▸ **Le Bugue (Tues & Sat)** The market is this town's raison d'être: find foie gras, goose and duck in all guises, and an excellent cheese stall. See p.209

▸▸ **Cahors (Wed & Sat)** Truffles and goat's cheese are the delicacies here, alongside the pride of the Quercy region, *agneau fermier* – tender lamb. See p.271

flowery nooks and crannies, and partly for views over the surrounding c… – for locals, though, the main reason to come to Pujols is gastronomic.

Immediately inside Pujols' main north gate, it's hard to tell where the fortific… tions end and the Gothic **church of St-Nicolas** begins. It contains nothing of particular note, whereas the **Église Ste-Foy** (open during temporary exhibitions, which take place most of the time between April and October; free), on the far side of the market square, is decorated with fifteenth- and sixteenth-century frescoes. Though faded, many are still visible, such as St George poised over the dragon and St Catherine with her wheel of torture, both around the apse. And look out, too, for a painting in the baptismal chapel (first on the left as you enter), depicting the old bridge at Villeneuve-sur-Lot sporting its three towers.

Top of the list for **restaurants** is the Michelin-starred *La Toque Blanche* (ⓣ05.53.49.00.30, ⓦwww.la-toque-blanche.com/uk; closed Sun eve, Mon & lunchtime Tues), just south of Pujols with views back to the village. Dishes include lobster, truffle and foie gras salad, and stuffed pigs' trotters, but it's not outrageously expensive: weekday menus start at €25, rising to €39 at weekends and holidays. The panorama is even better from the terrace at *Lou Calel* (ⓣ05.53.70.46.14; closed Tues eve & Mon), in Pujols itself overlooking the Lot valley; from around €20 you can enjoy beautifully cooked traditional but light menus. For somewhere smaller and less formal, try *Aux Délices du Puits* (ⓣ05.53.71.61.66, closed Oct–April, Sat lunch & Wed), next to the well on rue de la Citadelle. It serves basic salads and mains, with a €14 lunch menu.

The bastide country

Although *bastides*, or medieval new towns (see box, p.306), are by no means unique to this stretch of country north of the Lot, it's here that you'll find the two finest examples. The more southerly of the pair is **Monflanquin**, which makes a good place to start because of its museum outlining the history, architecture and daily life of the *bastides*. The route then heads northeast, skirting round the flanks of the imposing **Château de Biron**, before reaching **Monpazier**. This is the most typical of the *bastides*, with virtually no modern development around. There's a small museum here, too, but Monpazier's prime attraction is its atmosphere, "like a drowsy yellow cat, slumbering in the sun" as Freda White so aptly describes it in the *Three Rivers of France* (see p.369).

Nevertheless, some effort is required to reach it. Neither the Château de Biron nor Monpazier is accessible by **public transport**. The best on offer is the **bus** from Villeneuve to Monflanquin, but even that is aimed at the school run.

Monflanquin

Some 17km north of Villeneuve-sur-Lot, pretty **MONFLANQUIN**, founded in 1252 by Alphonse de Poitiers, is nearly as perfectly preserved as Monpazier, though less touristy and impressively positioned on top of a hill that rises sharply from the surrounding country, visible for miles. Despite being constructed on a steep slope, it conforms to the regular pattern of right-angled streets leading from a central square to the four town gates. The ramparts themselves were demolished on Richelieu's orders in 1630, but otherwise Monflanquin has experienced few radical changes since the thirteenth century.

The main square, tree-shaded **place des Arcades** – where the **market** still takes place on Thursdays as decreed in the *bastide*'s founding charter – derives a special charm from being on a slope. Its grandest building is the Gothic **Maison**

Bastides

From the Occitan *bastida*, meaning a group of buildings, **bastides** were the new towns of the thirteenth and fourteenth centuries. Although they are found all over southwest France, from the Dordogne to the foothills of the Pyrenees, there is a particularly high concentration in the area between the Dordogne and Lot rivers, which at that time formed the disputed "frontier" region between English-held Aquitaine and Capetian France.

That said, the earliest *bastides* were founded largely for **economic and political** reasons. They were a means of bringing new land into production – this was a period of rapid population growth and technological innovation – and thus extending the power of the local lord. But as tensions between the French and English forces intensified during the late thirteenth century, so the motive became increasingly **military**. The *bastides* now provided a handy way of securing the land along the frontier, and it was generally at this point that they were fortified.

As an incentive, anyone who was prepared to build, inhabit and defend the *bastide* was granted various perks and concessions in a founding **charter**. All new residents were allocated a building plot, garden and cultivable land outside the town. The charter might also offer asylum to certain types of criminal or grant exemption from military service, and would allow the election of **consuls** charged with day-to-day administration – a measure of self-government remarkable in feudal times. Taxes and judicial affairs, meanwhile, remained the preserve of the representative of the king or local lord under whose ultimate authority the *bastide* lay.

The other defining feature of a *bastide* is its **layout**. They are nearly always square or rectangular in shape, depending on the nature of the terrain, and are divided by streets at right angles to each other to produce a chequerboard pattern. The focal point is the market square, often missing its covered *halle* nowadays, but generally still surrounded by arcades, while the church is relegated to one side, or may even form part of the town walls.

The busiest *bastide* founders were **Alphonse de Poitiers** (1249–71), on behalf of the French crown, after he became count of Toulouse in 1249, and **King Edward I of England**, Edward Plantagenet (1272–1307), who wished to consolidate his hold on the northern borders of his duchy of Aquitaine. The former chalked up a total of 57 *bastides*, including Villeneuve-sur-Lot (1251), Monflanquin (1252), Ste-Foy-la-Grande (1255) and Eymet (1270), while Edward was responsible for Beaumont (1272), Monpazier and Molières (both 1284) amongst others.

du Prince Noir in the northeast corner, where the Black Prince is said to have stayed. On this north side you'll also find the high-tech **Musée des Bastides**, above the tourist office (Ⓦbastides.free.fr/nouvelle3.htm; same hours – see below; €4), which is full of information about the life and history of *bastides*; most of the text is translated into English, but unfortunately not the audio-tapes. Then, after a quick wander through Monflanquin's old centre, it's worth heading north past the **church**, which took on its pseudo-medieval look in the early twentieth century, to end up on a terrace with expansive views northeast to the next stop, Château de Biron (see opposite).

Practicalities

Buses from Villeneuve-sur-Lot stop on the main road below the *bastide* in modern Monflanquin; simply walk uphill until you hit rue St-Pierre heading north to place des Arcades, where you'll find the **tourist office** (mid-May to June & mid-Sept to Oct Mon–Sat 10am–noon & 2–6pm, Sun 3–5pm; July to mid-Sept daily 10am–7pm; Nov–April Mon–Sat 10am–noon & 2–5pm, early May also Sun 3–5pm; Ⓣ05.53.36.40.19, Ⓦwww.cc-monflanquinois.fr); they

can furnish you with details of the many **events** taking place here in summer (see box, p.266). In summer, regular tours are led by the costumed jester Janouille la Fripouille. The tours are in French only, but it's worth following along for the antics.

As regards **hotels**, your best bet is the *Moulin de Boulède* (Ⓣ05.53.36.16.49, Ⓦlemoulindeboulede.monsite.orange.fr; ❸), just west of Monflanquin on the D124 to Cancon, which has a handful of pleasant rooms, all en-suite. The owner's real passion, though, is his restaurant, where he specialises in fish dishes (closed Wed, menus from €14).

Otherwise, eat at one of the **cafés** and **restaurants** on place des Arcades. Pick of the bunch is the welcoming *Le Bistrot du Prince Noir* (closed Jan–March, Tues & Wed March–May & Oct–Dec, Wed in June & Sept) in the southwest corner of the square. It's both a wine bar – with an excellent choice of local wines (from €2 for a glass) – and restaurant. Another good option on the square is the British-run *La Bastide* (closed Mon), which serves crêpes and salads from around €7.50, while their terrace offers splendid views down the length of rue Ste-Marie. Alternatively, head 10km northeast to **Gavaudun**, where you'll find *Le Café de Gavaudun* (Ⓣ05.53.40.99.34, open daily except Wed in July & Aug, also Tues in May, June & Sept, open Fri–Sun only Oct–April; menus from €12), an unassuming little place on the main road, serving delicious local cuisine.

The best place for picnic fodder is the Thursday-morning **market** on place des Arcades, though you can also buy provisions at the **supermarket** on the main road immediately south of town. The neighbouring **wine co-operative**, the Cave des 7 Monts (Ⓣ05.53.36.33.40; closed Mon morn, Sat pm & Sun), represents some two hundred local vineyards producing some very palatable and reasonably priced wines; tastings are available free of charge.

Château de Biron

Twenty-two kilometres northeast of Monflanquin, via a picturesque route along the River Lède, the vast **Château de Biron** (Feb, March & Nov to mid-Dec Tues–Thurs & Sun 10am–12.30pm & 2–5.30pm; April–June & Sept to mid-Nov daily except Mon 10am–12.30pm & 2–6pm; July & Aug daily 10am–7pm; €6; Ⓦwww.semitour.com) dominates the countryside for miles around. It was begun in the eleventh century and added to piecemeal over the years by the Gontaut-Biron family, who occupied the castle right up to the early twentieth century. The biggest alterations were made in the fifteenth and early sixteenth centuries, when Pons de Gontaut-Biron started reconstructing the eastern wing. The result is an architectural primer, from the medieval keep through flamboyant Gothic and Renaissance to an eighteenth-century loggia in the style of Versailles.

Rather than the guided tour (in French only; 45min–1hr), at busy times it's better to borrow the English-language text from the ticket desk and wander at will. The most striking building in the grassy **lower court** is the Renaissance chapel, where the sarcophagi of Pons and his brother Armand, bishop of Sarlat, lie. Though their statues were hacked about during the Revolution, the Italianate biblical scenes and three Virtues carved on the sides still show fine craftsmanship. On entering the cobbled and confined **inner courtyard** around its twelfth-century keep, the route takes you to a dungeon and through the lord's apartments, with their Renaissance chimney and wood-panelled hall, to a vast reception room and an equally capacious stone-vaulted refectory. If the rooms decked out as a tannery, torture chamber and weavers' workshop make you feel as though you're walking through a film set, you are – Biron is a favourite for period dramas, the most recent being *Le Pacte des Loups* in 2000.

If you're looking for somewhere to **eat**, you could try the *Auberge du Château*, beside the path up to the castle, which serves decent menus from €13 (Ⓣ05.53.63.13.33; closed eves except Fri & Sat, except in July & Aug when open daily). Or, better still, head back southeast 5km – by road or on the GR36 footpath – to **LACAPELLE-BIRON**, where *Le Palissy* (closed Tues except mid-June to Aug), on the main road, is a friendly, locals' place offering excellent-value menus from €14. The village also boasts one of the region's best **campsites**, *Le Moulinal* (Ⓣ05.53.40.84.60, Ⓦwww.lemoulinal.com; closed late Sept to early April; €), beside a leisure lake and with four-star facilities including a shop, restaurant and bar and an internet café.

Monpazier

From the Château de Biron it's only another 8km north to **MONPAZIER**, the finest and most complete of the surviving *bastides*, made up of a lovely warm-coloured stone on a hill above the River Dropt. Founded in 1284 by King Edward I of England on land granted by Pierre de Gontaut-Biron, and picturesque and placid though it is today, Monpazier has a hard and bitter history, being twice – in 1594 and 1637 – the centre of **peasant rebellions** provoked by the misery that followed the Wars of Religion (see p.360). Both uprisings were brutally suppressed: the 1637 peasants' leader was broken on the wheel in the square and his head paraded around the countryside. In an earlier episode, Sully, the Protestant general, describes a rare moment of light relief in the terrible **Wars of Religion**, when the men of Catholic Villefranche-de-Périgord planned to capture Monpazier on the same night as the men of Monpazier were headed for Villefranche. By chance, both sides took different routes, met no resistance, looted to their hearts' content and returned home congratulating themselves on their luck and skill, only to find that things were rather different. The peace terms were that everything should be returned to its proper place.

Arrival and information

Monpazier's **tourist office** (Sept–June Tues–Sat 10am–12.30pm & 2–6.30pm, Sun 2–5pm; July & Aug daily 10am–12.30pm & 2–7pm; Ⓣ05.53.22.68.59,

▲ Monpazier

www.pays-des-bastides.com) is located on the east side of place des Cornières. Amongst all sorts of useful information, they produce a free DIY tour of the town, with information in English and games for children, and a book of eleven waymarked **walks** in the area (€2.50).

Accommodation

Camping de Véronne 3km northwest in Marsalès ⓣ05.53.22.65.50. Very basic campsite pleasantly located next to a lake. Open July & Aug.

Hôtel Edward 1er ⓣ05.53.22.44.00, ⓦwww.hoteledward1er.com. Housed in a nineteenth-century château, the luxurious rooms offer peace and quiet, while the restaurant downstairs books out quickly (menu €29.50, closed Wed). Closed mid-Nov to mid-March. ❻

Hôtel de France 21 rue St-Jacques ⓣ05.53.22.60.06, ⓦwww.hoteldefrancemonpazier.fr. Occupies a lovely medieval building on the southwest corner of place des Cornières. It has a fine regional restaurant (menus from €17; same closing as hotel), while in summer it also offers lighter brasserie-style fare. Closed mid-Oct to Easter, and Tues eve & Wed except in July & Aug. ❷

Le Moulin de David ⓣ05.53.22.65.25, ⓦwww.moulin-de-david.com. Luxurious, four-star campsite in the Dropt valley. Reserve well in advance. Closed early Sept to end April.

The Town

After such a turbulent past, it comes as something of a surprise to find Monpazier has survived so well. Three of its six **medieval gates** are still intact and its central square, **place des Cornières**, couldn't be more perfect with its oak-pillared *halle* and time-worn, stone-built houses, no two the same. Deep, shady arcades pass beneath all the houses, which are separated from each other by a small gap to reduce fire risk; at the corners the buttresses are cut away to allow the passage of laden pack animals. On Thursday mornings the square comes to life for the weekly **market**, which expands on the third Thursday of each month into a fair. In mushroom season (roughly Aug & Sept depending on the weather) people also come here in the afternoons to sell their pickings, while in December there's a truffle market.

Monpazier's main north–south axis is **rue Notre-Dame**, which brings you in to the northeast corner of place des Cornières, past the much-altered **church**. The thirteenth-century building opposite is a bit battered, but this is Monpazier's oldest house, where the tax collector received his share of the harvest. Of more interest is the local museum, the **Ateliers des Bastides** (May–Oct Wed–Mon 10am–12.30pm & 2.30–7pm; free), west of the square along rue Jean-Galmot. It boasts a few prehistoric remains and other historical bits and pieces, but is largely devoted to local adventurer Jean Galmot, who was born here in 1879 and was assassinated in 1928 in French Guiana, then a penal colony, where he was aiding its fledgling independence movement. There is, however, no information in English.

During the summer months the museum also hosts a number of temporary **art exhibitions**, and the town puts on all sorts of other events to draw the tourists, from book fairs to medieval jamborees (see box, p.266). Outside these occasions, however, there's not much else to do in Monpazier beyond soak up the sun at a café on the market square.

Eating

You'll eat very well in the two hotel **restaurants** (see above). Otherwise, browse around place des Cornières, or head north of the square along rue Notre-Dame, where *Le Privilège du Périgord* (ⓣ05.53.22.43.98; closed Nov to Easter, and Tues year-round) at no. 58 is a good bet, comprising a number of cosy dining rooms plus a few tables in the courtyard, and offering lunch *formules* from around €15, or menus from €21.50. Just outside the town walls, *Bistrot 2*

(☎05.53.22.60.64, closed Mon & Fri eves and Sat lunch, except in July & Aug) is owned by the same people as the *Edward 1er*, and you can sit out on the terrace watching the world go by as you sample their not-so-traditional use of the local ingredients.

Travel details

Trains

Cahors to: Brive (7 daily; 1hr–1hr 10min); Gourdon (6 daily; 30min); Montauban (6 daily; 40–50min); Paris-Austerlitz (6 daily; 4–5hr); Souillac (6 daily; 45min); Toulouse (7 daily; 1hr–1hr 20min).
Figeac to: Assier (4–7 daily; 25min); Brive (5–6 daily; 1hr 10min); Cordes (4–5 daily; 1hr 20); Gramat (4–7 daily; 50min); Laguépie (3–6 daily; 1hr); Najac (3–6 daily; 1hr 10min); Paris-Austerlitz (1 overnight; 7hr); Rocamadour (4–6 daily; 40min); St-Denis-lès-Martel (5–7 daily; 55min); Toulouse (3–5 daily; 2hr 20min); Villefranche-de-Rouergue (3–5 daily; 45min).
Gourdon to: Brive (6 daily; 40min); Cahors (6 daily; 30min); Montauban (3 daily; 1hr 30min); Paris-Austerlitz (2 daily; 4hr 30min); Souillac (6 daily; 15min); Toulouse (6 daily; 1hr 45min).
Gramat to: Assier (3–7 daily; 10-15min); Brive (6 daily; 45min); Figeac (4-8 daily; 30min); Paris-Austerlitz (1 overnight; 7hr); Rocamadour (4–6 daily; 8min); St-Denis-lès-Martel (4–6 daily; 25min); Toulouse (1 daily; 3hr).
Monsempron-Libos to: Agen (up to 8 daily; 40–55min); Le Bugue (4–6 daily; 50min–1hr); Les Eyzies (4–6 daily; 55min–1hr 10min); Penne-d'Agenais (6–7 daily; 15–20min); Périgueux (4–6 daily; 1hr 30min).

Buses

Cahors to: Albas (4–10 daily; 30min); Bouziès (3-5 daily; 30min); Cajarc (3–5 daily; 1hr); Figeac (3–5 daily; 1hr 45min); Fumel (4–8 daily; 1hr–1hr 15min); Gramat (Mon, Weds, Thurs & Sat 1 daily; 1hr 10min); Luzech (4–10 daily; 20min); Monsempron-Libos (4–8 daily; 1hr 15min–1hr 30min); Puy-l'Évêque (4–10 daily; 45min); St-Céré (Mon, Wed, Thurs & Sat 1 daily; 1hr 45min); St-Martin-Labouval (3–5 daily; 45min); Tour-de-Faure (3–5 daily; 40min); Vers (4–8 daily; 15–20min); Villefranche-de-Rouergue (weekdays 1 daily; 1hr 15min).
Figeac to: Assier (Mon–Thurs 1 daily; 25min); Cahors (3–5 daily; 1hr 45min); Cajarc (3–5 daily; 30–35min); Gramat (Mon–Thurs 1 daily; 50min); St-Céré (school term Tues–Fri 1 daily, school hols Tues, Thurs & Sat 1 daily; 50min–1hr 10min); Tour-de-Faure (3–5 daily; 1hr); Villefranche-de-Rouergue (1–2 daily; 40min).
Fumel to: Cahors (4–8 daily; 1hr–1hr 10min); Condat (4–8 daily; 5min); Duravel (4–8 daily; 10min); Luzech (4–8 daily; 45min); Puy-l'Evêque (4–8 daily; 25min); Touzac (2–3 daily; 20min).
Gourdon to: Souillac (school term Mon–Fri 1 daily, school hols Tues 1 daily; 1hr).
Gramat to: Assier (Mon–Sat 1 daily; 25min); Cahors (Mon, Wed, Thurs & Sat 1 daily; 1hr 10min); Figeac (Mon–Sat 1 daily; 50min); St-Céré (school term Mon–Fri 1 daily, school hols Tues, Thurs & Sat 1 daily; 1hr 15min).
Luzech to: Albas (4–10 daily; 10min); Cahors (4–10 daily; 25min); Monsempron-Libos (4–10 daily; 1hr); Puy-l'Évêque (4–10 daily; 20min).
Monsempron-Libos to: Cahors (4–8 daily; 1hr 15min); Condat (4–8 daily; 10–15min); Duravel (4–8 daily; 20min); Fumel (4–8 daily; 6–10min); Luzech (4–8 daily; 50min–1hr); Puy-l'Évêque (4–8 daily; 30min); Touzac (2–3 daily; 25min).
Puy-l'Évêque to: Albas (4–10 daily; 15min); Cahors (4–10 daily; 1hr); Condat (4–8 daily; 15–20min); Duravel (4–8 daily; 5–10min); Fumel (4–8 daily; 15–20min); Luzech (4–10 daily; 25–30min); Monsempron-Libos (4–8 daily; 20–25min); Touzac (2–3 daily; 10–15min).
Villeneuve-sur-Lot to: Agen (8–10 daily; 45–50min); Monflanquin (school term Mon–Fri 1 daily).

7

South of the River Lot

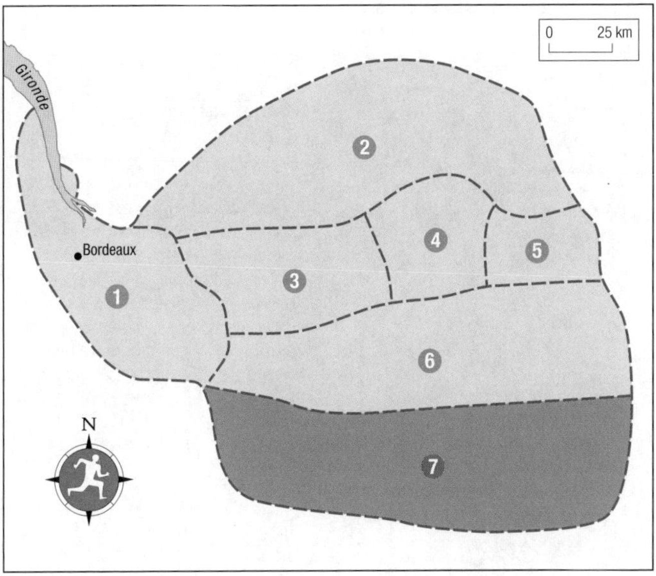

CHAPTER 7

Highlights

* **Moissac** The carvings decorating the south porch and cloister of Moissac's abbey church are masterpieces of Romanesque art. See p.325
* **Quercy Blanc** Take time to savour the bucolic countryside north of the Garonne dotted with vines, sunflowers and sleepy hilltop villages. See p.329
* **St-Antonin-Noble-Val** A compact medieval town set against the limestone cliffs of the Gorges de l'Aveyron. See p.340
* **Cordes-sur-Ciel** Perched on its knuckle of rock, this fortified town is a favourite haunt of artists and artisans. See p.342
* **Najac** Climb the castle tower for vertiginous views over the Aveyron valley. See p.344
* **Villefranche-de-Rouergue** The arcaded central square makes a superb setting for the weekly market. See p.346

▲ Moissac church carvings

7

South of the River Lot

The southern border of the Dordogne and Lot region is defined by the River Garonne in the west and by the Tarn and Aveyron in the east. On the whole this area to the south of the Lot offers less dramatic scenery than further north, but by the same token it sees fewer tourists. It is a fertile land, full of sunflowers and fruit orchards, particularly along the Garonne and spreading over the hills to the north: plums, pears, peaches, cherries, apples and nectarines all grow here, as well as melons, strawberries and the succulent chasselas grapes.

The first of the region's two gateways is **Agen**, the only major town on the Garonne between Bordeaux and Toulouse and more pleasant than it first appears, with an old centre built of pink-mottled brick and a fine local museum. Southwest of Agen, what's left of **Nérac**'s castle and its riverside pleasure gardens – where King Henri IV misspent his youth – still exudes a slightly decadent air. The river here is the Baïse, which flows north to join the Garonne near **Buzet-sur-Baïse** in the centre of a small wine region, from where it's worth continuing northwest again to see a tiny painting by Rembrandt in the church of **Le Mas-d'Agenais**.

Upstream from Agen, the region's unmissable sight is the abbey church at **Moissac**, with its wonderful carvings. The Garonne valley here is at its flattest and most featureless, but north of Moissac things improve as you climb up onto the low, rolling plateau of the **Quercy Blanc**, which stretches north almost to Cahors. It's a region of white-stone farmhouses, sun-drenched hilltop villages, windmills and *pigeonniers* – pigeon houses often raised on stilts – by the hundred. Of these, the prettiest is **Lauzerte**, but **Montpezat-de-Quercy** also merits a visit for its display of religious art, including a series of superb tapestries.

Near Montpezat the N20 and the A20 autoroute mark the eastern extent of the Quercy Blanc and funnel traffic south to **Montauban**. This brick-red city, not far north of Toulouse and on the Paris main line, is the region's second gateway, and justifies a few hours' exploration thanks to its art museum and central square surrounded by elegant town houses. It sits on the banks of the Tarn in the midst of an alluvial plain, which, in the east, gives way abruptly to hills. Running through them, the stunning **Gorges de l'Aveyron** are punctuated with ancient villages perched high above the river,

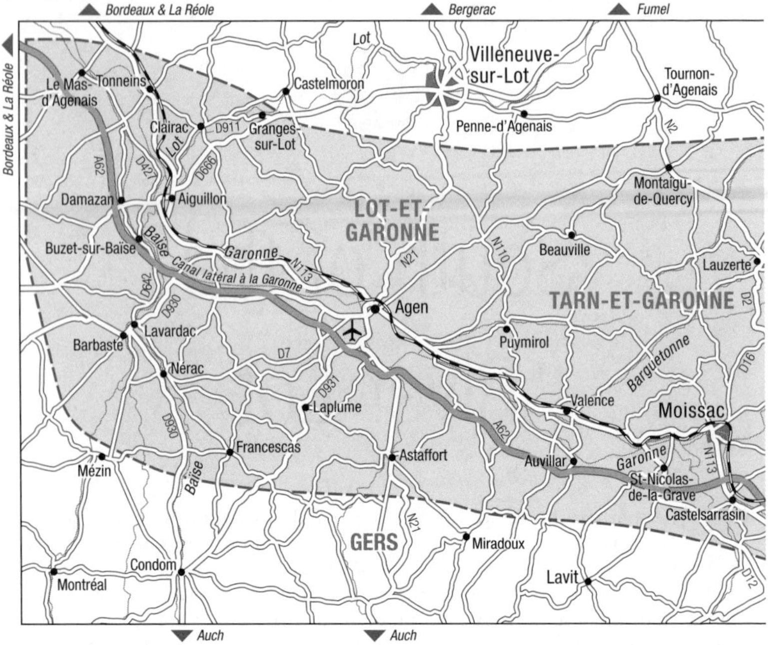

while **St-Antonin-Noble-Val**, with its core of medieval lanes, lies in the valley bottom caught between soaring limestone crags. Beyond St-Antonin, it's worth making a short detour south across the plateau to the aptly named **Cordes-sur-Ciel**, where noble facades line the steeply cobbled lanes, before rejoining the Aveyron beneath **Najac**'s much-contested fortress. The gorge opens out to the north of Najac, but it's worth continuing the last few kilometres to **Villefranche-de-Rouergue**, in the centre of which, in the monstrous shadow of its church tower, lies a perfectly preserved arcaded market square.

Three major **train** lines fan out across this region from Toulouse: along the Garonne valley to Montauban, Moissac and Agen; north via Montpezat to Cahors; and northeast through Cordes, Najac and Villefranche en route to Figeac. **Bus services** in the region are limited, and often only run at school times, but there is a regular service between Agen and Nérac, while Montcuq, Montauban and Villefranche-de-Rouergue all link up with Cahors. Another way to get about is by **boat** on the Canal latéral à la Garonne, which shadows the Garonne for nearly 200km from near Langon in the east (see p.99), passing through Buzet, Agen and Moissac, among other places, to Toulouse, where it joins the Canal du Midi.

Agen and around

AGEN, capital of the Lot-et-Garonne *département*, lies on the broad, powerful River Garonne halfway between Bordeaux and Toulouse. Close to the A62 autoroute and connected to both cities by fast and frequent train services, and to Paris by train and plane, it provides a useful gateway to the southern

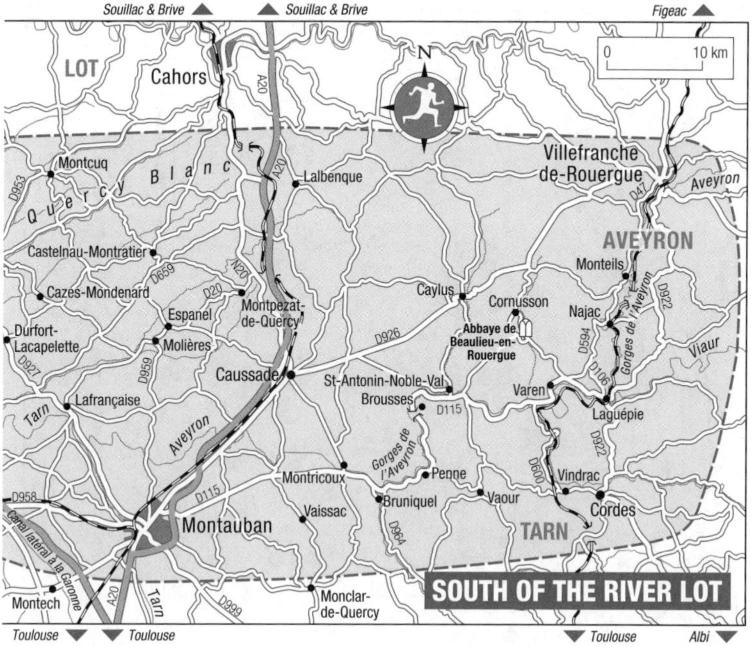

reaches of the Dordogne and Lot region. However, Agen is more than just a transport hub. Inside the ring of hypermarkets and industrial estates lies a core of old lanes lined with handsome brick houses, several churches worth a look and a surprisingly good fine arts museum. Add to that a number of excellent restaurants and a good choice of hotels, and Agen makes for a pleasant half-day's exploration, or a base from which to cover the surrounding country. The most interesting jaunts take you southwest to **Nérac**, where kings and queens disported themselves on the Baïse's wooded banks, and west to the wine town of **Buzet-sur-Baïse**. Further down the Garonne, **Aiguillon** provides a clutch of picturesque medieval lanes, while **Le Mas-d'Agenais** hides a few surprises inside its church.

Of these places, only Nérac and Aiguillon are accessible by **public transport**: the former by bus from Agen, and the latter by train. However, since they all lie on navigable and interconnected waterways – the Baïse, Garonne and the Canal latéral – renting a **boat** would provide a leisurely way of exploring the area.

Arrival and information

Flights from Paris arrive at Agen's La Garenne **airport**, around 3km southwest of town; a taxi into the centre costs roughly €15. The **gare SNCF** and **gare routière** are located next to each other on the north side of town. From in front of the station, boulevard du Président Carnot leads south to place Goya, where it crosses the town's other main thoroughfare, the east–west boulevard de la République. For drivers, free car **parking** can be found along the riverbank and on place du 14-Juillet. You'll find the **tourist office** in the town centre at 38 rue Garonne (July & Aug Mon–Sat 9am–7pm, Sun 9.30am–12.30pm; Sept–June Mon–Sat 9am–12.30pm & 2–6.30pm; Ⓣ05.53.47.36.09, Ⓦwww.ot-agen.org).

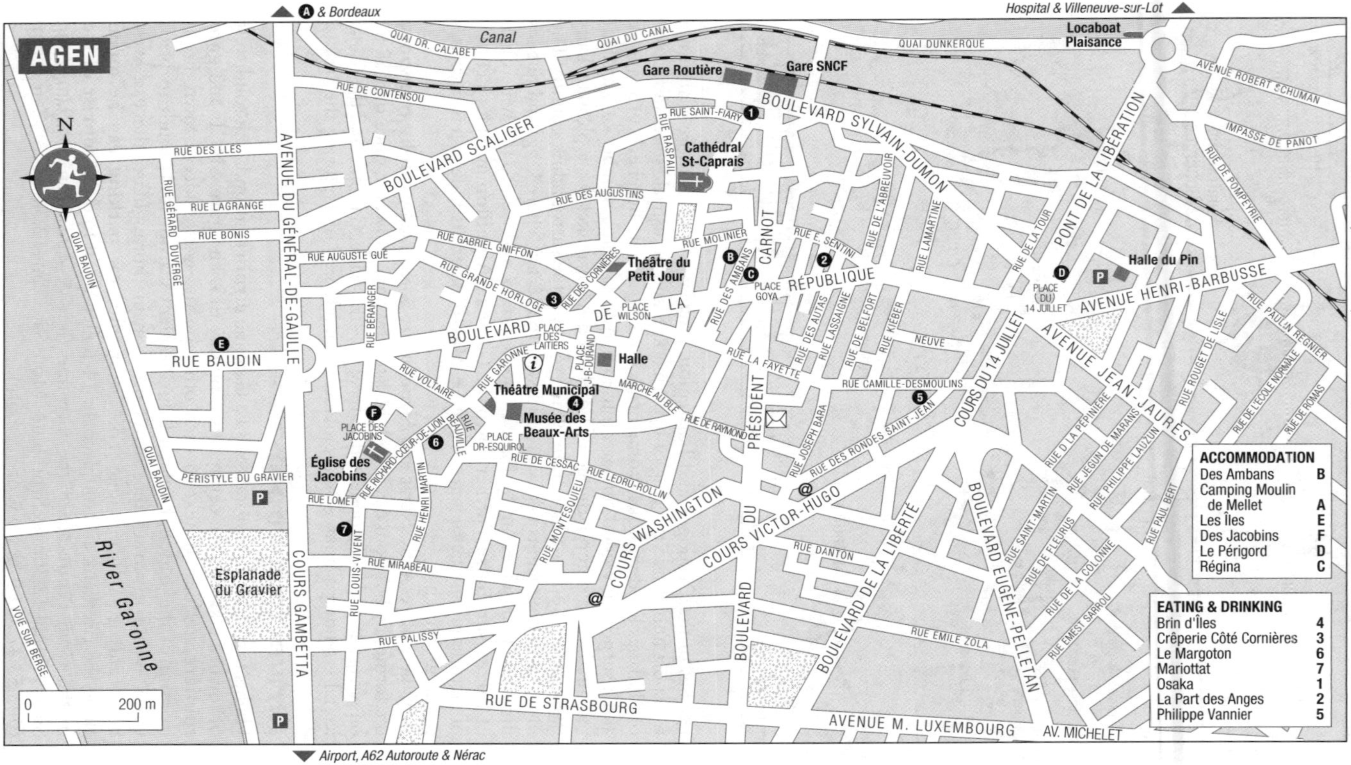
AGEN
A & Bordeaux
Hospital & Villeneuve-sur-Lot
Théâtre du Jour, Moissac, Cahors & Toulouse
Moissac
Airport, A62 Autoroute & Nérac
Canal
Locaboat Plaisance
Gare Routière
Gare SNCF
Cathédral St-Caprais
Théâtre du Petit Jour
Halle du Pin
Halle
Théâtre Municipal
Musée des Beaux-Arts
Église des Jacobins
Esplanade du Gravier
River Garonne
BOULEVARD SYLVAIN-DUMON
BOULEVARD SCALIGER
PONT DE LA LIBÉRATION
AVENUE HENRI-BARBUSSE
AVENUE JEAN-JAURÈS
BOULEVARD DE LA RÉPUBLIQUE
BOULEVARD PRÉSIDENT CARNOT
COURS DU 14 JUILLET
COURS VICTOR-HUGO
COURS WASHINGTON
BOULEVARD DE LA LIBERTÉ
BOULEVARD EUGÈNE-PELLETAN
AVENUE DU GÉNÉRAL-DE-GAULLE
COURS GAMBETTA
RUE BAUDIN
RUE DE STRASBOURG
AVENUE M. LUXEMBOURG
AV. MICHELET
QUAI BAUDIN
QUAI DU CANAL
QUAI DUNKERQUE
QUAI DR. CALABET
VOIE SUR BERGE
0 200 m
ACCOMMODATION
Des Ambans B
Camping Moulin de Mellet A
Les Îles E
Des Jacobins F
Le Périgord D
Régina C
EATING & DRINKING
Brin d'Îles 4
Crêperie Côté Cornières 3
Le Margoton 6
Mariottat 7
Osaka 1
La Part des Anges 2
Philippe Vannier 5

Accommodation

Agen has some good **hotel** options scattered around its centre, especially at the budget end, though you'll also find four-star luxury at a reasonable price. There's a clutch of chain hotels (such as *Formule 1*, *B&B* and *Campanile*) at the exit from the autoroute.

Alternatively, you can rent **houseboats** from Locaboat Plaisance on quai Dunkerque (ⓣ05.53.66.00.74, ⓦwww.locaboat.com), and make your way northwest from Agen along the Canal latéral to Buzet, Aiguillon, and Le Mas-d'Agenais, from where you can enter the River Lot. Prices vary from €860–1500 per week for a three-to-five-person boat, depending on the season and level of comfort.

Des Ambans 59 rue des Ambans ⓣ05.53.66.28.60, ⓕ05.53.87.94.01. The best value of the budget hotels, with nine small, tidy rooms; note that all but the most expensive lack an en-suite toilet. It's clean, friendly and central, which means you need to book well ahead for the summer season. Oct–March occasionally closed weekends. ❶

Camping Moulin de Mellet Eight kilometres west of Agen in Colayrac-St-Cirq ⓣ05.53.87.50.98, ⓦwww.camping-moulin-mellet.com. Friendly campsite that boasts two swimming pools and a small restaurant.

Des Îles 25 rue Baudin ⓣ05.53.47.11.33, ⓦwww.hotel-des-iles.fr. This family-run hotel boasts ten lovely, individually decorated rooms, some with a small balcony and all en suite. ❶

Des Jacobins 1 place des Jacobins ⓣ05.53.47.03.31, ⓦwww.chateau-des-jacobins.com. Oozing character, Agen's top hotel occupies an elegant nineteenth-century town house swathed in greenery beside the Jacobins church, and its rooms are decked out with antique furniture, gilt mirrors and plush fabrics. ❼

Le Périgord 42 cours du 14-Juillet ⓣ05.53.77.55.77, ⓦwww.leperigord47.com. This large hotel is stuck in a bit of a traffic island, however the rooms, decked out in country florals, are spacious, comfortable and reasonably priced. ❷

Régina 139 bd Carnot ⓣ05.53.47.07.97, ⓦwww.hotelreginagen.com. Rambling and welcoming hotel on the main road south of the station; it's best to ask for a quieter room at the back. The cheaper rooms don't have toilets, but the rest have good-sized bathrooms and modern, pale-wood furnishings, and the buffet breakfast is better than most. If you are arriving outside of reception opening hours (4–8pm weekdays, variable at weekends) call in advance to get the door code. ❶

The Town

The old centre of Agen lies on the east bank of the Garonne. It is quartered by two nineteenth-century boulevards – **boulevard de la République**, running east–west, and north–south **boulevard du Président-Carnot** – which intersect at place Goya and make for easy navigation. To the northeast stands **Cathédrale St-Caprais**, somewhat misshapen but worth a look for its finely proportioned Romanesque apse and radiating chapels. However, Agen's foremost sight lies southwest on place Dr-Esquirol: beside the exuberant, Italianate municipal theatre, the **Musée des Beaux-Arts** (daily except Tues: Oct–April 10am–12.30pm & 1.30–6pm, May–Sept 10am–6pm; €4.10; ⓣ05.53.69.47.23, ⓦwww.ville-agen/musee) is magnificently housed in four adjacent sixteenth- and seventeenth-century mansions adorned with stair turrets and Renaissance window details. Inside you'll find a rich variety of archeological exhibits, furniture and paintings – among the latter, a number of Goyas and a Tintoretto rediscovered during an inventory in 1997. Best, though, are the basement's Roman finds, which include intricate jewellery and a superb white-marble Venus.

To the west of place Dr-Esquirol, a clutch of brick and timber houses – the bricks forming neat zigzags within the timber frame – represent Agen's most attractive corner. From here a short and narrow alley, **rue Beauville**, cuts through

Festivals, events and markets

Mid-May Montauban: Alors, Chante! ⓣ05.63.63.66.77, ⓦwww.alorschante.com. Over Ascension weekend various well-known, and not-so-well-known, artists take part in this festival of French song (tickets required).

Late May or early June Moissac: Fêtes de Pentecôte ⓣ05.63.04.63.63. A traditional fair on the banks of the Tarn over the Whitsun weekend, with fireworks on the Monday night.

July and August Moissac: Les Soirs de Moissac ⓣ05.63.04.06.81. Varied programme of concerts, choral works and recitals, including world music, held in the cloister or the church of St-Pierre (tickets required).

Mid-July Villefranche-de-Rouergue: VISA Francophone ⓣ05.65.45.41.12, ⓦwww.visa-francophone.com. A one-week competition of French song held in the streets of Villefranche. Some ticket-only events, proceeds go to charity.

Mid-July Cordes-sur-Ciel: Fête du Grand Fauconnier ⓣ05.65.56.34.63, ⓦwww.grandfauconnier.com. This two-day medieval festival converts the town into a costumed extravaganza, complete with exhibitions on medieval crafts and falconry. Daily admission to the old town is €8, and you can hire medieval costumes for the occasion.

Early July to early August Montauban and around: Jazz à Montauban ⓣ05.63.63.56.56, ⓦwww.jazzmontauban.com. International jazz and blues artists play in Montauban (mostly in the Jardin des Plantes) and various other towns around the *département* (tickets required for most events). There's also a "festival off" with free concerts in the cafés and streets of Montauban.

Late July Cordes-sur-Ciel: Musique sur Ciel ⓣ05.63.56.00.75, ⓦwww.festivalmusiquesurciel.fr. Ten days of classical concerts, some by featured contemporary composers, in the church of St-Michel.

Late July to mid-August Lauzerte and around: Festival du Quercy Blanc ⓣ05.65.31.83.12. Concerts of classical and chamber music held mostly in churches around the region, including Lauzerte, Montcuq, Montpezat-de-Quercy and Castelnau-Montratier. Tickets available from local tourist offices.

End of July or start of August Lauzerte: Les Nuits de Lauzerte ⓣ05.63.94.61.94, ⓦnuitsdelauzerte.free.fr. Over the space of a weekend, Lauzerte becomes an art installation and performance space, through which you walk at night, taking your time and wandering at your own pace past street theatre, contemporary dance, music and projections. Tickets from the tourist office (€10).

Early August Villefranche-de-Rouergue and around: Festival en Bastides ⓣ05.65.45.76.74, ⓦwww.espaces-culturels.fr. Five days of contemporary theatre and performance art animate the streets of Villefranche and Najac, amongst other places. Some ticketed events, information from any participating tourist office.

Third weekend in September Moissac: Fête du Chasselas and Fête des Fruits et des Légumes ⓣ05.63.04.63.63. Every year the Fête du Chasselas celebrates the local grape, with tastings on offer and a competition to find the pick of the bunch; the event takes place in the market hall. Every two years (in the odd years) the whole range of local fruits plus vegetables are also on display and there are all manner of related events throughout the town.

Second weekend in October Auvillar: Marché Potier ⓣ05.63.39.57.33 Some forty exhibitors take part in this important pottery fair held on the place de la Halle.

Markets

The main **markets** in the region are at Agen (Sat & Sun); Aiguillon (Tues & Fri); Cordes (Sat); Laguépie (Wed & Sun); Lauzerte (Wed & Sat); Moissac (Sat & Sun); Montauban (Weds & Sat); Montcuq (Sun); Nérac (Sat); St-Antonin-Noble-Val (Sun); St-Nicolas-de-la-Grave (Mon); and Villefranche-de-Rouergue (Thurs).

to rue Richard-Coeur-de-Lion, with more eye-catching facades and the **Église des Jacobins**. This big, brick Dominican church was founded by Dominican monks in the thirteenth century, then served as the Protestants' headquarters before being used as a prison during the Revolution. It now forms an annexe of the Musée des Beaux-Arts and hosts temporary art exhibitions (daily except Tues 2–6pm; prices vary). Inside, you can see unusual Gothic frescoes of leaves and geometric patterns in trompe-l'oeil on the walls and ceiling.

Continuing westwards you reach the river and the public gardens of **Esplanade du Gravier**, where a footbridge crosses the Garonne – from it you can see a 550-metre **canal bridge** dating from 1843 further downstream.

Eating, drinking and entertainment

The best place to look for somewhere to **eat** in Agen is within the rough semi-circle between boulevard de la République, rue des Cornières and rue Emile Sentini, plus along rue La Fayette and its extension rue Camille Desmoulins running east from boulevard Carnot. Ethnic restaurants and fast-food outlets sit on rue Voltaire and rue Garonne further west, while there are a couple of decent cafés on boulevard de la République and at its western junction with avenue du Général-de-Gaulle.

With no fewer than three **theatres**, Agen has a reputation for its thespian activities. The main Théâtre Municipal, place Dr-Esquirol (Ⓣ05.53.66.26.60, Ⓦwww.agen.fr), puts on a varied programme of theatre, dance, concerts and opera by local and national artists, while the Théâtre du Jour, 21 rue Paulin-Régnier (Ⓣ05.53.47.82.08, Ⓦwww.theatredujour.fr), stages more innovative works and doubles as a drama school. Last but not least, the Théâtre du Petit Jour, 49 rue des Cornières (Ⓣ05.53.47.82.08, Ⓦwww.theatredujour.fr), offers a variety of children's entertainment.

Brin d'Îles rue des Cailles Ⓣ05.53.87.79.65. This restaurant is popular for its smattering of Creole dishes, including particularly good desserts such as fruit kebabs and carpaccio of pineapple. The menu changes weekly. Daily menu €17.50. Closed Sun, Mon & Sat lunch.

Crèperie Côté Cornières 5 rue des Cornières Ⓣ05.53.66.52.37. Simple restaurant serving a range of sweet and savoury *crêpes* from about €7.40. Their speciality is a sweet pancake with caramel made from salted butter.

Le Margoton 52 rue Richard-Cœur-de-Lion Ⓣ05.53.48.11.55, Ⓦwww.lemargoton.com. Stylish little place near the Jacobins church, serving a good range of seafood in addition to rich game dishes such as guinea fowl, pigeon and venison. Menus range from €16.50 to €35, or around €30 from the *carte*. Closed lunchtime Sat & Sun, & Mon, also late Dec to early Jan & the last two weeks in Aug.

Mariottat 25 rue Louis Vivent Ⓣ05.53.77.99.77, Ⓦwww.restaurant-mariottat.com. Agen's most elegant restaurant occupies a grand old villa with sumptuous interior to the south of the Jacobins church. They concentrate on mostly local produce, including duck in all its guises, with beautifully presented menus starting at a very reasonable €27 at lunchtime on weekdays, rising to €40 and above in the evenings and at weekends. Eating à la *carte* will set you back about €70. Closed Sun eve, Mon & lunchtime Wed & Sat. Also closed Feb school hols.

Osaka 38 bd Sylvain Dumon Ⓣ05.53.66.31.76, Ⓦwww.osaka-agen.com. Japanese place opposite the station serving good sushi, *teppanyaki* and noodle soups. Menus start at just €8.90 at lunchtime, though à la carte is reasonably pricey. Closed Mon.

La Part des Anges 14 rue Emile Sentini Ⓣ05.53.68.31.00, Ⓦwww.lapartdesanges.eu. This refined little restaurant is the place to go for well-prepared and presented local dishes, such as black Gascon pork, beef from Duras and cheeses aged on the premises. In summer they put a few tables outside in the pedestrian-only street.

Philippe Vannier 66 rue Camille Desmoulins Ⓣ05.53.66.63.70, Ⓦwww.philippe-vannier.com. A stylish restaurant with a cool, art-lined dining room. There's a good-value lunchtime *formule* for €20 and the inventive menu includes langoustines marinaded in lime, and a range of terrifically indulgent desserts such as chocolate mousse with orange and mango jam. Closed Sun eve and Sat lunchtime.

Pruneaux d'Agen

Agen grew rich at first on the trade of manufactured goods, such as cloth and leather, flowing through its river port, but the industrial revolution put paid to all that and since then the town's prosperity has been based on agriculture – in particular, its famous **prunes** and **plums**. Plums (*prunes* in French) were introduced to France by Crusaders returning from Syria in the eleventh century. It is believed that Benedictine monks at Clairac, near the confluence of the Lot and Garonne, were the first to cultivate the fruit, a variety known as *prune d'Ente*, which thrives on sun, high humidity and chalky soils and is also excellent for drying thanks to its size and high sugar content. Though plums now grow throughout the region, the dried fruit (*pruneaux*) were originally exported via the port at Agen – and are thus known as **pruneaux d'Agen**.

Nowadays **prunes** are one of the region's principal money-spinners and in late August the orchards are a hive of activity as the ripe fruit are shaken from the trees. They are dried slowly in hot-air ovens to retain the flavour – during which process they lose three-quarters of their weight. Even so, the biggest prunes weigh in at 20g.

You can learn more facts and figures about prune production in the specialist *confiseries* of Agen (see below) and also at an enjoyable **farm-museum**, Au Pruneau Gourmand (daily, mid-March to mid-Oct 9am–noon & 2–7pm, Sun 3–7pm; mid-Oct to mid-March Mon–Sat 9am–noon & 2–6.30pm, Sun 2–6.30pm; closed last 2 weeks in Jan; €3.60; Ⓦwww.musee-du-pruneau.com), near the village of Granges-sur-Lot, 10km northeast of Aiguillon (see p.324). In mid-September, nearby St-Aubin hosts a fair devoted to the prune, lasting several days. Call Monflanquin tourist office (Ⓣ05.53.49.55.80) for information.

Markets and shopping

A fresh produce **market** takes place daily (except Mon) in the covered market on place Jean-Baptiste Durand. There is also a large farmers' market held on Wednesday and Sunday mornings in the Halle du Pin, beside place du 14-Juillet, as well as a smaller one on Saturday mornings on the Esplanade du Gravier, and an organic market, also on Saturdays, on place des Laitiers, off boulevard de la République. The most interesting of several agricultural fairs are the *foire de la prune* (first or second Mon after Sept 15), devoted to plums and prunes, and the *foire aux oies et canards gras* (second Sun in Dec) for foie gras and all manner of products made from duck and goose. The fairs take place in varying locations around the town centre; contact the tourist office for further information.

For picnic supplies there is a lovely bakery at the junction of boulevard Carnot and cours Washington, and although there is also a boucherie a few doors down from there you're better off heading to the charcuterie at 39 rue Voltaire near the museum, which has a wide range of tempting salad options.

The main **shopping** streets are boulevard de la République and boulevard du Président-Carnot, while pedestrianized rue Molinier, south of the cathedral, has a few smarter boutiques. *The* thing to buy in Agen is prunes (see box above). You'll find them in the markets and at a number of specialist shops, including Confiserie P. Boisson (20 rue Grande-Horloge; closed Sun), southwest of the cathedral, which opened in 1835 and still uses traditional methods to produce chocolate prunes, truffle prunes, prunes in armagnac and stuffed prunes, amongst other delicacies. You can also ask to see a short explanatory film in English.

Listings

Airport Airlinair (ⓦwww.airlinair.com) operates flights to Paris from Agen's La Garenne airport, 3km southwest of centre.
Bike rental Méca Plus, 18–20 av du Général-de-Gaulle ⓣ05.53.47.76.76, ⓦwww.comptoir-du-deux-roues.fr; closed Sun.
Bus information For up-to-date bus schedules ask at the tourist office or phone the transport desk of the Conseil Général on ⓣ05.53.69.42.03.
Car rental Avis, 12 bd Sylvain Dumon and at the airport (ⓣ05.53.47.76.47), and Europcar, 120 bd du Président-Carnot (ⓣ05.53.47.37.40), have outlets near the train station.
Hospital Centre Hospitalier, rte de Villeneuve, located 1.5km northeast of central Agen on the N21 to Villeneuve-sur-Lot (ⓣ05.53.69.70.71).
Internet Nauteus, 83 Cours Victor Hugo ⓣ05.53.87.96.55; Mon–Fri 10am–8pm, Sat 2–8pm, Sun 2–6pm, or more cheaply at the library nearby on place Armand Fallières, though opening hours are limited especially in July & Aug.
Police Commissariat de Police, 4 rue Palissy, to the south of the old quarter (ⓣ05.53.68.17.00).
Post office 72 bd du Président-Carnot.
Taxis There is a taxi stand at the station or call Agen Taxis 9 on ⓣ06.09.37.07.74.

Nérac

Thirty kilometres across high, rolling hills to the southwest of Agen, you come to the castle town of **NÉRAC** on the banks of the River Baïse. It's hard to believe that this drowsy backwater, seat of the **d'Albret** family, once matched the Parisian court in its splendour and extravagance, or that the bitter rivalries between Protestant and Catholic were played out here. Nowadays, it's an attractive and prosperous little place, where you can happily spend a few hours wandering the riverbanks and what's left of the d'Albrets' **castle**.

The d'Albrets first came to Nérac around 1150 and over the next three centuries grew to become one of Aquitaine's most powerful dynasties – largely through a talent for marrying well. First they gained the Pyrenean kingdom of Navarre by marriage, and then in 1527 Henri II d'Albret wed **Marguerite d'Angoulême**, sister to King François I of France. Intelligent and cultured, Marguerite filled her Nérac court with scholars and proponents of the new Protestant faith, including Jean Chauvin (John Calvin) who stayed here briefly in 1534. Neither Henri nor Marguerite converted, but their determined and ambitious daughter, **Jeanne d'Albret**, did so in 1560, thus making Nérac an important Protestant stronghold. Jeanne's son, also Henri, for his part married the young and beautiful **Marguerite de Valois**, sister of the king of France and Catherine de Médicis, in 1572 and so ushered in Nérac's golden era. Their court glittered with eminent writers, diplomats and nobles, poets and musicians, while Henri indulged in the innumerable amorous conquests that earned him the nickname *Le Vert Galant*; Queen Margot, as she was called, was no retiring violet either, and the marriage was eventually annulled in 1599, by which time Henri had become **Henri IV** of France and removed his court to Paris.

Arrival and information

Buses from Agen (Citram ⓣ05.56.43.68.43) stop on the central place de la Libération next to the château, while the **tourist office** is located opposite on avenue Mondenard (May, June & Sept Tues–Sat 9am–noon & 2–6pm, Sun 10am–noon & 3–5pm; July & Aug Mon–Sat 9am–7pm, Sun 10am–12.30pm & 3–5.30pm; Oct–April Tues–Fri 9am–noon & 2–6pm, Sat same hours but closing at 5pm; ⓣ05.53.65.27.75, ⓦwww.albret-tourisme.com). In summer you can rent pleasure **boats** at the port through Les Croisières du Prince Henry (ⓣ05.53.65.66.66, ⓦwww.croisieresduprincehenry.com), for €90 for half a day or €130 for a whole day for 2–7 people. If you don't want to captain, take a cruise with commentary on a traditional *gabarre* a short distance up the Baïse to the first lock and back (1hr; April–Oct; €7.50). There's also a **tourist train**, the Train Touristique de l'Albret (ⓣ06.85.62.77.47, ⓦwww.lafrancevuedurail.fr/ttalbret) that runs the thirteen kilometres southwest from the **gare SNCF** to the medieval village of Mézin. The journey takes an hour and a half and there's a guided commentary in French (July & Aug daily 10.30am except Mon & Sat, 2.30pm & 4.45pm; April–June & Sept–Oct times vary – call for details; €6.50 single, €8.50 return). You can check **internet** in the Espace d'Albret overlooking the quay.

Accommodation

Hôtel d'Albret 40 allée d'Albret ⓣ05.53.97.41.10, ⓦwww.logis-de-france.fr. On the wide boulevard a couple of minutes' walk southwest of the centre, this welcoming, family-run place has a wide choice of rooms and a cheerful restaurant serving well-priced regional menus from €11 (closed Fri & Sun eves). ❷

Hôtel du Château 7 av Mondenard ⓣ05.53.65.09.05, ⓦwww.logis-de-france.fr. Centrally located on the main road west of the Pont-Neuf, and the most comfortable accommodation in Nérac. Quieter rooms are at the back. It also has a swanky restaurant with menus from €12.50 (Sept–June closed Sat lunch and for dinner Fri & Sun). Closed 2 weeks in winter. ❸

Auberge du Pont Vieux 19 rue Séderie ⓣ05.53.97.51.04, ⓦwww.vieux-pont.com. Comfortable, old-fashioned rooms with wooden shutters and flower-draped balconies overlooking the river, as well as a restaurant with good-value menus from €15 (restaurant closed Mon and eves Sat & Sun from Jan–March). ❹

The Town

Throughout their glory days, the d'Albrets added to their **château** (daily 10am–6pm; €4) on the river's west bank, at the far end of the bridge coming into Nérac from Agen. By the sixteenth century they had made it into a comfortable palace, of which only the north wing with its Renaissance gallery still exists, the other three having been partially destroyed in 1621 and finished off during the Revolution. It now houses a local history museum, of which the most interesting displays relate to Henri, Queen Margot and their larger-than-life relatives.

To the north of the château stands the Neoclassical **Église St-Nicolas** which was built in the mid-eighteenth century and contains some attractive nineteenth-century stained-glass windows, depicting scenes from the Old and New Testaments. From the terrace here you get good views of the triple-arched **Pont-Vieux** and the ancient roofs of the area known as **Petit-Nérac** on the opposite side of the river. It's worth wandering over the bridge and turning right along rue Séderie, where the wooden balconies of old tanneries overhang the river, to come out beside Nérac "port", now bustling with cruise boats in summer, below the Pont-Neuf.

Continuing south from the port across the main road, avenue Georges Clemenceau, a shady woodland path, leads 1.5km along the riverbank. **La Garenne**, as the area is known, was laid out as a royal pleasure park in the sixteenth century. The aviaries of exotic birds, the arbours and minstrels have long gone, but it's still a pleasant place to stroll or picnic. Not far from the entrance, look out for the **Fontaine de Fleurette**, marked by a statue of a prostrate and scantily clad young woman. According to legend, Fleurette was a gardener's daughter who had the misfortune to be seduced by *Le Vert Galant* and, when his attentions drifted elsewhere, drowned herself in the river. The inscription reads: "She gave him all her life. He gave her but one day."

For the more adventurous, Cap Cauderoue (ⓣ05.53.65.52.74, ⓦwww.cap-cauderoue.com) just outside Nérac is home to a treetop adventure playground, where visitors make their way, via ropes and swings, around an obstacle course high above the ground. The site also offers **mountain biking**, archery and **canoeing**.

Eating and drinking

For delicious, beautifully made chocolatey goodies, head for *Chocolaterie Artisanale la Cigale,* 2 rue Calvin, a couple of minutes' walk south of the *gare SNCF* (Tues–Fri 9am–noon & 2–6.30pm; ⓣ05.53.65.15.73).

L'Escadron Volant 7 rue Henri IV ⓣ05.53.97.19.04. Salads and sweet *crêpes* in addition to the standard duck-based dishes, in a prime spot facing the château entrance. Nov–April weekdays open for lunch only.

Le Relais de la Hire 10km southeast of Nérac in the lovely village of Francescas ⓣ05.53.65.41.59, ⓦwww.la-hire.com. Probably the best place to eat in the area, where you can feast on such dishes as roast spiced turbot with caramelised onions in an elegant eighteenth-century house or its flower-filled garden; the lunch menu starts at €14.50, or you can eat à la *carte* for around €50. They also offer cookery classes, and it's worth allowing the time to wander round the village. Closed Tues, Wed & Sun eves & Mon.

Le Vert Galant 11 rue Séderie ⓣ05.53.65.31.99. Does a nice line in *tartines* – toasted bread with a huge range of things to pile on top – accompanied by regional produce (the speciality of the house is *tartine* with duck confit, pear and bacon). It also serves over fifty flavours of ice cream, including tomato and basil, Camembert, and pumpkin.

Downstream from Agen

East of Agen the Garonne is sandwiched between the autoroute, two busy main roads, and the Bordeaux train line, which doesn't make for a particularly scenic journey. If you're headed this way, however, there is a clutch of interesting places to stop en route. Near the confluence of the Baïse and the Garonne lies the wine town of **Buzet-sur-Baïse**, where the local wine co-operative merits a visit, while over on the Garonne's east bank, **Aiguillon**'s eighteenth-century château presides over the junction of the Garonne and Lot rivers. From Aiguillon it's worth continuing downstream as far as attractive **Le Mas-d'Agenais**, which overlooks both the Canal latéral and the Garonne from the west, and has wonderful carvings and a little oil painting inside its church.

Buzet-sur-Baïse

BUZET-SUR-BAÏSE lies roughly 30km west of Agen, in the shadow of the Château de Buzet (not open to the public), which stands high on the green hillside, now separated from its village by the autoroute. Buzet itself is rather dull, but as the vines on this south bank of the Garonne indicate, you're back in wine country and you shouldn't miss the chance to visit the local **wine co-operative**, Les Vignerons de Buzet (July & Aug Mon–Sat 9am–12.30pm & 2–7; Sept–June Mon–Sat 9am–noon & 2–6pm; ⓣ05.53.84.74.30, ⓦwww.vignerons-buzet.fr), east of the village on the D642. Founded in 1953, this is France's largest wine co-operative, with around three hundred growers producing fourteen million bottles on average per year. The majority are strong red wines which benefit from ageing – Grande Réserve, Baron d'Ardeuil and Château de Gueyze stand out among the many award-winning wines produced by the co-operative (free **tastings** available). It's also well worth arranging for one of their exceptionally informative **guided tours** of the vinification plant and *chais* (July & Aug daily 10am & 3pm; Sept–June by appointment only; visits in English on request ⓣ05.53.84.17.16).

The other reason to visit Buzet is to rent a **boat** for a trip along the Canal latéral, the Baïse or the Lot. Aquitaine Navigation (ⓣ05.53.84.72.50, ⓦwww.aquitaine-navigation.com), based at the *halte nautique* on the canal below Buzet village, has small pleasure boats for rent hourly and by the half-day or day, as well as houseboats for longer excursions (prices vary seasonally).

Before setting off, you might want to refuel at one of Buzet's **restaurants**. The nicest option is *Le Vigneron*, on the broad main street (ⓣ05.53.84.73.46; closed Sun eve & Mon), which offers well-priced menus, kicking off with a four-course *menu du jour* at €14.80 (€20.80 on Sun) including an hors-d'oeuvre buffet and a dessert trolley stacked with delectable home-made desserts – the house special is a confection of *crêpes* layered with *crème patissière*, coated in meringue and baked.

Aiguillon

Six kilometres north of Buzet on the opposite bank, the hilltop town of **AIGUILLON** stands guard over the confluence of the Lot and Garonne rivers as it has done at least since Roman times. Nowadays Aiguillon's most imposing building is the eighteenth-century, Neoclassical **Château des Ducs** – now a school – which dominates the western approach to the town. It was built by the duc d'Aiguillon who, having served as an army chief and governor of Brittany under Louis XV, returned to transform his medieval château into a mini-Versailles, though the grand balls and other festivities were soon cut short by the Revolution. The small area of medieval lanes with their half-timbered houses to the north of the château is worth a wander, and the church next to the Château boasts a lovely, delicate organ.

Aiguillon's **gare SNCF**, on the Agen–Bordeaux train line, lies a couple of minutes' walk below the château to the southwest along avenue de la Gare. You'll find the **tourist office** beside the château on the central place du 14-Juillet (opening times vary but open daily in summer; ⓣ05.53.79.62.58, ⓦwww.ville-aiguillon.eu). If you want to **stay**, *La Terrasse de l'Étoile*, 8 cours Alsace-Lorraine (ⓣ05.53.79.64.64, ⓦwww.logis-de-france.fr; ③), occupies a handsome stone and brick building at the east end of place du 14-Juillet; they have a small pool and a good traditional restaurant (menus from €12). The market takes place on Tuesdays and Fridays.

Le Mas-d'Agenais

From Aiguillon, rather than taking the dreary N113, cross to the Garonne's west bank and follow the D427 northwest for 15km through orchards and poplar plantations to find another ancient village perched above the Garonne, **LE MAS-D'AGENAIS**. Traces of its ramparts still remain, but Le Mas' pride and joy is its cobbled central square with its old wooden *halle* and Romanesque **Église St-Vincent**. At first glance, the church's muddle of brick and stone and its truncated tower don't look like much, but there's a surprising amount to see inside. Firstly, the exceptionally expressive carved capitals all around the choir and the triple-vaulted nave, depicting scenes such as Daniel in the lions' den, Abraham's sacrifice and David and Goliath. Then, in the southwest corner of the nave, there's a white-marble sarcophagus covered with geometric designs, which is said to have held the remains of St Vincent, the third-century evangelist, to whom the church is dedicated. But what most people come to see is a tiny painting in the north apsidal chapel: the *Crucifixion* by **Rembrandt**. Dated 1631, the painting was donated to the church by a former parishioner in 1804; it belongs to a series of seven Stations of the Cross, the other six of which are in Munich. Christ is caught in a ray of light against an almost black background, his upturned face revealing the full agony of his question, "My God, why have you forsaken me?"

The Canal latéral runs immediately below Le Mas to the east, between the river cliffs and the Garonne. Here, beside the lock just north of the bridge over the Garonne, you'll find another **boating** centre, where Crown Blue Line (Ⓣ04.68.94.52.72, Ⓦwww.crownblueline.com) has houseboats for rent. The canal itself makes a pretty route westwards, but otherwise there's little reason to stop beyond Le Mas until you reach La Réole, 30km downstream (see p.106).

Moissac and around

There is little of historical interest left in the modern town of **MOISSAC**, some 40km southeast of Agen, largely because of the terrible damage wreaked by the flood of 1930, when the Tarn, swollen by a sudden thaw in the Massif Central, burst its banks, destroying 617 houses and killing more than a hundred people. Luckily, the cloister and porch of the Benedictine **abbey church of St-Pierre**, a masterpiece of Romanesque sculpture and model for dozens of churches throughout the region, survived to make Moissac a household name in the history of art. The flat plains to the south and west of Moissac are less exciting, not least because of the looming presence of a nuclear power plant, but there are, nevertheless, a couple of places worth visiting along the banks of the Garonne: **St-Nicolas-de-la-Grave**, for its nature reserve and little museum devoted to the founder of Detroit, after whom Cadillac cars were named, and **Auvillar** for its exquisite market square.

Moissac is well served by **public transport**, with train connections to Toulouse and Agen. For the rest of the region you'll be reliant on your own transport or taxis.

Arrival and information

Moissac's **gare SNCF** lies about 500m west of the centre along avenue Pierre Chabrié; from the station follow this road east and, where it curves northwards, you'll see steps leading down to the church square. The **tourist office**, 6 place Durand-de-Bredon (daily: April–June & Oct 9am–noon & 2–6pm; Sept 9am–6pm; July & Aug 9am–7pm; Nov–March 10am–noon & 2–5pm; Ⓣ05.63.04.01.85, Ⓦwww.moissac.fr), at the west end of the church, has details of Moissac's festivals (see box, p.318) and of concerts taking place in the church and cloister in the summer months. You can rent **bicycles** from Moissac-Loisirs, 29 rue Malaveille (Ⓣ05.63.04.03.48), on the north side of the market square. **Internet** is available at Video Pilote, 8 rue Camille Delthil (Tues–Fri 3–8pm; Sat 10.30am–noon & 3–8pm).

Accommodation

Le Chapon Fin 3 place des Récollets Ⓣ05.63.04.04.22, Ⓦwww.inter-fr.com. Situated on the south side of the market square, this comfortable hotel offers clean, simple rooms. ❸

Ile du Bidounet Ⓣ05.63.32.52.52, Ⓦwww.camping-moissac.com. A good-value, shady three-star campsite on a little island 2km from central Moissac across the Pont-Napoléon. Closed Oct–March.

Le Luxembourg 2 av Pierre Chabrié Ⓣ05.63.04.00.27, Ⓦwww.hoteluxembourg82.com. A nicely old-fashioned place halfway along the road to the station, though it suffers slightly from road noise and the train tracks running behind, despite double-glazing. Even if you're not staying here, the restaurant is worth a visit for its good-value traditional meals (menus €12.50 lunchtime, €20–30 in the evenings; closed Sun & Mon eves). ❷

Manoir Saint Jean Saint-Paul d'Espis Ⓣ05.63.05.02.34, Ⓦwww.manoirsaintjean.com. Nine kilometres north of Moissac, the manor is set in its own attractive grounds and offers nine suites, all individually decorated with plush furnishings, paintings and chandeliers. There is also a first-rate restaurant (menus from €38) serving delicious

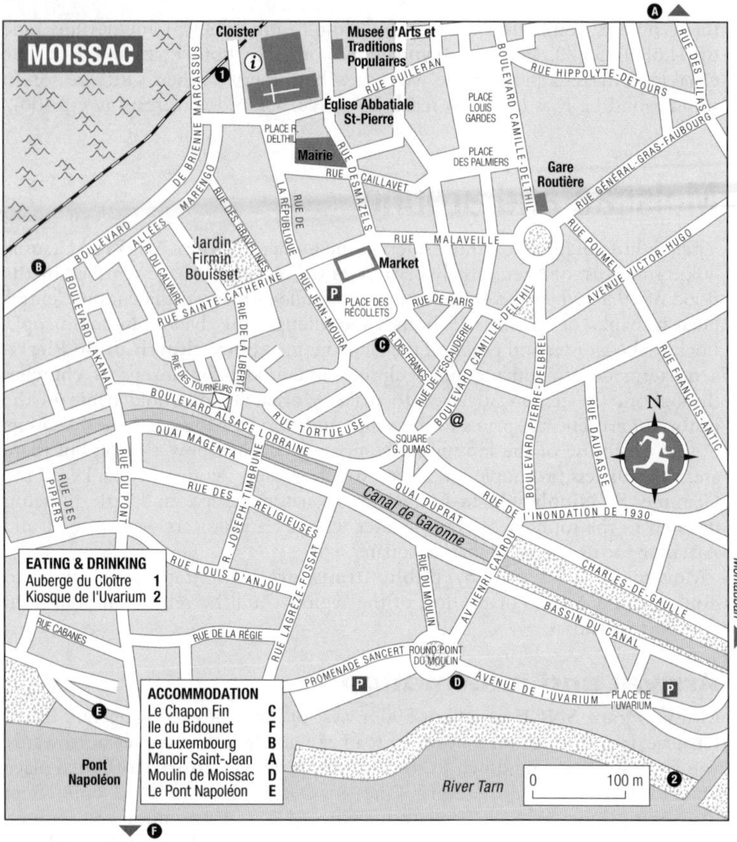

seasonal produce – organic wines, meat and wild fish with fresh herbs from the garden. ❽

Moulin de Moissac Esplanade du Moulin ☎05.63.32.88.88, Ⓦwww.lemoulindemoissac.com. Occupying a former water-mill just east of the Pont-Napoléon, this is the nicest hotel in town. It's a large, not hugely attractive building, but inside has been beautifully refurbished and the rooms have very comfortable beds, swish bathrooms and mod-cons such as DVD players. It also boasts a spa and a decent restaurant (lunch menus from €23, eves from €28; closed Sat lunch & Sun). ❺

Le Pont Napoléon 2 allée Montebello ☎05.63.04.01.55, Ⓦwww.le-pont-napoleon.com. A few very classy rooms above a fine restaurant (menus from €28, or around €46 à la carte; closed one or two days a week Oct–March), beside the bridge. The hotel overlooks a busy road, but inside, all is calm. ❸

The Town

Moissac sits with its back to the old river cliffs on the north bank of the Tarn just before its confluence with the Garonne. The town's compact centre is bordered to the south by the Canal lateral, to the east by boulevard Camille Delthil and to the west by boulevard Lakanal, at the south end of which Pont-Napoléon carries road traffic over the Tarn. Moissac's main east-west thoroughfare, named rue Gambetta in the west, rue Ste-Catherine and then rue Malaveille, brings you into the central market square, **place des**

Récollets, where you'll find the most convenient car park. From this square, rue de la République leads north towards the red-brick belfry of the **Église Abbatiale St-Pierre**.

Eglise Abbatiale St-Pierre

Legend has it that Clovis first founded a church here in 506, though it seems more probable that its origins belong to the seventh century, which saw the foundation of so many monasteries throughout Aquitaine. The first Romanesque church on the site was consecrated in 1063 and enlarged the following century when Moissac became a stop on the Santiago de Compostela pilgrim route. Since then the church has survived countless wars, including siege and sack by Simon de Montfort in 1212, during the Crusade against the Cathars. Indeed, the fact that it is still standing at all is something of a miracle. During the Revolution the cloister was used as a gunpowder factory and billet for soldiers, who damaged many of the carvings, while in the 1850s it only escaped demolition to make way for the Bordeaux–Toulouse train line by a whisker.

Apart from the dumpy, red-brick belfry, the first thing you see approaching from the town centre is the great stone arc of the **south porch**, with its magnificent tympanum, completed in 1130. It depicts Christ in majesty, right hand raised in benediction, the Book resting on his knee, surrounded by the Evangelists and the 24 elders of the Apocalypse – every one different – as described by St John in the Book of Revelation. Below, the central pillar bears the figures of St Paul and St Jeremiah, the latter with the most beautifully doleful face imaginable, in the same elongated style as at Souillac (see p.237).

There is more fine carving on the capitals inside the porch, and the **interior** of the church, which was remodelled in the fifteenth century, is painted with intricate patterns and filled with interesting wood and stone statuary. The most outstanding are those in the second chapel on the right as you enter: a lovely stone pietà in which Mary, enveloped in pastel blue, holds her son gently in her arms, and an equally compelling statue of Mary Magdalene with one arm outstretched and a thick tress of hair falling round her knees.

The adjoining **cloister** (same hours as tourist office – see p.325; €6) is accessed through the tourist office, behind the church to the west, where you can see a ten-minute video (in English on request) describing its main features. The cloister surrounds a garden shaded by a majestic cedar, and its pantile roof is supported by 76 alternating single and double marble columns. Each column supports a single inverted wedge-shaped block of stone, on which are carved, with extraordinary delicacy, all manner of animals and plant motifs, as well as 46 scenes from the Bible and the lives of the saints, among them Daniel in the lions' den, the Evangelists, fishermen on Lake Galilee, St Peter being crucified upside down and the decapitation of John the Baptist. Despite the damage done during the Revolution, they are in amazingly good shape. An inscription on the middle pillar on the west side explains that the cloister was constructed in the time of the Abbot Ansquitil in the Year of Our Lord 1100.

Musée d'Arts et Traditions Populaires

The same ticket for the church gains you entry to the rather less interesting **Musée Marguerite Vidal d'Arts et Traditions Populaires** (open daily except Mon, Nov–March 2–5pm, April–June & Sept–Oct 10am–noon & 2–6pm, July & Aug daily 10am–1pm & 3–7pm), housed in the former abbots' palace on rue de l'Abbaye immediately northeast of the church. Apart from a good collection of local ceramics, including faïence from Auvillar (see opposite), it contains a hotchpotch of furniture, ecclesiastical robes and religious treasures, portraits of old Moissac residents and a mock-up of a Quercy farmhouse interior.

Eating and drinking

The square outside the abbey boasts a variety of **restaurants**, though most are only open at lunchtimes. In fine weather, **eat** at the magnolia-shaded *Auberge du Cloître*, on place Durand-de-Bredon beside the tourist office (closed Mon & Wed & Sun eves), serving incredibly fresh local produce, some from the chef's own garden (weekday lunch menus from €8.50, others from €21). The *Kiosque de L'Uvarium*, on avenue de L'Uvarium by the river, has a large terrace and serves grills, salads and pastas, all at around €10.50. The adjoining outdoor entertainment space hosts a variety of events on summer evenings, such as theatre, Latin dance displays and even hip-hop. You'll find other good eating options at the hotel restaurants mentioned on p.325.

For picnic fodder, there's a small fresh produce **market** in the covered hall on place des Récollets daily except Monday, while on Saturday and Sunday mornings farmers' stalls fill the whole square, a marvel of colour and temptation. You'll also find a boulangerie and boucherie at the bottom of rue Jean Moura, near the Square G. Dumas.

St-Nicolas-de-la-Grave

Eight kilometres southwest of Moissac, the small *bastide* of **ST-NICOLAS-DE-LA-GRAVE** is dominated by a four-square château atop a low rise on the far side of the Garonne. Its oldest tower – the fattest of the four, on the northeast corner – is attributed to Richard the Lionheart, who passed through here on his return from the Third Crusade in the late 1100s. Nowadays, however, it houses the *mairie*, and there's nothing to see inside.

St-Nicolas is prouder of its second claim to fame as the home town of **Antoine Laumet**, founder of Detroit in America, who was born here in 1658. His birthplace, just southwest of the central square, now contains the **Musée Lamothe-Cadillac** (July & Aug daily 10am–12.30pm & 3–6.30pm; Sept–June ask the tourist office – see below; free), worth a quick look in passing as much for the story of Laumet's life as for any of the exhibits, which comprise mock-ups of a period bedroom and kitchen, and masses of documentation, some of it in English. Laumet was an adventurer who, on leaving for Canada in 1683, adopted the upper-crust name of de Lamothe-Cadillac. He later turned up in America in the service of King Louis XIV, where he founded a number of forts, among them a cavalry outpost called *le détroit* between lakes Erie and Huron in 1701. Two hundred years later, a Detroit car company was looking for a name at the same time as the city was celebrating its anniversary. They decided to honour Detroit's founding father, and thus were Cadillacs born.

The **tourist office** is on place du Platane in front of the château (July & Aug daily 10am–12.30pm & 3–6.30pm; Sept–June Mon 8am–12.30pm, Tues–Fri 2–6pm, outside these hours the *mairie* will provide information; ⓣ05.63.94.82.81, ⓦwww.stnicolasdelag.online.fr). St-Nicolas has no hotels, but the tourist office has details of *chambres d'hôtes* and there's a decent two-star **campsite** (ⓣ05.63.95.50.00, ⓦwww.cg82.fr/?page=sport; closed mid-Sept to mid-June) 2km north of the village where the Garonne and Tarn rivers form a large lake; the campsite is part of a leisure complex with **canoe** and **bike rental** amongst other facilities, and you can also go **bird-watching** in the adjacent nature reserve. If you need somewhere to **eat**, try *Le Cadillac*, on the village's northwest corner; it's a simple place serving pizzas, grills, salads and a good hors-d'oeuvre buffet on the €12 *menu du jour* (closed Mon).

Auvillar

AUVILLAR, 14km west of St-Nicolas, is perched on a cliff on the Garonne's south bank. Its feudal château and ramparts were demolished in the eighteenth and nineteenth centuries, but thankfully the wonderful old village centre remains. From the main road skirting south of the village, you duck under the seventeenth-century **Tour de l'Horloge** to find yourself in the gently sloping triangular-shaped **place de la Halle** surrounded by a harmonious ensemble of brick and timber buildings with arcades running all around. At the square's cobbled centre stands a pleasing circular stone-pillared market hall, built in the early nineteenth century. While you're here it's worth poking your nose into the **Musée du Vieil Auvillar** (mid-April to mid-Oct daily except Tues 2.30–6.30pm; mid-Oct to mid-April Sat & Sun 2.30–5.30pm; €2), on the square's north side, for its collection of local pottery. Auvillar was already known for its pottery production in the sixteenth century, but in the following century they began making *faïence* of sufficiently high quality to rival that imported from Holland and Italy. Local potters still have a good reputation, as witnessed by the big pottery fair held every October (see box, p.318).

Auvillar's **tourist office** is on place de la Halle next to the museum (daily: April to mid-Oct 10am–12.30pm & 2–5.30pm, mid-June to mid-Oct till 7pm; mid-Oct to March 2–5.30pm, closed Mon; Ⓣ05.63.39.89.82, Ⓦwww.auvillar.com). For somewhere to **stay** or **eat**, head for the *Hôtel de l'Horloge* (Ⓣ05.63.39.91.61, Ⓦmonsite.wanadoo.fr/horlogeauvillar; ❸; restaurant closed Fri & lunch on Sat except in July & Aug; hotel closed Fri mid-Oct to mid-April) beside the gate tower: in addition to a clutch of spacious en-suite rooms, they run a restaurant with menus from €27.

Quercy Blanc

As you head north from Moissac, the land gradually rises to gently undulating, green and woody country, cut through by parallel valleys running down to meet the Garonne and planted with vines, sunflowers and maize, as well as apple and cherry orchards. It's a very soft landscape, the villages are small and widely scattered and the pace of life seems about equal with that of a turning sunflower. This is the **Quercy Blanc**, named after the area's grey-white soils and building stone, a region with few sights, but one which lives up to the image of deepest rural France. The single most interesting place to head for is **Lauzerte**, atop a river bluff 25km north of Moissac. Further north again, **Montcuq** distinguishes itself with its solid square keep, the remnants of a twelfth-century fortress, standing guard over the medieval village, while way over to the southeast, **Montpezat-de-Quercy** is home to a Gothic church with a surprising collection of art treasures, including a beautiful and complete set of Flemish tapestries.

Public transport around Quercy Blanc consists of three separate bus services. You can reach Lauzerte from Moissac, and Montcuq from Cahors, while Montpezat is a stop on the route between Cahors and Montauban.

▲ Quercy Blanc countryside

Lauzerte and Cazes-Mondenard

The first of the sleepy hilltop villages that you reach travelling north from Moissac is **LAUZERTE**. It stands on a promontory between two rivers, a press of white-walled houses contained within its medieval ramparts, with the "new" town spilling down the south and eastern slopes. The site's strategic importance was not lost on the counts of Toulouse, who took control of Lauzerte in the late twelfth century and granted it the status of a *bastide*, with all the rights and privileges that entailed, in 1241. The other notable event in its history took place fifty years later, when the townspeople threw out the English occupiers. In reward the French king, Philippe IV, elevated Lauzerte to capital of the Bas Quercy (Lower Quercy) region and seat of the royal Seneschal. However, its heyday came to an end in the late sixteenth century when Lauzerte was demoted to a mere district capital in the aftermath of the Wars of Religion.

Nevertheless, a few vestiges of its glory days remain in the old town, which lies clustered around the pretty, arcaded central square, **place des Cornières**, and the church of **St-Barthélémy**. The church's origins go back to the thirteenth century, but it was largely rebuilt after the Protestants wreaked their havoc, and its main point of interest nowadays is the gilded Baroque altarpiece, dedicated to the Virgin Mary and depicting scenes from her life, which fills the north chapel. Behind the church, there are good views of the patchwork landscape all around from the **place du Château**, where the castle once stood on the promontory's northern tip. From here **rue de la Garrigue**, and its extension **rue de la Gendarmerie**, double back south of the church, running along the ridge past a number of thirteenth- and fourteenth-century merchants' houses with their big ground-floor arches and colonnaded windows above.

Once you've explored Lauzerte's compact centre, it's worth venturing 8km southeast to visit a quirky museum near **CAZES-MONDENARD**, a village with a pretty Gothic church. The core of the **Musée Yvan Quercy** (opening times vary, so phone to check ⓣ05.63.95.84.02; €5), at the end of a long lane signed off the D16 Molières road 2km east of the village, is its collection of hearses, which was kick-started in 1970 when Monsieur Quercy was given an old hearse. Once he'd acquired a second one, word spread, and nearby parishes rushed to offer him theirs. By the time of his death, he had amassed nearly a hundred different models, some horse-drawn, others pulled by hand, from the seventeenth century up to the first motorized model manufactured by Peugeot in 1949. His family now continue his work. The collection also includes a large number of regular carriages, all in excellent condition, and some early farm machinery. After the tour, you are offered tastings of wine, pâtés and other local produce, and in season they also serve regional meals if you book in advance.

Practicalities

There is a bus service to Lauzerte from Moissac, but it only runs on Wednesdays and Saturdays, returning to Moissac at 2pm. Buses (ⓣ05.63.04.55.50) leave from outside the Crédit Agricole bank. Otherwise, Lauzerte is only accessible by taxi or with your own transport. There is car parking in the lower section of the town, from where you can walk up to the medieval town via a series of steps, or you can drive to the top and park just outside the ramparts; from here the **tourist office** is a couple of minutes away on place des Cornières (July & Aug daily 9am–7pm; Sept–June Mon–Sat 9am–noon & 2–6pm; ⓣ05.63.94.61.94, ⓦwww.lauzerte-tourisme.fr).

The **hotel** on faubourg d'Auriac, the *Hôtel du Quercy* (ⓣ05.63.94.66.36; ❷; closed Sun evening & Mon, also Tues eve in low season, other than for reservations), has a handful of old-fashioned but perfectly comfortable rooms, and an excellent **restaurant**. In addition to traditional local dishes, such as *cassoulet*, farm chicken cooked in Cahors wine and *confit de canard*, the latter also stuffed with foie gras, they serve a good range of fish and seafood dishes and game in season; menus start at €11 at lunch and €18 in the evening; reservations are recommended. The next closest hotel is *Le Luzerta*, north of the village beside the Cahors road (ⓣ05.63.94.64.43, ⓦleluzerta.free.fr; ❷), which consists of several bungalows – functional but clean and en suite – around a pool. They also run a decent restaurant (closed Sun eve & Tues, also Nov–Feb; menus from €18).

In addition, there is another good option in the countryside around Lauzerte, the Belgian-run *Aube Nouvelle* (ⓣ05.63.04.50.33, ⓦaubenouvelle.chez.com; ❸; good restaurant from €20), in a handsome brick-built manor house 9km south of Lauzerte on the D2, just before the village of Durfort-Lacapelette.

Montcuq

Thirteen kilometres northeast of Lauzerte along the Petite-Barguelonne valley, **MONTCUQ** – pronounce the "q" if you don't want to be saying "my arse" – is built around the flanks of a conical hill, on top of which stands a huge square keep. Like Lauzerte, Montcuq guarded the ancient road to Cahors and lies on the Santiago de Compostela pilgrims' route, but it seems to have had the knack of picking the wrong cause: it sided with the Cathars, was condemned for collaborating with the English and later became a Protestant stronghold. As a result, there's not much in the way of sights, though it's an attractive little place and less touristy than Lauzerte.

To get the lie of the land the best thing to do is climb up to the newly renovated **tower** (see the tourist office for opening hours; approx €2). Any of the lanes leading uphill from rue de la Promenade, the wide boulevard to the south of the old town, will take you there. It was built at the turn of the eleventh century as part of a larger fortress, and although Louis IX ordered the ramparts destroyed, the ditches filled in and the tower's top knocked off in the aftermath of the Cathar Crusades, at 24m, it's still a fair climb. The effort is rewarded with

Montcuq Monopoly

In 2007, Hasbro, makers of **Monopoly**, opened an internet voting site to decide which towns would feature on a new French version of the game. As a joke, web users started a campaign to feature Montcuq, reasoning that most foreigners would rudely mispronounce the name. It took off, and Montcuq won – but Hasbro decided to overrule the popular vote and use Dunkerque instead. The outcry was, predictably, huge. To make up for the lack of democratic proceeding, Hasbro agreed to issue a special Montcuq version of Monopoly. The town was allowed to choose which streets would be used, and a local artist provided images. Look out for this unusual souvenir in shops around town.

all-round views; even when the tower is closed, the pinnacle of rock it stands on is high enough to give a good panorama. Wandering back down the slope through the maze of stone and half-timbered houses, the church of **St-Hilaire** stands out with its octagonal, brick tower, though there's nothing of particular interest inside.

Practicalities

Buses run to Montcuq from Cahors (Raynal Voyages; ⓣ05.65.23.28.28), stopping on rue de la Promenade near the **tourist office** (July & Aug Mon–Sat 9am–12.30pm & 3–6pm, Sun 10.30am–1pm; Sept–June Mon–Sat 9am–noon & variable afternoons; ⓣ05.65.22.94.04, ⓦwww.tourisme-montcuq.com). For a place to **stay**, try the welcoming *Hôtel du Parc* (ⓣ05.65.31.81.82, ⓦwww.hotel-restaurant-du-parc.fr; ❸; closed Nov–March), 500m west of Montcuq on the Belmont road, with old-fashioned but comfortable rooms, a big, quiet garden and a decent, resident-only **restaurant**. Should you need a new supply of reading matter, Montcuq is also home to Chiméra, an English-owned **bookshop** selling new and secondhand French and English titles; it's just off place de la République along rue du Faubourg-St-Privat – the road to Castelnau-Montratier.

Castelnau-Montratier and Montpezat-de-Quercy

The route southeast of Montcuq takes you on a roller-coaster ride across the valleys and intervening hills, on one of which stands **CASTELNAU-MONTRATIER**, 20km from Montcuq, with its incongruous neo-Byzantine church and spacious market square. Twelve kilometres further on through more country lanes you come to another, rather more interesting hilltop village, **MONTPEZAT-DE-QUERCY**. Traces of its medieval heyday remain in the arcaded central square and lanes of half-timbered houses, but the main reason to stop here is the **Collégiale St-Martin**, with its unusually rich hoard of treasures, standing at the southeast end of the promontory on which the village is built.

The church was founded in the early fourteenth century by Cardinal Pierre des Prés (1281–1361), a native of Montpezat, who grew wealthy in the service of the Avignon popes. With its high and severe single nave, the interior is unexciting, at least in comparison with the fourteenth- to sixteenth-century artworks arrayed in the side chapels. Best are the battered but still lovely *Vierge aux Colombes*, her face framed by golden ringlets, in the second chapel on the left, a polychrome pietà in the first on the right, and, next door, an English alabaster triptych depicting the Birth, Resurrection and Ascension of Christ – in the last only his feet are visible as he's whisked heavenwards. The church's finest treasures, though, are the five Flemish **tapestries** grouped around the choir. They were made specially for the church in the early sixteenth century, a gift from Jean IV des Prés, bishop of Montauban, and portray events from the life of St Martin de Tours, to whom the church is consecrated. The most famous scene is that in the first panel, where the future saint – at the time in the service of the Roman army – shares his cloak with a crippled beggar. The workmanship throughout is of superb quality, while the colours remain amazingly vibrant. Also in remarkably good condition is the white-marble sarcophagus and statue of Pierre des Prés, to the right of the choir, with his feet resting on a lion while his well-fed face is bathed in a contented grin.

Practicalities

The **tourist office** is on the west side of the town (April & Oct Tues–Fri 10.30am–12.30pm & 1.30–5.30pm; May Tues–Fri 10am–1pm & 2–7pm; June & Sept Tues–Thurs & Sun 10am–1pm & 2–7pm; July & Aug Mon 2–6pm, Tues–Sun 10am–1pm & 2–7pm; Nov–March Tues, Thurs & Sun 11am–5pm; Ⓣ05.63.02.05.55, Ⓦwww.tourisme-montpezat-de-quercy.com). Unlike many other tourist offices in the region they have plenty of information about sights outside their *département*, and the office also doubles as a Maison des Vins where you can buy the local Côteaux du Quercy wines and pick up a brochure listing vineyards to visit, though they don't offer tastings.

While there are no hotels in Montpezat, there is a very comfortable **chambre d'hôte** under French-English ownership. *Les Trois Terrasses*, rue de la Libération

▲ A Quercy Blanc *pigeonnier*

(Ⓣ05.63.02.66.21, Ⓦwww.trois-terrasses.com; ❽; closed Jan & Feb) has terraced gardens overlooking the Collégiale and inside is an intriguing mix of the contemporary and the traditional, with one bathroom occupying a former chapel. Evening meals are available on request for groups of four or more, at €28 a head all-inclusive. You'll also **eat** well at the *Ferme Auberge de Coutié* (Ⓣ05.63.67.73.51; menus €17–32), on the D20, 9km southwest of Montpezat, signed to the east of Espanel hamlet, on a Quercy farm surrounded by ducks and orchards. In July and August there's a well-tended two-star municipal **campsite**, the *Camping Révéa le Faillal* (Ⓣ05.63.02.07.08, or 08.25.80.14.40 out of season, Ⓦwww.revea-vacances.fr) in a leisure park on Montpezat's northern outskirts.

Montauban

Lying 20km east of Moissac and 50km north of Toulouse, **MONTAUBAN** is a prosperous middle-sized provincial city, the capital of the largely agricultural *département* of Tarn-et-Garonne. Its beautiful old centre sits on the north bank of the River Tarn, a harmonious ensemble of warm, pink brick which looks its best at sunset, or at night when the steeples, massive old bridge and riverside facades are illuminated. The layout follows the typical *bastide* pattern: a regular grid of streets around an arcaded market square, the glorious **place Nationale**, but between the main streets lie enticing alleys, covered passages and interior courtyards. The greatest delight is simply to wander – the centre is only a ten-minute stroll from end to end – taking in the scattered sights as you go, of which the highlight is the **Musée Ingres**, dedicated to Montauban's most famous son.

The city's origins go back to 1144 when Alphonse Jourdain, count of Toulouse, decided to create a *bastide* here as a bulwark against English and French royal power. Indeed, it is generally regarded as the first *bastide*, the model for the medieval new towns found throughout this region (see p.306). Montauban has enjoyed various periods of great prosperity (as one can guess from the proliferation of fine houses), mainly based on trade in silk and other textiles. The first followed the suppression of the Cathar heresy and the final submission of the counts of Toulouse in 1229 and was greatly enhanced by the building of the Pont-Vieux in 1335, making it the best crossing point on the Tarn for miles. The Hundred Years' War did its share of damage, as did Montauban's opting for the Protestant cause in the Wars of Religion, but by the time of the Revolution it had become once more one of the richest cities in the southwest.

Arrival and information

Montauban's **gare SNCF** lies roughly 1km west of centre across the Pont-Vieux at the far end of avenue Mayenne. There's no central *gare routière*, so you'll need to ask at the tourist office (see below) for information about **buses**. While central Montauban is eminently walkable, you might want to hop on a **city bus** from the train station to the centre (line A), stopping on allée de l'Empereur near place Prax-Paris, on the northeast side of town; tickets can be bought on the bus.

The **tourist office** is located nearby on rue du Collège (July & Aug Mon–Sat 9am–6.30pm, Sun 10am–12.30pm; Sept–June Mon–Sat 9.30am–12.30pm & 2–6.30pm; Ⓣ05.63.63.60.60, Ⓦwww.montauban-tourisme.com). Staff will phone round for accommodation for you, at a charge of €1.60. This may still be time and money well spent in high summer, when rooms are hard to come by.

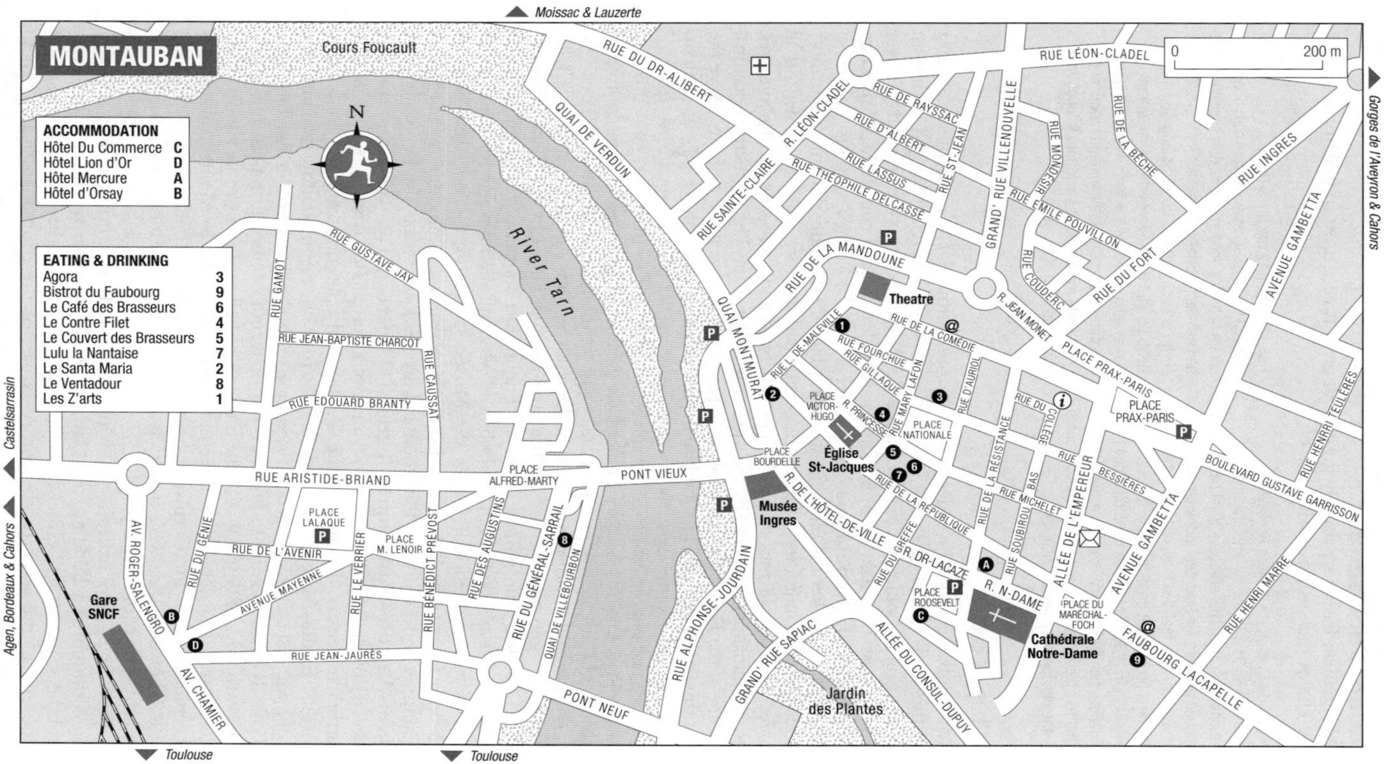

MONTAUBAN
ACCOMMODATION
Hôtel Du Commerce C
Hôtel Lion d'Or D
Hôtel Mercure A
Hôtel d'Orsay B
EATING & DRINKING
Agora 3
Bistrot du Faubourg 9
Le Café des Brasseurs 6
Le Contre Filet 4
Le Couvert des Brasseurs 5
Lulu la Nantaise 7
Le Santa Maria 2
Le Ventadour 8
Les Z'arts 1
Moissac & Lauzerte
Gorges de l'Aveyron & Cahors
Castelsarrasin
Agen, Bordeaux & Cahors
Toulouse
Toulouse
0
200 m
N
Cours Foucault
River Tarn
Theatre
Église St-Jacques
Musée Ingres
Cathédrale Notre-Dame
Jardin des Plantes
Gare SNCF
PONT VIEUX
PONT NEUF
QUAI DE VERDUN
QUAI MONTMURAT
RUE DU DR-ALIBERT
RUE LÉON-CLADEL
R. LÉON-CLADEL
RUE DE RAYSSAC
RUE D'ALBERT
RUE LASSUS
RUE ST-JEAN
RUE THÉOPHILE DELCASSE
RUE SAINTE-CLAIRE
GRAND' RUE VILLENOUVELLE
RUE MONDÉSIR
RUE EMILE POUVILLON
RUE COUDERC
RUE DE LA BÈCHE
RUE INGRES
RUE DU FORT
AVENUE GAMBETTA
RUE HENRI TEULÈRES
RUE DE LA MANDOUNE
R. JEAN MONET
PLACE PRAX-PARIS
RUE DE LA COMÉDIE
RUE L. DE-MALEVILLE
RUE FOURCHUE
RUE GILLAQUE
RUE MARY LAFON
R. PRINCESSE
RUE D'AURIOL
PLACE VICTOR-HUGO
PLACE NATIONALE
PLACE BOURDELLE
RUE DU COLLÈGE
RUE DE LA RÉSISTANCE
RUE BESSIÈRES
BOULEVARD GUSTAVE GARRISSON
RUE MICHELET
RUE BAS SOUBIROU
ALLÉE DE L'EMPEREUR
RUE DE LA RÉPUBLIQUE
R. DE L'HÔTEL-DE-VILLE
RUE DU GREFFE
R. DR-LACAZE
R. N-DAME
PLACE ROOSEVELT
PLACE DU MARÉCHAL-FOCH
RUE HENRI MARRE
FAUBOURG LACAPELLE
ALLÉE DU CONSUL-DUPUY
GRAND' RUE SAPIAC
RUE ALPHONSE-JOURDAIN
RUE GUSTAVE JAY
RUE GAMOT
RUE JEAN-BAPTISTE CHARCOT
RUE CAUSSAT
RUE EDOUARD BRANTY
RUE ARISTIDE-BRIAND
PLACE ALFRED-MARTY
PLACE LALAQUE
PLACE M. LENOIR
RUE DE L'AVENIR
AVENUE MAYENNE
RUE LE VERRIER
RUE BÉNÉDICT PRÉVOST
RUE DES AUGUSTINS
RUE DU GÉNÉRAL-SARRAIL
QUAI DE VILLEBOURBON
RUE DU GÉNIE
RUE JEAN-JAURÈS
AV. ROGER-SALENGRO
AV. CHAMIER

Accommodation

Montauban has a surprisingly limited range of hotels, most of which are owned by chains such as Ibis or Kyriad.

Hôtel du Commerce 9 place Roosevelt ⓣ05.63.66.31.32, ⓦwww.hotel-commerce-montauban.com. This attractive hotel beside the cathedral offers the best deal in the centre. It boasts en-suite facilities in all its rooms; they also lay on a good buffet breakfast (€9). ❸

Hôtel Lion d'Or Av Mayenne ⓣ05.63.20.04.04. Friendly, family-run place down near the station that has basic, spacious but slightly shabby rooms – the cheapest are not en suite. ❷

Hôtel Mercure 12 rue Notre-Dame ⓣ05.63.63.17.23, ⓦwww.mercure.com. Town-centre hotel with modern, reasonably spacious rooms and excellent facilities. Restaurant from €15. ❻

Hôtel d'Orsay 29 rue Roger Salengro ⓣ05.63.66.06.66, ⓦwww.hotel-restaurant-orsay.com. Opposite the train station, this hotel has dated but comfortable enough rooms and a great restaurant (closed bank hols & lunchtime Sat; from €24). ❹

The Town

Montauban couldn't be easier to find your way around. The most interesting area is the small kernel of streets based on the original *bastide*, enclosed within an inner ring of boulevards between **allée de l'Empereur** to the east and the river to the west. The main shopping streets are pedestrianized **rue de la Résistance** and **rue de la République**, which intersect in the *bastide*'s southern corner.

In the centre lies the city's finest point, **place Nationale**, the hub of the city's social life. Rebuilt after a fire in the seventeenth century, it is surrounded on all sides by a double row of arcades beneath two- and three-storeyed townhouses, their uniformity tempered by the square's irregular shape. The distinctive octagonal belfry of the **Église St-Jacques**, a couple of minutes' walk away, shows above the southwestern rooftops. First built in the thirteenth century on the pilgrim route to Santiago de Compostela, the church bears the scars of Montauban's troubled history, not only in its mix of architectural styles, but in the holes gouged out of the belfry's fortified base by cannonballs during an unsuccessful siege by twenty thousand Catholic troops – held off by just six thousand locals – in 1621.

On the banks of the river south of the church stands a massive half-palace, half-fortress, begun by the counts of Toulouse, then continued by the Black Prince in 1363. He left it unfinished when the English lost control of the town, and so it remained until 1664 when the bishop of Montauban chose this very prominent spot for his residence. It is now the **Musée Ingres** (Tues–Sun 10am–noon & 2–6pm; July & Aug 10am–6pm daily; €4 or €6 during exhibitions), which houses paintings and more than four thousand drawings left to the city by locally born **Jean-Auguste-Dominique Ingres** (1780–1867). The collection includes several of the supremely realistic, luminous portraits of women, which are the artist's trademark. It also contains a substantial collection of works by another native, **Émile-Antoine Bourdelle** (1861–1929), the ubiquitous monumental sculptor and student of Rodin, alongside a hotchpotch of other exhibits, from Gallo-Roman mosaics to fifteenth- and sixteenth-century European fine art. In the early days of World War II, the museum hosted more illustrious visitors when the Louvre dispatched over three thousand works of art to Montauban for safe-keeping prior to the German invasion. When southern France was occupied in 1942, however, they were moved again to more remote locations, including the Château de Montal (see p.258).

Providing a stark exception to Montauban's red-brick homogeneity is a cold, sore-thumb of a building, the **Cathédrale Notre-Dame**, ten minutes' walk southeast up rue de l'Hôtel-de-Ville. It was erected on the city's highest spot at the end of the seventeenth century as part of the triumphalist campaign to reassert the Catholic faith, following the defeat and harsh repression of the Protestants. Inside the dazzling white Classical facade lies an echoing nave, whose main point of interest is another Ingres painting, *Le Voeu de Louis XIII*, hanging in the north aisle. Specially commissioned for the cathedral, the vast canvas depicts Louis offering France, symbolized by his crown and sword, to a Virgin and Child, and is strongly influenced by Raphael's romantic style.

Eating and drinking

The best place for a **picnic** is the Jardin des Plantes, a pleasant green space south of the cathedral along the banks of a small tributary of the Tarn. You can buy provisions at pâtisseries and delicatessens on rue de la République and rue d'Auriol. While you're at it, keep an eye open for the **local speciality**, *Montauriols*, a chocolate-coated cherry preserved in armagnac; you'll find them at pâtisseries all over town.

A few stalls sell fresh produce every day on place Nationale, but the main farmers' **markets** take place on Wednesday morning on place Lalaque on the station side of the river, and on Saturday mornings on allées Consul Dupuy, near the Jardin des Plantes.

Restaurants

Agora 9 place Nationale. Serves salads and *plats* at around €7.50, and menus from €12. Closed Sun eve & Mon lunchtime.

Bistrot du Faubourg 111 faubourg Lacapelle ⓣ05.63.63.49.89. Popular place offering tasty, good-value traditional meals: at lunch you can eat for €9.30, rising to €19 in the evening. Closed Sat & Sun, also first two weeks in Aug & one week at Christmas.

Le Café des Brasseurs 22 place Nationale ⓣ05.63.63.54.56. Sit on the *terrasse* under the arches and watch the world go by on Montauban's famous square.

Le Contre Filet 4 rue des Princesses ⓣ05.63.20.19.75. Superb French cooking with a twist at this small restaurant. They are known for their beef in its signature sauce, but you can also feast on a kilo of mussels. Reservations recommended. Closed Wed & Sun.

Le Couvert des Brasseurs 27 place Nationale ⓣ05.63.91.30.61. Sister concern to *Le Café des Brasseurs* (see above), serving more upmarket food, including plenty of fish, in smarter surroundings.

Le Ventadour 23 quai Villebourbon ⓣ05.63.63.34.58. Montauban's top restaurant, magnificently sited in an old house on the west bank near the Pont-Vieux: *the* place for a splurge. Menus €22–40. Closed Sat lunchtime, Sun & Mon, also two weeks in both Jan & Aug.

Bars

Lulu la Nantaise Rue de la République. Busy café cum bar, frequented by a large number of locals. Closed Sun.

Le Santa Maria quai de Montmurat. Sip your drinks on a terrace overlooking the Tarn; they also serve tapas and more substantial Tex Mex meals. Closed Sun & Mon.

Les Z'arts Rue Gillaque. Tiny little place with a pub-like feel; it occasionally hosts live music – gig dates are posted outside.

Listings

Airport The nearest airport is Toulouse-Blagnac ⓣ08.25.38.00.00, ⓦwww.toulouse.aeroport.fr.

Car parks The most convenient option is the underground pay parking on place Prax-Paris or place Roosevelt. Free parking is available along the riverbanks beneath the Pont-Vieux and north of the theatre on rue de la Mandoune.

Car rental Both Avis, 23 av Mayenne ⓣ05.63.20.45.73, and Europcar, 21 av Roger Salengro ⓣ05.63.20.29.00, are located near the train station.

Hospital Centre Hospitalier, rue Léon Cladel ⓣ05.63.92.82.82, to the north of the old quarter.

Internet access Arob@ze, 112 faubourg Lacapelle (Tues–Thurs 10am–9pm, Fri & Sat 10am–11pm), on the southwest side of town.

Police Commissariat de Police, 50 bd Alsace-Lorraine ⓣ05.63.66.76.50, northeast of the centre, off blvd Alsace-Lorraine.

Post office Allée de l'Empereur, 82000 Montauban.

Taxis There are taxi stands at the station and the north end of allée de l'Empereur, or call ⓣ05.63.66.99.99.

The Gorges de l'Aveyron and around

In its lower course the Aveyron glides across the dull flood plain surrounding Montauban, offering little reason to stop other than the village of **Montricoux**, with its museum dedicated to a forgotten artist. The scenery becomes more interesting, however, about 30km east of Montauban where the river has sliced a narrow defile through the hills. The entrance of the **Gorges de l'Aveyron** is guarded by the fortress village of **Bruniquel**, its ancient houses assembled higgledy-piggledy on steep cobbled streets, while further east **Penne** perches beneath a crumbling castle. From here on the gorge gets increasingly dramatic as you work your way upriver to **St-Antonin-Noble-Val**, an excellent base for exploring the gorge and surrounding sights. The most compelling of these is the partially ruined **Abbaye de Beaulieu-en-Rouergue**, located 14km northwest, where the Gothic church has been converted into a contemporary art gallery. Beyond St-Antonin, **Laguépie** is less interesting but provides another possible base, from where you can hop south to the beguiling – if very touristy – hilltop town of **Cordes-sur-Ciel**. At Laguépie the Aveyron valley turns abruptly north, and its sides close in again to form a second increasingly deep, thickly wooded gorge, dominated by the ruins of **Najac**'s mighty fortress. It stands guard over the frontier of the former province of Rouergue, now the Aveyron *département*, and the southern approach to the *bastide* of refreshingly unprettified town of **Villefranche-de-Rouergue**.

Buses run along the Aveyron between Montauban and Laguépie (GAU Autocars; Ⓣ05.63.30.44.45), though they cater mostly to schoolchildren, which means they don't necessarily run every day and tend to be at inconvenient times. The best way of travelling between Laguépie, Najac and Villefranche is the Toulouse–Brive **train** line; these trains also stop at Cordes, further south.

Montricoux

Just before you leave the flat alluvial plains, 25km west of Montauban, **MONTRICOUX** would hardly be worth the stop if it weren't for its intriguing art museum, the **Musée Marcel-Lenoir** (May–Oct daily except Tues 10am–6pm; €5; Ⓦwww.marcel-lenoir.com), on the west side of the village. Like Ingres (see p.336), Marcel Lenoir was another prolific local artist, who was born in Montauban in 1872 and died in Montricoux in 1931. He was much fêted during his early years, when he was at the forefront of Pointillism and Cubism, and he even presaged Art Deco as he searched for new means of expression. But Lenoir was also an irascible character and managed to offend so many critics, dealers and galleries that he was eventually cast into oblivion. And there he stays, despite the best efforts of the owner of this collection of 140 works spanning Lenoir's whole career. One of the most revealing is the *Kiss of Judas*, in which you see Picasso profiled in blue and Van Gogh cutting off Gauguin's ear, while Judas is portrayed as a well-known art critic of the time.

Buses from Montauban and Laguépie stop on the main road across from the village on the river's south bank. As you walk into the village, you'll pass the entrance to a very swish riverside **restaurant**, *Les Gorges de l'Aveyron* (Ⓣ05.63.24.50.50, Ⓦwww.gorges-aveyron.com; closed two varying days a week except in July & Aug; menus from €25), along a lane beside the bridge. For comfortable **accommodation**, head 8km southwest to *Chez Terrassier* (Ⓣ05.63.30.94.60, Ⓦwww.chezterrassier.net; ❷; closed Sun & Fri eves; menus from €22), a pretty, modern place with a pool in the middle of **VAISSAC**.

There's also a very friendly **campsite**, *Aicí sèm pla* (Ⓣ05.63.30.98.01, Ⓦwww.aicisempla.com), on a farm in Revel, 2km from Vaïssac.

Bruniquel

East of Montricoux the hills rise suddenly and 5km later the **Gorges de l'Aveyron** really get into their stride as you sight the first of several fortified villages along these rocky crags. Once a Protestant stronghold, **BRUNIQUEL** shelters in the lee of its **castle** (daily: March–June & Sept–Oct 10am–6pm, July & Aug 10am–7pm, Nov 10am–5pm; closed mid-Nov to March; €2.50, or €3.50 for guided tour), teetering on the edge of a hundred-metre cliff. In fact there are two adjacent castles, since the original twelfth-century fortress had to be divided between rival cousins in 1484, but both are rather knocked about, although there is an impressive carved wooden fireplace in the "new" castle.

More engaging is the **Maison des Comtes de Payrol** (April–Sept daily 10am–6pm; July & Aug till 7pm; Oct Sat & Sun 10am–5pm; Nov–Feb by appointment only; Ⓣ05.63.67.26.42; €3) to the west of the castle entrance. The thirteenth-century home of a wealthy merchant family, its vaulted cellars and panelled and frescoed rooms now house an unusually good local history museum, including an interesting collection of oil lamps and candle holders.

Practicalities

Buses stop about 250m below Bruniquel to the south, beside a road leading up to the church and the **tourist office** (April–Sept daily 10am–1pm & 2–6pm; rest of year same hours but variable closing days; Ⓣ05.63.67.29.84, Ⓦwww.bruniquel.fr) at the entrance to the village; all practical information, including accommodation details, is listed outside. For an overnight **stay**, Marc de Baudouin runs a very good *chambre d'hôte*, to the right of the church (Ⓣ05.63.67.26.16, Ⓦwww.chambres-bruniquel.fr; ❸; closed Dec & Jan; evening meals on request €20), and is also a mine of information on local walks and mountain-bike trails. Alternatively, the swanky, Dutch-run *Cornelia* (Ⓣ05.63.67.75.68, Ⓦwww.cornelia-bruniquel.com), located 200m from the tourist office, has four rooms, including the "Romantique" with a round bed and the hammock-strewn attic. Rooms are available dorm-style per person (€25–29), but you can also book out half or all of it for a group. Opposite, the **restaurant** *L'Étape du Château* (closed mid-Nov to March, lunchtimes only in April) serves traditional menus from €13.

Penne and on towards St-Antonin

Six kilometres upriver from Bruniquel you come to the even more beautiful ridge-top village of **PENNE**, once a Cathar stronghold, with its ruined **castle** perched on an impregnable pinnacle. Everything is old and leaning and bulging, but holding together nonetheless, with a harmony that would be impossible to create purposely. There's just one cobbled street leading from an arch under the church belfry and through a second gate – where ancient grain measures are cut into the wall – to a footpath scrambling among the castle ruins. There's not much left, although restoration work is being undertaken, and it's an atmospheric spot, the piles of stones overrun with dog-roses, clematis and honeysuckle, with a panorama taking in the village roofs and the wooded country beyond. If that's worked up an appetite or a thirst, head for the **bar-restaurant** *La Terrasse* (daily for lunch and eves on Sat; menus from €12 in the week and €20 at weekends), at the north end of the village, from the back terrace of which you get a first-class view of the castle's airy crag.

Beyond Penne the gorge becomes deeper and more dramatic. To appreciate it at its best, turn off the main road just after Cazals, 6km from Penne, following signs for the **Corniche**, a single-track road which climbs steeply for a kilometre or so on to the cliff's edge. You'll be rewarded with tremendous views and, a little further on, a superbly sited **restaurant**, *La Corniche* (ⓣ05.63.68.26.95; menu at €29; reservations recommended; closed Sun eve & Mon) offering generous country dishes, in the hamlet of **BROUSSES**. Six kilometres later, you drop down to the river again to the west of St-Antonin-Noble-Val.

St-Antonin-Noble-Val and around

The finest and most substantial town in this lower stretch of the Aveyron valley is **ST-ANTONIN-NOBLE-VAL**, 16km northeast of Penne. It sits on the river's north bank beneath the beetling white cliffs of the **Roc d'Anglars**, where it developed in the ninth century around an abbey said to house the remains of the evangelizing **St Antonin**. According to legend, his body was carried here in a boat guided by two white eagles from Pamiers, in the Ariège, where the saint met his death. Since then the town has endured all the vicissitudes of this region's history: it sided with the Cathars, then the Protestants and each time was walloped by the alien power of the kings from the north, until it eventually sank into oblivion after the seventeenth century. Yet, in spite of it all, a marvellous heritage of houses endowed by wealthy merchants remains from its medieval glory days, when St-Antonin was an important commercial centre, manufacturing linen and leather goods.

Arrival and information

Buses on the Montauban–Laguépie route stop near the Crédit Agricole bank on avenue Paul-Benet, the boulevard to the north of the old centre. The **tourist office** is in the *mairie* next to the church (Nov–Feb Tues–Fri 10am–12.30pm & 2–5pm, Mon & Sat 2–5pm; March & Oct Mon 2–5.30pm, Tues–Sun 10am–12.30pm & 2–5.30pm; April–June & Sept daily 10am–12.30pm & 2–6pm; July & Aug daily 9.30am–12.30pm & 2–7pm; ⓣ05.63.30.63.47, ⓦwww.saint-antonin-noble-val.com). St-Antonin is also the starting point for canoeing down this lower stretch of the Aveyron: you can rent **canoes** from a number of outlets, including Variation (ⓣ05.63.68.25.25, ⓦwww.variation82.eu), on the town's eastern outskirts, who also rent out **bicycles** and organize **caving** and **rock-climbing** expeditions in the area. There's an English bookshop on rue de Pélisserie (ⓣ05.63.68.22.66, times vary but open Fri–Sun in summer).

Accommodation

Camping des Gorges de l'Aveyron 1.5km out of town on the Marsac road ⓣ05.63.30.69.76, ⓦwww.camping-gorges-aveyron.com. Friendly place next to the river, overlooked by the cliffs. Facilities include a pool, bar, restaurant and childrens' play area.

Hôtel du Commerce 58 av Paul Benet ⓣ05.63.30.62.25. Situated above a café, this basic hotel has shared toilets but en suite bathrooms. ❶

Jardins des Thermes 7km upstream in Feneyrols ⓣ05.63.30.65.49, ⓦwww.jardinsdesthermes.eu. Former spa that's now a comfortable hotel set in its own grounds with modern rooms and a good restaurant (menus €18–45; July & Aug daily; Sept–June closed Wed & Thurs). Closed Nov–Feb. ❸

Le Ponget 500m from the town centre on the Caylus road ⓣ05.63.68.21.13. Quiet and well-kept campsite with great views of the cliffs and rivers. Closed Oct–April.

La Résidence 37 rue Droite ⓣ05.63.67.37.56, ⓦwww.laresidence-france.com. A smart and welcoming Dutch-German-run *chambre d'hôte* on the road leading northwest out of place de la Halle. The rooms are large and light, with tiles or wooden floorboards and high ceilings – one even has its own roof terrace. Evening meals on request. ④

Les Trois Cantons 6km north up onto the *causse* Ⓣ05.63.31.98.57, Ⓦwww.3cantons.eu. Spacious and well-organized campsite with three-star facilities including a heated pool, shop and snack bar. Closed Oct to mid-April.

The Town

The easiest landmark to head for is the spire of the large but uninteresting neo-Gothic **church**, towards the town's southeast corner. Along the church's west wall rue du Pont-de-l'Aveyron leads south to the bridge, while rue Guilhelm Peyre curves northeast to **place de la Halle**. This square is St-Antonin at its most picturesque, with its cafés and pint-sized *halle*, the focus of an important Sunday-morning market, and the town's finest building, the **Maison des Consuls**, whose origins go back to 1125. The facade is pierced with arcades, pairs of colonnaded openings and a contrastingly severe oblong window on the first floor, on one pillar of which Adam and Eve hide their modesty; the old man on the pillar to the left, holding some books and a staff, is Emperor Justinian (483–565), who codified Roman law. The building's most striking feature, however, is the tower with its top-heavy loggia and too-perfect machicolations added by the controversial nineteenth-century architect Viollet-le-Duc (see p.100) – though he did save the building from collapse. It now houses the **Musée du Vieux St-Antonin** (July & Aug daily except Tues 10am–1pm & 3–6pm; Sept–June by appointment only, Ⓣ05.63.68.23.52; €2.50), with an uninspiring collection of objects to do with the former life of the place, including various prehistoric finds.

Eating

If you're after picnic fodder, there's an excellent boulangerie on place Buoc, with a boucherie opposite. The **restaurant** *L'Auberge Côté Pont*, 6 bd des Thermes (closed Sun eve to Tues lunch; menus from €24), offers traditional but interesting dishes, along the lines of duck with raspberry vinegar sauce. For more basic food, head to *Gazpacho* on avenue Paul Benet, which serves large portions of brasserie fare with menus from €10. It's very popular with local expats, and you're as likely to hear English spoken as French.

Abbaye de Beaulieu-en-Rouergue

Apart from exploring the gorge itself, the best excursion from St-Antonin takes you 14km northwest to the beautiful Cistercian **Abbaye de Beaulieu-en-Rouergue** (April–Oct daily: 10am–noon & 2–6pm; €5; Ⓦwww.art-beaulieu-rouergue.com), which lies deep among wooded hills. The abbey was founded in 1144, though the present buildings date from the thirteenth century, and are remarkably unscathed considering it was sacked and burnt during the Wars of Religion, looted again during the Revolution and then used as a barn until the late 1950s; in 1844 Viollet-le-Duc even wanted to rebuild the whole caboodle in St-Antonin but had to give up through lack of funds. The present owners have now restored the church to create a superb exhibition space for their collection of **contemporary art**; displays change several times a year, in combination with temporary exhibitions. The high, light nave with its clean lines and lack of ornamentation, save for the delicate rose windows and a few sculpted capitals, provides the perfect foil for works by Jean Dubuffet, Simon Hantaï and Henri Michaux, amongst others.

Upstream to Laguépie

Upstream from St-Antonin, the Aveyron valley widens out for a while and is spoilt by stone quarries. The only reason to stop is the village of **VAREN**, 16km from St-Antonin on the river's north bank. Its Romanesque **church** and tiny area of old streets repay a quick wander, but the prime attraction is another excellent though fairly upmarket **restaurant**, this time a converted mill on the riverbank just east of the village. The *Moulin de Varen* (ⓣ05.63.65.45.10; closed Sun eve & Mon except in July & Aug) serves a *menu à choix*, from which you select the number of courses you want; the choice is good and the food beautifully presented. Prices start at €17 for a main course and dessert, and the owner prides himself on his carefully selected wine list.

LAGUÉPIE, 9km east of Varen, where the cliffs begin to close in again, guards the confluence of the Viaur with the Aveyron. The village has nothing in the way of sights, but is pretty enough and provides a useful base, served both by occasional buses from Montauban and by trains on the Toulouse–Brive line. The **church** pinpoints the village centre occupying a spit of land between the two rivers. The **gare SNCF** lies 500m northwest on the north bank of the Aveyron; **buses** terminate either here or beside the church. There's a small **tourist office** (daily 10am–noon & 3–5pm, closed Wed afternoon & Sun afternoon; ⓣ05.63.30.20.34, ⓦwww.laguepie-en-rouergue.fr) on place du Foirail, a big open space with a café and a grocery to the southwest of the church.

Laguépie's one and only **hotel** is the friendly and well-priced *Les Deux Rivières* (ⓣ05.63.31.41.41, ⓦwww.logis-de-france.fr; ❶; closed three weeks in Jan or Feb), on the north side of the bridge across the Aveyron. It is also a good place to **eat**, offering a choice between a brasserie and a formal restaurant with menus from €19.70 (closed all day Fri, Sat lunch & Sun eve). You'll find a one-star municipal **campsite**, *Les Tilleuls* (ⓣ05.63.30.22.32; closed Nov–April), in a shady spot beside the Viaur roughly 1km to the east of Laguépie.

Cordes-sur-Ciel

While you're in this part of the world it would be a shame to miss out on the spectacularly sited fortified town of **CORDES-SUR-CIEL**, 15km south of Laguépie on the D922 (it's also accessible by train). The origins of the suffix *sur-ciel* ("in the sky") become obvious as you approach the foot of the sudden hill on which the town is built, girded by several concentric walls and endowed with a score of medieval houses. It is something of an open-air museum and artisan centre, hugely crowded during July and August, but otherwise an atmospheric place to spend a few hours.

Founded in 1222 by Count Raymond VII of Toulouse, Cordes grew rich on **leatherworking** and in the following century the walls had to be enlarged no fewer than seven times to contain the expanding population. Things took a downturn, however, with the arrival of the plague in the fifteenth century, but Cordes later recovered, and developed a notable lace industry in the nineteenth century. However, its real renaissance came in the 1970s, when hippies, including the **craftsmen** and **artisans** whose studios now cram the upper town, arrived to put Cordes back on the map, attracted by its beauty and abandon.

Arrival and information

Trains stop 5km to the west of Cordes at **Vindrac** (ⓣ05.63.56.05.64 for the station), from where it's a pleasant hour-long walk, or you can call ⓣ05.63.56.14.80 for a taxi, which will cost around €4.50, more at weekends. **Buses** from Albi arrive near the **tourist office** in the lower town (Jan Sun 2–5pm; Feb, March,

▲ Cordes-sur-Ciel at dawn

Nov & Dec Tues–Fri & Sun 2–5pm; April–June Mon, Sat & Sun 2–6pm, Tues–Fri 10.30am–12.30pm & 2–6pm; July & Aug daily 9.30am–1pm & 2–6.30pm; Sept Mon 2–6pm, Tues–Sun 10.30am–12.30pm & 2-6pml; Oct Mon & Sat 2–6pm, Tues–Fri & Sun 10.30am–12.30pm & 2–6pm; ⓣ05.63.56.00.52, ⓦwww.cordesurciel.eu). There's also an information point in the upper town in the Musée d'Art Moderne et Contemporain (same hours as the museum – see below). If you're driving, **parking** can be a challenge – in the summer months the area a few metres east of the tourist office soon fills up and cars line the roads leading into town. Don't be tempted to drive into the old town.

Accommodation

Famed Tarnaise pastry chef and chocolatier Yves Thuriès is the enlightened despot of Cordes' hotels, presiding over all three establishments.

Le Garissou ⓣ05.63.56.27.14, ⓦwww.aquadis-loisirs.com. Decent campsite located in Les Cabannes, on the west of town. Closed mid-Oct to May.

Grand Écuyer Haut de la Cité ⓣ05.63.53.79.50 ⓦwww.thuries.fr. Lavish four-star hotel housed in Raymond's former palace, with a suitably high-class restaurant. Closed Nov–March. ❽

Hôtel de la Cité Haut de la Cité ⓣ05.63.56.03.53 ⓦwww.thuries.fr. Very pleasant two-star option, with large, clean rooms. Closed mid-Oct to May. ❸

Le Vieux Cordes Haut de la Cité ⓣ05.63.53.79.20 ⓦwww.thuries.fr. The most atmospheric of Thuriès' hotels, with stone walls, spiral staircases and elegant rooms. Closed Jan. ❸

The Town

The traveller who, from the terrace of Cordes, watches the summer night knows that he has no need to go further and that, if he so wishes, the beauty of this place, day after day, will lift him from all solitude.

Albert Camus

Camus' words give some idea of the town's allure, and hard though it may be to achieve such a placid state when the streets are packed during summer days, in the evening or out of season the romance of Cordes returns. It's worth rising early to view the sunrise from the ramparts, and with every other building a medieval mansion, walking the town before the crowds arrive is a delight.

Its layout is simple: the old citadel – the "**upper town**" – runs along and down the sides of the long and narrow ridge which juts up from the plain, while the modern "**lower town**" consists of a clump of streets at the foot of the old town's eastern tip. The best route to the upper town is the knee-cracking Grande Rue de l'Horloge ascending from the tourist office (see p.342), although at busy times it is more pleasant to take one of the picturesque but less crowded side-streets. Alternatively, a **petit train** (May–Sept; €2.50) makes frequent trips from outside the tourist office.

The main sights are arranged along the old town's axis. Heading straight up from the tourist office, you'll pass through progressively older gateways towards the heart of the city. En route, you'll come across the **Maison de l'Art du Sucre et du Chocolat** (daily 10.30am–12.30pm & 1.30–7pm, closed Dec–Feb; €3), an exhibition of sculptures made entirely out of sugar or chocolate. They have a couple on display in the shop, so it's worth sticking your head round the door even if you don't want to see the full museum. Further along on Grande Rue Raymond VII, the elegant and symmetrical arcaded face of the fourteenth-century **Maison du Grand Fauconnier** conceals the **Musée d'Art Moderne et Contemporain** (Feb–March & Nov–Dec 2–5pm; April–May & Oct 11.30am–12.30pm & 2–6.30pm; June–Sept 11am–12.30pm & 2–7pm; €3.50), which features works by the figurative painter Yves Brayer, who lived in Cordes from 1940, a French-only audio presentation explaining the town's lace-making tradition and a motley collection of modern art, including minor pieces by Picasso, Miró and Klee. Across the street squats the ancient covered market, where you can peer down one of the town's famously deep wells. Continuing along Grande Rue, you'll see the **Maison du Grand Veneur** ("House of the Great Hunter") – whose otherwise plain stone facade is festooned with amusingly sculpted and extremely well-preserved medieval caricatures of beasts and hunters. A few doors down is the impressively carved frontage of Raymond of Toulouse's old palace, now home to the *Grand Écuyer* hotel (named after the finely sculpted horse figure). Just before the last of the fortified entrances is the **Musée Charles Portal** (Sept & June Sat & Sun 2–6pm, Oct & May Sat & Sun 2–5pm; July & Aug daily except Tues 2–6pm; €2.50), housing a display on the medieval wells that riddle the town, and which were used in time of siege for water supply or to store grain. Carry on along the street to leave the old town via the **Porte des Ormeaux** ("Gate of the Elms").

There are more than forty **boutiques** in Cordes, including some which are thinly disguised as "museums". If you would like to shop for leatherwork, metal and handicraft items and price is not an issue, you could easily spend an afternoon or two (and a considerable sum) here. Many of the stores double as workshops, so even window-shopping is quite interesting.

Eating

The best **restaurants** are in the town's hotels, including that in the *Grand Écuyer*, a one-star Michelin restaurant known for its foie gras and other regional dishes (menus €49–84). There are plenty of cheaper options around the central place de la Halle and adjacent place de la Bride, while for lighter meals head to the *J-P B Salon de Thé* on place Brayer, where you can enjoy excellent savoury tarts, salads and pastries (€10 for a main and dessert) as well as views over the valley.

Najac

Back at Laguépie, the Aveyron valley sits northwards and the river flows through a wooded defile. The most picturesque route along the valley bottom is either the train or the GR36 footpath, while road users should take the D106 and

D594 along the western line of hills. Either way, you eventually arrive at a bridge – 15km by road and slightly less on foot – beneath the brooding towers of **NAJAC**'s semi-ruined **castle**.

The castle occupies an extraordinary site on the peak of a conical hill isolated in the river's wide meander – a site chosen in the mid-1200s by **Alphonse de Poitiers** who wanted to bring the area's Cathar sympathizers to heel. He enlarged the original fortress and laid out a new town to the east in an elongated version of a *bastide* with its arcades and central market square. For a short while Najac prospered as the region's capital, but the site proved too restrictive and by the end of the thirteenth century it had lost out to Villefranche-de-Rouergue (see p.346), leaving the castle to be fought over endlessly in the conflicts that ensued. The Protestants pillaged it in 1572 and the revolutionaries had their turn in 1793, but, in spite of all this, Najac survived.

Arrival and information

Najac's **gare SNCF** lies on the north side of the old bridge, 2km by road below the village; call ⓣ05.65.81.12.92 for a taxi. The daily **bus** from Villefranche terminates on the square to the east of the village, while the **tourist office** is on the south side of the *faubourg*, the market square that forms the heart of Najac (April–June & Sept Mon–Sat 9am–noon & 2–6pm; July & Aug daily 9am–noon & 2–6pm; Oct–March Mon–Fri 9am–noon & 2–5pm, Sat 9am–noon; ⓣ05.65.29.72.05, ⓦwww.tourisme-najac.com).

Accommodation

Le Belle Rive ⓣ05.65.29.73.90, ⓦwww.lebellerive.fr. Welcoming, old-fashioned and in a lovely riverside position near the train station. From the garden you get an ant's-eye view of the château towering above. They also run an excellent restaurant serving good-value regional cooking with weekday lunch menus from €10, or €19 at other times. Closed Nov–March. ❸

Maison Authesserre place du Faubourg ⓣ05.65.29.73.47. A lovely, blue-shuttered *chambre d'hôte* owned by an artist, at the west end of the *faubourg*. The rooms are all en suite, spacious and packed with character; there's also a peaceful courtyard garden at the back. Closed occasionally in winter. ❸

L'Oustal del Barry 2 place Sol del Barry ⓣ05.65.29.74.32, ⓦwww.oustaldelbarry.com. At the *faubourg's* east entrance you'll find this very comfortable hotel, whose restaurant is renowned for its subtle and inventive cuisine (closed Mon & lunchtime Tues out of season; menus from €19). Closed Nov–March. ❸

Le Païsserou ⓣ05.65.29.73.96 or 04.73.34.75.53 off season, ⓦwww.lescledelles.com. Najac's four-star riverside campsite, to the southwest of the old bridge, is spacious and very well equipped. There's also a *gîte d'étape* (€15) at the adjacent leisure centre (ⓣ05.65.29.73.94, ⓦwww.aagac.com), where you can rent canoes and bikes, go white-water rafting, climb, or swing through the tree-top obstacle course. Campsite closed Nov–April, *gîte* open all year.

Relais Mont Le Viaur 1km east of Najac ⓣ05.65.65.08.08, ⓦwww.montleviaur.fr. Lovely stone building housing calm, simply decorated rooms with en suite bathrooms. The best bit about saying here is its wonderful restaurant – see p.346. ❷

The Town

The heart of modern Najac consists of a big, open square lying to the east of the medieval village, where grey-tiled houses tail out westwards in a single street along the narrow spur connecting the valley side to the castle hill. Entering from the east you come first to the **faubourg**, the elongated market square bordered by houses raised on pillars. It slopes gently downhill towards a cobbled street, overlooked by more ancient houses, which leads past a fountain to the **château** (daily: April, May, Sept & Oct 10am–1pm & 3–5.30pm; June 10.30am–1pm & 3–6.30pm; early July 10.30am–1.30pm & 3–6.30pm; end July

& Aug 10.30am–7pm; last week in Aug 10.30am–1.30pm & 3–7pm; closed Nov–March; €4). The castle is a model of medieval defensive architecture: its curtain walls reach to over 20m in places, within which five round towers supplement the square twelfth-century turret, and the castle is equipped with unusual multistorey loopholes for archers. However, the main reason to visit is for the magnificent all-round view from the top of the keep, a full 200m above the river.

Just below the castle, in what was the original medieval village, stands the huge, very solid-looking and austere **church of St-Jean** (April–Sept daily 10am–noon & 2–6pm; Oct Sun only; free), which the villagers were forced to build at their own expense in 1258 as a punishment for their conversion to Catharism. In addition to a collection of reliquaries and an extraordinary iron cage for holding candles, the church has one architectural oddity: its windows are solid panels of stone from which the lights have been cut out in trefoil form. Below the church, a surviving Roman road leads downhill to where a thirteenth-century bridge spans the Aveyron.

Eating

While the hotel restaurants mentioned above (see p.345) are all good options, *the* place to **eat** in the area is a friendly, family-run restaurant-hotel in **St-André-de-Najac** – just one kilometre east from Najac – the ★ *Relais Mont Le Viaur* (Ⓣ05.65.65.08.08, Ⓦwww.montleviaur.fr). They serve beautifully presented food, combining traditional and modern cuisine, with menus from €17–24. Reservations are essential. They also have a handful of peaceful little rooms, see p.345.

Villefranche-de-Rouergue

The second stretch of the Aveyron gorge peters out about 10km north of Najac, but it's worth continuing upstream the same distance again to the laid-back market town of **VILLEFRANCHE-DE-ROUERGUE**, which boasts one of the most atmospheric central squares in the whole region. As its regular form and the die-straight streets indicate, this is a *bastide*, founded in 1252 by the ubiquitous **Alphonse de Poitiers**, as part of the royal policy of extending control over the recalcitrant lands of the south. Villefranche became rich on trade and on copper from the surrounding mines. In 1369 it was also made the seat of the Seneschal, the king's representative, with the right to mint money. While its wealthy merchants built the ornate houses that grace the cobbled streets to this day, conditions in the surrounding countryside were so desperate that in 1643, more than ten thousand peasants, known as **Croquants** (see p.361), besieged the town for a week. As elsewhere, the rebellion was harshly put down and the leaders strung up in the market square.

Arrival and information

The **gare SNCF** and **gare routière** are located together a couple of minutes' walk south across the Aveyron from the old centre, while **car rental** is available from Location U (Ⓣ05.65.65.15.47) on avenue de Toulouse, on the north side of town. The very helpful **tourist office** sits on the river's north bank, on promenade du Giraudet (May, June & Sept Mon–Fri 9am–noon & 2–7pm, Sat 9am–noon & 2–6pm; July & Aug also open Sun 10am–12.30pm; Nov–April Mon–Fri 9am–noon & 2–6pm, Sat 9am–noon; Ⓣ05.65.45.13.18, Ⓦwww.villefranche.com), beside the new bridge.

Accommodation

Given its size, Villefranche is rather lacking in **accommodation** options, though there are some further out of town.

Auberge de la Poste 45 rue Prestat ☎05.65.45.13.91. Friendly, labyrinthine old place opposite the post office, with decent rooms, though the cheapest share bathrooms. If you can brave the stairs, room 23 is a portholed eyrie on the top floor with views over the town rooftops. ❶

Camping du Rouergue ☎05.65.45.16.24, ⓦwww.campingdurouergue.com. Huge but friendly three-star municipal campsite, 1.5km to the south of Villefranche, signed off the D47 to Monteils. Closed Oct to mid-April.

Le Claux de la Bastide 8 rue Ste Emilie de Rodat ☎05.65.45.54.79, ⓦwww.leclauxdelabastide.fr. Peaceful, elegant *chambre d'hôte* just north of the tourist office, with large bright rooms overlooking a lovely garden. ❹

Foyer des Jeunes Travailleurs 23 rue Lapeyrade ☎05.65.45.09.68, ⓦwww.fjtvillefranche.fr. HI-affiliated hostel providing some of the best-value accommodation you'll find anywhere, in a wood-faced building next to the train station. It offers individual, double or family en-suite rooms – some of which are huge, with mezzanine floors and separate seating areas – kitchen facilities and canteen meals. You must either be or become an HI member to stay here (€10 for membership). ❶

Relais de Farrou Route de Figeac ☎05.65.45.18.11, ⓦwww.relaisdefarrou.com. Smart hotel about 20 minutes out of town on the Figeac road. Guests have use of a small spa and gym, and the hotel also provides bicycles and other activities. ❹

The Town

Villefranche's medieval quarter lies on the north bank of the Aveyron, accessed by a modern road-bridge beside its pedestrian fourteenth-century counterpart. From the old bridge, the town's main commercial street, pedestrianized **rue de la République**, runs northwards up a gentle incline into the heart of the *bastide*. It is attractive enough, but no preparation for the central square you come out into, **place Notre-Dame**. The square, too, is built on a slope and is surrounded by unusually tall houses, arcaded at ground-floor level, some of which bear elaborate window surrounds. If possible, try and visit on a Thursday morning when local merchants and farmers spread out their produce at the weekly **market**, presided over by the colossal porch and bell tower – nearly 60m high and fortified – of the **Collégiale Notre-Dame**, which dominates the square's east side. The church was started in 1260 but wars and fires intervened and it was not finally completed until 1519. Behind the altar are two fine mid-fifteenth-century stained-glass windows: the one on the left depicts the Creation; that on the right portrays sixteen characters from the Old and New Testaments. Also worth noting are the oak choir stalls alive with a superb array of beasts and demons, as well as scenes from daily life – they took the craftsman, André Sulpice, fifteen years to complete in the late fifteenth century.

On boulevard Haute Guyenne, which forms the northern limit of the old town, the seventeenth-century **Chapelle des Pénitents-Noirs** (April–June Tues–Sat 2–6pm, July–Sept daily 10am–noon & 2–6pm; €4) boasts a splendidly Baroque painted ceiling and an enormous gilded retable – resplendent after its recent renovation. Another ecclesiastical building worth the slight detour is the **Chartreuse St-Sauveur** (same hours; €4), in the grounds of a hospital about 1km south of town on the main D922 to Najac and Laguépie. It was completed in the space of ten years from 1450, giving it a singular architectural harmony. The highlight is the second of the two cloisters, a minuscule quadrangle of white, sculpted stone, while the church itself contains more examples of André Sulpice's craftsmanship on the screen and choir stalls.

Eating

L'Assiette Gourmande Place André Lescure ☎05.65.45.25.95. Smart restaurant one block north of the church serving traditional meals in a pleasant stone-vaulted room or out on the square in fine weather. Menus from €15. Closed Sun in July & Aug; rest of year closed Tues eve, Wed & Sun eve, also two weeks in March & Nov, and one week in June & Sept.
L'Epicurien 8bis rue Raymond Saint-Gilles ☎05.65.45.01.12. Just down the road from the station, Villefranche's most upmarket option specialises in fish, with menus from €15 at lunch or €29.50 in the evenings. Closed Sun eve, Mon & Tues.
La Gabelle 10 rue Belle-Isle ☎05.65.45.57.13. Cheap and cheerful place one block south of the church, where you can eat pizzas, home-made pastas and grills from around €5. Closed Sun lunch & Mon.
Le Globe 1 place de la République ☎05.65.45.23.19. Bustling, modern brasserie just across the old bridge, serving simple but decent fare. Menus from €11 including wine.

Travel details

By plane

Agen to: Paris Orly (3 daily Mon–Fri, 1 on Sun; 1hr 30min).

By train

Agen to: Aiguillon (7–8 daily; 15–20min); Bordeaux (up to 19 daily; 1hr–1hr 20 min); Moissac (5–9 daily; 25–45min); Monsempron-Libos (4–8 daily; 35–45min); Montauban (6–9 daily; 40–50min); Périgueux (3–5 daily; 2hr–2hr 20min); La Réole (7–8 daily; 50min); Toulouse (12–14 daily; 1hr–1hr 15min).
Cordes-sur-Ciel (Cordes-Vindrac) to: Figeac (4–6 daily; 1hr 20min); Laguépie (4–6 daily; 20min); Najac (4–6 daily; 30min); Toulouse (3–5 daily; 1hr); Villefranche-de-Rouergue (4–6 daily; 50min).
Laguépie to: Cordes-sur-Ciel (4–6 daily; 20min); Figeac (4–6 daily; 1hr); Najac (4–6 daily; 10min); Toulouse (3–5 daily; 1hr 20min); Villefranche-de-Rouergue (4–6 daily; 25min).
Moissac to: Agen (6–8 daily; 30min); Bordeaux (1 daily; 1hr 50min); Montauban (5–8 daily; 20min); Toulouse (4–5 daily; 45min).
Montauban to: Agen (10–12 daily; 45–50min); Brive (2–5 daily; 1hr 50min); Cahors (3–8 daily; 40–50min); Moissac (7 daily Mon–Sat, 1 on Sun; 20min); Toulouse (every 30 min or less; 25min).
Najac to: Cordes-sur-Ciel (4–6 daily; 30min); Laguépie (4–6 daily; 10min); Figeac (4–6 daily; 50min); Toulouse (3–5 daily; 1hr 30min); Villefranche-de-Rouergue (4–6 daily; 15min).
Villefranche-de-Rouergue to: Cordes-sur-Ciel (4–6 daily; 50min); Figeac (4–6 daily; 45min); Laguépie (4–6 daily; 25min); Najac (4–6 daily; 15min); Toulouse (3–5 daily; 1hr 40min).

By bus

Agen to: Nérac (Mon–Fri 4 daily, 5 in school times; 40min); Villeneuve-sur-Lot (5–10 daily; 45min).
Cordes-sur-Ciel to: Albi (Mon–Sat 1–2 daily; 40min–1hr).
Laguépie to: Bruniquel (school term Mon–Fri 1 daily; school hols Tues, Thurs, Sat 1 daily; 1hr); Montauban (as for Bruniquel; 1hr30min); St-Antonin-Noble-Val (as for Bruniquel; 25min); Villefranche-de-Rouergue (Mon–Sat 1 daily; 35min).
Moissac to: Lauzerte (Wed & Sat 1–2 daily; 30min).
Montauban to: Bruniquel (school term Mon–Fri 4 daily, school hols Tues, Thurs & Sat 1 daily; 40min–1hr 10min); Cahors (Mon–Fri 1 daily; 1hr 15min); Laguépie (school term Mon–Fri 1 daily, school hols Tues, Thurs & Sat 1 daily; 1hr 40min); Montricoux (as for Bruniquel; 35–45min); St-Antonin-Noble-Val (as for Laguépie; 1hr 10min); Villefranche-de-Rouergue (Mon–Sat 1 daily; 1hr 45min).
Montcuq to: Cahors (school term Mon–Fri 1 daily, school hols Wed & Sat 1 daily; 35–45min).
Najac to: Villefranche-de-Rouergue (Mon–Sat 1 daily; 30min).
Villefranche-de-Rouergue to: Cahors (Mon–Fri 1 daily; 1hr 25min); Figeac (1–2 daily; 40min); Laguépie (school term Mon–Fri 1 daily; 40min); Montauban (Mon–Sat 1 daily; 1hr45min); Najac (Mon–Sat 1 daily; 45min).

Contexts

Contexts

History

The **history of the Dordogne and Lot** region is a fascinating illustration of how the political entity that is now a unified France in fact consists of numerous components of entirely distinct historical character. The southwest's vigorously independent cultural identity was forged millenia ago in the artistic endeavours of mysterious but highly gifted **cavemen**, and hundreds of years ago in the influence of **English rule** and in the poetry of the **Troubadours**, written in a language now virtually extinct. Even from the fifteenth century onwards, when the region was officially part of metropolitan France, it remained a distant territory, at least a week's travel from Paris, and one where local interests and powerful families held far more sway than the voice of the king. To this political detachment must be added the entirely secluded nature of the life led by the vast majority of the region's population, barely 15 percent of whom lived in towns even as late as 1910. Communicating in myriad local dialects, worshipping the gods of local folklore, and working on the land in the same manner as their ancestors had for centuries, the rural poor of the Dordogne and Lot, largely oblivious to the causes – though certainly not the devastating consequences – of the political and religious conflicts going on around them, were only in the twentieth century dragged into the familiar historical timeline.

The beginnings

Primitive flint tools found in the Dordogne indicate human presence dating back at least 400,000 years. However, the region's archeological treasure trove really gets going with the **Neanderthal** people, who arrived on the scene some 100,000 years ago. Despite their brutish image, evidence now suggests that Neanderthals were surprisingly sophisticated. They developed not only an increasingly elaborate range of stone tools but also complex burial rituals. This didn't, however, equip them to compete with the next wave of immigrants sweeping across Europe between 30,000 and 40,000 years ago, and Neanderthals gradually died out.

Early archeologists named the newcomers **Cro-Magnon** after a rock-shelter near Les Eyzies where the first skeletons were identified. Now they are better known as *Homo sapiens sapiens* – in other words, our direct ancestors. While Cro-Magnons developed ever more sophisticated tools, they also began to scratch fertility symbols into the rock, made various pigments and then took the great leap into abstraction that led to drawing, painting and carving. The earliest evidence of **prehistoric art** dates from around 30,000 years ago, but reached its apogee during the **Magdalenian** era (10,000–17,000 years ago) – also named after a shelter in the Dordogne's Vézère valley. It was during this era that Cro-Magnon people covered the walls and ceilings of the region's caves with art of a quality that would not be seen again for several millennia (see *Cave art* colour section for more).

Around 10,000 BC the all-important reindeer herds, the Cro-Magnons' one-stop source of meat, fat, skin, bone and sinew, began to move north as the climate grew warmer and wetter. Over the next three thousand years these nomadic hunter-gatherers were gradually replaced by settled **farming and pastoral communities** who left hundreds of **dolmen** (megalithic stone tombs) scattered over the region. This Neolithic era in its turn made way for the great metal-working cultures, culminating in the Iron Age, from around 700 BC. About the same time **Celtic** people began to spread into the region from north and central Europe, establishing trade routes and building towns and hilltop fortresses. They were skilled manufacturers and had their own coinage, but instead of a cohesive entity, comprised individual or loosely allied clans, continuously fighting amongst themselves. It was these disunited tribes that the Roman legions encountered when they arrived in what they called **Gaul** – roughly equivalent to modern France – in the second century BC.

The Roman occupation

At first the **Romans** contented themselves with a colony along the Mediterranean coast, but in 59 BC the threat of a Germanic invasion and various Celtic uprisings prompted **Julius Caesar** to subjugate the entire area. It took him just eight years. By 56 BC he had pacified southwest Gaul and the only real opposition came from a young Arvenian (modern-day Auvergne) chieftain called **Vercingetorix** who managed to rally a united Gaulish opposition in 52 BC. The Gauls had some initial victories, but in the end were no match for Caesar's disciplined armies. Vercingetorix was taken back to Rome in chains in 52 BC and the following year the Gauls staged their final stand at **Uxellodunum**, generally believed to be the Puy d'Issolud, to the east of Martel (see p.247).

The battle was one of the major turning points in the region's history. In 16 AD Emperor Augustus established the new Gallo-Roman province of **Aquitania**, stretching from Poitiers south to the Pyrenees. Its capital was Burdigala (Bordeaux), and regional administrative centres were set up in Vesunna (Périgueux) and Divona Cadurcorum (Cahors), each with its forum, amphitheatre, law courts and temples. During more than three centuries of peace – the **Pax Romana** – that followed, the Romans built roads, introduced new technologies, traded, planted vineyards and established an urbanized society administered by an educated, Latin-speaking elite. Today, the physical traces of this practically and culturally sophisticated society are most visible in the Roman ruins in Périgueux and in the exceptional examples of ancient sculpture in Bordeaux's Musée d'Aquitaine (see p.72). Just as durable, though, has been the linguistic impact: as well as being the language of the rulers, Latin penetrated rural areas and eventually fused with the local Celtic dialects to form two broad new language groups: the *langue d'Oïl* (where "yes" is *oïl* – later, *oui*), spoken north of the Loire, and the *langue d'Oc*, or *Occitan* (where "yes" is *oc*), to the south.

By the third century AD, Roman authority was starting to crack. Oppressive aristocratic rule and an economic crisis turned the destitute peasantry into gangs of marauding brigands, who were particularly rampant in the southwest. But more devastating were the incursions across the Rhine by various restless **Germanic tribes**, starting with the Alemanni and Franks, who pushed down as far as Spain, ravaging farmland and looting towns along the way. In response, urban centres such as Périgueux were hurriedly fortified while the nobles hot-footed it to their country villas, which became increasingly self-sufficient – economically, administratively and militarily.

The crunch came, however, in the fifth century when first the Vandals and then the **Visigoths** stormed through the region as the Roman empire crumbled. For nearly a hundred years the Visigoths ruled a huge territory extending across southern France and into Spain, with its capital at Toulouse.

Christianity and independence

The Visigoths' destructive and mercenary temperament did not induce sustained rule, and in 507 AD they were driven out of the region by the **Franks**, a northern tribe who gave their name to modern France. The end of the Visigoths marked the beginning of a long period of relative independence for Aquitaine and the southwest. Although the Frankish king, Clovis, was to found the **Merovingian dynasty** whose power technically extended to this region, he failed to re-establish the same over-arching authority as the Romans.

The power vacuum had been filled, in part, by representatives of the early church. **Christianity** had arrived from Rome in the early fourth century and was spreading slowly through France, but the invasion of the Vandals and Visigoths had put its advance on hold. It fell to **bishop Chronope**, active in the region between 506 and 533 AD, to re-establish the faith by a prolific programme of church building, most notably the first cathedral of St-Etienne in Périgueux. Chronope is also thought to have played a role in the creation of the legend of St-Front, after whom Périgueux's modern cathedral is named. Clovis himself had embraced Christianity around 500 AD and thereafter was happy to devolve a great deal of everyday administration to local bishops, such as those at Cahors.

The Merovingian empire began to disintegrate in the late seventh century, leaving the way clear for their chancellors, the Pepin family, to take control. One of their most dynamic scions, **Charles Martel**, defeated the Spanish Moors when they swept up through the southwest as far as Poitiers in 732. His grandson, **Charlemagne**, continued the expansionist policy of the **Carolingian** dynasty – so called for their fondness for the name Charles, or "Carolus" – to create an empire which eventually stretched from the Baltic to the Pyrenees.

Charlemagne and his descendants, however, had no more genuine control over the southwest region than the Merovingians, preferring, like them, to rule from a distance. In 781 Charlemagne created the quasi-independent **kingdom** of Aquitaine – an area extending from the Loire to the Cévennes and from the Rhône to the Pyrenees. Within the kingdom, the Carolingians delegated administrative power to royally appointed bishops, now joined by a growing number of counts – Quercy and Périgord for example – who had been awarded territory in exchange for their loyalty. In theory, the king retained feudal authority, but in reality the bishops and counts did largely as they pleased.

The royal position became weaker still in the ninth century, in part due to a long-drawn-out **battle of succession** following Charlemagne's death in 814, but also thanks to a series of extravagantly destructive raids by the **Vikings**, who sailed their longboats down from Scandinavia. They had been raiding coastal areas for decades, but in 844 they penetrated deep inland along the Garonne, Dordogne, Isle and Lot rivers, plundering towns and churches. Bordeaux was sacked in 848, Périgueux razed in 849. The annals of one monastery recount matter-of-factly, "the devastating Normans put fire to Périgueux and, without further ado, got back on their boats".

In the face of these destabilizing invasions the Carolingians were obliged to delegate ever more autonomy to the provincial governors until these

The Way of St James

According to the Bible, **St James the Apostle** was decapitated in Jerusalem in 44 AD. There is nothing to suggest how his remains came to be buried in northwest Spain, but in 820 it was declared that they had been discovered there, and during the fervent religious revival of the Middle Ages millions of pilgrims began flocking to his supposed tomb in **Santiago de Compostela**. The route took on a life of its own: monasteries, churches and hospitals were founded and villages grew up along the way to cater for the pilgrims wearing their distinctive cockleshell badge.

The pilgrimage faded out during the sixteenth century, partly because of the wars sweeping France and partly because the cathedral canons rather carelessly lost the saint's remains; the relics were allegedly hidden to keep them out of the hands of Sir Francis Drake, who was then sniffing around Galicia, but later no one could remember where they'd put them. By another "miracle" they were rediscovered by archeologists in 1879, declared by the pope to be the genuine article, and the pilgrimage revived, though on a far more modest scale.

In 1998 the whole system of paths and associated buildings was inscribed on the UNESCO World Heritage list. As a result, to walk the **chemin de St-Jacques** (Way of St James) – or at least some of it – is becoming increasingly popular again, partly as a spiritual quest, but also simply as a walking holiday. Three of the four main routes – from Vézelay, Le Puy-en-Velay and Arles – have been waymarked as long-distance footpaths (*grandes randonnées*, or GRs). Of these the GR654 from Vézelay and the GR65 from Le Puy pass through the Dordogne and Lot region; booklets outlining the routes are available in the Topo-guide series (see p.370 for more).

eventually grew more powerful than the king. So it was that when **Hugues Capet** succeeded to the French throne in 987, founding a 400-year dynasty that in theory ruled the whole of France, he in practice had authority only over a small area near Paris. Around the turn of the millennium, Aldebert I, one of the Counts of Périgord, is supposed to have rebuked a royal demand for payment of feudal dues with the question "*Qui vous a fait roi?*" – "Who made you king, then?" By this point, the local aristocratic families were more embroiled in jostling for power with one another than with the king. In the tenth century Périgord was carved up into four **Baronies** (Beynac, Mareuil, Bourdeilles and Biron), while Quercy was divided between five powerful families (Turenne, Gourdon, Cardaillac, Castelnau and St-Sulpice). At the same time, the counts of Poitou (based at Poitiers) and Toulouse were fighting for control of what was once again the **Duchy of Aquitaine**. The former emerged victorious, thus creating a vast territory that by the twelfth century reached from the Loire to the Pyrenees. The Poitou counts also ushered in a period of relative peace, rapid economic growth and renewed religious vigour, demonstrated in a wave of church building. To them we owe the lovely Romanesque churches (see box, pp.358–359) seen throughout the region to this day. At least some of this building activity was spurred and financed by the great procession of **pilgrims** passing along the route to Santiago de Compostela in Spain (see box opposite).

English rule

It was the huge kingdom created by the amalgamation of the territories of the counts of Poitou and the dukes of Aquitaine that indirectly allowed the whole of the Dordogne and Lot region to fall into the hands of the **English crown**. The cause of this catastrophe for the French royal family, the Capetian dynasty, was the strong-willed **Eleanor of Aquitaine** (1122–1204; see box, p.356), who inherited the domains of Aquitaine and Poitou in 1137 at the tender age of 15. Fifteen years later, she ditched her first husband, the French king, to marry **Henry of Anjou**, thereby creating an empire comprising Anjou and Normandy in addition to Eleanor's possessions. This in itself was a disastrous blow to the Capetians, but it was compounded in 1154 when Henry succeeded to the English throne (as Henry II). As a result, almost half of France fell under English rule. Much of it would remain so for the next three hundred years.

For the southwest region itself, however, English rule ushered in a period of peace, stability and impressive economic progress. With the major exception of **Richard the Lionheart** (Richard Coeur de Lion), Eleanor's third son, who plundered the region ruthlessly, the **English overlords** proved to be popular. For the most part they ruled from a distance, often preferring to stay put in England, and ensured the loyalty of their southern subjects by granting a large degree of independence to many of Aquitaine's rapidly growing towns and their local lords. Peasants lived under relatively privileged feudal conditions, helped by the fact that local lords were often in competition for their services. An important factor here was the building of dozens of **new towns**, the *bastides*, designed to secure border areas and accommodate the rapidly expanding population. In order to attract peasants to inhabit the new towns and cultivate the surrounding land, feudal lords had to offer enticing terms and considerable freedom.

The region continued to produce wheat and oats, but the real sensation of the era of English rule was the transformation of **wine** production into a lucrative and international industry. Merchants exporting the beloved claret of the English to London and other British ports grew wealthy, and the proceeds filtered through to the whole region. **Urban life**, too, began to take off, with the towns of Périgueux, Bergerac and Sarlat growing to populations of around five thousand each, while Bordeaux experienced the first of its golden ages.

Eleanor of Aquitaine

The life of **Eleanor of Aquitaine** (1122–1204) is an incredible tale of romance and tragedy, of high farce and low intrigue that rivals any modern-day pot-boiler. As Duchess of Aquitaine and Countess of Poitou she was already a key figure in twelfth-century Europe. She then married two kings and gave birth to three more, effectively ruled England for a time and died at the grand old age of 82.

In 1137, at the age of just 15, Eleanor inherited the domains of Aquitaine and Poitou. These assets, combined with her intelligence and beauty, gave her a healthy list of suitors, at the head of which was the future King Louis VII of France. They were married in Bordeaux's St-André Cathedral, and just a week later, the death of Louis VI made the young couple king and queen of France. The marriage, however, was not a success: it bore no male heirs, and the vivacious Eleanor found her attentions wandering elsewhere. In March 1152, they were divorced.

Just two months later, Eleanor married the handsome, charismatic and extremely ambitious **Henry of Anjou**, who was eleven years her junior, but far closer in temperament. The following year she bore him the all-important heir and, when Henry II succeeded to the English throne in 1154, Eleanor found herself queen of England.

Although Eleanor spent much of her time in France, she and Henry produced at least eight children. Of these Richard, Geoffrey and John all became kings of England, while only two, John and Eleanor, outlived her. In the meantime, since Henry proved reluctant to delegate power, his sons rebelled against him in 1173, supported by both Eleanor and her former husband, Louis VI; the latter hoped to put a more compliant neighbour on the English throne – and was possibly also out for a spot of revenge.

But the rebellion soon collapsed and Henry placed his wife under house arrest. She remained closely guarded until his death in 1189, but her problems had by no means ended. Richard I (the Lionheart), Eleanor's favourite son, was next in line. All went well until he was captured in 1192 while returning from the Third Crusade. The indomitable seventy-year-old waded in as unofficial regent, while also keeping her French possessions under control, for the next two years.

Eleanor withdrew from public life after Richard's release, and even more so after his death in 1199. She retired to the Abbey of Fontevraud, in the Loire valley, where she died almost unnoticed in 1204, to be remembered as a popular, shrewd and effective ruler, well able to control her notoriously hot-blooded southern vassals.

As English rule was delivered from across the Channel and therefore somewhat removed, it did not mean any perceptible invasion of the English language. On the contrary, independence from northern France allowed local language and culture to flourish, creating perfect conditions for the high-culture phenomenon of the **Troubadours** (see box opposite).

The Cathar Crusades

While the English ruled in Aquitaine, an audacious bid for independence from the political and religious dictats of the French crown was also being made over to the east, by the powerful **counts of Toulouse**. From the mid-twelfth century on, the so-called **Cathars** (also known as Albigensians) had won a great deal of support in the area, which extended as far as the Dordogne valley, by preaching that the material world was created by the Devil and the spiritual world by a benevolent God. They also believed in reincarnation and that the only way to escape the mortal coil was to lead a life of saintly self-denial. All of which completely undermined the role of the clergy. To put an end to such

heresy, Pope Innocent III unleashed a **crusade** against the Cathars in 1209, starting off with a particularly murderous attack led by **Simon de Montfort** in which the entire population of the Mediterranean town of Béziers, estimated at twenty thousand people, was slaughtered; the papal legate in charge of the assault is famously supposed to have proclaimed, "Kill them all. God will know his own."

A series of crusading armies, composed largely of land-hungry northern nobles, then proceeded to rampage through the region on and off for the next twenty years. This was followed by an equally vicious **inquisition** designed to mop up any remaining Cathars, which culminated in the siege of Montségur, in the eastern foothills of the Pyrenees, in 1244, when two hundred people were burnt alive.

As a result of the Cathar Crusades, the French Crown now held sway over the whole of southwestern France, including Toulouse. The new count of Toulouse was **Alphonse de Poitiers**, brother of the future Louis IX, whose lands stretched north through Quercy into Périgord, and west along the Garonne as far as Agen. Like his English neighbours, Alphonse started establishing a rash of *bastides* in order to impose his authority over his new domains.

The Hundred Years' War

Though the English had lost their possessions north of the Loire by the mid-thirteenth century, they remained a perpetual thorn in the side of the French kings thanks to their grip on Aquitaine. Skirmishes took place throughout the century, followed by various peace treaties, one of which, in 1259, took Quercy and Périgord back into the English domain. But the spark that ignited the ruinous – and misnamed – **Hundred Years' War** (1337–1453)

The language of love

The **Troubadours**, poets and musicians of the twelfth century, were early pioneers of Western Europe's cultural renaissance. Their love poetry, written in **Occitan**, elevated the vernacular of the rural peasantry to the status of high culture and, for the first time since Roman occupation, language was used for something other than essential, practical communication. Troubadour poems focus on courtly love, an idealised, noble emotion which might be romantic, tender, familiar, feudal, patriotic – or, in the best poems, a combination of all these. Thus the Troubadours not only reintroduced art to the region, they also gave it a linguistic and cultural identity – when Troubadours talk about their *pays*, they do not mean France as a whole, just the southwest.

The aggressive campaign of unification and standardisation waged by the state following the 1789 revolution outlawed the everyday use of the Occitan **language**, causing its gradual disappearance as a native tongue. It continued to inspire poets, however, most notably **Frédéric Mistral**, an early winner of the Nobel prize for literature, who wrote in Occitan. Today, the language described in 1900 by the visionary politician Jean Jaurés as "a noble language of courtship, poetry and art", is being revived. Basing their strategy on the models for revival of the Welsh and Irish languages, regional authorities have established a number of Occitan-speaking **schools**, known as *Calandretas*, including one in Périgueux. The Toulouse-based newspaper *Dépêche du Midi* has started printing a regular column in Occitan.

was a Capetian succession crisis. When the last of the line, Charles IV, died without an heir in 1328, the English king, **Edward III**, leapt in to claim the throne of France for himself. It went instead to Charles's cousin, **Philippe de Valois**. Edward acquiesced for a time, but when Philippe began whittling away at English possessions in Aquitaine, Edward renewed his claim and embarked on a war.

The major battles of the war were almost all fought in the northern half of the country, where Edward won an outright victory at **Crécy**, before his son, the **Black Prince**, took the French king, Jean le Bon, prisoner at the Battle of Poitiers in 1356 and established a capital at Bordeaux. The resulting treaty appeared to give the English victory, but the French fought back, banishing the English entirely but for a toehold in Bordeaux. In 1415, though, the tables turned again as Henry V inflicted a crushing defeat on the French army, against all odds, at the legendary battle of **Agincourt**. Once again, France seemed on the verge of unravelling at the seams, until **Jeanne d'Arc** (Joan of Arc) arrived on the scene. In 1429 she rallied the demoralized French troops, broke the English siege at Orléans and tipped the scales against the invaders. The English were slowly but surely driven back to their southwest heartland until even that was lost at the **Battle of Castillon** in 1453 (see box, p.180). Within months, the English surrendered Bordeaux, and their centuries-long adventure in France came to an end.

Although Castillon was the only major battle fought in the southwest, the region did not spare itself from **bloodshed**. The region's powerful families,

Churches and castles: the *vieilles pierres* of Périgord

In spite of the many conflicts that have ravaged the countryside since the Middle Ages, the Dordogne and Lot region has preserved an impressive wealth of medieval **churches**, at the heart of almost every village in some areas, and **castles**, which seem to crown the crest of each hill, especially along the golden stretch of the Dordogne valley.

Churches

Few traces now remain of the earliest churches, one exception being in St-Front in Périgueux, where the enthusiastic nineteenth-century restoration conceals traces of the original chapel built by bishop Chronope (see p.353) in the early sixth century. The region's golden age for church-building, however, came in the twelfth and thirteenth centuries, when the style of architecture and sculpture known as **Romanesque** (or sometimes Norman, in England) was dominant. In terms of architecture, these churches are characterized by round arches, sometimes domes (particularly in the Périgord region) and simple, graceful lines, but the highlights are often the sculptures that adorn the key structural points: the tympanum above the main entrance, the capitals at the top of supporting pillars, the keystones in their vaults – these all formed a blank canvas for craftsman to forge the most beautifully humane and unglorified depictions of saints, prophets and biblical stories. In no other architectural style are religious teachings so organically integrated into the physical structure of the church. The best examples include the churches in Souillac (see p.237) and Beaulieu (see p.253), in the upper reaches of the Dordogne, and the world-famous cloister at Moissac (see p.327) in the Lot valley, but it's the range and variety of styles, from the Byzantine touches in Périgueux and Souillac to the unembellished purity, almost austerity, of the church at Cadouin (see p.187), which make the region such a goldmine.

Rarer, but of all the more interest for that, are the region's **Gothic** edifices. While in Romanesque architecture the charm lies in the detail, in Gothic buildings it's the operating from their fortified bases (see box, p.355), sought to take advantage of the general chaos by attacking their neighbours and trying to strengthen their hands. Many nobles swapped sides repeatedly, fighting under English or French colours as it suited them. **Raymond de Montaut**, for example, a powerful baron based in Mussidan, initially swore allegiance to the French crown, but then fought with the English in the sieges of Bourdeilles (1369) and Limoges (1370). Only when he was captured by the French did he conveniently rediscover his patriotic sentiment and transfer his allegiance back. Most towns and castles were attacked at some point and many changed hands on numerous occasions, either by treaty or force. By the end of the war, farms and villages lay abandoned and roving bands of **brigands** terrorized the countryside, having abandoned all pretence of fighting for one side or the other. The population had been reduced by roughly a half to under twelve million, partly by warfare, but largely through famine and disease; millions died as the bubonic **plague** repeatedly swept through France during the fourteenth and fifteenth centuries.

Gradually the nightmare ended. Though the south now had to kow-tow to the hated northerners – the Counts of Périgord were particularly big losers, having their land and privileges confiscated by the crown – Louis XI proved to be an astute ruler who allowed some of the privileges granted by the English to remain. The Bordelais smarted for a while, but were eventually brought round with the establishment of their own parliament in 1462. Trade – particularly the wine trade – began to revive, towns were rebuilt and land brought back into production.

soaring, awe-inspiring ensemble that appeals. The cathedral of St-André in Bordeaux (see p.70) is one of the best illustrations, its pointed arches and vaults, the hallmarks of the Gothic style, giving a sense of imposing solidity rising into ethereal delicacy. If Romanesque churches evoke a humble, down-to-earth spirituality, their Gothic counterparts embody an awe-inspiring sense of elevation to a higher realm.

Castles

While the Hundred Years' War was raging, it was said that "towns were loyal to the king; castles were a law unto themselves". In both the conflict between the French and English and the later religious wars, the region's powerful families sought to strengthen their own positions and independence by fortifying their residences.

Invariably built on high ground, for strategic reasons, many castles would originally have covered a large area, with entire villages enclosed within their walls. In most cases, they were destroyed or dismantled when captured during various wars, so today it is often just a ruined keep that remains. From a military perspective, two of the most satisfying are those at Beynac and Castelnaud (p.224), squaring up to each other across the Dordogne river and offering commanding views over the surrounding countryside. For romance, it's hard to beat the rugged keep of Najac (p.345) rising above the village, shrouded in mist. In more peaceful centuries, the region's aristocracy set about making their residences more comfortable, and places like the Chateau de Hautefort (p.151) combined impregnability with stately grandeur, lavish furnishings and extravagant interior design.

In many cases, buildings were designed to serve both a religious purpose and a military one. The churches at Rocamadour (p.243), St-Amand-de-Coly (p.217) and Beaumont (p.186), to name just three, are notable for their imposing, fortified walls and slit windows, revealing them as buildings designed not just for worship, but to be defended.

The Wars of Religion

In the early sixteenth century the ideas, art and architecture of the **Renaissance** began to penetrate France. As elsewhere in Europe, the Renaissance had a profound influence on every aspect of life, engendering a new optimism and spirit of enquiry that appealed in particular to the new class of wealthy merchants. At the same time, increased trade and improved communications, including the invention of the printing press, helped disseminate ideas throughout Europe. Among them came the new **Protestant** message espoused by Martin Luther and John Calvin that the individual was responsible to God alone and not to the Church.

Such ideas gained widespread adherence throughout France, partly feeding on resentment of Catholic clergy who were often seen as closely linked to the oppressive feudal regime, but mainly because a handful of powerful families converted and, where the feudal overlord led, his subjects were bound to follow. On the national scale, the most significant families to convert were those of the **Bourbon-d'Albret** royal dynasty. In the southwest, the first Protestant (also known as **Huguenot**) enclaves were at Ste-Foy-la-Grande and Bergerac in the 1540s, followed soon after by Nérac, the fief of the **d'Albret** family (see p.321). As the Protestant faith took hold and Catholics felt increasingly threatened, the sporadic brutal attempts to stamp out Protestantism, such as a massacre in Cahors in 1560, erupted two years later into a series of bitter civil wars. Interspersed with ineffective truces and accords, the **Wars of Religion** lasted for the next thirty years.

On the Catholic side, a powerful lobbying group of traditionalists, organised mainly by the **de Guise** family, led an army against the Huguenots, who were in turn marshalled by the **Admiral de Coligny**. The two armies toured northern France, occasionally clashing directly, but more often capturing and converting towns that had taken one side or the other. The Duc de Guise was murdered in 1563, an act for which his allies held Coligny responsible. And in 1572, Coligny was among the victims of the war's bloodiest and most notorious date: the **St Bartholomew's Day Massacre**, when some three thousand Protestants, gathered in Paris for the wedding of Protestant **Henri d'Albret** to Marguerite de Valois, the sister of Henri III of France, were slaughtered.

Just as in earlier conflicts, the nationwide dispute was used as a pretext by **powerful families** in the southwest to consolidate their positions. Once again, private armies roamed the region, vying with each other in their savagery, but with only vaguely religious motives. Before his death, Coligny famously complained of Huguenot generals in the southwest who took no interest in the wider struggle and "refused to fight unless they could turn around and see their own chimney". One such general was the impulsive and ingenious **Geoffroi de Vivans**, who even succeeded in briefly capturing the staunchly Catholic towns of Sarlat and Périgueux. One of his most daring exploits, in 1588, involved hiding out in the caves beneath the hilltop town of Domme (see p.228) before scaling the formidable cliffs at dawn and taking the town with only a handful of men.

Some towns were attacked and changed hands repeatedly, either in violence or as a result of various **truces**, by which they were nominally declared either Catholic or Protestant. In reality, the majority of ordinary people, though cruelly affected by the fighting, saw little impact on their **notions of religion**, which remained a hotch-potch of rural paganism and local folklore, with only hints of orthodox Christianity, until several centuries later.

A twist of fate signalled the beginning of the end of the conflicts, when Henri d'Albret – king of Navarre and leader of the Protestant army – became heir to the French throne when Henri III's son died in 1584. Five years later, Henri III himself was dead, leaving a tricky problem, since a Protestant could not be king. After trying to seize the crown by force, Henri d'Albret eventually abjured his faith and became **Henri IV** of France. "Paris is worth a Mass," he is reputed to have said.

Once on the throne Henri IV set about reconstructing and reconciling his kingdom. Under the visionary **Edict of Nantes** of 1598 the Protestants were accorded freedom of conscience, freedom of worship in specified places, the right to attend the same schools and hold the same offices as Catholics, their own courts and the possession of a number of fortresses, including Montauban, as a guarantee against renewed attack.

The stirrings of discontent

The Dordogne and Lot region had barely drawn breath after the end of the Wars of Religion, when a different type of conflict erupted – this time one whose causes the ordinary peasantry could identify with all too easily. The countryside lay in ruins and the cost of the wars and rebuilding fell squarely on their shoulders. Ruinous taxes, a series of bad harvests, high prices and yet more outbreaks of the plague combined to push them over the edge in the late sixteenth century. There were **peasant rebellions** in Normandy and Brittany, but the worst of the "**Croquants'**" (yokels') uprisings broke out in the southwest. The first major revolt occurred in the winter of 1593, when a number of towns and castles, including Monpazier, Excideuil and Puy-l'Évêque, were attacked. After two years of skirmishes, nobles pulled together an army in 1595 and the rebellion was quickly and savagely put down by the allied forces of the local nobility. The same grievances resurfaced in more uprisings in May 1637, however, no doubt nourished in part by tales of the earlier failed rebellion, passed down by word of mouth from generation to generation. This time, the revolt was altogether more serious. In the face of one tax demand too many, a ten-thousand-strong **peasant army** tried unsuccessfully to seize Périgueux. Instead, they took Bergerac and then marched on Bordeaux. They were stopped, however, at Ste-Foy-la-Grande and the final show-down took place soon after against 3400 royal troops at La Sauvetat-du-Dropt, south of Bergerac, leaving at least a thousand Croquants dead. The leaders were executed, one in Monpazier (see p.308), while the surviving rebels returned to the land.

Thereafter, the long reign of **Louis XIV** (1643–1715) saw the French crown and Catholic religion begin to reassert control over the southwest. With the exception of the **Frondes** (of 1648–52), when aristocrats joined the lower classes in rebelling against royal taxes and when the army had to be brought in to crush demonstrations in Bordeaux, the state successfully reinstated military and feudal control. At the same time, the bishops of Sarlat and Périgueux set about the "Vendange des Âmes", the **Harvesting of Souls**, an aggressive campaign designed to eradicate strongholds of the Protestant faith. Protestant towns such as Bergerac were seized by the Catholics and Protestant rights were gradually eroded until in 1685 Louis revoked the Edict of Nantes, forbade Protestant worship and set about trying to eliminate the faith completely. Orders were given for the destruction of Protestant churches and of the castles of its most fervent supporters. Thousands of Protestants fled the southwest for the safety of the Netherlands, Germany and England.

At the same time, France began to establish a **colonial empire** in North America, Africa, India and the Caribbean, and, as trade from these places started to grow in the early eighteenth century, so Bordeaux and the other Atlantic ports prospered. Indeed, the late seventeenth and eighteenth centuries were something of a **golden age** for Bordeaux and its hinterland. On the back of colonial commerce and a booming **wine trade,** it grew to be the country's foremost port. The city centre was almost completely rebuilt and intellectual life flourished under the leadership of **Montesquieu** (see p.93) and other liberal visionaries.

Revolution

For the majority of people, however, little had changed. The gap between rich and poor grew ever wider as the clergy and aristocracy clung on to their privileges and the peasants were squeezed for higher taxes. Their general misery was exacerbated by a catastrophic harvest in 1788, followed by a particularly severe winter. Bread prices rocketed and on July 14, 1789, a mob stormed the **Bastille** in Paris, a hated symbol of the oppressive regime. As the **Revolution** spread, similar insurrections occurred throughout the country, accompanied by widespread peasant attacks on landowners' châteaux and the destruction of tax and rent records. In August the new National Assembly abolished the feudal rights and privileges of the nobility and then went on to nationalize Church lands.

In these early stages the general population of the southwest supported the Revolution, as did Bordeaux's elected deputies, known as the **Girondins**. However, as the Parisian revolutionaries grew increasingly radical and proposed ever more centralization of power, the Girondins found themselves in bitter opposition. Towards the end of 1792, as the **First Republic** was being declared, they finally lost out to the extremists and in October the following year **The Terror** was unleashed as mass executions took place throughout France; estimates run to three thousand in Paris and 14,000 in the regions. Amongst the victims were the Girondin deputies, the last of whom were tracked down and killed in St-Émilion in 1794.

Though revolutionary bands wrought a fair amount of havoc in the southwest, looting and burning castles and churches, hacking away at coats of arms and religious statuary, on the whole the region escaped fairly lightly; many aristocrats simply fled and their possessions were sold off at knock-down prices. Among many administrative changes following the Revolution, one of the most significant was the creation of **départements** in 1790 to replace the old provinces. Thus began yet another attempt at national unification, accompanied by efforts to draw the traditionally independent southwest into mainstream France. The campaign continued in the nineteenth century with moves to stamp out Occitan and other regional dialects (see box, p.357).

From Napoleon I to the Third Republic

By the end of 1794, more moderate forces were in charge in Paris. However, continuous infighting left the way open for **Napoleon Bonaparte**, who had made a name for himself as commander of the Revolutionary armies in Italy and Egypt, to seize power in a coup d'état in 1799. Napoleon quickly restored order and continued the process of centralization, replacing the power of local institutions by appointing a *préfet* to each *département* answerable only to the **Emperor**, as Napoleon declared himself in 1804. Nevertheless, the Dordogne and Lot *départements* supported the new regime by providing many military leaders – and more lowly troops – for Bonaparte's armies: the most notable examples were Périgueux's Baron Pierre Daumesnil (see box, p.133) and Joachim Murat (1767–1815), the son of a village innkeeper near Cahors, who was proclaimed king of Naples in reward for his numerous military successes. As elsewhere, however, it was the burden of the unceasing **Napoleonic wars** that cost the emperor his support. The economy of Bordeaux in particular and the southwest in general was hard hit when Napoleon banned commerce with Britain, to which Britain responded by blockading French ports in 1807.

Few tears were shed in the region when Napoleon was finally defeated in 1815. The subsequent restoration of the **monarchy**, on the other hand, saw opinions divided along predictable lines: the aristocracy and the emerging *bourgeoisie* (the middle classes) rallied to the king, while the working population supported the uprising in 1848 – a shorter and less virulent reprise of the 1789 Revolution – which ended in the declaration of the **Second Republic**. The new government started off well by setting up national workshops to relieve unemployment and extending the vote to all adult males – an unprecedented move for its time. But in elections held later in 1848 the largely conservative vote of the newly enfranchised peasants was sufficient to outweigh the urban, working-class radicals. To everyone's surprise, Louis-Napoleon, nephew of the former emperor, romped home. In spite of his liberal reputation, he restricted the vote again, censored the press and pandered to the Catholic Church. In 1852, following a coup and further street fighting, he had himself proclaimed **Emperor Napoleon III**.

Like his uncle, Napoleon III pursued an expansionist military policy, both in France's colonial empire and in Europe. And also like his uncle, this brought about his downfall. Napoleon III declared war on Prussia in 1870 and was quickly and roundly defeated by the far superior Prussian army. When Napoleon was taken prisoner the politicians in Paris – Cahors' Léon Gambetta among them (see box, p.271) – quickly proclaimed the **Third Republic**. Though it experienced a difficult birth, the Third Republic survived until 1940.

Into the twentieth century

Napoleon was more successful on the economic front, however. From the 1850s on, France experienced rapid **industrial growth**, while foreign trade trebled. The effect on the Dordogne and Lot region, however, was mixed.

Bordeaux and the towns along the region's great rivers benefited most from the economic recovery. Bordeaux in particular prospered once again thanks to its colonial trade. Although the region had no coal or mineral resources to stimulate large-scale industrialization (beyond metalworking around Fumel), industries were established along the navigable rivers – tanneries, paper mills, textile and glass industries. At the same time, agricultural areas within easy access of the rivers grew wealthy from exporting wheat, wine and tobacco. Many towns were given a facelift as their ramparts were torn down, wide avenues sliced through the cramped medieval quarters and a start was made on improving sanitation and water supply. Transportation was also modernized, although the **railways** came late to the Dordogne and Lot and were never very extensive. The region's first railway, the Bordeaux–Paris line, was completed in 1851, while the following year saw the opening of the **Canal latéral**, linking the Garonne with the Canal du Midi and thus the Mediterranean.

All this created pockets of economic growth, but the **rural areas** between became increasingly marginalized. Local industries dwindled in the face of competition from cheap manufactured goods and imports, while the railways simply provided the means for people to quit the country for the cities.

But by far the biggest single crisis to hit the area's rural economy in the late nineteenth century was **phylloxera**. The parasite, which attacks the roots of vines, wiped out almost one third of the region's vineyards in the 1870s and 1880s. For a while growers tried all sorts of remedies, from flooding the fields to chemical fumigation, before it was discovered that vines in America, where phylloxera originated, were immune and that by grafting French vines onto American root-stock it was possible to produce resistant plants. The vineyards were slowly re-established, but over a much smaller area. Many farmers turned to alternative crops, such as tobacco around Bergerac and sheep-rearing on the *causse* above Cahors.

The world wars

Such problems paled into insignificance, however, when German troops marched into northern France following the outbreak of **World War I** in 1914. The French government fled south to Bordeaux while thousands of southern men trekked north to lose their lives in the mud and horror of Verdun and the Somme battlefields. By the time the Germans were forced to surrender in 1918, the cost to France was 1.3 million dead, a quarter of whom were under 25 years of age, and three million wounded. Every town and village in the Dordogne and Lot, as elsewhere in France, has its sad war memorial recording the loss of this generation of young men.

In the aftermath of the war, agricultural and industrial production declined and the birth rate plummeted, although this was offset to some extent in the southwest by an influx of land-hungry refugees from Spain in the late nineteenth century and from Italy in the first decades of the twentieth. At the same time, however, Bordeaux's old-fashioned maritime industries were in terminal decline as the 1930s **Depression** hit home. The French government lurched from crisis to crisis while events across the border in Germany became increasingly menacing.

In April 1940, eight months after the outbreak of **World War II**, Hitler's western offensive began as he overran Belgium, Denmark and Holland. In June the French government retreated to Bordeaux again and millions of refugees poured south as Paris fell to the Germans. **Maréchal Pétain**, a conservative 84-year-old veteran of World War I, emerged from retirement to sign an armistice with Hitler and head the collaborationist **Vichy government**, based in the spa town of Vichy in the northern foothills of the Massif Central. France was now split in two. The Germans occupied the strategic regions north of the Loire and all along the Atlantic coast, including Bordeaux, while Vichy ostensibly governed the "Free Zone" comprising the majority of southern France. The frontier, with its customs points and guardposts, ran from the Pyrenees north through Langon and Castillon-la-Bataille to just south of Tours, and from there cut east to Geneva. Then, in 1942, German troops moved south to occupy the whole of France until they were driven out by Britain, America and their allies after 1944.

Resistance to the German occupation didn't really get going until 1943 when **General de Gaulle**, exiled leader of the "Free French", sent **Jean Moulin** to unify the disparate and often ideologically opposed Resistance groups. Moulin was soon captured by the Gestapo and tortured to death by Klaus Barbie – the infamous "Butcher of Lyon", who was convicted as recently as 1987 for his war crimes – but the network Moulin established became increasingly effective. Its members provided information to the Allies, blew up train tracks, bridges and factories. They undertook daring raids into enemy-held towns; the high, empty uplands of Dordogne and Lot *départements* afforded safe bases for many Resistance fighters. But for every action, the Germans hit back with savage **reprisals**. In May 1944 the SS Das Reich division, based at Montauban, set out to break the local resistance by massacring civilians and torching houses in some twenty towns and villages, of which the worst atrocities took place in Terrasson-la-Villedieu, Montpezat-de-Quercy, Mussidan and Frayssinet-le-Gélat.

Soon afterwards the Germans were being driven out, but the fighting didn't stop there. In the weeks following **liberation** thousands of **collaborators** were executed or publicly humiliated – women accused of consorting with the enemy had their heads shaved and were sometimes paraded naked through the streets. Not surprisingly, the issue of collaboration left deep scars in rural communities throughout the region, a bitterness which occasionally surfaces to this day in local disputes.

Into the new millennium

The new millennium sees the same issues that have dominated the last fifty years in the region remaining paramount. One of the main themes, as in much of rural France, is one of **depopulation**. On average there are now 25 percent fewer people living on the land than at the end of the nineteenth century, rising to thirty percent or more in the worst hit areas, such as parts of Lot-et-Garonne. Once again this has been partly offset by immigration, in this case by *pieds noirs* (black feet) – French colonialists forced to flee Algeria after independence in 1962 – many of whom settled on farms in the southwest, and by north Europeans in search of the good life. Agricultural production is in slow decline as the younger generation leave the land, though this has partly been offset by a massive push towards mechanization and the amalgamation of small farms into larger, more efficient holdings – albeit often propped up by subsidies from the European Union.

Agriculture remains the backbone of the region's economy, notably wine production but also poultry, maize, fruit, tobacco, fishing and forestry. The Bordelais vineyards alone account for around four percent of Aquitaine's GDP and six percent of its employment; some sixty thousand people in the region depend directly and indirectly on viticulture. **Industry**, on the other hand, employs around fifteen percent of the active population. The biggest industrial city is Bordeaux, with its aeronautical, electronic, optical and pharmaceutical businesses. Agen is also known for pharmaceuticals, while other main towns such as Périgueux, Figeac, Montauban, Fumel and Villeneuve-sur-Lot boast modest industrial sectors.

Besides agriculture and industry, **tourism** plays an increasingly important role in the regional economy. In recent years an enormous effort has gone into improving facilities and marketing the region, not just the honeypot attractions of Sarlat, Les Ezyies and the Dordogne valley châteaux, but also in the successful promotion of "green holidays", tempting people away from the Mediterranean and Atlantic coasts to discover all that the countryside has to offer. One of the largest such projects was the reopening of the River Lot and the Canal latéral to navigation, but at a local level almost every town and village now puts on a programme of summer events to lure visitors.

Across France, however, the economy continues to be hampered by the seemingly perpetual stand-off between advocates of economic reform to liberalise markets and stimulate growth, and uncompromising defenders of the "**French Model**", with generous social allowances and high job security. Almost every section of society seems to have seen this debate come its way in recent years: from teachers to car manufacturers, employees in all industries have taken action to block any reforms which might erode their privileges. Perhaps most emblematic of the battle lines was the controversy in 2006 surrounding the government's attempt to introduce the **CPE** or "First Employment Contract", aimed at encouraging the employment of young people by making them less costly to hire/employ (with fewer social security benefits and no guarantee that they would be kept on after two years). The intended beneficiaries, however, were less than grateful, and took to the streets in their thousands to protest against the new contract, arguing that it was the first step towards the hire-and-fire culture reviled in left-wing French circles.

In the **2007 presidential election**, it seemed as though momentum was swinging behind the arguments of the economic reformers, as former interior minister **Nicolas Sarkozy**, a member of the centre-right UMP party, was elected president having campaigned for a hard-line "rupture" with the French Model. In power, however, he has only fitfully pursued a free-market agenda, but has shown himself extremely adept at moderating his ideas in line with public opinion.

The **financial crisis** of 2008-09 hit manufacturing across France very badly, and its effects in the Dordogne and Lot region were most strongly felt in the wine business, with a partial collapse of prices and plummeting export sales. In the light of the general discrediting of liberal capitalism, Sarkozy shrewdly abandoned his rupturist rhetoric in favour of a new-found pride in the traditional French system. This impeccable tactical u-turn left the Socialist opposition lost for words and floundering in the polls: the **2009 European elections** saw Sarkozy's party come out on top with 28 percent of the vote, while across France, including in the southwest region, the Socialists were pushed into third place behind a green alliance – "Europe Ecologie" – led by Daniel Cohn-Bendit, familiar as the youthful leader of the 1968 student uprising.

Another consequence of the world's economic woes has been to make the situation of the thousands of **British residents** of the Dordogne and Lot region more difficult. Since the 1960s, low property prices, coupled with beautiful scenery and an enviable lifestyle, had attracted Brits, Dutch and other north Europeans to settle here in search of the good life. Now, though, volatile exchange rates and devalued savings and investments have caused what some are calling the biggest British exodus from France since Dunkirk.

Many locals hope that this will only be a short-term trend, as the region is in constant need of new settlers to restore its derelict farmhouses and pump money into the local economy. The British have been tolerated, indeed welcomed, too, because even after all these centuries, there still exists a vague and undoubtedly romantic sentiment among the resolutely independent, anti-Parisian southwesterners that they were better off under English rule, when at least the economy boomed and their forebears enjoyed a high degree of autonomy. Down the intervening years the region's strong sense of identity has been tested on many occasions, but has survived to resurface these days as a deep-burning pride in the land, its produce and its traditions.

Books

There are few English-language history books specifically devoted to the Dordogne and Lot region, and – apart from Jacquou the Rebel (see opposite) – a bit of a dearth of novels, whether in English or in translation. A few of those that do exist – and are worth recommending – are detailed below, along with a number of general history books and classic texts which provide the background to events that have occurred in the region. Books that are out of print are indicated by the abbreviation o/p.

History & biographies

Marc Bloch *Strange Defeat* (W.W.Norton). Moving personal study of the reasons for France's defeat in 1940 and subsequent caving-in to fascism. Found among the papers of this Sorbonne historian after his death at the hands of the Gestapo in 1942.

Lynn Haney *Naked at the Feast* (Robson Books). A lively warts-and-all biography of the cabaret star, Josephine Baker (see box, p.226), which traces the many setbacks and comebacks of her rags to riches tale, getting across her amazing charisma and just why France took her to its heart.

Colin Jones *The Cambridge Illustrated History of France* (Cambridge University Press). A political and social history of France from prehistoric times to the mid-1990s, concentrating on issues of regionalism, gender, race and class. Good illustrations and an easy, unacademic writing style.

Don and Petie Kladstrup *Wine & War* (Hodder & Stoughton, UK; Broadway, US). The role of wine in World War II and the often courageous and ingenious strategies used to prevent the best wines from being plundered by the German army; fascinating reading.

C.E. Lucas Phillips *The Cockleshell Heroes* (Pan). A thrilling, historically accurate account of what a German officer apparently called "the outstanding commando raid of the war". See box, p.74.

Marion Meade *Eleanor of Aquitaine* (Weidenfield & Nicholson, UK; Penguin, US). Highly accessible biography of one of the key characters in twelfth-century Europe. The author fleshes out the documented events until they read more like a historical novel.

Ian Ousby *Occupation: The Ordeal of France 1940–1944* (Cooper Square Press). Somewhat revisionist 1997 account looking at how widespread collaboration was and why it took so long for the Resistance to get organized.

Graham Robb *The Discovery of France (Picador).* A fascinating alternative history of France, in which Robb goes in search of the reality of life for the provincial, rural majority ignored by the currents of history, before recounting the way in which the nineteenth century saw this other France gradually discovered and "civilized". Contains some excellent sections on the southwest.

Theodore Zeldin *The French* (Harvill, UK; Kodansha, US). Urbane and witty survey of the French world view – chapter titles include "How to be chic" and "How to appreciate a grandmother".

Travel, art and literature

Patricia Atkinson *The Ripening Sun* (Arrow). The ultimately uplifting tale of an Englishwoman who struggles against all kinds of adversity to establish a well-respected vineyard near Bergerac.

Michael Brown *Down the Dordogne* (Sinclair-Stevenson, UK; Trafalgar Square, US). In the late 1980s, Michael Brown fulfilled a long-held ambition to follow the Dordogne from its source in the Massif Central to the Gironde estuary. The story of his journey – on foot, by canoe and bicycle – provides a lyrical introduction to the region.

André Chastel *French Art* (Flammarion). Authoritative, three-volume study by one of France's leading art historians. Discusses individual works of art – from architecture to tapestry, as well as painting – in detail in an attempt to locate the Frenchness of French art. With glossy photographs and serious-minded but readable text.

Arthur Conan-Doyle *The White Company* (Dover Publications). A far cry from Sherlock Holmes, here Conan-Doyle turns his talents to historical fiction, depicting a Hundred Years' War where the English have hearts of gold and all the rest are jolly rotters.

Freda White *Three Rivers of France* (Faber; o/p), *Ways of Aquitaine* (Faber; o/p). Freda White's classic books portray France in the 1950s before tourism came along to the backwater communities that were her interest. They are evocative books, slipping in history and culture painlessly, if not always too accurately, and still provide a valuable and vivid overview of the region.

Eugène Le Roy *Jacquou le Croquant* (EP Dutton o/p). This novel is one of the most important chronicles of the hardship of rural life in nineteenth-century France. The action takes place in the forest and villages around Montignac, home of the hero Jacquou who leads a vengeful revolt against the tyrannical local feudal lord.

Amanda Lawrence *White Stone, Black Wine* (Troubador Publishing). A readable and light-hearted account of an Englishwoman's experiences in the Quercy countryside, as she throws herself with gusto into local traditions and activities.

Michael Sanders *From Here You Can't See Paris* (Bantam Books). American Michael Sanders spent a year living in Les Arques (p.295), watching the inner workings of the local restaurant as it brought new life to this tiny village. A compelling glimpse behind the scenes and a tribute to the determination of the chef and his family.

Christian Signol *La Rivière Espérance* (Robert Laffont, UK; Pocket Presses, US). Set in the 1830s, this French novel – which was made into a hugely successful TV film – follows the adventures of a young sailor working the *gabarres* that then plied the Dordogne. This nostalgic tale commemorates the end of an era as the railways relentlessly destroy the romanticized river life.

Peter Strafford *Romanesque Churches of France* (Giles de la Mare). This scholarly guide to a handful of France's best churches contains a healthy section on those of the southwest, with several pages devoted to Moissac and Souillac alone. Strafford gives a somewhat dry but detailed account of the architecture and history of the churches featured, and an almost stone-by-stone description of some of the most important sculpture.

Guides

Glynn Christian *Edible France* (Grub Street). A guide to food rather than restaurants: regional produce, local specialities, markets and the best shops for buying goodies to bring back home.

Cicerone Walking Guides (Cicerone, UK). Neat, durable guides, with detailed route descriptions. Titles include *The Way of Saint James; A Walker's Guide* and *The Way of Saint James; A Cyclist's Guide*, both of which follow the route from Le Puy to Santiago (GR65), and *Walking in the Dordogne*.

Peter Knowles *White Water: Massif Central* (River Publishing). Don't be put off by the series title, this guide covers rivers suitable for a spot of gentle family canoeing and canoe touring, including parts of the Dordogne, Lot, Tarn, Vézère, Célé and Aveyron. Packed with good, practical advice.

Joy Law *Dordogne* (Pallas Athene). Erudite and accessible thematic guide-cum-history text written by a long-time resident of the *département*, packed with interesting anecdotes and local colour.

Helen Martin *Lot: Travels through a limestone landscape in southwest France* (Moho Books). It's well worth investing in this updated and expanded edition of Helen Martin's classic book about the Lot if you're going to be spending much time in the *département*. Her passion for the area, which she has known for more than 40 years, comes across loud and clear.

Hugh McKnight *Cruising French Waterways* (Adlard Coles Nautical). Essential reading for anyone going boating in France. It's not only a practical guide on navigating French rivers and canals, but also covers historical aspects and general tourist information.

Victoria Pybus *Live and Work in France* (Vacation Work). An invaluable guide, packed with ideas and advice on everything from job-hunting, tax and bureaucracy to health care.

Alain Roussot (ed) *Discovering Périgord Prehistory* (Sud-Ouest, France). Translated into English, this guide provides a solid introduction to the prehistoric caves of the Périgord. It covers the most significant caves in chronological order, while the illustrations give a taste of what's on offer.

Paul Strang *Wines of Southwest France* (Kyle Cathie). A bit dated now, but still by far the best English-language guide to the region's wines. In addition to the history of viticulture and brief reviews of recommended producers in all the wine-producing areas from Figeac to Bergerac (excluding the Bordeaux vineyards), the book gives a glimpse into local culture and traditions.

Topo-guides (Fédération Française de la Randonnée Pédestre, France). The best of the walking guides covering the long-distance paths, Topo-guides are widely available in France and not hard to follow with a working knowledge of French. The series includes guides to the GR65 St-Jacques pilgrimage routes, the *Tour des Gorges de l'Aveyron* (Topo-guide #323), the *Traversée du Périgord* (#321) and, for shorter walks, *Dordogne à Pied* (#D024) and *Lot à Pied* (#D046).

Language

Language

French

French can be a deceptively familiar language because of the number of words and structures it shares with English. Despite this, it's far from easy, though the bare essentials are not difficult to master and can make all the difference. Even just saying "Bonjour Madame/Monsieur" and then gesticulating will usually get you a smile and helpful service. People working in tourist offices, hotels and so on, almost always speak English, though, and tend to use it when you're struggling to speak French – be grateful, not insulted.

Phrasebooks and courses

Rough Guide French Phrasebook (Rough Guides). Mini dictionary-style phrasebook with both English–French and French–English sections, along with cultural tips for tricky situations and a menu reader.

Mini French Dictionary (Harrap/Prentice Hall). French–English and English–French Dictionary, plus a brief grammar and pronunciation guide.

Breakthrough French (Palgrave Macmillan). Excellent teach-yourself course including audio-cassettes.

French and English Slang Dictionary (Harrap); **Dictionary of Modern Colloquial French** (Routledge, UK). The key to French vernacular.

À Vous La France; France Extra; Franc-Parler (BBC Consumer Publishing/EMC Publishing). BBC courses, running from beginner's level to fairly advanced; each consists of a book and two cassettes. In addition, Ⓦwww.bbc.co.uk/education/languages/french has a range of online courses.

Pronunciation

One easy rule to remember is that **consonants** at the ends of words are usually silent. *Pas plus tard* (not later) is thus pronounced "pa-plu-tarr". But when the following word begins with a vowel, you run the two together: *les oranges* (the oranges) becomes "layzoronge". **Vowels** are the hardest sounds to get right. Roughly:

a	as in h**a**t	o	as in h**o**t
e	as in g**e**t	ô, au	as in **o**ver
é	between g**e**t and g**a**te	ou	as in f**oo**d
è	between g**e**t and g**u**t	u	as in a pursed-lip version of **u**se
eu	like the **u** in h**u**rt		
i	as in mach**i**ne		

More awkward are the **combinations** *in/im, en/em, an/am, on/om, un/um* at the beginning and ends of words, or followed by consonants other than *n* or *m*. Again, roughly:

in/im	like the **an** in **an**xious	**on/om**	like the **don** in **Don** caster said by someone with a heavy cold
an/am	like the **don** in **Don**caster when said with a nasal accent	**un/um**	like the **u** in **u**nderstand
en/em			

Consonants are much as in English, except that: *ch* is always "sh", *h* is silent, *th* is the same as "t", *ll* is like the "y" in yes, *w* is "v", and *r* is growled.

Basic words and phrases

French nouns are divided into masculine and feminine. This causes difficulties with adjectives, whose endings have to change to suit the gender of the nouns they qualify. If you know some grammar, you will know what to do. If not, stick to the masculine form, which is the simplest – it's what we have done in this glossary.

Basics

hello (morning or afternoon)	bonjour
hello (evening)	bonsoir
goodnight	bonne nuit
goodbye	au revoir
yes	oui
no	non
thank you	merci
please	s'il vous plaît
sorry	pardon/je m'excuse
excuse me	pardon
ok/agreed	d'accord
help!	au secours!
here	ici
there	là
this one	ceci
that one	cela
open	ouvert
closed	fermé
big	grand
small	petit
more	plus
less	moins
a little	un peu
a lot	beaucoup
cheap	bon marché, pas cher
expensive	cher
good	bon
bad	mauvais
hot	chaud
cold	froid
with	avec
without	sans
man	un homme
woman	une femme

Numbers

1	un
2	deux
3	trois
4	quatre
5	cinq
6	six
7	sept
8	huit
9	neuf
10	dix
11	onze
12	douze

13	treize	**70**	soixante-dix
14	quatorze	**75**	soixante-quinze
15	quinze	**80**	quatre-vingts
16	seize	**90**	quatre-vingt-dix
17	dix-sept	**95**	quatre-vingt-quinze
18	dix-huit	**100**	cent
19	dix-neuf	**101**	cent-et-un
20	vingt	**200**	deux cents
21	vingt-et-un	**300**	trois cents
22	vingt-deux	**500**	cinq cents
30	trente	**1000**	mille
40	quarante	**2000**	deux mille
50	cinquante	**5000**	cinq mille
60	soixante	**1,000,000**	un million

Days and dates

January	janvier	**Sunday**	dimanche
February	février	**Monday**	lundi
March	mars	**Tuesday**	mardi
April	avril	**Wednesday**	mercredi
May	mai	**Thursday**	jeudi
June	juin	**Friday**	vendredi
July	juillet	**Saturday**	samedi
August	août	**August 1**	le premier août
September	septembre	**March 2**	le deux mars
October	octobre	**July 14**	le quatorze juillet
November	novembre	**November 23**	le vingt-trois novembre
December	décembre	**2010**	deux mille dix

Time

today	aujourd'hui	**now**	maintenant
yesterday	hier	**later**	plus tard
tomorrow	demain	**at one o'clock**	à une heure
in the morning	le matin	**at three o'clock**	à trois heures
in the afternoon	l'après-midi	**at ten-thirty**	à dix heures et demie
in the evening	le soir	**at midday**	à midi

Talking to people

When addressing people you should always use *Monsieur* for a man, *Madame* for a woman, *Mademoiselle* for a young woman or girl. Plain *bonjour* by itself is not enough. This isn't as formal as it seems, and it has its uses when you've forgotten someone's name or want to attract someone's attention.

Do you speak English?	Parlez-vous anglais?	**What's your name?**	Comment vous appelez-vous?
How do you say it in French?	Comment ça se dit en français?	**My name is . . .**	Je m'appelle . . .

I'm	Je suis	**How are you?**	Comment allez-vous?/ Ça va?
...English	...anglais[e]	**fine, thanks**	Très bien, merci
...Irish	...irlandais[e]	**I don't know**	Je ne sais pas
...Scottish	...écossais[e]	**Let's go**	allons-y
...Welsh	...gallois[e]	**See you tomorrow**	À demain
...American	...américain[e]	**See you soon**	À bientôt
...Canadian	...canadien[ne]	**Leave me alone!**	Fichez-moi la paix! (aggressive)
...Australian	...australien[ne]	**Please help me**	Aidez-moi, s'il vous plaît
...a New Zealander	...néo-zélandais[e]		
I understand	Je comprends		
I don't understand	Je ne comprends pas		
Can you speak more slowly?	S'il vous plaît, parlez moins vite		

Questions and requests

The simplest way of asking a question is to start with *s'il vous plaît* (please), then name the thing you want in an interrogative tone of voice. For example:

Where is there a bakery?	S'il vous plaît, la boulangerie?	**where?**	Où?
Which way is it to the Eiffel Tower?	S'il vous plaît, la route pour la Tour Eiffel?	**how?**	Comment?
Can we have a room for two?	S'il vous plaît, une chambre pour deux?	**how many/ how much?**	Combien?
Can I have a kilo of oranges?	S'il vous plaît, un kilo d'oranges?	**when?**	Quand?
		why?	Pourquoi?
		at what time?	À quelle heure?
		what is/which is?	Quel est?

Getting around

bus	autobus/bus/car	**hitchhiking**	autostop
bus station	gare routière	**on foot**	à pied
bus stop	arrêt de bus	**Where are you going?**	Vous allez où?
train/taxi/ferry	train/taxi/ferry	**I'm going to...**	Je vais à...
boat	bâteau	**I want to get off at the road to...**	Je voudrais descendre à la route pour...
plane	avion	**near**	près/pas loin
train station	gare (SNCF)	**far**	loin
platform	quai	**left**	à gauche
What time does it leave?	Il part à quelle heure?	**right**	à droite
What time does it arrive?	Il arrive à quelle heure?	**straight on**	tout droit
a ticket to...	un billet pour...	**on the other side of**	de l'autre côté de
single ticket	aller-simple	**on the corner of**	à l'angle de
return ticket	aller-retour	**next to**	à côté de
validate your ticket	compostez votre billet	**behind**	derrière
valid for	valable pour	**in front of**	devant
ticket office	vente de billets	**before**	avant
how many kilometres?	combien de kilomètres?	**after**	après
how many hours?	combien d'heures?	**under**	sous
		to cross	traverser
		bridge	pont

Accommodation

a room for one/two people	une chambre pour une/deux personne(s)
a twin room	une chambre à deux lits
a double bed	un grand lit
a room with a shower	une chambre avec douche
a room with a bath	une chambre avec salle de bains
for one/two/three nights	pour une/deux /trios nuits
Can I see it?	Je peux la voir?
a room on the courtyard	une chambre sur la cour
a room over the street	une chambre sur la rue
first floor	premier étage
second floor	deuxième étage
with a view	avec vue
key	clef
to iron	repasser
do laundry	faire la lessive
sheets	draps
blankets	couvertures
quiet	calme
noisy	bruyant
hot water	eau chaude
cold water	eau froide
Is breakfast included?	Est-ce que le petit déjeuner est compris?
I would like breakfast	Je voudrais prendre le petit déjeuner
I don't want breakfast	Je ne veux pas de petit déjeuner
Can we camp here?	On peut camper ici?
campsite	un camping/terrain de camping
tent	une tente
tent space	un emplacement
youth hostel	auberge de jeunesse

Driving

car	voiture
service station	garage
service	service
to park the car	garer la voiture
car park	un parking
no parking	défense de stationner/ stationnement interdit
gas station	station service
petrol	essence
diesel	gazole/gasoil
(to) fill it up	faire le plein
oil	huile
air line	ligne à air
put air in the tyres	gonfler les pneus
battery	batterie
the battery is dead	la batterie est morte
plugs	bougies
to break down	tomber en panne
gas can	bidon
insurance	assurance
green card	carte verte
traffic lights	feux
red light	feu rouge
green light	feu vert

Health matters

doctor	médecin
I don't feel well	Je ne me sens pas bien
medicines	médicaments
prescription	ordonnance
I feel sick	Je suis malade
I have a headache	J'ai mal à la tête
stomach ache	mal à l'estomac
period	règles
pain	douleur
it hurts	ça fait mal
chemist	pharmacie
hospital	hôpital

Other needs

bakery	boulangerie
food shop	alimentation
supermarket	supermarché
to eat	manger
to drink	boire
camping gas	camping gaz
stamps	timbres
bank	banque
money	argent
toilets	toilettes
police	police
telephone	téléphone
cinema	cinéma
theatre	théâtre
to reserve/book	réserver

Food and dishes

See also *A Taste of Périgord* colour section for more food and dishes.

Basic terms

l'addition	bill/check
beurre	butter
bouteille	bottle
chauffé	heated
couteau	knife
cru	raw
cuillère	spoon
cuit	cooked
à emporter	takeaway
formule	lunchtime set menu
fourchette	fork
fumé	smoked
huile	oil
lait	milk
le menu	menu
moutarde	mustard
oeuf	egg
offert	free
pain	bread
poivre	pepper
salé	salted/savoury
sel	salt
sucre	sugar
sucré	sweet
table	table
tisane	a flower or herb infusion or tea
verre	glass
vinaigre	vinegar

Snacks and starters

un sandwich/ une baguette	a sandwich
au jambon	with ham
au fromage	with cheese
au saucisson	with sausage
au poivre	with pepper
au pâté (de campagne)	with pâté (country style)
croque-monsieur	grilled cheese and ham sandwich
croque-madame	grilled cheese and bacon, sausage, chicken or egg sandwich
panini	toasted Italian sandwich
tartine	buttered bread or open sandwich
oeufs	eggs
au plat	fried
à la coque	boiled
durs	hard-boiled
brouillés	scrambled
pochés	poached
omelette	omelette
nature	plain
aux fines herbes	with herbs
au fromage	with cheese

aux truffes	with truffles	**hors d'oeuvres**	combination of charcuterie, crudités, smoked fish and other cold starters
charcuterie	pâté and cold meats		
crudités	raw vegetables with dressings		

Pasta (pâtes), pancakes (crêpes) and flans (tartes)

nouilles	noodles		with anchovies and black olives
pâtes fraîches	fresh pasta	**tarte flambée**	thin pizza-like pastry topped with onion, cream and bacon or other combinations
crêpe au sucre/ aux oeufs	pancake with sugar/ eggs		
galette (de sarrasin)	buckwheat pancake		
pissaladière	tart of fried onions		

Soups (soupes)

bisque	shellfish soup	**potée**	thick vegetable and meat soup
bouillabaisse	Mediterranean fish soup	**soupe à l'oignon**	onion soup with a chunk of toasted bread and melted cheese topping
bouillon	broth or stock	**tourain, tourin**	garlic soup made with duck or goose fat served over bread topped with cheese
consommé	clear soup		
garbure	potato, cabbage and meat soup		
miques	dumplings of maize or wheat flour served in a thick soup		
potage	thick soup, usually vegetable		

Fish (poisson), seafood (fruits de mer) and shellfish (crustaces or coquillages)

alose	shad	**coquilles St-Jacques**	scallops
anchois	anchovies	**crabe**	crab
anguilles	eels	**crevettes grises**	shrimp
bigourneaux	periwinkles	**crevettes roses**	prawns
brandade de morue	puréed, salted cod with oil, milk, garlic and mashed potato	**daurade**	sea bream
		écrevisses	freshwater crayfish
		éperlan	smelt
brème	bream	**escargots**	snails
brochet	pike	**esturgeon**	sturgeon
bulot	whelk	**flétan**	halibut
cabillaud	cod	**gambas**	king prawns
calmar	squid	**hareng**	herring
carrelet	plaice	**homard**	lobster
colin	hake	**huîtres**	oysters
coques	cockles	**lamproie**	lamprey

langoustines	saltwater crayfish	**raie**	skate
limande	lemon sole	**rascasse**	scorpion fish
lotte de mer	monkfish	**rouget**	red mullet
loup de mer	sea bass	**saumon**	salmon
maquereau	mackerel	**sole**	sole
merlan	whiting	**thon**	tuna
moules (marinière)	mussels (with shallots in white wine sauce)	**truite**	trout
		turbot	turbot

Fish dishes and terms

aïoli	garlic mayonnaise served with salt cod and other fish	**grillé**	grilled
arête	fish bone	**hollandaise**	butter and vinegar sauce
beignet	fritter	**à la meunière**	in a butter, lemon and parsley sauce
darne	fillet or steak	**mousse/ mousseline**	mousse
la douzaine	a dozen	**pané**	breaded
frit	fried	**quenelles**	light dumplings
friture	deep-fried small fish	**thermidor**	lobster grilled in its shell with cream sauce
fumé	smoked		

Meat (viande) and poultry (volaille)

agneau (de pré-salé)	lamb (grazed on salt marshes)	**langue**	tongue
andouille/ andouillette	tripe sausage	**lapin, lapereau**	rabbit, young rabbit
bifteck	steak	**lard, lardons**	bacon, diced bacon
boeuf	beef	**lièvre**	hare
boudin blanc	sausage of white meats	**merguez**	spicy, red sausage
boudin noir	black pudding	**mouton**	mutton
caille	quail	**oie**	goose
canard	duck	**onglet**	cut of beef
caneton	duckling	**os**	bone
contrefilet	sirloin roast	**poitrine**	breast
dinde, dindon	turkey	**porc**	pork
entrecôte	rib steak	**poulet**	chicken
faux filet	sirloin steak	**ris**	sweetbreads
foie	liver	**rognons**	kidneys (usually lamb's)
foie gras	(duck/goose) liver	**sanglier**	wild boar
gibier	game	**steak**	steak
gigot (d'agneau)	leg (of lamb)	**tête de veau**	calf's head (in jelly)
grenouilles (cuisses de)	frogs (legs)	**tournedos**	thick slices of fillet
grillade	grilled meat	**tripes**	tripe
hâchis	chopped meat or mince hamburger	**tripoux**	mutton tripe
		veau	veal
		venaison	venison
		volaille	poultry

Meat and poultry dishes and terms

aiguillettes	thin, tender pieces of duck
aile	wing
au feu de bois	cooked over wood fire
au four	baked
blanquette, daube, estouffade, navarin, ragoût	types of stew
blanquette de veau	veal in cream and mushroom sauce
boeuf bourguignon	beef stew with Burgundy, onions and mushrooms
brochette	kebab
canard de périgourdin	roast duck with prunes, pâté foie gras and truffles
carré	best end of neck, chop or cutlet
choucroute	pickled cabbage with peppercorns, sausages, bacon and salami
civet	game stew
confit	meat preserve
coq au vin	chicken cooked until it falls off the bone with wine, onions and mushrooms
côte	chop, cutlet or rib
cou	neck
cuisse	thigh or leg
en croûte	in pastry
épaule	shoulder
farci	stuffed
garni	with vegetables
gésier	gizzard
gigot (d'agneau)	leg (of lamb)
grillé	grilled
magret de canard	duck breast
marmite	casserole
médaillon	round piece
noisettes	small, round fillets
pavé	thick slice
poêlé	pan-fried
poule au pot	chicken simmered with vegetables
rôti	roast
sauté	lightly cooked in butter
steak au poivre (vert/rouge)	steak in a black (green/red) peppercorn sauce
steak tartare	raw chopped beef, topped with a raw egg yolk
tournedos rossini	beef fillet with foie gras and truffles
viennoise	fried in egg and breadcrumbs

Terms for steaks

bleu	almost raw
saignant	rare
à point	medium
bien cuit	well done
très bien cuit	very well done

Garnishes and sauces

américaine	white wine, cognac and tomato
au porto	in port
béarnaise	sauce of egg yolks, white wine, shallots and vinegar
beurre blanc	sauce of white wine and shallots, with butter
bonne femme	with mushroom, bacon, potato and onions
bordelaise	in a red wine, shallot and bone-marrow sauce
chasseur	white wine, mushrooms and shallots
diable	strong mustard seasoning

forestière	with bacon and mushroom	**provençale**	tomatoes, garlic, olive oil and herbs
fricassée	rich, creamy sauce	**rouille**	a mayorraise of chillies and garlic
mornay	cheese sauce	**savoyarde**	with Gruyère cheese
périgourdine/ périgueux	rich wine sauce, possibly with truffles		

Vegetables (légumes), herbs (herbes) and spices (épices)

ail	garlic	**fèves**	broad beans
artichaut	artichoke	**flageolets**	white beans
asperge	asparagus	**haricots (verts, rouges, beurres)**	beans (French/string, kidney, butter)
avocat	avocado	**lentilles**	lentils
basilic	basil	**mange-tout**	snow peas
betterave	beetroot	**menthe**	mint
câpre	caper	**moutarde**	mustard
carotte	carrot	**oignon**	onion
céleri	celery	**persil**	parsley
champignon, cèpe, chanterelle, girolle, morille	types of mushrooms	**piment**	pimento
		poireau	leek
chou (rouge)	(red) cabbage	**pois, petits pois**	peas
choufleur	cauliflower	**poivron (vert, rouge)**	sweet pepper (green, red)
ciboulette	chives	**pommes de terre**	potatoes
concombre	cucumber	**radis**	radish
cornichon	gherkin	**riz**	rice
échalotes	shallots	**salade verte**	green salad
endive	chicory	**tomate**	tomato
épinards	spinach	**truffes**	truffles
estragon	tarragon		
fenouil	fennel		

Vegetable dishes and terms

à l'anglaise/ à l'eau	boiled	**jardinière**	with mixed diced vegetables
beignet	fritter	**mousseline**	mashed potato with cream and eggs
biologique	organic	**parmentier**	with potatoes
duxelles	fried mushrooms and shallots with cream	**pimenté**	peppery hot
farci	stuffed	**piquant**	spicy
feuille	leaf	**pistou**	ground basil, olive oil, garlic and parmesan
fines herbes	mixture of tarragon, parsley and chives	**râpée**	grated or shredded
garni	served with vegetables	**sauté**	lightly fried in butter
gratiné	browned with cheese or butter	**à la vapeur**	steamed
à la grecque	cooked in oil and lemon		

Fruit (fruits) and nuts (noix)

abricot	apricot
amande	almond
ananas	pineapple
banane	banana
brugnon, nectarine	nectarine
cacahouète	peanut
cassis	blackcurrant
cérise	cherry
citron	lemon
citron vert	lime
figue	fig
fraise (de bois)	strawberry (wild)
framboise	raspberry
fruit de la passion	passion fruit
grenade	pomegranate
groseille rouge/ blanche	red/white currant
kaki	persimmon
mangue	mango
marron	chestnut
melon	melon
melon d'eau	watermelon
mirabelle	small yellow plum
mûre	blackberry
myrtille	bluelberry
noisette	hazelnut
noix	nuts, walnuts
orange	orange
pamplemousse	grapefruit
pastèque	watermelon
pêche	peach
pistache	pistachio
poire	pear
pomme	apple
prune	plum
pruneau	prune
raisin	grape
reine-claude	greengage

Fruit dishes and terms

beignet	fritter
compôte	stewed fruit
coulis	sauce of puréed fruit
crème de marrons	chestnut purée
flambé	set aflame in alcohol
frappé	iced
macédoine	fruit salad

Desserts (desserts or entremets), pastries (pâtisserie) and related terms

bavarois	refers to the mould, could be a mousse or custard
bombe	moulded ice-cream dessert
brioche	sweet, high-yeast breakfast roll
charlotte	custard and fruit in lining of almond fingers
clafoutis	cake-like fruit tart
coupe/boule	a serving of ice cream
crème à l'anglaise	custard
crème Chantilly	vanilla-flavoured and sweetened whipped cream
crème fraîche	sour cream
crème pâtissière	thick, eggy pastry-filling
crêpe	pancake
crêpe suzette	thin pancake with orange juice and liqueur
fromage blanc	cream cheese
gaufre	waffle
gênoise	rich sponge cake
glace	ice cream
île flottante/ oeufs à la neige	soft meringues floating on custard
macaron	macaroon
madeleine	small sponge cake
mousse au chocolat	chocolate mousse
omelette norvégienne	baked Alaska

parfait	frozen mousse, sometimes ice cream	**sablé**	shortbread biscuit
pâte	pastry or dough	**savarin**	a filled, ring-shaped cake
petit-suisse	a smooth mixture of cream and curds	**tarte**	tart
poires belle hélène	pears and ice cream in chocolate sauce	**tartelette**	small tart
		tarte tatin	upside-down apple tart
		yaourt, yogourt	yogurt

Wine terms (*vin*)

barrique	oak barrel for maturing wine	**doux/moelleux**	sweet
blanc	white	**fin**	delicate
cave	wineshop/cellar	**fort**	strong
cépage	grape variety (e.g. Merlot, Pinot noir)	**léger**	light
chais	cellars	**millésime**	vintage
corsé	full-bodied	**mousseux**	sparkling
cuvé	vat for fermenting wine	**riche**	rich
cuvée	a specially blended wine	**rosé**	rosé
dégustation	tasting	**rouge**	red
		sec	dry
		vendange	harvest
		vignes	vines
		vignoble	vineyard

Glossary

General vocabulary and terms

abbaye abbey

abri prehistoric rock-shelter

appellation (Appellation d'Origine Contrôlée; AOC) wine classification indicating that the wine meets strict requirements regarding its provenance and methods of production

auberge country inn, frequently offering accommodation

auberge de jeunesse youth hostel

autoroute motorway

bastide new town founded in the thirteenth and fourteenth centuries, built on a grid plan around an arcaded market square (see box, p.306)

boules popular French game played with steel balls (see p.41)

cabane, borie or gariotte dry-stone hut, probably used by shepherds

Capétien Capetian royal dynasty founded by Hugh Capet, which ruled France from 987 to 1328

causse limestone plateau extending from Dordogne *département* south through Lot and into Aveyron

chai barn or storehouse in which wines are aged

chambre d'hôte bed-and-breakfast accommodation in a private house

chartreuse one-storey building typical of the Bordeaux wine region, slightly raised up and built on top of a half-buried *chai*; also a Carthusian monastery

château castle, mansion, stately home

château fort castle built for a specifically military purpose

collégiale church that shelters a community of priests

colombage traditional building style consisting of a timber frame filled with earth and straw or bricks

commune the basic administrative region, each under a mayor (very occasionally, a mayoress)

confiserie confectioner's (shop)

dégustation tasting (wine or food)

département mid-level administrative unit run by a local council – the equivalent of a county in Britain

dolmen neolithic stone structure, generally held to be a tomb, consisting of two or more upright slabs supporting a horizontal stone

donjon castle keep

église church

falaise cliff

ferme auberge farm licensed to provide meals in which the majority of the produce must come from the farm itself

Festival off fringe festival, set apart from the main programme, usually with free events

foire large market held once or twice monthly in some country towns

formule restaurant menu with two courses, usually comprising a choice of starter and main course or main and dessert

fouille archeological excavation

gabare or gabarre traditional wooden boat used to transport goods on the Dordogne and Lot rivers up until the late nineteenth century

gavage process of force-feeding ducks and geese to make foie gras

gisement deposit, stratified layers of an archeological excavation

gîte self-catering accommodation

gîte d'étape basic accommodation, usually restricted to walkers, pilgrims and cyclists

gouffre limestone chasm or sinkhole

grotte cave

halle(s) covered market (hall)

hôtel hotel, but also an aristocratic townhouse or mansion

lauze small limestone slabs, a traditional roof covering in the Périgord

navette shuttle-bus, for example connecting a town with its airport

Occitan language (and associated culture) formerly spoken throughout most of south and southwest France

pétanque variation of the game of boules (see p.41)

pigeonnier dovecote, often built on stilts and used to collect droppings for fertilizer

pisé traditional Périgordin floor made out of small limestone slabs inserted upright into a bed of clay or lime

porte gateway

retable altarpiece

seneschal chief administrator and justice in medieval times, the representative of the king

table d'hôte meals served to residents of a *chambre d'hôtes*. Also, a set menu with choices, at a fixed price.

tour tower

version originale (VO) film shown in its original language and subtitled in French

Architectural terms

ambulatory passage around the outer edge of the choir of a church

apse semicircular or polygonal termination at the east end of a church

Baroque High Renaissance period of art and architecture, distinguished by extreme ornateness

chevet east end of a church

Classical architectural style incorporating Greek and Roman elements: pillars, domes, colonnades, etc, at its height in France in the seventeenth century and revived in the nineteenth century as Neoclassical

flamboyant very ornate form of Gothic

fresco painting in watercolour on a wall or ceiling while the plaster is still wet.

Gallo-Roman period of Roman occupation of Gaul (1st century BC to 4th century AD)

Gothic architectural style prevalent from the twelfth to sixteenth century, characterized by pointed arches and ribbed vaulting

machicolations parapet on a castle, fortified church, gateway, etc, with openings for dropping stones and so forth on attackers.

Merovingian dynasty (and art, etc) ruling France and parts of Germany from the sixth to mid-eighth century

narthex entrance hall of church

nave main body of a church

Renaissance architectural and artistic style developed in fifteenth-century Italy and imported to France in the sixteenth century by François I

Romanesque early medieval architecture distinguished by squat, rounded forms and naive sculpture, called *Roman* in French (not to be confused with *Romain* – Roman)

stucco plaster used to embellish ceilings, etc

transept transverse arms of a church, at right angles to the nave

tympanum sculpted semicircular panel above the door of a Romanesque church

Regional names

Aquitaine Originally a Roman administrative region extending from Poitiers and Limoges south to the Pyrenees. It later became a duchy, which, at its apogee in the twelfth century, covered roughly the same area, though it fluctuated enormously. In the 1960s the name was resurrected with the creation of regional administrative units. Modern Aquitaine is based around Bordeaux and comprises the *départements* of Dordogne, Gironde and Lot-et-Garonne, amongst others

Gascony The region to the west and south of the River Garonne, named after a Celtic tribe (the Vascons). In the early tenth century it became an independent duchy but was soon subsumed into the duchy of Aquitaine, though still retained its own identity

Guyenne a corruption of the name "Aquitaine" originating during the period of English rule. Prior to the Revolution, the province of Guyenne extended from Gironde to Aveyron. Nowadays, it is occasionally used to refer to an area roughly encompassing Entre-Deux-Mers and St-Émilion, although there is no strict demarcation

Midi-Pyrénées the modern administrative region to the east of Aquitaine, based on Toulouse and incorporating the *départements* of Lot, Tarn-et-Garonne and Aveyron, amongst others

Périgord the confines of Périgord have changed little since pre-Roman times, when it was the home of the Gaulish tribe, the **Petrocori**. In the eighth century Périgord became a county, and then a province of France until the name was officially changed to Dordogne when *départements* were created in 1790 (each *département* was named after its principal river). However, Périgord is still used frequently, especially in tourist literature. These days it is often subdivided into Périgord Vert (Green Périgord; the *département*'s northern sector); Périgord Blanc (White; the central strip along the Isle valley including Périgueux); Périgord Pourpre (Purple; the southwest corner around Bergerac); and Périgord Noir (Black; the southeast, including Sarlat and the Vézère valley)

Quercy former province roughly equivalent to the modern *départements* of the Lot and the north part of the Tarn-et-Garonne. The latter is often referred to as Bas-Quercy, while Haut-Quercy comprises the Lot's northern region

Small print and

Index

A Rough Guide to Rough Guides

Published in 1982, the first Rough Guide – to Greece – was a student scheme that became a publishing phenomenon. Mark Ellingham, a recent graduate in English from Bristol University, had been travelling in Greece the previous summer and couldn't find the right guidebook. With a small group of friends he wrote his own guide, combining a highly contemporary, journalistic style with a thoroughly practical approach to travellers' needs.

The immediate success of the book spawned a series that rapidly covered dozens of destinations. And, in addition to impecunious backpackers, Rough Guides soon acquired a much broader and older readership that relished the guides' wit and inquisitiveness as much as their enthusiastic, critical approach and value-for-money ethos.

These days, Rough Guides include recommendations from shoestring to luxury and cover more than 200 destinations around the globe, including almost every country in the Americas and Europe, more than half of Africa and most of Asia and Australasia. Our ever-growing team of authors and photographers is spread all over the world, particularly in Europe, the US and Australia.

In the early 1990s, Rough Guides branched out of travel, with the publication of Rough Guides to World Music, Classical Music and the Internet. All three have become benchmark titles in their fields, spearheading the publication of a wide range of books under the Rough Guide name.

Including the travel series, Rough Guides now number more than 350 titles, covering: phrasebooks, waterproof maps, music guides from Opera to Heavy Metal, reference works as diverse as Conspiracy Theories and Shakespeare, and popular culture books from iPods to Poker. Rough Guides also produce a series of more than 120 World Music CDs in partnership with World Music Network.

Visit www.roughguides.com to see our latest publications.

Rough Guide travel images are available for commercial licensing at www.roughguidespictures.com

Rough Guide credits

Text editor: Lucy White
Layout: Pradeep Thapliyal
Cartography: Animesh Pathak
Picture editor: Emily Taylor
Production: Rebecca Short
Proofreader: Stewart Wild
Cover design: Dan May & Chloë Roberts
Photographer: Jean-Christophe Godet
Editorial: Ruth Blackmore, Andy Turner, Keith Drew, Edward Aves, Alice Park, Jo Kirby, James Smart, Natasha Foges, Róisín Cameron, James Rice, Lara Kavanagh, Emma Traynor, Emma Gibbs, Kathryn Lane, Monica Woods, Mani Ramaswamy, Harry Wilson, Lucy Cowie, Alison Roberts, Joe Staines, Peter Buckley, Matthew Milton, Tracy Hopkins, Ruth Tidball; **Delhi** Madhavi Singh, Karen D'Souza, Lubna Shaheen
Design & Pictures: **London** Scott Stickland, Dan May, Diana Jarvis, Mark Thomas, Nicole Newman, Sarah Cummins; **Delhi** Umesh Aggarwal, Ajay Verma, Jessica Subramanian, Ankur Guha, Sachin Tanwar, Anita Singh, Nikhil Agarwal, Sachin Gupta
Production: Liz Cherry
Cartography: **London** Ed Wright, Katie Lloyd-Jones; **Delhi** Rajesh Chhibber, Ashutosh Bharti, Rajesh Mishra, Jasbir Sandhu, Karobi Gogoi, Alakananda Bhattacharya, Swati Handoo, Deshpal Dabas
Online: **London** Faye Hellon, Jeanette Angell, Fergus Day, Justine Bright, Clare Bryson, Aine Fearon, Adrian Low, Ezgi Celebi; **Delhi** Amit Verma, Rahul Kumar, Narender Kumar, Ravi Yadav, Debojit Borah, Rakesh Kumar, Ganesh Sharma, Shisir Basumatari
Marketing & Publicity: **London** Liz Statham, Louise Maher, Jess Carter, Vanessa Godden, Vivienne Watton, Anna Paynton, Rachel Sprackett, Laura Vipond; **New York** Katy Ball, Judi Powers; **Delhi** Ragini Govind
Reference Director: Andrew Lockett
Operations Assistant: Becky Doyle
Operations Manager: Helen Atkinson
Publishing Director (Travel): Clare Currie
Commercial Manager: Gino Magnotta
Managing Director: John Duhigg

Publishing information

This third edition published May 2010 by
Rough Guides Ltd,
80 Strand, London WC2R 0RL
14 Local Shopping Centre, Panchsheel Park, New Delhi 110017, India

Distributed by the Penguin Group
Penguin Books Ltd,
80 Strand, London WC2R 0RL
Penguin Group (USA)
375 Hudson Street, NY 10014, USA
Penguin Group (Australia)
250 Camberwell Road, Camberwell, Victoria 3124, Australia
Penguin Group (Canada)
195 Harry Walker Parkway N, Newmarket, ON, L3Y 7B3 Canada
Penguin Group (NZ)
67 Apollo Drive, Mairangi Bay, Auckland 1310, New Zealand
Cover concept by Peter Dyer.

Typeset in Bembo and Helvetica to an original design by Henry Iles.

Printed in Singapore

400pp includes index

A catalogue record for this book is available from the British Library

ISBN: 978-1-84836-462-2

1 3 5 7 9 8 6 4 2

Help us update

We've gone to a lot of effort to ensure that the third edition of **The Rough Guide to The Dordogne and the Lot** is accurate and up-to-date. However, things change – places get "discovered", opening hours are notoriously fickle, restaurants and rooms raise prices or lower standards. If you feel we've got it wrong or left something out, we'd like to know, and if you can remember the address, the price, the hours, the phone number, so much the better.

Please send your comments with the subject line "**Rough Guide The Dordogne and the Lot Update**" to ⓔ mail@roughguides.com. We'll credit all contributions and send a copy of the next edition (or any other Rough Guide if you prefer) for the very best emails.

Have your questions answered and tell others about your trip at ⓦ www.roughguides.com

Acknowledgements

Laura Bennitt would like to thank Stuart Reed for the best restaurant information; to Edward and Elizabeth Corp for sheltering me from the rain, and Oscar for providing warmth; and to all the hotels, restaurants and tourist information offices who welcomed the cold, wet biker dripping on their floors.

Janet Cintas thanks the staff in the tourist offices in Dordogne, Lot and Corrèze.

Hugh Cleary would like to thank the staff of numerous tourist offices, museums – particularly Bordeaux's Musée d'Aquitaine – and châteaux, particularly Pichon-Longueville in Pauillac. I would also like to thank the British Library, Lucy White for her excellent editing, Jan Dodd for tips and suggestions, and Liz Cleary for chauffeuring.

The editor would like to thank all three contributors, Pradeep Thalipyal for typesetting and Emily Taylor for picture research.

Photo credits

All photos © Rough Guides except the following:

Title page
Dordogne geese, Aquitaine © A Demotes/Tips

Introduction
Bordeaux © Romain Cintract/Hemis/Axiom
Place de la Bourse in Bordeaux at dusk © Jean-Pierre Lescourret/Corbis
Hautefort castle gardens © Romain Cintract/Hemis/Axiom

Things not to miss
07 Local people wearing costumes during the Medieval weekend, Eymet © NYBoyd/Alamy
09 Man smelling truffle, truffles market © Karl Johaentges/PhotoLibrary
15 Najac Castle © http://www.flickr.com/photos/23203406@N06/3337940741/

A Taste of Périgord colour section
Cassoulet © Sudres Jean-Daniel/PhotoLibrary
Foie gras de canard entier – whole pieces of duck liver and pâté © Per Karlsson/Alamy
Truffles © PNS/Tips
Fishmongers in Périgueux, display of oysters © Peter Titmuss /Alamy
Sarlat Market © Ellen Rooney/Robert Harding

Cave art colour section
Lascaux Cave, Dordogne © Larry Dale Gordon/Tips Images
Cave painting Lascaux © Robert Harding
Lascaux II Cave, the Great Hall of the Bulls © Marc Dozier/PhotoLibrary
Grotte de Rouffignac © Courtesy of Grotte de Rouffignac
Prehistoric Museum © AFP/Getty

Black and whites
p.162 Meander of the Dordogne river at Tremolat, Dordogne © Philippe Body/PhotoLibrary
p.184 Old village of Limeuil, Dordogne Valley © David Hughes/Robert Harding
p.262 St Cirq Lapopie, Lot © http://www.flickr.com/photos/flissphil/2874836816/
p.290 Causse de Gramat, Lot Valley © Hemis/Alamy
p.300 Château de Bonaguil, Lot et Garonne © http://www.flickr.com/photos/flissphil/2889481764/
p.308 Market day, Monpazier, Lot-et-Garonne © http://www.flickr.com/photos/flissphil/2868678045/
p.343 Bastide hilltop town of Cordes sur Ciel © David Noton Photography/Alamy
p.354 Couple of pilgrims on the way from Le Puy to Aubrac – St James way, © Cro Magnon/Alamy

Index

Map entries are in colour.

D

E

F

G

H

I

J

O

P

Q

R

S

Y

Map symbols

maps are listed in the full index using coloured text

Chapter division boundary
Motorway
Major road
Minor road
Steps
Path
River
Ferry route
Railway
Cable car
Tourist train
Wall
Mountains
Cave
Bridge
Gate

Abbey
Windmill
Castle
Tower
Ruin
Viewpoint
Transport stop
Airport
Parking
Hospital
Post office
Internet access
Church
Building
Cemetery
Park/National park